Conquistadores

Conquistadores

*A New History of Spanish
Discovery and Conquest*

FERNANDO CERVANTES

VIKING

VIKING

An imprint of Penguin Random House LLC
penguinrandomhouse.com

First published in hardcover in Great Britain by Allen Lane,
an imprint of Penguin Books, a division of Penguin Random House Ltd., London, in 2020.

First North American edition published by Viking, 2021.

Illustration credits can be found on pp. xi–xiii.

LIBRARY OF CONGRESS CATALOGING-IN-PUBLICATION DATA

Names: Cervantes, Fernando, author.
Title: Conquistadores : A New History of Spanish Discovery and Conquest / Fernando Cervantes.
Other titles: New history of Spanish discovery and conquest
Description: First North American edition. | New York : Viking, 2021. |
Includes bibliographical references and index.
Identifiers: LCCN 2021029480 (print) | LCCN 2021029481 (ebook) |
ISBN 9781101981269 (hardcover) | ISBN 9781101981283 (ebook)
Subjects: LCSH: America—Discovery and exploration—Spanish. | Conquerors—Spain—History. |
Latin America—History—To 1600. | Conquerors—America—History.
Classification: LCC E123 .C47 2021 (print) | LCC E123 (ebook) | DDC 970.01/6—dc23
LC record available at https://lccn.loc.gov/2021029480
LC ebook record available at https://lccn.loc.gov/2021029481

Printed in the United States of America
1   3   5   7   9   10   8   6   4   2

Set in Sabon LT Std

To Brendan and Annabel

τὸ ἀργύριον αὐτοῦ οὐκ ἔδωκεν ἐπὶ τόκῳ

Contents

List of Maps   ix

List of Illustrations   xi

Introduction   xv

PART ONE
Discoveries, 1492–1511

1 The Ocean Sea   3

2 The Admiral   23

3 Hispaniola   55

4 A Question of Justice   69

PART TWO
Conquests, 1510–33

5 Cuba   93

6 Imperial Designs   104

7 The Lure of China   120

8 Tenochtitlan   150

9 Defeat and Victory   167

10 The Grand Chancellor's Dream   190

11 The World of the Mendicants   200

12 Spices and Gold   225

13 Cajamarca   249

PART THREE
Disenchantment, 1533–42

14 Cusco   273

15 Manqo Inka   293

16 The End of an Era   314

    Reassessment   346

    Notes   359

    Bibliography   437

    Acknowledgements   465

    Index   467

List of Maps

1 Early Modern Spain 4

2 Columbus's Four Voyages 24

3 Hispaniola 56

4 Darién 85

5 Fernandina (Cuba) 100

6 Cortés's Journey from Cuba, 1519 121

7 Cortés's March to Tenochtitlan, 1519 136

8 Cortés's Escape Route After the *Noche Triste* 169

9 Tenochtitlan and the Lacustrine Cities 181

10 Mendicant Foundations in Central Mexico
by the Middle of the 16th Century 212

11 The Route of Cabeza de Vaca 215

12 Alvarado's Invasion of Guatemala 229

13 Montejo in Yucatan 242

14 Inca Expansion 251

15 Pizarro's Route from Panama to Cusco, 1531–3 276

16 Cusco at the Time of Pizarro's Invasion 289

17 Quito and Tumipampa 294

18 Manqo Inka 302

19 The Hernando de Soto Expedition, 1539–43 321

20 The Expeditions of Jiménez de Quesada, Federmann
and Benalcázar 333

List of Illustrations

Photographic credits are shown in italics.

1. Monastery of St Mary of the Victory in Batalha, Portugal. *Alamy.*
2. Genoa, illustration from Sebastian Münster, *Cosmographia*, 1552. *Albion Prints.*
3. Coat of arms of Christopher Columbus, 1498. Archive of the Indies of Seville. *Juan Garcia/Dreamstime.*
4. Mapamundi, 1507, by Martin Waldseemüller. *Library of Congress, Prints and Photographs Division, Washington, D.C.*
5. The University of Alcalá de Henares, Spain. *Wikimedia Commons/ Superchilum CC BY-SA 3.0.*
6. Charles V, c.1515, Flemish School. Fitzwilliam Museum, Cambridge. *Bridgeman Images.*
7. Device and motto of Charles V on the reverse of a coin minted in Mexico, 1542–56. *Numisbids/Daniel Frank Sedwick LLC*
8. Portrait of a Man (Alfonso de Valdés), c.1531, by an associate of Jan Cornelisz Vermeyen. © *National Gallery, London.*
9. The Nuremberg Map of Tenochtitlan, from *Praeclara Ferdinādi Cortesii de Noua maris Oceani Hyspania narratio [. . .]*, 1524. *Newberry Library, Chicago, IL (Ayer 655.51 .C8 1524d).*
10. Stone disc depicting a dismembered Coyolxauhqui, c.1473, Aztec. Museo Del Templo Mayor, Mexico City. *Getty Images.*
11. Quecholli, from Juan de Tovar, *Historia de la benida de los yndios apoblar a Mexico [. . .]*, c.1585. © *John Carter Brown Library, Brown University, Providence, R.I. (Codex Ind 2, folio 154 r).*
12. Panquetzaliztli (*ibid*). © *John Carter Brown Library, Brown University, Providence, R.I. (Codex Ind 2, folio 154 v).*
13. Tititl (*ibid*). © *John Carter Brown Library, Brown University, Providence, R.I. (Codex Ind 2, folio 155 v).*
14. Tlacaxipehualiztli (*ibid*). © *John Carter Brown Library, Brown University, Providence, R.I. (Codex Ind 2, folio 147 r).*

15. Tonatiuh, depicted in the *Codex Borgia*, late Post-Classic period, Aztec. *Reproduced by permission of Biblioteca Apostolica Vaticana, with all rights reserved (Borg.mess.1, page 19).*

16. The Ahuehuetl of the Noche Triste, 19th century, by José María Velasco. Private Collection. *Alamy.*

17. Tzitzimtl, depicted in the *Codex Magliabechiano*, mid-16th century, Aztec. *Biblioteca Nazionale Centrale, Florence (CL. XIII. 3 (B. R. 232) fol 76r).*

18. Calmecac, depicted in the *Codex Mendoza*, 1541–1650. © *Bodleian Libraries, University of Oxford (MS. Arch. Selden. A. 1, fol. 61r).*

19. Telpochcalli (*ibid.*) © *Bodleian Libraries, University of Oxford (MS. Arch. Selden. A. 1, fol. 63r).*

20. Charles V, 1548, by Titian. Prado, Madrid. *Getty Images.*

21. Nezahualpilli, depicted in the *Codex Ixtlilxochitl*, Mexican, late 16th century. © *Bibliothèque nationale de France, Paris (Ms. Mex. 65–71, fol. 106r).*

22. Hernán Cortés, illustration from Christoph Weiditz, *Trachtenbuch*, 1529. Germanisches Nationalmuseum, Nuremberg. *Alamy.*

23. Friar Bartolomé de las Casas, 16th century, by an anonymous artist. Biblioteca Colombina, Seville. *Bridgeman Images.*

24. Monte Albán, Oaxaca, Mexico. © *Ben Pipe Photography.*

25. Detail from the *Lienzo de Quauhquechollan*, c.1530–40, Nahua school. Museo Regional Casa de Alfeñique, Puebla, Mexico. *Universidad Francisco Marroquín/Geosistemas y Tecnología Avanzada, S.A.*

26. Mask, turquoise mosaic on wood, 1400–1521, Mixtec. © *Trustees of the British Museum, London (Am,St.400).*

27. *The Mass of St Gregory*, feather mosaic, 1539, School of San José de los Naturales. *Musée des Amériques, Auch.*

28. Carving of an angel, 16th century, Mixtec. Convent of SS Peter and Paul, Teposcolula, Mexico. *Alamy.*

29. Hernán Cortés greets Friar Martín de Valencia, mural, mid-16th century. Parish of the Immaculation Conception, Ozumba, Mexico. *Wikimedia Commons/Alejandro Linares Garcia CC BY-SA 4.0.*

30. *Bridge of the Apurimac*, illustration from Ephraim George Squier, *Peru; incidents of travel and exploration in the land of the Incas*, 1877.

31. The Inca Road near Cuzco, Peru. *Shutterstock.*

32. Double ceremonial vessel, ceramic, 15th or early 16th century, Inca. *The Metropolitan Museum of Art, New York. The Michael C. Rockefeller Memorial Collection, Bequest of Nelson A. Rockefeller, 1979 (Acc. No. 1979.206.1149).*

33. Male figurine, gold-silver alloy, 1400–1533, Inca. *The Metropolitan Museum of Art, New York. Gift and Bequest of Alice K. Bache, 1974, 1977 (Acc. No. 1974.271.7)*

34. Juan de Pareja, c.1650, by Diego Velázquez. *The Metropolitan Museum of Art, New York. Purchase, Fletcher and Rogers Funds, and Bequest of Miss Adelaide Milton de Groot (1876–1967), by exchange, supplemented by gifts from friends of the Museum, 1971 (Acc. No. 1971.86).*

Introduction

'You are no city: You are a universe.' These are the words with which the Renaissance poet Fernando de Herrera addressed his native Seville in the middle of the sixteenth century.[1] With brilliant brevity, they evoke a change of unprecedented proportions: in a mere few decades this Andalusian city on the fringes of Europe had been transformed into the de facto capital of the greatest empire the world had yet seen. Under the rule of the Habsburg Charles V, it spanned medieval Christendom and, stretching across the Atlantic, the New World of the Americas. The story that underpins Seville's dramatic rise is very familiar to us. In 1492 an eccentric Genoese sailor named Christopher Columbus, hoping to sail to India across the Atlantic, stumbled across some islands in the Caribbean. A flurry of expeditions followed, culminating in the astonishing conquests of two formidable civilizations: the Aztecs of Mexico, conquered by Hernán Cortés in 1521, and the Incas of Peru, conquered by Francisco Pizarro just over a decade later. Both men styled themselves 'conquistadores', subduing, killing and establishing their dominion in the name of the Habsburg emperor and of God himself.

These vast, newly acquired territories quickly began to bear the marks of their energetic and often rapacious settlers. Monasteries, convents and cathedrals; churches and cemeteries; palaces, mansions and commercial enterprises – all cut through with networks of roads – soon dominated the landscape. The transformation happened swiftly, on a massive – and, from an indigenous perspective, often traumatic – scale, and with a solid grandeur that left little doubt that the invaders wanted to remain there and rule forever. The term 'conquistador' soon acquired an enduring resonance: for centuries, it became part of the imaginative mindset of informed readers. As Thomas Babington Macaulay once put it, 'every schoolboy knows who imprisoned Montezuma and who strangled Atahualpa'.[2] Redolent of its time, today Macaulay's phrase bears repeating only with a nagging discomfort. In the classroom, the view of the Spanish conquistadores as admirable adventurers has long since been dispelled: they are more often seen as brutal, genocidal colonists, culpable of a savage assault on innocent civilizations and perpetrators of the first great act of early modern colonialism – a shameful episode that should fill any European with a profound feeling of revulsion.

Yet, the way we view and condemn the conquistadores often tells us much more about our own sense of shame in the face of the devastating effects that the expansion of Europe has had on the world and its environment than it does about the people who first initiated those processes without an inkling of where they would lead. Our understandable sense of revulsion therefore runs the risk of hiding from us fundamental aspects of the late-medieval religious culture that nurtured the assumptions and behaviour of the conquistadores. It is easy to forget that these men evoked widespread admiration among their contemporaries – particularly their English contemporaries, who recounted the deeds of Cortés and Pizarro with unconcealed respect and approbation.[3] No matter how short-lived this attitude might have been, it survived residually in various forms and was reinforced in the nineteenth century, a time when travellers influenced by Romanticism often expressed a sense of charm at the quaintly exotic world that greeted them when they crossed the Pyrenees. 'What a country is Spain for a traveller,' exclaimed Washington Irving, 'where the most miserable inn is as full of adventure as an enchanted castle, and every meal is in itself an achievement!'[4] Something of the same spirit survived as late as 1949, when the travel writer Patrick Leigh Fermor jumped at the suggestion that he should contribute to a new series on travellers and explorers: in a letter to Edward Shackleton – the son of the Antarctic explorer – Fermor proposed a biography of Cortés's impetuous companion Pedro de Alvarado, framing his proposed subject in terms that sharply evoke William Prescott.[5] 'The story is so exciting,' wrote Fermor, 'that it would be impossible to turn it into a bore.' Indeed, 'it's got a wonderful dramatic completeness about it, one must admit!'[6]

Very little of this uncritically admiring enthusiasm survives nowadays – and that is all to the good. Our own perception of the conquistadores, however, has become entangled with a strangely persistent myth, one that sees in the history of Spain little but a record of cruelty at the service of political reaction and religious bigotry. The origins of this myth are to be found in the various reactions provoked by the portentous rise of the Spanish Habsburgs in the sixteenth century. Since the phenomenon coincided with the rapid spread of print, it is no surprise that the Spanish Habsburgs became the first victims of the propagandists. The trend reached a high point in 1581, with the publication of the *Apology* of William the Silent, Prince of Orange – a skilful diatribe in which the leader of the anti-Spanish Dutch revolt sought to rally support for his cause with a damning depiction of everything Spanish. His particular bête noire was Charles V's son and heir, Philip II, whose crimes were alleged to range from duplicity and adultery to incest and the murder of his wife and son.[7] And, of course, the conquistadores were always at the centre of these allegations: William himself took good care to plunder the damning accounts of the atrocities of the conquistadores that the Spanish 'defenders of the Indians' had been tirelessly producing with the specific aim of shocking the Castilian authorities into implementing reform. Foremost among them was Bartolomé de Las Casas's sensationalist polemic, *A Most Brief Account of the Destruction of the Indies*, destined to capture the European imagination for centuries to come, not least through the visual aid afforded it in vivid engravings by Theodor de Bry. But if anti-Habsburg propaganda was the basis of this distorted image, its persistence was due, even more importantly, to the lack of response to it in Spain itself; for by the time that the anti-Habsburg myths began to prevail, Spain, and those who wished to defend her interests, had become increasingly obsessed with the irksome question of decline. The soul-searching literature of those self-appointed analysts of the ills of the Spanish Habsburg monarchy, the *arbitristas*, hardly provided an answer to the negative polemics that became so dominant.[8]

It is important that we do not reduce the richly complex world of the conquistadores to a sweeping caricature. Our view of their many atrocities needs to be grounded in historical context. Their world was not the cruel, backward, obscurantist and bigoted myth of legend, but the late-medieval crusading world which saw the stamping out of the last vestiges of Muslim rule on continental Europe. In the wake of the capture of Granada and the expulsion of the Jews from Spain in 1492, Europeans were unexpectedly faced with the challenge, at first gradual but ultimately unavoidable, of having radically to redraw the map of the known world in order to accommodate a new reality – not the quick path to the riches of the 'Indies' for which cash-strapped monarchs had hoped, but an astonishingly large and hitherto unknown continent. The venal and acquisitive ethos that such circumstances engendered should not be dissociated from the powerful spirit of humanist and religious reform that marked late-medieval Spain.[9] This was a world that saw no inherent contradiction in the attempt to establish forms of governance that were simultaneously high-minded and shamelessly lucrative. The frequent claim among the conquistadores to have gone to 'the Indies' in order 'to serve God, the King, and to get rich' should evoke in our minds a 'disarming frankness' – to use J. H. Elliott's apt remark[10] – rather than a mere hypocritical pretext to hide base and immoral motives.

My aim in writing this book has been to place the conquistadores in just such a context. The experiment has entailed the reconstruction of a world that myth and prejudice have rendered almost as alien to us as the world of the Americas was to the conquistadores themselves. Our reluctance to take this difficulty into account largely explains the ease with which we subscribe to the condemnations that have become so common. More often than not, however, these attitudes are rooted in a profound ignorance of the religious culture of late-medieval Europe which formed and nurtured the conquistadores.

By attending to the diaries, letters, chronicles, biographies, instructions, histories, epics, encomia and polemical treatises produced by the conquistadores, their supporters and their detractors, I have tried to weave a familiar story in a way that often shows surprising and unfamiliar threads. With their late-medieval conflation of faith and glory, with their commitment to forms of political organization in which any separation of temporal and spiritual matters would have been considered absurd, the conquistadores can appear decidedly retrograde to us. Yet, for all their undeniable shortcomings, their story can only be adequately appreciated if we are open and receptive to a cultural world that, however alien it may appear to us, was just as human, and just as fallible, as our own.

Note on spelling: I have normally used accepted scholarly conventions in the spelling of Nahuatl, Maya, Quechua and Aymara words, with no accents. The few exceptions, such as the case of Coyoacán (Nahuatl, 'Coyohuacan'), relate to words that were Hispanized very early on and widely used in Spanish from the earliest years.

PART ONE

Discoveries, 1492–1511

I

The Ocean Sea

On a raw January day in 1492 a somewhat eccentric figure might have been spotted riding slowly through the Andalusian countryside on muleback. Tall and pale-eyed, the forty-year-old Christopher Columbus was making his way to the Franciscan convent of Santa María de la Rábida, near Seville, where he had befriended a number of friars. He had just visited Granada, a Moorish city for the best part of eight centuries, which had surrendered on 2 January to the reconquering Spanish monarchs, Isabel I of Castile and Fernando II of Aragon, whom Columbus hoped to persuade to support his proposed plan to sail to India across the Atlantic. Unfortunately, the monarchs were too busy with more pressing priorities after such a momentous victory, so Columbus, with years of royal pleading weighing heavily on his shoulders, decided to make his way back to the relative comfort afforded by his Franciscan friends.

His path to the court of Isabel and Fernando was a long and circuitous one. Adventuring, trading and moneymaking were in his blood. His native Genoa had long been one of Europe's most dynamic, most influential city states, establishing an extensive network of centres of production and exchange throughout the eastern and western Mediterranean. In particular, Genoa's dominance of the Iberian and North African sea routes gave it an unrivalled stake in the burgeoning trade between the Mediterranean and the Atlantic ports. When, some fifty years later, Sebastian Münster published his *Cosmographia*, he famously portrayed the republic of Genoa as an imposing, muscular male figure standing on two worlds, with a Janus face, holding a luscious bunch of grapes in his right hand and a huge key in his left. The image was a clear attempt to link the medieval legend associating the name of Genoa with that of Janus – or Ianos, its alleged Trojan founder – with

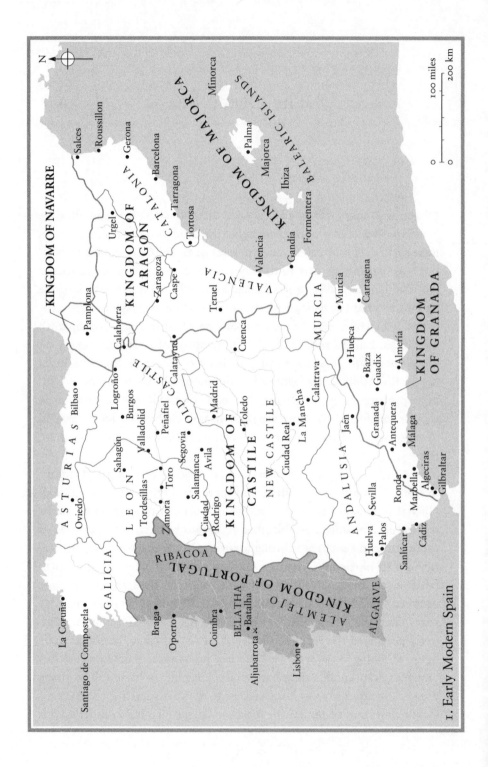

KINGDOM OF NAVARRE

KINGDOM OF MAJORCA

BALEARIC ISLANDS

Minorca
Majorca
Palma
Ibiza
Formentera

KINGDOM OF ARAGON

Salces
Roussillon
Gerona
Barcelona
Urgel
CATALONIA
Tarragona
Tortosa

Pamplona
Calahorra
Zaragoza
Caspe
Teruel

VALENCIA
Valencia
Gandia

Cuenca

MURCIA
Murcia
Cartagena
Huesca

KINGDOM OF GRANADA
Baza
Guadix
Almería

Bilbao
ASTURIAS
Oviedo

Logroño
Burgos
Valladolid
Peñafiel
OLD CASTILE
Calatayud
Madrid
Segovia
Avila
Toledo

NEW CASTILE
Ciudad Real
La Mancha
Calatrava

Jaén
Granada
Antequera
Málaga

LEON
Sahagún
Salamanca
Tordesillas
Toro
Zamora
Ciudad Rodrigo

KINGDOM OF CASTILE

ANDALUSIA
Sevilla
Ronda
Marbella
Algeciras
Gilbraltar

Huelva
Palos
Sanlúcar
Cádiz

GALICIA
La Coruña
Santiago de Compostela

RIBACOA
Braga
Oporto
Coimbra
BELATHA
Batalha
Aljubarrota
ALEMTEJO
KINGDOM OF PORTUGAL
ALGARVE
Lisbon

1. Early Modern Spain

100 miles
200 km

a more recent notion of Genoa as the door – *ianua* in Latin – to the Pillars of Hercules. This was the very place that for centuries had served as a warning to sailors to venture no further – *non plus ultra*.

For all the imposing size of Münster's figure, the source of Genoese strength was, paradoxically, to be found in its comparative weakness. Genoa had none of the characteristics that we have come to associate with a state, let alone an empire. Genoese traders prospered on the basis of their adaptability and family solidarity. They were happy to seek the patronage of foreign princes, so long as it did not erode the ties of friendship and kinship with their own countrymen. This was not, of course, a uniquely Genoese characteristic, but as in the example of the Turkish city of Galata, the Genoese had a distinctive ability to reproduce their city wherever they went. This made them particularly adaptable not only to different environments but also to widely diverse types of trade, from the slaves of the Black Sea, the alum of Phocaea and the grain of Cyprus and the Danube plains, to the mastic of Chios and the spices channelled by the Venetians through Alexandria and Beirut.

This adaptability was just as well. In 1453 the Genoese route – and, by extension, the European route – to the lucrative markets of Asia was abruptly severed by the Ottoman conquest of Constantinople, the great Eurasian city on the Bosphorus. Not only did the Ottomans now pose a military threat to Christendom, but they had also ripped through the supply lines – the 'silk roads' – on which so much Genoese trade depended, for it had transported everything from sugar and exotic textiles to alum, the dye-fixer so vital to the European cloth industry. This, in turn, brought to an end the former commercial pre-eminence of Caffa, the Genoese colony in Crimea.[1] Genoa had to look elsewhere for trade. Soon, Sicily and the Algarve began to produce good-quality silks and sugar under the guidance of Genoese merchants, and the kingdom of Granada – the one remaining Islamic enclave in Spain – began to prove especially enticing for Genoese merchants, not only for its silk, saffron, sugar and citrus fruits, but also for its privileged access to the Maghreb (north-west Africa) and the much-coveted supplies of gold from beyond the Sahara. In short, the Ottoman conquest of Constantinople led merchants and traders throughout Christendom to turn their gaze decidedly westwards. At their forefront were the Genoese, who found a welcome home from home in Portugal.

In the fifteenth century, Portugal would come to play a role that can be compared to that played by Genoa and Venice in the twelfth and Amsterdam in the seventeenth century. When the great depression that followed the Black Death in the fourteenth century forced Venice and Genoa to divert their interests to the land and to finance respectively, Lisbon remained a mercantile and maritime centre linking the Mediterranean to England and northern Europe. Great Italian merchant families like the Bardi of Florence and the Lomellini of Venice vied with entrepreneurs from Flanders and Catalonia in a race to set up a base in Lisbon. The city's preponderance turned Portugal into Europe's pre-eminent economic and maritime centre of the age. It became a key ally of England during the Hundred Years' War. The Anglo-Portuguese victory against Spain at Aljubarrota in August 1385 was brilliantly captured in the laborious construction of the great monastery of Saint Mary of the Victory in Batalha, roughly halfway between Lisbon and Coimbra, with its exuberant imagery of cables and anchors, corals, shells and waves. Here was an emphatic visual confirmation that Portugal had inherited the legacy of Italy. Soon, the Venetian Greek possessions of Chios and Crete would become the models for Madeira and the Canaries. In addition, the diplomatic alliance between England and Portugal agreed at the Treaty of Windsor in May 1386 would give English merchants, those based in Bristol in particular, ample experience of long voyages and a close connection to a country that had established itself as the most extensive seaborne empire of the age.[2]

Starting in the 1420s, under the leadership of Prince Henry 'the Navigator', the kingdom of Portugal had sponsored expeditions down the west African coast with the aim of establishing a direct maritime trade in gold, ivory and slaves from sub-Saharan kingdoms, thus bypassing the need to rely on the trans-Saharan caravan routes dominated by Arab traders.[3] By the end of the fifteenth century the Portuguese had charted the whole west coast of Africa as far as the Cape of Good Hope, in the process colonizing Madeira, the Azores and the Cape Verde Islands. Their enterprise was infectious. Far to the north, merchants in the English port of Bristol were launching Atlantic expeditions of their own. Although the bulk of their trade was with Ireland and Bordeaux, it was contact with Portugal that had piqued their interest. They could hardly muscle in on Portugal's own explorations, of course, but there was nothing to stop Bristolians from exploring 'lost' lands of their own. They knew about Iceland and Greenland, with which

England had traded liberally during the Viking era. Earlier in the fifteenth century, with Denmark – now effectively Iceland's ruler – showing little interest in the north Atlantic, Bristol had re-established contact with Iceland, exchanging European goods for the air-dried cod known as 'stockfish', mostly during the summer months when trade with Bordeaux and Portugal, which consisted mostly of wine, olive oil and fruits, was at its lowest intensity. As the sailing prowess of Bristol's merchants matured, so their horizons grew. The island of Brazil, believed to be to the west of Ireland, was the subject of much speculation among Europe's communities of merchant-adventurers. Mentioned by Catalan and Italian cartographers, it was described by the Basque chronicler Lope García de Salazar in 1470 not only as a real island but also as the burial place of King Arthur, no less. Here was the fifteenth century in all its bewildering glory, imagining the island of Brazil as a place of expansionist dreams, of hard-headed ambitions, of the foundational chivalric myth-histories that underpinned the identity of Christendom itself.[4]

So, when a youthful Columbus moved from his native Genoa to the Portuguese port city of Lisbon in the mid-1470s, he was following a path already well-trodden by his countrymen. Attracted by the exploration of the west coast of Africa, many of Columbus's compatriots began to take up jobs in Portugal, a trend that reached a peak during the reign of the energetic João II (1481–95), whose commitment to Atlantic exploration was often used by Columbus as an example to put the Spanish monarchs, Isabel and Fernando, to shame.[5] Columbus was driven by more than the simple desire to make money. He was on a quest of his own – and Lisbon suited him just fine.

Columbus was already an experienced sailor. He knew the Tyrrhenian sea – that part of the Mediterranean bounded by the coastlines of Provence, western Italy and the islands of Corsica, Sardinia and Sicily – like the back of his hand.[6] In Lisbon he quickly found work and participated in sailing expeditions to Madeira in order to buy sugar as part of a business transaction with the prosperous Genoese Centurione firm. He also got to know the well-worn trade routes with the Canaries and the Azores.[7] These three archipelagos, far to the west of the European mainland and – in the case of the Canaries – off the north-west coast of Africa, were part of a wide circle of Atlantic trade. By the 1470s, they had turned into jumping-off points for more adventurous and ambitious sailors, traders and explorers. Columbus himself claimed to have gone 'a hundred leagues beyond' Iceland on one trip from Bristol, via Galway in Ireland; later he had gone as far south as the recently founded fort of São Jorge da Mina, in what is nowadays Ghana, where the Portuguese gold trade in Africa was concentrated.[8] For Columbus, as for many of his fellow sailors, the Atlantic – the 'Ocean Sea' as it was known at the time – was becoming a compulsion.

The great bullion famine of the fifteenth century,[9] which drove explorers to seek the support of cash-strapped monarchs across Europe, went hand in hand with a race for wonders and novelties. Adventurers took a keen delight in challenging received wisdom with fresh empirical knowledge. The Portuguese explorations down the 'Gold coast' of Africa, for example, had shown all ancient preconceptions about the alleged impenetrability of the 'torrid zone' for the nonsense that they were. Columbus was obviously influenced by such speculations and they might have played a part in his growing conviction that it was possible to sail to India across the Atlantic, but there is no evidence that this was in his mind during his time in Portugal. In any case, the interests of João II were far too focused on the African coast and the possibility of reaching India via the Cape of Good Hope. Columbus's transatlantic project began to take clearer shape in the early 1480s. By this time he was preoccupied with supporting his son Diego, born in 1479, around the time of Columbus's marriage to the Portuguese noblewoman Filipa Moniz Perestrelo. This took him to Andalusia where he came across the convent of La Rábida sometime in the mid-1480s. There he found something far more interesting than a place to shelter and educate his young son, for one of the leading astronomers and cosmographers of the period was living there at the time. He was Friar Antonio de Marchena, and he warmed at once to the Genoese explorer.

It was Marchena who persuaded Columbus that the Antipodes and the Amazons mentioned in various classical sources might indeed be real. He also encouraged him to read the second-century Alexandrian astronomer Claudius Ptolemy, who had argued that the world was a perfect sphere, containing one continuous land mass stretching from the west of Europe to the east of Asia. Columbus was naturally enthusiastic about this theory, but he remained stubbornly unpersuaded by the Alexandrian's view that the known world comprised exactly half the globe. If this was the case, then crossing the Atlantic was beyond the capabilities of any contemporary vessel. This was something that Columbus simply did not care to imagine. His 'solution' was astonishing as much for its naivety as for its assuredness. First, he dismissed Ptolemy's calculation on the basis of the theories of one Marinus of Tyre – a figure who, in a delicious irony, had only survived because Ptolemy had taken the trouble to dismiss his patently erroneous calculation. Second, he used the evidence provided by the thirteenth-century Venetian traveller Marco Polo – in a book written at the request of the great Mongol ruler Kublai Khan – to argue that all the descriptions he found in the Venetian's account pointed well beyond Ptolemy's proposed limits. As far as Columbus was concerned, Ptolemy was wrong: the 'Ocean Sea' was much smaller than most of his contemporaries supposed.

Marco Polo's writings fuelled Columbus's imagination in other ways. He inhaled their exotic evocation of thousands upon thousands of islands beyond the continent of Asia, including 'Cipangu' with its gilded and watered gardens, allegedly 1,500 miles off the coast of China.[10] The marginal annotations found in his copy of the book suggest that Columbus read it not so much as a source of facts as of marvels and wonders.[11] The same is true of the similarly detailed annotations found in his copy of *The Travels of Sir John Mandeville*. Even Pierre d'Ailly's *Ymago Mundi* and the *Historia rerum ubique gestarum* by Enea Silvio de' Piccolomini (Pope Pius II), both of which attracted Columbus's more scholarly interests, were plundered by him for what they revealed about Asia's gold, silver, pearls, amber and 'manifold marvels'.[12] Columbus dreamed big: and he dreamed of untold and fabulous riches – fabulous, that was, until he led the expedition that turned these stories into reality.

But how would he, in turn, realize his own ambitions? Such adventuring was unfeasible without the support of a powerful patron. Money alone was not enough. A private venture, funded by rich sponsors, would instantly falter in the event that the expedition in question discovered a new territory, for it would have no authority with which to lay claim to it. To make such a claim of ownership – or what in those days was referred to as *dominium* – and, just as importantly, to defend that claim against hostile foreign princes, explorers needed the backing, as well as the funds, of a powerful sovereign state. Royal patronage, Columbus knew, was of the essence.

In later life he would claim that the choice of Castile had been entirely providential – a 'miracle' brought about by God's 'manifest hand' against competing offers from Portugal, France and England to sponsor him.[13] The reality was rather different, for there is no evidence of any interest in Columbus's plans, let alone offers of sponsorship by those other monarchies. Even in Castile, the progress he made proved frustratingly slow. It is true that Andalusia was showing great potential from Columbus's perspective. His own compatriots had been settling there in such droves that, by the late fifteenth century, more than half the nobility of Seville had Genoese surnames.[14] Isabel and Fernando had not been slow to take advantage of this regional dynamism. Since the mid-1470s they had been issuing licences to Andalusian privateers, seeking to encourage them to break into the lucrative Portuguese monopoly of trade in the Gulf of Guinea. A flurry of activity ensued during which the wealth of the Canaries proved increasingly enticing. In 1483 Andalusian privateers, among whom the Genoese of Seville and Cádiz were especially conspicuous, conquered Grand Canaria. La Palma and Tenerife (respectively conquered much later, in 1493 and 1496) would have followed swiftly, had Isabel and Fernando not been distracted by more pressing priorities in the mainland.

The fame of Isabel and Fernando, solidly based as it is on their many impressive achievements, should not make us forget how weak and precarious their circumstances were during the early years of the reign. When in December 1474 Henry IV of Castile died, his crown was contested by his daughter Juana – backed by Portugal – and his half-sister Isabel. Civil war soon broke out. The four-year-long conflict led to the definitive union of the kingdoms of Aragon and Castile. 'Spain' was now to be Castile and Aragon, *not* Castile and Portugal. With the civil war over, Portugal safely at bay, and their respective titles to the thrones of Castile and Aragon now beyond dispute (Fernando had succeeded his father, John II of Aragon, in 1479), the priority of the monarchs was to consolidate the new but still frail union of the two kingdoms as one. This called for an initiative that would bring about the final reunification of the whole kingdom under the aegis of the Christian faith. So it is hardly a surprise that in 1482 Isabel and Fernando turned their attention away from the Canaries and decided to concentrate on the war against Granada. If successful, the war would at last wrest the southern kingdom from Islamic control – and the monarchs could only see Muslims as an enemy within and potential allies of the encroaching Ottoman Turks. But it was a demanding and expensive enterprise, one that – as it turned out – would absorb the energy of the monarchs and that of the bulk of the Castilian aristocracy for the next ten years.

In the event, the long and costly campaign would immeasurably aid Columbus's prospects. In the settlement of the civil war, Castile had been excluded from the gold-prospecting grounds around the mouth of the Volta river (in what is now Ghana), which remained under Portuguese control. Now the war against Granada created a further and even more urgent need for alternative sources of gold, for it entailed the loss of the tribute that the monarchs had traditionally collected from the Islamic enclave. During the 1480s Columbus was only too aware of these propitious circumstances and he took particular care to keep his options open. He kept an eye on Castile as well as Portugal. He flirted with rich aristocrats like the Duke of Medina Sidonia or the Count of Medinaceli, both of whom had invested large sums of money in the conquest of the Canaries and the evolving sugar industry there. He played hard to get, threatening to take his project elsewhere: now to France, now to England. In late spring 1486 his strategy began to pay off. Isabel and Fernando even offered to meet Columbus's expenses, often as a member of their itinerant court. In the following year he presented his project to a panel of experts commissioned by the monarchs and chaired by Isabel's Hieronymite confessor, Friar Hernando de Talavera, the future Archbishop of Granada. Assessing it, the panel was sceptical and, in September 1487, royal support duly dried up. Now, Columbus had little option but to look elsewhere: in 1488 he again turned his attention to Portugal and then sent his younger brother Bartolomé to England and France the following year.[15]

Little is known about the actual views expressed by the panel of experts other than that, as Rodrigo Maldonado de Talavera, who had until recently taught law at the prestigious University of Salamanca, put it, 'all agreed that what the Admiral argued could not possibly be true'.[16] The lack of evidence has since generated a good number of nonsensical conjectures, among which is the absurd but strangely persistent canard that the members of the panel thought the world was flat. Yet the widespread image of Columbus during these years as the romantic hero of a lone and resolute struggle against ignorant and derisive forces is not remotely in line with the available evidence. For although he was now looking elsewhere for patronage, his time at the Castilian court had not been wasted. During these years, indeed, he had succeeded in winning the support of influential groups of power brokers and financiers whose lobbying at Isabel and Fernando's court would ultimately prove irresistible. Many, unsurprisingly, were Columbus's own countrymen.

Foremost among them was the powerful Genoese group that had lent its support to Alonso de Quintanilla, Isabel and Fernando's most influential financial strategist during the conquest of the Canaries. Also in their midst were members of the Rivarolo and Pinelli families, who would figure prominently as Columbus's sponsors, and some non-Genoese investors like the Florentine Gianotto Berardi. Columbus also managed to ingratiate himself with members of the court of the young heir to the throne, Prince Juan. He did this through his friendship with the prince's tutor, the Dominican friar Diego de Deza – who would eventually become inquisitor-general and Archbishop of Seville – and with the prince's nurse, Juana Torres de Ávila, who would prove a useful asset in Columbus's dealings with Isabel. A further influential group of contacts included his good friend from La Rábida, Friar Antonio de Marchena, who was now claiming the rare and somewhat questionable honour of actually believing Columbus's calculations. Another of La Rábida's guardians was one of Isabel's close advisors, Friar Juan Pérez, whose intervention with the queen in 1491 would be decisive in securing for Columbus a further audience with her. By this time, he had also managed to win the support of Luis de Santángel, a treasury official of the Crown of Aragon with a firm foot in Castile through his contacts with the royal financial strategist Quintanilla. Santángel was exceptionally useful to Columbus, drawing up a convincing plan with carefully worked-out calculations that enabled the Genoese to present a financially viable project to the monarchs, one which was, moreover, sharply focused on Asia as the exclusive goal.

Columbus had clearly realized that Isabel and Fernando were unenthusiastic about the prospect of searching for the Antipodes or any other undiscovered islands populated by Amazons. Exploring for its own sake was all very well, but what the monarchs really needed was cash: access to the lucrative, gold- and spice-rich markets of Asia. As Columbus had become all too aware during his time lobbying for access to the Catholic monarchs, Fernando had a longstanding interest in the trade routes to the Orient – and in Fernando's mind, money, commerce and

God were inextricably linked. The king's piety found its most charac-teristic expression in his ambition to conquer Jerusalem. This was no mere pious hope: the Aragonese monarch had inherited a rightful claim to the title of King of Jerusalem after his grandfather, Alfonso V, known as 'the Magnanimous', conquered Naples in 1443. Given that Jerusa-lem had been treated as a tributary to the crown of Naples since the late thirteenth century, Alfonso's conquest gave renewed power to the mil-lenarian prophecies of Arnau de Vilanova. A thirteenth-century Aragonese polymath, Vilanova had foretold that the monarchs of Aragon were destined to conquer Jerusalem, following which a sequence of events would lead to a universal Christian empire that would lay the groundwork for the second coming of Christ.[17]

Vilanova's own source of inspiration was the late-medieval chiliastic tradition epitomized in the writings of the twelfth-century Calabrian Cistercian abbot, Joachim of Fiore. Joachimism, as the movement would come to be known, had had a profound impact on early Franciscan spir-ituality, which in the late fifteenth century was undergoing a revival among the group of Franciscans of La Rábida whom Columbus had befriended. During his time at the Spanish court, moreover, Columbus came to appreciate the power of Fernando's commitment to the conquest of Jerusalem. Courtiers hailed Fernando in unmistakably crusading terms as a potential 'Last World Emperor'. Among them was Isabel's court composer, Juan de Anchieta, author of a motet about a vision of the coronation of the monarchs by the pope in front of the Holy Sepulchre.[18] As the war against Granada progressed, so this imperial cult around Fernando strengthened. By 1485, after the strategically important capture of Ronda, a city long considered 'impregnable',[19] the monarchs felt ready to begin to put pressure on the pope to grant them some signal reward for their efforts on behalf of the faith.

The reward came in a papal bull dated 13 December 1486. In it, Pope Innocent VIII granted Isabel and Fernando the notorious *patro-nato real*: the right of patronage and presentation, which effectively meant the right of the monarchs to appoint whomever they wished to any major ecclesiastical benefices established in any territories they might conquer. This was a unique privilege, one that would never have been granted had the pope had any inkling of what was about to hap-pen. Isabel and Fernando, of course, would have no qualms about extending the *patronato* by degrees to all their dominions. They also began to be seen by many as the long-awaited monarchs destined to destroy all the enemies of the Christian faith,[20] so it is understandable that in the late 1480s, still unsure about the support of the monarchs, Columbus began to insist that any profits derived from his proposed voyage should be devoted to the conquest of Jerusalem. It was in this unmistakably medieval, crusading spirit that we should understand the build-up towards what would soon become known as 'the enterprise of the Indies'.[21]

In the autumn of 1491, Isabel and Fernando's court and army were stationed at Santa Fe, six miles west of Granada. This austere town had been built quickly, in a mere eighty days, in the shape of a gridiron within a cross, by soldiers under instruction from the monarchs. Today, over the entrance to the sixteenth-century church of Santa María de la Encarnación, there remains a sculpture of a lance next to the words *Ave Maria*. It was carved in memory of Hernán Pérez del Pulgar, known to his contemporaries as *el de las hazañas* – 'he of the valiant deeds'. He had famously entered Granada in secret a year before the final conquest in order to pin a parchment, with his own dagger, inscribed with those very words – *Ave Maria* – over the entrance to the main mosque.[22]

Pérez del Pulgar was only one of many outstanding leaders of the Granada wars. Also among them was Rodrigo Ponce de León, Duke of Cádiz, who had captured the rich city of Alhama in 1482, and was immortalized by his contemporary, the chronicler Andrés Bernáldez, as the epitome of chivalric honour, generosity and courtesy.[23] The Granada wars captured the crusading imagination of knights throughout the Iberian peninsula and beyond. They also imbued the heterogeneous mass of the Castilian population with a sense of purpose and an esprit de corps that were as impressive as they were unexpected. The Italian historian Peter Martyr d'Anghiera, chaplain to the Catholic monarchs, was dumbfounded at this display of unity. 'Who would have believed,' he exclaimed, 'that Asturians, Galicians, Basques and Cantabrians, men accustomed to deeds of atrocious violence and to domestic brawls that they initiate on the basis of the silliest pretext', should mingle quite amicably, 'not only amongst themselves but also with Toledans and temperamental and jealous Andalusians, and live together in harmony as members of one family, speaking one language and acquiescent to a common discipline?'[24]

This discipline was all too evident in the final stages of the war, marked by a methodical succession of campaigns carefully geared to cope with the mountainous nature of the terrain. It was primarily a war of sieges, with infantry and artillery – rather than cavalry – playing the key role. With its skirmishes and surprise attacks, the experience allowed Castilian soldiers to develop not only a peculiarly individualistic style of warfare but also a remarkable ability to endure extremes of heat and cold, attributes that would make them such a formidable proposition on the battlefields of Europe and the New World.[25]

This sense of unity and common purpose could not have contrasted more sharply with the internal feuds that rent the Nasrid kingdom of Granada. As Isabel and Fernando confidently prepared for the final assault on Granada from their stronghold in Santa Fe, dismay spread across the Islamic bastion. With it came the realization that an honourable surrender would be preferable to the humiliation of what was now looking like inevitable military conquest. Nasrid foreboding lay at the heart of the negotiations that began in October 1491. Terms were quickly agreed the following month, and Granada finally surrendered on 2 January 1492, when the Nasrid ruler Boabdil, in a gesture whose symbolism was lost on no one, personally presented Fernando with the keys to the Alhambra.

The exhilarating sense of divine favour that spread across the peninsula in the wake of the Christian conquest of Granada is impossible to overstate. The culmination of centuries of struggle, the conquest brought with it a profound conviction that the kingdom of Castile had been entrusted with a divine mission to protect Christendom from the advancing threat of Islam. The sentiment gave renewed impetus to that sense of questing adventure captured in the chivalric romances that were consumed at court and by an increasingly literate public. One of the best of these – the 'best book of its kind in the world', according to Miguel de Cervantes[26] – was the Valencian knight Joanot Martorell's *Tirant lo Blanch*, whose popularity was given an added boost by the new technology of print. Published in 1490, it was the first of a myriad of such romances to be printed in Spain over the next century. The staggering popularity of these works indicates a society in which reading was becoming much more of a leisure habit than a scholarly pursuit, even though books were still largely regarded as objects to be read aloud.

Chivalric romances also reflected a world in which political frontiers were much looser than we tend to assume. There was nothing local or circumscribed about chivalry, which was a supranational cultural phenomenon.[27] Even in Arthurian Britain, which overwhelmingly provided the setting for these works, chivalry was part of an international court culture. It had arrived with the Normans from the disorderly society of the post-Carolingian world of the tenth century, where the focus of political life was not the sovereign kingdom but the fragmented feudal states to which it had given way, fiefdoms carved out by military adventurers and rebellious vassals. Gradually, the duchies of Normandy, Burgundy, Flanders, Champagne, Blois and Anjou came to play a role in medieval Europe comparable to that played by the Greek city states in antiquity or the Italian principalities during the Renaissance.[28] In the process, the blatantly un-Christian code of honour and the spirit of revenge that had characterized the early feudal world were gradually transformed. The tribal bonds of kin and the law of the blood feud remained dominant, but the new society was now also imbued with a sense of a wider spiritual loyalty that transcended blood ties. The knight had become a consecrated person in whom loyalty to the warlord could find its natural completion in the defence of the Church alongside the widow and the orphan.

By the fifteenth century, the romances of chivalry came to define a new idea of nobility. Their unique blend of savagery, courtesy and virtue was the result of a creative tension at the heart of medieval culture between the secular ideal of courtly love, on the one hand, and the austere and otherworldly values of the crusading era, on the other. The tension was reflected well in the dualism at the heart of the work of writers like Geoffrey of Monmouth and Chrétien de Troyes in, for instance, the sharp contrast between the knights Lancelot and Galahad: a worldly and adulterous chivalry on the one hand, and a virtuous and heavenly quest for the Holy Grail on the other.

It is tempting to see in this tension an incompatible divergence between a concern with lineage and a concern with virtue, between gentility and social exclusiveness on the one hand, and the obligations to uphold justice through the protection of the poor, the widow and the orphan on the other.[29] But this would be a crass anachronism. In fact, the moral code at the heart of the romances saw no opposition between lineage and virtue, or, indeed, between humility and magnanimity. Far

from being mutually exclusive, humility and magnanimity were partners in their opposition to the vices of pride and pusillanimity. What the
truly magnanimous knight despised, in other words, was not anything
that he perceived as inferior to himself. Rather, it was petty-mindedness.[30]
It comes as no surprise that the woman who persuades the 'ignoble'
Melibee to become 'magnanimous' in Chaucer's *Canterbury Tales* is
none other than Dame Prudence, a sentiment that would be eloquently
captured and transmitted to the world of the Renaissance by the humanist scholar Giovane Buonaccorso da Montemagno (1391?–1429), among
others.[31]

These long descriptions of barely conceivable exploits by knightly
heroes in exotic and enchanted lands inhabited by monsters and wonders, presented to the reader a new notion of human existence in which
virtue and passion acquired a transcendent character.[32] They exerted a
profound influence on the ethics and ideas of the age – but they were
also a reflection of it, and the tensions that seem like clear contradictions to the modern mind were easily reconciled. Columbus himself
had the age's characteristic concern with lineage. Sometime between
1477 and 1480 he had married Filipa Moniz Perestrelo. This was a
huge social leap forward for Columbus, the son of a Genoese weaver.
Filipa descended, on her mother's side, from a family of upwardly
mobile landholders with a good record of service to the Portuguese
Crown. Her father, Bartolomeo Perestrelo, had been honoured with the
grant of the fief of Porto Santo – admittedly a small and remote island,
but it served to show Columbus the kind of rewards that could be
obtained by royal service.[33] The same spirit had been splendidly per-
sonified in the legendary Count Pero Niño, immortalized by Gutierre
Díez de Games as a knight whose greatest battles were fought at sea
and who was never vanquished in either love or war. The tradition was
still a source of inspiration at the time of Columbus.[34] Although we
have no evidence that he ever read any work of maritime chivalry, it
would be impossible to think of his life's work, and, indeed, of the
evocative groups of islands that he would lovingly place in his coat of
arms, without reference to this genre.

But on his journey back to La Rábida, Columbus had different
worries in mind. Would all his dreams and ambitions come to nothing?
Of all the cases presented by plaintiffs at Isabel and Fernando's court,
his own must have looked especially hopeful: after the conquest of

Granada, what was there to stop the monarchs from granting his request? Exasperatingly, however, yet another panel of experts summoned by the monarchs during his visit to Granada had declared itself against him. And then, almost miraculously, after Columbus had ridden for a day, a rushing royal messenger caught up with him and urged him to return to Isabel and Fernando's camp in Granada. Something had changed their minds.

Informing the monarchs' caution towards Columbus's plans was their awareness of a delicate issue that the conquest of Granada had brought to light. If Spain was now in theory unified under one faith, there remained one obvious group of non-Christians whose presence began to look ever more incongruous in the new dispensation. When, centuries before, other European states had expelled their Jews – England in 1290, France in 1306 – Spain had refused to follow their example. Yet by the second half of the fourteenth century, the devastating combined impact of the Black Death and Spain's involvement in the Hundred Years' War had given rise to social tensions that erupted in urban violence. As usual, the Jews became scapegoats. Compounding the problem was the size of Spain's Jewish population, then the largest in the world;[35] their concentration in the larger urban centres; and their enviable success as merchants, traders, artisans, financiers and doctors.[36]

These factors help to explain the speed with which, in 1391, one of the most horrifying of medieval anti-Jewish pogroms spread across the Iberian Peninsula. Many Jews tried to escape from the big cities into the relative anonymity of smaller villages and rural communities. Those who chose to stay in the larger cities often only managed to survive by converting to Christianity.[37] From the perspective of the Christians, the rise in the number of conversions after 1391 made good sense. As was widely emphasized, especially by the members of the mendicant orders, if faith and reason went together, then when reason was properly applied the truth of Christianity would become irresistible.[38] This had been the aim of the most charismatic preacher of the time, the Dominican friar St Vincent Ferrer, a formidable driving force behind the conversions of thousands of Jews and Muslims during the 1410s.

Yet the unprecedented number of conversions did not take long to begin to generate further, often even more intractable, problems. For the Jewish converts – *conversos* as they were known – continued to be disproportionately successful in Iberian society. What was more, while *conversos* naturally preserved many of their old Jewish contacts and traditions, their new Christian faith meant they were now free to join the ranks of the nobility and the Church hierarchy, where they rapidly became influential. The resentment shown against Jews in the fourteenth century began to be directed against *conversos* in the fifteenth, and it would express itself all the more bitterly because *conversos* seemed to have usurped many of the privileges and prerogatives that in the past had been the preserve of those who now began to refer to themselves as 'Old Christians'.[39]

Inevitably, the pogroms flared up again. They culminated in a number of horrific riots and massacres throughout Spain in the 1460s and 1470s, coinciding with the civil war over the disputed succession of Isabel of Castile. After the war was settled in Isabel's favour in 1475 – and, especially, after her 1477 visit to Seville, where she heard the Dominican friar Alonso de Hojeda preach about the alleged dangers posed by the large number of 'false' *conversos* – the monarchs began seriously to consider the need to establish a national Inquisition, which began its activities in 1480 with the remit of dealing precisely with the problem of false *conversos*. Yet Isabel and Fernando desperately needed the backing of both *conversos* and the kingdom's remaining Jews. Indeed, the monarchs had received vital financial support from many Jews during the campaign against Granada. The eminent Jew Samuel Abulafia was in charge of supplies for the Christian troops; Abulafia's colleagues at court included the Rabbi Abraham Seneor and the distinguished scholar Isaac Abravanel.[40] Moreover, the political support that the monarchs had received during the civil war had come primarily from the urban governing classes, among whom there was a clear *converso* presence.

By all accounts, the monarchs regarded the Inquisition as a temporary emergency measure, intended to ensure religious orthodoxy. Soon, however, the sheer complexity of the problem began to overwhelm even those who had supported the initiative, among whom, perhaps not surprisingly, were a large number of *conversos* who assumed that the new institution would help to resolve their situation. To begin with, most of the inquisitors appointed in the 1480s possessed a very inadequate knowledge of Jewish religious practices. They therefore often became easy instruments of a judicial system in which social pressures and prejudices were given too much weight. The Inquisition's acceptance of anonymous denunciations during the early years often made it almost impossible for those accused of 'Judaizing' to prove their innocence. Not surprisingly, many *conversos* began to use their considerable influence in city councils to obstruct the work of inquisitors. Then, from the mid-1480s, city councillors and local officials began largely to disregard Crown policy and to implement openly anti-Jewish ordinances, arguing that it was the Jews rather than the 'new Christians' who needed to be removed from positions of influence. In the process, *conversos* managed to enlist the support of a significant proportion of 'Old Christians' among urban oligarchies resentful of the continuing protection afforded to Jews by Isabel and Fernando. The relentless passage of anti-Jewish ordinances by city councillors throughout Spain led to a process of expulsions of Jews from many towns and provinces. The problem became so intractable and the anti-Jewish opinion so pervasive that the monarchs were pushed reluctantly to take the most radical option. On 30 March 1492, barely three months after the final conquest of Granada and going against their natural inclinations, they issued an edict ordering the departure, within three months, of all Jews in their dominions who refused to convert to Christianity.[41]

This calamitous decision came exactly a month before the monarchs finally agreed to support Columbus's Atlantic project. At long last, Columbus could reap the benefits of years of pleading and feel relieved to see the end of Isabel and Fernando's cautious trepidations. He could also afford to reassure his sovereigns: Granada had been conquered and the situation of the Jews resolved, at least in theory. Both the long war against Granada and the forced departure of some of the monarchy's staunchest financial supporters had left the treasury depleted. Why not prioritize a venture that could conceivably bring much-needed wealth? Besides, the project was of crucially strategic importance in the crusade against Islam: it would bring Castile into contact with Asia, whose inhabitants were still widely believed to be willing to help Christians in their struggle against Islam. The tradition went back a long way and was vividly captured in the legend of Prester John, a mythical figure whose support could now be invoked against the threat of the Ottoman Turks.[42] As Columbus had repeatedly insisted, the project might include plans to return to Spain via Jerusalem, thus opening a rear route of attack. From this perspective, Columbus couched Isabel and Fernando's long-awaited support for his project as an act of gratitude to God for the victory in Granada. At long last, the monarchs were free to renew their commitment to the unfinished business of the war against Islam, a clear divine calling for which Castile was uniquely well equipped.

Columbus felt so confident, in fact, that he proposed to the monarchs exceptionally ambitious conditions. Foremost among them was the request, in perpetuity, of the post of governor-general and viceroy of any newly discovered territories for himself and his descendants. This amounted to a right to set up feudal domains in any overseas possessions – precisely the sort of thing that Isabel and Fernando had been trying to prevent in Castile since they emerged victorious in the civil war and realized the importance of promoting the interests of towns against the seigneurial demands of the aristocracy.[43] Not surprisingly, the monarchs came up with a very different plan. In drawing up their agreement with Columbus, they reached for a set of practices that had been well tested during the *Reconquista* and the occupation of the Canaries, when it had become customary for the Crown to make contracts with leaders of expeditions. These binding contracts, agreed directly with the Crown, known as *capitulaciones* ('chapters' or conditions present in the contract), reserved rights for the Crown in any new territory while guaranteeing to those who undertook to lead the expeditions their due rewards (*mercedes*). Expedition leaders would expect to enjoy the spoils of conquest, grants of land and even a title of nobility. The last of these usually came after the conferment of special military powers and rights of government over a certain territory, normally accompanied by a hereditary title on the basis of which the holders became known as *adelantados* (an untranslatable term meaning 'those who go forward'). These very considerable powers were highly attractive to potential explorers. As a proviso, the monarchs were always careful to underline that expeditions were primarily undertaken for the purpose of spreading the Christian faith, and that the *capitulación* was their only legal basis. The *capitulaciones*, moreover, safeguarded the rights of the monarchs – regarded as the fountainheads of justice – over any emerging feudal enclaves. Thus Isabel and Fernando took careful steps to avoid any insubordination by insisting upon the Crown's fundamental right to organize any distribution of land among the settlers of the new territories, and by making all the rights and privileges of new towns built in them directly dependent upon a royal charter.

Columbus had to content himself with the title of Grand Admiral and a right to a tenth of any produce or merchandise in an agreement signed on 30 April 1492. It was still a very substantial concession which meant that, in effect, what the monarchs had granted him was not strictly speaking a *capitulación*. So, for the time being, Columbus was happy to swallow the pill, but he never abandoned his original ambitions. In the 'Prologue' to his account of the first voyage, for example, he included a pointed reminder to Isabel and Fernando that they had agreed to 'ennoble' him, and that from that day forward he was to be called 'Don' and 'High Admiral of the Ocean Sea and Viceroy and Governor in perpetuity' of any territories he might discover. If this was not enough, Columbus insisted that his eldest son should succeed him and his heirs 'from generation to generation, for ever and ever'.[44]

These were privileges of an unmistakably feudal nature. Columbus thought that he had a solid legal basis for claiming them. After all, what had been signed on 30 April was not so much a *capitulación* as a letter of privilege, and therefore revocable. By insisting on them after the success of his first voyage, however, the Admiral only succeeded in making the monarchs apprehensive and increasingly disposed to attempt to curtail his powers. The episode marked the beginning of an arduous struggle between a reforming monarchy and the remnants of a feudal military aristocracy to which, ironically, Columbus did not even remotely belong. But all these trials lay in the future. On 30 April 1492, Columbus could at last begin the preparations for an adventure that would soon be described as 'the greatest event since the creation of the world, excluding the Incarnation and Death of Him Who created it'.[45]

2

The Admiral

Just over three months were to pass between the signing of Columbus's long-coveted contract with Isabel and Fernando, and the morning of 3 August 1492, when he sailed out of the port of Palos de la Frontera on the coast of Huelva. There was still a high degree of scepticism about the feasibility of the adventure, especially since most experts knew Columbus's calculations about the size of the globe to be chimerical. Not surprisingly, the monarchs had assumed that the project would be met with widespread indifference, so, in order to help their newly named Admiral recruit an adequate crew, they promised to issue a royal pardon to any condemned man willing to join the proposed expedition to Asia. In the event, such guarantees proved unnecessary. To their surprise, the three Pinzón brothers – the most prestigious sailors along the coast of Huelva – were persuaded by Columbus and signed up. Their presence on the expedition was enough to bring others flocking to the Admiral; so, he had reached his quota. The expedition was small: three cramped, ill-equipped vessels with a combined capacity of ninety men. The *Santa María* was the largest of the three, albeit not by much, and was assigned to Columbus's command. The other two we know by their nicknames: the *Niña* (literally 'girl' but so called because her owner was one Juan Niño), and the *Pinta*, probably referring to her captain, one of the Pinzón brothers, Martín.

In addition to the usual provisions common on most Mediterranean voyages – wine, water and olive oil, biscuit and flour, bacon and salt fish – the Admiral loaded a great store of trinkets which he hoped to exchange for Asian gold and spices.[1] The three caravels sailed swiftly along the familiar route to the Canaries. Once there, they replenished their provisions, and made running repairs, hoping that they would suffice for what was likely to be the longest open sea voyage in recorded

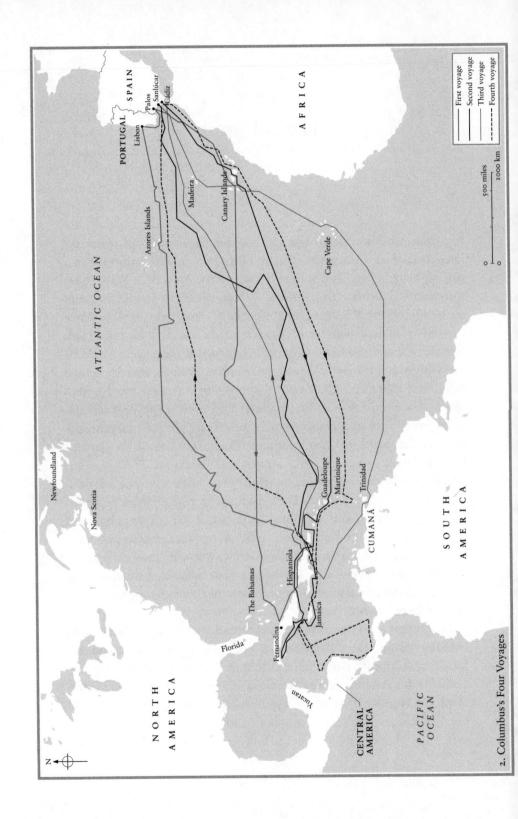

2. Columbus's Four Voyages

history. The *Pinta*'s rudder was replaced and Columbus gave instructions to convert the *Niña* to square rigging, which was more efficient in high seas. He then waited for favourable winds until the morning of 6 September when he raised sail out of El Hierro and into the unknown.[2]

The Admiral was determined to maintain a westerly direction until he struck land. The most logical way to do this, following contemporary navigational practice, was to keep the sun during the day and the Pole Star during the night at a constant angle of elevation. But Columbus was also determined to collect as much evidence as possible to confirm his theories. He not only used a chart (which was utterly pointless in uncharted seas), but also tried to take readings of latitude while verifying them by timing the length of the solar day. He clearly expected to be able to verify his theory of the relatively small size of the globe. The mistakes he made in his calculations correspond to a method of trying to work out the length of the day by reference to the hours of sunlight, and then reading this alleged latitude into the charts he had prepared on the basis of Pierre d'Ailly's *Ymago Mundi*.[3]

But Columbus was not a complete crank. He also kept a careful eye on the Pole Star and made a series of observations, meticulously recorded, of the difference between the direction suggested by the compass needle and that indicated by the position of the Pole Star. He was naturally very familiar with a slight variation to the east, which had long been observed in the Mediterranean; but then, on 13 September, he recorded a slight variation in both directions. From 17 September onward he began to notice a strong and very puzzling variation to the west. His immediate response was to try to begin to take readings when the Pole Star was at its most westerly position. On 30 September he wrote, with a strength of conviction only matched by the utterly erroneous nature of his conclusion, that 'the Star of the North moves, just like the all the other stars, but the compass needle always points in the same direction'.[4]

This authoritative tone belies nagging doubts that had been distracting the Admiral for some time. From around 10 September, in order to reassure his increasingly anxious and potentially mutinous crew, he had been manipulating the ship's log, deliberately undercutting the distance the caravels had travelled. When, on 22 September, an adverse wind hit the vessels he exclaimed with some relief: 'I was glad because I could now persuade the crew that there were indeed winds in those seas by which we could return to Spain.'[5] This, however, was little consolation to a crew who had good reasons to doubt the Admiral's faith in the 'map of islands', and whose hopes had by this time been repeatedly dashed by a number of phoney landfalls. In early October, Columbus had a tense meeting with Martín Pinzón, now increasingly under pressure from a crew he had largely recruited himself. Pinzón was sharply aware that, according to the Admiral's own calculations, they ought by then to have found land. He urged Columbus to change course to the south-west in the hope of finding the island of Cipangu. At first Columbus refused, arguing that it was 'better to go to the mainland first'.[6] Had he not eventually given in to Pinzón, the caravels would have taken them to Florida, and to a rather different future. In the event, after observing the flight of a flock of seabirds, Columbus altered the course to the south-west on 7 October. Finally, at two o'clock on the morning of Friday 12 October, with the crew on the brink of despair, an ecstatic cry of 'land, land!' from the crow's nest of the *Pinta* was answered on all three vessels with sighs of relief and joyful acts of thanksgiving to God.[7]

The Admiral's ships finally made landfall on one of the many islands off the north-east coast of Cuba, naming it San Salvador, in honour of Our Lord. Which island it was, is impossible to know for sure. All we know is that its inhabitants, whom Columbus described as 'naked people', called it something that sounded like 'Guanahaní'.[8] Nor do we know for certain which islands he explored in the days that followed, naming them – with an impeccable sense of priority – Santa María de la Concepción, in honour of Our Lady, and Isabela, after his patron, the Queen of Castile.[9] But there is no doubting that the great mass of land he came across on 24 October – which he immediately identified with 'Cipangu' and which he would eventually name Fernandina, after his other patron, Fernando of Aragon – was in fact Cuba. When it quickly became clear that what he saw there did not coincide with what he had read about Cipangu, Columbus optimistically persuaded himself that he had in fact reached the Asian mainland of 'Cathay', even dispatching an embassy, with a 'Chaldean-speaking' interpreter, to seek the court of the Great Khan.[10]

On 20 November, some days after the embassy had returned from its fruitless mission, an increasingly despondent Pinzón sailed off – without leave from Columbus and to his great chagrin – on a quest for gold. Three days later, Columbus, equally frustrated at the realization that this new land was not Cathay, began to look for a favourable wind to get away from Cuba. The wind came at last on 5 December. With a sudden – and, as it turned out, extremely fortunate – change of direction, the wind blew him to an island called Haiti, 'the mountainous land'. The Admiral renamed it La Española ('The Spanish One') – latinized as Hispaniola. His disappointment at finding that, again, the new island bore no resemblance to Cipangu was soon alleviated by the discovery of abundant sources of gold, and of inhabitants who enjoyed a relatively advanced way of life in comparison to what he had observed in Cuba. There was even some evidence of sophistication and wealth, and Columbus was quick to establish a strong personal link with the local chief (*cacique*), the charismatic Guacanagarí, who seems to have developed a soft spot for the trinkets that Columbus had brought with him. Although he had failed to find any convincing trace of China, Hispaniola filled the Admiral with hope. With characteristic hyperbole, he claimed that it was bigger than Castile and Aragon combined; in reality, it was a fraction of the size. He had collected many samples of gold, discovered the pineapple, the hammock, the canoe and 'some leaves which the Indians esteem very much' – a clear reference to tobacco. True, the new island was not Cipangu, but in Columbus's words it was nonetheless a 'marvel', reminiscent of the land of Sheba or of those exotic regions from where the Magi had brought their gifts to the baby Jesus.[11]

With all these assets, Columbus began to make definite plans to return to Spain. In one of his last attempts to gather gold and spices, however, the *Santa María* struck a sandbank in the middle of the night of 24 December and was damaged beyond repair. The haste with which the Admiral decided to erect a stockade in the north of the island, at what was to become Puerto Navidad (Christmas Port, so named because of the date of the wreckage), with the use of the timber amassed from the damaged ship itself, has led some historians to believe that the plan was premeditated.[12] But this is sheer speculation. The event nonetheless gave Columbus the opportunity of appointing thirty-nine men to garrison the stockade. He instructed them to remain there, collecting gold samples while awaiting a new expedition from Castile. With the *Santa María* now out of circulation for good, the men could hardly object to the plan.[13]

Meanwhile, Martín Pinzón had also been busy exploring the island

and rejoined the expedition on 6 January 1493. Columbus's anger at his insubordination was tempered when he realized that Pinzón had also found plenty of gold as well as pods of chilli and cinnamon, which raised the Admiral's hopes about the existence of exotic spices. Pinzón also claimed to have been told about the existence of extensive pearl fisheries further south. Although the rift between the two men was never healed, ten days later they were seaborne again. The weather was fair. On board the *Niña*, Columbus sailed north in search of the westerlies – the Atlantic winds that, blowing from west to east, would take them home – followed by the Pinzón brothers in the *Pinta*. Picking up these winds on 5 February, they swiftly made their way towards the Portuguese-ruled Azores. Soon after, however, near-disaster struck: Columbus and the *Niña* got lost, then ran into a storm that split up the small fleet. On 18 February a dishevelled *Niña* made it into the harbour of Santa Maria in the Azores, but there was no trace of the *Pinta*.[14] With tensions between Castile and Portugal running high, Columbus had little choice but to continue his journey despite the threatening weather. After a brush with the Portuguese authorities – ten of Columbus's crew, going ashore to give thanks at the nearest Marian shrine, were briefly arrested – the Admiral set sail again. An ill wind took him straight to Lisbon where, exhausted, he had little choice but to disembark on 4 March.

King João quickly had Columbus detained, attempting to use him as a diplomatic pawn in negotiations with Castile: the Portuguese king wanted to make concessions in the Atlantic to Castile, in exchange for the unequivocal respect of Portugal's rights in west Africa. A week later, after Columbus agreed to try to persuade Isabel and Fernando to accept João's proposal, he was allowed to leave. On 15 March he arrived back in Palos to find the *Pinta* already there. Escaping the storm, the vessel had limped into the northern Galician port of Baiona, near Vigo, before, remarkably, returning to Palos on the same day as Columbus. We do not know how the Admiral felt about this, but any sense of relief was probably mixed with a feeling of apprehension. After all, Pinzón had a claim to have discovered Haiti before Columbus and could use his knowledge of the existence of pearl fisheries to mount a convincing challenge to Columbus's own claims. As it turned out, Pinzón had obviously suffered much more from the crossing, for even before he had had time to tell his story, he was dead. His two brothers survived him, but they seem to have been more tolerant of Columbus's ambitions. With nobody to contradict him, the Admiral styled himself 'Don Cristóbal Colón, Admiral of the Ocean Sea, Viceroy and Governor of the Islands he discovered in the Indies', and set off to the royal court, currently residing in Barcelona.

Isabel and Fernando received Columbus magnificently. Yet, the questions and doubts provoked by the evidence he brought back with him were overwhelming. Most educated people rightly refused to abandon the traditional estimates of the size of the globe. They could not, therefore, concede that Columbus could possibly have reached Asia, as he still claimed and continued to do until his dying day. His close friend, the priest and chronicler Andrés Bernáldez, told the Admiral that he could have sailed 'another twelve hundred leagues' without reaching it.[15] On the other hand, the samples he had brought back with him – not least of them, a group of suitably feathered natives – were enough to persuade the monarchs that Columbus had discovered something of importance. Accordingly, they granted him the honour to sit in their presence, and to ride beside them at ceremonies and in procession. These were significant marks of favour, and courtiers, following the lead of their sovereigns, scrambled to praise Columbus, comparing him to a deified ancient hero, and even to one of Christ's apostles, doing in the west what St Thomas, who was widely believed to have been responsible for the evangelization of India, had done in the east.[16] In return, the monarchs expected Columbus to deliver on the promise of his first voyage.

Late that May, Isabel and Fernando authorized Columbus to prepare a much larger and grander expedition than the one that had first taken him across the Atlantic the previous year. By the time he set off on his second voyage, on 25 September 1493, Columbus had amassed an impressive fleet of seventeen vessels – including the well-tested *Niña*, which he would now command himself. He was accompanied by his youngest brother Giacomo – much better known by his Spanish name, Diego Colón.[17] Many thought the voyage a risk worth taking: over 1,300 men had enrolled, of whom only 200 were not in receipt of a royal salary; the group included twenty horsemen and the first priest to sail to the New World. This was Friar Bernardo Buil, entrusted with the evangelizing mission outlined in the bull *Piis fidelium* of 25 June

1493, in which Pope Alexander VI had appointed King Fernando 'Vicar Apostolic of the Indies'. This time, Columbus was given a royal send-off: the gun salutes and music to mark the departure were such, noted one onlooker, that 'even the Nereids and the Sirens were mesmerized': proof positive of the confidence bestowed by the Spanish monarchs on their Admiral. But the high expectations they had placed on him would inevitably have an effect on Columbus's own self-perception and behaviour.[18]

The voyage followed the same route he had taken to the Canaries the previous year; then, on leaving El Hierro on 13 October, Columbus took a markedly more southerly direction. This was the shortest and swiftest route across the Atlantic. Whether or not Columbus had established this on his first voyage is uncertain; it was more likely prompted by an urge to explore the islands to the south of Hispaniola, which, according to the late Martín Pinzón, were full of riches. It was thus that on 3 November, a Sunday, the fleet landed at an island that Columbus promptly named Dominica, after the Lord's day, or *dies domini* in Latin.

If they saw anything of the island's outstanding beauty, with its hot springs and imposing mountain ranges, no record survives. After a brief rest, the fleet moved swiftly northwards. The first island they encountered was Guadalupe (now Guadeloupe), named in honour of the Marian shrine of the same name in Extremadura, which Columbus had visited before departing. There, they came across evidence of cannibalism, recorded in chilling detail by Dr Diego Álvarez Chanca, the expedition's physician.[19] It was a disturbing experience, especially given that Columbus had taken good care to depict the Taínos, the indigenous people of the Caribbean, to Isabel and Fernando as innocent and peace-loving people who would readily become good Christians. This growing sense of unease was reinforced on their return to Hispaniola.

Sailing from Puerto Rico – named San Juan, in honour of St John the Baptist – the fleet anchored on 22 November on the south of Hispaniola. Heading north towards the stockade at Puerto Navidad, they were greeted a week later by a group of canoeing natives, sent by Guacanagarí to welcome them. They did not bring good news. Navidad had been burned to the ground. The thirty-nine men who Columbus had left behind to garrison the stockade had all been massacred by a group of natives under the leadership of Caonaobó, a *cacique* of the interior who was Guacanagarí's principal rival and an alleged cannibal to boot. However, it soon became clear that the Spaniards had hardly been entirely blameless. They had quarrelled constantly among themselves, and had organized many raids to steal gold and women from the increasingly enraged inhabitants.[20]

Even in the face of such unpalatable evidence, Columbus reassured himself with the thought that savagery and, indeed, cannibalism, confirmed that he was in Asia. Had not Pliny and Mandeville spoken about anthropophagous peoples in the Far East? Columbus also consoled himself with a more practical thought. The killing of his men constituted a clear offence against 'natural law' – which would make it rather easier to enslave the indigenous peoples without fearing any objections from moral theologians back in Spain.[21] It was no doubt with these thoughts in mind that Columbus presented Guacanagarí with a large gift of trinkets that made the *cacique* believe he had become very rich.[22]

But for all Columbus's optimism, the situation was dire. His prime motive for showering Guacanagarí with gifts was to buy time: Columbus's apparent ally was himself rumoured to have been involved in the massacres. Wisely, Columbus decided that this was no time for retaliation. As Bartolomé de Las Casas later put it, since 'the Christians' were already dead and the seizure of the *cacique* would 'neither restore them to life nor ensure their entry into paradise, if they were not already there', any act of vengeance would have been pointless and even counterproductive. This was an opinion with which Friar Bernardo Buil was sharply at odds. He tried to persuade Columbus to punish the *cacique* and grew increasingly enraged at the Admiral's unwillingness to do so.[23]

But magnanimity with the *cacique* did not mean that urgent action was not needed to provide a safe garrison and to punish the natives responsible for the massacre. Columbus thus commissioned his close associate, Alonso de Hojeda, to go in search of both the culprits and mineral wealth. He also put his Aragonese companion, Pedro Margarit, in charge of a new inland fortress – the first of many to be built in order to facilitate the recruitment of workers for the development of gold mining – calling it Santo Tomás (today's Jánico). In January 1494, Columbus also hurriedly founded a new town, La Isabela, in a harbour to the east of the destroyed Puerto Navidad. He soon became frustrated with the hot and humid climate: illness was rampant among his men, and the livestock they had brought from Spain began to sicken and die.

In a desperate letter he sent to Isabel and Fernando he makes no mention of gold. Complaining about the dreadful reality of having to survive on the edge of a savage frontier, he stated that the only way forward was to plant wheat, vines and sugar cane, and let European livestock graze the land. To do this, Columbus explained, he needed more resources from Spain. The monarchs would need to send a suitable labour force: men committed to long-term success rather than short-term exploitation. To cap it all, the natives would first need to be subjugated and only then evangelized. To imagine that evangelization could come first was a fantasy, but after subjugation it should be a requirement. If the natives refused – he proposed in a manner that would never be accepted by the monarchs or their advisors – they could then be legitimately enslaved and returned to Spain.[24]

Late in April 1494, still obsessed with proving that what he had discovered really was Asia, Columbus left Hispaniola in charge of Margarit and sailed west in an attempt to ascertain whether Cuba was indeed part of the mainland. Once in Cuba – which he reached in late May after making a fruitless and exhausting stopover in Jamaica in search of gold – he imagined things that give us a good idea of his desperation to confirm his theories. He claimed to have seen footprints of large animals, including griffins. When one of his crew reported the sight of a man dressed in white, Columbus immediately concluded that he must be the legendary Christian king Prester John, and tried to reassure his followers that they could return to Spain via Calicut and Jerusalem. Then, towards the end of June, he ordered the boat's scrivener to draw up an oath that all members of the crew were made to take; namely, that no island of such magnitude had ever been seen before; that, consequently, Cuba was an extension of Asia; and that, if they continued on their journey, they would soon encounter the Chinese.[25] This done, Columbus returned to Hispaniola.

A heartening surprise awaited him there. After six years in France and England, where he had been sent by Columbus in one of his fits of doubt over Isabel and Fernando's support, his brother Bartolomé had decided to join the Admiral and was waiting to greet him. Unfortunately, Bartolomé brought bad news. Friar Bernardo Buil had returned to Spain, overcome with anger, shortly after Columbus had set off for Cuba. As we have seen, Buil's rage had been fuelled by Columbus's refusal to comply with his request to punish Guacanagarí for his alleged participation in the massacre at Puerto Navidad. Back in Spain, Buil had been eagerly confirming other, even more serious charges against Columbus. An anonymous memorandum informed the monarchs that the Taínos were incapable of providing the labour demanded of them and that, though there was good evidence of gold in the ground, there were no spices of any worth on the island.[26] What most seems to have worried the sovereigns, Isabel in particular, was Columbus's policy of enslaving recalcitrant natives, which she saw as a hurdle to effective evangelization. In her mind (and in the minds of those at work in the evangelization of the Muslims of Granada) it was axiomatic that converts could never be made by force.

This statement is likely to surprise modern readers, accustomed as they have become to thinking about this period as one of increasing religious bigotry and violence. As we saw in chapter 1, however, the decision to establish the Inquisition had been taken reluctantly as a way of dealing with false *conversos* and was envisaged as a temporary measure to deal with a problem that had grown out of control. As the Inquisition began its activities in the 1480s, Isabel and Fernando were faced with further difficult challenges. The inability of inquisitors to solve the problem of false *conversos* had led the monarchs to take the even more reluctant decision to expel the Jews. By the time that Buil began to rage against Columbus, Isabel and Fernando were busy dealing with large numbers of newly converted Jews who had chosen to become Christian in order to avoid exile or had returned and converted shortly after departing. The monarchs were also deeply concerned with the situation of the Muslims of Granada. Now subjects of Christian sovereigns, they should in theory also be given the choice to convert or to depart. Yet Isabel and Fernando had opted to follow the example of their predecessors with an agreement to guarantee freedom of worship. A saintly Hieronymite friar, Hernando de Talavera, who had been Isabel's confessor, was appointed Archbishop of Granada after the conquest in 1492 and did his best to convert the Muslims by example rather than coercion. He made sure that any clergyman entrusted with Muslims should learn Arabic and he worked hard towards the establishment of a native Granadan clergy. There was no room for any inquisitorial activity in the newly conquered kingdom and the Inquisition was formally excluded from the region. It is hardly surprising, in such a climate, that Isabel – speaking now in her role as Queen of Castile, the kingdom to which all the newly discovered lands had been assigned – should have been particularly alarmed to receive from Columbus some Taíno slaves. As she began to insist at this time, any inhabitants of newly discovered territories were *her* subjects and therefore free. She hastily had them freed and ordered that they be transported back to Hispaniola. Isabel also commissioned a judicial inquiry into Columbus's activities, clearly worried that his exaggerated seigneurial claims were about to cause her more problems than she had envisaged.[27]

Columbus despaired about not being able to defend himself effectively against such accusations. Yet, his response showed unbending determination. From late 1494 onwards he, his brother Bartolomé and the loyal Alonso de Hojeda led a series of campaigns against the hostile Taínos. At the end of March 1495 he led 200 Spanish troops with twenty horses, a pack of dogs and a good number of Taínos under the leadership of Guacanagarí into the heart of Hispaniola, inflicting a comprehensive defeat on his enemies. After building a new fort there, Concepción de la Vega, he received promises of tribute and acts of submission from most of his former enemies. Although the fatalities were horrendous – Las Casas would claim that the campaigns had wiped out two-thirds of the population[28] – Columbus could claim to have brought to an end a war that he had had no conscious part in creating.

In the meantime, the official appointed by Isabel to investigate Columbus, Juan Aguado, set off for Hispaniola in October 1495. When he arrived, Columbus had turned his attention to the central region of Maguana, determined to exterminate Guacanagarí's fierce enemy and alleged culprit of the massacre of Puerto Navidad, the *cacique* Caonaobó. Aguado at once made his way there, raising the hopes of Columbus's enemies, and of some Taíno leaders, that he had come to replace the Admiral. According to Las Casas, Aguado's arrival made it clear to Columbus that any struggle to impose his authority would need to be fought not simply in Hispaniola, but back in Spain, at the court of his now-sceptical patrons Isabel and Fernando. He decided, Las Casas said, to return immediately – though other accounts claimed that he was ordered to return by Aguado himself. Whatever the truth of the matter, it was at this time that Columbus took the bizarre decision to dress up as a Franciscan friar and grow a beard.[29] He then raised sail on 10 March 1496 and, after a fair crossing on board the *Niña*, disembarked in Cádiz on 11 June. He was greeted coolly. The contrast with the obsequious reception he had last experienced in Spain was confirmation of a worrying change of heart at the court of Isabel and Fernando.

As he made his way from Cádiz to Seville – still dressed, feigning humility, in a grey Franciscan habit – Columbus heard about preparations of a fleet due to sail to Hispaniola on 16 June. The venture had been fully masterminded by Juan Rodríguez de Fonseca, a royal official who had helped to organize Columbus's second voyage in 1493 and who, since then, had gained increasing influence over the affairs of the Indies. At Seville, Columbus received a summons from the monarchs, sent from Almazán, near Burgos.[30] Still in his Franciscan habit, Columbus set off at once to meet them. Arriving in Burgos in early October, he was received in the splendid fifteenth-century palace known as the Casa del Cordón, with its imposing Gothic façade. Among the complaints that the monarchs had received about him were the dissatisfaction of the colonists that Buil and others had reported; the dearth of resources, especially spices; and the persistent doubts about whether the new islands were indeed in Asia. While they received him graciously enough, Isabel and Fernando had no option but to deal seriously with all these concerns.

At court, Columbus found out that a year had already passed since the monarchs had issued a decree authorizing Castilians to organize expeditions of discovery, so long as they left from Cádiz after registering themselves with the appropriate officials there,[31] a decision that effectively broke Columbus's monopoly.[32] Now, Columbus was handed a letter from the monarchs, ordering him to divide the supplies that, according to a complaint they had received, had not been shared out among the new settlers.[33] The initiative was the exact opposite of what Columbus had been trying to persuade the monarchs to do in order to turn Hispaniola into a successful fortified training station. He wasted little time in reiterating the point: all would be well, he told his sovereigns, if only they authorized trustworthy people to go to Hispaniola.

This was an almost unassailable argument, and Columbus made it both with due humility and with the authority of having experienced the situation first-hand. Before long, he managed to secure the authorization of the monarchs to take back enough people to bring the population of the island to over 300 settlers. They were to include forty military officers, one hundred enlisted men, thirty seamen, thirty ship's apprentices, twenty goldminers, fifty farmers, ten vegetable gardeners, twenty masters of all trades and thirty women. All these emigrants were to be Columbus's salaried employees. He was to take mining and construction implements, draft animals and millstones, wheat and barley, ploughs and spades, and enough flour, dried beans, biscuit and any other provisions he deemed necessary to survive until the first crop could be used in a flour mill.[34] Unfortunately for Columbus, recruitment would not be so easy. Indeed, the disillusioned reports of all those who had made it back from the second voyage made it so difficult for him to recruit emigrants that, in clear desperation, he was forced to ask for permission to recruit convicts. In view of the situation, Isabel and Fernando also decided, putting Columbus's requests to one side, to grant the petition of the Spanish settlers in Hispaniola that 'they be given and allocated land . . . on which they can sow grain . . . and plant vegetable gardens, cotton and flax, grapevines, trees, sugar cane . . . and build houses, mills and other necessary structures'.[35] What is at first sight surprising is that the monarchs did not provide any guidelines to Columbus himself about how the new settlements should be governed. But this was not an oversight. Given that the new settlement would be a typical Castilian municipality, it was more than likely that they assumed he would find any such guidelines incomprehensible. Isabel and Fernando, in other words, understood only too well that what they had heard about Columbus's inept management of the island so far was the result of his pitiful ignorance of Castilian political traditions.[36]

Their growing unease with Columbus's plans coincided with the origins of an imperial policy which, in its early stages, bears all the hallmarks of the influence of Isabel's new confessor, the austere Franciscan reformer Francisco Jiménez de Cisneros. He had succeeded Cardinal Pedro González de Mendoza as Archbishop of Toledo and Primate of Spain in January 1495. The new prelate had been persuaded by Rodríguez de Fonseca, who, as we have seen, was at the time preparing a fleet to sail to Hispaniola, that Columbus was not to be trusted.[37] Fonseca had by now been appointed Bishop of Badajoz and took pleasure in looking down his nose at Columbus as a typical Genoese merchant, bent on exploiting his royal monopoly to build his own private fortune of Oriental riches. Echoing wider opinion, Fonseca believed that Columbus's ambitions were a clear threat to the interests of the vast majority of potential emigrants, not to mention a flouting of existing protocols. As we have seen, when settling newly discovered lands, people tended to reach for the tried-and-tested principles developed during the *Reconquista* and the conquest and colonization of the Canaries.[38] In sharp contrast, Columbus seemed to have no understanding of the tradition of relying on existing models of municipal government for local administration in Hispaniola – models that most Castilian settlers would instinctively try to reproduce in the new territories: that is, the age-old tradition of living in municipalities and the implicit assumption of citizenship that this entailed.[39]

This helps to explain the tentative and paradoxical treatment that Columbus received from Isabel and Fernando. Weighing his achievements and promises against the complaints about him, the monarchs found – much to Columbus's relief – that the scales came down in his favour. They not only confirmed the privileges they had granted him in 1492 but they also seemed sympathetic about his plans to return to Hispaniola as soon as possible. They suggested that he took a fleet of eight ships and encouraged him to explore more of the mainland – something which Columbus was only too eager to do.[40] On the other hand, the monarchs were unwilling to overrule Fonseca's reluctance to authorize any further voyages at this time.

As a result, Columbus spent the next few months trailing around Spain after the monarchs, from Burgos to Valladolid and from Tordesillas to Medina del Campo, attempting to drive his argument home. He insisted with undisguised bitterness that the 'evil words' about his enterprise and its consequent 'denigration' had been made entirely on the basis that he had not at once dispatched vast quantities of gold to Spain. This, he claimed, was an outrage. His accusers were wilfully blind to the many problems he had faced. That was why he had decided to come to court in person: only in this way could he explain, with typical bullishness, that 'I was right in everything.' His obsession with having reached Asia came pouring out once more as he reassured his sovereigns that gold would be forthcoming, for he had seen the very land from which Solomon had procured his many riches, 'which Your Highnesses now possess in Hispaniola'. The new lands were in fact 'another world which the Romans and Alexander and the Greeks had tried to conquer with great feats of arms'.[41]

But Columbus was not bereft of more practical advice to offer his sovereigns. He talked to them about the various settlements in Hispaniola and the way to administer them, the licences needed for mining and the way to encourage farming, what to do with the estates of settlers after their deaths, and the urgent need to provide able missionaries.[42] But, always susceptible to prophecy and mystical revelations, by now he had become obsessed. Columbus had grown convinced that what he had seen, or imagined, in 'the Indies', confirmed Isaiah's prophecy that God's 'Holy name would be spread abroad from Spain'.[43] He based this claim on the common identification of Spain with Tarshish, and a clear reference to it in Isaiah 60:9: 'Surely the isles shall wait for me, and the ships of Tarshish first, to bring thy sons from far, their silver and their gold with them, unto the name of the Lord thy God, and to the Holy One of Israel.'[44]

It was around this time that Columbus sent for information from England about John Cabot's 1496 crossing to Newfoundland from Bristol, and for other materials to supplement his reading.[45] He obtained his own printed copies of *The Travels of Marco Polo*, St Albert the Great's *Philosophia Naturalis* and Abraham Zacuto's *Almanach Perpetuum*, which, as he toured Spain with the monarchs, he studied at leisure alongside old favourites like Pierre d'Ailly and Pius II. His overriding concern remained the same: to defend his theories about the relatively small size of the globe and the accessibility of Asia against the claims of the bulk of contemporary opinion.

If ever there had been method in his madness, by now it had more or less evaporated. To prove his theories, Columbus lumped together the most disparate authorities: with a confidence that might seem acceptable to us but which would have made no sense in the early sixteenth century, a Roman playwright and an apocryphal prophet were treated with the same respect as St Augustine and St Jerome.[46] The acerbity with which he denounced his critics, moreover, was symptomatic of a deep scholarly insecurity. He did, however, have one argument which no one at the time could easily disregard, and it was one that he repeated over and over again: the relatively small size of the globe was not a question of books, it was a question of experience. He had demonstrated the size of the globe empirically. 'The more one travels,' he proudly averred, 'the more one knows.'[47] It was a trump card: no one would dare refute Columbus's delusions, because no one else had sailed west to Asia.

He spent some time during the summer of 1497 in retreat at La

Mejorada, Isabel and Fernando's favourite Hieronymite monastery, near Medina del Campo. The monarchs were also there, and Columbus, very probably, was working away on them as usual.[48] As part of his attempt to gain favour, he penned a small memorandum to support the monarchs in their attempt to challenge the Treaty of Tordesillas, signed in June 1494. In it, the Portuguese had agreed to a line of demarcation at a point 370 leagues beyond the Cape Verde islands. This line was rather more favourable to the Portuguese than the one proposed a year before by Pope Alexander VI in the bull *Inter caetera* – eventually, it would help secure Brazil for Portugal – and the Spanish monarchs wanted it quashed. More in tune with his convictions, Columbus also wrote proposals for a crusade against Mecca and an expedition to Calicut, both – naturally – west via the Atlantic.[49]

His persistence began to pay off. By the end of 1497 Isabel and Fernando no longer seemed in doubt about the sanity of their discoverer's claims. Early 1498 saw Columbus preparing for a voyage that he planned both as a venture to continue the colonization of Hispaniola and to expand the radius of exploration into Asia. A sign of the renewed trust that Isabel and Fernando had placed in him came with their permission to allow Columbus to draw up an entail. This legal device allowed for the inheritance of an individual to be honoured over a number of generations; as a rule, it was only conceded to aristocratic families whose dynastic wealth the monarchs had an interest in preserving. But while such documents were normally written by notaries in a well-tested, formulaic style, there was little of the formulaic in Columbus's entail. The document laid bare all his eccentricities: it was obsessed with lineage; it dwelt to excess on the extent of his discoveries; it was marked by seriously exaggerated monetary ambitions; it contained a puzzling cryptic signature which has since led scholars into labyrinthine attempts to decipher it; and, it was tinged with a note of bitterness about the long time that it had taken the monarchs to grant him what he was convinced he justly deserved. The tone of the document was also influenced by Columbus's realization that the support of the monarchs was henceforth to be strictly conditional; for this time, they expected some tangible evidence of success.[50]

The weight of this expectation sheds light on what was otherwise a peculiarly puzzling decision. Some months before embarking on his third voyage, Columbus wrote to his brother Bartolomé in a tone of genuine sincerity, conveying his hope of seeing him in Hispaniola very soon. Yet, shortly before his departure, Columbus divided his fleet into two squadrons: one would sail directly to Hispaniola along the quick route he had established on his second voyage; the other, led by himself, would take a huge diversion into an unknown area of the Atlantic.

The decision was more than likely fuelled by the demands of his monarchs and by the various criticisms Columbus had endured. It was a commonplace at the time – one that even his critics would have readily conceded – that all lands located along the same latitude would exhibit strikingly similar characteristics. Columbus had seen rich deposits of gold at the mouth of the Volta (in what is now Ghana). Why not attempt a crossing along the same latitude? By the spring of 1498 this was precisely what Columbus had made up his mind to do. His mood was captured well in the instructions he wrote for the vessels he sent ahead to Hispaniola: 'May Our Lord be my guide and lead me to something that will be of service to Him and to our lord and lady the King and Queen, for this way has never been travelled before by any other man and this sea is completely unknown.'[51]

The fleet set off on 30 May 1498 from Sanlúcar de Barrameda, north of Cádiz. After the customary stop in the Canaries, Columbus split the fleet in two according to his plan, sending one squadron to Hispaniola and leading the other one south towards the Cape Verde islands. He reached Boa Vista on 30 June. The next day he arrived at São Tiago, where the air was insalubrious. 'With all my crew falling ill,' he wrote, 'I did not hang around.'[52] Following his plan, he sailed further south, towards what he expected to be the latitude of the mouth of the Volta, but he soon hit that unpredictable region near the equator known as the doldrums. For eight long days the squadron found itself becalmed in a brutal heat; when, on 22 July, a lucky south-easterly wind came their way, Columbus swiftly set the course to the west. Whether or not he knew that he had reached the desired latitude is difficult to establish: his account is contradictory. By the end of July, however, he was probably feeling optimistic. He had not spotted any land – which, this time, was a positive sign: since Columbus knew he was approaching the meridian that cut through Hispaniola, the lack of land meant that, at least along the parallel he was traversing, the Portuguese had no claim to any new discoveries. If, as Portugal's King João is said to have believed, there was an unknown southern continent in the Ocean Sea, Columbus had yet to see it.

The eight days in the doldrums had, however, taken their toll. Wine had turned to vinegar, much of the water had evaporated, and the bacon and salt cod were threatening to turn. Knowing that Hispaniola was to the north, Columbus decided to change course northwards, blissfully unaware that he was a very short sail indeed from an enormous continent. Then, on 31 July, he caught sight of what looked like 'three mountains', which could all be seen at once 'in a single glance'.[53] Columbus had dedicated his third voyage to the Holy Trinity, so this 'great miracle', as Bartolomé de Las Casas would describe it, seemed uncannily like what has been aptly described as 'a nicely calculated piece of theological semiotics'.[54] It also explains why the island in which the three mountains were spotted is to this day known as Trinidad.

As he explored the fertile island, Columbus's sense of awe and bewilderment grew by the minute. The natives were not the Black people he was expecting at that latitude, nor did they resemble the Taínos. Intoxicated by his unswerving belief that he was now in Asia, Columbus saw them as 'Moors', and convinced himself that the cotton bands they wore on their heads were 'turbans'. Then, as he made his way into the Gulf of Paria, he heard something that he could not fit into any of his preconceptions: 'a deafening roar, like the noise of an enormous wave crashing against rocks . . . and currents going from east to west with all the mighty fury of the Guadalquivir in full flood'. No European had ever seen anything remotely comparable to the estuary of the Orinoco. 'To this day,' Columbus wrote a few months later, 'I can feel the fear spreading through my veins that I felt with the thought that, with such force, we were in danger of capsizing.'[55]

In some respects these unexpected phenomena led Columbus to conclusions of surprising objectivity. On 13 August, for instance, when he was just off the island he called Margarita (off the north-eastern coast of what is now Venezuela), he wrote that all the evidence suggested he was 'in a very large continent which has hitherto remained unknown'.[56] This was not a claim he could have made enthusiastically, for it did not tally with his computations about the size of the world nor with his seemingly unwavering conviction that, if he was not actually in it, he must be very close to Asia. Not surprisingly, he kept falling back on reflections derived from Pierre d'Ailly's belief that the remotest parts of the Asiatic land mass could well be populated by antipodean peoples. Yet all the evidence around him suggested that he was somewhere genuinely 'new' and not a part of Asia. Perhaps, here, his own aphorism now came back to him with ironic force: 'The more one travels, the more one knows.'

In other respects, Columbus was clearly anxious to remain in the comfortable security of his own familiar intellectual world, untrammelled by the unknown and inexplicable. The temperate air and sweet water he had noticed in the Gulf of Paria seemed to him so perfect that there was even a hint of the supernatural about them. The fact that its river mouths were four in number was unmistakably reminiscent of the descriptions of the Garden of Eden in the book of Genesis. Of course, it would have been unacceptably presumptuous to claim that he had reached the earthly paradise, 'a place,' he wrote, 'where no one may go save by the grace of God'.[57] But there was no doubt in his mind that he was near Eden. This was in perfect agreement with the traditional interpretations that located the earthly paradise in the extreme Orient. It also helped to explain the otherwise inexplicable changes in climate he had detected about a hundred leagues west of the Azores, and his observations that the Pole Star deviated from the position traditionally assigned to it while the angle of elevation diminished progressively, irrespective of latitude. From Columbus's obsessively empirical perspective, this could only mean one thing: he was sailing uphill. Consequently, he concluded, the world was not round, but rather 'in the shape of a pear' – or, he fantasized, 'it was as if somebody had a very round ball and somewhere on its surface it was as if a woman's breast had been placed there, so that the point at which we might imagine the nipple would be the most prominent part and the nearest to the heavens'. What more apt location could there be for the earthly paradise?[58]

This extraordinary theory, a product of Columbus's increasingly untethered mind, obscured his real inkling that he might have found something genuinely new. Around this time his metaphorical blindness was complicated by a very painful eye condition that he had first contracted four years previously while exploring Cuba, and which now returned to plague him. It was very difficult to continue his observations, and the affliction served to remind him of his neglected responsibilities in Hispaniola. In the hope of returning to 'the top of the world' as soon as possible, therefore, on 15 August, the Feast of Our Lady's Assumption, he took the decision to sail away from the Venezuelan coast, to go and reassure his anxious brother.

Without his painful eyes, Columbus would most probably have continued his explorations of the coast of Venezuela and his first intimations of its continental nature would have been reinforced. His decision to return to Hispaniola at this time, however, brought preoccupations of a much more urgent nature, preoccupations that put a definitive end to any such speculations.

As soon as he reached the island, on 19 August, he realized that the decision to split the fleet into two squadrons had been a mistake. The new arrivals had fallen in with his enemies. A worrying number of them had grown disillusioned with Columbus's misleadingly lofty descriptions of Hispaniola. According to Bartolomé de Las Casas, 'May God take me to Castile!' became the most recurring oath, amid insistent demands to be given free passage home.[59] This Columbus willingly did. Once back in Spain, however, his enemies began to organize unruly demonstrations whenever Isabel and Fernando gave a public audience, expressing their deep frustration with Columbus's false promises and denouncing his alleged duplicity.[60]

Among his most embittered enemies were the very men Columbus had chosen to strengthen his hand in Hispaniola. Francisco Roldán, whom Columbus had left in charge of the town of Isabela when he returned to Spain in 1496, was now the leader of the rebels. In a long letter to Cardinal Jiménez de Cisneros, written in a tone suggesting some degree of familiarity, Roldán explained that the whole project had got out of hand because of hunger. Many Spaniards had felt free to disobey orders in good conscience and go in search of food. He also complained bitterly about the incompetence and cruelty of Columbus's brother, Diego Colón, especially against the Taínos who had understandably retaliated by attacking the fortresses of Concepción and Magdalena, putting the settlers in grave danger. This had led to embarrassing atrocities, but Roldán was adamant that they had been perpetrated in self-defence. His explanations conveyed a deeply felt sense of alienation from Columbus. Before long, Roldán's correspondent, Jiménez de Cisneros, would communicate that sense of alienation to the monarchs.[61]

Roldán found it easy to recruit a good number of the hungry settlers to his cause, reminding them that their salaries were yet to be paid and that they were therefore perfectly justified in moving to other regions in search of food and wealth. Once there, they would find it easier to persuade the Taínos of their goodwill, especially if they were seen to oppose the tyrannical Diego. As the suspicion began to spread that Columbus's fleet had been shipwrecked and that the Admiral was probably dead, Roldán's arguments became almost irresistible. If Columbus had indeed died, Roldán was now on an equal footing with Diego, whose authority he felt increasingly free to flout.[62]

In late March 1498 two Spanish ships mistakenly anchored off Jaraguá on the south coast of Hispaniola. Commanded by Alonso Sánchez de Carvajal and other followers of Columbus, they carried a well-equipped military squadron that the Admiral had clearly intended as additional support for Diego against the Taíno aggressors. After their initial surprise at encountering so many Spanish rebels in the region, many of Columbus's allies decided to join Roldán who, if we are to believe Peter Martyr, easily enticed them with the promise that 'rather than wielding the mattock they would fondle maiden breasts'.[63]

In late August, however, Roldán's growing confidence was badly shaken with the news that Columbus had, after all, made it to Hispaniola. At first, Roldán played for time. Then, on 17 October, he sent Columbus a letter explaining his conduct. His reason for rebelling, he explained, had been simply to prevent the tyrannical Don Diego from egging on other settlers to commit further crimes. He had thereby hoped to keep the settlers 'in harmony and love', confident that Columbus would listen to both sides upon his return to the island. Nevertheless, since more than a month had passed since Columbus's arrival without him bothering to communicate with Roldán, he and his followers had been left with no option ('in order to safeguard our honour') but to request to be allowed to part company with him.[64]

The conciliatory tone with which Columbus replied, barely hours after receiving such a brusque affront to his authority, is a clear sign that he knew just how precarious his situation had become. Sorrowfully, he urged Roldán to try to restore harmony among the settlers. Several months of difficult negotiations followed until finally, in August 1499, Columbus agreed not only to withdraw any charges against his former friend but also to reward him and his followers with most generous grants of land.[65] A few days later, Columbus's old collaborator, Alonso de Hojeda, arrived from Spain along with a number of the

Admiral's old associates, including Juan de La Cosa and Amerigo Vespucci. Using the arguments that Columbus's detractors were deploying in Spain, however, Hojeda offered to side with Roldán. He was clearly unaware that Columbus had just managed to reach an agreement with him.[66]

Although Columbus had managed to damp down the rebellion, the episode served to confirm in the minds of many settlers that he was no longer in control – a view that was now taking hold back in Spain. Roldán alarmed Columbus with the news that he had seen with his own eyes a royal licence that Hojeda was brandishing. Signed by none other than Bishop Rodríguez de Fonseca, it gave Hojeda free rein to undertake expeditions of discovery. During Hojeda's stay in Hispaniola, the rumour was that the sole purpose of his voyage was to depose Columbus, or at least to force him to pay all the salaries he still owed to many a disgruntled settler.[67]

The stew of festering vendettas and resentments in Hispaniola at this time is encapsulated in the ambitions of Fernando de Guevara, one of Hojeda's associates, who soon demanded a grant of land from Roldán. He was duly granted lands in the region of Cotuy, next to the rich estate of his cousin Adrián de Múxica. On his way to claim his new possession, Guevara is said to have fallen in love with Higueymota, the daughter of the local princess, Anacaona. When Roldán heard the news that Anacaona had actually given away her daughter to Guevara, he responded with extreme jealousy – he himself had developed a liking for the young girl – and sent orders to Guevara to abandon the region immediately. Guevara plotted to have Roldán killed, but the latter imprisoned him and sent him off to Columbus for trial. Múxica then gathered a group of supporters bent on killing both Roldán and Columbus.[68]

If Columbus had previously trodden cautiously in his relations with his enemies, now the gloves were off. His response, at least according to Bartolomé de Las Casas, was brutal. He gave the order for Múxica to be put to death and for the uncompromising hunting down of those suspected of having offered refuge to Guevara, who was nowhere to be found. As they awaited their execution, sixteen convicted men were imprisoned down a well.

If Las Casas placed the blame for the reprisals at Columbus's door, others stated emphatically that he had nothing whatsoever to do with them. Fernando Colón, the Admiral's son and biographer, blamed the executions and repression entirely on Roldán. Until recently, most historians had chosen to believe Colón's account, but the recent discovery of an important document in the archive of Simancas has altered the picture dramatically. Las Casas wrote that the sixteen well-bound rebels were in fact never executed, due to an 'unexpected development'. The document in question tells us precisely what that development was: the arrival, in August 1500, of a royal official named Francisco de Bobadilla, entrusted by Isabel and Fernando with the task of investigating the administration of justice in Hispaniola. Arriving on the island, Bobadilla quickly appraised the situation and gathered evidence. His response was swift and shocking. Arresting Columbus and his brother Diego, he sent them shackled back to Spain, to be tried for the various accusations that had been made against them. We know all this now, because the document discovered at Simancas is the long-lost account of Bobadilla's trial of Columbus.[69]

Months before Bobadilla's arrival, Columbus had begun to regret some of his actions. Feeling betrayed and isolated, he was becoming more and more convinced that all the troubles in Hispaniola were the result of his misplaced earthly greed. 'Miserable sinner that I am,' he wrote after a profound religious experience on 26 December 1499. In a state of despair he had gone to sea in a small caravel; there, he had heard what he thought was the voice of God calling out to him as to another St Peter: 'Oh man of little faith, be not afraid, am I not with you?' What was the point, Columbus concluded, of putting 'all my trust in the vanities of this world'?[70]

For some time Columbus, apparently so bullish, had been aware of his inadequacies as an administrator. He had repeatedly pleaded in his correspondence with Isabel and Fernando to send 'a lettered man, able in judicial matters' to help him.[71] His style was – affectedly and incongruously, but characteristic of his pretensions – that of an old-fashioned aristocrat, unashamed of his inadequacies in the face of a growing and increasingly vulgar bureaucratic culture. It was doubly ironic, therefore, that when the official whom Columbus called 'the man preferred' by the monarchs at last turned up in Hispaniola, he seemed to him to be 'the very opposite of what the task demanded'.[72] Bobadilla was no pen-pusher, but a knight of Calatrava and a veteran of the wars of Granada. He could boast a learned background and a respectable ancestry. The allegations against Columbus in Spain were fresh in his memory, compounded by a growing anti-Genoese feeling which had even given rise to the rumour that Columbus, in cahoots with his compatriots – increasingly scapegoated as the cause of all the ills of the metropolis – was concealing the gold reserves with the intention of appropriating the new discoveries for the Genoese.[73] Faced with the evidence now accessible to us in the trial, the decision taken by Bobadilla, traditionally seen as extraordinary and unexpected, is now more readily understood.

On his way back to Spain, Columbus bore his shackles proudly, affecting the patience of Job in the face of unjust suffering. Isabel and Fernando were mortified to see him, wearily – but doubtless with his usual theatricality – shuffling chained into their presence. After all, they had sent Bobadilla specifically in response to Columbus's request, instructing him to 'find out who it was who rose against the Admiral and our magistrates, and then seize them, confiscate their goods, imprison them, and proceed against them'.[74] The last thing they expected was Columbus's own arrest.

But, as usual, Columbus worked his magic on the monarchs, who quickly found themselves reassured by him. He told them that his sufferings had transformed him in unexpected ways. He did not ask for justice or retribution but merely told his sovereigns that everything he had gained, even from his previous voyages, was by God's grace. He was therefore resolved to give it all back to Him 'in equal measure for the expedition to Arabia Felix, as far as Mecca'.[75] There was no doubt in his mind, Columbus continued, that the 'flash of understanding' which had led to his discoveries was the work of the Holy Spirit, urging him to persevere, wishing 'to bring about a most evident miracle out of my voyage to the Indies in order to console me and others and to encourage us about the Holy Temple'. What he was saying, he insisted, was based 'only on holy and sacred Scripture, and on the prophetic authority of certain holy persons who, through divine revelation, have said something about this'.[76]

Among the 'holy persons' Columbus had in mind was the twelfth-century Cistercian Joachim of Fiore, whose newly fashionable prophetic writings stipulated that 'only 155 years remain of the 7,000 years in which, according to the authorities mentioned, the world must come to an end'. Absorbing these and other prophecies, Columbus grew increasingly convinced that he was an instrument chosen by God to set in motion the events that would initiate the last stage of history.

One of Columbus's acquaintances – the Genoese Agostino Giustini-ani, who had spent some years in Spain before joining the Dominican Order in 1487, later becoming Bishop of Nebbio in Corsica – left a glimpse of the Admiral's state of mind at this time. In a marginal note to one of the Psalms, he provided a brief summary of Columbus's life and stated that he was convinced his discoveries had confirmed one particular biblical prophecy: just as King David had provided the wealth that allowed Solomon to build the original temple on Mount Zion, Giustiniani wrote, so now Columbus would provide the gold for the Spanish monarchs to recapture the holy places. In Columbus's mind, his voyages were wholly subordinated to that predestined end: the newly discovered lands were to redeem the Old World.[77]

By early 1502, it began to look as if Fonseca's policy of licensing voyages of exploration in defiance of Columbus's monopoly might have been a mistake. None of these expeditions had yielded any tangible results, while competition was leading to even more rivalry and tension. Hopes had initially been raised when one of the surviving Pinzón brothers, Vicente Yáñez, sailed to the north of Brazil in January 1500. The following year an expedition led by Luis Vélez de Mendoza had reportedly reached the mouth of the São Francisco river, between modern Recife and Salvador, but the area was clearly well beyond the Castilian line of demarcation and it was not in anyone's interests to upset relations with Portugal, where explorations of the area were already underway. It was clear that any future Castilian explorations would need to be directed west and north of Hispaniola. Columbus saw this as a good moment to propose a fourth voyage. Given Isabel and Fernando's cautious procrastinations, he began to look elsewhere. In February 1502 he wrote to none other than Pope Alexander VI, describing his discovery of 14,000 islands and of the location of the Garden of Eden. He also informed the pope candidly about his plans for the conquest of Jerusalem, which would be enormously facilitated by the possession of Hispaniola, an island that he now associated with 'Quittim, Ophir, Ophaz and Cipangu'.[78] Calling on the pope to appoint worthy missionaries to the newly discovered lands, Columbus omitted any mention of the *patronato real* which that same pope had conferred upon Isabel and Fernando after the conquest of Granada, giving the monarchs' effective authority over ecclesiastical matters in any territory they might conquer. Had Pope Alexander paid any heed to such requests, Columbus's letter would have amounted to nothing less than an act of betrayal of the Spanish monarchs. His apparent willingness to risk such a dramatic rift was probably influenced by the news he had received recently that a good amount of the gold to which he was entitled had accumulated and awaited him in Hispaniola.[79] He had also secured a substantial sum of capital from Genoese bankers in Seville and, on 2 April, had written a revealing letter to the bankers of San Giorgio, Genoa, reassuring his compatriots that 'while my body is over here, my heart is always in Genoa'. The letter included a guarded griev- ance about the way he had been treated by the Spanish monarchs before he signed himself, in rather inflated terms, 'Grand Admiral of the Ocean Sea and Viceroy and Governor General of the Island and Main- land of Asia and the Indies'.[80]

The Admiral's grievances were real enough. Already in September 1501 Isabel and Fernando had replaced him as governor of Hispaniola. The new governor, Nicolás de Ovando, had left to take up his new post on 13 February 1502 with a substantial fleet. This meant that Hispaniola was now strictly out of bounds to Columbus. Additionally, the mon- archs had insisted that, were the Admiral to be given leave to set off on a fourth voyage, he should neither stop in Hispaniola nor do anything that might threaten Ovando's authority.[81] It is small wonder that Col- umbus felt bitterly affronted. As is clear from a petition he composed at this time, affectedly written in the third person, Columbus was adam- ant that the titles of Admiral, Viceroy and Governor had been conferred upon him 'and not anyone else'. This seemed to him a question of elem- entary justice. Indeed, he continued, no other person would have 'undergone such suffering or risked so much' to ensure the satisfactory completion of the whole enterprise.[82]

On the other hand, it is impossible not to detect the sense of relief that Columbus felt at having been spared the burdensome obligations of government. For their part, Isabel and Fernando had endured for more than a year a succession of implicit reproaches, shrouded threats and whimsical projects from Columbus, and it was also with a sense of relief that, in February 1502, just at the time when the Admiral was flirting with the pope and the Genoese bankers, they granted him leave to set off on his fourth voyage. Despite his indignant tones, there is a sense of exhilaration in Columbus's correspondence as he prepared for the voyage. This was, after all, a most welcome opportunity to resume the explorations of the north coast of South America that he had been forced to interrupt in August 1498. Additionally, he now knew that the continental land mass he had discovered stretched over a huge area of the south Atlantic – and, also, that subsequent expeditions by Andalusian explorers in the region had proved dismally disappointing. Thus, he decided to make a virtue of being banned from Hispaniola. Rather than stop there, he would sail through the gap between Hispaniola and the southern continent, on a route that would take him directly to the fabled land of gold and spices. So strong was his confidence that he warned the monarchs before his departure that he might well come across Vasco da Gama, who at this time was making a second voyage to India along the route he had established in 1497. They seemed enthusiastic, replying that they had already informed the King of Portugal, 'our son-in-law', of the situation, and instructed Columbus that, in the event of meeting Vasco, they were to treat each other as friends 'as befits captains and subjects of monarchs between whom there is so much love, friendship and ties of blood'.[83]

On 11 May 1502, Columbus was again seaborne. With a fleet of four vessels he made the now-familiar crossing to the Canaries. From there, on 25 May he raised sail from Gran Canaria, reaching Martinique on 15 June, his fastest Atlantic crossing yet. Two weeks later he was just off Hispaniola. Threatened by an approaching hurricane, he sent a message to the new governor, Nicolás de Ovando, asking permission to shelter in the harbour. When Ovando refused, Columbus sought refuge in a natural harbour he knew well. The new governor had chosen to ignore Columbus's warning about the hurricane, suspecting that it was a ruse to stop him dispatching a fleet to Spain with the largest consignment of gold bullion yet collected on the island. Ovando sent the fleet: no fewer than nineteen ships carrying about 500 men were lost in the storm. Among the dead were the two Franciscos who had given Columbus some of his worst headaches: Bobadilla and Roldán. Ironically, the only ship to reach Castile was the one carrying Columbus's revenues.[84]

With his fleet badly battered but still in one piece, Columbus set off again on his search for India. Towards the end of July he reached the coast of Belize. It had taken him nearly twice as long to make the crossing as it took him to reach Martinique from Gran Canaria – no mean feat considering the complexity of the currents, the dangerous shoals and reefs and the tempestuous weather that make the Caribbean treacherous even to those who know it well, and the Admiral made a point of bragging about it.[85] He was quick to notice that the coast seemed continental and was also struck by the comparatively civilized appearance of the inhabitants, who were skilled in the working of copper. If, as seemed quite likely, this coast was a continuation of the land he had discovered back in 1498, Columbus might have been expected to continue travelling west in his search for India. Instead, he turned east.

According to his son Fernando, among the crew on the voyage, Columbus's counter-intuitive move was made on the basis of local knowledge: the copper-skilled inhabitants of Belize had mentioned a narrow strip of land beyond which there was a large Ocean.[86] What they were talking about – or, rather, signing about, communication at this stage being mostly in sign language – was the Isthmus of Panama and the Pacific Ocean. Columbus, though, identified the description of this narrow strip of land with a narrow body of water: the Strait of Malacca. That he did so was not so surprising. After all, he had read how Marco Polo had travelled through one such strait at the foot of the Golden Chersonese, as the Peninsula of Malaysia was then known. The very same thought had crossed his mind during his second voyage, when he attempted to measure the longitude of Hispaniola, and he even wrote about it to Peter Martyr.[87]

The long search for this elusive strait took Columbus and his men nearly four hard months. Adverse winds impeded their progress; then, after turning south at the Cape that Columbus aptly named 'Gracias a Dios', on the northern frontier of what is now Nicaragua, they reached a region ravaged by torrential rain and malaria. By the end of September, Columbus and his crew were shattered; and while their spirits revived a month later on approaching the province of Veragua, just north of the modern border between Panama and Costa Rica, where there was good evidence of gold-rich deposits, gales drove the battered ships with their ailing crews away. They were, Columbus wrote, 'so utterly exhausted that we were barely conscious'.[88] It took a month to gather the required strength to begin their return to Veragua and then more than a month to reach it, which they did at long last on the feast of the Epiphany, 6 January 1503. The gold was indeed plentiful, but the torrential foul weather and the belligerent local inhabitants made things very difficult. With their ships riddled with termites, a swift return to Hispaniola was imperative. The explorers made their way along the coast, pumping and bailing as they went. They reached the end of the long isthmus on 1 May, thereby verifying that the mainland was indeed continuous from Belize to Brazil.

Sailing north to Hispaniola, they ran into a heavy storm: 'It was only by a miracle,' Columbus recalled, 'that we were not smashed to smithereens.' Finally, with the ships 'with more holes than a honeycomb', everyone working hard with pumps, buckets and even the odd saucepan to stay afloat, they reached the southern coast of Cuba. Making a last desperate effort to reach Hispaniola, they ran into adverse winds and were marooned on the northern coast of Jamaica.[89]

Survival was now the top priority. Good relations with the local Taínos were essential, but they deteriorated as the Spaniards grew disgruntled with the meagre diet of cassava bread and the meat of rodents. Faced with a mutinous crew Columbus persuaded one of his most trusted companions, Diego Méndez de Salcedo, to try to reach Hispaniola by canoe with the help of a group of friendly Taínos. Arriving at Hispaniola after five days of hard paddling against the current, Méndez confronted a recalcitrant Ovando, who – loath to give the Admiral, now widely referred to as 'the Pharaoh', any opportunity to regain control of his precious discovery – refused to send help. Eventually, he was persuaded to send a rescue vessel; it reached Columbus and what remained of his crew in June 1504, almost a year after his termite-ridden ships had been marooned in Jamaica.

With so much time on his hands, the Admiral had ample opportunity for self-pity. 'Now let the heavens pity me and the earth cry out for my sake!' he wrote in his logbook in Jamaica. 'Here I am, marooned in the midst of this dreadful anguish; ill, waiting for death at any moment, surrounded by a million savages who seethe with hatred and enmity against us, and so deprived of the sacraments of our holy mother church that my soul will be lost if it departs my body in this island.' He then implored 'all those who love charity, truth and justice to weep for me now'.[90] And yet, Columbus was also convinced that he had discovered the earthly paradise and the mines of Solomon, that he had seen the gold-bridled horses of the Massagetans – only just avoiding being bewitched by their sorcerers – that he had caught sight of the Amazons and reached a place that was only a few days' sail from the River Ganges. It was fitting, therefore, that everyone should be made aware of the urgent need to persevere in the quest for a safe passage to India. Only this would make possible not only the conquest of Jerusalem for Christendom but also the conversion of the emperor of China to the Christian faith.[91]

Thus, in Jamaica, Columbus reasserted all the elements of his much-derided theory about the size of the planet and his obsessive insistence that Cuba was part of mainland China. The insistent strength of his vision blinded him completely to his very real and tangible scientific achievements: the decoding of the wind system of the Atlantic; the observation that there was a magnetic variation in the western hemisphere, leading to the inkling that the world was not a perfect sphere; the intuitive navigational talent that allowed him to make such an epic crossing of the treacherous Caribbean sea; and, especially, the demonstration that the land mass stretching from Belize to Brazil was continuous. Any of these would have immortalized his memory; together they make up an unrivalled achievement.[92] Yet remarkably, to Columbus, none of these things were even worth mentioning next to his unwavering conviction that all his discoveries were in Asia. 'The world is small,' he insisted; 'experience has proved it.'[93]

Columbus made landfall back in Spain on 7 November 1504, coming ashore again at Sanlúcar de Barrameda. Less than three weeks later, on 26 November, Queen Isabel was dead. Columbus felt her loss deeply but consoled himself that 'we can be confident that she has gone to heaven and that she is now free of all the anxieties of this ungrateful and tiresome world'.[94] The ring of personal experience in these words is hard to miss. Despite the material prosperity he was enjoying at this time – especially after the remittances in gold owed to Columbus had arrived from Hispaniola – his health was in tatters. He had also lost trust in the king, whose mind, he was convinced, was immersed in priorities in which the passage to India and even the conquest of Jerusalem did not figure. The faint possibility that the new Castilian sovereigns, Philip the Handsome of Burgundy and his wife Doña Juana, might revive the support of the late queen for Columbus's project, faded in his mind as his health declined. By the time Philip and Juana arrived in Castile, on 26 April 1506, Columbus was too ill to travel to meet them from his bed in Valladolid. 'I trust you will believe me,' he told them in what was to be his last letter, 'that I never hoped so passionately for the health of my frail body as when I was informed that your Highnesses were to come to Spain . . . so that I could place myself at your service . . . But Our Lord in His wisdom has disposed matters otherwise.'[95] Columbus died a few weeks later, on 20 May 1506.

3

Hispaniola

The appointment of Nicolás de Ovando as the new governor of Hispaniola in September 1501 neatly encapsulated Isabel and Fernando's growing misgivings concerning Columbus's vision about how the recently discovered territories should be governed. The fifty-two-year-old nobleman was a member of one of the ancient Spanish chivalric orders, the Order of Alcántara, which was both a military and a monastic institution. It traced its origins to the twelfth century, particularly to the pressing need to resist the onslaught of the Almohad Caliphate, which by 1172 had overthrown the rule of the Almoravids in Berber North Africa and successfully extended its power over the whole of Islamic Spain. Since the principal task of the chivalric orders was to maintain the vulnerable frontier lands, its members were accordingly granted large swathes of land in areas of strategic importance behind the front lines. These areas were soon heavily militarized, dominated by fortresses and monasteries, in which communities of knights led a way of life that was both military and religious.[1]

The role of the military orders was understood in crusading terms: to fight the infidel. There was, however, another incentive for warring knights: the opportunity for self-enrichment. In a society in which the highest praise was reserved for men who were demonstrably courageous and honourable, knights naturally came to see conquest and plunder as legitimate means to wealth. In this way, the military orders encouraged the development of the notion of *hidalguía* – a term derived from the Castilian noun *hidalgo* (literally 'son of somebody') – according to which the most honoured members of society were those who had won their riches by force of arms. This idea saturated the *Reconquista* – primarily a southward movement of migration in the wake of conquering armies – and encouraged a widespread feeling of contempt for the

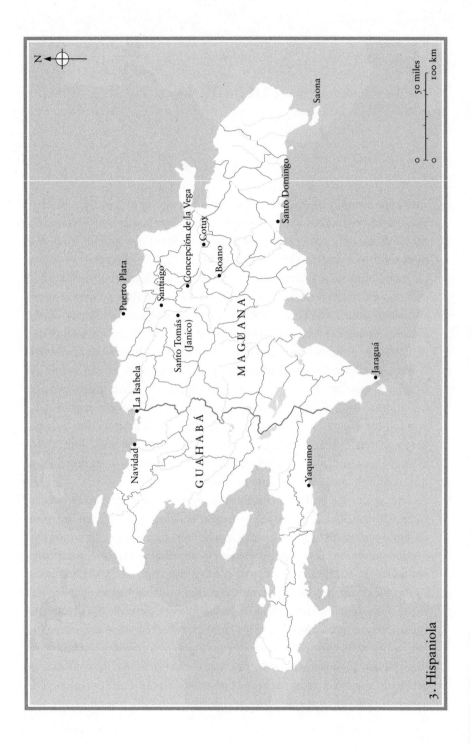

3. Hispaniola

established and fixed wealth of those who led a sedentary life. Consequently, large swathes of the Castilian population were soon imbued with ideals derived from a frontier ethos now given further impetus by the growing popularity of chivalric romances, with their tales of impossible feats carried out through sheer strength of character and constancy in virtue.[2]

It was an ethos deliberately encouraged by Isabel and Fernando, who threw Granada open to the ambitions of precisely such men. Yet the monarchs had also shown a deep sympathy for the growing anti-aristocratic feeling that had been spreading in Castilian towns and cities: during the civil war that erupted as a result of Isabel's disputed claim to the throne, for instance, they had been quick to realize that the urban masses were among their most fervent supporters.[3] The rivalry between aristocrats and Castile's burgeoning urban centres – whose expansion had been fuelled by the growth of the kingdom's wool industry and associated textile trades – had been bubbling for well over a century. The resulting widespread network of national markets and fairs led to a vastly improved system of roads and the wide circulation of money. By the mid-fifteenth century, the aristocracy found itself confronted by vigorous urban elites at a time when the cost of everything that concerned the bearing of arms – horses, weapons and armour – had trebled over the course of half a century.[4]

Many of these aristocrats did not have particularly long ancestries. Some of the great names on the eve of Columbus's voyages – the Mendozas, the Ayalas, the Velascos, the Ponce de Leóns – were hidalgo families, rewarded with titles and lands by the House of Trastámara (the royal dynasty governing Castile since the rise to power of Henry II in 1369). Rising prices forced these new aristocrats to diversify and seek other sources of wealth. They were drawn to cities by the attractions of urban living and the possibility of exerting a tighter political control over the urban elites. In this, however, they often came up against increasingly self-assured urban patriciates who, in control of key local government positions, were more than ready to call on the Crown to defend them against the increasingly unpalatable encroachments of the aristocracy.[5] Isabel and Fernando soon became aware of the huge advantages they could derive from these circumstances during the civil war of 1474–9. In particular, Fernando had fresh memories of the key role that towns had played in the fight against royal tyranny in Aragon; so why not use them against aristocratic abuse in Castile?

This would be one of the key innovations of their reign. The monarchs promoted the idea of the importance of the Crown in the administration of urban justice with the use of three key institutions: the *hermandades* (literally, 'brotherhoods'), a kind of urban police force; the *corregidores* (literally, 'co-regents', though in Spanish the word can also be translated as 'correctors'), royal officials chosen to represent the Crown in urban areas; and the *ayuntamientos* (literally the place of adjoining, or bringing together), town halls, which replaced the previous, more informal, urban institutions and were made directly answerable to royal authority. Of course, aristocrats who had been loyal to the Crown during the civil war were lavishly rewarded; yet the monarchs also took care to control them, forbidding the waging of any private wars. Lords soon became uncomfortably aware that their own possessions and authority were dependent on royal backing. For both the aristocracy and the urban elites, a strong monarchy was thus seen as essential.[6]

The preparations for Ovando's departure highlight many of these tensions. The very choice of official points sharply to the hope of the monarchs that a compromise between the two conflicting traditions at loggerheads in late-medieval Spain might be resolved in the New World. Ovando was both a member of the old nobility and a faithful royal servant, willing to implement the new policy of urban justice. Likewise, the official appointed to assemble his fleet – the largest fleet yet to have crossed the Atlantic – was Don Diego Gómez de Cervantes. As *corregidor* of Cádiz, Don Diego was precisely the kind of official on whom Isabel and Fernando had relied in their efforts to increase royal authority in urban areas. Don Diego, however, also happened to be a member of one of the oldest and most illustrious noble families of Andalusia, whose forebears had participated in every subsequent episode of the *Reconquista*.[7] This tension is perhaps best appreciated in the work of one of the *corregidor*'s most illustrious descendants. More than a century later, with a clear sense of nostalgia, the author of Don Quixote evoked a world in which the values of the old nobility still held sway. In a famous passage, Don Quixote laments that the poor and the afflicted can expect no help from 'gentlemen' who have 'never ventured beyond the boundaries of their locality', nor from 'slothful courtiers' who seem 'more concerned to find news fit only for gossip than to perform deeds and feats for others to talk and write about'.[8] This was a clear indictment of the obvious mediocrity of the new aristocrats, especially those who had recently returned from the New World with easily acquired fortunes and little idea of how to use them. Don Quixote's efforts to make the world understand the delusion under which it laboured, in not attempting to return to 'those most happy days when the order of knight-errantry reigned supreme', chime beautifully with the preoccupations at the back of the minds of Isabel and Fernando when they decided to appoint Ovando. Knights were no longer interested in 'the chastisement of the proud and the rewarding of the humble'; they 'rather rustle in damask and brocade and the other fine clothes they wear than they rattle in chain mail'. Not a single knight was left who was willing to sacrifice his comfort. Instead, everywhere 'sloth triumphs over diligence, idleness over work, vice over virtue, arrogance over courage, and the theory over the practice of arms'.[9]

Many of the complaints against Columbus had focused on the growing dislike among the Castilian nobility of Genoese merchants who had been acquiring wealth in a way that the new aristocracy was beginning to find enticing. These independent, upwardly mobile lords, hungry for wealth at the expense of honour and loyalty to their monarchs, and oblivious of the rights of the Crown and of their obligations to the poor, were the last people Isabel and Fernando wanted in charge of their remote and problematic new territories.

So, while Ovando was given the 'government and magistracy' of the recently discovered islands and the right to appoint subordinate 'magistrates, mayors and constables', the instructions he received from the monarchs put a marked emphasis on the exclusively Castilian nature of the enterprise. Any journey to the new territories would henceforth, on pain of severe punishment, require a royal licence. Any non-Castilians found in the islands were to be expelled. Gold mines were not to be established (or even sought) without Ovando's permission. As far as legal gold mines were concerned, half of the product would go to the Crown (an unrealistically high percentage which was then reduced, first to a third and finally to a fifth, the so-called *quinto real*).[10] In tune with Isabel's renowned piety, the instructions made clear her wish that 'the Indians be converted to our holy Catholic faith'. To that end, Ovando was to ensure that friars 'inform and admonish' the Indians 'with much love and without using force, so that they may be converted as swiftly as possible'. There were only a handful of friars in Hispaniola at this time, the majority of whom were Franciscans who had gone on Columbus's second voyage with Friar Bernardo Buil and, unlike their leader, had chosen to remain there. Ovando's expedition would carry many more and their numbers would begin to increase significantly from then on.[11] On a more practical note, Ovando was to reassure the Taíno *caciques* of the goodwill of the monarchs and of their protection, which, as befitted their new status as 'subjects', would be given in exchange for the payment of tribute, to be negotiated with the *caciques* themselves. In this way, so Isabel hoped, the *caciques* would be persuaded that the monarchs had their welfare in mind and in no way wished to harm them.[12]

With approximately 200 families, twenty friars (many of them ordained priests), groups of slaves who had been brought to Spain from Hispaniola and were now being sent back with strict instructions not to allow anyone to resell them, sixty horses, and enough mulberry shoots and sugar cane to begin sizeable silk and sugar industries, the clear objective of Ovando's expedition was the creation of a stable society of settlers.[13] Almost half of them came from Extremadura and most of them took their wives, children and a good retinue of servants. There was a good proportion of *hidalgos* among them, many of whom had been adversely affected by the royal decision to favour the wool monopoly, known as the Mesta, which gave priority to transhumant sheep at the expense of arable agriculture, and by a succession of bad harvests. A good number were old friends of Ovando, like Cristóbal de Cuéllar, the expedition's accountant, and Francisco de Monroy, who acted as factor. The supervisor was Diego Márquez, from Seville, and the official *fundidor* – in charge of melting down gold – was Rodrigo del Alcázar, who hailed from a prosperous Sevillian family of *conversos*. The treasurer was Rodrigo de Villacorta, from Olmedo in the Castilian province of Valladolid; the chief magistrate was Alonso de Maldonado, a native of Salamanca, who, unusually, would be praised by the authors of the two most diametrically opposed versions of the early history of the explorations – Gonzalo Fernández de Oviedo and Bartolomé de Las Casas – as one of the most able and honourable of Spanish judges in the New World. Bartolomé himself was on board, along with his father Pedro de Las Casas and Cristóbal de Tapia, both natives of Seville. At the last minute one of the company was forced to stay behind after badly injuring his leg while jumping from the balcony of a lady in Seville he had been trying to court. His name was Hernán Cortés.[14]

On 15 April 1502 Ovando landed in Hispaniola with half his fleet; the rest of the ships finally limped in two weeks later. Six weeks previously, on the way to the Canary Islands, the fleet had been dispersed. When many chests and lots of discarded merchandise was washed up on the Andalusian coast, rumours reached the court that the whole fleet had sunk. Deeply saddened by the news, Isabel and Fernando withdrew into a sombre silence for a week.[15]

It soon transpired that only one ship, *La Rábida*, and 120 passengers had been lost in the storm. It was, nevertheless, a significant loss, especially given there were only about 300 Spanish settlers in Hispaniola. Most were established at Santo Domingo, with small communities at Concepción de la Vega, Santiago, Boano and Jaraguá. Many maintained large numbers of Taíno servants, and the way in which these groups soon became linked to particular Spaniards rather than to particular functions gave rise to one of the most maligned of institutions: the so-called *encomienda* system, in which individual Spaniards, *encomenderos*, enjoyed the unlimited personal services of the large number of Taínos allotted to them.

This new system of exploitation was distinct from existing practices in Castile. While grants of land (together with lordship, jurisdiction and tribute) have clear precedents in previous colonizing activities carried out by Spaniards both in Andalusia and in the Canaries, nothing in late-medieval Castilian practice resembles the *encomienda*.[16] While there is nothing to suggest that Columbus himself actively instituted it, it may possibly have stemmed from his practice of gathering groups of Indians into work parties to extract gold and till the soil under Spanish supervision. It is probable that the system developed in the almost casual, ad hoc manner described by Bartolomé de Las Casas, who observed that the 300 Spaniards who had stayed in Hispaniola used to take the 'head women of the villages or their daughters as lovers, or servants as they call them', and, since their relatives believed that they had been taken 'as legitimate wives', they happily endorsed the practice.[17]

Ovando's difficulties after his arrival in Hispaniola prevented him from placing an effective check on the spread of this abusive practice. First came his refusal to heed Columbus's warnings about the hurricane that led to the loss of twenty-three ships together with 200,000 gold pesos and all the documents relating to the government of his predecessor, Bobadilla. Then, those would-be settlers who headed for the goldfields in the region of Cibao, in the north-west of the island, died of dysentery in large numbers; the survivors returned to Santo Domingo in the realization that, as Las Casas wryly put it, 'gold was not the fruit of trees, ready to be picked upon arrival'. Equally irksome was the habit of their Taíno servants to flee when they could, leaving their Spanish masters 'on their knees, loading carts and carrying burdens on their shoulders'. Fatigue, heat and hunger soon took their toll. By the end of 1502, some eight months after Ovando's arrival, 1,000 Spaniards had died, 500 were ill, and, to Ovando's chagrin, 300 veteran settlers remained very much in charge of their *encomiendas*.[18]

Ovando was determined to bring any remaining indigenous enclaves under his control. In late 1502, around the same time he began to build the port of Puerto Plata on the north coast, he started to explore the region around Concepción de la Vega. He then sent another expedition to the east of the island, during which a Spanish mastiff accidentally killed the *cacique* of Saona. Things quickly escalated. When the Taínos retaliated by killing eight Spaniards, Ovando sent 400 men to restore order: many of the defeated Taínos were enslaved 'legally' because they had been captured in a 'just war'.[19] In autumn the following year, with seventy horsemen and 300 foot soldiers, Ovando set off for Jaraguá, where former allies of Roldán were resisting his authority. There the indigenous leader, Queen Anacaona (the mother of the attractive young girl who had set Roldán and Guevara at loggerheads during Columbus's third voyage), received the new governor with a three-day display of entertainment. Suspecting a plot, Ovando offered to put on a display of Castilian horsemanship. Corralled into a house from which to watch the spectacle, the queen and local indigenous leaders were deliberately trapped by Ovando, whose men set the house on fire, slaughtering whoever survived. Queen Anacaona herself was taken back to Santo Domingo and hanged as a rebel in the central square.[20]

It was a deeply tragic moment – not the first of the many atrocities that would mar the early decades of the Spanish presence in the Caribbean – which filled the natives with dread and the Spanish court with sadness and shame. One eyewitness was Diego Méndez, sent by Columbus from his plight in Jamaica, who had recently reached the coast of Jaraguá after his epic five-day canoe crossing. The whole affair was bitterly recounted by Méndez to all and sundry in his attempt to stir the consciences of the Spanish settlers in Santo Domingo. Among them was the young Bartolomé de Las Casas who would, years later, famously recount such incidents in chilling detail in his tireless efforts to horrify the Spanish court.

Las Casas would describe the treatment of the indigenous people of the New World by Europeans in diabolical terms: packs of tyrants and thieves who tortured and murdered their way across the entire continent, leaving a trail of destruction of apocalyptic proportions. If historians might expect to find an uncompromising condemnation of Ovando's actions in Jaraguá, the writings of Las Casas would be the best place to start. Yet, throughout his narrative, Las Casas rarely mentioned individual names in conjunction with atrocities. Spaniards were depicted impersonally as 'ravening wolves', 'tigers and savage lions who have not eaten meat for days', who slaughtered those 'gentle lambs grazing peacefully in green pastures', bringing about a 'chaos worthy of Lucifer himself'.[21] Elsewhere, Las Casas remembered Ovando as a good and pious man who 'loved justice' and whose honesty was manifest in both 'word and deed'. An avowed enemy of 'both greed and avarice', Las Casas described the governor as exuding an air of authority that made him an excellent ruler. His only criticism was that, unfortunately, Ovando never understood the Indians. It was an observation that spoke volumes.[22]

The Jaraguá massacre drove home to Ovando the great hurdles that he faced in implementing Isabel and Fernando's plans for a community of settlers. He had arrived with the intention of imposing himself on the existing settlers, the veteran community that had first come to Hispaniola with Columbus back in 1493. But those settlers were proving themselves indispensable; among them, his new deputy in Jaraguá, Diego Velázquez de Cuéllar, had been a willing participant in the atrocities there. Somehow, in order to square their fierce independence from royal control with the demands of the Spanish monarchs, Ovando had to conciliate. Soon he would be able to reassure the monarchs that his conciliation was paying off, with the gold-mining industry beginning to yield the quantities of bullion that Columbus had predicted: 15.3, 17.5 and 16.8 million *marvedís* respectively in the years 1504, 1506 and 1507.[23]

By this time, the Casa de Contratación de Indias – a house of trade to deal with the affairs of the Indies – was well established. Founded in Seville by royal edict on 20 January 1503, this new institution, through which all trade with the New World was required to pass, would function as a market, a registry of ships and captains, a magistracy, and a centre of information. Modelled largely on the Portuguese Casa da Guiné, which had organized all foreign trade with Portugal until the Casa da India was established in 1498 to deal specifically with the newly discovered territories, the Casa de Contratación also owed a good deal of inspiration to the Consulado de Burgos. This had been established in 1494, along the lines of similar institutions in Barcelona, Valencia and Palma de Mallorca, to organize shipments of wool from Basque and Cantabrian ports. The Casa de Contratación, though, was handed greater powers, including the authority to impose fines, imprison malefactors and demand bail. No other institution reflected so clearly the determination of Isabel and Fernando to establish a solid grip on their new territories – which made it all the more ironic that it was precisely during these years that the Castilian settlers of Hispaniola began to reap handsome benefits for themselves.

The frenzy of construction in Santo Domingo during the first decade of the sixteenth century was evidence that the Crown and the settlers were starting to develop a working relationship in which symbiosis was more prominent – and profitable – than jealous confrontation. Among the buildings that symbolized the new dominance, and permanence, of the Spanish settlers on Hispaniola were the Governor's Palace, the hospital of San Nicolás de Bari, the Fortaleza de Santo Domingo (an imposing triple-towered fortress), and the handsome residences of Ovando himself and a host of other adventurers, notably the Genoese merchant Jerónimo Grimaldi: all solid stone structures that endure to this day.

Queen Isabel's death in November 1504 deprived the natives of Hispaniola of their most devoted defender. It also threw her Castilian subjects into some confusion. Technically, Fernando was only King of Aragon and now a mere former king-consort in Castile. The power vacuum led to tensions that soon erupted into riots across the kingdom, with nobles seizing towns and city councils splitting into factions. Isabel, however, had appointed Fernando 'administrator and governor' of her realms, and stipulated that if her daughter Juana, rightful heir to the throne but widely believed to be mentally unstable, should be deemed incapable of governing, then Fernando was to be declared 'permanent Regent'. Swift to consolidate his position, Fernando issued Castilian coins bearing the legend 'Fernando and Juana, King and Queen of Castile, León and Aragón' – a move that only served to vex Juana's husband and rightful heir to Castile, the Habsburg Duke Philip of Burgundy. But Fernando was widely distrusted in Castile – not least because, hoping to produce male heirs of his own, he had quickly decided to marry the eighteen-year-old niece of the King of France, Germaine de Foix, a clear reversal of the long-standing Castilian policy of alliances against France.[24]

The wedding took place in the small town of Dueñas, a few miles north of Valladolid, on 8 March 1506. Two months earlier, Philip and Juana had embarked at the Flemish port of Vlissingen on their way to Castile, but ran into heavy storms in the English channel. Shipwrecked on the south English coast, Philip was trapped by the incessant hospitality of the English king, Henry VII, who refused to let Philip leave until he had signed a new Anglo-Burgundian treaty, which included trade terms that heavily favoured the English. It was not until 16 April – over a month after Fernando and Germaine's wedding – that Philip and Juana were allowed to resume their journey to Castile; they reached the Galician port of La Coruña ten days later.[25]

On 20 June, Fernando and Philip met at a remote farmhouse in Remesal, in the valley of Sanabria in north-west Spain. The tense atmosphere soon lifted, the two monarchs swiftly reaching the mutually satisfactory agreement that Juana was unfit for government.[26] Barely a week later, Fernando agreed to abandon his claim to the Regency and Philip was confirmed as the rightful King of Castile at the *Cortes* – the Castilian parliament – of Valladolid on 12 July. Free to concentrate his energies on the affairs of the Crown of Aragon, Fernando set off for Italy on 4 September, to reorganize the political structure of the Aragonese kingdom of Naples.[27] Meanwhile Philip and Juana travelled to Burgos where, in a typical display of hubris that had already been noticed by his English hosts,[28] Philip decided to impress his new subjects by over-exerting himself in a game of *pelota* at the Carthusian monastery of Miraflores. He played again on a very hot day, on 25 September, and then avidly downed a large jug of iced water, which sent him into violent convulsions. He was dead before sunset.[29]

Philip's death sent the unfortunate Juana into a deep depression, which served to confirm the rumours of her insanity. A provisional Regency was then set up under the leadership of Isabel's former Franciscan mentor, Cardinal Francisco Jiménez de Cisneros, and word was sent to Fernando urging him to return urgently to Castile. With a serenity that would impress Niccolò Machiavelli,[30] Fernando continued his journey to Naples, replying that he would return in good time and endorsing Cisneros's regency. He finally returned in August 1507, eleven months after his departure, and took control of Castilian affairs. Nearly three years had passed since the death of Isabel and hardly a thought had been spared for the affairs of the New World. In the meantime, the population of Hispaniola had grown.

By 1507 the island was home to several thousand settlers who had been given the privilege to import, free of tax, all kinds of clothing, food, cattle and horses. Ovando wrote back to Spain, requesting a temporary stop to the immigration. He was also being criticized at court for an unacceptable level of favouritism. When these complaints reached the returning King Fernando, his response was dramatic.

As soon as he arrived from Italy the king appointed the thirty-year-old son of Columbus, Diego Colón – now succeeding his father as Admiral – to take over the government of Hispaniola. The decision was not entirely unexpected. Ovando himself, growing increasingly weary of the endless conflicts and divisions on the island, had been asking to be replaced for some time – although, typically, when the decision did come, he claimed to be surprised. Fernando's favourable disposition towards Colón, often to be seen at court, was no secret. Even Columbus's old rival, Juan Rodríguez de Fonseca, now Bishop of Palencia and the de facto minister of the affairs of the Indies, was happy with the appointment. This was no doubt influenced by the fact that Colón had recently married María de Toledo y Rojas, the niece of the Duke of Alba, not a man that Fonseca, or anyone else in Castile for that matter, would have been tempted to antagonize.[31]

Receiving his royal instructions on 3 May 1509, the new governor arrived in Santo Domingo some two months later, with a huge entourage to grace his aristocratic wife. But not all was as it seemed. Although he had been recognized as hereditary Admiral, only a handful of the other privileges granted in Columbus's original 1492 contract were now honoured. The king's instructions advised the new governor to defer to the treasurer, Miguel de Pasamonte – who had been sent ahead of Colón with the specific remit to keep a check on the new governor's authority – on all financial matters. The king also stated that Ovando, Colón's predecessor, was known to have had 'a very commendable way of conducting his affairs' and that Diego should therefore obtain from him an advisory document about the government of the island, which he should carefully heed. In other respects, Fernando's instructions faithfully continued many of the policies initiated by his late queen; in particular, to prioritize the conversion of Taínos and to ensure that they remained good Christians. To facilitate this, the *caciques* were to be reassured that the Spaniards would treat them well.

There were, of course, other preoccupations. The governor was to forbid any foreigners – which included Moors, Jews or heretics – to establish themselves in 'the Indies'. The Taínos were to be forbidden to feast in any way other than that 'styled by the people of our realms'. With the close assistance of Pasamonte, the new governor should endeavour to maximize the production of gold. The problem with this – one that had not so far been much in evidence – was that the Taíno population seemed to have entered a worrying decline. The governor was therefore urged to carry out a census of Hispaniola and to take accurate measurements of any fluctuations in population.[32] Meanwhile, physical labour would have to be imported to the island.

In February 1510, Fernando authorized the transport of 200 African slaves to Hispaniola to work in the gold mines. It is not clear whether this act was to make up for the shortfall in Taíno workers who, as the king put it, 'are feeble at breaking up rock'.[33] At this point, however, there was no sense of urgency – from Diego Colón, at any rate – about the catastrophic collapse in the population that would soon become a central object of concern. Uppermost in the governor's mind was the progress of a lawsuit against the Crown that he had filed on his departure from Spain, demanding his rightful inheritance according to the terms his father had secured in 1492. Finally, on 5 May 1511, the Council of the Realm in Seville declared that the new governor's hereditary rights would be recognized – but not, as Colón had demanded, over all the territories west of the line of Tordesillas. Only Hispaniola and the other lands discovered by Columbus were declared to be rightfully under Diego's jurisdiction. While not what the new governor had hoped for, it was nonetheless a substantial improvement. He immediately commissioned new seaborne expeditions, among them a fleet captained by his friend Juan de Agramonte, who was instructed, no doubt with Columbus's memory vividly in his mind, to sail towards and beyond Panama.[34]

Diego Colón's renewed sense of entitlement can be seen in his reaction to the establishment of the first *audiencia* – or court of justice – in Santo Domingo in 1511. In contrast to the Spanish *audiencias*, which were strictly judicial institutions, many of the judges appointed to the new body in Hispaniola felt empowered to engage in commercial transactions and the administration of the new territories. If Colón was affronted by these potential incursions on his authority as governor,[35] he was less bothered by the business interests of the new judges, which he viewed with an air of cool realism. Soon, the new judges established themselves as the most determined entrepreneurs dealing in pearls and native slaves.

This unprecedented pattern of judicial involvement in commercial affairs did no favours to the reputation of the Spanish legal system. It came at a time of increasing tension in Hispaniola, provoked by trenchant criticisms of the administration. These were voiced by some Dominican preachers, who denounced the maltreatment of Indians from the pulpit. One sermon, in particular, had left many of the settlers aghast. It was preached on the fourth Sunday of Advent (21 December) 1511, by Friar Antonio de Montesinos, to a crowd of settlers who had become great admirers of the Dominicans for their abilities as preachers. The last thing they expected was to be denounced by an eloquent friar for being in a state of mortal sin. But this, according to Bartolomé de Las Casas, was precisely what Friar Antonio had done.

4

A Question of Justice

On that Advent morning the settlers filed expectantly into church in their best attire and took their places with due deference. Some perhaps detected an irony in the name they had chosen for their town – Santo Domingo (after St Dominic, founder of the Order of Preachers) – for a Dominican sermon was a novelty there. Yet the fifteen friars who had recently arrived from Spain were eloquent preachers. Their leader, Friar Pedro de Córdoba, was a man of learning and impeccable manners who had preached a remarkable sermon – 'divinely inspired', according to Bartolomé de Las Casas – to the settlers in Concepción de la Vega, shortly after being greeted warmly by Diego Colón himself. As soon as he had finished, Friar Pedro had asked the settlers to send any natives in their care to the church. The settlers sent them all, Las Casas recounted, 'men, women, old and young', and then, with the help of some interpreters, Friar Pedro preached to them about sacred history, 'from the creation of the universe to the crucifixion of Christ Our Lord', in a manner 'so inspiring that none of those present had ever heard the like'.[1]

As they took their seats in the church on that fourth Sunday of Advent, the settlers assumed that what they were about to hear would be reassuring words from a friar sent by the Spanish Crown to help bring about the proper evangelization of the Taínos. Could anything augur better? As attested by the many sets of royal instructions, issued since news had arrived of the first landings on Hispaniola, a properly evangelized native was, by definition, a properly civilized one. The friars were there to help the settlers teach the Taínos their proper place, as faithful subjects of the Crown and subordinate members of a hierarchically ordered community. All the tensions, all the grievances suffered by the different groups of settlers, from the many old hands who had come to Hispaniola with Columbus to those who had disembarked with Ovando and, more recently, with Diego Colón, paled in the face of such high expectations. Or such was the hope.

Ego vox clamantis in deserto, exclaimed Friar Antonio de Montesinos: 'I am a voice crying in the wilderness.' These were the words of the prophet Isaiah, which that particular Sunday came from the Gospel of St Matthew (3:3), and the Santo Domingo congregation would have heard them often enough. But that morning, Friar Antonio decided to deploy what Las Casas would later refer to as his 'cholerical' style, in order to shake his flock out of any possible complacency.[2] Friar Antonio cast himself as the voice crying in the wilderness of Hispaniola, and he was determined to make the settlers listen 'not lightly and half-heartedly but with all your hearts and senses'. The words they were hearing were the 'freshest, sharpest, heaviest, most dreadful and dangerous' they had ever heard. After a dramatic pause during which, as Las Casas would describe it, many of those present felt as if they were about to hear the voice of Christ himself at the Last Judgement, the friar declaimed with righteous fury: 'This voice says that you are living and may die in mortal sin because of the cruelty and tyranny with which you deal with these innocent people.' He then demanded by what right or under what deluded understanding of justice the settlers kept their charges in such 'cruel and horrible servitude'. To what authority could they possibly appeal in order to justify 'such detestable warfare' against such 'gentle and peaceful' people? How could they not care about the state of 'oppression and exhaustion' in which the indigenous people were kept, with inadequate food and comfort, never mind teaching them about the faith? 'Are they not human?' he concluded with a torrent of questions designed to shake their consciences. 'Do they not have rational souls? Are you not bound to love them as you love yourselves? Do you not understand this? Do you not feel this? How is it,' he thundered, 'that you linger so obliviously in a slumber of such deep lethargy?'[3]

Our only source for this famous episode is Bartolomé de Las Casas, whose rendering is reminiscent of his famous *Brief Account of the Destruction of the Indies*, written years later in an attempt to shock the ministers at the Council of the Indies into implementing reform.[4] Despite Las Casas's tendency to embellishment, there is no ignoring the genuine sense of outrage that Friar Antonio's sermon provoked.[5] No sooner had the Mass ended than Governor Diego Colón and the king's treasurer Miguel de Pasamonte rushed over to confront Friar Antonio's superior, Pedro de Córdoba, and asked him to bring the deluded friar back to his senses. Fray Pedro's reply was calm and – to the two men – shocking: Friar Antonio had preached nothing other than the truth of the Gospel, 'the one thing necessary for the salvation of everyone in the island, whether Indian or Spanish'.[6] To drive the point home, Montesinos preached again the following Sunday, reiterating the same message in even more uncompromising terms.

Furious that their instructions had been ignored, Colón and Pasamonte wrote directly to the king, accusing the friar of sowing scandal and discord in the island. In their rage they put a spin on Montesinos's sermon, a copy of which they enclosed. They claimed that the friar's attack on them amounted to an unacceptable challenge to the king's own authority: it was nothing less than an attempt, they wrote, 'to deprive him of his rightful lordship and rents in these lands'.[7]

The king felt deeply offended by the apparent ingratitude of a group of friars in whom he had invested his own authority. Replying to Colón in April 1512, some four months after Montesinos's first sermon, Fernando referred to the friar's 'scandalous' words, which had 'greatly astonished' him, not least because they seemed to have no basis whatsoever in theology or law.[8] The king had good reasons for such confidence: a few weeks earlier the head of the Dominican order, Friar Alonso de Loaysa, had written to Montesinos with a stern reprimand for daring to preach outrageous 'novelties' that were clearly at odds with the opinions of innumerable 'prelates of learning and conscience' and of the pope himself. Such opinions, Loaysa continued, could only have been suggested to Montesinos by the Devil himself in order to endanger all the good work done on behalf of the Crown. 'Because of your words,' he concluded, 'all of this might have been lost' and 'all of India rebelled, so that neither you nor any other Christian could have been able to stay there.'[9]

The heated exchange between Loaysa and Montesinos points to a tension within the Order of Preachers that emerged in the late Middle Ages – and in the context of a movement of reform rooted in the extraordinary legacy of a most remarkable young woman, Catherine Benincasa. Born in Siena in 1347, Benincasa was only thirty-three when she died in Rome, but her influence was such that in 1461 she was declared a saint by Pope Pius II (himself a proud Sienese and renowned man of learning). By this time the life and writings of St Catherine of Siena, as she was by then known, were very influential across Christendom – and nowhere more so than in the Order of Preachers, of which she had been a lay member. St Catherine's teachings were in themselves conventional enough. What was new was the passionate vigour with which she expressed herself about the mystery of the Incarnation, the belief that in the person of Christ the divine nature had been united with the human.

St Catherine put a deeply personal emphasis upon God's revelation of himself as infinitely loving. In her letters, and in the candour and genuineness of her many friendships, this notion emerged vividly as a statement about the human condition. Above all, Catherine communicated a profound sense of the radical goodness of all things considered in themselves. Since this included human nature, it followed, according to St Catherine, that evil could only manifest itself either as an absence of being or as a disordered human desire. The key role of human self-knowledge, therefore, was precisely to unmask that insidious disorder at the heart of something fundamentally good.

Catherine did not try to bring about this unmasking through elaborate psychological recommendations. Rather, she placed a very particular emphasis on the central role of love in creation, expressed through her unwavering conviction that the human creature was loved even before it was brought into being. This, in turn, meant that God had literally fallen 'madly' in love with the creature-to-be – an idea of which Catherine was so certain that she often resorted to what otherwise might have seemed a scandalous use of imagery: talking of God, for example, as 'drunk' with love for his creatures.[10] God's love, she insisted, was not confined to the act of creation, or even to sustaining the creature in its 'being': His love was such that – as Catherine glossed the unfathomable mystery of the Redemption – he had recreated his creatures even after they had misused their inborn freedom and refused their share in the divine life. Seen in this light, the Incarnation was indeed a union of God and humanity animated by the 'maddest', 'most drunken' form of love imaginable. In the person of Christ, God himself had communicated infinity to humanity, to the very point of making human nature divine. The redeemed, in the striking words that Catherine put into the mouth of Christ himself, are 'another me, for they have lost and drowned their own wills and have united and conformed themselves with mine'.[11]

These were daring words. At first sight, it is difficult to understand how they could have been so readily accepted by Catherine's contemporaries, accustomed as they were to an understanding of Creation that necessarily entailed an unbridgeable chasm between the Creator and his creatures. Catherine herself was hardly oblivious to this chasm, but the candid vigour with which she expressed herself came as a breath of fresh air to a Europe that, already shaken by the effects of the Black Death, was wearily used to high levels of corruption – especially in ecclesiastical circles – and a Church still suffering from the effects of scandalous papal schism: between 1378 and 1417 there were two, and at one time three, rival claimants to the papacy. Catherine reminded her contemporaries with an authenticity that triggered a great wave of enthusiasm – and still suffused the sermons of Montesinos that December 1511 in Santo Domingo – that humans could in fact imitate God's utterly unconditional love in the way they loved their fellow human beings.[12]

The Dominican association with St Catherine was there from the very beginning. Her confessor and biographer was the Dominican Raymond of Capua. Although old enough to be her father and a man of considerable weight within the Order of Preachers, he called his new charge 'mother', submitting himself to her spiritual direction. He became Master of the Order in 1380, the year of St Catherine's death, and soon found himself leading a movement of spiritual renewal – or 'reform'. However, its very vibrancy made the movement difficult to manage, and it began to pose a danger to the unity of the Order. Although Raymond had undoubtedly encouraged reform, his successors considered his measures far too timid to meet the needs of the time. They therefore began to appoint a raft of new officials, the vicars-general, to bypass the authority of the more conservative Provincials – the Order's superiors in each province.[13] Rifts inevitably grew between reformed and non-reformed houses. In Italy many reformed convents sought to break all links with their Provincials – now seen as lacking power and authority – by forming independent corporations. Such was the case of the Congregation of Lombardy in northern Italy, which was under the sole jurisdiction of the Master of the Order.[14] The same spirit spread to Spain, where the baton of reform was taken up by the Dominican cardinal Juan de Torquemada, who had witnessed the fervour of religious renewal in Italy and had enormous intellectual prestige. He succeeded in obtaining from Pope Pius II similar privileges for his own convent of Valladolid as those already enjoyed by the Congregation of Lombardy.[15]

By the late fifteenth century, when Isabel and Fernando began giving their unconditional support to religious reform, many Dominican convents in Spain had already succeeded in flouting the authority of their Provincials by placing themselves under the jurisdiction of the vicars-general appointed directly by the Master of the Order in Rome. Although this was a delicate situation, by the late 1480s the movement of religious renewal was, with royal backing, in the ascendant.[16] Predictably, the growing popularity of the reformist party put the monarchs at loggerheads with the more conservative members of the Order. When, after his return from Naples in 1507, King Fernando showed an interest in sending a group of reformed Dominican friars to Hispaniola, he had to rely on the direct intervention of the Master of the Order, the distinguished theologian Tomas de Vio, more commonly known as Cajetan, after his place of birth. Cajetan wrote to his vicar-general in Spain, Tomás de Matienzo, ordering him in no uncertain terms – and under pain of one of the most severe penalties that the Constitution of the Order reserved for a friar – to help the king put together a team of reformed Dominicans to go to Hispaniola. The implication was that Matienzo was showing undue respect for the more conservative members of the Order, who regarded any favouritism towards their reformed brethren as an uncomfortable affront. Yet Cajetan himself, eager to help Fernando, was already busy licensing Dominican reformed friars to go to Spain in order to be sent to 'the Indies'.[17]

In the background of these tense negotiations a rather bizarre development acquired a pointed relevance. It was the prolonged trial of an illiterate peasant woman named María de Santo Domingo. Born in Aldeanueva, in central Castile, around 1485, María had come into contact as a teenager with the reformed Dominican convent of Santo Domingo in the town of Piedrahíta. Sometime between 1502 and 1504, following the example of St Catherine of Siena, María had become a lay member of the Order. Her various alleged prophecies, mystical trances and bodily raptures soon raised the suspicions of Cajetan who, in 1507, obtained Pope Julius II's permission to launch an investigation. In the four trials that followed, between 1508 and 1510, Dominican judges exonerated María – now widely known as 'the holy woman (*beata*) of Piedrahíta' – of all charges of feigned sanctity and declared that her doctrine and life were 'exemplary' and should be 'widely recommended'. Thereafter, she became prioress of a magnificent convent, built for her in her home town of Aldeanueva by her most important patron, the powerful Duke of Alba.[18]

Alba had introduced the *beata* to Fernando himself, the king having summoned her to his court at Burgos in 1507 in the company of Cardinal Jiménez de Cisneros. At this point, Fernando's political status in Castile was precarious: the rightful heir to the throne, Philip I, had died the previous year; Philip's wife, Juana, was regarded by many as the next rightful heir and the controversy over her alleged madness was not fully resolved; and a good number of Castilian nobles were making no secret of their discomfort over the unwelcome meddling of Fernando, merely King of Aragon, in the affairs of Castile. These circumstances are key to understanding why Fernando felt so easily drawn into the spiritual world of an unlettered woman whose many pronouncements seemed to fit neatly into the prophetic traditions that Columbus himself had so ably exploited. Among her many prophecies, the *beata* declared that Fernando would not die before he had conquered Jerusalem.[19] The care with which she adorned her language in the imagery of religious renewal played an important part in convincing the powerful Cardinal Jiménez de Cisneros – an influential promoter of the cult of St Catherine of Siena – that María de Santo Domingo was not merely genuine but a truly providential presence at a time of great anxiety and political instability in Castile.[20] Cisneros himself had long been a crusader: following the fall of Granada in January 1492, he had planned a great crusade aimed at conquering and evangelizing the Moors, and was determined to put his own life on the line, willing to die a martyr.[21] His unswerving faith ran ahead of Fernando's own: in 1509, Cisneros raised an army with his own resources and led it himself across to North Africa, to besiege the port of Oran. Fernando refused to back him financially, and there was a general air of trepidation around the expedition. Only the confident voice of the *beata* of Piedrahíta remained resolute. The news of the expedition's victory worked wonders for her reputation. Here was a true representative of genuine religious revival: not only a saint and a visionary but also a stalwart supporter of the established authorities.[22]

Despite his faint-heartedness over Cisneros's North African crusade, it was in this same spirit that King Fernando had supported the fifteen reformed Dominicans who first sailed to Hispaniola. In her staunch support of the cardinal's crusade, the *beata* of Piedrahíta was about to show that religious revival was not only desirable but also a useful political tool. Most reformed Dominicans had become her zealous defenders, seeing her as an exemplary representative of a movement that was as rigorous in its observance as it was submissive to the constituted authorities. Emboldened by her enthusiasm, on 11 February 1509, a few months before learning about Cisneros's victory in Oran, Fernando signed an order allowing fifteen reformed friars of the Order to leave for Hispaniola. If he seemed undeterred by the widespread reservations about the initiative expressed by the more conservative Dominicans, he was triumphant after the news of Cisneros's victory arrived.[23]

It is in this context that we can best make sense of the shock and sense of betrayal that spread around the court when the complaints about Montesinos's sermons arrived from Hispaniola in early 1512. The last thing that the king expected was for the very group of reformed Dominicans that he had so eagerly supported to question the rights of the Crown in the New World. Fernando must have dreaded the predictable reactions that flooded in from conservative Dominicans. But they were missing the point. Montesinos had done no such thing: he had merely shaken the consciences of the Spanish settlers in Hispaniola by alerting them to St Catherine's teaching about the obligation to imitate God's utterly unconditional love, stressing that the only way to do this was to show it in the manner in which they loved their fellow human beings – which of course included the exploited and maltreated Taínos. Nowhere did Montesinos question the king's authority or the rights of the Crown in the New World. Nor did he question their implicit basis upon Pope Alexander VI's bulls of donation, from which lawyers and theologians had concluded, in 1504, that indigenous peoples could be given to Spaniards without contravening human or divine laws.[24] In a quite delicious irony, however, it was the spin that Diego Colón and Pasamonte chose to put on Montesinos's words, with their provocative suggestion that they constituted an attack on the rights of the Crown, that ultimately opened the door to the real question about the validity of the papal bulls.

The Castilian Crown had never felt confident about its rights to enslave the indigenous peoples of the New World. As we have seen, when Columbus sent back to Spain some Carib captives to be sold as slaves in Seville, Isabel asked the advice of lawyers and theologians on the matter;[25] a year later, following their advice, she ordered that all of them be sent back to where they had come from.[26] Of course, there was no question in Isabel's mind, or that of any of her contemporaries, that slavery was a legitimate institution. But whereas all slaves sold in Spain came from areas of the world where the Spanish Crown had no jurisdiction, the indigenous peoples of the New World came from regions that the Crown had claimed to possess legitimately. As subjects of the Crown, therefore, they needed 'to be treated in the same way as our subjects and our vassals', as Isabel had written to Nicolás de Ovando in 1501.[27] This was a fundamental distinction: it could not be ignored.

Colón and Pasamonte evidently did not make this distinction. They followed up their complaints about Montesinos's sermons by persuading the superior of the Franciscan Order in Hispaniola, Friar Alonso de Espinar, to travel back to Spain to lobby the Crown on their behalf. Responding to this move, Hispaniola's Dominicans scraped together funds to send Montesinos back too, to defend himself in person. After some wrangling at court – where, according to Las Casas, Montesinos was clearly not welcome, Colón's sniping having made its mark – Montesinos managed to gain access to Fernando when the door to the royal chamber had been inadvertently left open; in front of the astonished king, he launched into an impassioned defence of the Taínos. Fernando was impressed and convened a council of civil lawyers, canonists and theologians at Burgos and ordered them to consider the problem. On 27 December 1512 the council – perhaps predictably – came down on the side of Colón and Pasamonte in a document known as 'the Ordinances'. By that time, however, Friar Pedro de Córdoba had also reached Spain and was quick to expose the dubious motives of this document, dominated as it was by Columbus's old rival, Juan Rodríguez de Fonseca, and a number of officials with clear interests in protecting the valuable income from the *encomiendas*. Despite his council's conclusions, when Friar Pedro spoke, Fernando listened.

Friar Pedro's indignation at the so-called 'Ordinances' is unsurprising, for they began with the dubious assumption that the failure of the settlers to ensure the welfare of the natives was due to fundamental deficiencies in the natives themselves. They were, the document stated, 'by nature inclined to sloth and many vices' and had no love for the

Spanish or 'our holy faith'. In other respects, however, the solutions proposed by the 'Ordinances' indicate the Spanish legislators were beginning to take on board the various complexities of the situation. They proposed that the natives be moved closer to Spanish settlements, thereby bringing them nearer to the churches in which they could be more easily instructed and where their babies could be baptized as soon as possible after birth. Cases of illness could also be more readily dealt with, and the many deaths caused by the long journeys that the natives were currently expected to make to the mines would be avoided. Fines were imposed on Spaniards who failed to instruct the natives in the Christian faith, and clear instructions were given for churches to be built near the mines to minimize the current neglect of the spiritual welfare of native workers. Other recommendations suggest that the complaints of the Dominicans were not entirely dismissed. The natives should work in the mines in five-month stints, after which they should be given a period of forty days' rest. They should never be made to work on Sundays or feast days, when they should be given meat and permitted their customary cultural activities. Mineworkers should be given a pound of meat every day and fish on Fridays. Pregnant women were not to work in the mines after their fourth month and should be allowed to nurse their babies for three years. All Indians were to be given hammocks. And crucially – a sign of the Crown's growing awareness of the issue – the 'Ordinances' stipulated that all births and deaths were to be monitored in order to determine to what extent the native population was declining.[28]

Friar Pedro persuaded King Fernando that these 'Ordinances' did not even begin to tackle the most urgent issues. The king therefore formed a further *junta* entrusted with revising the proposed regulations. On 28 July 1513, Fernando witnessed the 'Clarification of the Ordinances' duly proclaimed in the city of Valladolid, though they continued to be known as the Laws of Burgos.[29] Additionally, he asked two members of the Burgos *junta* to prepare more detailed opinions on the matter: Matías de Paz, a canon – or church – lawyer, and the civil lawyer Juan López de Palacios Rubios. Paz saw the problem from the perspective of the theory of a just war, the secular authority of the papacy and the sovereign rights of pagan peoples, and he limited himself to reiterating the legality of Pope Alexander's bulls. Palacios Rubios also dealt with these well-trodden topics, but with a clear eye to the interests of the settlers in Hispaniola, he opened his discussion with a consideration of what he called 'reliable accounts'. These would allow him to establish whether the natives were in fact barbarians or, as Aristotle had put it in his well-known discussion in *The Politics*, 'slaves by nature'.[30] Most of these accounts described the Taínos in terms that suggested they were 'rational, gentle, peaceful' and perfectly capable of understanding the Christian faith. They displayed no cupidity or hunger for riches, and there was no evidence that they ever took their enemies prisoner: Palacios Rubios reasoned that both these signs showed that 'the primitive law', by which human beings were born free, had endured undisturbed in 'the Indies'.[31] Yet it was not long before Palacios Rubios began to find the evidence he was looking for. Native nakedness, he argued, was no sign of innocence but a clear enticement to promiscuity. Small wonder that the natives recognized their offspring exclusively through the female line, for only women were able to know who the father was.[32] This was evidence that the natives were in a state of ignorance that rendered them mentally incapable, 'so stupid and inept that they have no knowledge about how to govern themselves'. In Palacios Rubios's view, therefore, the natives could be described as 'almost born to be slaves'.[33]

The word 'almost' is revealing. Palacios Rubios was careful not to abandon his claim that the natives were free and independent; at the same time, however, he argued that they had lost their authority to conduct their own affairs rationally after coming into contact with civilized Europeans. This was an argument that infuriated Las Casas, who could not resist scribbling an irate note in the margin of Palacios Rubios's account: 'false opinion, dishonestly contrived to promote tyranny'.[34] Palacios Rubios, though, was in a bind. A loyal subject of Fernando, he was more or less constrained to arrive at a legal conclusion that protected the king's rights in the New World at a time of increasing financial demands in the Old. Yet an ambiguity ran through his opinion: a fundamental unease with Aristotle's notion of natural slavery, a notion that would have denied the indigenous peoples of America any capacity for self-improvement. After all, to define them as such would in effect have prevented them from attaining the ultimate end that now overwhelmingly justified the Spanish presence in America: conversion to Christianity.[35]

Palacios Rubios, who proved himself a useful mouthpiece of the

Spanish Crown, was in all probability the author of one of the most widely reviled documents of the era: the infamous *Requerimiento* – a lengthy and rather convoluted manifesto which, from 1513 onwards, the Crown ordered to be read by a notary to any indigenous peoples before the Spaniards could legally open hostilities against them. A confection of religious idealism and naked self-interest, the document pays lip service to the idea of a common humanity: although all humans descended from 'one man and one woman', 5,000 years of history had dispersed them into many nations. Of these nations, some were more equal than others. St Peter invested his successors, the popes, with the authority to 'judge and govern all Christians, Moors, Jews, Gentiles, and all other sects'. It so happened that one of St Peter's successors 'made donation of these isles and Terra-firma' and everything they contained to King Fernando, Queen Juana and their successors, 'as is made clear in copious writings pertaining to the subject, which you can see if you so wish'.

The document goes on to explain that practically every native who had so far been made aware of this truth had 'received and served' the Spanish monarchs 'with good will, without any resistance, immediately and without delay'. If those now being addressed chose to do the same and freely to become Christians, then the monarchs would be bound to treat them as their 'subjects and vassals', and the settlers would – as the representatives of the Crown – 'receive you in all love and charity' and would not force conversion to Christianity upon them. All of which was, inevitably, followed with a 'but'. If natives failed to acknowledge the monarchs as their sovereign lords, then 'we shall make war against you in all ways and manners' and 'subject you to the yoke and obedience of the Church and of Their Highnesses' and 'shall do all the harm and damage that we can', and all the 'deaths and losses' that will result from this will be 'your fault, and not that of Their Highnesses, nor ours, nor of these gentlemen in our company'.[36]

Unsurprisingly, the *Requerimiento* has been held up as an example of the hypocrisy at the heart of the motives of Spanish settlers.[37] People also felt uneasy about the document at the time. Indeed, at its very first reading, delivered by the notary Rodrigo de Colmenares at what is now Santa Marta, Colombia, on 19 June 1513, the chronicler Gonzalo Fernández de Oviedo, who was present, warned 'it would seem that these natives will not listen to the theology of the *Requerimiento* and we have no one here who can help them to understand it'. He wryly

suggested that it would be more sensible for the leader of the expedition, Pedrarias Dávila, to put the document away 'until we have put
one of these natives in a cage, so that he might have the leisure needed
to learn it and then my lord bishop might want to explain it to him'. He
then handed the document back to Dávila, who burst into hysterical
laughter, as did everyone else who had heard it read; even Palacios
Rubios allegedly laughed when Fernández de Oviedo recounted this
story to him.[38] Later, Bartolomé de Las Casas, after subjecting it to a
sustained critique, blasted that the *Requerimiento* was 'unjust, impious,
scandalous, irrational and absurd'.[39]

It is hardly surprising that Las Casas's impassioned condemnation of
the document has carried the day. The bulk of modern readers regard the
Requerimiento as a reflection of a 'useless legalism' unworthy of serious
consideration, and Las Casas's own analysis of it has gone largely unchallenged.[40] This is unfortunate, and it has fostered a misleading blind spot
in our perception. For at the heart of Las Casas's critique is the mistaken
assumption that Palacios Rubios based his argument on the opinion of
the thirteenth-century Italian canon lawyer Henry of Susa, better known
as Hostiensis, who had endorsed the theories of one of the most extreme
defenders of papal power in the early thirteenth century, the English
canon lawyer Alanus Anglicus.[41] According to this view, Christ's Incarnation had brought about a transfer of all true authority, first to Christ
himself and then, through Christ, to St Peter and his successors. From
this it followed that infidel rulers could not possess any authority and,
therefore, could not rule legitimately – or in the legal jargon of the time,
possess *dominium* – over any other human group. If this theory was correct, then Christians were perfectly within their rights to conquer any
infidel society in good conscience.

But this was never a widely accepted view and it was categorically
rejected in the middle of the thirteenth century, after the first contacts
with the Mongols of Central Asia led Pope Innocent IV to declare that
all rational creatures, whether Christian or infidel, by their very nature
possessed *dominium*.[42] Hostiensis was Innocent IV's pupil, but he
clearly did not like his master's opinion on this issue. He reverted to the
views of Alanus, arguing that in the same way as Christ's Incarnation
had brought an end to the power of the Jewish priesthood, so too it had
rendered the *dominium* of all infidel rulers invalid.[43] This amounted to
affirming that *dominium* was the effect of grace rather than nature.

This argument was almost identical to the long-condemned heresy of St Augustine's rivals, the Donatists. The issue was widely debated at the Council of Constance, which met between 1414 and 1418. Among more urgent issues, like trying to end the papal schism, the Council considered the opinions of John Wyclif, which had found an echo in Bohemia in the person of Jan Hus. If, as Wyclif had asserted, civil lords, prelates and even bishops lost their *dominium* while in a state of mortal sin, then it was perfectly acceptable to justify the conquest of any infidel territory on the grounds that their rulers could not be in a state of grace. Wyclif's theory was unambiguously condemned at the Council. From then on, the theories of Hostiensis were deeply steeped in heresy and no canon lawyer worth his salt would have felt even remotely tempted to use them in defence of anything.[44]

The idea that Palacios Rubios actually did this is therefore bizarre in the extreme. Even more surprising is how resilient Las Casas's mistaken assumption has proved.[45] The central point of the *Requerimiento* was, precisely, that the natives had *dominium* regardless of their not being in a state of grace. If the author of the document had any doubts about this, he would have abandoned the effort. What was the point of presenting an ostensibly free choice to people who had no *dominium*?[46] Clearly, we need, then, to see the *Requierimento* in a different light. Rather than a 'useless legalism', it was a sign that the Spanish Crown was becoming all too aware of its obligations to the natives – and, in response, was attempting to cover itself legally. As today, contemporaries were appalled by the greed and venality of the conquistadores. Yet the *Requerimiento* indicates the emergence of another process, one which – by many convoluted and contradictory stages – was involved with the recognition and protection of the rights of indigenous peoples. Uneven as it was, this was a singular commitment, one for which it is not easy to find parallels in the history of European expansion.[47]

Even Fernández de Oviedo's scathing humour has its roots in a contractual understanding, prevalent in late-medieval Spain, where the relationship between rulers and their subjects allowed for different levels of resistance.[48] Implicit in the *Requerimiento* was the possibility that the indigenous peoples would be gradually assimilated into the same traditions, the most significant of which was the formula *obedezco pero no cumplo* – 'I obey but I do not implement'. Embedded in the medieval Castilian legal tradition, this formula was commonplace in situations where a royal order was considered unjust, or even inappropriate.[49] Here, the official entrusted with the execution of the royal order was entitled to place it symbolically on his head while declaiming the ritual words *obedezco pero no cumplo*, thereby expressing his 'obedience' while asserting his better understanding of the particular circumstances that made the order inapplicable. Non-compliance, in this sense, was done in the name of the monarch and in the wider interests of both the Crown and the community. It was so effectively deployed that it was incorporated into the laws of the Indies as early as 1528.[50] It furnished the conquistadores with an ideal mechanism for containing dissent and for giving time for reflection to potentially confrontational groups. It also, of course, allowed them to continue to enslave indigenous peoples for local use and even to ship them back to Spain, where scattered complaints about non-compliance with royal edicts can be found as late as the 1540s.[51]

It must be stressed, too, that there is very little evidence in these sources of any genuine concern for the spiritual or material welfare of peoples generally deemed to have brought their ill-fate upon themselves. Fernández de Oviedo, who had ridiculed the *Requerimiento*, peddled the typical line that 'by nature' the natives are 'completely devoid of any piety, have no sense of shame whatsoever, are marked by the vilest desires and deeds, and show no inkling of any good intention'.[52] For his part, the Dominican friar Tomás de Ortiz was astounded by the chilling indifference that the natives seemed to show towards the sick and the dying: 'Even if they are their close relatives,' he wrote, 'they show no natural pity and take them to the mountains to die.'[53] No one at the time seems to have wondered whether these attitudes might have had something to do with the loss of social cohesion brought about by the dissolution of tribal structures in the wake of the forceful imposition of European patterns of behaviour. The prohibition of polygamy, to give an obvious example, could only wreak havoc in a society where, as the Hieronymite friar Bernardino de Manzanedo noted with undisguised amazement in 1516, 'if an Indian man marries an Indian woman, the new household belongs to the family of the woman'.[54] It is more than likely that it was such unbearable demands which led to the very developments that so often shocked the sensibilities of the Spanish settlers: suicide, abortion, infanticide and the willing abandonment of the sick and the old. Very similar developments have been observed whenever a society's sense of social cohesion is dislocated by the forceful imposition of alien patterns of behaviour.[55]

Of course, the Spanish settlers were hardly unusual in their lack of appreciation of cultural difference. Not even the most committed European defenders of the indigenous peoples registered the slightest protest against the need to impose a Christian way of life upon them. Moreover, given that most of the Spanish settlers came from a stratum of society where *hidalgos* prospered through fighting and plunder, it is hardly surprising that very few attempts to compel them to comply – even when accompanied by threats of excommunication or the withholding of absolution – had the desired effect. The year after the promulgation of the 1513 Law of Burgos, for example, Diego Colón financed a slave-raiding expedition led by Pedro de Salazar to the islands of Curaçao, Aruba and Bonaire, off the coast of Venezuela, with ships staffed by sailors recruited from the streets of Santo Domingo and with the explicit approval of the king. Two hundred captured natives were sent back to Hispaniola in August. In the following months Salazar, who had remained in Curaçao, sent hundreds more. The few Indians who survived the crossing and the shock of displacement were sold at auction.[56]

Although many Spaniards continued to behave as if the indigenous peoples were their personal property, they were also being made aware that, at least in theory, they were free. This soon made the lure of previously undiscovered riches more enticing than slave raiding. The pearl fisheries spotted by Columbus just off the coast of Venezuela on his third voyage were a case in point. Among those who made a beeline for them at the first opportunity was Amerigo Vespucci.[57] Not long after, in 1501, an expedition led by Rodrigo de Bastidas and Juan de La Cosa sailed along the continental coast into the Gulf of Urabá, on the northern coast of present-day Colombia, where there were rumoured to be abundant seams of gold. In 1504, La Cosa had been authorized by Isabel and Fernando to lead an expedition and establish a settlement there; instead, he and his followers plundered and sacked the towns of Urabá and Darién and raided the surrounding countryside in search of booty and treasure. In 1508, most probably responding to the evidence of treasure that La Cosa had taken back to Spain in 1506, two further concessions were issued to Alonso de Hojeda and Diego de Nicuesa to

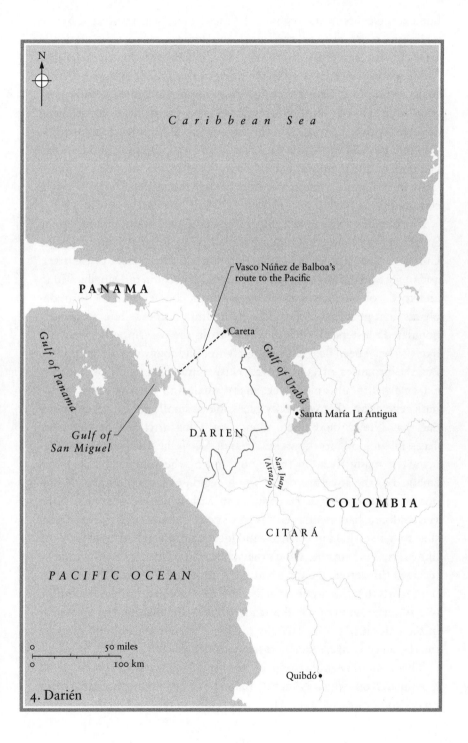

N

Caribbean Sea

PANAMA

Vasco Núñez de Balboa's
route to the Pacific

•Careta

Gulf of Panama

Gulf of Urabá

*Gulf of
San Miguel*

•Santa María La Antigua

DARIEN

*San Juan
(Atrato)*

COLOMBIA

CITARÁ

PACIFIC OCEAN

0   50 miles
0   100 km

Quibdó •

4. Darién

build settlements in the region. The experiment was frustrated by the stubborn resistance of the local inhabitants, who systematically attacked the Spaniards after every raid. There were many casualties. Those who survived moved to the town of Darién under the leadership of the daring Andalusian explorer Vasco Núñez de Balboa who, in contrast with Hojeda and Nicuesa, saw the importance of securing alliances with the *caciques* of the region. Successfully settled, the town was renamed Santa María la Antigua in 1510. Here, in modern-day Panama, at last there was a solid base – the first city founded by Spaniards in mainland America – from which the search for gold might continue.[58]

The obvious route to take for this purpose was to sail inland, up the San Juan, as Núñez de Balboa had called the River Atrato, from the Gulf of Urabá. Rumours of very rich mines on both sides of the river, and of vast quantities of gold in the legendary region of Dabeiba, led to an expedition that first put the Spaniards in contact with the formidably resilient peoples of Citará. Contemporary accounts refer to densely populated clusters of villages which, from the descriptions given, are likely to have been near the extremely wet and foggy region of Quibdó. But the promises of gold proved elusive and navigation of the river extremely difficult among the 'many small and narrow arms', dense with vegetation, that were only accessible in small canoes.[59] Small wonder that Núñez de Balboa soon turned his attention to the more accessible regions to the west of Santa María la Antigua. He outmanoeuvred many rivals in the region and by the summer of 1511 had emerged as the governor of the whole region of Darién. Núñez de Balboa would soon regret the enthusiasm with which, in a letter to King Fernando, he had mentioned 'rivers of gold' – it was, he said, even possible to fish for gold in Darién – and local chiefs who had 'gold growing like maize in their huts which they collect in baskets'.[60] By the time he received this letter, the king had been informed by some of the governor's rivals that the situation in Darién left a lot to be desired. According to Las Casas, rumours had already reached Castile that the Spaniards in the isthmus lived in 'anarchy' and had no interest in administering the region or converting the indigenous peoples.[61]

The rumours would soon be confirmed by witnesses from Santo Domingo, from which Núñez de Balboa had fled in disgrace after being unable to pay his creditors. The king decided to replace him as governor, but no amount of hostility would be enough to distract him from Núñez de Balboa's enticing evocations of rivers flowing with gold. They also had an intoxicating effect in Castile. King Fernando and the man in charge of what would eventually become the Council of the Indies, Bishop Juan Rodríguez de Fonseca, renamed the region 'Castilla del Oro' (Golden Castile, literally 'Castile of the Gold') and began to plan the most important expedition that had yet set sail for the New World. Indeed, after Columbus's second voyage of 1493, this was to be only the second expedition directly financed by the Crown. It would be led by the man appointed to replace Núñez de Balboa, the aforementioned Pedrarias Dávila, the first man to carry a copy of the *Requerimiento* with him. The fleet of twenty-three ships left Sanlúcar de Barrameda on 11 April 1513 at a cost of more than 10 million *marvedís* – equivalent approximately to the king's annual household income[62] – the most expensive expedition yet mounted to the New World.[63] A clear majority of the roughly 2,000 people on board were from *hidalgo* families and included what Pascual de Andorga – one of Pedrarias's captains – considered some of the most 'distinguished people who had ever left the shores of Spain'.[64] With a reputation for arrogance and impetuosity, Pedrarias himself hailed from a distinguished family of Segovia; his wife, Isabel de Bobadilla, a lady with royal connections, was the daughter of the ill-fated governor of Hispaniola, Francisco de Bobadilla. She was also intrepid: when Pedrarias suggested leaving her behind, she said that she 'would rather be eaten by fish in the sea or devoured by cannibals on the land than to sink into the endless mourning and intolerable sorrow that would be engendered by having to wait, not for my husband but for his letters'.[65]

Hearing he was about to be replaced in his post, Núñez de Balboa threw caution to the winds. In a further, desperate effort to find the land of gold, and perhaps win back King Fernando's favour in the process, he set off by sea on 1 September 1513 with fewer than 200 men, sailing north towards Careta in Panama. There, the expedition disembarked and scaled rugged mountain ranges and crossed large rivers, passing through thick, exhausting jungles of a density they had never imagined possible, subduing indigenous people as they went with gunshot and packs of hungry dogs. Finally, in late September 1513, they reached the summit of a 'bare hill'. There, surrounded by his companions – who included a sturdy man from the Extremaduran town of Trujillo called Francisco Pizarro – Núñez de Balboa was dumbfounded by a sight that was as awesome as it was unexpected. Kneeling down, he raised his hands, gave thanks to God, and 'prouder than Hannibal showing Italy and the Alps to his soldiers . . . he promised great riches to his men, saying: "Behold . . . all you men who have endured so much, behold the land of which . . . the natives have told us such wonders." '[66] In front of them lay the Pacific Ocean.

To these men, the awesome sight was indeed a wonder: one that they somehow had to fit into a European understanding of the world as it had been explained for thousands of years by the likes of Strabo, Ptolemy and Pomponius Mela. Curiously, although in some respects the Renaissance was prompting Europeans to extend their mental and geographical horizons, in other respects it had encouraged a closing of the mind. The veneration of received wisdom often became more slavish. Authority staked fresh claims against experience and classical texts were endowed with more authority when they were fixed on the printed page.[67] Indeed, this adherence to classical learning even restored faith in a host of ideas and phenomena that had been severely questioned even by medieval Christian authors: prodigies, freaks of topography, monsters, enchanted places. As Pliny the Elder had argued when imagining people beyond the sea: 'I have no doubt that some facts will appear . . . incredible . . . Is there anything that does not seem marvellous, when first we hear about it? How many things are judged impossible, until they are judged to be facts?'[68] These remarks were followed by a long list of monsters, including the Arimaspi, the Nasamones, the Megasthenes, the Cynocephali, the Troglodytes, the Choromandae and the Astomi, as well as races of giants and anthropophagi, all of which worked their way into popular travelogues. Griffins and amazons routinely made an appearance in accounts that otherwise read like perfectly factual narratives. Romance, travel and hagiography became so intermingled that readers routinely mistook the fictional for the historical. Othello's reference to 'Cannibals that each other eat; / The Anthropophagi, and men whose heads / Do grow beneath their shoulders' – among the marvels he had seen on his adventures to win the love of Desdemona – has a ring of realism that we now find fanciful.[69]

As for the Pacific, we should not forget that transatlantic navigators persisted in their belief that they were bound for Asia well into the 1520s. Ferdinand Magellan himself could not have made this clearer during the audience he managed to arrange with Charles V's chancellor, Jean Sauvage, in Valladolid in March 1518. According to Las Casas, who claims to have been present at the meeting, Magellan took with him a painted globe with which he explained to Sauvage that if the line dividing the world between Portugal and Spain was continued around the earth, Spain had a clear claim to the Moluccas, the fabled land of spices. He then argued that he would reach those coveted islands by sailing across the strait shown in the famous map of America drawn by Martin Waldseemüller in 1507. Las Casas claims to have asked Magellan, clearly with the benefit of hindsight, 'and what if you do not find the strait that will allow you to cross over to the other sea?'[70] But this did not seem to deter the Portuguese captain. He knew from correspondence with his cousin Francisco Serrano, a commander in the Moluccas, that it was common knowledge in those islands that a route existed between them and the West Indies.[71] In fact, finding the strait also seems to have been the intention of Juan Díaz de Solís, who had succeeded Vespucci as chief pilot in 1512, when he set out to explore the southern continent in October 1515. His hopes were raised when he discovered the estuary of the River Plate in 1516, shortly before being tragically captured, along with the majority of his companions, and more than likely eaten by Guaraní Indians.[72] One of the survivors of that ill-fated expedition was Alejo García, who became the first European to make contact with the Incas after reaching the southern continent in an improvised canoe. He then set off in search of a mythical figure called 'The White Man' whom the natives believed to possess enormous riches. It is all too easy to forget that this was still very much the mental world of the Spanish adventurers at the time of King Fernando's death in January 1516. The author of the sixteenth-century chivalric romance *Amadís de Gaula* could not have done better.[73]

PART TWO

Conquests, 1510–33

5

Cuba

With the enduring lure of riches came the gradual erosion of some stubborn preconceptions. In 1507 the Galician *hidalgo* Sebastián Ocampo – who had first come to the New World with Columbus on his second voyage fourteen years earlier – led an expedition to circumnavigate Cuba, and to establish beyond doubt that it was either (as Columbus had thought) an extension of Asia or an island. With two ships, Ocampo took eight months to circumnavigate Cuba and confirmed that it was indeed an island – and, predictably, that there was some evidence of gold along its eastern mountain range.[1]

Following in the wake of Ocampo and other explorers – who, by expanding Spanish rule to the nearby islands, were rewarded with promotions and high office – was another grizzled *hidalgo*, Diego Velázquez de Cuéllar. Born in 1464 in Cuéllar, an ancient Castilian town halfway between Segovia and Valladolid, Velázquez's ancestors included a co-founder of the military order of Calatrava, as well as several judges, commanders of castles and distinguished royal functionaries.[2] Formed during the years of Castile's civil war, Velázquez had fought in the last years of the *Reconquista* before sailing to Hispaniola with Columbus's 1493 expedition, and had since made a name for himself, ruthlessly subduing the Taínos whenever they threatened to revolt. His interest in Cuba was more than likely piqued by the flight to that island of Hatuey, the *cacique* of the Guahabá region – on the top western peninsula of what is nowadays Haiti. Velázquez's request to be permitted to hunt Hatuey down was backed by the powerful royal treasurer, Miguel de Pasamonte, through whom he established direct contact with King Fernando himself. These negotiations were followed with interest by Velázquez's secretary, the thirty-year-old Hernán Cortés, who had a good grounding in the law, having spent time studying it at the University of Salamanca before his departure for Hispaniola.³ With such powerful backers, Velázquez easily brushed aside the authority of the new governor of Hispaniola, Diego Colón, who wanted his own uncle Bartolomé to lead the expedition.⁴

Characteristically, the enterprising Velázquez financed the expedition himself. Sailing to Cuba in 1511, he founded a settlement in Baracoa, on the far eastern side of the island, swept aside local resistance and captured Hatuey. Facing his inevitable execution, Hatuey was approached by one of the four Franciscan friars in the expedition to persuade him to accept baptism if he wanted a decent Christian burial. Also on the expedition was Bartolomé de Las Casas, who related how Hatuey declined the offer: accepting baptism, the *cacique* replied, would mean having to spend eternity in the company of Spaniards; hell would be preferable to such a fate. After this, Hatuey was promptly burned at the stake.⁵

Hatuey's execution set a pattern for the swift subjugation of the island. Cuba was not as densely populated as Hispaniola; its inhabitants, used only to sporadic Carib raids that they would repel with stones and arrows, were no match for Spanish steel. In the company of another veteran, Pánfilo de Narváez, who had helped crush resistance in Jamaica, Velázquez advanced relentlessly through Cuba. By the end of 1513 resistance had been more or less eradicated. Massacres abounded: in response to a suspected ambush, Narváez slaughtered about a hundred Taínos, pursuing the rest to the town of Camagüey, where he killed their leader Caguax. At a nearby settlement, which Las Casas later referred to as Caonao, a crowd of around 2,000 Taínos gathered to stare at the Spaniards and the astonishing animals they rode. According to Las Casas, an unnamed Spaniard went berserk and started killing the Taínos; this was the trigger for many of Narváez's captains to follow suit in an orgy of further killing: the streets, wrote Las Casas, ran with blood. The scene was watched by Narváez who stayed on his horse, 'still as a marble statue'. It was, Las Casas recalled, 'all so cruelly done, and all so easily dismissed and forgotten'.⁶

Las Casas was himself an ordained priest – the first, in fact, to have been ordained in the New World. Before reaching Hispaniola, in 1502, he had attended the cathedral school in his native Seville, where he acquired a good knowledge of classical literature and proficient Latin.⁷ In Hispaniola, however, he readily settled into the lifestyle characteristic at the time of the average 'secular' priest – that is, one unaffiliated to any religious order – marked neither by piety nor by learning. Although he embraced the preaching of the reformed Dominicans, who urged the humane treatment of indigenous peoples, Las Casas seems to have seen no contradiction between a Christian sense of justice and the practice of de facto slavery – even after the dreadful events at Caonao. Indeed, his participation in the conquest of Cuba had earned Las Casas an *encomienda*, and he threw himself enthusiastically into the system, using native labourers to extract gold from the mines and – taking advantage of a growing culinary penchant among Cuba's Spanish settlers – developing a prosperous green-turtle farm in a lagoon near Cienfuegos.[8]

Yet it was in Cuba that Las Casas underwent a dramatic change of heart about the conquest and the *encomienda* system. Exactly when it was that a Dominican friar refused him absolution, on the basis that he had natives in *encomienda*, is unclear. It may have been two of the Dominicans in Velázquez's expedition to Cuba who stirred the conscience of Las Casas, before they returned to Hispaniola to inform Friar Pedro de Córdoba about the atrocities they had witnessed.[9] But the change in Las Casas was glaringly clear by the time he was preparing his Easter sermon in 1514. The scriptural reading for the solemn occasion was poignant and hard hitting: 'Who robs the poor and then brings sacrifice, is of their fellowship that would immolate some innocent child before the eyes of his father' ran the piercing text from the book of Ecclesiasticus. 'Poor man's bread is poor man's life; cheat him of it and thou hast slain him; sweat of his brow, or his life's blood, what matters?'[10] It was then that Las Casas began to denounce the conquest openly. A few months later, on 14 August 1514, he spoke to the settlers of Sancti Spiritus about 'their blindness, their injustices, their tyrannies, their cruelties'.[11] Soon afterwards, he abandoned his property to Velázquez and returned to Spain, to campaign on behalf of the Taínos. There, the indefatigable Las Casas secured an audience with King Fernando and won the goodwill of Cardinal Francisco Jiménez de Cisneros. Hispaniola, he explained to them, was practically depopulated: out of an estimated two million Indians on the island when Columbus first landed in 1492, barely 15,000 remained. Although the figures were, in the manner of the time, wildly inflated – the most authoritative estimates suggest a population of approximately 200,000 at the time of Columbus's arrival and 90,000 when Las Casas was making his case[12] – the situation was gravely concerning. The only solution, he insisted, was the outright abolition of the *encomienda*. Once this was achieved, the

Taínos should only be made to work for Spaniards in return for a just wage. They should, moreover, be gathered into villages, each with a hospital and a church, where the relations between settlers and natives could be carefully monitored so that no more than a third of men aged between twenty-five and forty-five should be summoned to work at any one time. Additionally, those thus summoned should only be made to work for a maximum of two months each year and should never be moved further than twenty leagues away from their allotted villages. To compensate for any losses to the Crown, Las Casas recommended a substantial increase in the import of African slaves.[13]

If Las Casas was driven, he was also practical in his recommendations. His aim, clearly, was to convince the Spanish authorities that the proposed reforms would benefit the lives of the Taínos and the Crown in equal measure, while still keeping an eye on his own personal profit. He was not against further Spanish settlers, so long as those authorized to go were 'farmers rather than adventurers' – proper settlers, in other words, who would be willing to teach the Taínos practical skills and even enter into marriages with them.[14] For all this, Las Casas was – with the notable exception of the Dominican friars under Pedro de Córdoba – the first Spaniard to go on record as having any genuine concern for the spiritual and material welfare of the Taínos. Many friars and priests who had gone to the New World had since returned to Spain, demoralized by the lack of home comforts and their manifest failure to convert more than a handful of people. Even those who lived among the Taínos, like the Catalan Hieronymite friar Ramón Pané, were utterly baffled both by their language and their culture. The garbled accounts that have come down to us from the pen of Pané – amended at various stages by the courtier Peter Martyr and Las Casas himself – read like strained efforts to make sense of stories he was told by his Taíno interlocutors. Although they all worshipped sculptural objects called *zemís* that were believed to contain spirits, Pané was disarmingly quick to assume that they also had some knowledge of the Creator: 'They believe,' he wrote with charming optimism, 'that he is in heaven and is immortal, and that no one can see him, and that he has a mother, but he has no beginning.' The name of this deity was translated by Pané as 'giver of cassava, master of the sea, conceived without male intervention'. The name of his mother was 'mother of the waters, lady of the moon . . . universal mother'.[15]

Bewilderingly for Pané, the Taínos seemed to have no sense of history in the way they understood their origins. Past and present, the living and the dead, humans and animals, all seemed inextricably intertwined. They kept no records of past rulers or even of exceptional natural phenomena. They did, however, have a clear notion of some primeval world in which creatures underwent dramatic transformations, or metamorphoses. For instance, one of the men who emerged from the primordial Cave of the Jagua Tree – from where the Taínos believed that mankind had emerged – was transformed by the sun into a bird resembling a nightingale. Alarmed by this portent, a friend of the transformed caveman decided to take all the women in the island to safer lands, and so he sailed with them to an island called Matininó, 'without fathers'. Finding themselves without female company, the men grew restless until one day, while bathing, they saw some strange creatures falling from the skies. The creatures, though enticing, were neither male nor female, so the men fetched a woodpecker to help them make a hole 'in the place where the sex of women is generally located'. Such beliefs were, according to Pané, the result of the reprehensible teachings of *behiques* (the Taíno word for a type of shaman), who passed down these mythical fables in the form of songs that were never written down. These *behiques* functioned essentially as intermediaries, both with the dead and with the *zemís*, with whom they thought they could communicate after inhaling a powder that put them in a trance in which 'they do not know what they are doing'.[16]

Often described as an innovative work of anthropology, Pané's short treatise is the only source of information we have about the mythological world of the Taínos – a priceless account of a tragically vanished people. In fact, Pané was working within a long-established tradition, stretching back at least to the time of the great Majorcan friar Raymond Lull (c. 1235–1316), one of the most significant figures in the medieval study of Islam. A Franciscan, Lull was convinced that it was possible to bring the Christian faith to unbelievers through the use of reason. This required studying the languages and cultures of non-Christian peoples, as well as sending missions among them. Lull's recommendations were incorporated into the official policy of the Western Church at the 1312 Council of Vienne, which called for the establishment of schools of Arabic, Greek, Hebrew and Syriac at the Universities of Paris, Oxford, Salamanca, Bologna and Avignon. In practice, neither the personnel nor the financial means was available to bring this dream to reality.[17] But Lull's way of thinking nonetheless survived, not least among Pané's Catalan predecessors who had for two and a half centuries studied the texts and languages of Islam and Judaism in preparation for preaching expeditions.[18]

Nor was this a Catalan monopoly. As Pané was learning the Taíno language, the first Archbishop of Granada, Hernando de Talavera, also a Hieronymite friar, was insisting that Christians should respect the agreements of 1491 which, as we saw in chapter 1, guaranteed Muslims the free exercise of their religion. Talavera had both a genuine interest in Arabic studies and a deep respect for the Muslim cultural achievements in Spain. Conversion, he maintained, should never be imposed: it had to be a gradual process of gentle assimilation, requiring good knowledge of the languages and customs of the recently conquered 'infidels'.[19] It is hardly an accident that, when studying at the University of Salamanca, Talavera had been a pupil of Juan de Segovia, who, tired of papal politics, eventually retired to a remote monastery in Savoy where he engaged in a laborious new translation of the Qur'an that aimed to avoid the various misrepresentations of Islam he had detected in previous translations. Talavera inherited Segovia's concern for textual accuracy and criticism, as well as his sympathy for Islam.[20] In a long letter, Segovia had argued that war would never solve the problems between Christianity and Islam. What was needed was the kind of confrontation with the enemy that could only be achieved through what he termed a friendly 'con(tra)ference'. Even if it did not achieve the desired result of conversion, such a procedure was bound to produce much more positive results – as well as being incomparably cheaper – than any resort to violence.[21]

If Pané was drawing on a tradition that sought to understand the cultures of non-Christian peoples, with the Taínos he encountered an unprecedented problem: a total absence of written texts. The chasm between an oral culture – where supernatural forces interacted with humans (both living and dead), as well as with animals, vegetables and natural forces, in what seemed to Pané a seamless way – and the mental world of literate Western Europeans, was far wider than Pané could possibly have expected. For him, differences between Christianity and Judaism and Islam – or even Buddhism, or the religious expressions of the Tartars, or the Canary islanders – paled beside such a strange world. In Hispaniola, Cuba and the other Caribbean islands, Europeans had yet to find familiar points of reference. There was no evidence of organized religious ceremonies, no temples, no sacrifices. Faced with such unprecedented phenomena, European information-gathering easily gave way to the more congenial task of elaborating fables. When Pané reported the myth of the island of Matininó, rumours of its actual existence spread like wildfire among European settlers. Columbus immediately thought of the famous legend of the Amazons. Matininó itself became a source of endless fascination, leading the mythical world of the Taínos to be linked to the imagery of Marco Polo and the fictions that went under the name of Sir John Mandeville. As Columbus would write with candid enthusiasm, 'there is an island called Matenico [*sic*] where there are only women'.[22]

After the conquest of Cuba, Diego Velázquez sent King Fernando a full report of the island. Among other things, it referred to the sporadic visits to Cuba of 'certain Indians who come from the north, after about a five- or six-day crossing by canoe, and give news of other islands in those regions'.[23] Where and what these other islands were, nobody quite knew. The conqueror of Puerto Rico, Juan Ponce de León, had taken an expedition up the Bahamas in March 1513, and on Easter Sunday had made landfall near what is now Palm Bay, in Florida – hence its name ('Pascua Florida', Spanish for Easter Sunday). From there, he had sailed south and then turned into the Gulf of Mexico, in search – if we are to believe Peter Martyr – of the 'Fountain of Youth' described in the travels of Sir John Mandeville and mentioned again in the popular romance of chivalry, *Palmerín de Oliva*, which had been published in Salamanca barely two years previously.[24] Failing to find this source, the disappointed Ponce de León returned to Puerto Rico in October, having made a brief stop in Yucatan, which other explorers had already visited back in 1507. Ponce de León and his crew, their heads full of chivalric romance, assumed both Yucatan and Florida to be islands. There was as yet no inkling of the existence of a continental land mass anywhere north of Nicaragua.

Meanwhile, Velázquez and his companions were quickly becoming acclimatized to Cuba in a way that had not yet happened in Hispaniola. There was, it seemed, no repeat in Cuba of the anxieties Columbus had expressed about the dearth of produce, which resulted in Europeans falling ill due to poor diet.[25] Not only turtles – which, as we have seen, Las Casas had been quick to appreciate – but cassava bread, iguanas and even parrots had become part of the staple diet. In early 1515,

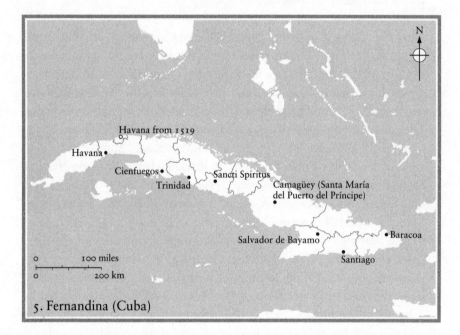

N

Havana from 1519

Havana

Cienfuegos

Trinidad

Sancti Spiritus

Camagüey (Santa María
del Puerto del Príncipe)

Salvador de Bayamo

Santiago

Baracoa

0   100 miles

0   200 km

5. Fernandina (Cuba)

moreover, Velázquez moved his capital from Baracoa in the east to a splendid bay on the south coast, which he and his right-hand man Cortés had already graced with the name of Spain's chief patron saint.

Santiago de Cuba was not the most strategic location Velázquez could have picked for the island's seat of government. Yet the conqueror of Cuba had come to the conclusion that he did not need to keep a firm grip on the islanders – or, put another way, he had little interest in what was going on outside the dozen or so *encomiendas* that he had set up with royal licence across Cuba.[26] Largely dedicated to the breeding of turtles, pigs, horses and different kinds of game, these prosperous enterprises were usually run in conjunction with other settlers and administered by a *majordomo*, who received a share of the profits.[27] Such rural businesses were closely monitored from urban centres which, slowly but relentlessly, established themselves in the landscape along the predictable pattern of central squares, churches, palaces and town halls: Asunción de Baracoa, founded in 1511, had been swiftly followed by San Salvador de Bayamo in 1513, Trinidad, Sancti Spiritus and Santa María del Puerto del Príncipe (as they renamed Camagüey) in 1514, and now Santiago and Havana in 1515.[28]

Established in Santiago, Velázquez and his compatriots comfortably settled into the business of extracting a fortune from the lands they had conquered. Velázquez certainly felt entitled to enjoy a life of leisure rather than attempting any more 'deeds of heroism'. Had he not, he was fond of asking, done more than enough on that front? He often recalled his participation in the last campaign against Granada in the early 1490s, an adventure that had left him 'ill and poor'.[29] Now, after more than two decades of hard toil in the New World – and happy in the knowledge that, as he had candidly written to King Fernando a few years previously, the natives of Cuba were 'much better disposed to the matters of our holy faith than those of Hispaniola or Puerto Rico'[30] – he felt at last able to enjoy a lifestyle worthy of his proud ancestry.

In his new Cuban capital, Velázquez began to build the imposing house of stone that still stands in the centre of Santiago and which soon became a venue for reunions with old friends, some of whom, like Juan de Grijalva and Velázquez's treasurer, Cristóbal de Cuéllar, were also natives of Cuéllar. Amid the banter and jollity that so often mark old friendships in new environments, in these *tertulias* Velázquez and his friends reminisced about the customs and traditions of Old Castile.

Prominent among these were the chivalric romances with which the vast majority of Castile's knightly classes identified. The phenomenally popular *Amadís de Gaula*, first printed in Zaragoza in 1508, was avidly read in the New World. Amadís is the son of the secret union of Perion, King of Wales, and Princess Elisena who, to protect her honour, conceals the birth by placing the baby in a boat that floats out to sea. The baby is rescued by a Scottish knight who brings him up in the court of his king. There, Amadís falls madly in love with Princess Oriana. The inevitable knight-errantry swiftly follows: a sequence of extraordinary adventures through exotic lands, enchanted islands, strange peoples and hidden wealth – all of which resonated with *Amadís*'s settler readership – in order to win the hand of his beloved Oriana.[31]

Amadís's success spawned many imitators, but the original – recasting ideals of late medieval chivalry in elevated Renaissance prose – remained the epitome of good taste, valour and nobility, and the model of worthy conversation.[32] Its author, Garci Rodríguez de Montalvo, capitalized on the book's success with a follow-up recounting the exploits of Amadís's son, Esplandián. *Sergas de Esplandián*, which went through at least ten editions in the sixteenth century, was far inferior to *Amadís*; yet it was this book in particular that caught the imagination of the Spanish settlers. That it did so was down to the way in which its plot lines could not but resonate with the world in which the settlers found themselves. The son of Amadís, now King of Wales, and Oriana, now Queen of England, Esplandián falls in love with Leonorina, daughter of the deposed Christian emperor of Constantinople and, as his father had done, undertakes a series of adventures in order to win her love. These adventures are interspersed with recognizable historical episodes. Esplandián summons the Christian rulers of Europe to the aid of Leonorina's father, urging none other than Isabel and Fernando to protect the Christians who live in Persia against those who are putting pressure on them to renounce their faith. Voices sound as though they come straight from the early sixteenth century: a pagan convert to Christianity has no qualms about criticizing Christian knights for fighting among themselves; the author himself intervenes with his own voice to urge the pope and the Catholic monarchs to work together in peace and in pursuit of justice.[33] Although Esplandián still battles against the odd giant, the enemies of Christendom are overwhelmingly depicted as real. Conversion is presented in a surprisingly pragmatic light: pagans convert because they are impressed by the behaviour of Christians, especially their humility and benevolence, and become rationally convinced of the truth of the Christian faith.[34]

So, when Velázquez and his friends came across a depiction of Calafia – the Amazon-like queen of a wealthy island inhabited solely by a tribe of warlike women – in *Sergas de Esplandián*, they would have hardly considered this a fantasy. After all, the description of Calafia was remarkably close to one of the Taíno legends – in Ramón Pané's description, at any rate. Could Pané's story have travelled to the Old World and been re-exported to the New, dressed in a chivalric romance steeped in historical realism? It certainly seemed so. Then, in Montalvo's work, Calafia herself enters history: ignorant of Christianity, she takes the pragmatic decision of siding with the Turks in the battle for Constantinople, after observing that in the eastern Mediterranean fortune always seems to favour the pagans. She sets griffins against the Christians, but the griffins fail to distinguish them from the Turks and attack the latter instead. Calafia is then captured by Christian forces and taken to Esplandián, with whom she falls in love. After Esplandián marries Leonorina, Calafia converts to Christianity, marries a Christian knight, and turns her once man-hating island into a Christian society of exemplary men and women.[35]

What is undoubtedly the case is that these stories were read and commented on by the Spanish settlers in the New World. When we recall that the islands that Velázquez had so recently mentioned to King Fernando were still firmly believed to be in Asia and inhabited by pagans that would soon be persuaded of the truth of the Christian faith, the influence of these romances in the imaginative world of the Castilian adventurers becomes immediately compelling. For Velázquez and his friends, these stories, the subject of endless conversations in the *tertulias* of Santiago de Cuba, carried equal weight with the narratives of Taíno myth, and profoundly influenced the way in which they viewed the new lands and their place, and role, in them. Early in 1516, however, the talk took on a more urgent edge, when news came from Spain that King Fernando was dead.

6

Imperial Designs

King Fernando had been ill for some time. He had tried hard to keep up with the demanding schedule of an itinerant monarch: in early January 1516 he even managed to attend the wedding of a daughter of one of his many illegitimate children in Plasencia. He was making his way from there to Seville when, on 20 January, he reached a small town in Extremadura called Madrigalejo. Exhausted, he realized that he could not go on. The Dominican friar Tomás de Matienzo heard his last confession and the king amended his will. His second grandson, the *Infante* Fernando, had been his original choice as successor to the kingdom of Castile. Now, however, Fernando chose his first: the son of Philip of Burgundy and Juana of Castile, Charles of Ghent.

There had been a clear logic in his original choice. Raised in Spain, the *Infante* was familiar with the languages and customs of the peninsula in a way that could not be said about Charles, who had been born and brought up at his father's court in Burgundy. This plan was more in tune with the King of Aragon's widely known but frustrated efforts to secure a male heir for his kingdom after his marriage to Germaine de Foix in 1506. Indeed, in the months before his death, the rumour began to spread that the reason for Fernando's illness was a mysterious potion made out of a bull's testicles that Queen Germaine was giving him in a curious effort to increase his fertility.[1]

On his deathbed, however, the king was ready to heed the advice of his ministers, who overwhelmingly favoured Charles. Most felt that a Burgundian heir would ease the tensions between the ministers of the Crown and a belligerently anti-Aragonese Castilian nobility that – rather naively, as it turned out – expected great things to come from northern Europe. For their part, the Burgundians were only too aware of the close ties created between the two economies by the growth in

Castilian wool production and the key role that the Low Countries had played in it, ties made all the more enticing by the fresh commercial opportunities now afforded by the New World. These circumstances had created a constant traffic of secret agents and place-hunters between the Netherlands and Castile, all determined to engineer Charles's succession.[2]

Leaving careful instructions for the regency of Castile to be entrusted to Cardinal Francisco Jiménez de Cisneros (and that of Aragon, Catalonia and Valencia to his own illegitimate son Alonso de Aragón), Fernando dictated an unusually affectionate letter to Charles, regretting that 'it had pleased God' not to allow them to meet before his death, and entrusting his wife Germaine to Charles's care.[3] The day after, 23 January, King Fernando died, in what Peter Martyr described as 'an ill-provided and unworthy little house'.[4] He was sixty-three.

The news reached Burgundy on 10 February. Immediately, Charles went on a charm offensive: summoning all the Spanish officials in Flanders to court, he tripled their salaries.[5] Yet even these Spanish supporters had their doubts about Charles as the future King of Castile: one among them, the future inquisitor-general, Alonso Manrique, warned its regent Jiménez de Cisneros on 8 March 1517 that Charles was very ignorant of Spain and completely under the thumb of Flemish officials. Manrique was worried about the openly pro-French bias of Charles's principal advisor, Guillaume II de Croÿ, the Sieur de Chièvres, who had already brokered a marriage between Charles and Louise, the then one-year-old daughter of Francis I of France. More immediately worrying to the Castilians was Manrique's revelation that Charles was soon to be proclaimed King of Spain in distant Brussels.[6] Although nominally united under the rule of Isabel and Fernando, Castilians were fiercely opposed to the Aragonese ministers who, under Fernando's rule, had dominated Castile's affairs; indeed, they had looked to Burgundy to provide a solution to their anti-Aragonese grievances. Now, they were hopeful that Fernando's death would allow Castile to regain some measure of independence. The Council of the Realm in Castile had already written to Charles requesting him politely to leave Castile alone. There was, the council advised, 'no need, while the queen, our lady and your mother, is alive, for you to use the title of king'. To do so would be an affront to 'the honour and reverence' that belonged to Juana 'by divine and human law'. If this was not clear enough, the

Council reminded Charles that, 'by virtue of the death of the Catholic King, your grandfather, you have not acquired any rights that you did not already possess; for these kingdoms did not belong to him.'[7]

The plea fell on deaf ears. Charles himself was already in the grip of his Aragonese grandfather's advisors. Those whom he had recently rewarded included Aragonese ministers who were widely resented in Castile for their perceived corruption. Yet they had flocked to the Burgundian court in the knowledge that Fernando's death had made Charles the undisputed King of Aragon – as he was not of Castile. Among their number was Fernando's most influential secretary, Lope Conchillos y Quintana. They also included a good number of *conversos*, who were at the time deeply resented in Castile. The last thing the Castilian nobility would have wanted when they looked to Burgundy for a solution to their anti-Aragonese grievances was to be given a government of Flemings, Aragonese and *conversos*, but this was now looking extremely likely. As the secretary of Jiménez de Cisneros wryly put it, he would rather entrust the affairs of Castile to the proudest Frenchman than to such a bunch.[8]

This state of affairs put the regent in a delicate position. Faced with groups of bellicose aristocrats who could still use the *Infante* Fernando as a valuable trump card and were determined to discredit the cardinal in the eyes of Charles's Burgundian ministers, Jiménez de Cisneros had no choice but to resort to repression. Separating the *Infante* from his supporters, Cisneros set about organizing a militia. With the support of Castile's cities, each of which was expected to make a contribution proportionate to its population – Ávila and Segovia provided 2,000 men; Toledo 3,500 – he quickly assembled a well-equipped force of about 30,000 men. Any complaints that his enemies made to Charles's ministers in Brussels foundered on Cisneros's firm conviction that Charles should be Fernando's undisputed successor as King of Castile.[9]

As this drama of high politics unfolded, that indefatigable defender of the Taínos, Bartolomé de Las Casas, had been characteristically busy. The death of Fernando – who had listened to him sympathetically during their short meeting in Plasencia – might have seemed like a setback, but Las Casas was undeterred. He sent Cisneros a translation of a long memorandum in Latin that he had already sent to Charles's ambassador in Spain, his old tutor Adrian of Utrecht, detailing the many atrocities that the settlers of Cuba and Hispaniola had been perpetrating against the indigenous peoples. It is not entirely clear whether Cisneros's decision to dismiss the de facto minister of the Indies, Juan Rodríguez de Fonseca (with whom Las Casas had famously clashed), had any connection with the contents of this memorandum, but Las Casas certainly saw the cardinal's move as a clear endorsement of his arguments. Adrian of Utrecht had been deeply shocked by Las Casas's allegations and made sure to express his horror to the cardinal. The latter did not need much persuading. He had been paying little heed to two of Las Casas's detractors, Pánfilo de Narváez and Antonio Velázquez, who had returned from Cuba to file a complaint against the campaigning cleric: they accused Las Casas of being 'lightweight, with little authority' and unworthy of trust because he was fond of 'speaking about things he does not know and has not seen and giving reasons that, in themselves, contradict one another'.[10] But Cisneros had already made up his mind to embrace Las Casas's campaign, appointing a group of Hieronymite friars with the task of implementing reform in 'the Indies'. He had also penned a letter to Charles himself, explaining this decision with reasoning that bears all the marks of Las Casas's influence: the instructions prepared for the friars, signed by Cisneros and Adrian of Utrecht on 18 September 1516, asked the friars to ensure that the natives of the New World were 'properly instructed in our Christian religion' so that they can 'live as men of reason'.[11]

In other respects, the cardinal's choice of religious order is not, at first sight, so easy to explain. While there had been a handful of Hieronymites in the New World – notably Friar Ramón Pané, who wrote about the Taínos of Hispaniola – the ethos of the Order was not particularly concerned with the evangelization of non-Christians. This put them at odds with the mendicants, for whom evangelizing was more or less their stock in trade. Yet the Hieronymites had strong connections with Cisneros's own order. From their earliest years in Spain the Hieronymites had developed a keen interest in Franciscan lay spirituality, in turn reflected in their enthusiastic championing of the classic *Laudi* of the popular thirteenth-century Italian Franciscan Iacopone da Todi.[12] This tradition had been enormously influential in the development of the late-medieval movement of Netherlandish spiritual revival known as the *devotio moderna*, which was most characteristically captured in the spiritual classic *The Imitation of Christ*, attributed to Thomas à Kempis. The movement lay very close to the heart of Charles of Ghent through the influence of his childhood tutor, Adrian of Utrecht.

It is more than likely, therefore, that Cisneros's choice of the Hieronymites was part of a wider effort to win the sympathy of the incoming regime. Las Casas's project could be easily construed as integral to the same movement of spiritual reform that Charles and his advisors were encouraging in Burgundy and which, for want of a better term, has become generally known as 'Erasmianism'. The term captures the manner in which the thought of Desiderius Erasmus, the influential sage of Rotterdam, succeeded in gaining the allegiance of the best minds of his time. Erasmus's secret was the deceptively simple way in which he managed to fuse into a single intellectual tradition the main conflicting currents of the late fifteenth century: the Netherlands piety of the *devotio moderna* and the Windisheim reform movement, Florentine Neo-Platonism, humanistic textual scholarship, and the various anxieties of what we might anachronistically call a growing 'middle class' increasingly aware of its needs and its potential for social action.[13] Much had been done already in this direction in Spain itself, not least by Cisneros himself. A mere glance at the Plateresque façade (meaning in the manner of a silversmith) of one of his most enduring foundations, the Complutense University in Alcalá de Henares, immediately transports us to a world as remote from the purity of the Gothic as it is from the Renaissance insistence on the subordination of detail to unity and harmony. Yet the style is nonetheless steeped in both traditions. It is therefore sharply suggestive of the intellectual eclecticism that would make Spain so uniquely receptive to Erasmus's writings: commercial contacts with Flanders had brought marked Flemish influences; ties between Italy and the Crown of Aragon had prepared the ground for the dissemination of Italian humanism; the introduction of the printing press in 1473 had helped to popularize humanist learning by making classical texts widely available to the interested public; and the Italian-inspired humanism patronized by the court soon found keen adherents among the growing 'middle classes' in urban areas – the very groups whom Isabel and Fernando had shrewdly chosen in their efforts to offset the destabilizing influence of an independent-minded aristocracy.

Not surprisingly, it was in Spain that the most wholehearted reception of 'Erasmianism' in Europe was staged. All the cultural and social trends that the movement addressed were not only present but also officially patronized and encouraged there. And it is not altogether fanciful to suppose that Cisneros saw in the Hieronymites a welcome group of allies in the much-needed encouragement of this trend. Erasmus's insistence that a return *ad fontes* – that is, a return to Scripture and the early, especially Patristic, sources of Christianity – was an essential remedy against the decay of contemporary society, was expressed above all in his *Enchiridion militis Christiani*, a work which enjoyed enormous popularity in Spain, especially after the accession of Charles of Ghent.[14] Its central message found strong echoes in the Hieronymite ethos, with its love of Scripture and manual labour, its distrust of philosophical speculation and its stress on the need for greater affectivity in spirituality.[15]

In late October 1516 the group of friars chosen for the mission arrived in Seville; there, they were unexpectedly met by Las Casas, demanding to travel in the same ship so that he could inform them properly about what was going on in 'the Indies'. Las Casas was worried: he had got wind that some of the Hieronymites had been won over by supporters of his opponent Miguel de Pasamonte, the influential treasurer in Santo Domingo. Moreover, the friars appeared to be ill-disposed towards the Taínos with whose conversion they had been entrusted. When Las Casas voiced his fears to an ailing Cisneros, he allegedly declared: 'In whom are we to trust? Go back there yourself and watch over everything!'[16] For all that, the Hieronymites refused to allow Las Casas to travel with them when they raised the sails of the *San Juan* on 11 November; his presence, they explained, would do little to help their peace of mind.[17] A few days later, Las Casas managed to board the *Trinidad*, on which a young man from Extremadura called Gonzalo de Sandoval, who was destined for a rather illustrious future, was also travelling.[18]

Reaching Santo Domingo on 20 December, the Hieronymites, distancing themselves from both settlers and officials, immediately set about implementing Cisneros's instructions. Freeing any Taínos belonging to absentee *encomenderos*, they travelled to the gold mines, attempting to resettle the workers into nearby towns where they could be taught the basics of agriculture. Their travels around the island confirmed that the Taíno population was in sharp decline. Many of the cities founded by Nicolás de Ovando had practically vanished, and those that remained seemed to be little more than labour camps to service the mines; there was, moreover, considerable evidence of slaving expeditions and of the continued capture of natives on the unlikely pretext that they were cannibals.[19] They confirmed, besides, that the bulk of Spanish settlers were contemptuous of the Taínos, considering them unworthy of instruction. Diagnosis, though, was easier than pre-scription. Explaining their views to Cisneros, the friars could only offer one practical piece of advice: the urgent need to import African slaves to Hispaniola in order to replace the ravaged Taíno population.

Las Casas was gratified that his recommendations had at last begun to bear some fruit, but the rift with the Hieronymites was never healed and it was made all the more irritating by Las Casas's insistence that the friars were not showing enough compassion for the Taínos or any willingness to address their spiritual and material needs. It was not long before he decided that his influence would be much more effective at the Spanish court, where he returned in early June.[20] After a swift crossing, he went at once to Aranda del Duero to meet Cisneros, but the cardinal's health had taken a turn for the worse. Now in his eight-ies, bedridden and in pain, Cisneros was too ill to meet Las Casas. Characteristically, the champion of the Taínos decided that he needed to go straight to the top and take his message directly to Charles him-self. He had made up his mind to travel to Charles's court in Burgundy when he was saved the trouble: in September 1517, Charles was, finally, on his way to visit his new Spanish kingdoms, having secured a loan of 40,000 ducats from his uncle, Henry VIII of England, to help with his expenses.[21]

Forced by bad weather to disembark on an isolated stretch of the Can-tabrian coast near San Vicente de la Barquera, Charles made slow progress with an entourage of 200 companions, wearily reaching Tord-esillas on 4 November 1517. There he had a brief meeting with his mother, Juana, whom he had last seen more than a decade before. After obtaining her consent – or claiming to have done so – to assume sole control of the kingdom, he summarily dismissed the ageing Cisneros. Charles's letter reached the gravely ill cardinal on 8 November; he died the same day.[22]

Ten days later, Charles entered Valladolid in triumph. In the days and weeks that followed, his trusted Burgundians were installed in key government roles, while Charles's rival for power in Castile, the *Infante*, was hastily shipped off to Flanders, thereby depriving the restive Cas-tilian nobles of a potential figurehead. Charles's key advisor, Sieur de Chièvres, was made chief accountant of Castile, a post so lucrative that he sold it to the Duke of Béjar for 30,000 ducats. Chièvres's wife, and the wife of the king's chief equerry Charles de Lannoy, received licences allowing them to take 300 horses and eighty pack mules laden with bullion, jewels and other luxuries out of Spain. Chièvres's sixteen-year-old nephew, meanwhile, was made Archbishop of Toledo – the successor of none other than Cisneros himself.[23]

Adapting quickly to the change of regime in Castile, Las Casas petitioned Charles's new chancellor Jean Sauvage, whom he conveniently found to be 'a most admirable man, most prudent and able'.[24] Initially his approaches met with success, Sauvage asking him to submit a detailed memorandum about the affairs of the Indies. But on 7 June, not long after Las Casas had sent the chancellor an outline of a plan for the peaceful evangelization of the north coast of South America, Sauvage died of typhus. Although his death was not particularly regretted in Spain, where he was widely regarded as a determinedly venal individual, it proved an unwelcome setback for Las Casas. With Sauvage out of the way, Juan Rodríguez de Fonseca swiftly tempted Chièvres with a suitable bribe that allowed him to recover his influence over the affairs of the Indies. Uninterested in the question of reform, he began to grant many new licences for slave raids. On 18 August he signed a decree giving permission to a Fleming, the governor of Bresse, Laurent Gorrevod, to import 4,000 black slaves to the Indies. Gorrevod soon sold the lucrative privilege to the chief accountant of the Casa de Contratación, Juan López de Recalde, who in turn resold it to Genoese merchants. Fonseca also successfully briefed against Cisneros's Hieronymite mission, persuading the king to bring it to an end on the grounds that it had failed to achieve the desired results. In order to shut down any further talk of reform, Fonseca installed his own protégé, Rodrigo de Figueroa, as governor of Hispaniola. He proposed that the new governor's assistant should be none other than Las Casas himself – a plan doubtless concocted to remove the troublesome cleric from the Spanish court.[25]

Las Casas was not tempted by Fonseca's ruse. Nor was he particularly perturbed by the end of the mission of the Hieronymites who had never, after all, shown much interest in his proposals. What was more, Las Casas knew from his correspondence with the eloquent Dominican friar Pedro de Córdoba that the Hieronymites had been totally overwhelmed by the first serious outbreak of smallpox in 1518. The Taínos had no immunity to the disease and the effects had been devastating. It was this situation that had made the demand for black slaves all the more urgent. Las Casas was not at this stage opposed to the idea, but he was appalled by the shameless venality of Fonseca and his cronies in the wake of the steady depopulation of Hispaniola. When, on 10 September 1518, Fonseca promulgated an order allowing all who lived in poverty in Spain the right to emigrate to the New World – offering them free passage, medicine, land, animals, seeds, and a delay of twenty years on the payment of any tax[26] – Las Casas turned to Adrian of Utrecht, now a cardinal and Grand Inquisitor. In chilling detail he related to him all the information he had been receiving from Friar Pedro about the continuing maltreatment of the Taínos.[27] It did not take Las Casas long to win the unconditional support of Charles's old tutor, who in turn won for him the authorization to reserve the continental land mass stretching from the Gulf of Urabá to the island of Margarita, known as Cumaná, exclusively for the mendicant orders. Las Casas wasted no time in setting off from Zaragoza, where Charles's court was in session, to persuade people in various parishes in Old Castile to leave their poverty behind and migrate to the New World. He returned to Zaragoza in October 1518, having recruited, to Fonseca's utter astonishment, 3,000 volunteers. Las Casas boasted that the figure could have easily been more than trebled had he not opted for caution in the face of a possible reaction by local aristocrats, who would deeply resent being deprived of cheap labour.[28]

These promising developments were to be temporarily eclipsed early in 1519. Having secured the agreement of the Aragonese *cortes* to accept him as king, Charles was on his way to Barcelona when, at Lérida, the news reached him that his grandfather, Emperor Maximilian I, had died on 12 January. The news was momentous, for Charles had a good claim to succeed him. The possibility was not, of course, a foregone conclusion, for the coveted post was elective and three other candidates – the French king Francis I, Henry VIII of England and the Elector of Saxony Frederick III – had thrown their hats into the ring. The front runner was Francis, who was supported by Pope Leo X, clearly uneasy about the unpalatable prospect of having Charles as emperor when he was already King of Aragon and, therefore, of the whole of southern Italy, Sicily and Sardinia. Francis had already secured the support of the Electorate of the Palatinate and the Archdiocese of Trier and was offering a tempting 300,000 guilders as election money.

But Charles was determined to put up a brave fight. He had been keenly groomed for the purpose by many of his close advisors, not least of them the very man he had recently chosen to replace Sauvage as Grand Chancellor: Mercurino Arborio, Marquis of Gattinara. The appointment of this part-Burgundian, part-Piedmontese statesman signalled a radical reversal of the Francophilia of Sauvage and Chièvres. No sooner had the news of Maximilan's death reached the Spanish court than Gattinara seized upon the recently discovered 'Indies' as a powerful portent of a growing belief: that Charles would be, as he put it, the 'last world emperor'.[29]

The idea was not new. The recently discovered *Oratio Supplicatoria* addressed by Gattinara to Charles in 1516 – the moment the young Habsburg succeeded to the Spanish throne – sheds valuable light on the slow gestation of Gattinara's imperial vision. A curious document, it begins with a short sonnet in Italian outlining the various supernatural sources of his belief in 'the true universal monarchy'.[30] The phrase loudly echoes an old idea popular among those who believed that the supreme authority of the Holy Roman Emperor trumped even that of the pope.[31] Its deployment allowed Gattinara to set out what amounted to a job application for an exceptionally lofty role: to help the future emperor understand his divine mission, which was nothing less than to bring about the culmination of Christian history. Charles, Gattinara wrote, was destined to subdue the infidel, travel to Jerusalem, climb Golgotha, remove the crown from his head, place it on the very spot where Christ was crucified, and offer Christendom to God the Father.[32] Gattinara, in other words, urged Charles to accept a divinely ordained mission in a spirit immediately reminiscent of Columbus's messianic exhortations to Isabel and Fernando. To this end he juxtaposed themes from the imperial tradition of prophecy with apocalyptic themes associated with the Crown of Aragon – in particular the writings of the thirteenth-century Aragonese polymath Arnau of Vilanova, whose writings had met with a resurgence of interest at Fernando's court.[33] The death of Emperor Maximilan served as a trigger to reinforce the efforts of imperial panegyrists to tell the story of the *Reconquista* – now almost three decades past – in imperial terms: the recovery of the ancient Roman province of Hispania from Islam was glaring proof that the Spanish Crown was God's chosen instrument to bring about the final unification of the world. Now in the possession of the Habsburgs, the heirs of Augustus, the Spanish Crown would become the new focal point of the empire, the God-appointed scourge of Islam, and the bearer of the *pietas* that had been the source of the greatness of ancient Rome.[34]

The new spirit evoked by Gattinara was at once classical and romantic, imperial and Christian, and it was put to full effect in the race to beat Francis I to the imperial Crown. The most immediate hurdle was financial, but Charles turned to Jakob Fugger for help. This fabulously rich German banker had very substantial investments in Habsburg territories, which made Charles the obvious candidate in his mind. In a few months Fugger raised a staggering 850,000 guilders, after which Charles was unanimously elected Holy Roman Emperor at the Church of St Bartholomew in Frankfurt on 28 June 1519. The news reached him in Barcelona on 6 July, after which Gattinara hailed him as 'the most important emperor' since Charlemagne, for he was now able to gather the world into 'the care of a single shepherd'.[35] This ethos would be memorably captured in Titian's equestrian portrait of Charles. Evocative of antique Roman equestrian statues of stoic Roman emperors, most notably that of Marcus Aurelius in the Roman Capitol, Titian's Charles is also a chivalrous Christian emperor, wearing the collar of the Burgundian Order of the Golden Fleece. It was precisely through his endorsement and extension of this prestigious Burgundian Order that Charles reasserted his role as a veritable knight-emperor, pledging to maintain the unity of Christendom by defence of the faith and the practice of the imperial virtues, which he and his successors would spread throughout the world alongside the gospel of Christ. It was in just this spirit that Charles would be hailed by Ludovico Ariosto as the ruler who would spring from the union of the houses of Austria and Aragon, and succeed to the diadem of Augustus, Trajan, Marcus Aurelius and Severus, bringing Christendom into a new Golden Age.[36]

Las Casas had been following these developments with interest. He eagerly welcomed Charles's election, seeing it as a new opportunity to win the chancellor's backing – and that of the new emperor – for his Cumaná project, and to sidestep Fonseca's plans in the process. For their part, the new emperor and his chancellor saw Las Casas's plans as an early opportunity to implement the vision of Charles as a pastoral 'world emperor'. They proposed setting up a committee to assist Las Casas, even allowing him to choose its members. Moreover, the project was refined with the new imperial vision clearly in mind: the proposed settlers were given knightly titles hitherto reserved for the official elite of the Holy Roman Emperor and would be known as Knights of the Golden Spur. They were to be accompanied by twelve mendicant friars and ten native interpreters, and they were to be allowed to trade in pearls and to have African slaves at their service.[37]

The imperial election had transformed Las Casas's fortunes: now he basked in the favour of Emperor Charles. When Juan de Quevedo, a Franciscan who had accumulated a considerable fortune in Darién and was at odds with Las Casas's positive opinion of the Taínos, disputed with him in front of Charles and Gattinara, both the emperor and his chancellor brushed Quevedo's opinions aside.[38] Notwithstanding that the only source we have for this exchange is Las Casas himself, who preened at Charles and Gattinara's evident goodwill towards him, their support spoke volumes. The unconditional imperial backing he received for a scheme to entrust 1,000 leagues of fertile land to fifty Knights of the Golden Spur – in the face of the understandable scepticism of, among others, Fonseca and the chronicler Gonzalo Fernández de Oviedo – suggests that, for now, Las Casas's vision for the New World had won the day.[39]

Charles, however, had urgent matters to attend to and they were not in Spain. Early in 1520 the court began to make progress northward, towards La Coruña, from where it would sail to Charles's new imperial domains in northern Europe. In preparation for his departure, Charles signed a decree, endorsed, among others, by Gattinara and Adrian of Utrecht – the latter had been appointed Regent in Charles's absence. The decree concerned the government of the new territories in 'the Indies' and the obligation of settlers to care for the material and spiritual welfare of its native inhabitants. The detailed guidelines could have been penned by Las Casas himself. The decree also reinstated Diego Colón, who had been recalled by King Fernando in 1514 after Diego had fallen foul of royal officials sympathetic to Fonseca. The influence of Las Casas was clearly behind this decision too. In gratitude, Colón invested handsomely in Las Casas's Cumaná project.[40]

This wholehearted embrace of Las Casas's principles by Charles's ministers had as much to do with self-interest as reforming zeal. A few months previously, in the autumn of 1519, two messengers had reached Seville carrying some objects of great beauty. They had been sent by

Hernán Cortés, secretary to Diego Velázquez, the governor of Cuba. Velázquez had given Cortés permission to lead an expedition to the 'island' of Yucatan, with very modest aspirations, but had grown suspicious of his secretary when he saw the magnitude of the operation he had mounted. Cortés, who had managed to leave Cuba swiftly before Velázquez had the chance to apprehend him, now stood condemned of rebellion by Velázquez for leading the expedition well beyond the terms of the original contract. Fonseca had been informed and was ready to arrest the two envoys and have them executed. Then, on 30 April 1520, the Council of the Realm, headed up by Gattinara and Adrian of Utrecht, ruled that Cortés be allowed to continue his expedition, free now of any obligations to Velázquez. The decision came after the emperor had granted an audience to the messengers sent by Cortés. Reaching the imperial court at Valladolid in early April, during Holy Week, they presented Charles with a long letter, claiming to be composed by members of the town council (*cabildo*) of Villa Rica de la Vera Cruz, a town founded by Cortés in Mexico. An elaborate justification of Cortés's act of rebellion, it argued that the decision to break with Velázquez was taken under pressure from the popular will as represented by the army, composed, as they claimed, of 'noble *hidalgos*, jealous of the service owed to Our Lord and Your Royal Highnesses',[41] an argument that, ironically, Velázquez himself had used when bypassing the authority of Diego Colón and communicating directly with King Fernando.[42] Cortés, however, added an additional, irresistible, argument. His insubordination was justified, the letter continued, because it was done in the service of the king. Mexico was a land of great wealth, beauty and sophistication, and its peoples had shown a remarkable willingness to accept the sovereignty of Castile and convert to the Christian faith.[43] Of these arguments, one in particular lodged in Charles's mind after he had had a chance to inspect the stunning objects that Cortés had sent. It was now clear to Charles that the lands across the Ocean Sea were of far greater importance, both culturally and materially, than anyone had hitherto realized. In a speech, made shortly after, to the *cortes* of Santiago de Compostela, Charles made reference to Mexico: a new 'gold-bearing world', which had just been added to his domains.[44]

On 29 May 1520, Charles finally set sail from La Coruña. Nine days later rebellion broke out in Castile, sending a clear signal that although the new imperial vision had been embraced at court, the people were not so keen. The root of the *comunero* revolt – as it came to be known – was a deep sense of grievance at what was widely perceived as an affront to the independence of the parliamentary institutions known as *cortes*. The general anger was directed against the erosion of the privileges of the Castilian towns, which the rebels claimed had the right to assemble the *cortes* on their own initiative every three years. In sharp contrast to this principle, Charles had asked for money twice in the space of three years, while his venal ministers had shipped vast quantities of money abroad.[45] More generally, Charles had not come across well to his new subjects. He appeared to know little about Spain and was unable to speak the language, while his physical appearance was remote from any-body's idea of a 'last world emperor'. Unprepossessing and gawky, with a jutting jawline, he was – in the words of the Venetian ambassador Piero Pasqualigo – 'thin beyond belief, pale, melancholy, his mouth always open and drooping, as are his eyes, which seem stuck onto his face and not his own'.[46]

The imperial agenda had thus left a bad impression across the towns of north and central Castile, producing a furious indignation that expressed itself in the demands of the Junta of Tordesillas, the highest organizational body of the revolt, on 20 October: no town officials (*corregidores*) should in future be appointed without the specific consent of the town concerned, while the emperor should commit to residing in Castile, bring no foreigners with him, and conform in all things to the customs of his grandparents, Fernando and Isabel. In this way the rebels raised the banner of revolt in what has been aptly described as 'a gallant but hopeless attempt to prove to themselves that, although everything had changed, it could still be the same'.[47] Las Casas was quick to take advantage of Charles's distracted ministers to consolidate his conces-sions. He gaily reassured Adrian of Utrecht, preoccupied with the revolt, that in two years his scheme would provide the new emperor with approximately 10,000 new tax-paying vassals who, after three years, would yield a revenue of nearly 6 million *marvedís*; a figure that would rise to 11 million after six years and 23 million in the course of a decade.[48]

As the *comunero* revolt continued to rage across Castile, Las Casas raised sail from Seville on 14 December, reaching Puerto Rico on 10 January 1521. There, Las Casas began to realize that the followers he had gathered in Castile were to prove much less amenable to his designs than he had imagined. Some fell ill and died; some settled so well that they became reluctant to leave Puerto Rico; others were enticed by Juan Ponce de León, who was mounting yet another expedition to Florida, to join him.[49] When, at long last, Las Casas set off for Cumaná from Santo Domingo in July, he had only a handful of his original companions with him. And it was not long before things began to go awry. When he reached Cumaná on 8 August, the group barely had time to build a settlement when they were attacked by groups of Indians who killed a Franciscan and five settlers and then burned the wooden house that Las Casas had built for himself.[50] Two months later Las Casas was back in Santo Domingo, having been shipwrecked in the southern port of Yáquimo, on what is now Haiti, after a desperate escape. Deeply disillusioned, he sought the help of the Dominicans. The new Provincial in Santo Domingo, Friar Domingo de Betanzos, suggested that Las Casas had done enough to defend the indigenous peoples and that he now needed to think about his own spiritual welfare. The inevitable mockery that the disastrous experiment provoked only served to convince Las Casas that the failure was a divine punishment for the element of greed still present in his scheme. From now on he convinced himself that any future venture could afford no flirtation with Mammon. A prolonged period of self-examination followed, during which he made up his mind to enter the Dominican order.[51]

If Las Casas had succeeded in eradicating Mammon from his mind, it had become firmly entrenched in the imagination of the imperial court. Charles had taken the objects sent by Cortés with him on his travels, reportedly making great show of them to his fellow princes.[52] They were put on display in Brussels, where they were seen by one of the greatest artists of the day, Albrecht Dürer. On 27 August 1520, Dürer described in his journal the experience of seeing them. His account yields the sense of a growing consciousness in Europe that the New World was far more important than anything hitherto imagined. The great artist went from exhibit to exhibit in a state of mesmerized fascination: 'a sun all of gold a whole fathom broad, and a moon all of silver of the same size' were flanked by 'two rooms full of armour of the people there, and all manner of wondrous weapons of theirs, harness and darts, very strange clothing, beds, and all kinds of wonderful objects of human use, much better worth seeing than prodigies'.

Frustration coloured his wonder: frustration at not being able adequately to describe the objects he was seeing, and the impression they made on him. To read this passage is to enter the mental world of someone fully conscious that a new age had dawned: 'All the days of my life I have seen nothing that rejoiced my heart so much as these things, for I saw amongst them wonderful works of art, and I marvelled at the subtle Ingenia of men in foreign lands.'[53]

7

The Lure of China

With the objects that so moved Albrecht Dürer, Cortés had sent a series of dispatches. One of them spoke with conviction about the sophistication of the peoples in the newly discovered lands and of the stunning beauty of the landscape, 'as pleasing to behold as it is fertile'. It was therefore eminently suitable 'for cultivation . . . and all manner of livestock'. A mere five leagues inland there was a magnificent mountain range, with peaks unlike anything known in the Old World. One was so high that its summit could only be seen on very clear days, hovering above the clouds, 'and so white that we think it might be covered in snow, and even the natives assure us that it is snow; but since we have not seen it properly, and taking into consideration the warmth of this climate, we do not dare affirm that it really is snow.'[1]

What Cortés described was an imposing peak called Citlaltepetl in Nahuatl, meaning 'Star Mountain' and nowadays commonly known as the Pico de Orizaba, the highest mountain in Mexico and the highest volcanic peak in the world. It crowns a mountain mass of vast proportions; so vast that, as Cortés's description suggested, the explorers had no way of understanding the physical magnitude of what now confronted them, not least because Velázquez's instructions to Cortés gave no indication that the expedition would come across anything but islands. What the explorers thought they were charting was a long line of coast to the west, divided by a strait from the 'islands' of Yucatan and Ulúa, beyond which there was an unknown territory that many imagined to be China.

The aim of Cortés's expedition, at least in theory, was to search for the expedition led by Juan de Grijalva, which had set off from Cuba a year before Cortés, in April 1518, and had not returned. In the process, and in tune with the conversations that the settlers had become used to

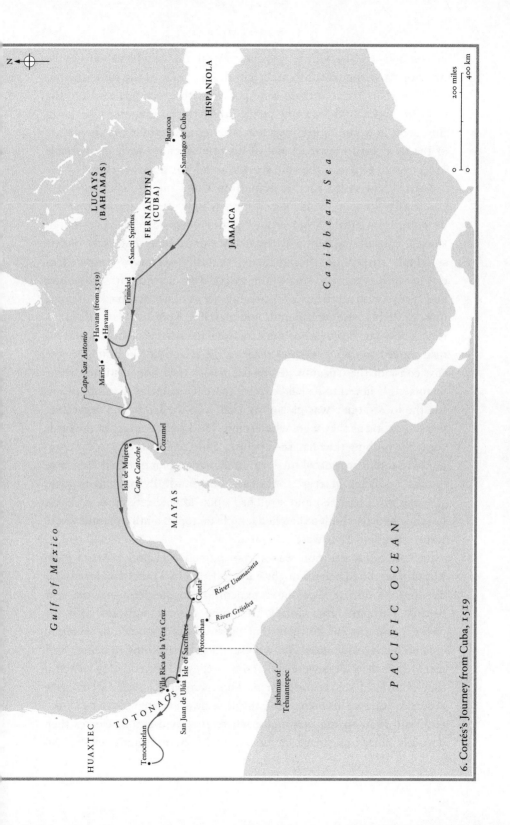

6. Cortés's Journey from Cuba, 1519

in Santiago de Cuba, Cortés was also to establish the whereabouts of the Amazons and endeavour to ascertain the accuracy of the rumours that somewhere in Yucatan there were people with enormous ears and the faces of dogs.[2] By the time he penned his letter to Emperor Charles in July 1519, however, Cortés was much better informed about the nature of the new territories than any of his predecessors, with the possible exception of Grijalva, the man for whom he was now searching.

Cortés had sailed for Yucatan from Cuba on 18 February 1519, studiously ignoring Velázquez's increasingly desperate attempts to decommission him. The governor had first entrusted the expedition to Cortés, considering him a trustworthy subordinate, but grew understandably suspicious after realizing that the operation consisted of eleven ships, 530 men – of whom thirty were armed with crossbows and twelve with arquebuses – sixteen horses and several packs of dogs, most probably Irish wolfhounds and mastiffs. This was blatantly far in excess of what the governor's instructions required. But Cortés and his men moved swiftly and soon reached the island of Cozumel, off the east coast of the Yucatan peninsula, where they hoped to find some Spaniards believed to be held captive there. Cozumel was full of promise: the local honey was gloriously rich, and the fruits and vegetables were as exotic as they were wholesome. The bright colours of the birds were like nothing they had seen before, a suitable corollary to the comparative sophistication of the local inhabitants. Not only did they have 'books', as Peter Martyr would call the beautifully painted pictures smeared with bitumen and stretched upon long sheets made of bark, but they had also built a thatched temple on top of a tall pyramid where some intriguing idols were venerated.[3]

In Cortés's expedition was a man named Melchor, a Maya from Yucatan who had been brought back to Cuba by Francisco Hernández de Córdoba during his ill-fated expedition to the peninsula the year before. Through him, Cortés attempted to communicate with the natives, pointing out to them that there was only one God, who had created heaven and earth and who sustained everything in being. This meant that their idols were evil and that they all risked going to hell if they continued to venerate them. This peroration over, Cortés gave orders to some of his men to roll the idols down the temple steps and to build an altar on the very place where they had stood. Cortés then devoutly placed an image of the Virgin Mary on it and ordered two carpenters to build a tall cross to be placed on the high tower of the pyramid.[4] The reaction of the Mayas to these blatant affronts is difficult to fathom, for no reliable record survives. It is nonetheless remarkable that a few weeks later, when, on his onward journey around Yucatan, Cortés decided to return to Cozumel to fix a brigantine carrying vital supplies that had begun to leak near Isla Mujeres, just off the north coast of the peninsula, he was gratified to find the image of the Virgin and the cross still in place and duly honoured by the Mayas.[5]

For good reasons, historians tend to give short shrift to such accounts. But this was only the first of many incidents in which Spanish explorers destroyed indigenous idols and replaced them with Christian images without any apparent opposition. The practice set a pattern of so puzzling a consistency that it demands an explanation. What, then, was going on? First, we need to remember that Cortés was working within a long-established tradition in which attitudes towards non-Christians had been remarkably consistent. Since at least the time of Emperor Constantine's conversion to Christianity in 312, no one had seemed in any doubt that the universalism of the Christian Church made her the ideal spiritual ally of the universal empire. As Constantine's official panegyrist, Eusebius of Caesarea, had put it, 'by the express appointment of the same God, two roots of blessing, the Roman Empire and the doctrine of Christian piety, sprang up together for the benefit of mankind'.[6] This meant that as the Church came to take the place of the Empire's old civic organization as the organ of popular consciousness, so Christians grew in the conviction that Jesus's instruction to his apostles had already been accomplished: the gospel had indeed been taken to the ends of the – then – known world. And if this was so, it followed that conversion was not a matter of going out into the wilderness to compel pagans to accept the truth; it was, rather, a matter of inviting those already inside the universal society to enter into the sacramental life of the Church. There might still be a few fringes here and there where the gospel had yet to take root, but the advantages of belonging to the universal Christian society were plain to everyone. Christianity and civilization went hand in hand.

Over the centuries, this attitude remained surprisingly unchallenged. Even encounters with peoples who could never have had the chance to hear the gospel are marked by a disarming confidence. In the thirteenth century, for example, the Franciscans John of Plano Carpini and

William of Rubruck took the gospel into the lands of the pagan Tartars and Mongols. Their accounts are full of descriptions of practices sharply at odds with the most elementary tenets of the gospel; yet these practices are described with the solid conviction that pagans will readily become Christians as soon as they are made aware of their twisted ways. 'If an army of the Church were to come,' wrote Rubruck, 'it would be a very easy thing to subjugate all these countries . . . and take possession of the whole world.' And the bull of Pope Innocent IV to the emperor of the Tartars candidly reprimanded him for 'laying waste many countries in a horrible desolation' through his deliberate turning away from an 'innate law', which unites 'not only men, but even the irrational animals . . . after the manner of the celestial spirits, all of which God the Creator has divided into choirs in the enduring stability of peaceful order'.[7]

In much the same way, Cortés seemed just as certain that as soon as the Christian message was announced to the Mayas, they would realize the error of their ways, remember their true origin, and set their spiritual house in order. There was, after all, no question about their humanity; there could therefore be no question about their innate susceptibility to divine grace. As humans, moreover, they already belonged to the universal society of Christendom; indeed, the gospel must have reached them at some stage in the past.[8]

If Cortés was convinced that the Mayas would receive the gospel gratefully, what about the ostensive willingness of the Mayas to do so? The simple answer is that their apparent tolerance was only to be expected. In a polytheistic pantheon, new deities were not apt to arouse jealousy, particularly if they were the deities of powerful people. The Mayas had often adopted foreign deities in the past and they were more than willing to do it now. What Cortés and his men did not realize was that the acceptance of the Christian God into the densely populated pantheon of the Mayas actually reinforced rather than challenged their polytheism. This particular problem, however, would not emerge with any clarity for some time. For now, Cortés took their 'conversion' at face value.

His optimism was reinforced by another significant development. As the expedition was getting ready to leave once again for Isla Mujeres, Cortés and his men spotted a canoe coming towards them from the mainland. It carried three men wearing only loincloths, their hair 'tied as women's hair is tied', and armed with bows and arrows. On reaching the shore, one of them approached the Castilians and asked, in Spanish: 'Gentlemen. Are you Christians? Whose subjects are you?' On hearing their reply, the man burst into tears and asked them to give thanks to God, just as he himself was doing. He recounted how he had been on a ship making its way from Darién to Santo Domingo in the spring of 1511, entrusted to inform the governor about the intractable enmity that had developed between the settlers there when, on its approach to Jamaica, their ship struck shoals. He and about twenty others had set off in a rowing boat but were caught in a strong westerly current that eventually brought the few who survived to the Yucatan coast, where they had been captured. Five had been sacrificed and eaten; the man and some others had been put in cages to be fattened. They had managed to escape and had been received by a rival *cacique* called Xamanzana, who had enslaved them.[9]

This was Gerónimo de Aguilar, a man of remarkable resilience and strength of character. He had taken religious vows as a Franciscan friar in his youth: vows which, during his period of enslavement, he had managed to keep, resisting the many women offered him by the natives and keeping up with the daily recitation of the divine office. This had allowed him to keep an impressively accurate record of the time: he was only three days out. By contrast, another survivor, Gonzalo Guerrero, had taken a Maya wife with whom he had fathered three children. With his face and hands tattooed and his nose and ears pierced, Guerrero was in no mood to return to the Spanish way of life; but Aguilar was more than willing to do so. Cortés was delighted, for Aguilar was by now fluent in Maya, and his Castilian, though understandably rusty, was incomparably better than Melchor's. Using Aguilar as an interpreter, Cortés again preached to the Mayas about the danger they were in if they – as he explained with clear poetic licence – did not abandon their ridiculous idols with their damnable demands for human sacrifice. He then ordered his men to complete the destruction of the idols. Far from antagonizing the Mayas, the initiative seems to have inspired their affectionate devotion. They even implored Cortés to leave behind a preacher who might continue their instruction in the Christian faith.[10]

Cortés left Cozumel elated, convinced that the inhabitants of these 'islands' would be admirable Christians and loyal subjects of the kingdom of Spain. Stopping once again at Isla Mujeres to replenish their supplies, they caught a shark that bore evidence of the now regular

European activity in the Caribbean: cutting it open, they found in its belly over thirty rations of pork, substantial amounts of cheese, a tin plate and three leather shoes.[11] They then sailed around the Yucatan in late March 1519, stopping between the mouths of two navigable rivers: the Usumacinta and the Grijalva. Cortés decided to explore, sailing up the Grijalva with about 200 men in brigantines. Soon they came across settlements with houses of stone which gave every indication that the local builders had, as Peter Martyr would put it, 'real talent'.[12] Tense negotiations ensued, with the Spaniards demanding large quantities of food and the Indians urging them to leave immediately. Cortés then ordered the notary, Diego de Godoy, to read a proclamation – which Aguilar translated to the bewildered Indians – asking them to submit to the authority of the monarchs of Castile. Instead, the Indians attacked.[13] They used bows and arrows, stones flung from slings, and swords with obsidian blades. Although the Spaniards were greatly outnumbered and about twenty of them were wounded, Cortés managed to put ashore some of his cannons. The noise frightened the Indians, who began to flee. In the middle of the confusion, the tempestuous Pedro de Alvarado led a surprise attack that allowed the Spaniards to take possession of the town. Despite the wounded, their only loss had been the now undoubtedly embittered Melchor, who had fled in the confusion. Aguilar subsequently discovered, while questioning some of the prisoners, that Melchor had been urging the Indians not to give up, for the Spaniards were mortal, just like them.[14]

Called Potonchan by its inhabitants, the captured town was renamed by Cortés, with characteristic fanfare, Santa María de la Victoria.[15] Cortés was gratified to have tested the effect of artillery, confirming that it gave the Castilians a huge advantage even against comparably sophisticated enemies who greatly outnumbered them. Fighting resumed a few days later, as the expedition made its way back to the coast. The Castilians were confronted along the fields of Centla, a flat expanse of richly fertile land with ample supplies of maize. Again outnumbered, Cortés decided to bring out some horses. The effect was even more immediate and decisive than the noise of the cannons. The sight of a horse is impressive at any time; but to a group of people who had never seen such animals – and who saw them mounted by men who seemed inseparably fused to them – it was a terrifying experience.[16] It is no surprise that the ensuing days brought conciliatory gestures: Cortés and his men were visited by emissaries carrying food and gifts, including some objects of gold and turquoise, and twenty women to serve and cook for them. Communication was difficult, for the Maya spoken in the region was not the one Aguilar was familiar with, but Cortés seemed happy to conclude that the emissaries were eager to accept the authority of the monarchs of Castile. He thus arranged for them formally to accept their vassalage in front of the notary Pedro Gutiérrez and then sternly instructed them to abandon their human sacrifices and demonic idols, which were suitably smashed and replaced by a Christian altar and cross.[17] Cortés also arranged for the twenty women to be baptized and given Christian names. One, called Malinali, became Marina. She would soon become Cortés's mistress. A woman of sharp intelligence and practical good sense, whose loyalty to Cortés seems to have known no bounds, Marina had the added advantage of speaking both Maya and Nahuatl, the lingua franca of central Mexico; she was able, therefore, to speak in Nahuatl with the Mexica and then in Maya with Aguilar, who would then speak in Castilian to Cortés. It would not be long, however, before Marina mastered enough Castilian to make Aguilar redundant. She and Cortés would thus come to constitute what has aptly been described as a 'duet . . . which often combined eloquence with subtlety, piety with menace, sophistication with brutality'.[18] If, as the humanist scholar Antonio de Nebrija had famously told Queen Isabel on presenting her with his seminal Castilian Grammar back in 1492, 'language has always been the companion of empire', then Cortés could not have made a better choice of companion.[19]

Rested and well fed, the explorers resumed their journey along the Gulf of Mexico. On 21 April 1519, Maundy Thursday, they reached an island that had been named San Juan de Ulúa by Juan de Grijalva the year before. The next day, Good Friday, Cortés and about 200 men, equipped with horses, dogs and artillery, set off in brigantines for the mainland, landing in the Totonac town of Chalchicueyecan, the site of the modern port of Veracruz. The Totonacs, who remembered Grijalva fondly, greeted the Castilians with food and presents. On Easter Sunday another emissary arrived. He introduced himself as Tendile, governor of Cuetlaxtlan (present-day Cotaxtla) – a nearby province on the eastern edge of the area controlled by the great Mexica city state of Tenochtitlan.[20] He had been sent, he announced, by none other than Moctezuma himself. Tendile seemed at ease with the intruders and Cortés soon warmed to him, asking him to greet the Mexica emperor on his behalf and entrusting him with some presents to take back to him. The great Mexica emperor was the ninth *tlahtoani* or ruler of the powerful triple alliance that dominated central Mexico. He had been in power since 1502 and is more than likely to have heard about the strange intruders ever since they had first settled in Darién, renaming it Castilla del Oro, nearly a decade before. He had been informed of their recent arrival in Yucatan, of the ease with which they had defeated the inhabitants of Potonchan, and of the deep aversion they seemed to harbour for human sacrifice, the linchpin of the religious system that Moctezuma represented. If the memories of the Nahua informers of the Franciscan chronicler Bernardino de Sahagún, written down a generation later, are to be believed, Moctezuma seems to have been utterly bewildered by the relentless advance of the Castilians. Indeed, he seemed anxious in the extreme, filled with a 'swooning' dread. 'His soul was sickened and his heart was anguished', and he repeatedly asked his courtiers, 'What will happen to us?'[21] The emperor's mood is not likely to have improved with the reports, sent back by Tendile to Tenochtitlan, describing the deafening sound of the Castilian artillery and the damage it caused, splintering large trees to smithereens. The reports described the horses as 'deer . . . as tall as roof terraces'; the dogs, meanwhile, were like nothing they had ever seen, with 'ears folded over, great dragging jowls' and 'fiery yellow eyes'. When Moctezuma heard all this, he was 'terrified. It was as if he fainted away. His heart saddened; his heart failed him.'[22]

The ill portents continued to pile up. Among the presents sent to Moctezuma by Cortés was a helmet that, by an uncanny coincidence, bore a marked resemblance to the headgear sported by Huitzilopochtli, the god who had led the Mexica to their promised land in the valley of Mexico and whose statue was venerated in the great temple at Tenochtitlan. Equally disturbing for Moctezuma, the blue colour of Cortés's personal flag was exactly the same as the colour associated with Huitzilopochtli. This cast Moctezuma's worship of Huitzilopochtli's rival god, Quetzalcoatl, in a worrying light. As recently as 1505 the Mexica emperor had built an unusual round temple in honour of Quetzalcoatl, placing it in the sacred precinct at Tenochtitlan.[23] According to legend, Quetzalcoatl had been among the founders of the sacred Toltec city of Tollan, from where he was expelled by enemy gods, Huitzilopochtli among them, possibly as a result of his alleged opposition to human sacrifice. It was said that he had fled first to the city of Cholollan before vanishing across the eastern sea on a raft of serpents. Now, yet another disturbing coincidence presented itself to Moctezuma. The year of Cortés's arrival, 1519, was the year I-Reed in the Mexican calendar. Quetzalcoatl was believed to have been born in I-Reed and to have died, after an exact 'century' of fifty-two years, according to the Mexica sacred calendar, also in I-Reed. As an indigenous source noted, I-Reed was a particularly bad year for kings: 'according to the signs . . . I-Crocodile . . . strikes the old men . . . I-Jaguar, I-Deer, I-Flower . . . the children . . . I-Reed . . . strikes at kings . . .'[24] It was also widely accepted that the east was the direction associated with the sign of the Reed. Not only had the Castilians come from the east, the direction in which Quetzalcoatl had disappeared on his raft of serpents, but they had also come dressed in black, one of Quetzalcoatl's colours – for Cortés and his men, of course, landing on Good Friday, the colour had an altogether different connotation. Everything, in other words, seemed to Moctezuma to indicate that the arrival of these bearded intruders who opposed human sacrifice heralded the return of Quetzalcoatl.

This is the story that began to circulate in the wake of the fall of Tenochtitlan and which, by the middle of the sixteenth century, had become firmly entrenched in conquistador myth-history.[25] Yet there is nothing to indicate that this is what Moctezuma himself thought. It is just as likely that he may have believed the Castilians were led by the god Tezcatlipoca, the 'smoking mirror', who had tricked Quetzalcoatl into leaving Tollan and who specialized in bringing about confusion, misery and disease.[26] Far from being morbidly obsessed with ill omens, the scanty available evidence suggests that Moctezuma felt in control of the situation. Determined to appease the intruders, he sent another envoy, Teoctlamacazqui – whom he had dispatched the previous year to meet Juan de Grijalva – with presents of great munificence: it was this gesture that later interpreters understood as a sign that Moctezuma thought he was dealing with deities, for the gifts included offerings related to the legends of Quetzalcoatl and Tezcatlipoca.[27] According to the subsequent testimony of the Dominican Diego Durán, Moctezuma went as far as ordering Teoctlamacazqui to allow himself to be eaten in the event that the Castilians did not like the food on offer and appeared keen to eat human flesh: 'I promise to look after your wife and children if you do,' Moctezuma reassured his envoy.[28]

Yet Moctezuma's displays of munificence, intended to dissuade Cortés from advancing towards Tenochtitlan, had precisely the opposite effect: if Moctezuma could afford to lavish these gifts on them, the Castilians reasoned, what riches might await them in the Mexica capital? The temptation grew even stronger sometime in May, when Moctezuma sent the stunning objects that Dürer would see in Brussels. They came with plenty of good food, some of which some later sources claimed, rather incongruously, to have been ceremoniously sprinkled with the blood of recently sacrificed humans. This deeply deferential gesture did not have the desired effect. On seeing the gifts, some Nahua nobles later recalled, the Castilians 'closed their eyes tight. They shut their eyes. They shook their heads . . . Much did it revolt them. It nauseated them.'[29]

Before taking their leave, Moctezuma's envoys presented the Castilians with a litany of reasons for the inadvisability of going to Tenochtitlan: the route was full of deserts, insurmountable obstacles and dangerous enemies.[30] But any qualms that Cortés might have harboured about making the onward journey vanished with the arrival of a group of Totonacs from the city of Cempohuallan (present-day Cempoala). What they told Cortés could not have been more reassuring. The Mexica, they said, were intolerable tyrants who gave little in return for the heavy tribute they extracted from their vassals.[31] Around the same time Cortés reportedly received messengers from Ixtlilxochitl, a noble lord of Tetzcoco (present-day Texcoco), one of the three city states in the Valley of Mexico that made up the dominant Triple Alliance, of which Tenochtitlan was the most important member. Ixtlilxochitl also informed Cortés that the Mexica were deeply resented.[32] Cortés realized that in any attack on Tenochtitlan he might be able to call on allies. In the deep disaffections between these neighbouring cities, he saw the irresistible opportunity to divide and conquer: an important first step on the inexorable road to China.

For all this, the Spaniards were divided too. Many were still loyal to Velázquez and felt that Cortés, in planning to stay in the region, was overstepping his authority. The expedition, they argued, had already achieved its objectives: it had found Aguilar, knocked down idols, amassed plenty of gold, and acquired much more detailed knowledge of the new territories than any previous expedition. It was high time to return to Cuba.

Shrewdly, Cortés gave every sign of agreeing with their reasoning: his mission, he concurred, had indeed been accomplished, and he had no power to act outside his remit. At this point arguments broke out. Those who, eager for gold, wanted to stay, reminded Cortés that before they had set off from Cuba, he had spoken about the possibility of implementing the Castilian tradition of founding towns.[33] In what was a consummate performance, Cortés pretended to toy with the idea. He knew that even those who wanted to return to Cuba would hardly be averse to founding towns in a land that was much richer and much larger than they had imagined, and whose people were more civilized than anything they had seen in the Caribbean: all unmistakable signs of the proximity of China. From such new towns they would be able to trade with those states resentful of the Mexica – and get rich in the process. Such a plan, indeed, more or less followed what Velázquez had done in Cuba; a process with which Cortés, who had often personally confirmed the notarial details of new settlements, was deeply familiar.

Cortés's first step, a small one, reassured both sides. He proposed an expedition to look for a better site for a harbour than San Juan de Ulúa. He sent two brigantines, each carrying around fifty men, down the coast.[34] Even the captains were intended to balance the different views in his camp: one, Francisco de Montejo, was a firm supporter of Velázquez; the other, Rodrigo Álvarez Chico, was close to Cortés. At the same time, Cortés dispatched Juan Velázquez de León, a relative and keen supporter of the governor of Cuba, on an expedition into the interior.[35] There was a further reason why Cortés sent Montejo and Velázquez de León on their respective explorations: to get these two key opponents of his plans out of the way while he made his move. Calling a meeting, he proclaimed that his chief aim was to serve the Crown. Then, with carefully crafted reluctance, he gave in to the petitions of those who wanted to stay in Mexico, and agreed to found a town, to be called Villa Rica de la Vera Cruz. All those present at the meeting would thenceforth become *vecinos* (citizens) of the new town, with a right to vote in the elections of the *cabildo* (municipal council). Those closest to Cortés were named *alcaldes* (magistrates) or *corregidores* (councillors) of the new town. In a planned move these newly appointed officials promptly asked Cortés to show them the original instructions he had received from Velázquez. After examining the documents, the newly appointed councillors formally declared that, since Cortés had accomplished his mission, he no longer had any legitimate authority. Cortés then dutifully resigned. No sooner had he stepped down than the municipal council solemnly nominated him chief justice of the town and captain-general of the royal army – until, of course, such a time as 'the monarchs' (at this time Cortés and his followers still assumed that Juana remained the rightful Queen of Castile) could have a say in the matter.[36]

In the eyes of Cortés's enemies, this move was a blatant act of rebellion. Although he might claim to have acted in the name of the monarchs, his flouting of Velázquez's authority made his legal position highly questionable. Even Cortés's modern admirers have often needed to cite in his defence arguments that the conquistador never in fact used himself: for instance, that he was invoking the 'democratic traditions of free Spaniards', which gave them 'the right to found towns wherever they liked', or 'the common doctrine . . . which stipulates that, in the absence of an authority constitutionally invested with its original legitimacy, such authority reverts to the community, which can then use it to elect legitimate representatives'.[37] Another scholar insists that Cortés's step was 'uniquely original' and done in 'the supreme interest of the common good in the service of God and the Crown'.[38]

Yet clues to Cortés's thinking do exist – and they can be found in the letter that he sent to Charles and Juana along with the gifts that would so astonish Dürer. The letter's wording reveals that Cortés based his move on a centuries-old medieval legal tradition, one compiled during the late thirteenth-century reign of Alfonso X, 'the Wise', of Castile, in a work called the *Siete Partidas* (literally 'The Seven Divisions'). Cortés's legal studies in Salamanca and his long experience as a notary in Hispaniola and Cuba had given him plenty of opportunity to become intimately acquainted with this work, so the letter followed aspects of the *Siete Partidas* closely.[39] Although there is little doubt that he was its author, the letter was allegedly written by all the new *vecinos* (citizens) of Villa Rica de la Vera Cruz. Portraying the letter as a collective effort allowed Cortés to map his actions onto the justifications given in the *Siete Partidas* – and thereby coat them in a convincing veneer of legality.

The letter opened with a statement from its authors, who, as noble *hidalgos*, were therefore 'zealous servants of Our Lord and of Your

Royal Highnesses and desirous of extolling your royal crown, of enlarging your dominions and of increasing your income'.[40] The wording alluded unmistakably to a law in the second *Partida*, which established a very close link between Crown and *hidalgos* – for it was through the latter that monarchs made their conquests and upon them that they always relied, both in peace and in war.[41] In justifying their act of disobedience against Velázquez the authors emphasized that, had they decided to follow the governor's instructions in the particular circumstances in which they found themselves, such an action would have amounted to looking after their exclusive private interests at the expense of those of the Crown and the wider community.[42] This argument drew on a law in the third *Partida*, which states that the common interest should never be displaced by that of a few. This principle, which informs the whole lengthy compilation, derives from the formula that laws should under no circumstance be broken unless they can be shown, with the general consent of 'all the good men of the land', to have reached a point where they actually defeat their own purpose.[43] In cases where this could be demonstrated, then laws should be 'broken in their totality'.[44] This, of course, was a point that served Cortés's purposes perfectly.[45] In insisting that the interests of the Spanish Crown would be best served by founding new towns in Mexico – for this was the only way in which justice could be established and proper lordship exercised[46] – the letter drew on another passage in the third *Partida*, which proposes that any situation in which naked force and barbarism prevail should be countered by a protected zone of laws and local privileges.[47] Meanwhile, the carefully orchestrated charade of Cortés's resignation and subsequent nomination as chief justice and captain-general – justified in the letter as an effort to find 'peace and concord among us in order to govern our affairs well'[48] – chimed perfectly with the 'law of nations' (*ius gentium*) as laid out in the first *Partida*. This was defined as a universal law, common to all peoples and based upon reason, without which concord and peace among peoples is impossible, and through which all peoples know what belongs to them and are able to determine the limits of the land and of the villages.[49]

The legal language and tone of the letter conveyed that this was no hasty and self-aggrandizing act of rebellion, but a carefully considered decision, one necessary to protect the interests of the Crown and the wider community. Moreover, it was a decision based not on civil law – about which only the monarchs could have the last word – but upon the universal 'law of nations'. The letter made a special point of reiterating the obligation that any worthy vassal had to speak the truth, especially when addressing the monarchs – an observation unmistakably reminiscent of laws set out in the second *Partida*.[50]

A masterly and legally watertight argument to justify Cortés's actions, the letter was presented in the form of a 'true' story, specifically crafted to set the record straight in the face of the 'lies' that Velázquez and his cronies had criminally inflicted upon the royal ears. When reading the letter, the monarchs would realize that everything they had hitherto been told about the newly discovered lands 'is not nor could possibly be true, because no one until now has known these things as they are told here, in which we write and will narrate to your royal highnesses what has happened from the very beginning of the discovery of these lands until their present state'.[51] Far from constituting an act of rebellion, the decision to found the town of Villa Rica de la Vera Cruz had been a reluctant but necessary initiative to bring a great evil to an end. With Cortés in command, the monarchs could count on a group of disinterested vassals who were so full of zeal to serve God that they were willing to risk all their possessions and their very lives in the noble enterprise of incorporating the native peoples – who were, according to this logic, already nominally vassals of the Crown – into the Catholic monarchy.

The letter went on to argue that Velázquez – in contrast to Cortés and his group of loyal subjects – had given every indication of being guilty of one of the most heinous vices against which the *Siete Partidas* specifically fulminated: greed.[52] In a clear echo of the language of the *Partidas*, the letter claimed that Velázquez was 'moved more by greed than by any other passion'.[53] Such an accusation, with its far-reaching religious and legal implications, was used to justify Cortés's request that under no circumstances should Velázquez be granted any further favours or be given any more powers – and if he had been, such powers 'should be immediately revoked, because they could only work to the detriment of your royal Crown'.[54]

This curious insistence needs some context. When Cortés founded the town, he did not know that the Council of Castile, at its meeting in Zaragoza on 18 November 1518, had granted Velázquez a new licence to explore. Cortés only found out about this on his return to Villa Rica de la Vera Cruz in June 1519 from a visit to the nearby Totonac towns of Quiahuiztlan and Cempohuallan, where further evidence of deep resentment against the Mexica had filled him with confidence. The news was brought by Francisco de Saucedo, who had come from Cuba with reinforcements. Tensions boiled over when a plot was revealed. The two envoys (now carefully called *procuradores* – that is, members of a properly established town council) entrusted by Cortés with escorting Moctezuma's treasure and the explanatory letter to Spain, were being persuaded to go via Cuba in order to consult with Velázquez first.[55] Cortés could barely afford to dither. The suspects were court martialled under Cortés's eagle eye: some were hanged, others scourged, one had his toes cut off. Then, to end any further defeatist talk of returning to Cuba, Cortés ordered the masters of nine of the twelve anchored ships to sail them aground. To ensure that they were entirely unseaworthy, all the rigging, sails, anchors and guns were removed, and the materials used to build houses in the new town of Villa Rica de la Vera Cruz.[56] In time, this astonishing decision would be compared to Caesar crossing the Rubicon; years later, Cortés's lawyer would refer to it as 'the most remarkable service rendered to God since the foundation of Rome'.[57] It is not difficult to see why. Now there was only one viable option open to Cortés and his group of explorers: 'to conquer the land or to die'.[58]

Cortés wasted little time preparing for a march on Tenochtitlan. The expedition set off in early August 1519. It consisted of about 300 Spaniards,[59] each divided into companies of fifty, captained by Pedro de Alvarado, Juan Velázquez de León – now ably won over to Cortés's side – Cristóbal de Olid, Alonso de Ávila, Gonzalo de Sandoval and Cortés himself. With them were some 150 Cuban servants and 800 Totonacs from Cempohuallan – a clear sign that Cortés's policy of forming alliances was bearing fruit. As they made their way towards nearby Jalapa, they had an unwelcome reminder of how precarious their situation had become. News reached them that a flotilla led by Alonso Álvarez de Pineda – an old acquaintance of Cortés in Cuba who, on a previous expedition, had seen the mouth of the Mississippi – had reached San Juan de Ulúa armed with trumped-up documents that ordered Cortés to share the new territories with the governor of Jamaica, Francisco de Garay.[60] Cortés again showed a knack for decisive action: he returned to the coast with about a hundred companions, arrested several of the envoys, and persuaded the others to join him.

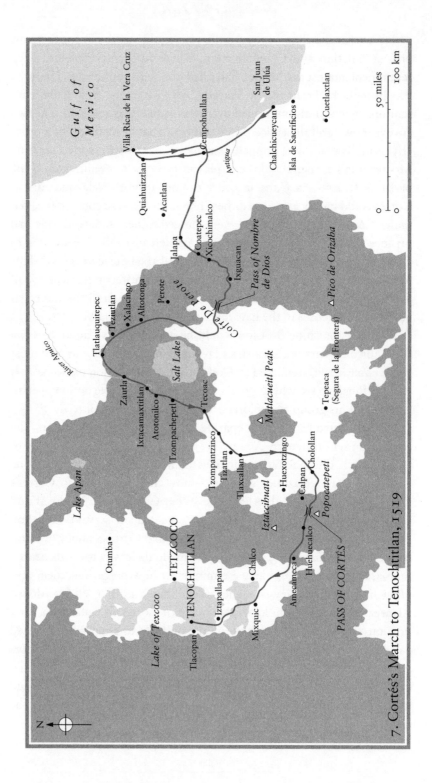

7. Cortés's March to Tenochtitlan, 1519

On 16 August they were on their way again, rising gradually past Coatepec, Xicochimalco and Ixguacan, from where their views were dominated by the mysterious, snow-capped volcanic peak that they had seen from the coast. In the following days their route took them through an imposing mountain range now known as the Cofre de Perote, where the extreme cold took the lives of some of the Cubans. Then they descended into an inhospitably bleak plain dominated by an impenetrable salt lake and another snow-capped peak known to the natives as Matlacueitl. In Nahuatl this means 'she who wears a jade skirt', a clear association with the goddess of the same name believed to be the source of the 'living waters' of the region.[61] Then, they took the route to the north, via Altotonga, Xalacingo, Teziutlan and Tlatlauquitepec – a decision they soon regretted, for the country was desolate, and water and food were scarce.[62] Turning south, they faced mountainous territory leading to a high pass; beyond it, they took a winding and seemingly interminable path through a pine forest. Eventually, it gave way to a beautiful valley along the River Apulco, leading to the town of Zautla, which they reached on 24 August. 'As we saw the bright gleam on the white rooftops,' a foot soldier would later recall, 'we could not but think how closely it resembled some of the towns in our Spain; and we called it Castil Blanco because some Portuguese soldiers said it looked just like the town of Castel Blanco in Portugal.'[63]

The *cacique* of Zautla, a man called Olintecle, was a loyalist of Moctezuma, and received the Spaniards with caution. When Cortés asked him if he was a vassal of the great Mexica emperor, Olintecle appeared flummoxed by the question. It was strange that Cortés could possibly doubt it, he replied: was not Moctezuma the ruler of the whole world?[64] He seemed equally unperturbed by Cortés's insistence that it would be in his interest to become a vassal of the Spanish monarchs, and to desist at once from the execrable practice of sacrificing human beings and eating them. Olintecle, who had no qualms about sacrificing fifty men at a festival, made it clear that he would do nothing without Moctezuma's consent, for he was the greatest lord in the world. Olintecle elaborated for Cortés's benefit: the Mexica emperor had thirty major vassals who owed him fealty, each of whom had 100,000 men under his command; his capital was the best defended and most beautiful in the world: 20,000 men were sacrificed there every year.[65] Olintecle was less forthcoming about the best route to the Mexica capital. When he suggested the route through Cholollan, the leader of the Cempohualteca in Cortés's entourage warned him that this was probably a trap. The best route, he continued, was obviously by way of Tlaxcallan (present-day Tlaxcala). Even had Olintecle's advice been heeded, however, Tlaxcallan was on the way to Cholollan, so Cortés made up his mind to head that way and probably kept an open mind.[66]

While both the description of Olintecle's enthusiastic human sacrifice and the alarming figures of Moctezuma's military strength are the exaggerations of later chroniclers, Cortés nonetheless left Zautla much better informed about the dominant power in the region. He sent four of the Cempohualteca chiefs ahead of the main expedition, to inform the rulers of Tlaxcallan about the imminent arrival of envoys of the monarchs of Castile, who were coming to assist them in their heroic resistance against the tyrant of Tenochtitlan.[67] Moving south along the valley of the Apulco, Cortés reached Ixtacamaxtitlan, where he was impressed by the mountain fortress that surrounded the house of the *cacique*: 'as good as the best fortress to be found in the middle of Spain, and even better defended'.[68] After waiting there a week for the return of the messengers, who failed to turn up, he moved on again, reassured by the Cempohualteca about their friendship with the Tlaxcalteca. The advice, though, was incorrect. As the Castilians approached Tlaxcallan, they were ambushed by a huge cohort of face-painted warriors armed with obsidian-bladed swords; their deafening cries terrified some Spaniards.[69] Despite killing two horses, the warriors proved no match against Spanish steel, artillery and the remaining horses. Cortés's new worry, that Tlaxcallan, far from being friendly, was actively opposed to him, was largely dispelled when his envoys eventually reappeared, explaining that the attack had been led by a group of autonomous Otomí tribes in the region, who were not from Tlaxcallan. The Tlaxcalteca, in fact, were eager to welcome the Spaniards and had even offered to pay for the dead horses.[70]

Tlaxcallan was a densely populated chain of settlements, housing approximately 120,000 people divided among a cluster of autonomous states loosely united in a military federation hostile to the Mexica. These hostilities had isolated the Tlaxcalteca economically: they had no cotton, precious stones or gold. Most frustratingly – despite the proximity of the salt lakes controlled by the Mexica – they had no salt. Yet they had managed to maintain their independence and valued their freedom proudly. They were, moreover, able cultivators of the land and had developed a tradition of consultation that led Cortés to compare their society to the free republics of Venice, Genoa and Pisa, 'for there is no one general lord of all but several lords, all residing in this city'.[71]

Cortés would need to wait a few weeks before taking advantage of these seemingly auspicious circumstances. The Cempohualteca envoys soon revealed that their account about the Otomí attacks was in fact a ruse concocted by the Tlaxcalteca to lure the Castilians into danger. They themselves had barely escaped with their lives from the Taxcalteca, who had tried to fatten them up before sacrificing and eating them.[72] These frustrating revelations were confirmed when, in early September, more attacks from alleged Otomí tribes, now widely suspected by the Spaniards to be working in cahoots with the Tlaxcalteca, forced Cortés to take refuge in the nearby hilltop of Tzompachtepetl. In retaliation, he carried out a series of punitive expeditions, terrorizing the surrounding towns with great cruelty, but morale among his men began to slump. Some had died, either from the wounds of battle or from disease; many more were ill; and all were hungry. As dissent grew, Cortés was visited in mid-September by another deputation from Moctezuma, with the message that the Mexica emperor had decided to become a vassal of the monarchs of Castile and pay them tribute, provided that Cortés did not go to Tenochtitlan. Moctezuma would, the envoys continued, have been delighted to welcome Cortés and his men, but the road was treacherous, and the capital lacked the necessary provisions. Moctezuma was anxious that the Spaniards should not suffer unnecessarily. Additionally, the messengers warned Cortés not to trust the Tlaxcalteca, who were incorrigible traitors and were setting a trap to kill all the Spaniards.[73]

Again, Moctezuma's efforts proved counterproductive. Cortés seemed greatly heartened by the message brought by the emperor's envoys. It was far better, he told his disgruntled followers, to die in a good cause than to live in dishonour. Besides, was it not clear that these obvious divisions between the Mexica and the Tlaxcalteca were greatly to their advantage? As he later put it in another letter to Charles V, the situation made him recall Jesus's words, when he declared that no kingdom at war with itself can avoid being laid waste: *omne regnum in se ipsum divisum desolabitur*, Cortés cited in shaky Latin from memory.[74] His tactic paid off: even as Moctezuma's envoys were still with him, Cortés was honoured by a visit from the Tlaxcalteca leader Xicotencatl the younger. He begged the conquistador for forgiveness, asking him to understand why the Tlaxcalteca had never submitted to the authority of any emperor, preferring instead to suffer 'great evils', such as a lack of salt or cotton, rather than submit to the yoke of Moctezuma. Now, however, if Cortés deigned to 'admit us to your alliance', they would readily submit to the Spanish monarchs. Although they had no gold or silver, they came to offer their friendship. In an episode that would capture the European imagination for centuries to come, further messengers then arrived bringing slaves, incense and feathers, turkeys and fruits of the forest.[75]

Whether or not Cortés suspected what was going on, he played his hand inscrutably. It later emerged that when his Cempohualteca envoys arrived in Tlaxcallan late that August, the Tlaxcalteca leaders consulted together, as was their custom. Maxixcatzin, ruler of Ocotelulco, was in favour of accepting Cortés's offer of peace: he was, perhaps unsurprisingly, backed by the merchants of the community. But the proposal clashed with the interests of the military leaders. Xicotencatl the elder was joint ruler with Maxixcatzin, but he was frail and blind and had delegated powers to his son, Xicotencatl the younger, who resolutely supported the military commanders in their desire to fight the Spanish. A compromise was reached. The Spaniards would be welcomed with caution while any formal agreement was delayed; in the meantime Xicotencatl the younger would plan a series of concerted attacks with the use of Otomí warriors. If these attacks proved successful, they would be celebrated by the Tlaxcalteca with the traditional sacrifices and sumptuous banquets. If not, then they could blame the Otomí warriors and revert to Maxixcatzin's original proposal – which, in the event, was precisely what happened.[76]

In the face of these machinations, Cortés was impassive – or so he portrayed himself in his second letter to Charles V, which most subsequent historians have chosen to follow. In it he appears the cool possessor of an uncanny foresight that allowed him to play a masterly game of divide and rule: he welcomed and appeared genuinely magnanimous towards Xicotencatl the younger, while ensuring that the Tlaxcalteca leader witnessed his close ties with the envoys of Moctezuma – now self-described vassals of the Castilian monarchs – who were still with him. Cortés made a point of waiting for Moctezuma's reply before accepting the invitation to visit Tlaxcallan. When word came from the Mexica emperor, it was accompanied by the customary deferential presents – 3,000 pesos worth of gold and 200 pieces of cloth, according to an unusually observant foot soldier – and further warnings about the unreliability of the treacherous Tlaxcalteca.[77] This only served to stoke tensions in Tlaxcallan: the next day, in an attempt to trump Moctezuma's offerings, an entourage of potentates from the city, including Maxixcatzin and Xicotencatl the elder, came to Cortés personally to reiterate the invitation and to offer the Spaniards gifts of golden jewels and stones. Cortés received them warmly, taking particular care to dismount from his horse and embrace Xicotencatl the elder before solemnly delivering an elaborate and no doubt carefully planned oration in which he pledged to defend the liberty of Tlaxcallan. The Spaniards – still, astonishingly, in the company of Moctezuma's ambassadors – were then welcomed into the city on 18 September 1519, where they were handsomely regaled.[78]

Cortés and his men stayed in the city for about three weeks. It was valuable respite, allowing them to rest and gather much-needed strength, but also giving Cortés the chance to establish what was to be his most important and lasting alliance. This was – or so it was later described – founded on a firm friendship between Cortés and the two older chiefs, Maxixcatzin and Xicotencatl the elder. Cortés, moreover, came across as a man of his word: genuine in his insistence that he had come to defend their liberty, and robust in disciplining his own troops when they threatened to misbehave. Friendships were cemented when one of Xicotencatl's daughters, who took the name of Doña María Luisa, was given to Pedro de Alvarado, while a daughter of Maxixcatzin, christened Doña Elvira, went to Juan Velázquez de León.[79]

Characteristically, Cortés was reluctant to encourage any such intimacy before the Tlaxcalteca had given convincing proofs that they were willing to become proper Christians. Yet, there is little doubt that the city made a positive impression on the Spaniards. Even the lack of cotton did not stop the Tlaxcalteca creating beautiful clothes made of henequen fibre. Other impressions were more disturbing. Among those who had greeted Cortés on arrival were a number of priests who seemed to resemble all the others that the Spaniards had encountered on their journey: their hair long and messy, horribly tangled with clots of blood – clear evidence of the practice of human sacrifice – their nails dirty and unseemly long.[80] Meanwhile, the presence of Moctezuma's ambassadors, whom Cortés was adamant to keep on side, was an ongoing source of tension. The Mexica were now urging Cortés to leave Tlaxcallan as soon as possible and head for Cholollan where they would not be attacked, for the leaders of that city were allies of Moctezuma. The Tlaxcalteca, for their part, were busy advising Cortés to avoid Cholollan and continue the march to Tenochtitlan by way of Huexotzingo, a nearby city with whom they were friendly. Cortés made one of his characteristic compromises: he would go by way of Cholollan, as Moctezuma wanted, but he would take Tlaxcalteca warriors with him. In the meantime Pedro de Alvarado and Bernardino Vázquez de Tapia would go directly to Tenochtitlan to try to prepare Moctezuma for their arrival.[81]

One native source, however, puts Cortés's apparent imperturbability in an entirely different light. It was written by one of the sons of Quauhpopocatzin, a Mexica nobleman whom Moctezuma had sent to the coast as soon as he heard about the arrival of the Spaniards. As a young man, his son had been an eyewitness to the main events in Tenochtitlan after the arrival of the Spaniards: he claimed, astonishingly, that his father had 'brought, guided and protected' the Castilians along all the stages of their journey to the great Mexica city. Later, he took the name Don Juan de Guzmán Itztlolinqui and converted to Christianity: his account – written in the Renaissance Latin that he had learned from his Franciscan teachers in the 1530s – was part of a petition to Charles V to put a stop to the ill treatment of natives by Spanish settlers.

Itztlolinqui's account, clearly partisan, has been dismissed by historians precisely because it conflicts with most other narratives. Yet its depiction of Moctezuma seems in many respects much more realistic than the hackneyed European accounts of him as a terrified and indecisive leader, paralyzed by superstitious forebodings and the conviction that the Castilians were supernatural entities. Rather, Itztlolinqui tells us that Moctezuma was doing to the Castilians exactly what the latter had done to all the indigenous peoples they had encountered: to place them firmly within familiar mental parameters. He referred to the Spaniards as 'Caxtilteca', from the word Castilian, rendered as Caxtillan in Nahuatl, thus giving them a recognizable identity as members of an *altepetl* – or 'ethnic state'[82] – with their leader, Cortés, as their *tlahtoani.*

Itztlolinqui painted a picture of Moctezuma as intelligent, pragmatic and firmly in control, eager to establish communication with and to obtain information about the 'Caxtilteca'. Far from the master of realpolitik he claimed to be, Cortés emerges from this account as a gullible ingénu who naively trusted the promises of his Cempohualteca intermediaries – who, far from arranging for the Spaniards a friendly welcome in Tlaxcallan, instead led them into a trap. All of which squared with Moctezuma's own wishes, for he stood to benefit from violent encounters between the 'Caxtilteca' and the Tlaxcalteca. Just as Cortés embraced a strategy of divide and rule, so did Moctezuma himself. While the Mexica emperor was clearly not anticipating that the encounter would lead to a Caxtilteca-Tlaxcalteca alliance, even so it is unlikely that, secure in his own military might, he was unduly bothered by the outcome.[83]

Leaving Tlaxcallan on 10 October,[84] the Castilians reached Cholollan the following day. Ostensibly, they were received well – 'with the rich sound of trumpets and kettledrums'.[85] As in Tlaxcallan, Cortés was awestruck by the city: 'more beautiful than any to be found in Spain'. Nestling on a fertile plain, its centre consisted of some 20,000 buildings, not including its sprawling suburbs, and was punctuated by towers that graced the city's many temples. Climbing to the top of one of them, Cortés himself had counted 'about 430 such towers'. Cholollan was clearly a lordship in its own right, being subservient to no one, and governing its own affairs just like the people of Tlaxcallan; yet the Chololteca dressed more elegantly. It was, in short, the finest city they had yet seen.[86]

In his account of Cholollan, Cortés's choice of words merits some attention. What I have translated as 'kettledrums' Cortés called 'atabales': Moorish drums used by the Berbers of North Africa. Similarly, in describing the elegantly dressed Chololteca, he noted that the well-heeled among them wore a gown, Cortés's word for which was 'albornoz': a woollen overcoat used by Berber shepherds. Most revealingly, the term I have rendered as 'temples' he consistently called 'mosques'. Clearly, for Cortés and his fellow explorers there was a seamless link between the *Reconquista* and what they were doing in the New World, and Cortés was determined to make full use of it in his attempt to win the goodwill of the monarch at a time when he still had no idea whether the mission of his envoys – with Moctezuma's rich gifts and the letter allegedly authored by the new municipality – had had the desired effect.

Cortés made a point of reassuring Charles – whom he now knew, with an acute sense of the workings of Providence, to have been elected Holy Roman Emperor – that the people of Cholollan had readily become, and remained, 'faithful vassals of your majesty, and very obedient to whatever I, in your royal name, have told them and requested of them, and I have no doubt that they will remain so in the future'.[87] Yet there were some glaring omissions from Cortés's account. Events in Cholollan were to leave him with some of his most disturbing memories – so disturbing, in fact, that he chose rarely to refer to them in writing.

The city was ruled by two men: Tlaquiach ('lord of the here-and-now') and Tlachiac ('lord of the world below the earth'), who lived in houses attached to the temple of Quetzalcoatl.[88] In sharp contrast to what had happened in Tlaxcallan, despite the musical reception, neither ruler turned out to greet the Spaniards. Food was available grudgingly and in insufficient quantities – and, after a couple of days, not at all, with only fuel and water provided. The Spaniards saw, moreover, that stones were being piled on roofs, ready to be hurled at the intruders, and that the streets were being blocked, to prevent their escape. All of which was exactly what the Tlaxcalteca had warned would happen in Cholollan.

With the help of the dutiful Marina, Cortés decided to question a group of Chololteca priests. The picture that emerged was worrying. Such precautions were being taken, the priests alleged, because Moctezuma seemed incapable of making up his mind. One day he was planning a peaceful reception and the next he was thinking of killing the Spaniards. All the evidence seemed to indicate that the warnings of the Tlaxcalteca had not been misplaced: the Chololteca were likely to be in hock to Moctezuma and the Castilians were in great danger. According to later Spanish accounts, Cortés consulted with his captains. Some urged a swift retreat to Tlaxcallan, others a resumption of the advance to Tenochtitlan via the allegedly friendlier city of Huexotzingo. The prevailing option, however – and one which received the overwhelming support of the bulk of the Tlaxcalteca warriors who had accompanied Cortés – was to make a pre-emptive attack on the Chololteca.[89]

Cortés sent a message to the leaders of the city, informing them that he had taken the decision to leave at once for Tenochtitlan and that he wanted to say his goodbyes in the courtyard of the temple of Quetzalcoatl. Once they had gathered there, the Spaniards closed the doors of the courtyard and Cortés announced that he knew about their treason, a crime punishable by death.[90] This unleashed a frenzy of 'stabbing, slaying and beating of people' throughout the city. The violence lasted two days; all the Chololteca leaders were killed.[91] By all accounts Cortés's allies, the Cempohualteca and the Tlaxcalteca, revelled in the opportunity to massacre their Chololteca enemies: they methodically sacked the city, taking, as they did so, many prisoners for sacrifice back in Tlaxcallan.[92]

The sack of Cholollan was to become one of the most controversial episodes in the history of the Spanish conquest, largely through Bartolomé de Las Casas's chilling account of events, written decades later in an attempt to shock the Spanish court. Cortés as described by Las Casas was another Herod: as he slaughtered, he gaily sang a popular ballad about Nero's nonchalant enjoyment of the screams of the young and the old while Rome burned.[93] This damning and highly influential portrait, however, must be set alongside the opinions of the vast majority of eyewitnesses, all of whom regretted the unintended excesses but nonetheless thought that the episode had constituted a 'suitable punishment', one that had instilled so much fear that from then on the Chololteca 'had dared not commit any such treason'.[94]

Cortés himself claimed to have used the massacre to intimidate Moctezuma's ambassadors, telling them that he knew Chololteca treachery had been instigated by Moctezuma himself. As a result, he told the ambassadors, he could hardly go to Tenochtitlan with peaceful intentions – a message he instructed the ambassadors to report unambiguously to their lord. Departing, the ambassadors returned to Cortés within the week, laden with ten plates of gold, 1,500 cotton cloaks and plenty of good food: a goodwill gesture from Moctezuma, who, they told Cortés, was profoundly sorry about the incident but was nonetheless adamant that he had had nothing to do with it. Moctezuma now offered to send anything that the conquistadores might need – provided they did not go to Tenochtitlan: provisions, the ambassadors explained, were running low and Moctezuma would regrettably not be able to welcome them as they deserved. To this Cortés replied with calculated imperturbability that he was obliged to render an account of Tenochtitlan to the Holy Roman Emperor; he therefore had no choice but to continue the march.[95]

Again, this account was the work of later narratives. Itztlolinqui argues that Cortés and his captains were in fact much more afraid of Moctezuma – who, far from trying to dissuade them, was luring them towards the capital – than the self-assured emperor was of them. This makes good sense if we consider that there were some curious similarities between Tlaxcallan and Tenochtitlan. They were both alliances of unequal partners, Tlaxcallan's being Huexotzingo and Cholollan. The former had eagerly joined the Tlaxcalteca against the Spaniards in the series of bloody ambushes described above, but the Chololteca had recently abandoned the alliance and become willing tributaries of Tenochtitlan. So the decision to advance towards Cholollan, which was a pointless detour by comparison with Huexotzingo, makes good sense as a Tlaxcalteca tactic deployed to test their new alliance with the Castilians and to punish the Chololteca for their disloyalty. It was a decision that Moctezuma was only too happy to manipulate to his own ends, but it also sheds light upon the ferocity of the massacre.[96]

The expedition was on its way again in early November 1519. Their route to Tenochtitlan took them through a high mountain range, dominated by two peaks of astonishing beauty: the volcanoes Iztaccihuatl ('White Woman) and Popocatepetl ('Smoking Mountain'). It was not the most obvious way. The most direct route – one that would become the main road from Mexico City to Veracruz (as Villa Rica would soon begin to be called) – followed the River Atoyac, north of the Iztaccihuatl, from Huexotzingo to the outskirts of Chalco; other more leisurely routes went north towards the Valley of Mexico, near Otumba, from Lake Apan, and south of the Popocatepetl (a road already taken by Pedro de Alvarado and Bernardino Vázquez de Tapia, the Spanish emissaries whom Cortés had sent on ahead). Cortés himself, though, did not choose any of these routes; the information he had gathered from the priests of Cholollan suggested that the routes would have been blocked by the Mexica. The path he took was much more demanding, rising to the col between the two great volcanoes – a route now known as the Paso de Cortés. Ahead, he dispatched a smaller group to investigate the 'secret' of the Popocatepetl, which was smoking dangerously and throwing out hot rock. The heavy snowstorms and extreme cold drove them back, but they did get a view of the astonishing lake on which the cities of the Valley of Mexico seemed to be nestling, with the great Tenochtitlan ensconced on an island in the middle. They returned 'full of joy at having discovered such a good route, and God knows just how much that pleased me', Cortés later wrote to Charles V.[97]

As they approached the col, the Spaniards were met by some lords from Huexotzingo to the south of Calpan. They warned Cortés against going to Tenochtitlan but, seeing his determination, advised him, when the route split just after the col, to take the blocked path rather than the clear one: the Mexica, they said, would be sure to have planned an ambush along the clear one.[98] As the expedition progressed, the weather threatened to turn – there would surely have otherwise been descriptions of the views from the col, truly breathtaking on a clear day – and it soon began to snow. Navigating the precarious blocked path, they stayed overnight at the town of Huehuecalco and, with improved weather, began the descent into the fertile lands leading to the city of Chalco. Along the way they were met by yet another group of messengers from Moctezuma, including a nobleman who, it was said, pretended to impersonate the Mexica emperor himself in the unlikely hope that the Spaniards might choose to return to the coast after seeing him. But the Castilians, so the legend continued, were not fooled. 'Whom do you take us to be?' a subsequent indigenous source recalled Cortés exclaiming. 'You cannot mock us, nor make us stupid, nor flatter us, nor become our eyes, nor trick us, nor misdirect our gaze, nor turn us back, nor destroy us, nor dazzle us, nor cast mud in our eyes.' An unbending sense of determination had clearly left its mark on the memory of the Mexica.[99]

The following day, in the town of Amecameca – where they were well received, fed, and presented with gifts of gold and forty slave girls[100] – Cortés heard various complaints about Moctezuma's tax collectors, and reassured the people of Amecameca that he was keen to help them against such intolerable oppression.[101] They continued onwards through a succession of Mexica towns, each more beautiful than the last, their march punctuated by gift-bearing delegations from Moctezuma – which the Spaniards interpreted as ever more desperate attempts to dissuade them from their march.[102] Their reception at Iztapallapan (present-day Iztapalapa) – whose houses, according to Cortés, 'were as good as the best in Spain, because of their size and artistry, both in terms of masonry and carpentry' – was especially sumptuous. The apartments in which they were housed were splendid, with ceilings of cedar wood and courtyards covered with cotton baldachins, surrounded by verdant, scented gardens filled with exotic birds and ponds teeming with fish.[103]

On 8 November the expedition set off on the final advance along the main causeway to Tenochtitlan. From Iztapallapan they moved west towards the peninsula of Culhuacan, after which they joined the main north-south causeway leading to the capital from Coyohuacan (present-day Coyoacán). In his letter to Charles V, Cortés did not mention this town by name, which he would later choose for himself, but he did refer to its 'very good constructions of houses and towers, especially the houses of the lords and principal people, and of their mosques and oratories where they keep their idols'.[104] As they approached the capital, Cortés formed his men into a procession, himself adopting an air of lordly gravitas worthy of a Renaissance potentate. Decades later, some Mexica nobles recalled the horsemen in armour, the infantrymen with drawn swords and lances gleaming in the sun, the crossbowmen with their quivers, the arquebusiers, the feathered helmets, the standard-bearers, and the thousands of indigenous allies, dressed and painted for battle and dragging artillery on wooden carts. The horses and dogs, in particular, filled the natives with fascination and wonder.[105] But the sense of awe that struck the seemingly unperturbed 'Caxtilteca' was, if anything, even more pronounced. What now opened up ahead of them was like nothing they had ever seen.

In terms of size, both in extension and population density, no city in western Europe came close to Tenochtitlan. As they crossed the causeway into the city, the Castilians were staggered by the tens of thousands of canoes – some, like great barges, carrying up to sixty people – that dotted the vast lake, inevitably prompting references to the city as 'another Venice' or even 'great Venice' or 'Venice the rich'.[106] Progressing into the city, the Spaniards were astonished by the beauty of the many towers, all 'stuccoed, carved and magnificently adorned with merlons, painted with colourful animals and sculpted on stone', which seemed to one observer to resemble the enchanted 'castellated fortresses' of chivalric romance: 'glorious heights that were a marvel to behold!'[107]

Something of this sense of enchantment was preserved in what has been described as 'one of the most beautiful maps in the history of cartography'.[108] This was the map of Tenochtitlan printed in the Latin edition of Cortés's Second Letter to Charles V, published in Nuremberg in 1524. Based on a sketch that Cortés might have used to illustrate his letter (which was itself embellished and printed in Seville in 1522), the detailed beauty of the Nuremberg Map, as it has come to be known, is a good indication of the sense of fascination which Cortés's news created in Europe.[109]

Cortés and his men were greeted by a group of splendidly dressed noblemen at the end of the causeway, a place called Acachinanco, and escorted into Tenochtitlan where, at long last, they came face to face with the magisterial figure on whom their lives now depended. Moctezuma appeared on a litter, borne by noblemen, with a baldachin of green feathers, fitted with jade and beautifully adorned with gold and silver embroidery.[110] As the emperor stepped down from the litter, Cortés dismounted, wanting to embrace him 'in the Spanish fashion', but was stopped by the guards.[111] Formalities were exchanged, Cortés presenting Moctezuma with a necklace of pearls, the emperor reciprocating with a golden one.[112] The Spaniards were both awestruck and uneasy at their new surroundings. They admired their imperial host's splendidly exotic plumed headdress, but the blue figure of a hummingbird encrusted on the emperor's lower lip, his earplugs and turquoise nose ornament, and the jaguar costumes of the chief warriors, clashed sharply with their sensibilities.[113] They were gratified by the thousands of canoes that had paddled to the edge of the lake to greet them, a spectacle remembered decades later by a foot soldier 'as if it were yesterday', along with rooftops crowded with 'countless men, women and children'.[114] Yet the Castilians cannot have failed to realize the hopelessly vulnerable situation in which they had unwittingly put themselves. If Tenochtitlan was a beautiful city, it was also one engineered for defence: the various stretches along the causeway were flanked by bridges of removable wooden beams. Used primarily to allow canoes to pass from one side of the lake to the other, their potential use for defensive purposes was equally obvious. So too was the fact that the Spaniards were, should the situation deteriorate, hopelessly outnumbered. In the annals of conflicting emotions aroused by unprecedented human encounters, this episode has few if any rivals.

8

Tenochtitlan

Over the winter months, as the Spaniards settled into life in Tenochtitlan, these conflicting emotions deepened. Their admiration for the city increased in proportion as they came to know it. Few places in the world were as graced by nature as Tenochtitlan. Nestling on an island near the shore of a great lake in the middle of a broad valley, the city was surrounded by magnificent mountains and volcanic peaks covered in snow. The air was pure, the weather temperate, the colours intense, the scents mesmerizing; time passed in a succession of sunlit days. Moctezuma's cordial welcome reassured Cortés and his men, who were housed in the splendid palace of Axayacatl: 'a wonder to behold', as one soldier put it. The building had 'countless rooms, antechambers, sumptuous halls, large cushions covered in fine cloth, pillows of leather and hemp, excellent bed linen, white robes of fur, admirably crafted wooden seats'. Even the attention of the servants 'was worthy of a great prince'.[1]

Yet the Spaniards were not at ease. There was something about the aloof attitude of Moctezuma's companions – Totoquihuatzin, the ruler of Tlacopan, Cacama, ruler of Tetzcoco, and Itzquauhtzin, ruler of Tlatelolco – that unsettled them. None of these princes had greeted the Castilians with anything like the deference displayed by Moctezuma; indeed, some Mexica guides had told the explorers about the conviction of these potentates – which was, it seemed, well known among the Mexica – that the only way to deal with the intruders was to finish them off. Uncomfortable reminders of this attitude came at regular intervals, in particular the frequent beating of the drum atop the round temple of Quetzalcoatl, signalling the performing of human sacrifice.

This mixture of Spanish wonder and dread permeates the sources. A visit to the market of Tlatelolco, on the north of the island, left Cortés reaching for superlatives. He thought it twice the size of the great square at Salamanca, and many of his companions – some of whom had travelled throughout Europe, and even as far as Constantinople – had seen nothing like it.[2] The market was extremely well organized: divided into orderly sections for the exchange of an endless supply of goods ranging from precious metals, clothes and pottery to whitewash and mats, and including every kind of trader, from butchers, fishmongers and grocers to barbers, tanners and paint merchants. Cortés filled several long paragraphs of a letter to Charles V with a detailed description of the place, concluding breathlessly that one could find in it 'every imaginable thing that can be found on this earth . . . In addition to the ones I have mentioned, there are others, so numerous and so varied in their qualities that, wishing to avoid prolixity and because of the difficulty of bringing them all to mind, and even because I do not know their names, I do not mention.'[3]

Then there was a visit to the great temple, with its permanent staff of priests, their earlobes disfigured by frequent sacrificial piercing, their hair long, knotted and clotted with human blood. Cortés and his captains climbed the steep staircase that rose from the relief portrait of the dismembered moon goddess Coyolxauhqui, the sister of Huitzilopochtli, set into the stone floor in front of the staircase, and onto which the bodies of the sacrificed victims were thrown from the top of the pyramid.[4] Once at the top, in dramatic contrast with the stunning views of the city – including what was then perhaps the largest menagerie on the planet – the Castilians were confronted by the strange reclining figure of a humanoid *chac-mool*, supporting itself on its elbow and holding a *cuauhxicalli* – the stone bowl that received sacrificed human hearts. Further along, in front of the shrines, stood the *techcatl*, a green execution stone, overlooked by the statues of Huitzilopochtli and Tezcatlipoca, encrusted with human blood and flanked by braziers in which lay the still-warm hearts of human victims sacrificed earlier that day.[5] Appalled, Cortés delivered what was by now a well-rehearsed admonition to his imperial host: 'I fail to understand,' he allegedly told Moctezuma, 'how such a great lord and wise ruler as yourself has not worked out by reasoning that these idols are not gods but bad things called devils.' His suggestion that they should be replaced by a cross and an image of the Virgin did not meet with the friendly response he had observed in Yucatan. Moctezuma was angry. The uncharacteristic compunction that, according to Bernal Díaz del Castillo, Cortés showed for his rashness, is an eloquent reminder of a feeling of dread and insecurity.[6]

Such feelings were conspicuously absent from Cortés's account of Tenochtitlan, written for Charles V, in which Cortés recounted an extraordinary exchange between him and the Mexica emperor. Moctezuma supposedly told his guest on the evening of their arrival that the Mexica had originally come to the Valley of Mexico as foreigners, led by a lord who had brought them to Tenochtitlan before returning to his native land. When, some years later, the same lord returned, the Mexica refused to follow him, having grown fond of the place and intermarried with its native inhabitants. However, as Moctezuma explained, 'we have always believed that those who descend from him [the spurned lord] would one day return to subdue this land and make us vassals'. Since Cortés and his companions had come 'from where the sun rises' and had spoken at length about 'that great lord or king who sent you here . . . we have no doubt that he is indeed our natural lord'. For all these reasons, Moctezuma told Cortés, 'we shall obey you and hold you as our lord in representation of that great lord about whom you have spoken to us'. The Mexica emperor went on to reassure Cortés that he should feel free 'to order whatever you will; it will be obeyed and put into effect, since all that we possess is for you to dispose of at your will'.[7]

By any standards, this is an incredible account. From the earliest days it was given the short shrift it deserves: 'more of a story, a means of inventing a fable to serve his purpose by an astute, wise and artful captain', as the chronicler Gonzalo Fernández de Oviedo famously remarked.[8] Nevertheless, it is important to take into account the context in which Cortés was writing. Although he now knew that Charles had been elected Holy Roman Emperor, Cortés still did not know what decision, if any, had been reached at the Spanish court over his plea for retrospective authorization of his act of rebellion against the governor of Cuba. Unsurprisingly, he opted to give his account a predominantly 'imperial' theme, presenting Moctezuma's offer in such a way that it supported the legal rationale of his rebellion against Velázquez, as set out in his previous letter.[9] In short, Cortés's chief aim was not to represent the reality of the situation in Tenochtitlan, as he and his companions had encountered it, but to present Charles V as the lawful sovereign of this vast new empire, and to persuade him that his Castilian subjects were merely attempting to recover what was already, rightfully, a possession of the Holy Roman Emperor.

Second, Cortés's account is not wholly fictitious. It is certain that from their very first meeting Moctezuma's behaviour went well beyond the traditionally courteous Mexica hospitality: at times, indeed, it was strangely deferential. Cortés's cunning deployment of the massacre of Cholollan as the regrettable consequence of Moctezuma's instigations had clearly left the Mexica leader in a state of some perplexity. Nor would any well-informed observer have failed to notice the uncanny coincidences of the arrival of the Spaniards in the year of the god Quetzalcoatl, I-Reed, and their choice to enter the capital on the day I-Wind, whose glyph depicted the same god with the attributes of a whirlwind and was widely believed to make it possible for wizards to terrorize the people in the night.[10] It is true that nobody seems to have mentioned Quetzalcoatl at the time, and that the coincidences were more than likely embellished by later interpretations. Yet, the profound sense of unease that the Spanish presence in the capital unleashed is undeniable. As a group of interlocutors who witnessed the event would recount to Fray Bernardino de Sahagún some decades later, 'there was a scattering from one's sight, a jumping in all directions'. A dreadful feeling spread across the city, 'as if one had lost one's breath; it was as if for the time there was stupefaction, as if one were affected by [hallucinogenic] mushrooms, as if something unknown were shown one'. As fear took hold, it felt 'as if everyone had swallowed his heart. Even before it had grown dark, there was terror, there was astonishment, there was apprehension, there was a stunning of the people.'[11]

In mid-November, a week or so after his arrival, Cortés took full advantage of Moctezuma's state of mind when he heard the news that Cohualpopocatzin (more commonly rendered as Qualpopoca), the ruler of Nauhtla, a town north of Villa Rica de la Vera Cruz, had been involved in a squabble with the local Totonacs after he demanded tribute. In the ensuing battle, during which a group of Spaniards turned up to defend their Totonac allies, Cortés's lieutenant had been killed alongside six of his companions. One of them had been captured and sacrificed, and his head sent to Moctezuma as a prize. An indignant Cortés at once sought an audience with the emperor, taking with him most of his senior captains alongside the resourceful Marina, through whom he expressed his astonishment to Moctezuma. Reminding the emperor that it was his meddling at Cholollan that had led to the tragic massacre, Cortés then offered to forgive Moctezuma on condition he accompany him back to his quarters at the palace of Axayacatl – thereby effectively taking him prisoner – without making the slightest fuss. If he did not, Cortés exclaimed, his captains would kill him on the spot.[12]

If we are to believe this account, Cortés had put the Mexica emperor in an impossible predicament. The prospect of being killed by Cortés's captains was not much better than the alternative: 'My person,' Moctezuma explained to Cortés, 'is not of the kind that can be imprisoned. Even if I consented to such an action, my people could scarcely tolerate it.'[13] Insisting that he had had nothing to do with the attack at Nauhtla, Moctezuma ordered a group of officials to carry out a detailed inquiry and then punish the culprits. Cortés agreed to this, on condition that three of his men – Andrés de Tapia, Alonso de Aguilar and Pedro Gutiérrez de Valdelomar – went along too.[14] To Moctezuma's claim that 'his person' could not be imprisoned, Cortés retorted by reminding him that he was now subject to a much higher authority, the Holy Roman Emperor. As the exchange broadened into a negotiation, Cortés's captains began to lose their nerve, Juan Velázquez de León reprimanding Cortés for wasting words: 'either we take him prisoner,' he exclaimed in what a foot soldier remembered as a 'loud and terrifying tone', 'or we stab him senseless'. Understandably alarmed by the heated words that he could not understand, Moctezuma turned to Marina who, with characteristic wit and grace, advised the emperor to do as Cortés demanded without the slightest protest, for he would be greatly honoured at the palace 'as the great lord that you are'. After a desperate offer to send his son and daughter as hostages failed to persuade the Spaniards, Moctezuma at last agreed to go willingly. He explained to his guards and noble entourage that he had reached such an eccentric decision after praying to none other than Huitzilopochtli himself, who had revealed to him in a vision that it was convenient for him to spend some time in the company of his bewildering guests.[15] This seems to have convinced at least his courtiers, some of whom were seen carrying the emperor in a litter to the palace of Axayacatl.[16]

A more astonishing triumph for Cortés could hardly be imagined. Apart from increasing the sense of confusion and insecurity among the Mexica – who, as some indigenous eyewitnesses would report decades later to Sahagún, were left feeling 'as if everyone had lost their heart . . . all huddled in frightened, awed, thunderstruck groups'[17] – it also reinforced Cortés's conviction that he was doing a great service, not only to God and his king but also to the Mexica themselves. As he would soon describe the episode to Charles V, the conqueror of Mexico, like a new Moses, had brought the Mexica out of their long exile in the demonic wilderness of their heathendom to the promised land ushered in by their acceptance of the Christian faith and their submission to the Holy Roman Emperor. Moctezuma's deference and docility were, in Cortés's mind, clear signs of precisely this process.

Having apprehended Cohualpopocatzin, the ruler whose capture and sacrifice of Spaniards had triggered Cortés's seizure of Moctezuma, Cortés ordered him put to death by burning in front of the great pyramid alongside his sons and just over two dozen accomplices. He took a fettered Moctezuma along to witness the execution, the fetters being a symbolic gesture that alerted everyone present that, since Moctezuma was implicated in the crime, he deserved the same fate. Cortés – or so he said – tempered harsh authority with magnanimity: as soon as the burnings were over, he pardoned Moctezuma, had the fetters removed, and solemnly announced that the emperor was free to go. But Moctezuma turned down the offer. He said that he was very happy to continue in the company of the 'Caxtilteca' and that, should he choose to return to his palace, it was likely that the lords of the land might put pressure on him to do something against Cortés's will – which would in turn amount to being disloyal to Charles V, to whom he had pledged unconditional allegiance.[18]

Again, by any standards, the spin that Cortés put on this episode is unbelievable, and is largely unsupported by the bulk of other sources.[19] It was precisely to prop up this theme of Moctezuma's vassalage to Charles V that Cortés painted an enduring portrait of the Mexica emperor as being too aware of the need to ingratiate himself with his captors. Not only was this a matter of elementary political expediency, but there is also the suggestion that Moctezuma felt quite comfortable in his new environment. Yet according to other accounts, Cortés was acutely aware of the importance of honouring Moctezuma's illustrious status, and went out of his way to acknowledge it, emphasizing that his act of submission to Charles V would turn him into a much greater lord than he already was.[20] Likewise, the Spanish guards entrusted to wait on Moctezuma paid him every courtesy, even going out of their way to make him laugh. He developed a particular affection for a young page known as Orteguilla, who had picked up enough Nahuatl to keep the Mexica emperor enthralled with his descriptions of Spain.[21] Moreover, Moctezuma was kept in contact with members of his supreme council, one of whom – Itzquauhtzin, the ruler of Tlatelolco – had moved in with him.[22] What was glaringly evident, however it might have actually happened, was that Moctezuma's continued house arrest had created a deep crisis whose resolution seemed to evade everyone.

In Mexica cosmology, Moctezuma was the linchpin of the universe. There was nothing comparable in contemporary Western thought to explain his exalted state, other than the theological concept of the mystical body of Christ, which gave the sacrifice of the Mass, as a re-enactment of Jesus's redeeming sacrifice on Calvary, a comparable sustaining function – not that anyone at the time would have dared fall into such sacrilegious comparisons. From the perspective of Moctezuma's supreme council, however, the capture of the emperor by a group of unpredictable strangers was a terrifying calamity. Yet even imprisoned, Moctezuma remained not merely *huey tlahtoani*, 'he who speaks', which was the same as 'he who commands', but the very 'substitute' and 'surrogate' of the gods. 'You are their seat (the throne from which they rule)', he had been told at the time of his accession; 'you are their flute (the mouth through which they speak) . . . they make you their lips, their jaws, their ears . . . They also make you their fangs, their claws, for you are their wild beast, you are their eater-of-people, you are their judge.' The Mexica gods, for whom Moctezuma acted as surrogate, were wilful, capricious and arbitrary. The emperor might be regarded as the father and mother of his people, 'the precious one', the 'heart of the community', 'a great cypress' and 'barricade', but he could also, just like the gods, bare his fangs and threaten with his claws. His task was a formidable one: not merely to govern but to keep the universe in being. And for this task, war was of the essence. Without war there were no captives; without captives there were no sacrifices; and without sacrifices the gods could not be fed.[23] And now, this great war-maker was himself in prison.

Cortés knew enough to understand that having Moctezuma under his grip gave him the power he needed to ensure the survival of Castilians against the awesome odds of being so overwhelmingly outnumbered in a city built with defence as a top priority. He was also quick to grasp that Moctezuma's power was inseparable from the propitiation of his gods – and that any interruption or threat to such a propitiation would deprive the emperor of value as Cortés's prisoner, rendering him dangerous and counterproductive. Cortés would have been quick to notice the change of mood in the relationship between Moctezuma and his inner council – 'no longer was he heeded', a group of indigenous witnesses would later recount to Sahagún[24] – and make every effort to give the impression that there had been no change in the emperor's pre-eminent position. Moctezuma continued to bathe regularly, to eat sumptuously, to surround himself with his advisors, and to meet discreetly with his women. He continued to govern, seeing countless suitors and nominating judges. And, however appalled Cortés might have been, Moctezuma continued to make sacrifices involving the ritual killing of men and boys. 'We could not,' one foot soldier would later recall, 'do anything under the circumstances but turn a blind eye to such things, for there were many stirrings in Tenochtitlan and other great cities among Moctezuma's nephews.'[25]

There was, moreover, not much to raise serious concern in the middle of November, known as Quecholli by the Mexica – the fourteenth month in the eighteen-month twenty-day calendar used by them. Quecholli – literally 'Precious Feather' – is rendered as 'War Lance' in one of the early Mexica codices; it is illustrated by a man with a bone through his nose, holding a spear and wearing a headdress of white feathers. Dedicated to the Chichimec hunting god Mixcoatl-Camaxtli, Quecholli was marked by much hunting, in which the Spaniards seemed to have participated with relish.[26] But it was also a time for war and capturing sacrificial victims: Quecholli, indeed, ushered in the month of Panquetzaliztli, literally 'the Raising of Banners', illustrated by an old man holding a banner decorated with blue stripes and pennants, the colours of Huitzilopochtli, in whose honour many sacrifices were performed. Atemoztli, literally 'the Descent of the Waters', was dedicated to Tlaloc and was followed by Tititl, literally 'the Stretching', illustrated by a man balancing an upright rope with a figure of eight symbolizing the way in which the gods 'stretch' and sustain the cosmos against the violence of the winds, which marks this time of the year.

It was the Mercedarian friar Bartolomé de Olmedo, Cortés's chaplain, who seems to have been the main restraining influence on Cortés's dogged insistence that the sacrifices should stop.[27] The friar's view, that forced conversion was undesirable, was very likely influenced by his recollections of the failed forced conversion of Muslims in the years following the fall of Granada in 1492.[28] The long-term aim, however, was of course the eventual conversion of all indigenous peoples to the Christian faith, and in this Moctezuma was a prime target. The Mexica emperor was even reported to have learnt the basic Christian prayers in Latin and to have been eager to be baptized as soon as practically possible. Indeed, the ceremony was alleged to have been scheduled for Easter so that it could be done 'with due solemnity'.[29]

If this was the case, it was hardly unusual. Moctezuma's behaviour was perfectly in tune with a well-established practice throughout Mesoamerica to accept new gods alongside existing deities. The practice was never, of course, accompanied by any indication of a willingness to abandon the other gods or the need to propitiate them through sacrifice. Inevitably, though, this was how the Spanish interpreted it, seeing in Moctezuma's apparent docility a first step towards the establishment of the Christian faith – which was indispensable if Moctezuma's alleged acceptance of the sovereignty of Charles V was to be made fully effective. This hope never seems to have faded in Cortés's mind. In one of his letters to Charles V, he gave an account of Moctezuma's response after he delivered one of his well-rehearsed sermons about the one true God and the consequent falsehood of their idols. 'And everyone replied,' wrote Cortés, 'that they had already told me that they were not natives of this land and that a long time had passed since their ancestors had come here.' It was therefore 'perfectly possible that they might be mistaken in their beliefs' and that the Spaniards, as recent arrivals, 'would know the things that they should hold and believe much better than them'.[30]

Again, to dismiss this story as complete fiction can blind us to Cortés's genuine belief that the Mexica would naturally realize the error of their ways as soon as the Christian message was explained to them. In any case, Moctezuma had shown himself most cooperative in other respects. He had supplied carpenters for the construction of the chapel where Cortés and his men heard Mass every morning, and for the building of some new brigantines with which the Spaniards explored the lakes around the city.[31] He had taken them to the *totocalli*, the treasure house, where, as Sahagún's informers later recalled, the conquistadores were offered 'brilliant goods, quetzal fans, shields, golden discs, neck-laces, golden nose crescents, golden leg bands, golden arm bands, golden head bands', which made them look 'eager and content . . . as if greedy and covetous'.[32]

As this indigenous account hints, all was not well with Cortés's men. Their greed for gold had led to some shameful squabbles and fallings out. Gonzalo de Mexía, the treasurer of the army, had quarrelled with Velázquez de León over a set of gold plates, and they had drawn swords and wounded each other. An indignant Cortés imprisoned both men in chains in a room close to Moctezuma's quarters. Alarmed by the groans, the Mexica emperor pleaded with Cortés to show clemency. Shortly after this incident, Moctezuma informed Cortés that he had at last been able to communicate with his gods, who had been uncannily silent of late. Now they were telling him that it was his duty to make war on the Spaniards, for they were clearly thieves who had upset the balance of the cosmos by imprisoning Mexica leaders and imposing their gods to the exclusion of the local deities.[33]

Moctezuma's change of attitude undoubtedly had much to do with the point in the ceremonial year. It was now mid-March 1520. On 14 February, I-Reed had become 2-Flint, and the propitiation of Quetzal-coatl gave way to the appeasement of the rain god Tlaloc in a series of festivals that involved the sacrifice of young children. This was fol-lowed by the month of Tlacaxipehualitzli, which runs from 6 to 25 March. Literally 'the Flaying of Men', it is illustrated in an early codex by the god Xipe Totec (literally 'Our Lord the Flayed One'), depicted with a protruding tongue and a tunic made of flayed human skin. Some of the most elaborate ceremonies of the year were performed at this time, including gladiatorial contests and the wearing of the flayed skins of sacrificed victims who had taken the roles of impersonating the gods. Moctezuma himself was expected to wear one such flayed skin.[34] The absence of the emperor at such an important event was unthinkable.

Moctezuma was also clearly under pressure from his advisors in the supreme council. They had by now had ample opportunity to witness the disorderly squabbling among the Castilians and were beginning to wonder how much longer they would need to put up with them, let alone continue to feed them. Even by the standards of Tenochtitlan, hosting an army of a few hundred Spaniards and over 2,000 indigen-ous allies was a tremendous drain on resources. By this time, moreover,

Moctezuma had received news about a development on the gulf coast that he decided to keep secret from the Castilians for as long as he could. A large Spanish fleet had made a landing there. Its leader claimed to be a faithful subject of Charles V and wanted Moctezuma to know that he had been entrusted with the mission of liberating him from Cortés, who was in fact a rebel and an outlaw.[35]

It was not long before Cortés got wind of the situation. Despite his control of the Mexica emperor, he was not as well informed as Moctezuma, who used the new knowledge as leverage to persuade Cortés to leave Tenochtitlan as soon as possible, offering whatever help he might need for the purpose.[36] Playing for time, Cortés dispatched his chaplain to the coast with a letter demanding to know the identity of the new arrivals, and whether they came as 'natural vassals' of Charles V. If this was not the case, then he would find himself obliged to treat them as enemies of his 'king and lord' and would arrest them and put them to death.[37] By this time a delegation from the recently arrived fleet had also reached Cortés's new city of Villa Rica de la Vera Cruz. They announced to the city's governor, Gonzalo de Sandoval, that the fleet, under the command of Pánfilo de Narváez, had been sent by Cortés's chief enemy, Diego Velázquez, the governor of Cuba. Velázquez had appointed Narváez captain-general of the region and, the envoys continued briskly, it would be in Sandoval's best interests to give himself up immediately. But Sandoval gave as good as he got. Such language, he replied, deserved a good beating, for there was only one captain-general in the region and his name was Hernán Cortés. Without more ado, Sandoval had the envoys arrested and sent to Tenochtitlan as prisoners.[38]

When they arrived, Cortés could afford to be magnanimous. Quick to take advantage of their disorientated state, dazzled by the Mexica capital, he released them, prepared a banquet in their honour, apologized profusely on Sandoval's behalf, housed them sumptuously, and soon 'turned the fierce lions that came into very tame ones'.[39] Cortés also learned much about Narváez and his army. The expedition, consisting of eleven ships and seven brigantines, had left Cuba on 5 March 1520. Among the 1,000-strong force were some ninety horsemen, eighty arquebusiers and 120 crossbowmen.[40] Yet Cortés felt reassured to learn that Narváez was not in control of his men; indeed, he had antagonized many of them by failing to redistribute the lavish gifts he had received from the Cempohualteca on landing. In particular, he had fallen out with Lucas Vázquez de Ayllón, a judge who had been sent by the judicial authorities in Santo Domingo to prevent any potential friction between Narváez and Cortés. This, of course, could not have been more at odds with the intentions of the governor of Cuba, who was keen to generate as much friction as possible, and Narváez duly ignored Vázquez de Ayllón. For his part, the judge saw this blatant insolence as an offence to the authorities of Santo Domingo and, in response, began to speak favourably about Cortés, even sending a letter to him expressing his support.[41]

After a few days Cortés felt confident enough to send the envoys back to Narváez, accompanied by a servant and a mare loaded with presents of gold.[42] With them, Cortés sent a letter to Narváez in which he expressed his delight at the arrival of an old friend, while also voicing some surprise that he had not had the delicacy to contact him directly. Cortés also expressed concern that Narváez was calling himself captain-general and had even appointed magistrates and councillors. Did he not know that the land had already been formally subdued and was the rightful property of Charles V? Cortés never received a reply. Instead, he soon heard that the Totonacs, including the chief of Cempohuallan – Tlacochcalcatl, whom Cortés believed to have been his first ally – had sided with Narváez. His only option now was to depart at once for the coast and face his old 'friend' in person.[43]

In what was one of the most unfortunate gambles of the campaign, Cortés placed his remaining men under the command of Pedro de Alvarado, whom he entrusted with the awesome task of keeping Moctezuma prisoner. He then set off for the coast in early May with about eighty men. At Cholollan he was joined by a further 260 men under the command of Rodrigo Rangel and Juan Velázquez de León, who had been sent there in search of gold. Any dissenters were ably won over by promises of gold and by Cortés's characteristic insistence on the importance of loyalty to Charles V above everything else. When he received a letter from an old acquaintance from Cuba, Andrés de Duero, warning him that he was leading his men into a slaughterhouse, Cortés had it read aloud. He then asked his captains to suggest a solution. As Cortés more than likely expected, they replied that they would do whatever he deemed best.[44] With this agreement, Cortés delivered one of his most memorable orations. He reminded everyone that he himself had had no qualms about going back to Cuba after realizing his commission from Velázquez had been accomplished; it was his captains – all now councillors of Villa Rica de la Vera Cruz – who had urged him to found a town and had then solemnly named him captain-general until such a time as Charles was able to make a decision on the matter. Until then, therefore, anything else was tantamount to high treason.[45]

Cortés never deviated from this argument. Years later, he insisted that he had never seen any papers that could be interpreted as the king's will on the matter. Had he done so, then of course he would have 'been obliged to obey them and would have obeyed them as coming from our lord the king'. The words were carefully chosen. They were used by Cortés in the Castilian legal tradition that allowed for 'obedience' to a royal order without necessarily having to 'comply' with it. Indeed, Cortés was careful to insist that 'it was clear' that if the king knew the truth, he would never have issued such an order, 'if, indeed, he ever did'.[46]

Cortés and his men now advanced towards Cempohuallan, where Narváez had taken refuge on top of the main temple and, on the night of 28–29 May, made a surprise attack before dawn and in heavy rain. In the squabble Narváez himself lost an eye and, with blood gushing out, begged for clemency; most of his captains promptly surrendered to Cortés, who again took advantage of the opportunity to show his magnanimity. He set most of the prisoners free and gave them back their horses and weapons on condition that they returned with him to Tenochtitlan. He then confiscated the welcome provisions of wine, flour, bacon and cassava bread, and beached the ships.[47]

Cortés's triumph was soon dampened by news from Tenochtitlan. Pedro de Alvarado, his deputy, was handsome, gallant, chivalrous and charismatic: his reddish-blond hair and beard had earned him the nickname *Tonatiuh*, the sun god depicted in one of the native sources as a red-faced warrior.[48] This was high praise anywhere, but supremely so in Tenochtitlan where metaphors of the setting and rising of the sun were reserved for the death of rulers and the accession of their successors.[49] Underneath such qualities, however, Alvarado was, to quote William Prescott, 'altogether destitute of that moderation, which, in the delicate position he occupied, was a quality of more worth than all the rest'.[50] He had none of Cortés's political skills, and all the prickly honour of a chivalrous knight.

Soon after Cortés left for the coast, the Mexica stopped feeding the Spaniards, forcing them to buy food in the market.[51] Then, in mid-May, as preparations for the important feast of Toxcatl got underway, many Tlaxcalteca allies began to express their concern, no doubt remembering fellow compatriots who had been sacrificed by the Mexica in previous festivals. Some of them even affirmed that the various stakes being placed in the main square were to tie up the Castilians before sacrificing them – and that the biggest stake, erected on the main temple, was reserved for the *Tonatiuh*, Alvarado himself. Others would insist that the Mexica were preparing to kill all the 'Caxtilteca'. There was an additional problem: one of communication. Cortés had taken with him his regular interpreters, Marina and Aguilar, so Alvarado and his men were reliant on the help of 'Francisco', a native lad who had picked up some Castilian but whose replies were invariably monosyllabic.[52]

When the festival began, therefore, the Spaniards were in a state of some anxiety. About 400 Mexica, holding hands, danced in large concentric rings.[53] Fearing that an attack was imminent, Alvarado instructed his men to block the three entrances of the main square: the gates of the Reed, the Obsidian Serpent and the Eagle.[54] When the gates were closed, Alvarado and his men wielded their steel swords against the dancers and the priests who were playing the drums. The repellent scene was later recalled by the indigenous informers of Sahagún in ghastly detail: 'The blood . . . ran like water, it spread out slippery and a foul odour rose from it.' The Spaniards surrounded the dancers, and 'struck off the arms of the one who beat the drums . . . and, afterwards, his neck and his head flew off, falling far away. They pierced them all with their iron lances, and they struck each with iron swords.' Of one group of dancers, 'they slashed open the back so that their entrails fell out'. Of another, 'they split the heads, they hacked their heads to pieces. Their heads were completely cut up.' Of yet another, 'they hit the shoulders . . . they struck in the shank and in the thigh'. And if this was not enough, they attacked another group and 'struck the bellies, and the entrails streamed out'.[55] Soon the drums on top of the great pyramid began to beat: a call to all the men who had survived the massacre to go to the armouries located at each of the four entrances to the main square and launch a counter-attack.[56] The Spaniards were forced to retreat; Alvarado, hit on the head by a stone, managed to escape to the palace of Axayacatl, covered in blood. In that state, he apparently complained to Moctezuma, who coolly replied that it was Alvarado's own fault: 'had you not yourself started this, my men would not have acted thus. You have brought ruin upon yourselves, and upon me too.'[57] Moctezuma, indeed, displayed an imperial calm, especially given that his Spanish guards had killed some of his noble companions, including Cacama, the ruler of Tetzcoco; the few who survived – Moctezuma himself, his brother Cuitlahuac, and Itzquauhtzin, the governor of Tlatelolco, to name the most prominent – were now held in chains.[58] Outside the palace compound, the Mexica grew increasingly threatening. In a state of desperation, Alvarado ordered Moctezuma at knifepoint to call off the battle. But the Mexica emperor seemed to have lost his authority. Anyone seen taking food to the palace was put to death; several bridges were pulled up and the roads were blocked. At night the air was filled with the sound of lamentation. The flower of the Mexica nobility was dead. Even the stones, an indigenous source reported, seemed to weep.[59]

As they returned to Tenochtitlan, Cortés and his men noticed that something was amiss: they encountered none of the messengers who had greeted them on their previous approach to the city.[60] Suspecting something, Cortés decided to take another way, skirting Tenochtitlan round the north side of the lake and entering the city from the west by the causeway of Tlacopan, which he knew to be the least conspicuous. He entered the city on the feast of St John the Baptist, 24 June 1520. The silence was deafening.[61]

Cortés realized that his hope of capturing Tenochtitlan for Charles V without a fight was in tatters. Although Moctezuma was ostensibly pleased that Cortés had returned, the conquistador knew that his possession of the emperor was practically useless now. Not only had Moctezuma's standing among his own people fallen to a worryingly low ebb, but Cortés also had reasons to feel betrayed by the emperor. 'Why,' he asked his captains, when they advised him to be more conciliatory towards his distinguished prisoner, 'should I be moderate to a dog who had secret relations with Narváez and does not even give us anything to eat?'[62] His only communication with the emperor was to demand the reopening of the food markets in order to feed his increasingly mutinous entourage. Knowing that his word no longer had any power, Moctezuma suggested sending another lord. They settled on

Moctezuma's brother, Cuitlahuac, lord of Iztapallapan, who was freed one day after Cortés's return, on 25 June. It was an atrocious tactical error on Cortés's part, for no sooner had he left the palace than Cuitlahuac set about organizing a concerted Mexica resistance.[63]

The next few days were extremely tense. The Spaniards could not leave the precinct without being attacked. Their horses, cannons and arquebuses were useless in street battles. Then, from their vantage point on the palace roof, they noticed a group of Mexica nobles, dressed in cloaks adorned with gold, silver and feathers and carrying gold-plated shields, followed by a large crowd. They seemed to treat one of their number with particular deference. Cortés naturally assumed that this must be Cuitlahuac, though Moctezuma said he very much doubted that the Mexica would have chosen a successor while he was still alive. Cortés urged the emperor to speak to his people from the palace roof and order them to disperse. While Moctezuma now wanted as little as possible to do with Cortés, he allowed himself to be persuaded. He was taken to the roof of the palace by Alonso de Aguilar – the future Dominican friar who would take the name Francisco and who was 'contemplative by nature' and 'brooded about the moral aspects of the conquest' – and by Leonel de Cervantes, a member of an old noble Sevillian family who had recently arrived with Narváez and transferred his loyalties to Cortés. Moctezuma had barely appeared before a volley of projectiles were fired from the streets: it seemed, Aguilar later recalled, 'as if the heavens had sent a shower of stones and arrows'. Hit three times, the emperor had to be carried back to his quarters in haste. He died on 30 June, probably of his wounds – though there were suggestions that the emperor, now demonstrably lacking any authority with his people, was killed by the Spaniards for whom he had no further use.[64]

That evening, it was clear that the Spaniards had no other option than to flee the city. The retreat began in the dead of night. Muffling the hooves of their horses, the Castilians moved quietly through rain-slicked streets. Using a pontoon put together with beams from the ceilings of the palace, they crossed the first four bridges of the western causeway leading to Tlacopan. Then, as they were most of the way across, they were sighted and at once the drum on top of the main pyramid began to beat. Almost immediately, the lake swarmed with canoes filled with warriors firing arrows with a fury and clearly oblivious to the traditional Mexica tactic to aim to capture rather than kill. Those at the front of the column, including Cortés, managed to swim across to the mainland at Popotla. Cortés returned to assist the others, but the causeway was now under heavy attack on both sides and all the bridges were up. Those not killed by arrows were drowning, sinking with the weight of cannons and gold. The few who managed to reach the mainland no longer needed to swim: they crawled frantically over a multitude of corpses. All in all, some 600 Spaniards and several thousand Tlaxcalteca had perished. Of the royal gold they were carrying, there was no sign.[65]

9

Defeat and Victory

The massacre of the Spanish as they fled Tenochtitlan came to be known as the *Noche Triste* – the 'Night of Sorrows' – when, as every school-child is still taught in Mexico, on the morning of 1 July 1520, Cortés shed bitter tears under the shelter of an imposing *ahuehuetl* tree that can still be visited in its current cadaverous state, or admired in the art it has inspired. He also allegedly said 'Onwards, for we lack nothing!' as soon as he established that his skilful but badly wounded shipbuilder, Martín López, had survived the ordeal alongside some 400 men.[1]

It was essential for their very survival that Cortés held what remained of his group together. But his uncompromising determination can only be properly understood by considering how he always assessed his indigenous opponents: the Mexica were already the subjects of monarchs of Castile, and now they were guilty of an unacceptable act of 'rebellion' against the legitimate rights of the Spanish king. As he lamented his losses, however, Cortés still did not know the fate of the mission on whose outcome his fate depended. He was painfully aware that he was still completely unknown in Spain and that any hope of royal favour was in the hands of the two envoys he had dispatched the previous year. Francisco de Montejo and Alonso Hernández Puertocarrero had reached Seville the previous autumn, but any news from them had yet to reach Cortés.

Almost immediately the two envoys had run into problems. Benito Martín, Diego Velázquez's influential chaplain, had reached Seville ahead of them and had persuaded the local authorities to impound the treasure that they had brought back with them, along with any funds. Montejo and Puertocarrero then journeyed around Spain in pursuit of the king. They arrived in Barcelona in late January 1520, only to find that Charles had left for Burgos; two months later they finally caught up with him at Tordesillas, near Valladolid. There, with the welcome help of Francisco Núñez – a royal official and cousin of Cortés whom they came across in Barcelona and who offered to act as Cortés's legal representative – they could at last petition Charles in person on behalf of the still-unknown adventurer and de facto rebel.[2]

The odds were against them. Velázquez's agents and the powerful Bishop of Burgos, Juan Rodríguez de Fonseca, were briefing against Cortés's interests. For all the whispering and lobbying on both sides, however, one irrefutable fact worked definitively in favour of Cortés's envoys: the sight of Moctezuma's treasure, which Charles had ordered to be sent to him from Seville, reaching him in early April. Despite deferring a final decision, it is significant that Charles declined to declare Cortés a rebel, dismissing the protests of Velázquez's allies and ordering the authorities in Seville to return the funds they had confiscated along with the treasure. If this was a clear triumph for Cortés's procurators, events in Spain would soon begin to work against them. As we have seen, no sooner had Charles sailed for England from La Coruña, on his way to claim his inheritance as Holy Roman Emperor, than the revolt of the *Comuneros* broke out. The leader of the royalist army was none other than Fonseca's brother, and he wasted no time in painting Cortés's act of rebellion with the same brush as that of the Castilian rebels. It is little wonder, in this context, that Fonseca had enthusiastically supported Narváez's expedition against Cortés. Although this had now been resolved in the conquistador's favour, the events of the *Noche Triste* had shattered all such hopes. Having so insistently promised to deliver Tenochtitlan to Charles, Cortés had now proceeded to lose it in the most spectacularly humiliating circumstances.

As he began his slow retreat from Tlacopan, Cortés seemed unable to accept what had happened: he was adamant that the dreadful defeat was no more than a temporary setback. Nonetheless, his situation did not look good. With the majority of his 400 men injured, his battered band was exceptionally vulnerable to attacks and ambushes. Taking the same route he had used to return to Tenochtitlan after his campaign against Narváez, along the north shore of the lake, he rested the first night in a temple at Otoncalpulco. The expedition then set off for Teocalhueycan, the wounded in the middle, and those who could still fight at the front and the rear. While Cortés got valuable respite at Teocalhueycan – whose Tepanec inhabitants, resenting the Mexica,

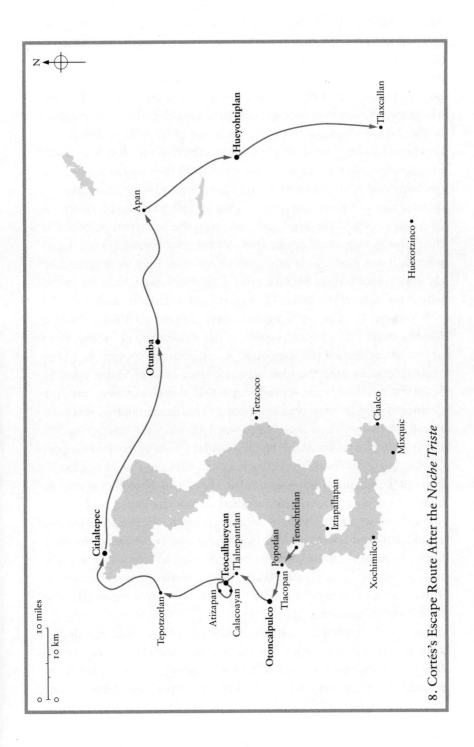

8. Cortés's Escape Route After the *Noche Triste*

received the Spaniards well – the expedition came under constant, wearing guerrilla attack as it made its way slowly north, via Tepotzotlan and Citlaltepec. Many of the wounded died; by one count, in a few days their numbers had been reduced to 340 men and twenty-seven horses.[3] In this state, exhausted and desperately hungry, they had to face a large force mounted by Moctezuma's successor, Cuitlahuac, at Otumba.[4] In the thick of the fighting Cortés made one of his boldest moves, one that he would later attribute to the intervention of the Holy Spirit: seeing a group of Mexica captains detached from the main army, he took five horsemen to attack them, himself spearing and killing Cuitlahuac's deputy, the so-called *cihuacoatl*. This spread confusion among the Mexica ranks and the army fled, allowing the Spaniards to continue their slow progress to Apan, from where they finally turned south towards Tlaxcallan. On 9 July, at Hueyohtiplan, they were greeted by the Tlaxcalteca leaders Maxixcatzin, Xicotencatl and Chichimecatecle, who came to offer the weary Castilians food and much-needed rest.[5]

It was not long before Cortés discovered that Cuitlahuac, the new Mexica emperor, had been in touch with the Tlaxcalteca, urging them to join forces against the Spaniards. Xicotencatl the younger had been eager to comply with the request, but he had been prevailed upon by Maxixcatzin. The latter was adamant that the Tlaxcalteca-Castilian alliance should be preserved at all costs. This determination was reinforced when the Tlaxcalteca discovered that Cortés was set on the reconquest of Tenochtitlan. The Tlaxcalteca then offered to support Cortés, but at the same time struck a hard bargain: should the reconquest of Tenochtitlan prove successful, the city of Chollollan was to be handed over to them, complete with the authority to establish a permanent military presence there. Moreover, any booty was to be divided equally between Spaniards and Tlaxcalteca, the latter being exempted from paying any tribute to Spain in perpetuity. Cortés was in no position to refuse: a deal was struck. The Spanish then moved on to Tlaxcallan where, over the next three weeks, they were finally able to rest and recuperate.[6]

Tensions remained. Many among Cortés's group, tired and disillusioned, were ready to give up. They did not trust the Tlaxcalteca, nor did they believe that they were capable of reconquering Tenochtitlan. They petitioned Cortés to abandon the whole enterprise, threatening to sue him for his failures of leadership if he refused.[7] With his characteristic agility, Cortés turned the question on his critics. Had it ever been known, he asked them, for any captain worthy of the name to give up after losing a battle? Was there anyone among them who would not feel deeply ashamed to be reminded in later life that he had given up? As for the Tlaxcalteca, he pointed out, they would much prefer to be under the authority of the Spanish than to continue being subdued and exploited by the Mexica.[8] As Cortés subsequently explained to Charles V, he persuaded his disgruntled followers that the worst thing they could do in the circumstances was to show any sign of weakness. They must not forget, he told them, that fortune always favoured the brave, and that they were Christians who should trust in the goodness and mercy of God. There was no way he could abandon the enterprise: apart from personal humiliation, such an act of cowardice would be an unforgivable 'act of great treason to Your Majesty'.[9]

Cortés had some reasons for optimism. He now knew much about Tenochtitlan, and his ecstatic descriptions of its size and wealth had not blinded him to some obvious weaknesses. One of these was the city's dependence on imported foodstuffs. Most of the labour force in the Mexica capital, he knew, consisted of occupational specialists, few of whom engaged in any form of agriculture beyond the tending of their gardens or *chinampas*.[10] There was, besides, a chronic shortage of wood and fuel. Despite the city's outward magnificence, it was in fact a fairly recent creation, barely 200 years old. In political terms, this brought its own problems: it remained one city in a mosaic of *altepeme* – city states – each of which was determined to uphold its own independence, identity and local gods against all others.[11] One of the key things that Cortés had noticed and tried to exploit was that subjugation at the hands of the Mexica rarely led to incorporation. This, in practical terms, meant that Tenochtitlan had no significant bureaucracy and hardly anything by way of a standing army. While, following their conquests of surrounding city states, the Mexica had tried to link the leading dynasties through marriage alliances, local rulers were normally left in place, largely undisturbed so long as they paid tribute regularly. When called on to fight for the Mexica, local rulers did so under their own banners, thus turning the whole system into what has been aptly described as 'an acrobats' pyramid, a precious structure of the more privileged lording it over the less, with those poised on the highest level triumphant, but nervously attentive to any premonitory shift or shuffle from below'. For all its imposing grandeur, Tenochtitlan was 'at once the forced fruit and the massive proof of a late-dawning greatness'.[12]

Cortés rarely missed an opportunity to exploit weaknesses. In early August 1520, having placated the potential rebels and backed by thousands of Tlaxcalteca warriors, Cortés moved swiftly against one of Tenochtitlan's most important dependencies.[13] This was Tepeaca, a mountain-top fortress and a centre for tribute collection, which dominated the flat expanse of land between the Popocatepetl and the Pico de Orizaba volcanoes, the best route between Tenochtitlan and the gulf coast (see Map 7).[14] Cortés was now determined to establish his ascendancy in uncompromising terms. After a brutal campaign in which some 400 Tepeacan warriors were killed, the Spanish-Tlaxcalteca force moved into the centre of the town and sacked it for days. Cortés was merciless. He allowed his followers to enslave the wives and children of those who had been killed, branding them on the cheek with a 'G' for *Guerra* (War); he allowed others to be torn to pieces by dogs, and even turned a blind eye when Tlaxcalteca warriors held cannibalistic feasts. From his new fortress in Tepeaca, Cortés set about subduing the surrounding area, setting a pattern of slaughter, mass mutilation and systematic enslavement of thousands of women and children. His enemies would later claim that he had killed up to 20,000 people in the region.

Even allowing for possible exaggerations in such a neatly rounded figure, there can be no question of Cortés's horrendous brutality during these campaigns. He himself admitted as much to Charles V: without a good dose of terror, he wrote, the Mexica could have easily dissuaded the whole region from acknowledging the emperor's authority.[15] What Cortés did not mention was that his brutality also allowed him to vent his frustrated anger in a way that appalled many of his followers.[16] But the strategy nonetheless paid off: by the autumn of 1520, Cortés had established himself as the most important and feared potentate in the large swathe of flat land separating the Popocatepetl from the Pico de Orizaba volcano, effectively cutting off Tenochtitlan from the gulf coast and winning the allegiance – be it willing or cajoled – of the bulk of the region. Following a well-established precedent, Cortés founded a new town in Tepeaca, now renamed Segura de la Frontera by him, and filled its town council with his friends and supporters. The time was ripe to begin to plan his next move: he turned to the shipbuilder

Martín López, whom he sent alongside several assistants to Tlaxcallan, where he would be assisted with the necessary provisions and the support needed for the construction of thirteen brigantines.

On arriving at Tlaxcallan, López and his assistants found the old chief, Maxixcatzin, on his deathbed. His illness had nothing to do with his age: he had contracted smallpox.[17] A disease previously unknown in the Americas, smallpox had been inadvertently introduced by Spanish explorers, and proved devastating to native populations, which had no immunity against it. Reaching epidemic proportions in Hispaniola and Cuba in 1519, it had been brought over to Cozumel in Narváez's fleet, soon causing havoc throughout Yucatan. Francisco de Eguía, one of Narváez's black porters, carried the disease to Cempohuallan; from there it spread fast, decimating the Totonac population.[18] The disease reached the Valley of Mexico in the autumn of 1520, taking the life of Cuitlahuac, Moctezuma's successor, and the kings of Tlacopan and Chalco, before spreading to Michoacán.[19] It is impossible to exaggerate the devastating physical and psychological impact of this merciless epidemic on indigenous communities. Decades later, those who could remember the episode recalled how 'there spread over the people a great destruction of men'. Its symptoms included pustules that 'spread everywhere, on one's face, on one's head, on one's breast'. People died in vast numbers. 'No longer could they walk; they only lay in their abodes, in their beds. No longer could they move, no longer could they bestir themselves, no longer could they raise themselves, no longer could they stretch themselves out on their sides, no longer could they stretch themselves out face down, no longer could they stretch themselves out on their backs.' Those who did not contract the disease began to die of hunger, for 'there was no one to take care of another; there was no one to attend to another.'[20]

Something that the natives did not miss in all this was that the disease did not seem to affect the Spaniards, who thus began to appear as endowed with a mysterious aura of invincibility. This in turn explains why a growing number of indigenous communities decided to pledge loyalty to Cortés as leader of a growing anti-Mexica alliance. Nor did fortune fail to favour Cortés. Many of the expeditions that kept arriving from Cuba and Hispaniola now came to support him, offering fresh supplies of men, horses, armaments and provisions. One arrived in a large ship sent from Spain at the request of Cortés's father and his business partners in Andalusia. It came laden with horses, muskets, gunpowder and crossbows. Now increasingly sure of Charles V's backing, Cortés relaxed enough to show some magnanimity to his opponents, even allowing several disgruntled captains and potential conspirators who had come with Narváez to return to Cuba: as far as Cortés was concerned, they were good riddance.[21] He could now focus on the next stage of the campaign. Leaving Francisco de Orozco in charge of operations at Segura de la Frontera, he set off for Tlaxcallan in mid-December to check up on Martín López's progress with the brigantines.[22]

On 27 December, as soon as the Christmas celebrations were over, Cortés was on the move again. He aimed to establish a base in Tetzcoco, facing Tenochtitlan on the eastern shore of the great lake, where the brigantines would be transported in pieces and assembled when ready. It was a brave decision: although Cortés had received some friendly gestures from Tetzcoco, the city was nonetheless, at least in theory, an ally of Tenochtitlan. Wary of ambushes along his route, Cortés decided to make the journey along the steeper and comparatively inhospitable northern pass of Xaltepec-Apan, instead of the route he had taken in 1519, along what is still known as the 'Paso de Cortés'. It paid off: although the expedition had to negotiate blocked paths and some minor ambushes, progress was swift. Two days later, the expedition reached Coatepec where Ixtlilxochitl, a royal lord of Tetzcoco, came during the night to offer his support.[23] Marching through Coatlinchan, they pressed on to Tetzcoco, reaching the city on New Year's Eve.[24]

Entering Tetzcoco, Cortés found its streets and gardens empty, and its palaces abandoned: it was completely deserted.[25] Cortés sent Pedro de Alvarado and Cristóbal de Olid to check out the lie of the land from the summit of the city's great temple. On a normal day they might have been awestruck by the palace gardens with their remarkable botanical variety and the sophisticated system of canals carved into solid rock;[26] now what caught their attention were the hundreds of canoes carrying the city's inhabitants across the lake to Tenochtitlan.[27]

Cortés turned his forces loose: they ran riot through Tetzcoco, sacking the city. His Tlaxcalteca allies, diehard enemies of Tetzcoco, did the most damage, setting fire to the royal palaces, along with the archives, codices and genealogies.[28] Cortés probably thought the destruction was a price worth paying: just as in Tepeaca, he soon received pledges of allegiance from the lords of surrounding cities. According to Cortés's

1. Monastery of St Mary of the Victory in Batalha, with the exuberant maritime imagery that would capture Columbus's imagination (see p. 6).

2. Sebastian Münster's depiction of Genoa as both Janus (Ianos) and Ianua – the door to the Pillars of Hercules (see pp. 3–5).

3. Columbus's coat of arms with the map of islands on the bottom left (see p. 17).

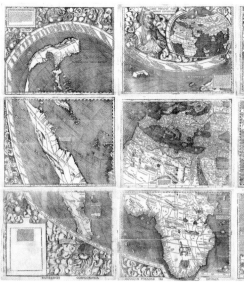

4. Map by Martin Walseemüller (1507) showing (*see detail, right*) the elusive strait that would lead to the Spice Islands (see p. 89).

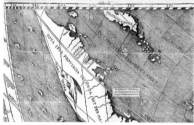

5. The Plateresque façade of the University of Alcalá de Henares, as remote from the Gothic and the Classical as it is evocative of both (see p. 108).

7. Charles V's hubristic motto, *Plus Ultra* (see p. 196).

6. A young Charles of Ghent, the future Charles V, as he would have been seen by Piero Pasqualigo (see p. 117).

8. Alfonso de Valdés holding a portrait of Charles V's Grand Chancellor – Mercurino Arborio, Marquis of Gattinara (*see detail, above*).

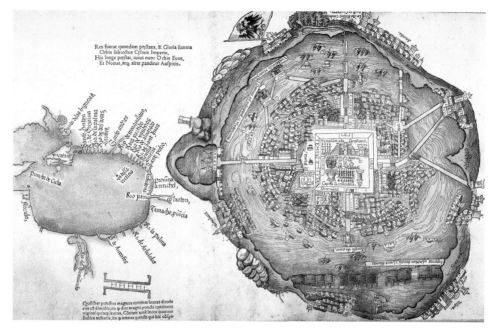

9. The Nuremberg Map of Tenochtitlan (see pp. 148–9).

10. Relief portrait of the goddess Coyolxauhqui, sister of Huitzilopochtli, onto which the bodies of sacrificed victims were cast (see p. 151).

11. Quecholli, 'Precious Feather' (see p. 157).

12. Panquetzaliztli, 'The Raising of Banners' (see p. 157).

13. Tititl, 'The Stretching' – the figure of eight symbolizes the way the gods 'stretch' to sustain the cosmos (see p. 157).

14. Tlacaxipehualiztli, 'The Flaying of Men', depicting a man wearing a tunic made of flayed human skin (see p. 159).

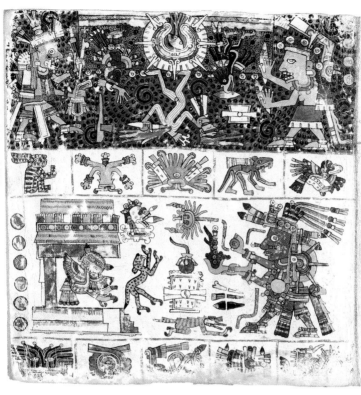

15. Tonatiuh, the sun god, depicted in the lower right-hand corner, leading to comparisons with Pedro de Alvarado, who was also dubbed Tonatiuh (see p. 162).

16. The Ahuehuetl tree at Tlacopan (Tacuba), as viewed by a nineteenth-century artist. To this day, its ancient trunk marks the spot where Cortés wept after the *Noche Triste* (see p. 167).

17. Tzitzimitl, the Nahuatl singular of Titzimime, those demonic monsters of Mexica mythology with which some mendicant friars were identified (see p. 204).

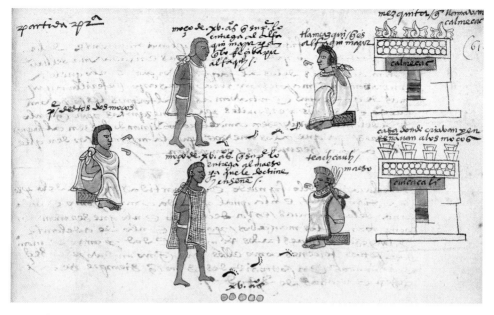

18. Calmecac, 'The House of Lineage', where the Mexica nobility received a rigorous religious and military training (see p. 182).

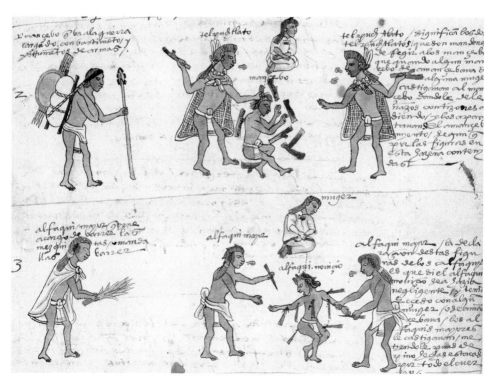

19. Telpochcalli, 'The House of Youth', where, as Mexica parents told their children, 'You will cut agave thorns … and draw blood with those spines' (see p. 182).

20. Titian's equestrian portrait of Charles V at Mühlberg, both Classical and Romantic, Imperial and Christian (see p. 114).

own account, many of them wept in his presence, explaining that they had fought against him in the past, not of their own volition but cajoled by the tyrannical Mexica; they then begged his forgiveness and swore loyalty to Charles V.[29] There was obviously plenty of poetic licence in Cortés's account: in reality, these lords were driven by practical and opportunistic motives, which Cortés later chose to spin into his 'imperial' theme. All these towns – Huexotla, Coatlinchan and Chalco – were sophisticated commercial centres that had recently come under the uncomfortable monopoly of Tenochtitlan. Any goods coming from the gulf coast necessarily had to pass through the Mexica. Now Cortés's subjugation of Tepeaca had made him master of that very monopoly, putting all the commercial networks under extreme pressure. For these cities to seek an alliance with Cortés made perfect sense.[30]

Yet Cortés was not quite as in control of the situation as most subsequent accounts would have us believe. The political situation in Tetzcoco was far too complex for Cortés or any of his captains to have been able to understand. It was rooted in a complex alliance forged in the middle of the fifteenth century, during the reign of the legendary Nezahualcoyotl, when Tetzcoco had joined forces with Tenochtitlan and Tlacopan. In 1472, Nezahualcoyotl was succeeded by Nezahualpilli, a ruler who sought to establish close dynastic links with the Mexica by taking wives who were related as closely as possible to the rulers of Tenochtitlan. He fathered well over a hundred children, at least six of whom had a solid claim to be his rightful heir. The three with the strongest claims at the time of Nezahualpilli's death in 1515 were Cacama, a nephew of Moctezuma, and his half-brothers Coanacoch and Ixtlilxochitl (who met up with Cortés in Coatepec), themselves great-nephews of Moctezuma's grandfather, Tizoc, who had ruled Tenochtitlan between 1481 and 1486. When Cacama was declared the rightful successor, most probably through the influence of Moctezuma, Ixtlilxochitl was furious and began to gather enough support to establish some control over the northern region of Tetzcoco. Moctezuma then played his cards adroitly, allowing a tripartite division of power: Ixtlilxochitl in control of the north, Cacama of the centre and Coanacoch of the south. This worked to Moctezuma's advantage, for a divided but peaceful Tetzcoco was essential to the continuation of Tenochtitlan's dominant position.[31]

This delicate balance of power was severely shaken by the arrival of the Spaniards. As we have seen, Cacama met Cortés in 1519, led him to meet Moctezuma, and stayed in Tenochtitlan until he was killed in the events leading up to the *Noche Triste*. The Tlaxcalteca were now in a position to begin taking advantage of the weaknesses and divisions in Tetzcoco, primarily by expanding their control over the east of the region with reinforcements from Huexotzingo and Cholollan. While Cortés might insist to Charles V that he was in complete command of the situation, it was clearly his Tlaxcalteca allies who held the initiative during these first months of warfare. Then, when Coanacoch escaped to the safety of Tenochtitlan, Ixtlilxochitl seized the moment, offering his support to the Castilian-Tlaxcalteca forces in order to tilt the balance of power against Tenochtitlan.[32]

The confidence with which Cortés claimed to have set about scoping out the surroundings of the great Mexica capital during the early months of 1521 deliberately underplays the crucial role of Ixtlilxochitl, now the undisputed lord of Tetzcoco and eager to lead the fight against Tenochtitlan. Cortés described how, leaving Gonzalo de Sandoval in charge at Tetzcoco (with barely a mention of Ixtlilxochitl), he led a force of some 200 Spaniards and nearly 4,000 indigenous allies on a raid across the lake to Iztapallapan, the neighbouring city state that the Mexica had used as a strategic base against Tetzcoco. There they were confronted by warriors from Tenochtitlan, who in a defensive move had breached the dyke between the salt and freshwater lakes, aiming thereby to flood the lower city and drown the intruders. But the Spaniards moved swiftly into the centre of the town, which was safely above the flood, looted it and terrorized the population. They withdrew before the water became too deep to prevent them returning to Tetzcoco.[33] With Iztapallapan subdued, Tetzcoca and Tlaxcalteca leaders could turn their attention to Tlacopan, and so bring about the effective isolation of Tenochtitlan. In their timing and purpose both these crucial campaigns were fought according to local tradition and precedent, their aim being not conquest but subjugation. What Ixtlilxochitl and his Tlaxcalteca allies wanted, in other words, was to force these city states from now on to recognize Tetzcoco or Tlaxcallan as the dominant regional powers to which tribute should be sent – a rather different outcome to the one Cortés had in mind.[34]

The image of Cortés as a presiding strategist in these early campaigns dissolves in the light of such evidence: quite clearly, at this time he had to mould his plans to the objectives of his indigenous allies. Yet the Castilians were being exposed to a steep learning curve – and they learned fast. Cortés soon started to turn the complex circumstances to his advantage. Within days of the campaigns against Iztapallapan and Tlacopan, the Castilians and their Tetzcoca and Tlaxcalteca allies were visited by several lords of nearby cities. While Cortés implausibly described these visits as grovelling expressions of guilt and a willingness to submit to Charles V, the lords had undoubtedly come to realize that their best bet was to side with the intruders and their allies, whose growing military strength had become all too evident.

It was within this increasingly favourable climate that Cortés launched a further destructive raid, similar in size to the ones that had succeeded against Iztapallapan and Tlacopan, this time led by Sandoval and Francisco de Lugo. The target was the city state of Chalco, on the extreme south-east of the great lake, which Cortés and his men had first had a chance to admire from a distance on their approach to Tenochtitlan in the autumn of 1519. Cortés later recounted how the expedition had been a resounding success. Several battles had been won with few losses, the Tlaxcalteca had shown themselves to be proficient in European methods of war, and he had personally received submission from some lords of Chalco, now free from Mexica oppression.[35] Again, however, behind Cortés's account is a rather different scenario, one in which the lords of Chalco were looking over the conquistadore's shoulder to seek alliances with his Tlaxcalteca and Tetzcoca supporters.

Nevertheless, as the year advanced, the initiative began to pass to the conquistadores. According to local custom, the campaigning season came to an end in April. As far as Ixtlilxochitl and his Tlaxcalteca allies were concerned, their aims had been more than satisfactorily accomplished: the Tlaxcalteca alliance with Huexotzingo and Cholollan was stronger than ever; Tetzcoco was at last unified under one leader, Ixtlilxochitl, who had shown himself triumphant in warfare; and Tenochtitlan was severely weakened and increasingly isolated. That spring, their plan was to suspend the war in order to consolidate their hold on their newly subdued tributary milch cows. But this was not at all what Cortés had in mind. He continued the reconnaissance trips with increasing confidence, edging ever closer to Tenochtitlan itself. He found an old causeway in Xaltocan, to the north of the great lake; he admired the great pyramid of Tenayuca, visited Azcapotzalco, and even ventured into the site of the *Noche Triste*. After learning from his indigenous allies that its inhabitants had been brutally defeated by the Mexica some seventy years previously, he tried to stir up these bitter memories to bring them on side. Failing in this attempt, Cortés allowed his Tlaxcalteca allies to burn the town.[36]

Cortés returned to Tetzcoco to more encouraging news. Another expedition – the seventh since the *Noche Triste* – had arrived from Hispaniola: three ships carrying 200 men, sixty horses, a large supply of gunpowder and plenty of arquebuses and swords. It had been financed by Rodrigo de Bastidas, the companion of Juan de La Cosa in the expedition to the Gulf of Urabá in 1500. Since then, Bastidas had amassed a good fortune, trading in pearls and slaves, and had subsequently become an important shipbuilder in Hispaniola in partnership with Genoese bankers in Seville.[37] This was a clear sign that the authorities in Hispaniola had become aware of just how significant the developments in Mexico were becoming. They had even appointed Julián Alderete – a man who, ironically, had once been Juan Rodríguez de Fonseca's personal steward (*camarero*) – to be Cortés's official treasurer.

Meanwhile, the indefatigable Gonzalo de Sandoval had continued to win allies. When he returned from a series of campaigns that had taken him to the south of the Popocatepetl volcano, from where he had descried a wonderful valley nestling a rich and densely populated city called Cuauhnahuac (present-day Cuernavaca), Cortés sent him to bolster the defences of Chalco, which was being attacked from Tenochtitlan. On arrival, Sandoval was reassured to find that the people of Chalco had held their own quite well against their former oppressors. Yet it was clear that the new Mexica emperor, the man who had succeeded Cuitlahuac after his death of smallpox the previous autumn, was showing no signs of being intimidated by the advance of the conquistadores. His name was Cuauhtemoc, a son of Ahuitzotl, Moctezuma's predecessor. He was very young but possessed an iron will – his bravery and ruthlessness making him an ideal choice to succeed Cuitlahuac.

One of Cuauhtemoc's first acts as emperor had been to execute Moctezuma's sons. The purpose of this ruthless measure was not so much to remove potential rivals as to make it plain that any form of negotiation with the Castilians – the very thing that had doomed Moctezuma – was completely out of the question.[38] It was not long before Cortés got a taste of the new emperor's character. Shortly after Easter, on 5 April, he set off to assess Sandoval's progress, reaching Cuauhnahuac a week later. On the way back, at Xochimilco, he was ambushed by a group of Mexica warriors sent by Cuauhtemoc. They had adopted many of the warring methods of the Spaniards and were now using the Toledo swords and lances that had been lost in the lake the previous year. The Mexica surrounded them and could easily have finished the Spaniards off, but they had been instructed to capture them for sacrifice. Cortés managed to escape but many of his followers were not so lucky: they were captured and sacrificed by Cuauhtemoc, who ordered their limbs to be distributed to the nearby towns as a portent of Mexica supremacy.[39]

By late April, Cortés decided it was time to put the brigantines to the test. The vessels, completed in January, had been brought to Tetzcoco in their constituent parts from Tlaxcallan by the shipbuilder Martín López. In mid-February the operation entered Tetzcoco in triumph. The pieces of shaped timber were borne by some 8,000 Tlaxcalteca allies, who formed a file almost six miles long. Drums and trumpets announced their entry, together with shouts of 'Long live the Emperor our lord' and 'Castile, Castile and Tlaxcallan, Tlaxcallan!'[40] Cortés, meanwhile, had been busy, directing the construction of an enormous channel to take the brigantines down to the lake – helped by a resigned Ixtlilxochitl, who conscripted thousands of men from the surrounding villages to help with the relentless digging. When finished, the channel was a mile and a half long, some twelve feet deep and twelve feet wide. It was, Cortés puffed to Charles V, 'a most splendid work and worthy of admiration'.[41] The assemblage of the vessels was done inland, in part to avoid any waterborne attacks by the Mexica while the work was in progress. Surviving a Mexica attempt to burn down the boatyard, the brigantines were finally launched on 28 April to the sound of music, the unfurling of flags and the firing of cannon.[42] Friar Bartolomé de Olmedo celebrated mass on the waterfront.[43] Cortés was, finally, ready to begin his assault.

He organized his men into four divisions. Three, which would fight on land under the leadership of Pedro de Alvarado, Gonzalo de Sandoval and Cristóbal de Olid, would each comprise about thirty horsemen, fifteen crossbowmen and arquebusiers, 150 foot soldiers, and a substantial detachment of indigenous allies.[44] The fourth, a seaborne division under the command of Cortés himself, consisted of the thirteen brigantines, each equipped with a cannon and carrying about twenty-five men and five or six crossbowmen and arquebusiers.[45] The three land divisions were to seize control of the three main entrances to Tenochtitlan: Alvarado was to move to Tlacopan, Olid to Coyoacán, and Sandoval to Iztapallapan. Alvarado and Olid left first, on 22 May. They reached Tlacopan on 25 May in the evening, 'the hour of vespers'.[46] The next morning, following Cortés's orders, they rode to the 'hill of the grasshopper', Chapultepec, inland from the west coast of the lake, where they broke the wooden conduits of the main spring that supplied Tenochtitlan with water across a great aqueduct. In the days that followed, they attempted to destroy the causeway to Tenochtitlan, but were eventually forced to retreat by detachments of canoe-borne Mexica warriors. With some thirty Spaniards injured, Olid withdrew, taking up a position about five miles south in Coyoacán, and leaving Alvarado in Tlacopan as planned.[47] By this time, early June, Sandoval was already installed in Iztapallapan; Cortés's plan was to sail straight there to join forces with him. His fleet of brigantines, it was said, was augmented by a 16,000-strong force of canoes led by Ixtlilxochitl – the numerical exaggeration intended to convey what was nevertheless a huge waterborne force. On the way, however, Cortés noticed smoke signals emerging from the top of the temple on the island of Tepepolco. Dropping anchor, he landed with a detachment of 150 men. When he realized that the people there were Mexica spies who were communicating with their compatriots in Tenochtitlan, he slaughtered all the menfolk in a 'most handsome victory' in which, as he would later boast to Charles V, only twenty-five Spaniards were injured.[48] A battle then ensued against enraged Mexica in canoes from which the Spanish again emerged triumphant.[49] Capitalizing on his unexpected gains, and realizing that the Mexica were more active in the lake than he had anticipated, Cortés changed his plans with a display of characteristic strategic flexibility. Rather than continuing to link up with Sandoval, he ordered the brigantines to head for the east side of the southern causeway and the fortress of Xoloc at Acachinanco, a strategic place which would secure control of the water routes between Acachinanco, Coyoacán and Iztapallapan, thus allowing Cortés to free one of the two divisions, otherwise restricted by the two-pronged shape of the causeway.[50] It was not long

N

to Tollan (Tula)

Citlaltepec

Tepotzotlan

Xaltocan

Teotihaucan

Cuauhtitlan

Tepexpan

Papalotla

Tenayuca

Tlalnepantla

Atzacoulco

Tetzcoco

Nonalco

Azcapotzalco

Tepeyac

Huexotla

Tlacopan

Tlatelolco

Coatlinchan

Popotla

Tepetzinco

Chapultepec

TENOCHTITLAN

Chimalhuacan

Acachinanco
(Xoloc)

Mixoac

Tepepolco

Coatepec

Iztapallapan

Coyoacan

Culhuacan

Iztahuacan

Cuitlahuac

Xochimilco

Xico

Chalco

Mixquic

0   5 miles
0   10 km

to Cuauhnahuac
(Cuernavaca)

Amecameca

9. Tenochtitlan and the Lacustrine Cities

before Cortés was safely installed as the undisputed master of the fortress. From there, he sent for reinforcements from Olid's division in Coyoacán, and then opened a bridge to the south of the fortress to allow some brigantines to sail to the west side of the lake; from there they could set off to support Alvarado, who was being attacked along the Nonaclo causeway to the north. Two other vessels went to assist Sandoval at Iztapallapan, soon allowing him to transfer his division to Coyoacán, just as Olid had transferred his to the fortress of Xoloc at Acachinanco. This shrewd manoeuvre gave Cortés a clear advantage over the Mexica.

Cuauhtemoc, meanwhile, seemed to be everywhere: directing operations from a canoe aimed at attacking Alvarado in Tlacopan and Cortés, Olid and Sandoval in Acachinanco. He unleashed wave after wave of warriors armed with javelins and archers with arrows made from the repurposed Spanish steel retrieved from the lake.[51] Under his command the Mexica dug defences; they reopened the holes and breaches along the causeway wherever the Spaniards and their allies had filled them in with rubble in order to allow their horses to cross. A foot soldier reported that most of Alvarado's men were wounded and that there was a general reluctance to take any horses into battle.[52] Despite the ease with which the brigantines managed to constrain the canoes, Cuauhtemoc's strategy made the progress of the conquistadores towards Tenochtitlan frustratingly slow.

Sometime in mid-June, Alvarado spotted something: with all the other causeways broken or blocked, there remained a constant stream of people along the northern causeway that led to the hill of Tepeyac from Tlaltelolco. Cortés had not given any attention to this route, perhaps – as he later claimed, rather implausibly – in the vague hope that if the Mexica chose to escape that way it would minimize the inevitable atrocities.[53] To Alvarado, however, it was clear that the Mexica were using the route to keep their troops resupplied. Cortés wasted no time: he ordered Sandoval 'with twenty-three horsemen, one hundred foot soldiers and eighteen crossbowmen and arquebusiers', to plug the gap. With the blockade reinforced a few days later by three brigantines, 'the city of Tenochtitlan was surrounded on all sides and along every causeway that they [the Mexica] could use to reach the countryside'.[54] The siege of the capital was in place.

By now Cortés had lost any hope – if indeed he ever had any – of being able to force the Mexica to flee the great city. Nor could he aim any longer to offer Tenochtitlan to Charles V as a prized trophy rather than a sacked ruin. In the third week of June, with Alvarado and Sandoval, he attempted two coordinated drives into the city, both of which were resisted fiercely. Although the Castilians could now penetrate to the heart of the city at will, Cortés was only too aware of the danger of being caught inside, as had happened the previous year. Reluctantly, he settled for a series of attritional assaults.[55] Not all of them paid off: on 23 June, Alvarado, having captured a number of bridges along the causeway, failed to repair breaches made by the defenders as they retreated and was unable to escape when his forces were ambushed, resulting in the capture and sacrifice of some of his men;[56] elsewhere, when one of the brigantines ran aground, its stranded crew was also captured.[57] Yet, slowly, the Castilians and their allies were gaining a stranglehold on the capital.

Under the circumstances, the resilience of the Mexica was astonishing. Their toughness and discipline had been imposed from an early age, through the education system of the *calmecac* ('the house of lineage'), which put the sons of the nobility through a rigorously disciplined religious and military training, and the *telpochcalli* ('the house of youth'), in which the commoners and the younger or illegitimate sons of the nobility received theirs.[58] A generation after the conquest, native nobles could still recall the stern words of their parents on the day they were packed off to school at an early age, warning them that they would not be honoured or esteemed, but 'looked down upon, humiliated, and despised'. This was a system designed to 'harden your body' and, as parents warned their children, 'you will cut agave thorns for penance, and you will draw blood with those spines'.[59]

Drugs very probably also played a role in the ferocity of the Mexica defence. As some Mexica noblemen recalled, those who ingested peyote, the hallucinogenic cactus, or sacred mushrooms, were filled with a 'drunkenness that lasted two or three days' and which 'gave them courage for battle, destroyed fear, and kept them from thirst and hunger'.[60] All of which helps explain how, every night, the Mexica would creep out of the city to redig those ditches in the causeways that the Tlaxcalteca had filled in the previous day; how they withstood the sequence of heavy assaults, on three fronts, with horses, guns and steel swords; and how they could cause more damage than seemed possible with arrows, stones, clubs and obsidian weapons. A month into the siege, the Spaniards were dumbfounded to see buildings they had recently burned or cleared in functional use again. Gradually, the Spanish patience began to wear thin: 'when the Spaniards were tired', when 'they could not break the Mexica', one native nobleman recalled, they 'were indeed afflicted'.[61] It was now that Cortés's captains urged him – against his better judgement, as he would explain to Charles V – to go for broke: to launch a concerted attack on the food market at Tlatelolco, and thereby leave the Mexica with a stark choice – to surrender or starve to death.[62]

The assault began on 30 June. Alvarado advanced from the west alongside Sandoval's men while Cortés's troops came from the south. They got inside the city easily enough and then divided into three. At that point things began to go awry. As Cortés's column crossed into Tlatelolco, he ran into an ambush. With his men attempting to retreat along the causeway, he noticed, to his horror, that one of the breaches had either not been filled properly or had been dug up by the Mexica, leaving a wide gap where the water was at least eight feet deep. Unable to use either guns or horses, the conquistadores were soon surrounded by canoes.[63] 'And when this had happened', some native noblemen would remember years later, 'the brave warriors who had lain crouched' threw themselves upon the Castilians, forcing them 'to run along among the houses'. They were 'just like drunk men'. Many of Cortés's men were captured and sacrificed, the Mexica stringing fifty-three heads on rack staves alongside the heads of four horses and proudly putting them on display.[64]

Cuauhtemoc and his generals exploited this horrifying spectacle to the full. Knowing that Alvarado and Sandoval were still in the city, they approached each general, displaying the severed heads of some of their compatriots. To Alvarado they said they would do to him what they had already done to Cortés and Sandoval; to Sandoval they said the same, substituting the name of Alvarado for his own.[65] Even though the Spaniards soon found out that this was a ruse, it was not much comfort: the groans of the wounded, mixed with the background noise of Mexica drums and horns, brought back vivid memories of the *Noche Triste* – whose anniversary, in an uncanny coincidence, it happened to be. Worse still, the bulk of their indigenous allies had suddenly vanished. Among the few that remained loyal were Ixtlilxochitl and some of his relatives from Tetzcoco, Chichimecatecle, a lord from Huexotzingo, with some faithful followers, two sons of Xicotencatl, and about forty Tlaxcalteca. Most of the valley's population, having pledged their loyalty to the Spanish-led coalition, now had second thoughts: if Tenochtitlan and Cuauhtemoc survived, they no doubt imagined, reprisals would be horrific.

Cuauhtemoc knew as much and did his best to capitalize on the situation. He sent messengers to important cities, notably Chalco, Xochimilco and Cuauhnahuac, with the severed heads of his victims and of some horses, claiming to have killed half the Castilians and emphasizing that all their indigenous allies had vanished overnight.[66] But the tactic did not pay off. Its exaggerations betrayed a clear weakness that Cortés was not slow to miss. After all, Cuauhtemoc had not mounted a single attack against the Spaniards since 30 June, while the Mexica themselves were obviously exhausted. True, five brigantines had been lost, but the remaining eight were still comfortably in control of the lake. Even in the absence of most of their allies, the Spaniards could maintain the blockade of the city. The shortage of food and water was becoming intolerable. Moreover, reinforcements to compensate Cortés for the wavering of his local alliances were already on their way from Tlaxcallan.[67]

Still, some of those alliances did hold firm: the city of Cuauhnahuac, which Cuauhtemoc had been trying to court, appealed to Cortés for help to resist an attack launched against them from the nearby city of Malinalco.[68] Although their cry for help certainly did not include pledging their loyalty to Charles V – as Cortés, as usual, claimed – it was nonetheless genuine, and Cortés immediately sent Andrés de Tapia with eighty foot soldiers and ten horsemen to their aid. Then Cortés himself defeated a force from the northern city of Tollan that had come in support of Cuauhtemoc. These advances emboldened the Tlaxcalteca leader, Chichimecatecle, to embark on a raid into Tenochtitlan supported by a small force of indigenous warriors; they easily captured a bridge and engaged in battle with the enfeebled Mexica before making a strategic retreat in the evening with many prisoners. This was the first time the Tlaxcalteca had fought the Mexica without Spanish assistance. The way they acquitted themselves was an indisputable morale booster to the allies.[69]

Although the tide seemed once again to have turned in Cortés's favour, the Spanish remained cautious. With the lessons of 30 June fresh in everyone's mind, they advanced slowly, razing all the buildings methodically as they went and using the rubble to fill in the defensive ditches for good. Yet the Mexica fought on. 'Not one of them lost courage,' recalled a Mexica nobleman.[70] The advance was strengthened by further reinforcements arriving on one of the ill-fated ships from Juan Ponce de León's expedition to Florida that had docked in Veracruz.[71] Apart from men and crossbows, it brought with it a good supply of gunpowder that proved especially useful for demolishing buildings. Combined with the blockade, the effects on Mexica health and morale were devastating. As some native witnesses would later recall, many died of hunger. 'No more did they drink good water, pure water. Only nitrous water did they drink.' Many more had developed what they described as 'a bloody flux'. In desperation they ate whatever they could find: 'the lizard, the barn swallow, and maize straw, and saltgrass'. And they gnawed 'colorin wood' and 'the glue orchid and the frilled flower, and tanned hides and buckskin, which they roasted, baked, toasted, cooked, so that they could eat them, and sedum, and mud bricks which they gnawed'. Meanwhile, the Spaniards advanced 'quite tranquilly'. They 'pressed us back as if with a wall; quite tranquilly they herded us.'[72]

In the next few weeks the city was systematically destroyed – a process punctuated by a number of brutal surprise attacks in which hundreds of Mexica were killed. According to Cortés, this allowed his Tlaxcalteca allies to 'dine well, for they carried all those that had been killed, sliced them into pieces and ate them'.[73] Their advance forced Cuauhtemoc and his entourage to retreat to Tlatelolco, which the Castilians finally reached 'on the feast of the Apostle Santiago' (St James), 25 July. There they systematically destroyed the city: 'on both sides of the main street', Cortés would later recount to Charles V, 'nothing else was done save the burning and razing to the ground of all the buildings, the sight of which in truth filled us with pity, but having no other option we were forced to continue'.[74] As their gunpowder ran low, the Spaniards constructed a large catapult in order to continue the demolition. The operation seems to have been an embarrassing failure: with no skilled workmen, the structure wobbled about – and, as it did so, one indigenous witness recalled, the Spanish argued among themselves: 'they jabbed at each other's faces with their fingers. There was much chattering.'[75] Cortés typically made moral capital out of the incident, explaining to Charles V that they had decided not to use the catapult because they had been moved to compassion by the plight of the Mexica and did not want 'to finish them off'.[76]

This is unlikely, but the sentiment cannot be too readily dismissed. Cortés seems to have been genuinely moved by the appalling suffering that – he would always insist – he had reluctantly been forced to inflict upon the Mexica. Had it not been for the unfortunate developments in Tenochtitlan the year before, during his absence as he dealt with Narváez, leading to the death of Moctezuma and the uncompromising belligerence of his successors, things might have been different. How Cortés wished he could have been spared the sorrowful spectacle he now encountered. Such was their 'extreme hunger', he wrote, that they had gnawed even the 'roots and bark of the trees'. He promised the defenders peace, if they could only persuade Cuauhtemoc to surrender; he even freed an influential Mexica prisoner, who promised to try to persuade the Mexica leader to do so. But Cuauhtemoc would not budge: after sacrificing the man in question, he launched a further defiant but by now pointless attack on the Spanish.[77]

Confronted with such resistance, Cortés had no option but to continue the attack. Pedro de Alvarado seems to have taken the lead in most of the final skirmishes. Now, in the early days of August, Cuauhtemoc took the desperate decision of nominating a quetzal-owl warrior – an initiative that, allegedly, had always brought the Mexica victory in the past. 'This device,' Cuauhtemoc declared, had been used by 'my beloved father Ahuitzotl. Let this man wear it. May he die with it . . . May our foes behold it; may they marvel at it.'[78] Decades later some indigenous witnesses remembered that the Spaniards had indeed been terrified at the sight: '. . . when our foes saw him, it was as if a mountain crumbled. All the Spaniards indeed were terrified; he terrorized them; it was as if they marvelled at something.' But the effect hardly lasted. The quetzal-owl did manage to capture a handful of men but then vanished after dropping from a roof terrace.[79] Then, on 12 August, Cuauhtemoc sent a messenger to Cortés, saying he was ready to negotiate a surrender. Cortés arrived in the marketplace of Tlatelolco, their prearranged meeting place, and waited. Hours later he was still waiting: Cuauhtemoc, having sued for peace, had failed to turn up. Livid, Cortés ordered Alvarado to continue the final assault.

With Tlatelolco sealed off – Sandoval had surrounded the precinct with the remaining brigantines – the Mexica could only escape by scrambling over the bodies of their own dead or over the remaining rooftops. They had no weapons with which to resist the Spaniards. The latter and their allies, by contrast, were armed with swords and bucklers, which the Tlaxcalteca wielded with a ferocity that shocked even the most hardened conquistadores. Cortés claimed, in another of his hyperbolic moments, that about 40,000 natives perished at their hands, 'and so loud was the shouting and the wailing of the children and the women that there was no one among us whose heart did not shatter at the scene'. Indeed, he continued, 'it became more difficult to prevent our allies from killing so cruelly than for us to fight against the Indians; for such fierce cruelty, so alien to any natural order, has in no generation been seen to flourish as it does among the natives of these parts.'[80]

Although he could no longer ignore the inevitable, Cuauhtemoc still did not surrender; everything he represented militated against any sort of negotiation. He held a final meeting with the few remaining Mexica leaders to discuss how they should proceed. The leaders then tried to smuggle Cuauhtemoc out of the city in a boat.[81] Cortés gave instructions to all his captains to ensure that Cuauhtemoc was captured alive. The Mexica emperor was then sighted by the commander of one of the brigantines, Garci Holguín, who drew up alongside Cuauhtemoc's boat and apprehended him.[82] After an embarrassing squabble between Holguín and his commander, Sandoval, Cuauhtemoc was finally brought to Cortés, who received the Mexica emperor under 'a many-coloured canopy' on the roof of a house he had sumptuously prepared with many rugs and chairs and plenty of good food.[83]

Cortés, wanting Cuauhtemoc to know that he held him in the highest esteem, received the emperor with signs of great affection.[84] For his part, Cuauhtemoc told Cortés tearfully that he had done everything in his power to defend his city and could do no more, 'and since I have been brought into your presence by force and imprisoned, take that dagger that you have in your belt and kill me with it'. To which Cortés replied 'very lovingly' that he admired him all the more for the exemplary courage he had shown in defending his city. Although Cortés regretted that Cuauhtemoc had not made peace sooner, thereby avoiding so much death and destruction, he assured the Mexica emperor that he could continue to rule over his dominions as before. Cortés then enquired after Cuauhtemoc's wife and asked for her and her companions to be brought over.[85] The war against the Mexica, 'which God Our Lord deigned to bring to an end on the feast of St Hippolytus, that is, the thirteenth day of August, 1521', had finally been won.[86]

Despite Cortés's rapprochement with Cuauhtemoc, the mood was not even remotely celebratory. After weeks of a siege punctuated by the crash of falling buildings, cannonfire and screams of pain, the silence was deafening and the stench of the rotting corpses overpowering. There was still no food or drinking water for the survivors. Responding to a plea from Cuauhtemoc, Cortés allowed the few remaining, emaciated Mexica to leave the city and seek refuge in the neighbouring towns. Their departure was a pitiful sight. The conquistadores themselves retreated to more salubrious quarters in Coyoacán, where a banquet was laid on: wine from a ship recently arrived in Veracruz washed down rations of pork from Santo Domingo, Mexican turkey and maize bread. Although a great victory had been won, the price was disproportionately high. The mood was marked by a melancholy that none of the sources was able to hide.

10

The Grand Chancellor's Dream

Back in the Old World, the news of Cortés's triumph was met by a marked lack of interest. This was not surprising: news was slow to travel, and the one thing that had previously managed to catch the emperor's attention – treasure – was conspicuous by its absence. This was odd, for Cortés had extracted a fair amount of treasure from Cuauhtemoc: indeed, with his third letter to Charles V, dated 15 May 1522, he had sent a colossal amount of treasure: 50,000 gold pesos, a wealth of jewels, plenty of jade, large quantities of assorted gifts for a range of dignitaries, churches and convents, three live jaguars, and even some bones of alleged giants. Cortés was clearly presenting himself as a Renaissance Maecenas, anxious to reward every member of the Council of Castile, even Bishop Juan Rodríguez de Fonseca himself. Cortés's gifts to this implacable enemy of his give us a good idea of his calculated munificence: two episcopal robes, one in blue, with a substantial gold border and a collar of sumptuous plumes, the other in green with a collar adorned with exotic masks; four ornamental shields, one of them with a ruby encrusted in the middle; a coat of arms made of large green feathers and golden quills; and a collection of golden-beaked parrots made out of real feathers.[1] Had the treasure reached its destination, it would have caused a sensation – but it did not.

The crossing was disastrous. At one stage one of the jaguars escaped, killed two sailors and badly mauled a third before jumping overboard.[2] Then, on the way to Spain from the Azores, the fleet was attacked by Jean Fleury, a French pirate from Honfleur operating under the command of Jean Ango of Dieppe.[3] Ango had been lying in wait for Cortés's ships since hearing about the treasures shown in Brussels in 1520. He had probably also been inspired by King Francis I's scornful remark that the papal grants to Spain and Portugal could in no way prejudice third parties: 'I should be very happy to see,' the king allegedly exclaimed, 'the clause in Adam's will that excluded *me* from my share when the world was being divided.'[4]

It is not difficult to imagine Cortés's desperation when the news of the loss of this great treasure reached him in the early months of 1523. Over a year had passed since the fall of Tenochtitlan, and he had yet to hear a word from Charles V. The emperor, though, had more pressing things on his mind. As his empire extended outward, Charles's silence on the objects that had so captivated Albrecht Dürer and, indeed, on the whole matter of 'the Indies', was the most puzzling omission from his memoirs.[5] True, he had been dealing with a Castile that had brutally turned in on itself – and, although the *Comunero* uprising had been quashed in April 1521, the underlying issues had not been addressed. Nor is this surprising, given that Charles was now confronted with a crisis of an unprecedented magnitude elsewhere in his dominions. Even as the *Comuneros* were being defeated, he was having to deal with a man who was changing the course of history. Martin Luther was himself conscious of being the harbinger of a new age, an awareness reflected in his deliberate change of name. His surname at birth was Luder, which in German has unfortunate associations with looseness and immorality. So, around the time when he formulated his famous ninety-five theses, in the autumn of 1517, he took on the Greek name 'Eleutherius' – meaning 'the freed one' – subsequently keeping the kernel of the name as 'Luther'.[6]

When Charles and Luther met at the Diet – or imperial council – of Worms on 18 April 1521, what had started as a run-of-the-mill dispute over the abuse of indulgences – those grants 'of remission of the temporal punishment still due to sin after sacramental absolution'[7] – had turned into a widespread revolt. Luther had already become the inescapable point of reference for Christian communities who defined themselves in terms at odds with the established Church. The indomitable passion with which he went about his business soon turned Luther into what was effectively the first great propagandist in the age of print.[8] By one count, 183 editions of his works appeared in 1523 alone, and the responses they elicited led to a staggering tenfold increase in the output of the budding German printing presses.[9] When combined with Luther's commitment to rendering the scriptures in a language intelligible to speakers of the wide range of dialects that spread from the Low Countries to Poland, his movement served to make the German language the ideal cultural vehicle through which the long resentment against ecclesiastical abuses could be expressed in tandem with Luther's bitter complaints against the papacy.[10]

If all this – inconveniently added now to the ever-growing threat of Ottoman expansionism – was not enough to keep Charles V from attending to Cortés's various claims, the defeat of the *Comuneros* had led to the return to imperial favour of Bishop Juan Rodríguez de Fonseca, the brother of the campaign's leader. Predictably, he wasted little time in attempting to frustrate Cortés's designs. Almost immediately he arrested Alonso Hernández Puertocarrero, one of Cortés's envoys, on trumped-up charges of seduction – charges so historical that they were alleged to have taken place even before his first trip to the New World nearly a decade earlier. Fonseca also managed to convince Charles V's regent, Adrian of Utrecht, whose attention was absorbed with events in Germany and the aftermath of the *Comunero* uprising, to appoint one of his protégés, Cristóbal de Tapia, as governor of 'New Spain', as Cortés had now called Mexico.[11] Tapia was then serving as a royal inspector in Hispaniola. Now, with the backing of both bishop and regent, he set off for Veracruz in December 1521, clutching instructions to arrest Cortés, who was being accused of greed and disobedience, and send him back to Spain to stand trial.[12]

Clearly Tapia did not know his opponent. Even before Cortés had received any written communication from the new governor, he had instructed the ever-reliable Sandoval to go to 'Medellín' – as he had decided to rename the Totonac town of Nahutla, to the north of Veracruz on the gulf coast – and found a municipality there, complete with the appointment of all the requisite councillors and magistrates. Meanwhile, Cortés himself was doing exactly the same thing in Tenochtitlan, transforming this great city state into the mirror of a Castilian municipality.[13] These initiatives were perfectly in tune with the strategy that Cortés had already deployed against Velázquez with the use of the medieval legal tradition of the *Siete Partidas*.[14] In addition to Veracruz, Cortés now controlled three other municipalities, including Segura de la Frontera, against which Tapia would need to contend. This gave Cortés a sufficiently strong legal foundation upon which to write to Tapia with an almost artless confidence, reminding him how well they had known each other in Hispaniola and remarking confidingly how glad he was that such a wise choice – he could not, in fact, think of a better one! – had been made for the post of governor.[15]

As so often with Cortés's interpretation of events, the reality was rather different. The conquistador was only too aware of the tensions and resentments caused by the meagre profits with which most of his followers had been forced to content themselves as a result of his insistence that the priority was to reward Charles V. Many of them might have considered Tapia's arrival as a good opportunity to redress this undesirable situation. In the circumstances, Cortés offered a masterclass in perfidious duplicity. Giving every impression of wanting to go personally to meet his 'good friend' Tapia in Veracruz, he claimed to have been prevailed upon by his close supporters who feared that leaving Tenochtitlan without its 'natural leader' might easily give rise to sedition and rebellion. He had therefore agreed to stay behind, sending Pedro de Alvarado and Gonzalo de Sandoval to meet Tapia on his behalf. Yet again, Cortés pretended to yield reluctantly to a scheme he had almost certainly concocted himself.[16]

What followed was a bravura deployment of legal principle, which Cortés later elucidated in a letter to Charles V. 'On arriving at the place where the said Tapia was staying', he wrote, his envoys 'all went to the city of Cempoal.' There, Tapia presented them 'with Your Majesty's instructions, which they all *obeyed* with the respect and deference which is due to Your Majesty. As far as their *implementation* was concerned, however, they said that they needed to appeal directly to Your Majesty, because that was in the best interests of the royal service, as would become clear in the reasons they had given in that same document of appeal ... which had been duly signed by a public notary.'[17] The Spanish words used by Cortés – *obedecieron* ('they obeyed') and *en cuanto al cumplimiento* ('as far as their implementation is concerned') – consciously echo the widespread legal formula *obedezco pero no cumplo*, 'I obey but I do not implement'.

It is difficult for modern readers not to feel a certain cynicism when confronted with Cortés's apparently recondite reasoning – often seen as a semantic excuse for sophistry and corruption. But this is to ignore two fundamental points. The first is that this formula had developed in late-medieval Spain as a mechanism to protect the interests – and, by extension, the *fueros*, or local laws and privileges – of the diverse regions and localities that retained a large degree of local autonomy under the overarching authority of the Crown. This was precisely the reason why Cortés had taken such special care to found two additional municipalities with which to confront Tapia; it also explains the confidence with which Alvarado and Sandoval could retort to Tapia's demands for 'obedience' with what was, for all intents and purposes, a foolproof legal argument: their refusal to implement Tapia's instructions did not amount to 'disobedience'. They said all this with the confidence of men who considered themselves knightly heroes of recent victories won in the most heroic of circumstances. And now, as representatives of legally established municipalities they could claim to be much better placed than Tapia to know what was best for the new territories and in the best interests of a distant monarch to whom they had a legal right to appeal. Given all this, Alvarado and Sandoval found no difficulty in persuading Tapia to return to Hispaniola and await Charles V's decision once the emperor had had the opportunity to consider their appeal.[18]

The second point is that the very notion of 'obedience' needs to be put in its contemporary context. Nowadays the term is primarily understood as an act of the will: to 'obey' is temporarily to give up one's will by submitting to the will of another. Thus, in the modern context, perfect obedience is especially well expressed when people agree to obey a command with which they might not in fact agree. But such an understanding would have made little sense to the conquistadores. For them the term 'obedience' was much closer to the original Latin root of the word: *obedire* comes from *ob audire*, to listen. This meant that obedience was not primarily an act of the will but of the intelligence. A bad command was not so much inconvenient as stupid; it led to a situation where neither the one in command nor the one who obeyed had learned anything from one another – and, therefore, a situation in which any 'implementation' would be detrimental to everybody, not least the one in command. Rather than submitting to a command regardless of what one thought, therefore, the principle of *obedezco pero no cumplo* allowed for an understanding of obedience as primarily a learning process, a matter of the practical intelligence, where those in command and those who obeyed had come to share a common mind. What mattered most, in other words, was not that those in command imposed their will on others but that they were widely perceived to be in the right. Whenever this was not the case, then those under 'obedience' could appeal directly to the king through legally constituted mechanisms. Among these, the locally elected

municipalities – municipalities that Cortés was busily and hastily repro-
ducing in his newly conquered territories – were fundamental.[19]

Tapia must have felt rather foolish to be reminded of this principle,
particularly because the *audiencia* of Hispaniola had expressly recommended that he apply it as soon as he received the instructions from the
authorities in Castile. He was warned before setting off for Veracruz
that if he chose to 'implement' Fonseca's instruction, he was likely to
'cause harm and break the thread' of what Cortés had achieved in New
Spain.[20] Tapia had not listened, preferring to put his trust in the distant
authority of the bishop. He would pay dearly for this misplaced trust:
soon after his return to Hispaniola, the *audiencia* declared itself in
favour of Cortés, not only giving him permission to allot indigenous
peoples to his followers in *encomiendas*, according to the practice that
had developed in Hispaniola, Cuba and Jamaica, but also authorizing
him to continue with any further conquests he might deem necessary.
The *audiencia* of Hispaniola also wrote directly to Charles V rather
than to Fonseca, explaining its position and the reasons why its recommendations now had the force of law – until such a time, of course, as
the emperor should decide otherwise.[21]

When he returned to Spain in July 1522, Charles V had decided to place
Castile at the centre of his imperial designs. He was therefore determined to address all the issues raised by the revolt of the *Comuneros*,
not least the need to ensure that a broad cross section of the local
power brokers – officials, middle and lesser nobles, merchants and artisans, in particular – once again identified their own interests with those
of the Crown. This was in fact precisely what the majority of the
Comuneros had wanted: a return to the policies of Isabel and Fernando,
a reversal of the political atrophy that had set in since Isabel's death,
and a restoration of a monarchy that people felt willing to respect.

Charles well understood the main causes of the revolt: the royal
courts had failed to provide adequate channels for conflict resolution,
with the result that people no longer felt able to look to the monarchy
as the fountainhead of justice. This failure had been compounded by
the lethargy of the Royal Council and the flagrant corruption and
aloof detachment of most royal officials, particularly those who had
come from Flanders. Wisely, therefore, Charles decided to issue special
pardons to the moderate *Comunero* leaders – a symbolic gesture

indicating the protective and caring nature of the monarchy. He also set about revitalizing and expanding the system of councils – advisory bodies that eventually took over most administrative matters in order to allow the emperor to concentrate more effectively on foreign policy; and the *audiencias* – supreme royal courts with jurisdiction over entire provinces, which now became the highest courts of appeal. The emperor also took care to strengthen the political and legislative role of the *Cortes* – parliamentary assemblies of representatives of the nobility, clergy and selected municipalities – to ensure that they regained their role as effective channels for limiting the impact of royal taxation, thus bolstering local commerce and industry. This initiative soon turned the *Cortes* into the key instruments for ensuring that the loyalties of powerful and potentially disruptive local leaders stayed firmly with the Crown.[22]

There was another development that would give Charles's reforms a more obviously imperial flavour, one which his contemporaries could not fail to see as providential. When Adrian of Utrecht was unexpectedly elected pope (as Adrian VI) in January 1522, Charles sent his close advisor, Charles de Poupet, Seigneur de La Chaulx, to congratulate him on his behalf.[23] A close friend of Archduchess Margaret in Brussels, La Chaulx had been as mesmerized as Dürer by the treasure sent by Cortés and had become a keen enthusiast. The new pope did not leave for Rome until August, conscious that his role as Regent could not be vacated without adequate preparations. A flurry of correspondence with Charles at this time gives every indication that Adrian was adamant that the main issues were to be addressed in a spirit that would strengthen the image of the emperor in a context that could only work in Cortés's favour.[24] Adrian even issued a Bull, *Charissimo in Christo*, dated at Zaragoza on 9 May, reiterating the decision of his predecessor, Leo X, to entrust the mendicant orders with the task of evangelizing the New World, 'and in particular' reformed Franciscans or, as he called them, 'the friars minor of regular observance'.[25]

This new imperial spirit contrasted sharply with the apprehension that had surrounded Charles's departure from Spain in May 1520. We catch a sense of it in some lines that the humanist poet Ludovico Ariosto composed at the time and then added to his great epic poem *Orlando Furioso*, first published in 1516, in a special edition that he presented to Charles V in 1532, two years after his coronation at the hands of Pope Clement VII in Bologna: 'A prince of Austrian and

Spanish blood / Born on the Rhine's left bank, behold, I see: / With valour such as his no valour could / Compare in legend or in history. / I see Astraea with new power endued, / From death restored to life and victory. / I see these virtues by the world exiled, / Return in triumph and all vice reviled.'[26]

These lines reveal a change of mood in humanist circles regarding the medieval tradition of empire, especially as it applied to the emerging empire of Charles V. At once an evocation of the medieval romances of chivalry – something humanists had hitherto tended to dismiss – and an implicit defence of the medieval political tradition that saw in Charlemagne's coronation by Pope Leo III, on Christmas day 800, a *translatio imperii* – a valid transfer of the legacy of the Roman Empire to the north of Europe. Now Charles V was being hailed in identical vein as the ruler who would spring from the union of the houses of Austria and Spain and succeed to the diadem of Augustus, Trajan, Marcus Aurelius and Severus.[27]

Ariosto was acutely aware of contemporary political sensibilities. He knew that the recently discovered lands across the Atlantic had been unknown to the Romans, and that in the popular European imagination they had themselves become a portent of a new empire. Not for nothing had the sixteen-year-old Charles chosen as his personal emblem the Pillars of Hercules – the straits of Gibraltar – which symbolized the known limits of navigation. And not for nothing had he turned the tables on their symbolism quite radically by removing the first word from the old motto *Non Plus Ultra*, which had been intended to set bounds to human pride.[28] Charles's hubristic *Plus Ultra* signalled a prince who brooked no limits.[29] Many of his contemporaries, not least Erasmus of Rotterdam, expressed reservations about the seemingly boundless ambitions encapsulated in the emblem.[30] Many others, however, saw it as a clear portent of the emergence of Charles as the last world emperor who would unite Christendom, conquer Islam and Jerusalem, and prepare the world for the Day of Judgement.[31] In many respects, these hopes were seen as a natural progression of the way history had been moving: the Aragonese Italian possessions, in particular, had already plunged Spain into a wider project for the creation of an empire that would defend Christendom against the Turk from without and, after the Reformation, from Protestantism from within.

The chief protagonist of these ideals was Charles's Grand Chancellor,

Mercurino Arborio di Gattinara, who had accompanied him to Spain.[32] There, Gattinara took a special interest in the Aragonese tradition of biblical prophecy. The Polish ambassador to the emperor at this time was Johannes Dantiscus, who penned the following revealing lines to his sovereign, Sigismund I: 'Here [in Spain] war is made on the basis of prophecies, which they believe, especially the Grand Chancellor who often speaks of them at table with evident pleasure.' Among these prophecies, Dantiscus singled out one about 'a hermit from the vicinity of Constantinople', which began with the strange words 'Arise, bat, arise!' It puzzled Dantiscus that Gattinara had no doubt that the prophecy referred to the emperor.[33] But there was indeed an Aragonese tradition of describing the king as a bat, a nocturnal animal associated with the West, and therefore with Spain, who was known to have a predilection for mosquitoes. When we consider that the word for mosque in Spanish is *mezquita*, the association of the king with a bat, devourer of mosquitoes – and, by association, of mosques – becomes clear. Gattinara's source was the Valencian doctor and astrologer Jeroni Torrella, who had specifically applied to Fernando of Aragon a prophecy attributed to a hermit from Constantinople beginning with those very words: '*Surge, vespertilio, surge*'.[34]

In such a mental climate, news from the New World could only be seen as powerful grist to Gattinara's imperial mill. Cortés himself claimed that the new territories he had recently acquired in the name of Charles were so large and important that the new emperor could reasonably assume a fresh imperial title, as worthy in its own right as his existing title of Holy Roman Emperor.[35] The imaginative transformation that such news provoked was seismic. It even gave a new and unexpected twist to the legacy of the *Comunero* revolt. With fresh memories of the profound social unrest unleashed precisely by Charles's imperial designs, the New World was portrayed by Gattinara in a light to attract the recent rebels. The new vision of empire had little in common with the one that had recently seemed so inimical to Castilian interests. The fact that a new empire across the Atlantic had appeared – coincidentally, and no doubt, in the minds of Gattinara and his contemporaries, providentially – at the same time as the new emperor's unavoidable role as defender of Christendom, should allow the national ambitions of the *Comuneros* to arise 'phoenix-like from the ashes to greet the glittering opportunities of a new imperial age'.[36]

There was no clearer signal of the importance that the New World was now acquiring at Charles's court than the decision to put Gattinara in charge of its affairs – a decision that would culminate in the creation of the Council of the Indies in August 1524. One of the Chancellor's first initiatives was to carry out a review of the existing situation, creating a special commission to investigate the claims of Diego Velázquez regarding Cortés's actions in Mexico. Concluding that Velázquez's mandate should be deemed to have expired as soon as he appointed Cortés commander of the Mexican expedition, the commission absolved Cortés from any accusations of rebellion, recognized his conquest of Tenochtitlan, and formally appointed him governor of 'New Spain'.[37]

The news reached the conquistador in the autumn of 1523. Although it delighted him, not everything was as he would have wished. Suspicious of his avarice and possible duplicity, the special commission, with the approval of Gattinara, had also appointed four persons to 'assist' Cortés – an obvious euphemism for keeping an eye on him – each with a salary of no less than 500,000 *marvedís* per annum. Cortés smelt a rat when he noticed that his own annual salary would be considerably less than each of his four 'assistants': 366,000 *marvedís*, approximately what Governor Nicolás de Ovando had received two decades earlier.[38]

This came as a humiliating blow, especially because Cortés's expectations had been very recently raised by the arrival, at the end of August 1523, of three Flemish Franciscans. Cortés had been calling for mendicant friars, and Franciscans in particular, for some time to spread the Christian gospel. This was certainly a good omen, therefore, and he was hardly expecting to be so sorely disappointed by the terms of the commission's proposals. The arrival of the Franciscans nonetheless marked the beginning of what was to become one of the most remarkable chapters in our story.

11

The World of the Mendicants

The Franciscans Johann Dekkers, Johann van der Auwera and Pieter van der Moere had journeyed to New Spain from their native Flanders. They had gone by way of England and Castile, in the company of Charles V himself, so they were, for all intents and purposes, imperial envoys. It is more than likely that they would have heard about, if not themselves seen, the treasures that had so captivated Albrecht Dürer in Brussels. But their interest in the New World went far beyond any desire for material gain.

Back on 25 April 1521, Pope Leo X had authorized two Franciscan friars to voyage to New Spain.[1] They were Jean Glapion, a renowned Flemish preacher and one-time confessor to Charles V, and the blue-blooded Enrique de Quiñones.[2] The pair never made it across the Atlantic: Glapion died unexpectedly the same year; Quiñones, better known as Francisco de Los Ángeles, the name he took when he joined the Franciscan Order, was elected commissary-general of the Ultra-montane Franciscans – in other words those north of the Alps – and subsequently minister-general of the Order.[3]

Despite his onerous new post, Friar Francisco kept an eye on the affairs of the New World. He undoubtedly had a hand in the redaction of the bull *Omnimoda*, issued a year later, by the new pope, Adrian VI.[4] Broadening the scope of Leo X's instructions, Adrian urged all mendicant orders – while expressing a preference for the Franciscans – to head to the New World. In language redolent of the late-medieval Flemish movement of mystical reform known as the *devotio moderna* – the most characteristic example of which was the supremely popular spiritual classic *The Imitation of Christ* attributed to Thomas à Kempis (c. 1380–1471) – the pope exhorted the mendicant orders to take up the challenge. The three Flemish Franciscans who arrived in Mexico in

1523 were steeped in this movement. They had an immediate impact – notably, on Cortés himself, who was soon enthused by their idea of establishing in the New World a Church suitably purged of European corruption. In October 1524 he wrote another long letter to Charles V from his mansion in Coyoacán, urging the emperor to send many more mendicant friars, especially Franciscans and Dominicans, rather than 'bishops and other prelates' who 'would not be able to resist the habit ... of using for themselves the goods of the church, that is, to spend them in pompous ceremonies and other vices'.[5]

Whatever the unswerving commitment of the three friars to their reforming project, they were not blind to the awesome challenges ahead of them. Pieter van der Moere, who became known in New Spain as Peter of Ghent, was a natural teacher with enviable linguistic abilities. While developing a great love for his neophytes, he nevertheless lamented that all the idols they worshipped were in fact so many devils, 'which are so numerous and so diverse that not even the Indians themselves can count them'. Horrified as he was by the persistence of human sacrifice, he explained the phenomenon as the result of the false belief that, if they stopped, 'their gods, which are naught but devils, would kill them and eat them'. He thus explained that his Christian neophytes performed their sacrifices 'not out of love, but consumed with fear'. All the same, he observed, 'those born in these parts are by nature extremely handsome and gifted in everything, especially in just the right aptitudes to receive our holy faith'. The main hurdle was to help them overcome 'their servile condition', which makes them do everything 'as if coerced rather than through love'. This was 'not due to nature but to custom, for they have never been taught to act out of a love of virtue but only through fear and dread'.[6]

This spirit was not peculiar to the Flemish Franciscans. In 1524 a further contingent of twelve Castilian friars, sent by Francisco de Los Ángeles with a set of instructions that reflect an identical spirit of ascetic fervour, arrived in New Spain.[7] 'The Twelve', as they came to be known, were welcomed by Cortés himself who, in a richly symbolic gesture, knelt in the dust before the assembled Spanish and indigenous nobility to kiss the hand of their leader, Friar Martín de Valencia.[8] Shortly afterwards, in October 1524, Cortés asked friars Johann Dekkers and Johann van der Auwera to accompany him on a long and testing expedition to Honduras. Perhaps piqued by the jarring supervision of those overpaid 'assistants' appointed by the Council of the Indies, who were more than ready to supervise affairs in Mexico City, as Tenochtitlan was now called, Cortés eagerly seized the opportunity to get away from the tedious task of government and engage again in his well-honed skills. Honduras had been claimed by one of his captains, Cristóbal de Olid, who had come under the influence of Cortés's perpetual rival, the governor of Cuba. As far as Cortés was concerned, this was an unforgivable act of insubordination that required his immediate attention.[9]

We know nothing about what the two scholarly friars made of the thick forests of enormous trees choked by lianas, with wreaths of moss trailing down their branches and howls of monkeys emanating from their shadows. A great twentieth-century writer, who traced the route on horseback at a time when the scenery was not so different from what it was in the sixteenth century, noticed shy tapirs taking refuge in the reeds. In the rivers, the 'logs that appeared to float' with 'their upper edges almost awash' turned into alligators that disappeared into the depths with a swirl of their tails. Hummingbirds flitted across the paths while parrots chattered in the clearings. Above the treetops, flights of red, blue and yellow macaws soared like hawks uttering harsh cries. In stagnant pools, herons and cranes stood fishing while toucans, with 'monstrous beaks' that gave them 'an air of birds that lived before the flood', flitted like kingfishers over the water's edge. As the forests grew thicker and the humid heat increased, a silence descended which sharpened the dread of any dangers that might lurk in the dense everglades. Only the humming of the insects broke the eerie stillness of a damp hot mist that shrouded everything and sapped energy and morale.[10]

Cortés returned triumphant to Mexico City in early January 1526, fourteen months after his departure. He had managed to subdue Olid, but the expedition had taken a heavy toll. Many men, including the two Flemish friars, had succumbed to exhaustion, starvation and disease and were never seen again. In the meantime, the Twelve had begun to make their mark in Mexico City and its surroundings. These friars had been recruited from the recently founded Andalusian province of San Gabriel de Extremadura, which was imbued with the spirit of reform that had been encouraged by Isabel and Fernando with the keen support of Francisco Jiménez de Cisneros.[11] There is a strangely persistent notion that the general outlook of these friars was 'millenarian', in the sense that they were conscious of living in the end of times and were inspired by the writings of the twelfth-century Calabrian abbot Joachim of Fiore. Joachim's prophetic writings stated that humanity was living on the cusp of a third age, governed by the Holy Spirit, whose coming would be announced by the emergence of two orders of 'spiritual men', a prophecy that received an uncanny confirmation in the foundation of the two great mendicant orders – the Franciscans and the Dominicans – in the early thirteenth century. It is not surprising that many friars chose to see in Joachim's writings a portentous harbinger of the dawning age.[12] Nonetheless, neither the conduct nor the opinions of the Twelve betray much influence of Joachim's writings.[13]

The nagging persistence of the idea that the Twelve were millenarian Joachimists has proved an unfortunate distraction from what is one of the most remarkable episodes in the history of Christianity. Far from showing any hint of an exalted millenarianism, these friars were a completely down-to-earth, well-prepared and committed group of evangelizers. In many respects they paralleled the movement of Dominican reform inspired by the legacy of St Catherine of Siena, which had proved so fruitful in the preaching of friars Pedro de Córdoba and Antonio de Montesinos in Hispaniola.[14] The outlook of the Twelve and their successors was marked by a similar affirmation of the goodness of creation, with its implicit trust in the innate susceptibility of human nature to divine grace. This was an attitude that had characterized Franciscan spirituality from its earliest beginnings, giving the message of St Francis of Assisi the characteristic spontaneity and freshness that provoked comparison with the gospels themselves.[15]

There can be no doubt that the Twelve, and those who followed them, were steeped in this tradition. The province of San Gabriel de Extremadura had also been influenced by the movement of scholarly and humanistic reform that took its cue from the great Dutch intellectual Erasmus, whose thought was hugely influential in the first years of the sixteenth century.[16] One aspect of 'Erasmianism' that especially attracted the Franciscans was the insistence that a return to 'the sources' (ad fontes) – by which Erasmus meant the Scriptures and the early Christian, especially Patristic, writings – was an essential antidote against the decay of contemporary society. The enthusiastic espousal of this ideal by the Twelve sheds a bright light on the peculiar sense of optimism permeating the first years of mendicant evangelization in the New World, years filled with an ardent hope that the early Church would be reborn in the newly discovered lands, unhampered by the pomp, wealth and corruption afflicting its European counterpart.[17]

The way in which the Twelve went about their business was marked by a dynamism that seemed submerged in ritual euphoria. The apparent lack of greed displayed by their indigenous neophytes and the consequent scarceness of their material possessions seemed to them to be clear signs of evangelical simplicity – an unmistakable sign, in fact, that Providence had more than adequately prepared these people for the reception of the gospel. 'In all the world there has never been a people more naturally willing or well-disposed to save their souls than the Indians of New Spain,' wrote the great seventeenth-century Franciscan chronicler Gerónimo de Mendieta. The indigenous peoples were a welcome reminder to the friars of the austere precepts of their founder, St Francis himself, and of the urgent need to put 'the pride and presumption of the Spaniards' to one side so as to make themselves 'Indians with the Indians: phlegmatic and patient as they are, poor and half-naked, gentle and humble as they are.' Not since the days of the Apostles, Mendieta averred, had the gospel been welcomed with such exemplary candour.[18]

Mendieta's mentor had been one of the Twelve. This was Friar Toribio de Benavente, better known as Motolinía – the Nahuatl nickname he adopted, meaning 'the poor one'. Motolinía had portrayed the early years of Spanish settlement as a new exodus, with New Spain as another Israel escaping from the Egyptian captivity of demonic idolatry. He never ceased to marvel at the docility of the natives and their eagerness to convert to Christianity: he himself claimed to have singlehandedly baptized more than 14,000 souls in under a week.[19] In tune with his companions, he was in no doubt about the intrinsic goodness of every cultural manifestation he came across. The devil might be busy at work trying to deceive the indigenous peoples and lead them astray, but 'that proud spirit' was powerless to offset that basic goodness. The friars therefore made a point of encouraging dances, feasts, and songs in the native languages, preserving their flavour and style, in order to help their neophytes to embrace Christianity. That they did this with undisguised eagerness in turn confirmed the optimism of the friars.[20] Motolinía was equally lavish in his praise of the converts. They were, he wrote, extremely talented: many of them had learned Spanish arts and crafts with exceptional ease under the supervision of Peter of

Ghent. Indigenous masons, carpenters and sculptors willingly collaborated in the construction of churches and monasteries, and displayed exemplary generosity in the care and attention they showed their mentors. As early as 1532 the German Franciscan and controversialist Nicolaus Ferber reported to his co-religionists at the general chapter of the Order, held that year in Toulouse, that in one Franciscan convent in Mexico there were fifty friars who claimed that the care and attention that the Indians paid to them would be enough for a thousand of them.[21] By the middle of the century the friars had succeeded in resettling most of the indigenous population of central Mexico, with scattered hamlets being concentrated into new towns, usually planned in a grid system leading out from a main square and dominated by a Gothic-style church.[22] Additionally, some of the children of the nobility showed intellectual gifts worthy of the very best European humanists. Now bearing Christian names like Antonio Valeriano, Martín Jacobita, Antonio Vejerano and Pedro de San Buenaventura, they had all become excellent Latinists, immersed not only in Patristic theology and the philosophy of Boethius but also in the writings of Pliny, Martial, Sallust, Juvenal, Livy and Cicero, as well as of Nebrija, Erasmus and Vives.[23]

Understandably, this mendicant narrative of the enthusiastic wholesale embrace of Christian culture is commonly dismissed as a rosy picture. After all, there is plenty of evidence that seems to contradict it. An indigenous source plainly argues that, in the past, it was the gods who kept the Indians healthy and the sacrifices which kept the gods happy – but 'after their conversion to Christianity and the loss of their gods . . . they began to die'.[24] Other sources describe the friars condescendingly as 'poor and ill' men, more worthy to be pitied than admired for preferring 'sadness and solitude' to 'pleasure and contentment'; or, fearfully, as 'dead men with shroud-like attire', who disintegrated at night in order to go down to hell, 'where they kept their women'.[25] On one occasion they were identified with those petrifying monsters of native mythology, the dreaded *tzitzimime* – plural for *tzitzimitl* – those enemies of the sun and emissaries of death and destruction who would come down to kill and eat the last human beings left on earth before the end of time.[26] The sunlit enthusiasm of the mendicant chroniclers seems to fade in the face of such comments. Were the friars painting a mendacious picture of what was a far more complex and at times hopeless task?

This is certainly a widespread opinion. Yet the mendicant chroniclers were not only sincere but also perfectly aware of the problems that came with their task. As they saw it, it was no surprise that the new Israel still hankered after the forbidden rites of Egypt. Just as the passage from Egypt to the Promised Land had been full of trials, so, the friars felt, it was fitting that the Indians should experience hardship in the form of ill-treatment and abuse, forced labour, the effects of famine, and the tragic incursions of disease. This, at least, was the way the friars justified the impact of European settlement to themselves and their readers. By 1540, Motolinía estimated that at least a third of the native population had been carried off by 'war, plague and famine'.[27] But, he reminded his readers, this was a necessary purgation. Motolinía spared no detail in his descriptions of the cruelties of indigenous rites, never passing up a chance to focus on the execrable practices of human sacrifice and ritual cannibalism. Were not these clear proofs that Mexico had been under the tyrannical dominion of Satan? As a vanquished enemy, moreover, that proudest of spirits would make every effort to return to his lost lordship. He needed to be kept at bay.[28]

Motolinía's words betray the influence of a fellow Franciscan, Friar Andrés de Olmos, who had accompanied Friar Juan de Zumárraga, also a Franciscan, to New Spain after Zumárraga was appointed the first Bishop of Mexico City by Charles V in 1528. Prior to this, Zumárraga had carried out one of the few witch-hunts to have afflicted the Iberian peninsula, in the remote mountains of the Basque country; Olmos had been his willing assistant.[29] No sooner had the pair arrived in Mexico than they began to paint 'idolatrous' Indians with the same brush. Alarmed at finding that human sacrifice lingered on, and that young men were being found with their legs cut open or with wounds in their tongues and ears inflicted with the purpose of providing blood for their idols, they initiated the first inquisitorial trials against native religious practices.[30]

Few moments in history seem tinged with a more bitter irony. The thought of a Franciscan friar – also a humanist and author of a treatise that spelled out Christian doctrine in clear and accessible language – acting as an inquisitor, engaged in a ruthless persecution of native apostates culminating in the burning at the stake of the charismatic lord of Tetzcoco and grandson of Nezahualcoyotl, Don Carlos Ometochtzin, in November 1539, would have seemed like a very bad kind of nightmare to the Twelve. Seen another way, however, Zumárraga was acting within the only parameters he understood. By this point the indigenous neophytes were no longer innocent pagans awaiting Christian enlightenment, but fully fledged Christians and therefore subject to the same punishments used in Europe against the crime of apostasy. It was evident to Zumárraga that just such a crime was widespread and thriving among the neophytes. Their deities were no mere false idols but, as another Franciscan put it, 'lying and deceitful devils' who 'neither sleep nor have forgotten the cult that these natives rendered them in the past'.[31]

It is often thought that the violence of Zumárraga's reaction was to a great extent the result of the shock of betrayal.[32] If this was the case, it was also the result of a misunderstanding. For it is more than likely that the initial enthusiasm with which the natives accepted and even demanded baptism sprang from a deeply rooted habit among them of willingly incorporating alien deities into their pantheon. As we have seen, a people whose glyph for conquest was a burning temple was likely to accept a victor's god as a matter of elementary prudence. In no way, however, would this entail the necessary abandonment of all non-Christian deities. Indeed, to do so would put the whole cosmos in danger of disintegration. As far as the indigenous peoples were concerned, negative and destructive forces were not the enemies of positive and constructive ones. Both were essential components of the universe: life came from death, creation from destruction; disharmony was as necessary as harmony. Entropy eroded order, but it also provided the energy and the substance for the re-establishment of order. This meant that opposite forces did not, as some friars maintained, engage in a cosmic battle of good against evil.[33]

From this perspective a more coherent picture emerges of what was going on. The neophytes accepted and honoured the Christian deity, but they could not fundamentally grasp the insistence of the friars that he was totally good. Any such being would have lacked the necessary power to disrupt that would enable him to create, and vice versa. Worse still, the idea of a single deity who demanded the exclusion of all others was an explosive liability that put the whole cosmic order in peril – particularly through the ban on sacrifice, which was at the heart of the indigenous understanding of the corporate relationship between the natural and the supernatural worlds.[34]

Given all this, there is a clear logic in what are at first sight puzzling opinions, such as the one provided by the indigenous neophyte Andrés Mixcoatl in 1537, after he was apprehended while wandering through the villages of the Sierra de Puebla, distributing hallucinogenic mushrooms and demanding to be worshipped as a god. During his interrogation, Mixcoatl agreed that he had been deceived by his friend, the devil. This reply echoed those of other indigenous 'apostates' like Tacaetl and Culoa Tlaspicue, both of whom candidly agreed that all their sacrifices were offered to the devil.[35] These were not necessarily Spanish mistranslations or even misunderstandings. Here we need to combine two seemingly contradictory perspectives: on the one hand, the insistence of the friars that sacrifices were the work of the devil; and on the other, the indigenous understanding of a deity as a compound of good and evil. Rather than seeing the devil as an enemy to be feared and avoided, often what the neophytes saw was a further deity that they could, and should, incorporate into their pantheon. Indeed, if, as the friars insisted, it was the devil to whom the sacrifices were offered, then the indigenous 'apostates' would not have failed to see him as a crucially important ally. The friars, in other words, had unwittingly encouraged a tendency among their neophytes to collaborate willingly in their own 'demonization'.[36]

Despite all this, it is a mistake to generalize from such instances. The evidence that we have from the trials initiated by Zumárraga was not the norm. As time went on, similar examples became increasingly characteristic of regions on the fringe, where Spanish immigrants were few and indigenous people less than fully sedentary.[37] In the more acculturated regions, where the Franciscans were soon joined by Dominicans (1526) and Augustinians (1533), indigenous 'apostasy' continued to be seen in a comparatively benign light. Often, for example, the neophytes were more readily associated with angels rather than demons.[38] The Dominican Diego Durán captured the mood most memorably, when he recounted the reply of an 'apostate' whom he had reproached: 'Father,' the man retorted, 'you should not be alarmed that we are still *nepantla*.' This term, Durán explained, means 'to be in the middle'. When he pressed the man to clarify what he meant by this, the latter replied that 'since they were still not yet firmly rooted in the faith . . . they were still neutral and held on neither to one law nor to the other; or, in other words, that they believed in God, but at the same time they still reverted to their old customs and rites of the devil.'[39] Exactly the same view can be read in the remarkable set of 'colloquies' composed in Nahuatl under the direction of the Franciscan Bernardino de Sahagún. After the friars had proclaimed the gospel and denounced the native deities as so many demons, the indigenous priests willingly acknowledged the Christian deity but continued to argue for the preservation of their own gods. Not for nothing, the new converts insisted, had the gods provided them with spiritual and material sustenance for so long.[40]

Clearly, mendicant repression and extirpation did not lead to the formation of an independent and resistant religious subculture among the indigenous converts. To think along these lines is to give too much authority to the extant official documentation and to ignore the widespread practice that we have already seen succinctly captured in the formula *obedezco pero no cumplo* – 'I obey but I do not implement'.[41] The difference between what was accepted by the indigenous converts and what was not, was almost invariably a difference that reflected social context rather than doctrinal truth.[42] The widespread acceptance of these developments by the friars shows their deep familiarity with early Christian, especially Patristic sources. This is especially evident in the many references they made to the similarities between their own circumstances and those of Christian evangelizers in European late Antiquity and the early Middle Ages. They often showed an almost instinctive awareness of what in Byzantium had been termed the 'Divine Theophany' – the miraculous interposition of Providence in daily human affairs. They depicted this phenomenon to their neophytes not through elaborate theological disquisitions but as something visually enacted every day in the liturgy, which was far more integral and public than any modern liturgy.[43] The idea of the supernatural was not, as it would become in the modern Christian understandings of the term, something that was not natural. Quite the reverse: it was the very thing that made it possible for human beings to relate to the divinity at all. As such, the supernatural was inseparable from *natural* gifts, especially intelligence and free will.[44] The friars made frequent references to the works of Pope Gregory the Great and the Venerable Bede, citing the famous letter of Gregory to Abbot Mellitus, in 601: 'Tell Augustine [of Canterbury] that he should by no means destroy the temples of the gods . . . For, if those temples are well built, they should be converted from the worship of demons to the service of the true God.' In invoking

Pope Gregory, the aim of the friars was clearly the incorporation of existing practices and rites wherever possible, rather than repression. What Gregory had come to realize was that if pagans noticed their places of worship had been preserved, they would more easily 'banish error from their hearts and come to places familiar and dear to them in acknowledgment and worship of the true God'. He concluded: 'if they are not deprived of all exterior joys, they will more easily taste the interior ones'.[45]

These sentiments echo throughout a statement made by a Synod in 1539 that the situation in Mexico was 'the same' as that in England and Germany at the time of Augustine of Canterbury and Boniface of Crediton, and that 'the same' practices should therefore be followed.[46] It is not coincidental that the name of a sixteenth-century church in Mexico City, Santa María la Redonda, should have consciously evoked Pope Boniface IV's consecration of the Roman Pantheon as Sancta Maria Rotunda.[47] Nor is it a shock to find the Dominican friar Diego Durán proposing that the dreaded *cuauhxicalli* – the sacrificial stone upon which many beating human hearts had been deposited – should become the baptismal font of the new cathedral: there was, after all, something truly 'sacramental' in the rituals of pagan religions, where many intimations of Christianity could already be discerned.[48] Even the Jesuit José de Acosta, who in the late sixteenth century penned the most damning condemnation of pre-Hispanic religions, asserted that 'on those points in which their customs do not go against religion and justice, I do not think it is a good idea to change them; rather . . . we should preserve anything that is ancestral and ethnic as long as it is not contrary to reason.'[49]

The persistent implementation of these perspectives was accompanied by a swift transformation of the landscape during the first decades after the conquest. A key innovation introduced by the mendicants was the construction of open chapels, where most of the Christian religious instruction of the neophytes took place. These spaces, which allowed for the instruction of far larger numbers than would have fitted into a church, were often presided over by large angels placed symmetrically around a crest. There can be little doubt about the importance attached to these figures, with their large, extended, beautifully sculpted wings and long belted tunics. They were much closer to the angels that adorned the temple of Jerusalem and the tetramorphic figure of Byzantine art than to the cherubs with tiny wings that were the result of Renaissance reinterpretations of ancient Erotes as Cupids.[50] They leave us in no doubt that the friars were trying to give their neophytes a vivid visual imagery of an intimate relationship between the natural and the supernatural worlds. For this purpose they eagerly encouraged the very same sense of the sacred with which the indigenous peoples had already imbued their landscape. As soon as the friars understood that sacred dance rituals had been associated with a sacred quincunx, for example, they began to preserve and replicate such structures and practices, thereby allowing the recent Christian converts to preserve their own indigenous sense of sacred space.[51]

There was nothing startlingly innovative or original in this. The performative elements in indigenous worship in fact find striking parallels in late-medieval European liturgy, with its deep roots in the allegorical exegesis of Scripture and the way it had developed in Patristic and Carolingian times. This tradition received its classic formulation in Guillaume Durand's thirteenth-century *Rationale divinorum officiorum*, a general treatise on the liturgy and its symbolism which circulated widely in sixteenth-century Mexico.[52] From this perspective the many, admittedly rather daunting, constructions that dotted central Mexico during the first decades after the fall of Tenochtitlan, so often seen as devices designed to cope with the alien and often threatening environment in which the friars found themselves, emerge in a new light. In their design and construction, the friars drew on a rich medieval tradition of surrogate Jerusalems, which in this new context became part of a sacred landscape with topographical references to the real Jerusalem, confirmed by the liturgy and meticulously conflated with native sacred spaces.[53]

The friars found this liturgical flexibility perfectly natural. Their approach, indeed, echoes that of Cardinal Jiménez de Cisneros who, in the decades following the reconquest of Granada, obtained a special dispensation from the pope to preserve the Mozarabic rite in his Missal and his Breviary. In the New World similar instances of free adaptability explain the development, to give but a handful examples, of Christian musical styles that fuse Andalusian elements with influences that sound as Angolan and Caribbean as they are peculiar to the various localities.[54] Similarly, the use of the aromatic smoke *copal* – which in pre-Hispanic ritual had associations with incorruptibility and immortality, acting as

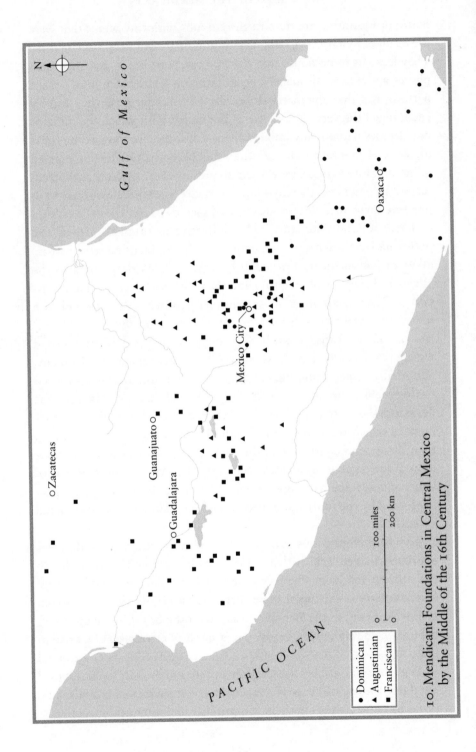

10. Mendicant Foundations in Central Mexico by the Middle of the 16th Century

N

Gulf of Mexico

PACIFIC OCEAN

Oaxaca

Mexico City

Guanajuato

Zacatecas

Guadalajara

Dominican
Augustinian
Franciscan

100 miles

200 km

a mediator between the material and the spiritual worlds – seemed not only natural but providential to the friars. Its billowing clouds were known in Nahuatl as *iztac teteo*, 'white gods'; as far as the friars were concerned, these supernatural entities made possible a dialogue between this world and the next, the natural and the supernatural, that could only be conceived as 'angelic'.[55] They were reminiscent of the ladder in Jacob's dream, set up on earth with its top reaching heaven; or as exemplifying and setting in motion the angelic hierarchies alluded to in Jesus's promise to Nathanael: 'you will see heaven laid open and, above the Son of Man, the angels of God ascending and descending'.[56]

Most of the surviving documentation paints a very different picture, with hardly any liturgical flexibility and plenty of dogmatic condemnation. The same Synod that had so openly recommended the imitation of St Augustine of Canterbury in England and St Boniface of Crediton in Germany, also advised caution in the incorporation of indigenous-style dances and songs in the Christian liturgy, and categorically forbade their performance in churches. By 1555 the First Provincial Council was laying down detailed guidelines to restrict the free use of indigenous songs and dances in order to avoid confusion between Christian and pagan practices.[57] These preoccupations were also at the heart of the decision to found the Franciscan College of Santa Cruz de Tlaltelolco, in January 1536, which aimed to instruct the indigenous nobility in the Christian faith.[58] While this college was the very place where 'putting the new religious message into the same vessels that had made the old religion attractive'[59] occurred, a more cautious approach was never far from the surface. Towards the end of the century this negative attitude seemed firmly entrenched among the intellectual elites. The distinguished humanist Francisco Cervantes de Salazar encapsulated the mood by explaining that the friars had encouraged the natives to continue with their songs and dances in the genuine hope that, 'in the same way that they used to sing praises to the devil, they would now sing praises to God'. Yet, he lamented, 'they are so much inclined towards their ancient idolatry . . . that they mingle pagan songs with holy prayers . . . the better to cover up their wicked act'. It would be much better, he concluded, 'to wean them completely from all traces and vestiges of their heathenism'.[60] Although the Provincial Councils of 1555 and 1565 reiterated the view that indigenous cultures were fundamentally good and naturally predisposed to receive the Christian faith, they also expressed the prejudices that had existed since the early days of conversion about the intelligence of the indigenous peoples and their capacity for genuine piety. In 1577 the Crown specifically forbade any further study of indigenous religions and withdrew all scriptural translations into Nahuatl from circulation. By the time of the Provincial Council of 1585, a widespread paternalistic attitude towards the natives reflected a more fundamental preoccupation with what was increasingly perceived as the demonic inspiration behind their recalcitrance.[61]

Despite all this, it can be said that the friars laid the foundations of an unofficial tradition that persisted into modern times throughout Spanish America and which allowed, and often actively encouraged, the incorporation of indigenous elements into the rites and ceremonies of Christianity and vice versa. *Obedezco pero no cumplo* is again a useful guide here. If an official decree or instruction did not fit the circumstances of a distant locality, it could be 'obeyed', in the sense of being suitably heeded, but not 'implemented', in the sense that those thus instructed understood the local circumstances much better, and therefore knew how to ensure that the interests of those in authority were properly respected. Whenever those in authority and those who 'obeyed' them had not managed to come to share the same mind, then those under 'obedience' were free to ignore the 'implementation' of the instruction.

This attitude was widespread. The fact that it does not come through in most official narratives is due to the understandable tendency to present the triumph of Christianity as a given. But when we go beyond these sources and delve into the more sparsely documented contacts of indigenous peoples with Europeans of widely different backgrounds through miscegenation, through immigration and trade, and through the comparatively unspectacular, often downright suspect, ministrations of a wide variety of itinerant preachers, a very different picture emerges. On this level the new religion with which the indigenous peoples were presented was not so much the religion of those who were bent on extirpating any vestige of idolatry as what has been called the 'local' religion of sixteenth-century Spain.[62]

One contemporary source offers a window on to the complex interactions that were constantly going on at this level. This is the journal of Alvar Núñez Cabeza de Vaca, a native of the Andalusian town of Jerez de la Frontera, who had been second in command on the expedition to

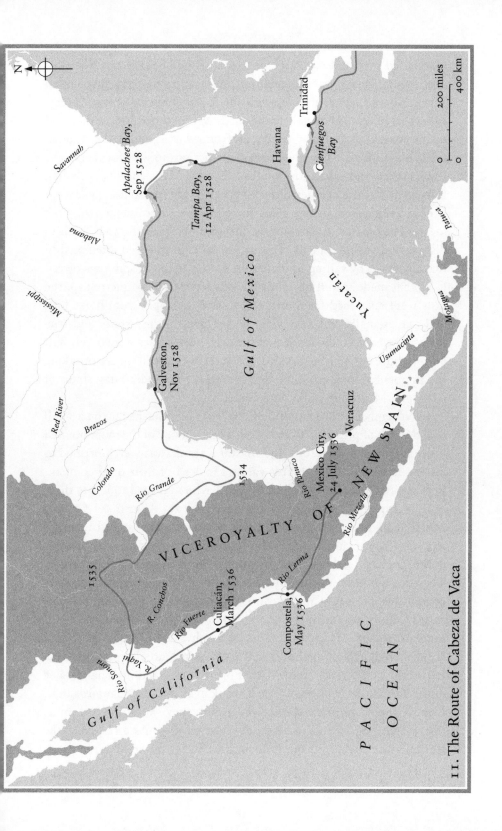

11. The Route of Cabeza de Vaca

Florida led by Pánfilo de Narváez in the spring of 1528, and who kept a record of events. It was a sizeable operation: 400 men and eighty horses. When Narváez, after talking with the local Timucua people, understood that he would find gold to the north-west of the region, he marched up the coast with 300 men, setting off from what is present-day Tampa, while his ships sailed on ahead with instructions to wait for them. The ships waited and waited, to no avail. Narváez's expedition, including Cabeza de Vaca, had entered the kingdom of the Apalachee, near what is now Tallahassee, before being forced to flee after antagonizing the locals. They suffered many losses, including Narváez himself, both to disease and Indian attacks. The 200 or so who survived attempted to reach Mexico by sailing in makeshift barges made of split logs of yellow pine, made watertight with tar extracted from palmetto sap; the sails were fashioned from torn shirts, and the ropes from horse tails and manes; nails and axes were forged from melted spurs and stirrups.[63] On board these inadequate vessels, whose sides were barely half a foot above water when loaded, the starving expedition set off along the impossibly long coastline that traverses the modern-day states of Alabama, Mississippi, Louisiana and Texas.

In November 1528 a handful of survivors were washed up on a small island south of present-day Houston. There, in one of the more pointed historical ironies on record, the coastal Karankawas were horrified to see the few starving Spaniards eating the flesh of their dead companions. Among them was Cabeza de Vaca, who managed to locate three other survivors: Andrés Dorantes de Carranza, Alonso del Castillo Maldonado, and a charismatic black Moroccan slave called Estevanico. The Karankawas, after recovering from the shock of Spanish anthropophagy, fell prey to a disease that carried off half their people. They did not jump to the obvious conclusion that the Spaniards were responsible, most probably because they had seen so many of them die. Instead, quite astonishingly, they sought to enlist the help of the Spaniards as healers. 'They tried to make us physicians,' Cabeza de Vaca remembered, explaining how the Karankawas 'cure illnesses by blowing on the sick person, and with that breath of air and their hands they expel the disease from him'. The Karankawas told the Spaniards that, if they wanted to make themselves useful, they should do the same. 'We laughed about this', Cabeza de Vaca recalled. As a response, the Karankawas 'took away our food until we did as they told us'. In short,

the Spaniards found themselves with little choice but to become healers. The manner in which they performed cures was by making the sign
of the cross over the sick, blowing on them, as they had been instructed,
'and praying a Paternoster and an Avemaria, and as best we could,
beseeching our Lord God that he grant them health and move them to
treat us well'. Mercifully, 'Our Lord God . . . willed that all those on
whose behalf we made supplication, after we had made the sign of the
cross over them, said to the others that they were restored and healthy,
and on account of this they treated us well, and refrained from eating
in order to give their food to us.'[64]

For several years they continued to live among the Karankawas,
working, trading and acting as healers.[65] Then, in 1534, they began a
southward expedition towards Pánuco, but soon headed west again in
search of safer and more straightforward routes. In the spring of 1536
they at last came across a group of Spaniards, who, Cabeza de Vaca
recalled, seemed to experience 'a great shock upon seeing me so strangely
dressed and in the company of Indians. They remained looking at me a
long time, so astonished that they neither spoke to me nor managed to
ask me anything.'[66] It was hardly surprising: 'They had not worn clothes
for years and were just as sunburned and longhaired as the barbarians
with whom they were travelling.'[67] Once the Spaniards realized what
had happened, they asked their interpreter to tell 'the local Indians'
that Cabeza de Vaca and his companions were 'of the same people',
that is, Spaniards, but that they had been 'lost for a long time' and were
now 'of ill fortune and no worth'. By contrast, the Spaniards remained
'the lords of the land whom the Indians were to serve and obey'. Fasci-
natingly, the 'Indians' would have none of it. They called the Spaniards
liars, Cabeza de Vaca recalled, 'because *we* came from where the sun
rose and *they* from where it set; and that *we* cured the sick, and that
they killed those who were well; and that *we* came naked and barefoot,
and *they* went about dressed and on horses and with lances.' The 'Indians' also made the revealing point that Cabeza de Vaca and his friends
'did not covet anything but rather, everything they gave us we later
returned and remained with nothing, and that the others [i.e. the Span-
iards] had no other objective but to steal everything they found and did
not give anything to anyone'. Under the circumstances, the 'Indians'
refused to believe that the people who showed so much empathy for
them were true Spaniards.[68]

Cabeza de Vaca was in a no man's land. He understood exactly where the 'Indians' were coming from, yet he had no wish to alienate his compatriots; indeed, he became their useful agent by persuading the 'Indians' to return to their villages – for they had fled to the *sierra* to escape the Spaniards – and to till and work the land. He also found little difficulty in persuading them to become Christians. If they did, he told them, they would be treated well; if not, they would be subjugated.[69] In all this Cabeza de Vaca made good use of a gift he had received from one of the indigenous healers he had befriended on his remarkable journey: a rattle gourd. These gourds were the specific insignia of the native healer, and the fact that Cabeza de Vaca was the proud possessor of one invested him and his companions with great spiritual authority.[70] The deployment of a powerful indigenous symbol to convert the natives to Christianity may seem incongruous, but it seems to have come as naturally to Cabeza de Vaca as it did to Diego Durán when he recommended the use of the *cuauhxicalli* as a baptismal font for the new cathedral; indeed, Cabeza de Vaca's success as a healer and his deployment of the gourd allowed him to become an iconic figure for both cultures.[71]

Although he is often singled out as unique, Cabeza de Vaca's actions were typical of someone steeped in the 'local' religion of sixteenth-century Spain. As was the case in the rest of Europe, religion in Spain was not an individual affair confined to the private conscience; it was very much a public, corporate affair, involving the propitiation of a host of supernatural beings who, just as in the New World, displayed benevolent and malevolent attributes.[72] Throughout Castile, saints were considered to be the resident patrons of their communities, and members of these communities had made vows to the saints as a response to some natural disaster. The saints, in turn, were considered capable of inflicting harm on communities if the latter did not observe their vows. Moreover, though the official Church might have liked to believe otherwise, not all magical practices stood outside official teaching. Many of them, indeed, were built into the very structure of the liturgy throughout western Europe, and formed the focus of some of its most solemn and popularly accessible rituals, such as the Rogation processions, the administration of baptism, and the blessings of salt and water.[73]

The way in which the Christian religion took root in the New World makes much better sense when placed in this 'middle ground' of corporate religious practice.[74] It was in this twilight world of mythology – of the cult of the saints and their miracles and their relics – that the friars succeeded in instilling a vision of the universe in which their neophytes came to understand their actions primarily as an act of praise. This presupposed that the 'natural' and the 'supernatural' were integral parts of the same reality. Unlike some influential strands in modern Christianity, in which the transcendence of 'the world' is often presented as a desirable goal, the friars saw transcendence as inescapably rooted in history. The eternal world could only be reached through time because it had already entered history and had given time consistency and purpose.[75] This was a deeply sacramental outlook where the 'supernatural' became present in time and space.[76] There was no room here for the dichotomies of objectivity and subjectivity that modern readers are likely to expect. The eternal world could never be 'objective' in that sense, since it could only be experienced in the very act of praise.[77] This is why the methods deployed by the mendicant friars never seemed to respond to any urgency to 'convert' their neophytes with reasoned arguments. Their task was not so much instruction as enactment. It required, above all, participation in the act of praise – the liturgy, which was nothing other than an expression of the strengthening of community.[78]

For all his dogmatism, even Bishop Zumárraga was part of this world. When he talked to his neophytes about the 'innocence' of the angels and their 'constant love of God', for example, he made them aware of the usefulness of thinking about the angels as 'neighbours' – beings who cared for them, just like the Archangel Raphael had cared for Tobias.[79] His frequent references to the overflowing happiness that the angels experienced when his neophytes went to Mass, and the 'silence, admiration, wonder, joy, thanksgiving and praise' which they felt when they saw them going to communion, evoke a closeness between the natural and the supernatural worlds that is difficult to fathom from a modern perspective.[80] A ritual song in Nahuatl, to be performed and danced in the indigenous style, states that after Christ rose from the dead, 'he told his faithful: as I am man, my kingdom is attained *now*, achieved *now*, in heaven and on earth.' This gave the indigenous neophytes, as much as the friars, a clearly inclusive sense of the kind of community they belonged to, thus preparing them for sharing, by grace, in the heavenly community that belonged to them as much as it did to the angels. As Sahagún put it in a passage most aptly entitled 'Bodily Bliss, known as the Blessing of Paradise', 'even more gifts are your due, your lot, which God, your King, will give you, will bestow upon you in the Empyrean Heaven'.[81]

These stories about the efficacy of prayer derived from well-known medieval *exempla*, in which angels came to the rescue of needy individuals. Sahagún recounted how St Mary Magdalen was fed by angels during her last years, while a Dominican friar recalled how, after praying for the soul of a man who died without confession, an angel had saved him from his encounter with demons.[82] In tune with this, a moving Nahuatl prayer, preserved by Peter of Ghent and composed specifically to be recited by the sick and the dying, begins by invoking the Virgin Mary but then goes on to say: 'May it be that I will joyfully hear the cries of the angels as they will call out to my spirit, my soul. They will say: ... Come, rejoice with us!'[83] Elsewhere, a sixteenth-century Nahuatl document composed for the feast of the Assumption – in which Mary is greeted by each of the nine hierarchies of angels as she goes to take her place above them – has echoes in the writings of Sahagún, who also accorded pride of place to angelic hierarchies on the feast of the stigmata of St Francis: 'The heavenly host of Thrones,' the third psalm begins, 'of Cherubim and Seraphim, of Dominions, of Principalities, of Powers, and Virtues, of Archangels and Angels, were St Francis's well-beloved.'[84]

This reference to the angelic hierarchies is another reminder that the mendicants drew on a rich Patristic tradition – a tradition that reached a high point in the work of the thirteenth-century Franciscan St Bonaventure, whose *Mystical Theology* was published twice in sixteenth-century Mexico.[85] In this work St Bonaventure dwells on the way in which the angelic hierarchies collaborate and participate in the inner life of Christians and their relationship with the Trinity.[86] This was merely one in a host of theological traditions that the friars deployed as they attempted to recreate as close a replica of the early Christian Church as they could manage in the New World. That it happened at all, and that it happened so consistently, is a good sign that the process was widely accepted and even encouraged, despite all the official misgivings which, by their very nature, are much more prevalent in the extant documentation available to us. There are endless continuities between the foundations laid down by the friars and the indigenous Christian cultures that flourished quite spontaneously in subsequent decades.[87]

How else could we explain the development of some of the most enduring and characteristic of Christian devotions in New Spain? The early development of the cult of Our Lady of Guadalupe on the site of the indigenous goddess Tonantzin is an obvious case in point. According to tradition, an indigenous neophyte called Juan Diego was passing by the hill of Tepeyac – to the north of what had been Tenochtitlan – in early December 1531, when he heard sweet music and saw a young woman radiant with light. The woman said to him, 'You must know, my son, that I am the Virgin Mary, mother of the true God. I want a house, chapel, and temple to be founded for me here, where I can show myself as a compassionate mother to you and to yours.' She then told Juan Diego to go to the bishop – at that time Juan de Zumárraga – with her message. Juan Diego obeyed, but Zumárraga, unconvinced by his story, demanded proof. The Virgin appeared to Juan Diego again, telling him to fetch some flowers from the hill to take to Zumárraga as a sign. At a time of year when the hill should have been covered with cactus scrub, Juan Diego found roses 'inviting with their beauty', lilies 'bearing milk', carnations 'their blood', as well as violets, jasmines, rosemary, irises and broom. He gathered the flowers in a cloak woven from cactus fibre and took them to the city. At Zumárraga's feet, Juan Diego let fall the 'miraculous spring', leaving imprinted on the coarse cloak an image of the Virgin, 'the holy image that today is preserved, guarded and venerated in her sanctuary of Guadalupe of Mexico'.[88]

This account was published by the Oratorian priest Miguel Sánchez in 1648, more than a century, that is, after the miracle is alleged to have taken place. By this time the devotion was firmly entrenched at the sanctuary of Tepeyac. Yet there is no documentary evidence of the apparition narrative in any other record. There have been several attempts since then to establish a link between Sánchez's account and a local tradition stretching back to 1531. The best known of these focuses on the work of the sixteenth-century indigenous humanist Antonio Valeriano, who is thought to have written an original Nahuatl account of the apparitions called *Nican mopohua*. But there is now little doubt that the author of the *Nican mopohua* was a fellow priest and friend of Miguel Sánchez, Luis Laso de la Vega. This conclusion has been reached after the meticulous scrutiny of Spanish loan words and spellings, which place the *Nican mopohua* quite neatly in the middle of the seventeenth century. Not only is there a clear identity between the account given by

Sánchez and the one embellished and adapted by Laso de la Vega, but there is also direct linguistic proof of the dependence of the Nahuatl on the Spanish version. No serious student of the *Nican mopohua* can doubt that its author was Laso de la Vega, who took the apparition narrative straight from Sánchez's treatise and published his own Nahuatl version in 1649.[89]

A comparable devotion concerns the cult of Our Lady of Ocotlán, to the north-east of Tlaxcallan, now Tlaxcala. The tradition recounts the story of another indigenous neophyte, also called Juan Diego. When he was fetching water for his family during an epidemic in 1541, Juan Diego came across a beautiful lady who promised to give him 'another water' with which he would quench not only the thirst of his relatives but also the more widespread contagious disease, 'for my heart is always inclined towards the downcast and I cannot endure to see their suffering without coming to their aid'. As she led Juan Diego to a miraculous spring, the lady told him that he would find an image in a nearby pine grove which was 'a true portrait not only of her perfections, but also of her piety and of her clemency', instructing him to tell the Franciscan friars to place it on an altar in the church.[90]

This account dates from 1750 and clearly borrows from the Guadalupe account, not least the name of the neophyte. Many attempts have also been made to establish a link between it and a local tradition stretching back to 1541, including a likely forgery claiming to date to 1547, in which a Franciscan friar addresses the issue of whether Juan Diego saw the Virgin Mary and not the indigenous goddess Xochiquetzalli. This was obviously a matter of concern in the sixteenth century, for Xochiquetzalli displayed very similar attributes to the ones with which Juan Diego depicted his beautiful lady. The alleged Franciscan, however, concluded that the likely association should be of no concern, so long as it gradually encouraged the indigenous neophytes to venerate the Virgin Mary, Mother of God; he then added that similar associations should be encouraged wherever possible.[91]

If we allow ourselves to be swayed by the documentary evidence, we shall be forced to conclude that both devotions were strongly opposed by the friars in the sixteenth century. There is a conspicuous absence of any mention of Our Lady of Guadalupe in any of Zumárraga's writings. In those cases where the devotion is mentioned, it comes with a clear warning. Even Sahagún complained that, despite the many Marian sanctuaries that existed throughout central Mexico, indigenous neophytes preferred instead to go to 'this Tonantzin', as they still called her, which seemed to him 'a Satanic invention' to 'dissemble their idolatry'.[92] On Our Lady of Ocotlán there is no surviving documentary evidence from the sixteenth century. It is not surprising that most historians have been sceptical of these accounts and dismissive of the whole tradition as a later, 'Baroque' invention. But this attitude misses a very important dimension: the transparent honesty of the accounts. Miguel Sánchez's treatise, in particular, is the product of a lifetime's study, solitary prayer and devotion, and his claim to have been working within an oral tradition that stretched back to the sixteenth century – a claim echoed by subsequent accounts of other devotions – has a sure ring of authenticity. His purpose was not to write an accurate historical account, but to present to his readers a story that would give a popular and well-established devotion spiritual and theological substance.[93]

Rather than evidence of an incomplete process of Christianization, these accounts are a clear testament to the success of the mendicant friars. Their achievement was remarkable by any standards. The foundations they laid have never been destroyed and their resilient influence is impossible to exaggerate.[94] The main reason why historians are often blinded to this is that the process can only be grasped from a perspective that gives the liturgy the central place it deserves. The extant material culture is often much more eloquent. A mere glance at the feathered depiction of the Mass of St Gregory dating from the 1530s, for instance, plunges us into an astonishingly free 'sacramental' world, one where Nahua symbols of life, such as human bones, skulls and ears of maize, were frequently used to depict Christ's resurrection without any apparent incongruity.

Normally we tend to focus far more closely – often almost exclusively – on belief and doctrine rather than on enactment and ritual. This is a symptom of a post-Reformation trend to draw a sharp line separating the natural and the supernatural worlds that did not exist in the world view of the friars – or, indeed, the conquistadores.[95] Their most typical cultural expressions were no mere formulaic rituals, but fully integrated cycles that would offer a principle of unity and a means by which the indigenous neophytes could become attuned to a new view of life. There might be innumerable similarities between the cult of the saints and the sacrificial propitiation of pre-Hispanic deities, but gradually the cult of the saints, with all its seemingly syncretic accretions, became part of the liturgical cycle; and the commemoration of the feasts of the saints would provide a sense of corporate identity and social continuity by which every community found its liturgical representative and patron. Understanding this world provides us with vital clues for understanding the attitudes and assumptions of the conquistadores, their ideals and ambitions.

12

Spices and Gold

Shortly after the fall of Tenochtitlan, Cortés dispatched his ever reliable sidekick Gonzalo de Sandoval to conquer Tuxtepec and then Coatza-coalcos, the regions linking Veracruz and Yucatan. This was richly fertile land, and Sandoval wisely distributed large swathes of it among many of Cortés's disgruntled followers, among them Francisco de Lugo, Diego de Godoy, Pedro de Briones and the talented chronicler Bernal Díaz del Castillo. The conquistadores now had a firm base for further expeditions into Yucatan and Guatemala. Then, in the spring of 1523, Sandoval set off in a different direction: the stunningly beautiful region of Chiapas. He took with him seventy foot soldiers and a sizeable group of indigenous allies, twenty-seven horsemen, fifteen crossbowmen, eight musketeers and a cannon, and soon gained the acquiescence of the people of the region.[1] His aim was to link up with a second mission there, led by another of Cortés's deputies, Cristóbal de Olid.

The previous summer Cortés had dispatched Olid to Michoacán, whose leaders had been flirting with the Castilians since before the conquest of Tenochtitlan. It was an enticing region, whose inhabitants were highly skilled in metallurgical techniques, allowing them to produce among other things the lethal weapons with which they had decimated the Mexica armies in the late fifteenth century, 'like flies that fell into the water'.[2] Backed by more than 5,000 indigenous warriors, mainly from Tlaxcallan, Olid and his 200 Spanish troops secured control of the region with little opposition, then moved west to the Pacific coast, which was still seen by Cortés and his followers as the gate to fabled China and the land of spices.[3]

Olid and Sandoval met at a place called Zacatula (just north of the present-day seaport of Lázaro Cárdenas), where they established a shipyard and named it Villa de la Concepción. Within weeks, brigantines and caravels were being assembled with the sole purpose of further expansion into what was still thought to be Asia. 'My ships,' Cortés wrote to Charles V in September 1526, 'are ready to start on their journey ... And I pray to Our Lord that by this voyage I shall render a great service to Your Majesty.' Even if the famous strait still proved elusive, he continued, 'I hope to discover a route to the Spice Islands, so that every year Your Majesty may be informed about everything that happens there.'[4]

Foremost in Cortés's mind at this time was the dispute then raging between Spain and Portugal over the possession of the Moluccas. The conflict stemmed from the terms of the treaty, signed at Tordesillas some three decades previously, in June 1494, which established a line of demarcation – a meridian 370 leagues west of the Cape Verde Islands – to define Spanish and Portuguese spheres of influence in the Atlantic. If the line were to be extended to include the Pacific, the obvious problem was to establish a place from which the 370 leagues could be measured. An expedition of seven ships, dispatched by Charles V and led by García Joffre de Loaísa, set off to the Moluccas from La Coruña in July 1525; its remit was to secure Charles's claim to the Spice Islands, and to keep an eye out for one of the lost ships of Magellan's expedition, the *Trinidad*. According to the survivors who made it back to Spain, this vessel had last been seen attempting to return by sailing east from the Spice Islands towards Patagonia.

Loaísa's expedition failed to find any trace of the *Trinidad*. Reaching the Strait of Magellan, to the south of present-day Chile and Argentina, the fleet was scattered by high winds and heavy rain. Two ships were wrecked, one deserted the expedition and sailed back across the Atlantic, one was driven south, and the three remaining vessels soon lost sight of each other. One, the *Santiago*, sailed north. Eventually, it reached the Pacific coast of Mexico and arrived at Villa de la Concepción in July 1526.[5] By the time Cortés wrote to Charles V two months later, therefore, he had first-hand knowledge of Loaísa's abortive expedition and he would more than likely have heard that, apart from consolidating Spanish control of Magellan's discoveries, it had been ordered to keep an eye out for 'Tarshis, Ophir, Cipango and Oriental Cathay'.[6] With all this in mind, Cortés made the emperor an irresistible offer: 'What I am proposing is to undertake the discovery of a route to the Spice Islands and any others, if there be any, between Maluco and Malaca and China.' His aim – though Cortés did not mention that it clearly echoed the orders given to Loaísa – was to ensure that Charles V would no longer need 'to take possession of the spices by way of trade, as is the case currently with the king of Portugal, but rather as Your Majesty's rightful possession, and that the natives of those islands recognize and serve Your Majesty as their rightful king and lord'. After this reassurance Cortés made a solemn pledge to go to the Spice Islands 'either in person or to send such a fleet as will subdue those islands, settling them with Spaniards and constructing fortresses that are so well equipped with solid defences and artillery that no prince of those parts, or of any other for that matter, will be capable of subduing them'.[7]

The ever-present lure of China was never strong enough to distract other Castilians from what was closer at hand. Sandoval might have moved swiftly from Coatzacoalcos to Chiapas and the Pacific, but it was not long before the Spaniards who stayed behind got wind of the attractions that awaited them to the south. Back in the autumn of 1523, Cortés had asked the intrepid Pedro de Alvarado to lead an expedition to Soconusco, in southern Chiapas, 'to learn the truth' about some rumours that the indigenous people of the region were being harassed by the inhabitants of Guatemala.[8] Alvarado, who had grander designs, managed to persuade Cortés to allow him to lead a full-scale conquest. With Cortés's agreement, he left Mexico City on 6 December in the company of 300 foot soldiers, 130 horsemen and about 3,000 'Nahuas' – the generic term for the Nahuatl-speaking people of central Mexico – who were joined by thousands more as the expedition marched south. Reaching the isthmus of Tehuantepec in January 1524, they entered Soconusco shortly afterwards. There they were met by an embassy of Guatemalans carrying gifts of gold, cacao and clothing. Brushing the embassy aside, Alvarado marched on. On crossing the river Samalá, the Castilians knew they were entering a region that had thus far successfully resisted Mexica incursions, and whose people were proud, independent – and fierce.

The natives of this area, the Maya, were representatives of the most advanced pre-Columbian civilization of the New World. In the thirteenth century the elite families of the highlands had successfully extended their control over the surrounding valleys to create two dominant political power blocs: the K'iche' and the Kaqchikel. By the early fifteenth century the K'iche' began an aggressive expansion from their newly founded capital, Utatlán – the 'town of the ravines' built out of 'stone and mortar', as the great K'iche' book of mythology and history, the *Popol Vuh*, describes it.[9] By the mid-fifteenth century, K'iche' power had spread to the west, across the highlands, and to the south, as far as the Pacific coast, only for the Kaqchikel to fight back, inflicting major damage on their former conquerors, even capturing and sacrificing one of their kings.[10] Along with other regional ethnic groups with proud identities – the Tz'utujil in the region of Lake Atitlán, the Mam to the west, the Poqomam to the east, and the Pipil to the south – these were warlike peoples, constantly fighting and seeking to undermine each other. Contrary to the impression that Alvarado and Cortés were eager to give, they did not seem in the least intimidated by Spanish technological superiority.

Indeed, the embassy that greeted Alvarado in Soconusco was hardly an expression of any willingness to submit. Sent by the Kaqchikel, it was more likely an attempt to persuade the conquistadores either to turn back or to engineer an anti-K'iche' alliance.[11] Whatever the case, as Alvarado marched deeper into Guatemala, the shrewd Kaqchikel military and diplomatic resistance made the Spanish advance painfully slow and often frustrating. In the early stages the Kaqchikel stood off, watching with interest as the Castilians and their allies battled to overcome the stiff resistance mounted against them by the rival K'iche'. A crucial turning point was the battle of El Pinar, on 12 February 1524, where the K'iche' were first routed by Spanish cavalry, then slaughtered by Spanish and Nahua foot soldiers. Alvarado, in what is probably a typical exaggeration, reckoned the K'iche' army to number 30,000; the general impression nonetheless suggests that the K'iche' had committed the entirety of their fighting force to the endeavour.[12] The expedition then progressed to the Quetzaltenango valley and defeated a further K'iche' contingent that Alvarado reckoned to number 12,000. In a town called Olintepeque legend has it that Alvarado killed the K'iche' king Tecún Umán in single combat – a description that fits European chivalric contests rather than guerrilla warring tactics used by the K'iche'. But there is no doubt that the Spaniards inflicted a comprehensive defeat on their rivals. The survivors begged for peace and invited their enemies to Utalán. Fearing a trap, Alvarado reacted in characteristic

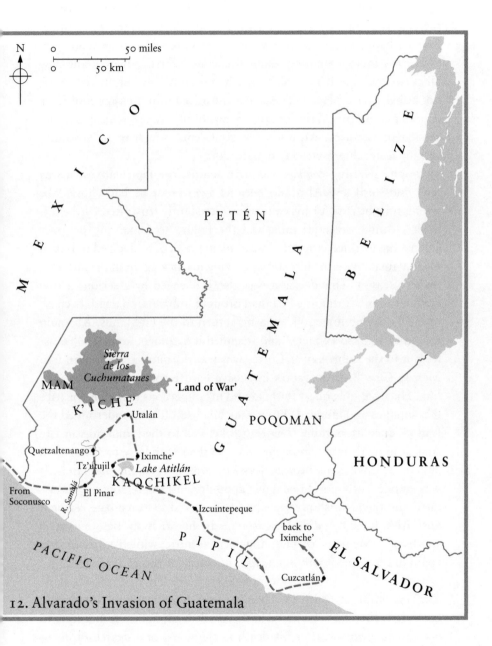

12. Alvarado's Invasion of Guatemala

fashion, executing two more K'iche' rulers and ordering his men and Nahua allies to destroy the city.[13]

So far, things had worked out exactly as the Kaqchikel had wished: the Spanish had effectively destroyed their K'iche' rivals. They therefore felt happy to seek a truce with Alvarado in order to persuade him to destroy their remaining regional enemies. First, however, the new allies ensured that K'iche' resistance had been utterly eliminated: those not killed were enslaved. Then, they advanced into the region of Lake Atitlán and destroyed the Tz'utujil army. In the wake of this quick succession of victories, Alvarado felt confident enough to move south, seeking to reach present-day El Salvador.

Despite winning decisive victories against the Pipil natives, it was now mid-April and Alvarado became aware that he had chosen the wrong time of year for his campaign. Constantly frustrated by the difficult terrain, torrential rain, and the failure to make any progress against the fortified cities of Cuscatlán and Izalco, he decided to return to Guatemala with the intention of trying his luck again in the autumn, the dry season. This decision was also influenced by a serious arrow wound to his left thigh, which had brought him close to death because of the spreading infection.[14] On his return to the highlands, Alvarado moved straight to Iximche' and renamed it Santiago, aiming to transform it in the same way as Cortés was transforming Tenochtitlan into Mexico City. But Alvarado's impulsive nature soon got the better of him. His insatiable quest for gold and his impetuous demands for tribute, supplies and labour led to a Kaqchikel revolt that undermined the frail alliance irreparably. The Kaqchikel fled to the mountains in late August and Alvarado took the city. He then withdrew to Chiapas in late 1524, leaving his brother Jorge in command of the highlands. It was emphatically not an enviable appointment: the region was devastated and the Spanish presence had only served to exacerbate regional hostilities. Jorge could do little to remedy the situation. Before long he was back in Mexico City planning his next move, while Pedro sailed to Spain in the hope of winning favour at court for future exploits.[15]

The reputation of Pedro de Alvarado as the conqueror of Guatemala could not, therefore, be more undeserved. It grew out of attempts to honour his memory after his death in the midst of a dearth of documentary evidence that is only just beginning to be remedied.[16] It is now clear that Alvarado's expedition was a dismal failure. It contrasted sharply with the piecemeal progression of alliances that Cortés and the other conquistadores had managed throughout Mexico. The most recent of these got underway just as Alvarado was approaching K'iche' territory early in February 1524. That month, back in Mexico City, Cortés sent Rodrigo Rangel and Francisco de Orozco with a force of 150 foot soldiers and four pieces of artillery to seek an alliance with the Zapotecs and the Mixtecs of Oaxaca. The Zapotecs populated much of the Oaxaca valley, and the Mixtecs were in control of its western reaches: between them, they dominated the dozen or so language groups in the region. All had been subject to a process of acculturation by the Mexica of Tenochtitlan and their Nahua allies for at least a century before the arrival of the Spaniards. The late fifteenth and early sixteenth centuries, during the reigns of Ahuitzotl and Moctezuma, had seen Nahua influence expand considerably through commerce, intermarriage, military alliances and warfare. By the time the conquistadores arrived in the region, the majority of the valley chiefs were fluent Nahuatl speakers, and Nahuatl became the lingua franca for the different indigenous groups and the Spanish alike.[17]

Reaching the Oaxaca valley, the Spanish force under Rangel and Orozco met with sporadic resistance, and only along the region's borderlands. They took control of the valley with a minimum of violence. About 4,000 Nahuas had accompanied the expedition, the majority of whom settled in and around Antequera – the name given by the conquistadores to the city that would later be renamed Oaxaca, after its native name (Huaxayacac).[18] A gratified Cortés soon came to regard the valley as his most treasured possession. He had a good eye: having already chosen for himself idyllic Coyoacán in Mexico City and 'the place of eternal spring', as Cuernavaca would come to be known, Oaxaca could not fail to catch his attention. Graced with a large temperate valley, high mountains with a cold climate, the humid lands of Papaloapan, and attractive tropical coastlands, the region was largely peaceful. Life was based on a settled agricultural economy supplemented by hunting and fishing, and while the religious rituals had strong parallels with Tenochtitlan, human sacrifice was not practised on anything like the same scale. The region was home to peoples of great sophistication. As any modern visitor to Monte Albán can attest, the Zapotecs were architects of genius, while the Mixtecs, the creators of Mitla and its magnificent palace, were widely known for the manufacture of exquisite gold and jade jewellery, hard stone carvings, polychrome pottery, turquoise mosaics, and extraordinary pictographic books. It was from the Mixtecs that the Mexica learnt to work with metal, and many of the objects that had so dazzled Albrecht Dürer would never have been produced without their influence.[19]

At first sight, this region could not contrast more sharply with the warlike territories that Alvarado had so impetuously brought into confusion. But this would be misleading. The mere existence of the K'iche' *Popol Vuh* is testimony to the depth of the poetic sensibilities of the people of old Guatemala. And despite Alvarado's exaggerations about the density of the population, the pyramidal mounds of the region would have been impossible to build without a sizeable supply of labour. Moreover, the presence of exquisite pottery, elaborate sunken ball courts with steep walls, and dance spaces for the performance of music dramas, were clear signs of a level of sophistication that rivalled the natural beauty of the region. The landscape and vegetation were astonishingly varied, especially along the well-watered plain on the Pacific coast. The temperate climate of the high fertile valleys, the volcanic stone and the availability of lime for mortar, the evidence of some gold and copper in the streams, the magnificently exotic birdlife, the plentiful supplies of fresh fish, silk and cotton, tobacco, pumpkins and delicious honey, all made Guatemala a much more enticing place than anything the Alvarados might remember of their native Extremadura. This varied beauty included the Sierra de los Cuchumatanes, the highest and most dramatic non-volcanic mountain range in Central America, the jungle lowlands of Petén, and the range of volcanic peaks lining the Pacific coast that inspired one of the most famous declarations made in England about Latin America before the Great War. Benjamin Disraeli compared the aged Whig Cabinet of 1870 to one of those landscapes: 'You behold a range of exhausted volcanoes. Not a flame flickers on a single pallid crest. But the situation is still dangerous. There are occasional earthquakes and, ever and anon, the dark rumbling of the sea.'[20]

Yet the whole region was now in tatters, and the rebellion of the Kaqchikel had given way to internecine warfare, exacerbating the rivalries and divisions that had existed before the arrival of the Spaniards. It was with these obvious weaknesses in mind that Jorge de Alvarado returned to Mexico City to seek support for his next move. Amassing a force of some 200 Spaniards and at least 5,000 indigenous allies, he marched again into K'iche' territory in March 1527. Setting up a base at Olintepeque, the town where Pedro de Alvarado had allegedly killed Tecún Umán, Jorge's forces launched an assault against the Kaqchikel, securing a further strategic base at Chimaltenango. From there they waged a series of campaigns against the various resistance leaders in the surrounding valleys. But Jorge soon realized that he had underestimated his rivals. It was difficult to fight against well-honed warriors who could use the landscape to their advantage and had learned how to neutralize Spanish horsepower and steel. The campaign developed into a laborious, prolonged and frustrating operation, leading to much bloodshed on all fronts. The reports that reached Mexico City were alarming enough for the *Audiencia* to embark upon a formal investigation. In August 1529, Jorge was instructed to hand over the government of the region to Francisco de Orduña, a judge sent from Mexico City. But it did not take long for Orduña to understand the complexity of the situation. During his eight-month stint in the region his actions differed little from those of his predecessors. He had no choice but to continue to endorse campaigns of conquest against indigenous warriors who had grown in confidence and gave no indication of any willingness to capitulate.[21]

Although the Spaniards claimed to have established control of the province of Guatemala by the early 1530s, the violence did not subside. It is no coincidence that one of the most damning descriptions of Spanish cruelty in Bartolomé de Las Casas's impassioned account, *A Most Brief Account of the Destruction of the Indies*, should concern this very region. By then a Dominican friar, Las Casas had first-hand knowledge of what he described, having spent several months between 1536 and 1538 attempting to establish a Dominican presence in what was known, aptly, as 'the Land of War' – the area of present-day Rabinal, Sacapulas and Cobán in central Guatemala – and claiming that the 'cruel tyrants' of Spain were responsible for the murders of 'four or five million' people. As usual, such numbers were gross exaggerations deployed for rhetorical effect and intended to convey the huge amount of suffering that had taken place.[22] They are also a neat reflection of the prevailing view at the time: the operation had become a veritable war of attrition in which the conquistadores made full use of their technological superiority and their access to fresh supplies of reinforcements. The high mortality resulting from constant warfare was fatally compounded by periodic massacres, waves of epidemics – in which indigenous peoples continued to succumb to diseases brought by the Spanish and against which they had no immunity – and the constant disruption of any organized resistance. Gradually but relentlessly, indigenous morale was sapped.

What most sources do not highlight is the scale of Nahua participation in the wars against the Kaqchikel – and, significantly, the increasing involvement of other Maya peoples against their detested former Kaqchikel overlords, whom they now took the opportunity to eliminate. These 'native conquistadores', as they have been called, played far more than a merely supportive role: they consistently outnumbered the Spaniards by at least ten to one, and on occasions by as much as thirty to one. Indeed, many battles were entirely indigenous engagements.[23] In the fascinating pictographic account known as the *Lienzo de Quauhquechollan*, the Guatemalan campaign is presented by the Nahua participants as a joint enterprise based on an alliance of equal partners, Spaniards and Nahuas, with the latter depicted throughout the painting as conquerors in their own right. Especially significant is the appearance, in the top left-hand corner, of a clever reinterpretation of the Habsburg coat of arms, depicting the conflation of Spanish and Nahua forces shown by the two swords – one Spanish and one Nahua – clasped by the Habsburg eagle. Immediately underneath is a depiction of a friendly embrace between a Spanish conquistador and a Nahua chief. Flanking them is another Spaniard, most probably Jorge de Alvarado with his indigenous wife, and a native lord presenting the gifts that symbolize the alliance. As the campaign sets off, Alvarado is depicted alongside four Nahua lords who, like the Spaniards, are incongruously but significantly painted white – a clear sign of the equality of the alliance. In the rest of the *lienzo* – Spanish for 'canvas' – the Nahua allies are all painted white; and, in the depiction of the various battles, it is again the collaborative nature of the enterprise that is highlighted. The *lienzo*, in short, is an apt reminder that any opposition to the Spanish, however fierce, would never be strong enough to overcome the pointedly local sense of identity that characterized the indigenous peoples. This was something, of course, that the Spaniards were never slow to realize. They knew from the start that any thought of conquest would be chimerical without indigenous support and the possibility of forming local alliances wherever possible.[24]

In November 1526 the Council of the Indies met in the seductive courtyards of the Alhambra of Granada to review the situation in the New World. Charles V was presiding – an unusual gesture, suggesting his particular interest in the topics to be discussed. These included the 'disordered avarice' of many of the Spaniards who had gone to 'the Indies' and the many abuses they had inflicted upon the indigenous peoples, particularly the 'heavy and excessive burdens that they lay upon them in order to extract gold from the mines and pearls from the fisheries', and depriving them of the necessities of life, including food and clothing. In so doing, they treated the natives 'far worse than if they were slaves', causing the death of 'a large number of the said Indians on a scale that has turned many of the islands and large swathes of the mainland into veritable wastelands, bereft of population'. Such appalling ill-treatment precipitated a spiritual crisis, for how could it be possible, in such circumstances, 'to see to the conversion of the said Indians to our Catholic faith?'

As an urgent remedy for this state of affairs, the Council issued a declaration to the effect that whenever Spaniards came across any new lands, they were under strict obligation to make it as clear as possible to their inhabitants that they came, in the name of the emperor, to 'teach good customs'. They were to do their very best to 'instruct the natives in the holy faith so that they could attain salvation' and 'dissuade them from any evil vices such as the eating of human flesh'. To this end, any expedition should in future be accompanied by at least two clerics specifically appointed by the Council, who were to instruct the indigenous peoples in the faith and to defend them against any act of cruelty or injustice. War was under no circumstances to be waged without the Council's written approval, and whoever dared to enslave a native would be punished by the confiscation of all his goods.[25]

There was nothing particularly new in any of this. The declaration merely reiterated a set of legislative measures dating back to the edicts of Isabel and Fernando and the Laws of Burgos of 1513, and they clearly echoed the many complaints that had been voiced by the Dominicans of Hispaniola and Bartolomé de Las Casas. Yet, the note of urgency in the Council's declaration and the presence of the emperor at the deliberations was a clear sign that the Spanish Crown now meant business in the New World. Not only was Charles now free of the many distractions that had absorbed his attention in the wake of the revolt of the *Comuneros* and the Lutheran crisis, but other developments had also forced him to pay much closer attention to developments in the New World. Not the least of these was the stunning victory of the Ottoman Sultan, Suleiman the Magnificent, at Mohács in August 1526, which left most of the Hungarian nobility, including the King of Hungary, Louis II, dead on the battlefield. Charles's brother, Fernando, now known as Ferdinand, was married to Louis's sister. He quickly claimed the crown of Hungary and requested urgent help from Charles. The emperor wryly replied to him: 'Don't you know that I already have a wearisome Turk to contend with?'[26] The 'Turk' in question was the King of France, Francis I, who had been defeated and imprisoned by the emperor's forces at the battle of Pavia in February 1525. The news of this victory had left Charles stunned, 'as if frozen' before 'falling to his knees before an image of Our Lady that he kept by his bed' and spending 'a good half-hour there'.[27]

Charles could only see this extraordinary victory as a clear sign of divine predilection. Before the news arrived his plans for securing his hold on Italy seemed in tatters. These plans dated back to the summer of 1522, when Duke Charles III of Bourbon had rebelled against Francis I after the latter announced that the entire Bourbon domain should revert to the French Crown on the death of the duke's mother, Louise of Savoy. The duke immediately appealed to Charles, who turned to his Grand Chancellor Gattinara for advice. Half-Piedmontese himself, Gattinara had always been adamant that Milan and Genoa were the key to Charles's control of Italy. Pope Adrian was in complete agreement with Gattinara on this issue, but his death in September 1523 threatened to upset this balance: Adrian's successor, Clement VII, was a Medici and unlikely to be sympathetic to Habsburg interests in Italy. Gattinara thus urged Charles to appoint the Duke of Bourbon as his lieutenant-general in northern Italy, in the hope that the plan would appeal to Charles's uncle and faithful ally against the King of France, Henry VIII of England. The latter, however, showed no interest, and this left Francis I free to direct his forces against the Duke of Bourbon. As the French king crossed the Alps into Lombardy in the winter of 1524, the republic of Venice and Pope Clement VII abandoned Charles and sided with the French king. A few weeks later, in the early days of 1525, Henry VIII followed suit.[28]

It is small wonder that the news of the victory at Pavia should have seemed miraculous to Charles. An official account written by Alonso de Valdés, Gattinara's humanist secretary, compared the victory to that of Gideon against the Midianites as recounted in the Book of Judges (7: 17–22), seeing it as a prelude to 'the conquest of the empire of Constantinople and the Holy City of Jerusalem, now occupied because of our many sins', in such a manner that, 'as so many have prophesied, under this most Christian of princes the whole world may accept our holy Catholic faith and the promise of our Redeemer be fulfilled: that may there be one flock and one shepherd'.[29]

But now all these hopes were in jeopardy. Not only had Francis I reneged on all his promises to Charles at the Treaty of Madrid, signed on 14 January 1526, but he had also been flirting with Suleiman. Indeed, it had been the French embassies dispatched to Istanbul during Francis's imprisonment in Madrid that had persuaded the Ottoman Sultan to advance against Hungary. Despite Charles's wry reply to his brother, therefore, there was no doubt in his mind that his top priority had become the halting of the Ottoman advance, now a terrifying threat to Austria. As he admitted to the distinguished papal nuncio Baldassare Castiglione, the emperor had made up his mind to seek the mediation of either Henry VIII or Pope Clement to reach an agreement with the King of France. As far as he was concerned, the latter could even 'take Spain if he deemed it fit; for, in order to defeat the Turk, he was now prepared to abandon everything'.[30]

The emperor's presence at the meeting of the Council of the Indies was undoubtedly driven by this new sense of urgency. Coincidentally, only a few days earlier Charles had received the handsome gift of 60,000 gold pesos from Hernán Cortés, a sum, the conqueror of Mexico explained in another long letter dated 3 September 1526, far in excess of what the emperor might reasonably expect; but the conquistador had sent it nonetheless 'because of the great need we knew that Your Majesty was passing'.[31] Cortés did not know about Mohács, but his gift could not have come at a more pressing time for Charles. Accordingly, the emperor felt only too pleased to be able to reward Cortés's envoy, Francisco de Montejo.

We last met Montejo on his mission to Spain in 1520, on behalf of

Cortés, entrusted with the treasure destined to dazzle Dürer in Brussels.[32] After the Crown decided to favour Cortés over Velázquez, Montejo had been named commander (*alcalde*) of Veracruz.[33] He had returned to Mexico in 1524 to be handsomely rewarded by Cortés with the grant of profitable *encomiendas*, before being sent back to Spain with the gift of bullion that he hoped might win the emperor's favour.[34] Very soon after the Council ended its deliberations, Charles agreed to grant Montejo a contract (*capitulación*) for the conquest of Yucatan. The document was signed on 8 December 1526, while the Council was still in Granada. Montejo was given the title of *adelantado*, governor and captain-general, with a salary of 250,000 *marvedís* per annum. He was, of course, instructed to heed all the stipulations in the ordinances of November 1526, which were repeated almost verbatim in the *capitulación*.[35] But despite this altruistic concern for justice, the Council's motives, just like those of the emperor, were clearly informed by the hope that many similar gifts of bullion would continue to arrive. Charles was desperate for cash. As the Polish ambassador Dantiscus wrote to his sovereign in 1525, 'the Emperor sends all the money that comes his way to his armies, and as a result has to endure extreme penury'.[36]

Once Montejo was granted his own *capitulación*, he busied himself recruiting followers. He left Sanlúcar de Barrameda in June 1527 in four ships transporting no fewer than 250 men, several horses, armaments and enough food to last a year.[37] Meanwhile, as Montejo was on his way to conquer Yucatan, Cortés was having to face one of his most difficult adversaries. This was Nuño Beltrán de Guzmán, a native of the Spanish city of Guadalajara. Guzmán's relatives had played an important role in Castilian politics, supporting Charles V during the revolt of the *Comuneros*, and the emperor was quick to show the family his gratitude. Guzmán himself was appointed one of Charles V's hundred or so bodyguards; then, in 1525, he was given the chance to prove himself in the New World by being appointed governor of the Mexican region of Pánuco. Two years later, after a difficult transatlantic crossing, he took up the post. At once he pursued a policy of enslavement of the indigenous population that was as extensive as it was brutal. Despite complaints and an investigation against him, Guzmán's star continued to rise: in 1528 he was appointed president of the newly created supreme court of New Spain: an institution set up to tackle the chaotically corrupt situation that had taken root in Mexico City during Cortés's expedition to Honduras.[38]

The choice of Guzmán was a clear indication of the Spanish Crown's determination to appoint an official with sufficient clout to oppose Cortés when he deemed it necessary – a response, in other words, to the widespread allegations sown by Cortés's many enemies at the imperial court. By this time Cortés himself had decided to return to Spain to plead his case in person. He arrived in May 1528, accompanied by forty indigenous people including many of the jugglers who had entertained Moctezuma and other distinguished nobles of Tenochtitlan and Tlaxcallan.[39] He found Charles in jubilant mood. The emperor had just emerged from a crisis that was even more alarming than the news of the battle of Mohács. Not only had Francis I's failure to honour his promises destabilized the position of the Duke of Bourbon – whose properties and revenues were confiscated by the French king – but it had also led to an alliance, the Holy League of Cognac, in which Venice, Florence, Pope Clement VII and the deposed Duke of Milan, Francesco Sforza – with Henry VIII acting as 'protector' – sided with the French king against Charles. In retaliation, the Duke of Bourbon led his mutinous troops south, first to Florence and then to Rome where, in a disorderly rampage that many Europeans saw as one of the most horrible in recorded history, between 6 and 12 May 1527, as many as 10,000 civilians are estimated to have been slaughtered, countless women raped, and hundreds of churches, palaces and homes plundered.[40] Embarrassingly, Charles's pamphleteers initially wrote about a glorious victory over a perfidious pope. It was only after the full horror of the tragedy began to sink in that they attempted to distance the emperor from what had happened, arguing that his will had been transgressed by groups of undisciplined and predominantly Lutheran mercenaries.[41]

In the wake of Charles's loss of reputation throughout Italy, Francis was quick to realize that his enemy was more vulnerable in Naples than in Milan. Under the leadership of the experienced commander Odet de Foix, Viscount of Lautrec, the French army moved south from Lombardy with more than 50,000 troops and, in April 1528, placed Naples under siege. Then, just as all the gains that Charles V had won at Pavia seemed irretrievably lost, his fortunes turned. The Genoese admiral Andrea Doria, who had offered to help Lautrec by intercepting imperial supplies and reinforcements during the siege, decided to defect to Charles V. He later explained that he had been appalled by what he called 'the shameful treatment' Francis consistently inflicted on the Genoese. With Doria out of the game, the French siege of Naples was rendered practically ineffectual. What is more, an outbreak of the plague took the life of Lautrec and decimated the French army, which had no option but to surrender. Doria then took his galleys up to his native Genoa, entering the city in triumph in September. The impact of this victory seemed even more astonishing than that of Pavia. As Gattinara put it, 'it exceeded all hope'. Naples and its kingdom and the republic of Genoa had been permanently and, it seemed, miraculously lost to France.[42]

Charles could therefore afford to receive Cortés magnanimously, treating him like a Renaissance prince and even asking him to sit at his side. He bestowed on him the title of Marquis of the Valley of Oaxaca, endorsing an enormous *encomienda* of approximately 23,000 vassals, and confirming him as captain-general of New Spain – though not governor, since that title had now been granted to Guzmán. As a consolation, Cortés was named 'governor of the islands which he might discover in the South Sea', as the Pacific was still called.[43] Charles also endorsed Cortés's marriage to Doña Juana Ramírez de Arellano, daughter of the Count of Aguilar and a niece of the Duke of Béjar, one of the most powerful men in Spain. It was around this time, too, that Cortés was sketched by the German medallist, sculptor, painter and goldsmith Christoph Weiditz, most probably on the recommendation of the Polish ambassador, Johannes Dantiscus. Weiditz was clearly having an off day, but he nonetheless left us the only real-life likeness we possess of the conqueror of Mexico.[44]

Despite all these honours, it is obvious that Charles was subtly planning to play off Cortés against Guzmán and the new governmental institutions recently established in New Spain. Cortés returned to Mexico City in the summer of 1530 to find that Guzmán had imposed almost total control. Cortés was personally humiliated: denied entry to his own mansion in Mexico City, he retreated to Cuernavaca, as Cuauhnahuac was now called, where he had built a handsome palace that still graces the centre of that city. In Cortés's absence, Guzmán had conducted an exhaustive investigation into his activities before, during and after the conquest of Mexico. This was the normal procedure for any high-ranking royal official, but the case of Cortés was made much more complex by the sheer number of old followers whom he had disappointed with disproportionately meagre financial rewards. A series of long inquests involving throngs of witnesses led to accusations ranging from illicit profiteering and unnecessary massacres to the murder of his first wife, Catalina Juárez. The witnesses did not produce enough evidence to have Cortés convicted, but they dwelt endlessly on the suspicious circumstances surrounding the convenient disappearance of some of his enemies. Nor could they find enough evidence to convict him of unacceptable maltreatment of indigenous peoples, yet accounts of his actions at Cholula, as Cholollan was now called, and Tepeaca suggested that Cortés was not immune to fits of outrageous brutality. It was also clear to many that the Marquis, as he was now generally known, was far wealthier than he claimed to be: had he, by any chance, conveniently forgotten the royal fifth owed to the Crown on all his profits?[45]

It soon dawned on Cortés that his ambitions in New Spain were doomed when confronted with the rising interest of the Spanish Crown in controlling the new territories. His own accumulation of so many lordships belied a desire for a degree of independence that would be unthinkable in Spain itself, even to the highest nobleman. To boot, Cortés's growing unpopularity in Mexico City and the suspicions that had been raised at the imperial court served to remind him that administration had never been his métier. On the other hand, in his grant of a governorship of all the islands that he 'might discover', Charles V had offered him a way out: a new opportunity to concentrate his energies where they were most effective. Shortly after his return to Mexico City, Cortés decided to take full advantage of his royal entitlement and set out on a quixotic quest for islands in the Pacific. Devoting large sums of his fortune to a search for the famous strait that would open the route to the Moluccas and, subsequently, to China, Cortés found what he thought was an island, which he named Santa Cruz. It was in fact the peninsula of Baja California.[46]

Meanwhile, Francisco de Montejo had been busy in Yucatan. His fleet had sailed there directly from Spain. It had taken the familiar route to Cozumel, where the Spaniards were well known. From there the expedition crossed to the mainland, where they founded a settlement that Montejo named Salamanca, after his place of birth. It was an

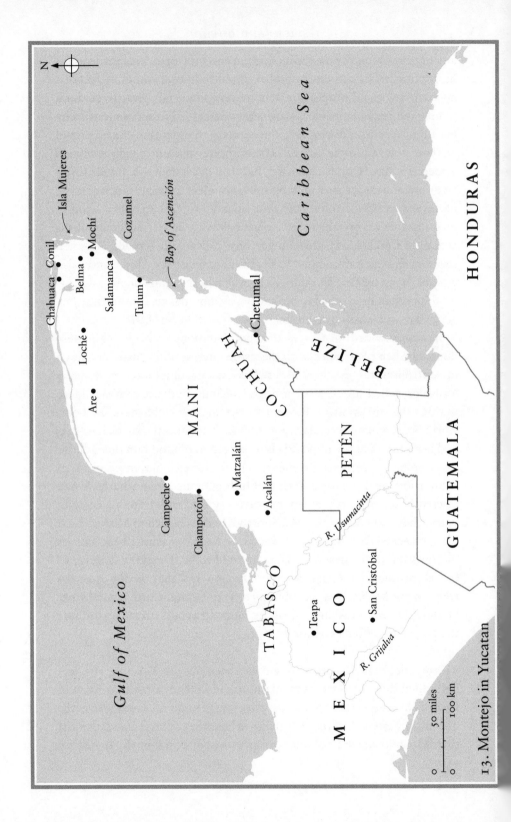

13. Montejo in Yucatan

unfortunate choice: 'in a palm grove near a swamp in the least whole-some place to be found in the whole region'.[47] Montejo quickly realized his error. In the first days of 1528 he began a northward journey to look for a better port. At Mochí and Belma the Castilians were welcomed by friendly *caciques*, and Montejo was impressed by Conil, a large town of about 500 houses in the north-east of the peninsula. From there they moved, via Cachí and Sinsimato, to Chahuaca. The latter was a very attractive place, with ponds of clear water and artificial watercourses and temples dating back to the classical Maya period. Montejo and his men were received well, but it soon turned out that they had walked into a trap. The next morning they awoke to find the town deserted. Surrounding it, local forces launched a fierce attack with bows and arrows. With the help of their horses and superior weaponry the Span-iards repelled the attack and moved on to Ake, there brushing off another attack and continuing via Loché towards Campeche. On the way Mon-tejo divided his forces into two. One group was to make its way back towards the prosperous port town of Chetumal across the interior of the peninsula; there, Montejo and his approximately sixty remaining men returned to the insalubrious settlement of Salamanca. From there they set off southwards towards the Bay of Ascención and Chetumal, where they came across Gonzalo Guerrero, the companion of Gerónimo de Aguilar who had gone native in the region, complete with piercings, tattoos and an indigenous wife who had produced several children. Despite Montejo's pious admonitions, Guerrero remained steadfast in his decision to stay put. Then, when the second contingent arrived, it brought disappointing news: there was no trace of any silver, gold, pre-cious stones or any commercial activity; all they had seen on their journey was a grim forest stretching out into the horizon.[48]

By now Montejo was becoming aware that circumstances in Yucatan were very different to what Cortés had experienced in central Mexico. In contrast to the short two years that it had taken to subdue Tenoch-titlan, it would take Montejo and his men several decades to begin to feel in control of Yucatan. Even then the conquest of the region never felt complete. The principal reason for this was the absence of an over-arching structure that could be targeted. The peninsula was home to at least sixteen autonomous provinces, each of which needed to be con-quered separately. Additionally, the pot-holed terrain that characterized the thick bush forests was hardly suitable for horse manoeuvrability and the type of fighting that favoured Spanish weaponry and tactics. This allowed for levels of resistance and fierce opposition that gradually sapped Spanish morale.

For these reasons the initial thrust of Montejo's expedition never penetrated further than the southern borders of Mani and Cochuah. The vast region stretching from the mountain district and the Petén to the foothills of Guatemala and Chiapas, the historic heartland of classical Maya culture, remained largely unknown. While the region had entered a sharp decline long before the arrival of the Spaniards, their presence unwittingly turned the very factors that had produced such good crop yields into terrifying liabilities. In particular, the climate proved mercilessly congenial to the Old-World pathogens against which the natives had no immunity. The effects were devastating, and they were compounded by the impact that Cortés's conquest of Tenochtitlan had on the economic prosperity of the region. Tenochtitlan's capture, and the incursions of the Spaniards into Guatemala and Honduras, had violently disrupted the network of vigorous commercial centres on which Yucatan had relied. These centres stretched from Chahuaca in the north down through Tulum to the Bay of Honduras, and from there across to the gulf coast.[49] Now, as Mexico City was constructed on the ruins of Tenochtitlan, even those regions that Montejo had considered promising along the east coast had been reduced to a handful of deprived settlements – an easy prey for the increasingly frequent attacks by French, Dutch and English pirates.[50]

In the summer of 1528, Montejo opted to return to Mexico City in search of reinforcements but in a mood of deep despondency. His visit coincided with the arrival of Nuño de Guzmán as president of the *Audiencia*. Despite his enmity with Cortés, Guzmán showed himself deferential, even obsequious towards the aristocratic Montejo, offering to help him and even naming him magistrate of Tabasco, a fertile and prosperous region on the gulf coast. This emboldened Montejo to return to Yucatan in a renewed mood of optimism that can be appreciated in a letter he sent to Charles V in the spring of 1529. He told the emperor that he had found 'many signs of gold and precious stones' in Yucatan, all of which gave him 'great hopes that with the help of Almighty God I shall pacify those lands in little time'. The greatest drawback so far had been the absence of a suitable port. Indeed, he had spent most of his time in Yucatan looking for one and had failed. For this reason he had discussed with Guzmán that he should be given possession of the Grijalva, a navigable river that flows from the Chiapas highlands to the Bay of Campeche.[51]

A few days later Montejo set off for Tabasco and from there he sailed up the Grijalva as far as Teapa at the foot of the mountains of Chiapas. He soon claimed to have 'pacified' all the provinces at the cost of the lives of about thirty Spaniards, but there was still no firm basis from which to carry out a concerted operation of conquest. From Teapa, Montejo sent Antonio de Ávila on a weary journey across the mountains, first to San Cristóbal, recently founded by Alvarado, and then to Acalán. This settlement had very good communications, but it was relatively small, there was no gold, and the supplies of food were poor. So Ávila moved on to Maztalán and from there to Champotón where Montejo caught up with him from Tabasco. Eventually, Montejo and Ávila took the decision to establish themselves further north, in Campeche, which was more suitable as a port. From there Montejo launched a series of campaigns over the next few years but never succeeded in gaining control of the region. The natives often mounted fierce resistance with weapons that could inflict serious damage. When they could not withstand the advance of the Castilians, they often destroyed their towns and fled into the forests. By the mid-1530s Montejo and his men had little more than a base in Campeche, and most of their followers were deeply demoralized. When news of a great empire that had been discovered along the south Pacific began to arrive, most of Montejo's followers understandably deserted him.[52]

We last met the conqueror of this great empire, Francisco Pizarro, on the journey across the isthmus of Panama that had led to the discovery of the Pacific in 1513.[53] He became closely associated with Pedrarias Dávila after the latter was appointed governor of Castilla del Oro in 1514. In January 1523 the aged Dávila allowed the ambitious Gil González de Ávila – who had quit his job as a royal accountant in Santo Domingo – to sail north in search of the fabled strait that would open up the wealth of Asia to the Spanish Crown. After his ships were irreparably damaged by termites, González de Ávila and his companions were forced to continue the journey by land. Crossing what is present-day Nicaragua, the Castilians were impressed by the ceremonial centres, commenting that their large palaces were in no way inferior to anything that they had seen in Spain.[54] On their return to Panama, where Pedrarias had moved his capital in 1524, they bragged about the thousands of indigenous people they had allegedly baptized; the latter, in turn, had reciprocated with plenty of gold. When Pedrarias, predictably, asked for the fifth he was entitled to, González de Ávila fled to Santo Domingo to seek reinforcements before returning to Nicaragua in a failed attempt to take control of the region.

The episode confirmed in Pedrarias's mind that the ambitions of his compatriots in Central America were far in excess of what such limited swathes of land could provide. With slave raids still considered the best and most reliable way to raise money, the chaos of Guatemala was being replicated in Honduras. Further south, Pizarro had grown disgruntled by the disappointing grant of indigenous labourers he had been allotted by Pedrarias for his *encomienda* in Panama. He therefore persuaded an old acquaintance, Gaspar de Espinosa y Luna, whom Pedrarias had appointed mayor of Santa María la Antigua, to provide the funds for an expedition down the Pacific coast. Pizarro set off from Panama in November 1524 but soon returned, having succumbed to bad weather and the hostility of the indigenous peoples along the coast of what is present-day Colombia. Undeterred, he set off on a second voyage on 10 March 1526, this time with a sizeable force of 160 men and several horses. After facing similar problems along the Colombian coast, the crew grew restless and demanded to return to Panama. On the way back, Pizarro made a stop on the island of Gallo, where he assembled his men on the beach and drew a line in the sand with his sword, asking those to cross it who preferred glory, honour and gold to the comparative misery and obscurity of Panama. Only thirteen men did so; the rest, unconvinced by Pizarro's bombast, returned home.[55] Defiantly, Pizarro stayed on in Gallo with the 'famous thirteen', as they came to be known, having convinced his pilot, Bartolomé Ruiz de Estrada, to come and fetch them in due course. Life in Gallo was uneventful and harsh. The Spaniards barely eked out a living on the scarce food available amid what a chronicler called 'enough mosquitoes to wage war against the Turk'[56] – yet their letters to Panama mentioning the 'very fine gold' they had seen began to cause a stir.[57]

When Ruiz de Estrada returned to Gallo a few months later, he found the Spaniards in a despondent mood. He tried to persuade Pizarro that it made sense to return to Panama. Pizarro agreed, but not before one final trip south. For a few months in 1527, therefore, Pizarro, Ruiz de Estrada, and those of the thirteen who felt strong enough, set off on a voyage that seems to have taken them as far as the mouth of the river Chincha, south of what is present-day Lima. After various adventures – two of their number opted to stay behind in the city of Tumbes, one falling in love with an indigenous woman, another with the culture – Pizarro and his men made it back to Panama with colourful tales of gold, exquisite textiles, llamas, and the astonishing beauty of the landscape. Of the powerful people that lay behind all these marvels, the Incas, they were still completely in the dark.

When, back in Panama, Pizarro was reunited with two old friends, Diego de Almagro and Hernando de Luque, the conversation inevitably turned to conquest and to dreams of at least equalling the deeds of Cortés. The more cautious Luque pointed out that any such plans would require the formal approval of the Crown, and after some debate they agreed that Pizarro should sail to Spain.[58] He departed in the company of Diego del Corral, a veteran of Pedrarias's 1514 expedition to Darién, and the Cretan artilleryman Pedro de Candia, reaching Sanlúcar de Barrameda in January 1529. From there they made their way to Toledo, where the emperor was busy making plans for a forthcoming trip to Italy.

It is not surprising that Charles V could not give Pizarro the treatment he had given Cortés the previous year. Despite the very good news he had recently received from Naples and Genoa, the emperor was under great pressure to avoid the mistakes he had made after Pavia. His most urgent task was to make amends with Pope Clement, still shocked by the scandalous Sack of Rome. He also needed to consolidate his hold on Italy, a policy that required the most delicate diplomatic negotiations with the different territories and republics as well as with the pope. After endless negotiations Charles finally boarded Andrea Doria's galley in Barcelona on 27 July 1529 and sailed for Italy to the jubilant shouts of *Plus Ultra!*[59]

This lack of attention to Pizarro by no means amounted to a lack of interest. In the background of the delicate diplomacy there lurked the spectre of Suleiman's threat to Austria, now compounded by the possibility of anti-Habsburg alliances with the Ottomans that not only the French king but also the Lutheran princes might well be tempted to forge. Charles knew that the consolidation of his power in Italy was merely the beginning of a problematic and, without substantial quantities of New World bullion, impossibly expensive set of military and naval campaigns. It would otherwise be very difficult to explain why, on the day before the emperor sailed from Barcelona, the Council of the Indies issued a *capitulación* stating that Pizarro was to be allowed to 'continue the said discovery and conquest and settlement of the province of Peru'. He was, besides, awarded the title of *adelantado mayor* of Peru and the captaincy-general and governorship of whatever lands he should conquer, with an enormous lifetime annual salary of 725,000 *marvedís* – almost twice what Cortés had been granted a few years earlier. Pizarro was given six months to prepare his expedition, and was allowed to recruit 150 men from Spain and 100 from the Americas.[60] Elated, Pizarro went to his native Trujillo in Extremadura, where he recruited four of his own brothers. By the time he reached Sanlúcar de Barrameda, where he bought four ships, Pizarro had recruited 185 men, including at least one Franciscan and six Dominican friars.[61]

13

Cajamarca

Pizarro set sail from Panama on 27 December 1530, and headed down the Pacific coast. He intended to make for Tumbes, but a strong south wind made that impossible. His first port of call was therefore the Bay of San Mateo, at the mouth of the river Esmeraldas, just south of the island of Gallo, which he had come to know so well. From there the expedition continued on foot across barren countryside intersected by large rivers that could only be crossed in rafts. The explorers were headed for the town of Coaque, which they had heard was rich in precious stones and metals. Reaching Coaque on 25 February 1531, they were pleased to find plenty of emeralds; they also seized a good amount of gold and silver. Heartened by his initial good fortune, Pizarro sent messengers back to Panama and Nicaragua with a sample of the treasure and instructions to show it off as a bait to entice others to join him.[1]

The elation did not last long. In a reversal of the usual epidemiological story, many Spaniards were struck down by a strange disease that began with aches in the bones, joints and muscles before the appearance of large, painful and unpleasantly disfiguring boils.[2] Several died of the mysterious affliction; the rest were forced to remain in Coaque for several months. In a tactic reminiscent of Cortés's treatment of Moctezuma, Pizarro seized the local chief and persuaded him to instruct his men to feed the Spaniards. The tactic worked for a while, but the natives soon grew weary of the Spaniards and fled to the forests.[3] When, eventually, reinforcements from Nicaragua arrived under the leadership of an entrepreneur named Pedro Gregorio, they included, amid approximately twenty men and thirteen horses, the royal treasurer, Alonso Riquelme, the royal accountant, Antonio Navarro, and the official supervisor, García de Salcedo, ample evidence that Pizarro's enticing gifts had caused a stir among people of standing in Central America.[4]

With renewed optimism the expedition resumed its southward march on 12 October. It headed for Tumbes – by far the most enticing settlement that Pizarro and 'the Thirteen' had come across back in 1527 – which Pizarro planned to make the capital of Peru; indeed, several of his men had already been promised appointments to the council of the prospected town.[5] On their way they reached what is present-day Puerto Viejo where, for the first time, they became aware that not all was well with the Inca realm. As they marched onward, deeper into Inca territory, the damage caused by the violent conflict between two great Inca leaders, Waskhar and Atawallpa (normally rendered as Huáscar and Atahualpa in the older literature), was palpable everywhere.[6]

These leaders were the sons of Wayna Qhapaq, who had died in 1527. His reign marked the culmination of a complex hundred-year-long process of concerted Inca expansion and unification. From what we can infer from various Inca legends filtered down to us through a range of confusing and contradictory Spanish and Andean voices, in the early fifteenth century the Inca first emerged from the Valley of Cusco as a power to be reckoned with, having previously incorporated the various tribes of the region through a combination of diplomacy and war. In the hundred years that followed, Inca influence reached far beyond Lake Titicaca, with successful expeditions on two fronts. To the west, the Inca gained control of the Pacific coastlands that had previously been under the influence of Nazca and Arequipa. To the east, they broke into the forests of the Chunchos and Mojos, described as a veritable land of horrors in many of the sources, while subduing the uprisings of the Qolla and Lupaqa lords of the Altiplano. During this confrontation, the Aymara-speaking peoples were split, with the Cana and Canche taking the side of the Inca. The subsequent events are shrouded in confusion, but when, eventually, the Inca emerged successful, they marked the occasion in a most dramatic fashion by flaying the defeated lords of the Altiplano and, after impaling their heads on poles, fashioning their skins into drums.[7]

The Inca also expanded north, into what is present-day Ecuador and south-west Colombia. Soon after they had gained control of the Titicaca basin and the Altiplano, first occupying Guasco and Coquimbo, before crossing over into what is present-day Chile in pursuit of mineral wealth at Porco, Tarapacá and Carabaya. This steady process of expansion was only halted by the ferocious resistance of the Mapuche

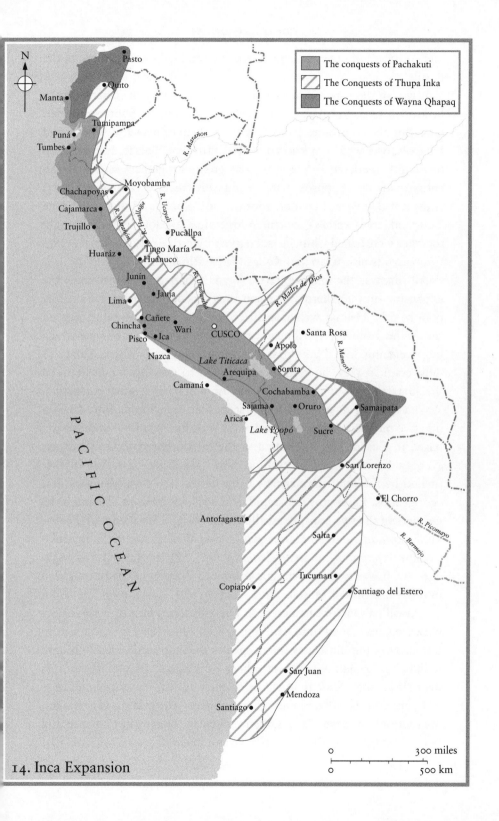

N

The conquests of Pachakuti
The Conquests of Thupa Inka
The Conquests of Wayna Qhapaq

Pasto
Quito
Manta
Puná
Tumbes
Tumipampa
R. Marañon
Chachapoyas
Moyobamba
Cajamarca
R. Ucayali
Trujillo
R. Marañon
Pucallpa
Huaráz
Tingo María
Huánuco
R. Huallaga
Junín
Jauja
R. Urubamba
Lima
R. Madre de Dios
Chincha
Cañete
Wari
CUSCO
Santa Rosa
Pisco
Ica
R. Mamoré
Nazca
Apolo
Lake Titicaca
Arequipa
Sorata
Camaná
Cochabamba
Sajama
Oruro
Samaipata
Arica
Lake Poopó
Sucre
San Lorenzo

PACIFIC OCEAN

El Chorro
R. Picomayo
Antofagasta
Salta
R. Bermejo
Copiapó
Tucuman
Santiago del Estero

San Juan
Mendoza
Santiago

0   300 miles
0   500 km

14. Inca Expansion

and Araucanian peoples, who emerged triumphant at the battle of the Maule.[8]

It was in the wake of these notable advances that the ruler came to be known as 'Sapa Inka', a term meaning 'Unique' or 'Supreme' leader, reflecting the control he exerted, with the help of his various heirs and relatives, over what was known as Tawantinsuyu. This term, which can be roughly rendered as 'the four parts brought together', referred to an entity made up of approximately eighty provinces encompassing what is present-day Peru, Ecuador, south-west Colombia, Bolivia, northern Chile and large swathes of northern Argentina. The four 'parts' it brought together were called Chinchaysuyu (north-west), Antisuyu (north-east), Cuntisuyu (south-west) and Kollasuyu (south-east).

All this was the inheritance of Wayna Qhapaq, who continued the expansion into northern and eastern regions despite being afflicted by poor health.[9] He may well have died of smallpox, a disease that reached the Andes from the Caribbean and Panama in the 1520s and which most certainly killed his eldest son, Ninan Cuyuchi. Wayna Qhapaq's most tragic legacy, however, was his plan to split his realm between Waskhar, the son of his first wife, and Atawallpa, the son of his second. Wayna Qhapaq apparently thought it sensible to divide his large domain into two more manageable realms, with Waskhar in control of the south, based in Cusco, and Atawallpa of the north, based in Quito. However, each son wanted everything. Their resulting clash was further fuelled by the long-simmering rivalry of the two royal dynastic descent groups, known in the singular as *ayllu* or *panaqa*. Through the mothers of the two sons, Atawallpa was closely identified with Pachakuti's *panaqa* – named *Hatun ayllu* – and Waskhar with Thupa Inka Yupanki's *panaqa* – named *Qhapac ayllu*.[10] What followed was a savage war. It was finally burning itself out as Pizarro's expedition sailed into the Bay of San Mateo.

Atawallpa's victory had come at a terrible cost. Hardly a settlement between Cusco and Quito had been spared a horrific dynastic confrontation. Nothing illustrates the deep rifts that the conflict had brought to light better than Atawallpa's otherwise unspeakable cruelty towards his half-brother. Shortly after the conflict ended, he sent his highest-ranking military officer and high priest, Kusi Yupanki, to Cusco, with instructions to supervise a sadistic spectacle of the slow torture and painful slaughter of all Waskhar's wives and children, making sure that the defeated leader was forced to watch. Although Atawallpa's victory had brought back some degree of stability and enhanced power and influence to his senior generals – Quisquis in Cusco, Rumiñawi in Quito and Challcochima in Jauja and Pachacamac – it was obvious to everyone that Tawantinsuyu's honourable nobility, upon which the system had largely relied, was now irreparably torn. The scars of the war were too fresh, too painful and only too obvious. It would not take Pizarro and his men long to notice.

Whether or not Pizarro appreciated the full extent of the crisis at this stage, his spirits certainly rose when, just south of present-day Guayaquil, he was joined by a further Spanish contingent from Nicaragua and Panama, led by Sebastián de Benalcázar, with a following of approximately thirty men and twelve horses.[11] They moved on south, before stopping for a much-needed break at the island of Puná, off the southern coast of what is now Ecuador. Their sojourn did not begin well. The island's chief at first appeared welcoming, but this was in fact an ambush in the guise of a ceremonial reception: a dance rehearsal soon turned into a fierce attack, in which a number of Spaniards were wounded, including Pizarro's brother Hernando. Finally, the conquistadores managed to seize the chief and several of his guards, imposing themselves on the indigenous forces with their superior weaponry and the strength and speed of their horses.[12] There was plenty of evidence in Puná of the war between Waskhar and Atawallpa, 600 prisoners having been brought over from the nearby port of Tumbes and held captive. While pondering what to do about these convicts, Pizarro was joined, on 1 December, by a further contingent led by the *hidalgo* Hernando de Soto. The pair had struck an informal deal during the preparations in Panama, whereby Soto would receive the governorship of 'the most important city in Peru' in exchange for financing some of Pizarro's ships.[13] With Soto's approximately 100 men and twenty-five horses, the expedition now counted nearly 300 Spaniards, around a hundred of whom were on horseback.[14]

Their swelling numbers, however, led to further hostility from the Puná islanders. Inviting the Spaniards on a deer hunt, they planned an ambush. Pizarro got wind of the plot from a bilingual native boy known as Felipillo, who had been captured by the Spaniards some years earlier and spoke their language. When the islanders attacked, the conquistadores fought them off effectively. Then, helping themselves to plenty of good cloth, and some gold and silver that had been laid out in sheets – most probably to be used as linings for the interior walls of palaces and temples – they set off for Tumbes with the 600 prisoners, with whom Pizarro hoped to allure his indigenous acquaintances there.[15]

He was soon to be disappointed, for the devastation caused by the war was even more evident in Tumbes than in Puná. Finding the town deserted, Pizarro ordered Hernando de Soto to find out where the people were hiding.[16] Taking some seventy horsemen, Soto tracked them down in the town of Piura, about a hundred miles south of Tumbes. There the Spaniards were presented by the native chiefs with a plentiful amount of silver, gold and precious stones. The town had good supplies of water as well as being comparatively well populated and near a bay that could act as a good port. Renaming the town San Miguel, the first Spanish settlement in Peru, Pizarro shrewdly offered the weakest members of his expedition, approximately forty of them, the opportunity to become citizens of the new foundation with grants of *encomiendas*.[17] He also learned much valuable information from the local chiefs about the great riches of Cusco and other Inca towns such as Vilcas and Pachacamac. Equally interesting was the news that the victor of the Inca war, Atawallpa, was resting in a spa near a highland city called Cajamarca.

Immediately Pizarro changed his original plan, which had been to march along the coast towards Cusco, and made up his mind to head for Cajamarca as soon as possible. On 16 May 1532 he and 170 men set off from San Miguel on a long and treacherous uphill march across bleak mountains that held much sand and little water. Passing scattered hamlets, in one settlement they were greeted by a young lad sporting a desert cloak and a shawl to protect his head and shoulders from the sun. His seemingly innocent curiosity endeared him to the conquistadores, but also made them suspicious. They were right: it would soon become apparent that the lad was a spy from Atawallpa. With hindsight, they also realized that he would have been easily identified as a member of the Inca nobility by the large earspools that caught their attention. It was then that they coined the term, later widely used, *orejón* (Spanish for 'the one with big ears'). They also kept the lad, whose name was Apoo, on friendly terms. The result was that Apoo formed the impression that the Spaniards were harmless, while also noticing their covetousness. He would relay this information to Atawallpa, describing the intruders as gullible bearded robbers who could be easily enslaved.[18]

According to some accounts, Pizarro at this time also received a message from the defeated Waskhar, asking him for protection, to which the conquistador replied in friendly terms.[19]

Their slow march continued across barren countryside, dotted here and there with isolated villages – Sarrán, Olmos, Motux – whose people wore cotton clothes and woollen shawls and tended llamas. Early in October they descended towards the altogether more attractive region of the Chimor valley, home to the industrious Chimú, arriving in the town of Saña on 16 October. After a final and difficult uphill ascent from Saña, on 15 November, six dreary months after their departure from Tumbes, the conquistadores crossed the cotton plantations around Cajamarca and entered the city.[20]

Cajamarca nestled in a fertile valley with a sophisticated irrigation system. It was graced with a Temple of the Sun and sacred buildings arranged around a large central square, each side of which was approximately 180 metres long. On three sides were buildings, each with twenty gates; the fourth side was bounded by a wall of adobe with a gate and tower in the middle.[21] Cajamarca itself was deserted. Atawallpa and his tens of thousands of men were resting, encamped a few miles away at a sophisticated spa in a place called Kónoj. Wasting no time, Pizarro sent Hernando de Soto and some of his best horsemen to invite the Sapa Inka to visit the conquistadores in Cajamarca. He soon feared for their safety and sent another force under his brother Hernando. Reports are conflicted as to what happened next. We know that Pizarro's ambassadors were accompanied by an interpreter – variously called Felipillo and Martinillo – who was clearly not as able as Cortés's Doña Marina, or even Gerónimo de Aguilar, for his stammering mistranslations succeeded in infuriating both Atawallpa and the Spaniards.[22] What transpired from the garbled exchange left various witnesses with the impression that the Sapa Inka considered the Spaniards to be divine messengers (Wiracochas), whose arrival had been predicted by his father, Wayna Qhapaq. It was for this reason, Atawallpa allegedly explained to the Spaniards, that he had let them come in peace. Without this knowledge he would most certainly have stopped them coming, something that his vastly superior army (an undeniable statement, in terms of numbers) would have accomplished without any trouble. He was, however, puzzled by the Spanish claim to want peace at all costs, for he had heard they had no qualms about pillaging and even killing people. To this, Hernando Pizarro reiterated a message of peace. His brother Francisco had great affection for the Sapa Inka; why else would he have travelled such a long and tortuous route to find him?[23]

Although much seems to have been lost in translation, Atawallpa was nonetheless deeply impressed by what he saw. To see a horse for the first time is quite an experience. But to see a group of Spanish stallions mounted by men in Renaissance finery, 'with their colourful hats, tight breeches, starched doublets, and capes with their long sleeves, almost in the Basque style', as an indigenous chronicler would later describe them, would have been astonishing.[24] Soto got so close to Atawallpa that his horse's nostrils stirred the red fringe on the Sapa Inka's forehead – the *llautu* that all Sapa Inkas donned when they formally assumed office after a four-day fast.[25] Soto then took a large gold ring from his finger and offered it to Atawallpa as a token of peace and friendship. Calling for another, specially trained, horse, he proceeded to entertain the dignified Sapa Inka with a stupendous display of Castilian horsemanship, running a drill of curvets, tight turns, skirmishes and charges that left the hitherto impassive Atawallpa agog with admiration. He even insisted that the Spaniards should stay the night. Perhaps fearing a trap, the Spaniards declined the offer, explaining that they needed to return to their companions in Cajamarca. Atawallpa then relented and promised to visit them the next day.

As soon as the Spaniards left, Atawallpa ordered a squadron of his own soldiers to be executed because they had shown fear at the approach of the horses. He also ordered the execution of 'their immediate superiors, who were there, and their wives and children' – done, so one Spanish account had it, 'in order to terrorize his people so that no one would run away when confronted with the Christians'.[26] Despite the poetic licence likely to have influenced the Spanish version of the episode, it nonetheless sheds light on the sense of dread that came over the Spaniards that night in Cajamarca. While they had put on a brave face in their encounter with Atawallpa, the terrible danger they were in now dawned on them. Before meeting the Sapa Inka, they had no idea of the sophistication of Tawantinsuyu. Now they had seen something of the splendour of Atawallpa's domains. Even in a remote spot like Kónoj, the Inca had access to a palace with towers and a courtyard with a pool equipped with cold and hot water pipes.[27] The very remoteness of the place reminded the Spaniards that they had unwittingly cut themselves off from the coast, from which they had journeyed by a long and difficult march over bleak mountains. Atawallpa, by contrast, was in command of a victorious army of tens of thousands of disciplined warriors.

When Atawallpa did not show up the following morning, as he had promised, tensions rose further. Pizarro began to fear an attack and prepared accordingly. Then, in the late afternoon, the Sapa Inka arrived in Cajamarca in ceremonial fashion, carried 'in a very fine litter with its handles covered in silver', and 'richly dressed, with a crown on his head and a collar of large emeralds round his neck'.[28] The Spaniards were mostly in hiding, awaiting a signal to attack, while Atawallpa simply presumed that they were afraid of his might: hundreds of his own soldiers surrounded him, and he had no idea that he might be in any danger. In addition to the reassuring information about the intruders that he had received from Apoo, had not the Spaniards themselves told him they came in peace? When he called out to them, he was met by the Dominican friar Vicente de Valverde, accompanied by one of the young interpreters. Friar Vicente allegedly told the Sapa Inka that he should repudiate his dreadful deities and pay tribute to Charles V; if he did not, then the Spaniards would have no option but to destroy him and all his followers, 'even as the Pharaoh of old and all his household perished at the Red Sea'.[29] Unperturbed, but rather intrigued, both by the extraordinary exchange and by the book that the friar was holding, Atawallpa asked to see it. There followed a confusing altercation and the book ended up on the ground. Visibly alarmed, Friar Vicente took cover. What happened next was an echo of Alvarado's tragic decision to slaughter the celebrating Mexica in Tenochtitlan: two salvos of artillery fire gave the signal for the horsemen to gallop out of their quarters, followed by foot soldiers. A savage butchery ensued. Within minutes, hundreds of Atawallpa's soldiers lay dead on the ground. Although his warriors outnumbered the Spaniards by at least ten to one, they soon broke ranks and fled, pursued and cut down by the horsemen. In just over two hours thousands were killed without a single Spanish casualty. In another echo of Cortés's capture of Moctezuma, Pizarro seized Atawallpa and took him to safety.[30]

The following morning Soto rode to Kónoj with thirty horsemen. The tens of thousands of troops there offered no resistance, something that can only be explained by the total subservience that every inhabitant of Tawantinsuyu was expected to show the Sapa Inka. Before noon the Spaniards were back in Cajamarca with all the objects of gold and silver, or adorned with precious stones, that they could lay their hands on. The booty exceeded their wildest dreams: 80,000 pesos of gold, 7,000 marks of silver and fourteen emeralds. Their exhilaration must have been evident.[31] As well as presumably anxious for his own welfare, Atawallpa was clearly both mystified and disdainful: how on earth could these familiar objects from his mountain retreat make the intruders look so foolish? Then he had an idea: surely these excitable strangers would agree to free him if he offered them more of these metals, of which he had practically endless supplies. Through the young interpreter he managed to convince Pizarro that, in a mere two months, he would fill the room where he was being held with similar objects, as high as his hand could reach. To drive the point home he drew a line on the wall. In typical Spanish fashion an agreement was written down by a notary. Whether or not Pizarro offered to free Atawallpa if he complied is not entirely clear from the sources, but this certainly seems to have been the implication.[32]

Again, just as Cortés had done with Moctezuma, Pizarro ensured that, even in captivity, Atawallpa continued to receive the honour due to the Sapa Inka. Accordingly, he was given the freedom to receive messengers, make new appointments, consult advisors, and give instructions. His nobles – now commonly referred to as *orejones*, the ones with big ears, on account of the large earspools the Spaniards had first noticed on Apoo – were also allowed to maintain their privileges. This situation suited Pizarro very well in two respects: it gave him ample time to wait for reinforcements; and it furnished him with a valuable opportunity to learn as much as he could about the political and military situation in Tawantinsuyu. As Atawallpa and his nobles befriended their captors, so this information grew to a deluge. With the Sapa Inka in their power, wrote one conquistador, everything was calm and in order: Atawallpa gave the impression of being 'the most refined and able [native] that we have yet seen, very keen to learn our ways, so much so that he plays chess extremely well'.[33] He could also, of course, manifest signs of callous cruelty, continuing to order the murders of a number of his rivals. When he heard that his own half-brother Waskhar was being escorted to Cajamarca from Cusco, rather than agreeing with Pizarro that Waskhar should be allowed to arrive in safety, Atawallpa ordered his execution. Pizarro pretended to believe Atawallpa's story that Waskhar had been killed by his own bodyguards, but he knew that no one would have dared kill the Sapa Inka's half-brother without Atawallpa's explicit command.[34]

As time dragged on, and Atawallpa's ransom – the treasure he had promised in return for his freedom – proved slow to materialize, the Spaniards grew irritated. To show his goodwill, Atawallpa agreed with Pizarro that three of his men – Martín Bueno, Pedro de Moguer and Juan de Zárate – should be allowed to go to Cusco, the Inca capital, to oversee the collection of a consignment of treasure, offering for them to be carried in litters by his soldiers. Leaving Cajamarca early in the new year, 1533, they arrived in Cusco two months later – no mean feat given that, as the crow flies, the distance between the two cities is a good 750 miles and the road cuts across the central Andes. Crossing the watershed between the Pacific Ocean and the Amazon basin, the expedition would have had to negotiate wild torrents and several subsidiary ranges of steep mountains – a journey that has been compared to travelling from Lake Geneva to the eastern Carpathians or from Pike's Peak in the southern Rocky Mountains all the way to the Canadian border.[35]

Atawallpa's general in Cusco had received strict instructions to allow the three Spaniards to take as much gold as they could manage from the Qorikancha, the Temple of the Sun, whose interior walls were lined with the precious metal. No information survives about what the three envoys thought of the Inca capital, other than Juan de Zárate's remark that the streets were well organized and paved and that, in the eight days they had spent there, they had not managed to see all the sights.[36] They were, of course, busy with a more pressing priority: they amassed so much gold and silver that they had no way of taking it back to Cajamarca. It is a measure of the overriding nature of the hold of the Sapa Inka over his subjects that the treasure was carried by no fewer than 700 porters who formed the escort of the three Spaniards on the return journey.[37]

In the meantime Hernando Pizarro had made it to Pachacamac, a city just to the south of what is present-day Lima, also with the support of Atawallpa. He returned to Cajamarca laden with gold and in the company of Challcochima, Atawallpa's most powerful commander in the region. Hernando had persuaded the commander – falsely as it turned out – that the Sapa Inka had asked to see him. Hernando insistently questioned Challcochima about the gold that he assumed the Inca general must have stolen from Cusco after the defeat of Waskhar. Embarrassingly, Hernando had to rein in his misplaced curiosity on the return of Bueno, Moguer and Zárate from Cusco, bearing vast quantities of gold. Pizarro's priorities now changed once more: the amassed treasure had to be converted into transportable form.

The melting down began in the first days of May. Over eleven tons were fed into the newly built forges. They produced a staggering 13,420 pounds of 22½ carat gold and 26,000 pounds of silver – incomparably the greatest quantity of bullion that had ever been seen in the New World. It was carefully divided into equal shares which were then apportioned according to what Pizarro and a small committee considered fair in relation to merit. In what was perhaps a rash decision the committee, which included Soto and the notary Miguel de Estete, made sure that neither Diego de Almagro nor any of his followers, approximately 200 foot soldiers and fifty horsemen, received any of the bullion. They had only recently made it from Panama to Cajamarca, arriving there on 15 April, and had taken no part in the capture of the Sapa Inka.[38] From Almagro's perspective, this could only appear as a betrayal of trust on Pizarro's part. After all, an agreement had been reached on Pizarro's departure from Panama that Almagro would stay behind awaiting instructions to recruit reinforcements when necessary.

Almagro's arrival gave Atawallpa good reasons to feel apprehensive. The conquistador's animosity was palpable, and it felt all the more jarring in the absence of some Spaniards who Atawallpa had befriended over the past few months, many of whom had chosen to sail hurriedly back to Spain with their newly acquired, extraordinarily large fortunes; among them was one of Atawallpa's favourites, Hernando Pizarro. By contrast to Hernando's comparatively diplomatic approach, Almagro was a man of rough manners whose numerous followers made the Sapa Inka realize that a steady feed of Spanish recruits, armaments and horses would continue to arrive in the region. Tensions escalated with the rumours that Atawallpa had ordered his commander in Quito, the skilled warrior Rumiñawi, to organize a military campaign against the intruders.[39] Whatever the truth of the matter, Francisco Pizarro certainly took the rumour seriously and doubled the number of sentries overnight. If, indeed, he had promised to free Atawallpa after the latter delivered the treasure in full, Pizarro now had good reasons for not doing so. The rumour also presented Pizarro with an unenviable dilemma. He was eager to move down to Cusco as soon as possible. How could the Sapa Inka be guarded in Cajamarca during his absence? The option of taking Atawallpa with him was even more problematic: the presence of the Sapa Inka would more than likely provoke indigenous attacks. Gradually, Pizarro reached the reluctant conclusion that the only viable course of action was to have the Sapa Inka executed as a traitor. A makeshift trial was conducted, with Pizarro and Almagro as 'judges' and Sancho de Cuéllar as notary. They found Atawallpa guilty of the typically Western crimes of usurpation, fratricide, idolatry, polygamy and insurrection, and sentenced him to death.[40]

On 26 July 1533 the Sapa Inka was brought to the central square in Cajamarca and tied to a stake. As was his duty, Friar Vicente de Valverde did his best to persuade him to accept baptism. This was expected practice, but eternal life was not the only thing on offer. If Atawallpa refused, he would be burned to death; if, on the other hand, he accepted baptism, he would be garrotted. Atawallpa's formal request for baptism, therefore, which Friar Vicente administered while the Spaniards around him sang the Creed,[41] needs to be understood in the context of the Inca belief that the body of the Sapa Inka had to remain intact if it was to undertake the journey to the permanent new existence that awaited him.[42] According to one of his brothers, Pizarro nonetheless felt a relative sense of relief after Atawallpa was garrotted rather than burned, for at least now he could give him a dignified Christian burial. But the tragedy would be impossible to exaggerate. According to a witness, Pizarro wept in the face of his victim, hoping that he might understand his dilemma.[43] It was not only Atawallpa who could not understand. Pizarro knew that his brother Hernando, now on his way to Spain, would have been horrified at what had happened. Then, when Soto returned from his frustrated search for the alleged threat posed by Rumiñawi in Quito, he made no effort to conceal his fury that such an important decision had been taken in his absence. Apart from anything else, Atawallpa's execution had left the conquistadores bereft of an Inca leader through whom to rule, and it had left the indigenous peoples without a sovereign. Would it not have been incomparably more sensible to keep Atawallpa alive after he accepted baptism?[44]

News of Atawallpa's killing spread quickly as the less adventurous conquistadores sailed to Panama and from there to Spain in a mood of contagious enthusiasm. Their message was that Peru was evidently a land of unimaginable plenty awaiting eager and long-frustrated adventurers from Panama, Nicaragua, Guatemala and Yucatan. On 5 December 1533 the first ship, carrying Cristóbal de Mena with the initial samples of Peruvian gold to reach the Old World, sailed up the Guadalquivir into Seville, soon to be followed by Hernando Pizarro in early January 1534. News of their arrival spread like wildfire across the peninsula and was met with reactions verging on the ecstatic. That very year saw the publication of Juan de Córdoba's *Lidamor de Escocia* in Salamanca and the anonymous *Tristán de Leonís el Joven* in Seville – books destined to be devoured by a reading public avid for tales of chivalrous heroism against mysterious, awesome and breathtakingly outlandish odds. Yet even these stories seemed to pale by comparison with the recent exploits that the new arrivals had recounted. In addition to unprecedented amounts of melted bullion, the conquistadores had brought with them a good supply of llamas and some eye-catching works of art. As the chronicler Francisco de Xerez remembered, these included 'thirty-eight recipients of gold and forty-eight of silver, among which was a silver eagle' into whose main cavity could be poured approximately eight gallons of liquid; 'two enormous urns, one gold and one silver, both of which could fit a whole quartered bullock; two very large golden pots . . . and an idol of solid gold the size of a four-year-old boy'.[45] If seventy ships had arrived in the northern port of Laredo with 10,000 Amazons on board, claimed a bemused observer, the tale, surely, would have been believed.[46]

The material benefit to Charles V was soon evident. The royal 'fifth' of the treasure to which the emperor was entitled allowed him to repay his Genoese creditors, and to mount the biggest military campaign that Christian powers had ever launched in the western Mediterranean, conquering Tunis from the Ottomans in 1535.[47] Yet when he learned about the execution of Atawallpa and the squalid manner in which it had been carried out, the emperor could not have been more appalled. Even if, as he was willing to concede, it was true that the Sapa Inka had been planning an attack against Pizarro and his men, a sovereign of Atawallpa's standing should never have been executed without a fair trial by competent authorities. As far as the emperor was concerned, the most embarrassing and unpardonable fact was that such a shameful decision had been taken 'in the name of justice'.[48]

*

Charles V was far from alone in his concern about the way in which Justice, one of the four cardinal virtues, had been abused. The news had certainly led to a great degree of anxiety and soul searching. On 8 November 1534 the brilliant theologian at the University of Salamanca, Friar Francisco de Vitoria, wrote to his Dominican co-religionist Friar Miguel de Arcos, that 'after a lifetime of studies and long experience . . . no business shocks or embarrasses me more than the corrupt profits and affairs of the Indies. Their very mention freezes the blood in my veins.'[49] Vitoria and Arcos were corresponding about a query from a *perulero* (a pejorative term combining the word 'Peru' and the suffix *lero*, added to suggest something ridiculous and worthy of mockery, to describe those returning from Peru with their enormous fortunes). This particular *perulero* wanted to legalize his various acquisitions through a process called *composición*; that is, the payment of a lump sum to the Crown in return for the right to repossess land that had been confiscated.[50] Vitoria began his reply by underlining the blatant contradiction in the request: no *perulero* could possibly claim to be repossessing anything; given that the property in question belonged to someone else – the Inca from whom it had been seized – 'they can allege no title other than the law of war'. But here, again, the *peruleros* had no leg to stand on. 'As far as I understand from eyewitnesses,' Vitoria continued, neither Atawallpa nor any of his people 'had ever done the slightest injury to the Christians, nor given them the least grounds for making war on them'.

Yet there were people in Spain who were happy to make excuses for the behaviour of the *peruleros*. One particularly egregious argument was that, since soldiers were expected to obey orders, they should not be held responsible for their actions. It was an argument that enraged Vitoria: 'I accept this response in the case of those who did not know that there was no other cause for this war than sheer robbery – which was all or most of them.' There had, after all, been other, more recent conquests that had been 'even more vile'. But Vitoria could not let the matter rest there. 'I grant that all the battles and conquests were good and holy, but we must still consider that this war, by the very admission of the Peruvian conquistadores, is not against strangers, but against true vassals of the emperor, as if they were natives of Seville.' The Inca were, in other words, patently innocent. Even if one were to grant that the justice in the war was on the side of the Spaniards, hostilities could only be waged 'for the good of the vassals and not of the prince'. From all this it was clear to Vitoria that there was no way to excuse the conquistadores of 'utter impiety and tyranny'. Alluding to the vacant and enticing archbishopric of Toledo, Vitoria asserted that if he were offered it on condition that he swore to the innocence of the conquistadores, he still would not do so. 'Sooner my tongue and hand wither than say or write a thing so inhuman, so alien to all Christian feeling! On their heads be it and let them leave us in peace. There will be no lack of men, even within the Dominican order, to salve their consciences, and even to praise their deeds of butchery and pillage.'[51]

The importance of this letter can hardly be exaggerated. Vitoria was one of the most influential thinkers of his time. Although he never published a word, famously explaining that his students had more than enough to read already, what has come down to us through student notes (given Vitoria's lecturing style, these were often fairly accurate transcriptions) and through the writings of his most brilliant disciples – men like the Dominicans Domingo de Soto and Melchor Cano and the Jesuits Luis de Molina and Francisco Suárez – is of the first importance for understanding how the news of the conquests of Mexico and Peru, the latter in particular, challenged and altered established notions of justice in Spain.[52]

In January 1539, Vitoria delivered a series of lectures on 'the Indies'. He began with the explosive claim that the arguments hitherto used to justify the Spanish presence in the New World were no longer valid. Up until recently, he asserted, it had been assumed that 'since the affair is in the hands of men both learned and good, everything has been conducted with rectitude and justice. But when we hear subsequently of bloody massacres and of innocent individuals pillaged of their possessions and dominions, there are grounds for doubting the justice of what has been done.'[53] Vitoria posed the question of what right (*ius*) the Spanish had to subject the indigenous peoples of the Americas.

In addressing this issue, Vitoria was opening up a legal and theological can of worms. For a start, the Latin term *ius* is not properly rendered by the use of the modern English word 'right' (though we often translate it this way). The term *ius* was inseparable in the sixteenth century from the ancient principle known as *suum cuique* – that is, the act of rendering to each individual what is his or her *due*. As St Thomas Aquinas, the authority that Vitoria and his contemporaries followed most closely, had defined it, the principle was 'the lasting and constant will' of rendering 'to each his [or her] due (*ius*)'.[54] Here Aquinas was drawing on a very long tradition, stretching back to Plato – who in turn was quoting the poet Simonides – and handed down through Aristotle, Cicero, Ambrose, Augustine and, above all, Roman Law. It was the most basic definition of justice. And yet, it was not without its obvious complications. Plato had put the problem quite neatly in the *Republic*, specifically in a dialogue between Socrates and Polemarchus. When the latter is asked by the former to clarify what Simonides meant by justice, Polemarchus replied: 'That it is just ... to render to each his due.' Unconvinced, Socrates retorts: 'I must admit ... that it is not easy to disbelieve Simonides, for he is a wise and inspired man. But just what he may mean by this you, Polemarchus, doubtless know, but I do not.' After raising his characteristic objections, Socrates concluded: 'It was a riddling definition of justice, then, that Simonides gave after the manner of poets, for while his meaning, it seems, was that justice is rendering to each what befits him, the name that he gave to this was "the due".'[55]

What then was this *due* that Aquinas called *ius*? How did anything come to belong to a person? As he addressed this question in January 1539, Vitoria was aware – in a way we might find puzzling – that the answer could not begin with the notion of 'Justice' itself. Once it was agreed that the act of justice was to give each person his or her due, then, as Aquinas had explained, 'the act of justice is preceded by the act whereby something becomes that person's due'. Justice could not come first simply because 'the act by virtue of which something comes to be due to a person cannot itself be an act of justice'.[56] Justice, in other words, came after *ius* (after 'the due'). In the absence of a 'due' there could be no justice.

But where exactly did this 'due', this *ius*, come from? Vitoria took it for granted that 'it is as much more evil as it is more shameful to do than to suffer wrong'.[57] This is the forceful reply to Callicles that Plato had put in the mouth of Socrates, and it left no one in any doubt that justice belonged to the very 'being' (*esse* or *ens*) of a person. Again, the Latin terms are important if we are to grasp the full significance of the notion. For Vitoria and his contemporaries, the inalienability of an obligation to a person had to be based on nothing other than the very 'being' of the person to whom the obligation was due. Appeals to anything else – agreements, treatises, promises, laws, and so on – were necessarily secondary to this. Beyond this acceptance that there were things due to a person because of that person's 'being', language had to fail – as it always did in the minds of Vitoria and his contemporaries whenever an attempt was made to render a self-evident concept more intelligible.

So it is no surprise that, in addressing the question of what 'right' (*ius*) Spaniards had to subject the indigenous peoples of the Americas, Vitoria began by addressing the question of *dominium* that was so central to the Laws of Burgos and the *Requerimiento*.[58] As we have seen, an often-overlooked motive behind the drafting of that extraordinary document was the realization that the peoples of the New World did indeed possess *dominium*. Despite coming to this conclusion, the authors of the *Requerimiento* still aimed to justify the Spanish presence in America on the basis of the bulls of donation that Pope Alexander VI had granted to Isabel and Fernando in 1493. Yet now, Vitoria categorically rejected that such a donation could be valid. He had already explicitly set out his thinking in his lecture series of some six years previously on the power of the Church, expressed in his pithy statement that the pope had no power whatsoever that he could 'donate' to kings or princes for the elementary reason that 'no one can give what he does not have. He [the pope] has no . . . *dominium* . . . and therefore cannot give any'.[59]

At a stroke, Vitoria had effectively deprived the Crown of the one prop for its actions in the New World that still carried some degree of respectability, even among passionate defenders of the indigenous peoples like Bartolomé de Las Casas. Vitoria went on to establish that there could be no doubt that the peoples of the New World were in undisputed possession of their property, both publicly and privately, and that the Spaniards 'carried with them no right at all to occupy their countries'. This left Vitoria with only four hypothetical grounds that might be used to justify their subjection: (1) that they were sinners; (2) that they were non-Christians; (3) that they were mad; or (4) that they were irrational. The first two grounds were given short shrift on exactly the same basis that the authors of the *Requerimiento* had used to avoid repeating the 'heretical' arguments of John Wyclif and Jan Hus – now, of course, widely known to have been endorsed by Luther. Aware of this tradition, Vitoria reminded his students that rights did not depend on grace, as these 'heretics' thought, but on law. This meant that Christians could never use heretical arguments to justify dispossessing natives of their property. He also easily brushed aside the second two grounds, on the empirical basis that there was no evidence whatsoever that the natives of America were either mad or irrational. Even if some of their customs indeed appeared 'barbaric', the fact that they lived in cities with magistrates and laws, that they engaged in industry and commerce, and that they possessed a recognizable form of marriage, all pointed clearly to the use of reason.[60]

Having demolished these justifications, Vitoria then turned his attention to a range of further arguments that were being deployed to justify the conquests. If claims to sovereignty made by either pope or emperor had been shown to lack foundation, any such claims were rendered equally invalid when applied to peoples who had never been under the jurisdiction of the former Roman Empire. The argument that the natives of America had voluntarily accepted Spanish rule, as Hernán Cortés had famously claimed, seemed spurious when one considered that they could not possibly have had a clear idea of what they were doing. There were some, Vitoria said, who wanted to claim that America had been given to Spain as a 'special gift from God'. To them, he replied with undisguised impatience: 'I am unwilling to enter into a protracted dispute on this argument, since it is dangerous to give credit to anyone who proclaims a prophecy of this kind contrary to common law and the rules of Scripture unless his teaching is confirmed by some miracle.' Besides, 'even if it were true that the Lord had decided to bring about the destruction of the barbarians, it does not follow that a man who destroyed them would thereby be guiltless'. 'And if only,' he concluded in a tone of exasperation, 'the sins of some Christians were less grave . . . than those of the barbarians!'[61]

Having considered the whole range of arguments being deployed at the time, the great Salamanca theologian had come to the conclusion that not one of them could be used to invest the Castilian Crown with *dominium* in the New World. No 'just title' could be drawn from either the divine or the natural law; nor, by extension, could it be drawn from any human or positive law. These were the three most important categories used by Vitoria and his contemporaries, following Aquinas, to understand the law. The first, divine or eternal law, pointed to the norms established by God in the act of Creation. The second, natural law, was, in the words of Aquinas, 'the participation in the eternal law by rational creatures'.[62] The third, human or positive law, was consti-tuted by laws enacted by human beings, and could therefore vary, sometimes quite radically, from community to community; but they had nonetheless to be derived from one or other precept of the natural law, which was a reflection of the divine law. To claim that any ruler of any kind had been invested with universal sovereignty was impossible on the basis of any of these. As Vitoria's former student Domingo de Soto would put it, a truly universal empire would have needed a general assembly of the whole world in which at least a majority consented to the election of the universal sovereign. This seemed quite absurd. But even if, as some jurists insisted, some such meeting could be plausibly imagined at some stage in the past, and that the rights established by such a meeting could have been passed on in some mysterious way to Charles V, it was nonetheless clear that 'neither the name nor the fame of the Roman Caesars ever reached the Antipodes and the islands dis-covered by us'.[63]

Vitoria had left Charles V with no claim to *dominium* in the New World, and no property rights whatsoever. Did this mean that the Crown should simply wash its hands of the whole affair, punish indi-vidual conquistadores for their crimes, and abandon the enterprise? This might seem like a logical conclusion to us, but in the sixteenth century the problem was rather more complex: as one of the four car-dinal virtues, Justice was intrinsically related to the other three: Prudence, Courage (or Fortitude) and Temperance.[64] It was evident to anyone working in this tradition that the world could not be kept in order through Justice alone. Indeed, there were at least some obliga-tions or relations of indebtedness that could not be acquitted in full and were therefore beyond the scope of Justice. This was particularly the case when it came to God, for there was simply no way for any human being to give God what was His due. Moreover, given that the Span-iards were already settled in the New World, and that a large number of indigenous peoples had been converted to Christianity, the cardinal virtue of Prudence ruled that 'it would be neither expedient nor lawful for our prince to abandon altogether the administration of those terri-tories'.[65] In defence of this position, Vitoria drew on a fourth category of law, which occupied a somewhat ambiguous place between the nat-ural and the human or positive law. This was known as the law of nations (*ius gentium*) and had originally been used by the Romans in their dealings with non-Romans (*gentes*). It was based on a set of customs that, as Cicero had observed, were 'extremely widespread' and 'shared by all with all'. From this, Vitoria derived his own notion of the *ius gentium* as a body of laws enacted by the whole world, 'which is in a sense a commonwealth'.[66]

The notion had undergone several transformations since Cicero's time, and the tradition that Vitoria inherited had endowed the *ius gentium* with the universality that was intrinsic to the natural law but not with its immutability. Unlike the natural law, the *ius gentium* was subject to history and contingency. Yet its participation in the natural law allowed Vitoria to argue that just as the 'commonwealth' took precedence over the nation, so the *ius gentium* should take precedence over the laws of individual societies. It is on this basis that some scholars have claimed that Vitoria should be considered the founder of international law – although at this stage the experiment looks a lot more like an 'interpersonal' law applied on a universal scale.[67] It nonetheless allowed Vitoria to maintain, without fear of contradiction, that even those societies that had never formed part of the Roman Empire were subject to the *ius gentium*, just as they were subject to the natural and divine laws. And it was on this basis that Spaniards could claim to possess the right (*ius*) of 'natural partnership and communication', which in turn gave them the right to travel, the right to trade, and the right to preach. Vitoria also conceded that the *ius gentium* allowed human beings to wage just wars when they involved the defence of innocent people against tyrants.[68]

Vitoria was under no illusions about how much influence his arguments would have on government policy. When Miguel de Arcos asked him why it was that those in power so rarely listened to the views of their advisors, Vitoria replied that princes were of necessity pragmatic creatures, 'whose thoughts often only travel from their feet to their hands, and their counsellors even more so'.[69] But the way in which Vitoria had come so close to arguing his emperor out of the larger portion of his empire had not gone unnoticed. His views soon became something of an orthodoxy, an inescapable point of reference for every subsequent effort to ensure that the indigenous peoples of the New World were treated as what they were: not just fully human, but fully fledged subjects of the emperor and of his rightful successors.

PART THREE

Disenchantment, 1533–42

14

Cusco

However much he dressed it up, Pizarro's execution of Atawallpa was informed by cold-bloodedly strategic motives. The conquistador knew well the extent to which the administration of Tawantinsuyu depended on the person of the Sapa Inka. He also sensed that a good number of the local inhabitants resented the oppressive rule of the victors and still mourned the killing of Atawallpa's half-brother Waskhar. Happily for the conquistadores, the eldest surviving son of Wayna Qhapaq, Thupa Wallpa, had not only been spared the murderous wrath of his triumphant half-brother but also accompanied him to Kónoj and happened to be in Cajamarca at that time. No sooner had Atawallpa been buried than Pizarro asked all the chiefs in the city to assemble in the main square to agree on a successor. Thupa Wallpa was the obvious choice: Pizarro could present him as a representative of the legitimate line of Cusco and a convincing figure to lend credence to his own condemnation of Atawallpa as a traitor and a usurper. The enthronement of the new Sapa Inka was carried out with what seemed to be complete unanimity. The ceremony took place as soon as possible, a mere day after Atawallpa's execution, on Sunday 27 July 1533.[1]

During the ceremony Pizarro was puzzled by an apparent incongruity: why was Thupa Wallpa not wearing the *llautu* – the red fringe that had marked Atawallpa as the Sapa Inka? Had not all the chiefs ceremoniously handed him the white plume that symbolized their vassalage? And why had he not taken the trouble to don a suitable attire, one worthy of the occasion? Pizarro was reassured that this was normal practice: the new ruler was expected to mourn for the old one by fasting for four days in seclusion; once that rite was over, he was certain to look the part. And indeed, on the fourth day, Thupa Wallpa emerged magnificently attired and accompanied by a great many chiefs, including

Atawallpa's brilliant commander Challcochima. They all accepted him as their lord and then placed a very fine *llautu* on him before sitting down to dine.

After this, according to the somewhat bewildered and more than likely fanciful account of an eyewitness, Thupa Wallpa expressed his earnest wish to do homage to Charles V, offering Pizarro one of the many white plumes he had received. This encouraged Pizarro to schedule another ceremony the following day in which, now in his own best attire, he informed all those present that the conquistadores had been sent by the Emperor Charles to bring the true faith to all the natives of Peru, so that they could be saved and inherit eternal life. Pizarro made a point of having the pronouncement, clearly a version of the *Requerimiento*, 'proclaimed word for word through an interpreter'. He then asked the Sapa Inka's followers whether they had understood it. When they all said that they had, Pizarro 'took the royal standard and raised it above his head three times' before instructing all the members of Thupa Wallpa's entourage to do the same. This they did 'to the sound of a trumpet blast' and the event was followed by celebrations that lasted several days.[2]

It is impossible to read such accounts without a dose of scepticism. Had the Inca nobles really understood the claims of such an odd document as the *Requerimiento*? How could a distant monarch, about whom they had never heard, claim to have any rights – or, to use the Salamanca theologians' term, *dominium* – over their territories and possessions? Even if such an abstract notion had been spelled out to them, 'word for word', would they have made any sense of it? More sharply ironic is the apparent earnestness with which Pizarro and his companions complied with the formalities of the process. It would be anachronistic to blame them for hypocrisy or duplicity: after all, this was the only legal basis at their disposal that still carried unanswerable authority. Not surprisingly, Pizarro made a point of having the whole process duly recorded and notarized. Little did he know it was precisely this tradition that was about to be dramatically demolished by the most competent and respected minds in Spain – and that they were to do so largely in response to news of his own actions. Were the Inca and the conquistadores talking at cross-purposes? How can we explain such goodwill and openly festive concord in such complex circumstances?

The case of Mexico sheds light on the problem, especially the way in which the indigenous peoples of Yucatan and the Gulf coast had willingly complied with Cortés's admonitions about idolatry, human sacrifice and anthropophagy, and with the consequent need for them to abandon their idols and begin to venerate Christian images.[3] Cortés's enthusiasm seems to us misplaced – but in this, as in so much, we have the dubious benefit of hindsight. In their particular circumstances, both groups had good reasons to behave as they did and, above all, to trust each other in good faith. The situation of Pizarro and the Inca nobility at Cajamarca mirrored that of Cortés and the Maya, and they behaved in a similar way.

From the Inca perspective, the conquistadores had given every sign of being invincible in military terms. An operation to defeat them would have needed the most careful orchestration – and, in any case, would have been impossible to plan without the initiative of the Sapa Inka. The latter had been under the control of the intruders for months and, after his execution, the conquistadores had wasted no time in appointing a successor who seemed equally, if not more, subservient to them. All sides, moreover, were aware that the aftermath of the wars had left Tawantinsuyu deeply divided. They had seen the death of Atawallpa greeted by large sections of the population with relief, yet they all knew that the absence of a properly recognized Sapa Inka would plunge the region into warfare once again. The best option for all concerned was to recognize Thupa Wallpa as the new Sapa Inka. As far as the conquistadores were concerned, the most immediate threat came from the north, from Rumiñawi, Atawallpa's loyal and skilled commander in Quito. A swift move to Cusco was therefore expedient for the conquistadores, and not just because of the treasures the city housed: while Quisquis, Atawallpa's commander in Cusco, might have been outraged at the murder of his leader, he was a known quantity and had proved himself unconditionally subservient to any instruction coming from the Sapa Inka. Besides, Atawallpa's third commander, Challcochima, was safely in Pizarro's custody.

The conquistadores marched out of Cajamarca, the city that had been their base for eight months, on 11 August 1533, in the company of the new Sapa Inka and a large contingent of Inca warriors who saw their new leaders in much the same light as the Tlaxcalteca had viewed Cortés and his followers. Passing Cajatambo and Huamachuco, they marched on to Andamarca, the town where Waskhar had recently been

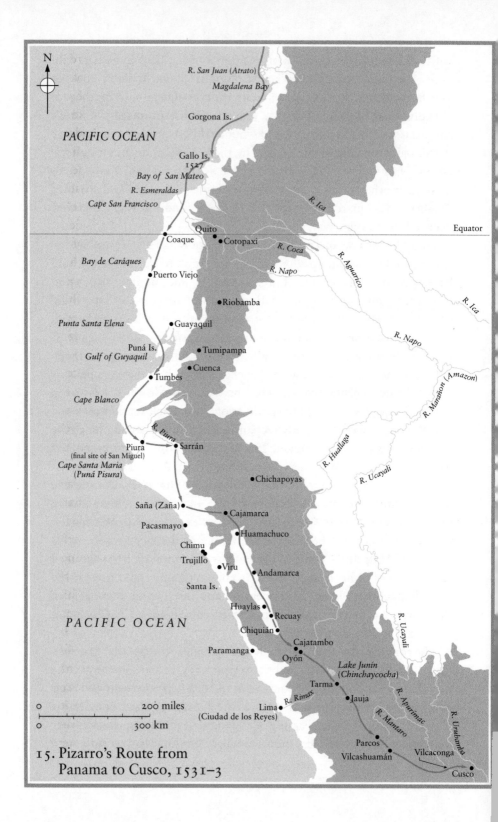

N

PACIFIC OCEAN

R. San Juan (Atrato)
Magdalena Bay

Gorgona Is.

Gallo Is.
1527
Bay of San Mateo
R. Esmeraldas
Cape San Francisco

Quito
Coaque ● Cotopaxi
R. Coca
R. Napo

Bay de Caráques
Puerto Viejo

R. Ica

Riobamba

Punta Santa Elena
Guayaquil

Puná Is.
Gulf of Guyaquil
Tumbés

Tumipampa
Cuenca

R. Napo

Cape Blanco

R. Piura

Piura
(final site of San Miguel)
Sarrán
Cape Santa Maria
(Puná Pisura)

Chichapoyas

R. Maranón (Amazon)

Saña (Zaña)
Pacasmayo

Cajamarca

Huamachuco

R. Huallaga

R. Ucayali

Chìmu
Trujillo
Viru
Andamarca

Santa Is.

Huaylas
Recuay
Chiquián
Cajatambo

PACIFIC OCEAN

Paramanga
Oyón

Lake Junín
(Chinchaycocha)

R. Ucayali

Tarma

Lima
(Ciudad de los Reyes)
R. Rimax

Jauja

R. Apurimac
R. Mantaro

R. Urubamba

Parcos
Vilcashuamán

Vilcaconga

Cusco

Equator

PACIFIC OCEAN

0   200 miles

0   300 km

15. Pizarro's Route from
Panama to Cusco, 1531–3

killed by Atawallpa's men. From there to Cusco the most direct route was along the main highway through the Conchucos, to the east of the breathtakingly imposing Cordillera Blanca, with its hundreds of glaciers crowned by the astonishing sight of the mountain of Waskaran (rendered as Huascarán in the older literature). The conquistadores opted for the longer and less daunting route along the valley of Huaylas. Not that it was free of challenges: Pedro Sancho de la Hoz left a memorable description of the terrifying suspension bridge they had to cross in order to reach Huaylas. This was at the point where the river Santa turns westwards towards the Pacific, slicing across magnificent gorges of pink rock, and is at its 'most petrifying'. The long span of the bridge made it sag. As they crossed it, 'suspended in mid-air and high above the turbulent waters', it shook with the weight of the men and the approximately seventy timorous and excitable horses, all of which naturally 'made the head of anyone unaccustomed to such things reel'.[4]

The expedition rested for a good week in Huaylas before making its way up the spectacular valley. Pizarro's men were in no hurry to get away from the scenery and spent a good two weeks resting at Recuay with its mineral waters and thermal springs. From there, they took the route that skirts the mountains to the south-east and climbed across the Pativilca and Huaura rivers towards Chiquián, Cajatambo and Oyón. From then on, things grew less straightforward. As far as Chiquián, the conquistadores had benefited from the overwhelming support that the people of the region had given the defeated Waskhar. Cajatambo and Oyón, by contrast, were almost deserted.[5] Soon, news arrived that a concerted resistance was being prepared at the Inca city of Jauja, the muster station for Challcochima's former army. Suspicious, and fearful that the former commander might try to escape to lead the resistance, Pizarro had him put in chains before continuing the march along the desolate pass that led to Bombón on Lake Junín (known then as Chinchaycocha).[6] There Pizarro took a decision that speaks eloquently about the extent of his suspicions. Determined that Jauja needed his immediate attention, he took Almagro, Soto, the best seventy-five horsemen, and twenty foot soldiers in charge of guarding the Sapa Inka and the chained Challcochima, leaving behind the rest of the infantry, artillery and basic equipment. They climbed over the hills and descended into the valley of Tarma. Fearing that its tight surroundings would provide an ideal location for an ambush, they pressed on and were forced to spend the night of 10 October in the open: it snowed and, in their hurry to depart, they had left their tents behind. A deep sense of foreboding hit them the next day as, damp and exhausted, they wearily made their way through Yanamarca, where they saw the corpses of thousands of Inca warriors killed in the recent dynastic wars. It was with a sense of relief as well as trepidation that, beyond the cool mountains, they at last looked down on the fertile Mantaro valley, with Jauja nestling in the distance.[7]

As they approached the city, the conquistadores grew increasingly apprehensive at the sight of forces that had only recently been commanded by their captive, Challcochima. Unusually, we have a good idea of the numbers involved, for they were recorded by the city's *khipu kamayuc*, the official responsible for keeping accurate information on knotted strings (*khipus*). Jauja contained a truly formidable 35,000 soldiers.[8] Just then, however, something unexpected happened. 'The natives,' an eyewitness remembered, had not been well treated by Challcochima's army of occupation, whom they resented as alien, so they 'came out to the road to see the Christians, and they rejoiced greatly about their coming, for they thought that the event marked an end to the slavery imposed upon them by those foreigners.'[9] This encounter encouraged the conquistadores to enter the city.

While the bulk of Challcochima's army was stationed on the far side of the river Mantaro, a large contingent of warriors had been sent into the city with orders to destroy the buildings that were part of the sophisticated system of road networks linked to thousands of storehouses which were replicated regionally.[10] Massively outnumbered, the conquistadores decided that the only option was speed. Attacking and driving the soldiers back to the far bank, they crossed the river on horseback and caught the Inca army by surprise. Many warriors fled into the hills; those who attempted to fight soon discovered that their arrows, sling-stones, javelins, maces, clubs and spears were no match for Spanish horses and swords.[11] As soon as Pizarro realized that the surviving leaders were making their way to Cusco, presumably to alert Quisquis's forces there, he sent eight of his horsemen in pursuit. Catching up with them, the Spanish killed the leaders and took their servants and the women with them captive.[12]

This was the first military confrontation that the conquistadores had faced since their arrival in Peru seventeen months earlier; its outcome filled them with confidence. Victory against allegedly mighty Inca forces had proved even easier than anything that they had encountered in Panama, Mexico, Yucatan, Guatemala or Nicaragua. How could this be? The simple explanation is that, unlike the peoples of Mexico and Central America, the Inca had virtually no experience of invading forces or how to prepare for them. While their recruitment mechanisms were highly sophisticated – based on an ascending decimal structure whereby ten heads of household (*hatun runa*) were placed under the command of an official known as the *chunka kamayuq*, 100 under a *pachaka kuraka*, 1,000 under a *waranka kuraka*, and 10,000 under a *hunu kuraka* – the end result was nothing that we could call a standing army in any sense of the word. It consisted mostly of nodular units of conscripts who had to provide their own weapons and were led by their own lords. The recent dynastic wars had been fought largely by farmers, peasants and herders pressed into duty. Nor did the vast majority of conscripts speak Quechua, the lingua franca of the leaders. This gave Inca armies very limited flexibility on the battlefield: once the fighting had begun, mutual incomprehension made tactical changes almost impossible.[13]

Inca warfare had evolved in tandem with a process of expansion based primarily on diplomacy and reward. The Inca were careful to show magnanimity towards those who submitted and brutality to those who resisted, but the effectiveness of the expansion seems to have owed as much to the perceptions of Inca power – always symbolically associated with homage to the Sun and loyalty to the Sapa Inka – as to any clear technical superiority (they tended to win through sheer weight of numbers).[14] Moreover, war was for the Inca deeply imbued with religious ritualism. It is true that the perception of some Spanish chroniclers, who imagined the Inca to believe that they had been given a divine mandate to spread the religion of Wiracocha to the rest of mankind, seems too much like a projection of their own understanding of religious warfare. Yet there can be little doubt that divination, fasts, feasts and sacrifices accompanied every campaign.[15] The battles themselves reflected these characteristics, with each regional group sporting distinctive vestments. Bernabé Cobo was intrigued when he noticed that Inca warriors wore 'their most attractive ornaments and jewels' while fighting.[16] Even in the midst of battle the Inca carried with them an extraordinary array of religious objects called *wak'a* (normally rendered *huaca* in the older literature). Each Sapa Inka also had his own named battle *wak'a*, and

capturing the *wak'a* of every subjugated region, followed by their transfer to Cusco, was a powerful symbolic act.[17] The practice was a fitting
tribute to a supreme ruler who began as a living warrior only to mature
into a dead deity.[18] And the theatrically belligerent gestures that preceded
the fighting, which often went on for days, were, from a Spanish perspective, anything but effective. As an indigenous chronicler recalled, the
warriors would pretend to intimidate their enemies with well-rehearsed
threats that included looking forward with keen anticipation to drinking
out of their skulls, adorning themselves ritually with necklaces made
from their teeth, playing music with flutes constructed from their bones,
and beating drums created from their flayed skins.[19] It was magnificent
theatre but totally ineffective against a brutally pragmatic enemy.

The swift victory at Jauja allowed Pizarro and his men to take possession of the city, whose inhabitants welcomed them as liberators, on
Sunday 12 October. The slower-moving infantry and equipment arrived
a week later. Following conquistador custom, Pizarro decided to establish a Spanish municipality in Jauja. This was designated as the first
Christian capital of Peru and plans were made for the building of a
church and a town hall. But then came a shock. Thupa Wallpa, the subservient Sapa Inka who was effectively the Spanish passport through
Inca lands, died.

Evidence suggests that the Sapa Inka died of an illness that had afflicted
him since the departure from Cajamarca on 11 August. The rough nights
they were forced to spend on their way to Jauja had probably not helped.
Nevertheless, the Spaniards were suspicious, imagining that Challcochima had poisoned him.[20] Even before the rumours that the great Inca
commander was secretly masterminding the resistance at Jauja, there
were signs that Challcochima had betrayed the trust of the Spaniards
by discrediting Thupa Wallpa's reputation among the Inca warriors,
encouraging them to disobey him while persuading Pizarro that such
disobedience was proof that Thupa Wallpa was a liability – that he was,
in other words, unable to command the respect of the Inca people.[21]

Pizarro soon came up against an even more intractable problem. The
Inca nobles he summoned to decide on a successor could not reach an
agreement. There was a clear rift between those who had supported
Waskhar, who favoured a successor to represent the line of Cusco; and
those who had supported Atawallpa, who favoured one of his sons in

Quito. In the absence of a Sapa Inka, regional leaders with conflicting interests could use a variety of means to reassert some level of autonomy. For example, some Lake Titicaca societies, like the Qolla and the northern Chachapoyas, were renowned for their attempts to reassert their independence whenever they could. To control them, the Inca had traditionally relied on loyal colonists faithful to the Sapa Inka. In his absence, however, the various regions found themselves in freedom to establish alliances with the conquistadores, who often effectively replaced the hegemony of the Sapa Inka. Aware of these rifts, Pizarro secretly encouraged both sides in the succession dispute. Nevertheless, scheming commanders like Challcochima were much better informed, and played a double game of their own. As they continued to pretend to be the faithful allies of the conquistadores, they simultaneously organized a resistance while pretending to Pizarro that the Inca warriors, with whom they themselves were in conflict, were disobeying the Spaniards.[22]

What the situation brought to light, above all else, was the dramatic loss of prestige that the office of the Sapa Inka had suffered. This development also inevitably entailed the decline of the entire ruling class, who depended directly on his overarching authority. While Pizarro and his followers were only dimly aware of these circumstances, they realized that their inability to do anything about the succession crisis made it all the more urgent to get to Cusco as swiftly as possible. Pizarro had been given detailed information of the route by the three messengers who had been sent from Cajamarca to Cusco in search of the treasure earlier that year.[23] He was therefore aware of a particularly challenging stretch of the journey between Parcos and Vilcashuaman: traversed by steep ravines, it could only be crossed on a series of suspension bridges that would be an obvious and easy target for enemy troops of the Atawallpa faction, who wanted to prevent them getting to Cusco. Anxious to secure the bridges, Pizarro sent his best seventy horsemen ahead under the command of Soto. They left Jauja on 24 October, followed four days later by Pizarro and Almagro in command of thirty horsemen, thirty foot soldiers entrusted with guarding their prisoner Challcochima, and the customary support of an unspecified but sizeable number of indigenous auxiliaries. The plan was for the two contingents to rendezvous at Vilcashuaman. The rest of the expedition stayed behind in Jauja, which, acquiring the status of a Spanish municipality, was the de facto Christian capital of Peru.

The route to Cusco from Jauja ran alongside the river Mantaro, which the conquistadores followed until it forked in an abrupt north-ward U-turn between Pucará and Parcos. From then on it cut across imposing mountain ranges, fiercely sliced by rivers plunging their way down towards the Amazon basin. It would have been practically impossible to cross without the stupendous Inca roads that so impressed the Spaniards: 'nowhere in Christendom,' wrote one of Pizarro's brothers, 'shall one ever find roads as magnificent as these'.[24] In the circumstances, however, roads proved a two-edged sword: they had been designed for pedestrians and llamas to cope with the challenging steep slopes of the Andes, but their many narrow tunnels and steep flights of steps could not have been less suited to the horses. Nor was it long before Pizarro found out that the strategy of sending Soto ahead of him to secure the bridges had been anticipated by the enemy troops: they had removed many of the bridges, and burned and sacked most of the towns en route. Progress was therefore painfully slow. Although the scattered skirmishes invariably resulted in Spanish victory, it was obvious that the indigenous warriors were quickly learning; and, as ever, they had the advantage of numbers. On reaching Vilcashuaman, Pizarro learned that Soto had pressed ahead, disregarding their original plan to rendezvous there. Ostensibly, Soto's reasoning was that he was desperate to secure the bridge over the Apurímac river and, even more pressingly, to stop the Atawallpa faction that had managed to flee Jauja from joining forces with Quisquis. Other eyewitnesses gave reasons that did not augur well for the future harmony of the Spanish leaders, pointing to the greed and misplaced pride that tempted Soto to forge ahead in order to 'enjoy the entry into Cusco' in the absence of Pizarro and Almagro.[25]

Yet Pizarro clearly believed Soto. He even split his own contingent once again, sending Almagro ahead to reinforce Soto with thirty horse-men, Pizarro himself following with only ten horsemen and twenty foot soldiers to guard Challcochima. By this time, Soto and his men had crossed the Pampas, Andahuaylas and Abancay rivers without any sign of local antagonism. But on Saturday 8 November, as they approached the massive canyon of the Apurímac, they realized in dismay that they had been too late to stop their enemies burning the bridge. They were, however, fortunate in another way: with early November a notoriously dry time of year, they managed to ford the river with the water only coming up to the necks of their horses. A few weeks later, they would have drowned in the fast torrents. Soto's feat became legendary: a triumph 'not since seen again', according to Philip III's official historian, 'and certainly not in the Apurímac'.[26]

The eastern bank of this mighty river is flanked by a series of steep hillsides. That evening, having forded the river, Soto finally reached the top of the colossal gorge. Both men and horses were exhausted by the gruelling ascent, not to mention the effects of altitude and the intense heat of the day. At the nearby mountain hamlet of Vilcaconga, the conquistadores stopped to rest, the locals giving them food and much-needed maize for the horses. As they ate, Inca warriors launched a surprise attack, first with slingshot, then hand-to-hand combat with their stone clubs, maces and battleaxes. Those few Spaniards who managed to mount the exhausted horses could not raise them even to a trot. For once the Inca had managed to catch the Spaniards in the one form of battle they excelled at, and they made the most of it. When, as night fell, the attackers retreated up the hill, they had left six dead and eleven wounded conquistadores, as well as fourteen wounded horses. That night, providence arrived in the shape of Almagro and his thirty horsemen. When, the next morning, the Inca warriors came down the hill to finish off Soto's badly battered force, they were faced by a fresh and redoubled contingent of horsemen who forced them to retreat up the hill, killing several.[27] The rest of the Inca forces were only spared by the sudden descent of a ground mist, of the kind that often clings to the edges of the Apurímac canyon on cool mornings.[28]

Three days later, Pizarro crossed the Apurímac, joining Soto and Almagro on Thursday 13 November. As soon as he heard news of the battle, Pizarro concluded that Challcochima was behind the resistance and decided to have him executed.[29] That very evening, at a place called Jaquijahuana, the great commander was given the unenviable opportunity of accepting baptism if he preferred to be garrotted rather than burned. Swearing that he had nothing whatsoever to do with the acts of resistance the Spaniards had encountered, Challcochima refused. He was burned alive as a traitor in the central square.[30] It was a rash act of bitter and unjust vengeance on Pizarro's part. If anything, the resistance had been pathetically ineffective: Quisquis, the Atawallpan loyalist in Cusco who had in fact been behind these ambushes, had missed many chances to surprise the Spaniards in countless steep hills and tight valleys where it would have been an easy task to eliminate them. When we consider that, in future years, native troops comprehensively defeated much larger Spanish forces in similar terrain, we can only conclude that the native armies were rendered indecisive by the portentous advance of these seemingly invincible horses and men.

The approach into Cusco from the north-west is unusual. The city nestles on the fold of a valley, keeping it concealed until one is practically above it. The first thing the conquistadores noticed on approaching the capital was a cloud of smoke above the hills. Moving onwards, they found Quisquis's army blocking the road into the city. A fierce battle followed: the Inca managed to drive the Spaniards back, wounding dozens and killing three horses, before the conquistadores escaped into the surrounding hills.[31] The next morning Pizarro assembled his cavalry and the infantry at dawn: all were aware that a potentially decisive confrontation was imminent. As they marched down from the hills towards Cusco, astonishingly, they encountered no resistance. Quisquis's forces had melted away. On Saturday 15 November 'of the year of the birth of Our Lord and Redeemer Jesus Christ MDXXXIII ... at the hour of high mass' Pizarro and his men 'entered the great city of Cusco with no further resistance or battle'.[32]

What had happened? Why had Quisquis allowed the conquistadores such an easy victory? The previous evening, the Inca forces had inflicted unprecedented damage on a Spanish army, even taking the lives of no fewer than three of those mighty animals that had hitherto filled them with awe. Surely, a well-orchestrated, determined resistance would have easily halted the Spanish in their tracks? A likely reason for this apparent timidity was the battle at Vilcaconga. The Inca knew that their enemies had re-emerged the following morning rejuvenated and redoubled. Was this about to happen once again? Quisquis was well informed by his contacts in Quito about the stream of Spanish galleons that were arriving in the ports around Tumbes. Even if he was victorious, such victory would only be temporary; moreover, it might invite terrible Spanish reprisals.

There is, however, another much more likely reason for Quisquis's decision not to engage. Among the indigenous forces that accompanied Pizarro's troops, Quisquis cannot have failed to notice a figure of enormous significance. This was Manqo Inka, a son of Wayna Qhapaq who had escaped Kusi Yupanki's murderous onslaught in Cusco – in which Waskhar's wives and children were tortured and killed on Ata-wallpa's instructions.[33] In what seemed to Pizarro and his men a truly miraculous occurrence, Manqo had turned up on the very evening of Challcochima's burning. He had confirmed Pizarro's fears, claiming that Atawallpa's commander had indeed been sending secret messages to Quisquis with details about various weaknesses of the Spaniards that might be exploited.[34] Manqo also made it clear to the conquistadores that, although he had been 'a constant fugitive' because of the need to stay away from Atawallpa's forces who were 'determined to kill him' – for which reason he was dressed 'to look like a common Indian' – he was in fact 'the greatest and most powerful chief in the land, whom all and sundry wanted as their lord'.[35]

When we remember Quisquis's scrupulous compliance with Ata-wallpa's orders during the visit of Bueno, Moguer and Zárate to Cusco, entrusted as they were with the otherwise scandalous pillage of the Qori-kancha, the most important temple in the city, it is not hard to imagine his sense of insecurity at the reappearance of the most obvious succes-sor as Sapa Inka, and the only figure able to command the loyalty of the majority of the indigenous people in the region. With Manqo now in the power of his Spanish opponents, Quisquis's position was untenable. The conquistadores would only appear to the locals as veritable libera-tors, friendly warriors sent to restore the ruler that they all fervently desired. It is no coincidence that, as soon as the conquistadores entered Cusco, Pizarro abandoned his strategy of playing off the two sides of the civil war against each other. From this point on, he would side unam-biguously with the Cusco faction of Waskhar's royal line. Scarcely a day after their peaceful entry into the city, Pizarro encouraged Manqo to put an army together in order to punish those loyal to Quiquis. Quickly assembling 5,000 fully armed indigenous soldiers, supported by fifty Spanish horsemen under Soto's command, Manqo set off in pursuit of Quisquis's troops. The size of Manqo's army made it clear to Quisquis that any attempt to remain in the region was pointless. His only con-ceivable plan of action was now to prepare his forces for a slow return to their homeland in the distant north.[36]

Towards the end of December 1533, Manqo took to the nearby mountains in order to carry out the customary four-day fast before his formal enthronement as the next Sapa Inka. He then made a triumphal entry into the main square at Cusco, much as Thupa Wallpa had done earlier that year in Cajamarca. But there was much more in Cusco to capture the imagination of the chroniclers; in particular, the many embalmed mummies of Manqo's ancestors that were removed from their tombs 'with great veneration and reverence, and brought into the city, seated on their thrones in order of precedence. There was a litter for each one, with men in its livery to carry it.' Manqo was also carried, alongside the embalmed mummy of his own father, Wayna Qhapaq, 'and the rest similarly in their litters, embalmed and with diadems on their heads'. Alongside each mummy was 'a reliquary or small altar with its insignia, on which were fingernails, hair, teeth, and other things that had been cut from its limbs'. The ceremony was attended by everyone in the city, and they drank so much *chicha*, the fermented ceremonial maize drink, that the two wide drains that emptied into the river 'ran with urine throughout the day . . . as abundantly as a flowing spring'.[37]

The relative circumspection and humour with which the Spaniards observed these rituals suggests that they were not as alien to them as we might be tempted to imagine. The mummies and their bodily insignia found ready parallels in Europe in the cult of the saints and their miracles and relics. Far from disapproving, Pizarro used the occasion to cement his friendship with the people of Cusco by reading the same version of the *Requerimiento* that had been read in Cajamarca after the enthronement of Thupa Wallpa. Again, he made sure that the whole ritual was duly recorded and notarized and, again, with the use of interpreters, he asked the Inca nobles whether they had understood it. When they replied that they had, once again Pizarro made each one of them raise the royal standard three times to the sound of a trumpet blast, after which Manqo Inka and the leading conquistadores drank copiously from a ceremonial golden cup.[38]

With this crucial ritual out of the way, Pizarro felt at ease to plunder the Inca capital with a clear conscience. He went about the long-anticipated task with extreme order and discipline; indeed, extant documents have allowed modern historians to reconstruct the whole process in minute detail. Pizarro instructed his men to gather all the precious objects in a room in the great residence he had chosen for himself, which became known as the Casana. This was the magnificent palace that the great Pachakuti Inka Yupanki had built for himself on the north-western corner of the main square, where the river Huatanay flowed, to mark the great Inca expansion out of Cusco in the mid-fifteenth century. As the treasure was collected, each item was recorded by Diego de Narváez, whom Pizarro had appointed acting treasurer in the absence of Alonso Riquelme, who had stayed behind in Jauja. Since the latter was in possession of the royal seals, Pizarro also authorized the fabrication of new seals bearing the royal arms. Various documents attest to the solemn oaths taken by the officers engaged in the melting down of the precious objects and the weighing of the bullion produced from them. The process began on 15 December, with the melting down of silver of varying quality, which was then redistributed by Pizarro himself, with the approval of Friar Vicente de Valverde, to his followers according to individual merit. The gold was then distributed in mid-March 1534. Since much of the Cusco gold had already been transported to Cajamarca, and then to Spain, there was a limited amount to go around. Silver, on the other hand, was more than four times as plentiful. On the whole, the monetary value of the Cusco melting was marginally higher than that of Cajamarca.[39]

Already an enormously wealthy man, Pizarro was in magnanimous mood. He ensured that the Crown received its 'fifth', which was sent to Charles V along with various precious objects: these included the figures of a woman and a llama, each weighing nearly thirty kilos in eighteen-carat gold. Fair shares were put aside for those who had stayed at Jauja. Pizarro even remembered to include the families and heirs of the six conquistadores killed at Vilcaconga, reserving for himself merely the share due to 'his person, two horses, the interpreters and his page'. Diego de Almagro, on the other hand, was amply compensated for the harsh deal he had been given after his late arrival in Cajamarca, receiving, in total, more than anyone else.[40]

The methodical sack of Cusco also allowed the conquistadores to savour the magnificent splendour of the Inca capital, even as they stripped it bare. The city was described to Charles V as 'the greatest and most splendid of all the cities ever seen in the Indies . . . so beautiful and graced with so many fine buildings that even in Spain it would certainly stand out'.[41] Despite its relatively small size, especially when compared with Tenochtitlan, Cusco had been fastidiously planned, within the constraints of its rugged setting, as a microcosm of Tawantinsuyu. Nestling in a high mountain valley, Cusco was fed by numerous springs channelled through the urban centre before merging into the river Huatanay. Well suited to the cultivation of highland crops, the valley was home to rich pasture lands enhanced by a stunning back-drop of rows of snow-capped peaks running from east to west to the north of the valley.

As is well known, though not necessarily well understood, these natural features had a life and even a consciousness of their own in Inca cosmology. The nearby Wanakawri peak, for instance, was a revered *wak'a* – the sacred resting place of a petrified ancestral deified ruler. It was only one in a myriad of similar landmarks, including springs, boulders, terraces and even fields, which had been given symbolic names: each was associated with a particular history and endowed with sacred powers, on the basis of which a careful modification of the landscape had been carried out to mark key moments in Inca history and mythology. The beauty that the conquistadores admired was therefore only the outward expression of a dynamic social, political and mythological space that acted as the linchpin of the organization of Tawantinsuyu and which, as a result, was the constant focus of political rivalries.[42]

All this was faithfully reflected in the capital itself. Cusco was a 'spatial metaphor' of the Inca world.[43] Its elaborate ceremonial life and the elegant symmetry of its architectural design were inextricably intermingled with the mythologically charged self-perception of Tawantinsuyu. The centre of the city was dominated by two adjoining squares separated by the river Huatanay. The *Aukaypata* ('terrace of repose') was flanked by imposing buildings on three sides and typically hosted open-air ceremonies, often involving the processions of mummies and other *wak'a* of deified rulers and their relatives seated according to rank. The *Kusipata* ('terrace of fortune'), on the other hand, was covered with a layer of sand from the Pacific coast, under which gold and silver objects from the various regions of Tawantinsuyu were buried. Some recent archaeological findings suggest that this organization was consciously replicated in the provinces, especially in the lodgings spread across the road system, known as *tampu* (usually rendered as tambo in the older literature), used by the Inca to exert their authority through elaborate ceremonies linked to ritual hospitality.[44] These rituals probably also replicated the division of the centre of Cusco into the *Hanan* or 'upper' sector, and the *Hurin* or 'lower' one, surrounded by twelve districts: three for each of the four *suyu* (or divisions) of Tawantinsuyu, corresponding to the four main roads that left the city in the direction of Antisuyu to the north-east, Kollasuyu to the south-east, Cuntisuyu to

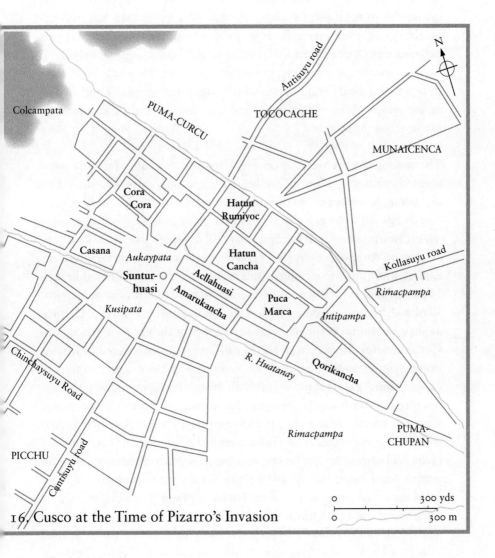

Colcampata

PUMA-CURCU

Antisuyu road

TOCOCACHE

N

MUNAICENCA

Cora Cora

Hatun Rumiyoc

Casana

Aukaypata

Hatun Cancha

Kollasuyu road

Suntur-huasi

Acllahuasi

Rimacpampa

Amarukancha

Puca Marca

Kusipata

Intipampa

Chinchaysuyu Road

R. Huatanay

Qorikancha

Cuntisuyu road

Rimacpampa

PUMA-CHUPAN

PICCHU

0   300 yds

16. Cusco at the Time of Pizarro's Invasion

0   300 m

the south-west and Chinchaysuyu to the north-west.[45] Additionally, a series of sacred agricultural fields surrounding the city were associated with hundreds of carefully located shrines that tied Cusco's organization to the landscape and the Inca cosmos.[46] This was the result of a long process whereby each region set aside lands for a particular ruler, giving rise to royal estates whose designs adapted to their natural surroundings in a manner reflecting the symbiotic relationship that was believed to exist between humanity and the powers of the cosmos. It was this symbiotic relationship that in turn kept the whole of Tawantinuyu in a delicate equilibrium which concentrated power and wealth in the hands of an endogamous and exclusionary ruling oligarchy at the heart of the system.[47]

The conquistadores were, of course, blissfully unaware of a set of complexities that are, after all, only just beginning to be elucidated by archaeological research in our own time, and rather tentatively at that. Nor is it such a surprise that the centripetal pull Cusco had exerted over Tawantinsuyu had become markedly weaker in the wake of the civil wars. Although by early 1534 Pizarro was firmly in control of the capital, and could count on the full support of the Cusco-based branch of the Inca family, now unambiguously associated with the memory of Waskhar, the recent construction of Tumipampa by Wayna Qhapaq along very similar principles was a reminder of the growing fragility of Cusco. During the civil war, the city of Tumipampa, located in what is present-day Ecuador, had emerged as a veritable 'New Cusco' and rival capital, sharing several toponyms with the original imperial city. Indeed, it is no exaggeration to suggest that Tumipampa had effectively replaced Cusco as the focus of political and military power.[48] Rumiñawi, Atawallpa's old commander in Quito, was firmly in control there and had given no indication that he was willing to defer to Pizarro or his new puppet Sapa Inka; that was the main reason why Quisquis was now making his way north to join him. Through Manqo's informers, Pizarro soon found out that Quisquis had been busy recruiting several contingents that had previously been under the command of Challcochima along the bank of the Apurímac. This recruitment posed a clear threat to the recently founded Spanish municipality at Jauja, and Pizarro wasted no time in sending reinforcements: in late January 1534, Diego de Almagro, Hernando de Soto and fifty Spanish horsemen left for Jauja in the company of approximately 20,000 indigenous warriors under the command of Manqo Inka and one of his brothers.[49]

Progress was frustratingly slow. Quisquis had taken good care to destroy any remaining bridges, and the rains had swollen the rivers. The Pampas, in particular, proved impossible to ford. Manqo's men were instructed to construct a new bridge, an impressive feat they completed in three weeks of intense labour. But the three-week delay was an enormous asset to Quisquis, who reached Jauja well in advance of his pursuers. The Spanish commander at Jauja, Alonso Riquelme, was comparatively inexperienced. But he was lucky: days before Quisquis attacked, the distinguished and vastly experienced military commander Gabriel de Rojas arrived in Jauja, along with a stream of reinforcements from the coast. Under his command, horses and steel again proved too much for the Inca forces. Despite the determined ferocity of Quisquis's men – Riquelme himself was knocked off his horse and swept downstream by the strong currents of the Mantaro, yet he survived – the conquistadores managed to push Quisquis's forces into the surrounding hills and even to dislodge them from the Tarma valley, where they had tried to take refuge. A decisive factor in the Spanish victory, too, was the staunch support they received from thousands of local inhabitants: tribes of the region, in particular the ferociously determined Wanka, were more than ready to play a key role in the defeat of the Inca. Their support was immediately reminiscent of the role that the Tlaxcalteca had played in Cortés's capture of Tenochtitlan.[50]

In late March, after the redistribution of the Cusco bullion was complete, Pizarro made his way to Jauja, reaching the city in mid-April. The following month he and Manqo put together an impressive army to drive Quisquis away from the region. By early June it was clear that Quisquis and his demoralized men were gone, making their long way back to Quito, some 1,200 miles away. Pizarro and Manqo marked their victory with a six-week fiesta, with various celebrations that included a great royal hunt organized by Manqo as a surprise treat for his valued ally. No expense was spared, tens of thousands of people taking part in a vast hunt in which some 11,000 head of game were slaughtered.[51]

Meanwhile, news of Pizarro's successes had triggered a fever of ambition among the Spanish population in Panama and the Caribbean. Peru had become so enticing that, as an exasperated group of officials in

Puerto Rico put it to Charles V, 'not a single Spaniard will be left here unless we tie them all down'.[52] Despite royal decrees stipulating that only substantial merchants or married men who were ready to take their wives and children with them should be given permission to go to Peru, every ship that left Panama seemed to be crammed to the hilt with impassioned adventurers determined to make their fortune. Not many of these, however, seemed ready to brave the long and treacherous overland journey to Jauja or Cusco. Pizarro himself had been struck by the absurdity of lines of native porters carrying supplies to the recently founded Spanish cities in the remote mountains. It was doubtless this inaccessibility, as well as his own personal preferences, that influenced Pizarro's decision to move his capital to the coast, to a climate and altitude more congenial to the immigrants. In late November 1534 he proposed the relocation to the citizens of Jauja. The following month he chose a site at the mouth of the river Rimac, 150 miles west of Jauja; shortly afterwards, on 5 January 1535, the eve of the Epiphany, the city of Lima was formally founded. Pizarro named it 'Ciudad de los Reyes' (City of the Kings) after the Three Wise Men, or Magi, whose solemnity was being celebrated across the Christian world.[53]

15

Manqo Inka

In late February 1534, soon after Riquelme's triumph against Quisquis's forces at Jauja, Gabriel de Rojas, the experienced commander who had masterminded the victory, hurried down to Cusco with news from the north. He was itching to tell Pizarro that the flow of Spanish immigrants was staying in the north because Tumipampa and Quito were now widely believed to exceed Cusco in wealth. Indeed, the rumour that Atawallpa had sent his best treasures to Tumipampa had caused a veritable fever throughout Central America and the Caribbean. Even one of the most celebrated of conquistadores, Cortés's old friend, the impetuous Pedro de Alvarado, was making his way to the north of Peru in twelve ships carrying an enormous force of 500 Spaniards, more than 4,000 indigenous Guatemalans, and over 100 horses. Rojas was also aware that as soon as Sebastián de Benalcázar – who had set up his headquarters in the Pacific port of San Miguel, as Pizarro had renamed Piura – had got wind of the news, he had set off for Tumipampa with a large force. Then, on his way to Cusco, Rojas came across Almagro, who immediately, deeming the situation too urgent to await Pizarro's instructions, set off for the north himself. In short, just as the Sapa Inka was preparing to entertain Pizarro so extravagantly at Jauja, there were three different Spanish operations heading for the northern region of Chinchaysuyu.[1]

Almagro moved fast. He reached the northern coast in early April and continued north towards Quito. On his way he soon became aware that Rumiñawi – Atawallpa's old commander in the region – had mounted a ferocious resistance, so he retreated to San Miguel to seek reinforcements.[2] Circumstances in the north had changed radically. The conquistadores no longer had any hostages in their power that might give the indigenous forces pause in their resistance; nor did they

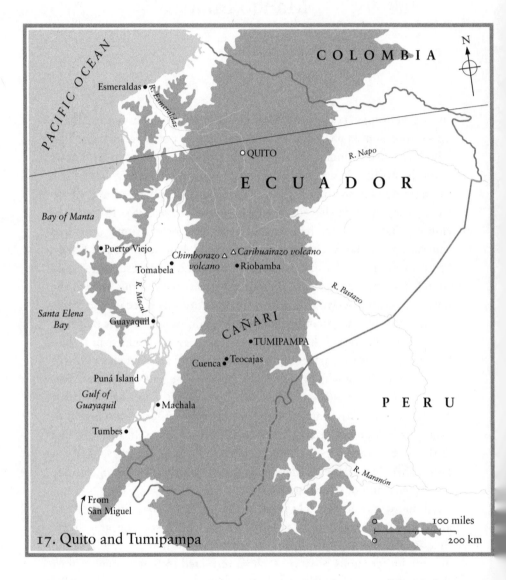

17. Quito and Tumipampa

attract Inca support in the way they had done in the south. All the same, Benalcázar had good reasons for optimism on his arrival at Tumipampa. Not only was he able to confirm that the city did indeed rival Cusco in splendour, but there were also clear signs that the local Cañari people had fresh and bitter memories of the violence with which the Inca had established themselves in the region and of the brutally cruel punishments inflicted on the Cañari for backing the Waskhar faction in the civil war.[3] They therefore seemed more than willing to offer their support to the Spaniards.[4]

The Cañari did not need to wait long to vent their anger on their Inca overlords. Rumiñawi was not far away. He was preparing his army for a pitched battle on the site of the remote *tampu* of Teocajas, situated on the highest point of the pass separating the Pacific watershed from Riobamba. It was a desolate spot, 'a land of tough, slippery ichu grass, mountain tarns, mossy swamps and lichen-covered boulders soaked by mists and rain'.[5] The terrain had served Rumiñawi very well in the past – but this time he did not know his enemies. Despite the unfamiliar surroundings and the inevitable effects of high altitude, the battlefield left ample room for manoeuvring horses. It was early May. Benalcázar led a surprise attack on Rumiñawi and the landscape was soon littered with Inca corpses.[6] As the conquistadores retreated, confident after inflicting such devastating damage, Rumiñawi led a counter-attack. Once more the Spaniards prevailed, but the horses were beginning to tire, and their attempt to retreat was met by yet another fierce attack that took the lives of several Spaniards and at least five horses. Nightfall came as a welcome relief. The next morning, refreshed and reorganized, the Spanish launched another cavalry assault on the Inca lines, driving them into the mountains.[7] Still the fighting continued for several months: it was more or less continuous from Riobamba to Quito.

When, at long last, Benalcázar reached Quito in early December, he found the city abandoned, stripped of everything from food to treasure, and the storehouses and the palaces burned to the ground, torched by Rumiñawi's men before they retreated.[8] Undeterred, Benalcázar dispatched Rui Díaz with sixty horsemen in pursuit of Rumiñawi. Atawallpa's old commander was prepared: with the support of local chieftains he ambushed the Spaniards in the middle of the night, thus preventing them from mounting their horses. The ensuing hand-to-hand combat lasted all night. At dawn a temporary respite allowed the Spaniards to bring out the horses with which they easily forced Rumiñawi's men to flee. The next morning, perhaps in defiance of Rumiñawi's wishes, the local chieftains came to surrender. They also formally abandoned their camp with its many women, and its cache of gold and silver, to the lustful whims of Benalcázar's men.[9] Meanwhile, Almagro had been making slow progress with the men he had managed to recruit in San Miguel. By the time he reached Quito there was little to do other than reprimand Benalcázar for failing to await orders from Pizarro. In response, Benalcázar reassured Almagro that he had acted in good faith and in the loyal interests of both men.[10] The one puzzling thing was that the man who had forced this otherwise rash initiative in the first place was nowhere to be found.

Alvarado had made an unwise choice of route. Landing to the north of Puná island on 25 February, he had taken a route via present-day Guayaquil, moving northwards along the river Macul towards Tomabela. From there the route to Quito follows the highest pass in the region, between the two mighty volcanoes of Chimorazo and Carihuairazo. This was a tall order in the best of circumstances, but the journey along the Macul had already taken a heavy toll on Alvarado's men, with its humid heat, insects and disease: even their steel swords had rusted. But the worst was yet to come. The famished and sickly expedition ran into snowstorms. Nearly a hundred Spaniards, countless Guatemalans, and most of the horses froze to death. When Alvarado and his surviving companions finally reached the highland Inca road, they encountered the tracks of the horses left by Almagro and Benalcázar, who had ridden into Quito some days earlier.[11]

Alvarado now had little choice but to follow these tracks. Despite the heavy losses he had endured, he could still count on a good number of crossbowmen and arquebusiers. He was, nonetheless, perfectly aware that control of Quito gave his rivals the upper hand. Almagro, indeed, took full advantage of the situation, making crafty use of his recently acquired wealth. Riding out to meet Alvarado along the road, he easily convinced him of the futility of a confrontation. Then he offered Alvarado a way out: he would buy his equipment and ships at a good price if he agreed to go back to Guatemala. A relieved Alvarado leapt at Almagro's offer. After founding a Spanish municipality in Quito, which they named San Francisco de Quito, the newly reconciled conquistadores moved down to the coast, leaving Benalcázar in control of Quito with a well-reinforced garrison.[12]

This is hardly what Quisquis and his men were expecting when they eventually made it back to their homeland. After a two-year absence they could think of little else than returning to their homes. To find Chinchaysuyu controlled by conquistadores sapped their morale. It is true that the experience they had acquired in Kollasuyu about avoiding cavalry charges allowed them to kill three horses, wound a further twenty, and behead no fewer than fourteen Spaniards, but on their first encounter with Benalcázar, early in 1535, they suffered a heavy defeat.[13] When his men asked him to seek peace with the Spaniards, Quisquis refused, accusing them of cowardice. The result was an open rebellion, which led to his killing at the hands of his own followers, armed with battleaxes and clubs.[14] The news came as a devastating shock to Rumiñawi, who was facing similar opposition among his own subordinates. Attempting to hide, he was recognized by a spy, captured by Spanish forces and brought to Quito, where he was executed in the main square.[15] Thus, by the summer of 1535, the Spaniards were in undisputed control of Atawallpa's former powerbase in the north.

The news that Almagro was sailing down the Pacific coast with his newly acquired fleet reached Pizarro in Lima, where he was still busy with the foundation of the city. He seemed genuinely pleased with the way in which his increasingly powerful partner had dealt with Alvarado. Accordingly, he suggested that Almagro move to Cusco and replace Hernando de Soto as governor of the Inca capital. Almagro did not hesitate. On his way to Cusco, however, he received some intriguing news. Pizarro's brother, Hernando, who had clearly played his cards very ably at Charles V's court in Castile, was sailing back with the emperor's agreement to award Pizarro the north and Almagro the south of Tawantinsuyu. The obvious question was: where did Cusco lie? Almagro's opinion was predictable: since the north was graced with Tumipampa and Quito, Cusco was unquestionably in the south. This was also the majority view among his followers, many of whom had originally come with Alvarado before transferring their loyalties to Almagro, and who were anxious to amass wealth as soon as possible.

When Almagro arrived in Cusco, the atmosphere was extremely tense, and grew worse when Soto decided to take Almagro's side. Two other Pizarro brothers, Juan and Gonzalo, were enraged, threatening Almagro and Soto with an armed opposition. By mid-March 1535 the situation was so unstable that Francisco Pizarro needed to rush from Lima to try to calm things down. Arriving in Cusco in late May, he managed to convince Almagro, with enticing tales of further treasure and riches, to lead an expedition to Chile. This plan seemed to capture the chivalric imagination of Almagro's disgruntled followers and tensions were temporarily diffused.[16]

Almagro set off for Chile in early July with nearly 600 Spaniards and 12,000 Inca allies supplied by Manqo, under the leadership of one of the Sapa Inka's own brothers, Paullu Tupaq, and the powerful priest Willaq Umu, a distinguished relative of Wayna Qhapaq. The expedition was not an edifying experience, by any standards. The Spaniards treated their Inca subordinates with unspeakable cruelty.[17] Not surprisingly, the latter began to put up a resistance, organizing ambushes and killing Spaniards whenever they could. Then, as the high passes leading into Chile began to take their toll on the Spaniards, the majority of their indigenous followers defected in disgust: by late October only Paullu and his followers remained on the expedition. Even Willaq Umu was making his way back to Cusco, leaving the Spaniards – in one chronicler's words – with no one 'even to fetch them a jar of water'.[18]

Back in Cusco, Willaq Umu's bitter complaints about the gratuitous cruelty of Almagro's men coincided with what Manqo had been hearing from various corners of Tawantinsuyu. He began to wonder whether Quisquis and Rumiñawi had not been right in their stubborn resistance to the intruders. This certainly seems to have been the view of Manqo's sole surviving military commander, Tisoq Yupanki, who told the Sapa Inka that, for the sake of their wives and children, whom the Spaniards constantly dishonoured, it would be better to die fighting for their liberty than to resign themselves to such a humiliating fate.[19] Persuaded by these arguments, Manqo summoned a clandestine meeting with the leaders of Kollasuyu and informed them of his decision to rebel. He himself then escaped from Cusco in the middle of the night, but a spy informed the Pizarro brothers, who immediately set out in pursuit. By early November they had successfully tracked the Sapa Inka down, leading him back to Cusco 'with a chain around his neck and irons on his feet.'[20] In the meantime, Tisoq Yupanki and some of the Kollasuyu leaders had made their way to the highlands north of Jauja, where the natives of Tarma and Bombón soon rebelled; other leaders did the same in various regions of Kollasuyu. Reports of the deaths of as many as thirty Spaniards soon began to arrive in Cusco, triggering a succession of cruel punitive expeditions led by the Pizarro brothers and their indigenous allies.[21]

This was the critical situation that greeted Hernando Pizarro in Cusco on his return from Spain in January 1536. The horror with which the news of Atawallpa's execution had been received in Spain haunted him as he discovered that the treatment his brothers had given the Sapa Inka would have appalled Charles V. Indeed, Hernando himself had come with specific instructions from the emperor, to ensure that Manqo was treated with the deference due to a legitimate sovereign. Accordingly, Hernando wasted no time in giving the young Sapa Inka every possible sign of friendship and respect. It was, alas, too late. Although Manqo showed signs of gratitude towards Hernando, he also followed the advice of Tisoq Yupanki and Willaq Umu, and came up with a plan. Telling Hernando that he needed to accompany Willaq Umu to the Yucay valley, where some important religious ceremonies needed to be performed, Manqo tempted him with an offer: if Hernando let him make the trip, he would bring him back a lifesize statue of his father, Wayna Qhapaq, made of solid gold. Few in Cusco believed Manqo's ruse, but Hernando, perhaps blinded by cupidity, was adamant that the Sapa Inka could be trusted. Then, on Holy Saturday 1536, the news reached Hernando that Manqo was indeed in the middle of a carefully concerted operation involving leaders from all four corners of Tawantinsuyu to drive the Spaniards out of Cusco. Hernando had no choice but to accept he had been fooled.[22]

Soon, indigenous troops surrounded Cusco in their tens of thousands. By night, their fires seemed to an eyewitness to resemble 'a very clear sky, filled with stars'.[23] Manqo and his commanders, who had learned valuable lessons from their previous encounters with Spanish horsemen, wisely chose to stay on the slopes of the surrounding hills. Unable to seize the initiative in such circumstances, the conquistadores, with their ineffective eighty horses, could only watch the swelling numbers of natives with dread. Manqo waited patiently until the sheer weight of numbers was overwhelmingly in his favour. Then, on Saturday 6 May, he launched a concerted attack on Cusco, in which the Inca combined the power of their slings with an innovative technique that was as unexpected as it was devastating: all the stones had been made red-hot in the campfires. Soon the thatched roofs of the city caught fire. The Spaniards almost suffocated in the dense smoke, managing to survive by huddling on the one side of the main square that had no houses.[24] Although Manqo's advance out of the hills and on to open ground technically brought the Spanish horses into play, he had again resourcefully anticipated the Spanish tactics with a new device: Inca warriors tied three stones to the ends of tight ropes connected to dried llama tendons, which, when thrown, twirled and tangled themselves around the legs of the horses, bringing most of them down.[25]

Realizing that they were doomed if they remained in the city, the Spaniards concentrated all their efforts on capturing the fortress of Saqsaywaman, situated on the northern outskirts. It was a risky operation, for the Inca had mined the approach to the fortress with lethal pits that had to be laboriously filled while the horsemen stood guard, dangerously exposed to attacks from the hillside. In a clever feint, the horsemen rode fast north-west, making their pursuers assume that they were fleeing and tempting them to cut across country to burn the suspension bridge on the Apurímac. Just then, the Spaniards doubled back to the right, approaching the fortress from the one angle that was free of obstacles.[26] The defenders of the fortress greeted them with a virulent rain of javelins and slingshots. Juan Pizarro, who had been struck on the jaw the previous day and was unable to wear a helmet because of the swelling, was dealt a mortal blow on the head. While the death of this feared enemy boosted Inca morale, the Spaniards now applied the well-tested methods of siege warfare that had been so effective in Spain during the campaigns against Granada. By night they climbed the high fortress walls with scaling ladders. By the end of May, after a few days of fierce fighting, they were in complete control of the fortress. This gave them a solid base from which to reassert their control of the old Inca capital.

Painfully aware that his situation was untenable, Manqo Inka withdrew to the relative safety of Ullantaytampu, a ceremonial centre some forty-five miles north-west of Cusco. Located at the point where the Yucay valley narrows as the Urubamba river descends towards the Amazon basin, the walled complex commanded the entrances of the valleys leading over the Panticalla Pass and down into the eastern jungles, thus serving as a safe stronghold from where to continue a determined resistance against the conquistadores.[27]

Back in Lima, Francisco Pizarro began to arrange for relief expeditions as soon as he heard about Manqo's revolt. A contingent was sent to Jauja under Francisco Mogrovejo de Quiñones, and another one to Huamanga under Gonzalo de Tapia. Against them the Inca had the clear advantage of the landscape, and they made full use of it. They adopted a lethal strategy of waiting for the conquistadores to enter the deep narrow gorges that abound in the central Andes. Blocking both ends, they then bombarded the trapped Spanish forces with heavy boulders from the hillsides. Hundreds of Spaniards were killed, forcing Pizarro to send for reinforcements to Panama and Nicaragua. As time passed, Spaniards in Lima began to think their situation was hopeless, even asking themselves how soon they would be forced to abandon Peru altogether.[28] Pizarro poured out his frustrations in a letter to Pedro de Alvarado, now back in Guatemala, telling him that the losses he had incurred had caused him such deep sorrow that he wanted to die.[29] None of this was lost on Manqo, whose commanders made several attempts to invade Lima itself in the autumn of 1536. This was symptomatic of overconfidence: Lima's location on a flat open plain was undoubtedly advantageous to the Spaniards. It is true that Manqo's commanders had acquired Spanish weapons and were already deploying them to great effect, but the Spaniards held on and were gradually reinforced by large numbers of enthusiastic compatriots who flooded into Lima from Central America, the Caribbean and even Spain.[30] The tide had turned by early November 1536, so much so that Pizarro dispatched a sizeable expedition to Cusco under the command of Alonso de Alvarado, a nephew of the famous conquistador. The latter left Lima on 8 November 1536 with 350 followers, including over a hundred horsemen and forty crossbowmen. As the Spaniards made their way to Jauja, showing no mercy towards any resistance they encountered, they were reassured that the Wanka people of the region north of Jauja continued to harbour deep resentments against Inca expansionism. They had therefore been very reluctant to support Manqo's rebellion and were more than willing to side with the Spaniards.[31]

As the young Alvarado began his advance into Cusco in the early days of 1537, Almagro's frustrated expedition was also making its way back from Chile to the old Inca capital. Almagro, adamant that Cusco remained unquestionably in the area of Tawantinsuyu allotted to him by Charles V, was determined to make up for his failure to find any

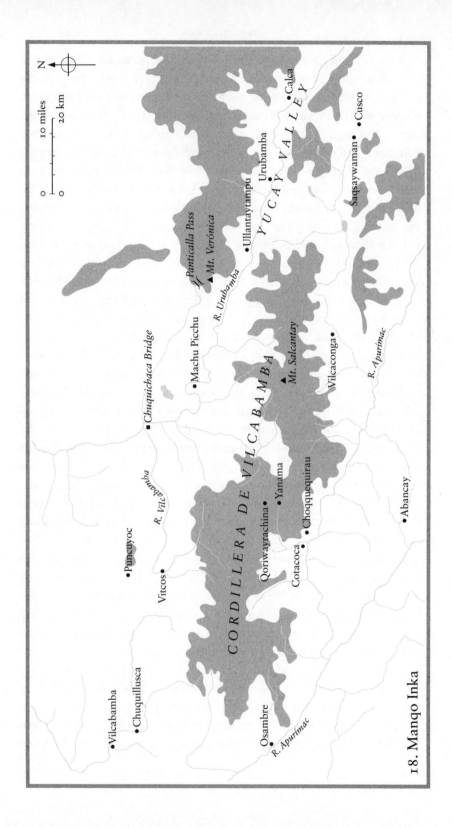

18. Manqo Inka

21. A romanticized portrait of Nezahualpilli, ruler of Tetzcoco (see p. 175).

22. Sketch of Hernán Cortés by Christoph Weiditz (see p. 240).

23. Portrait of the indefatigable 'Defender of the Indians', Friar Bartolomé de Las Casas.

24. Monte Albán, a jewel of Zapotec architecture (see p. 231).

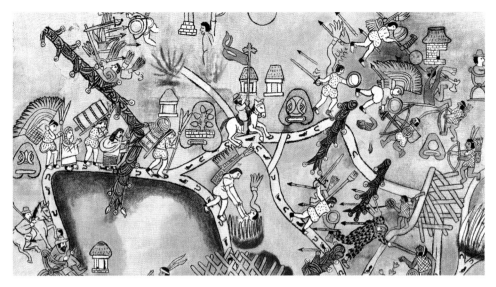

25. *Lienzo de Quauhquechollan* showing the advance of Spaniards and Nahuas as equal partners in the conquest of Guatemala (see pp. 234–5).

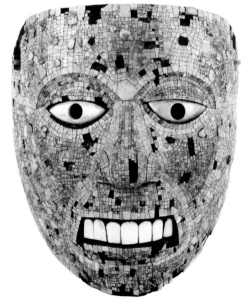

26. Mixtec turquoise mosaic mask (see p. 232).

27. Feathered depiction of the Mass of St Gregory, a window into the astonishingly free 'sacramental' world encouraged by the mendicant friars (see p. 223).

28. A Mixtec-style angel from the Dominican convent of SS Peter and Paul in Teposcolula, Oaxaca, much more reminiscent of the imposing Byzantine tetramorphs with their clear references to angels in Old Testament descriptions of the Temple of Jerusalem than to the chubby cherubs that would soon populate European Christian art (see pp. 210–11).

29. Cortés greets Friar Martín de Valencia, leader of 'The Twelve', in the company of Friar Bartolomé de Olmedo and a group of conquistadores. The discarded episcopal mitres point to Cortés's express request to Charles V to send worthy mendicant friars, especially Franciscans, who would not waste the goods of the Church 'in pompous ceremonies and other vices' (see p. 201).

30. Bridge crossing the colossal Apurímac gorge. After the Incas burned the bridge, the conquistadores were left with no option but to cross the Apurímac in a feat that became legendary (see p. 282–3).

31. Inca road near Cusco, clearly not designed for horses (see p. 282).

32. Inca ceremonial vessel (*above*) for pouring libations.

33. One of the Inca figures (*left*) of gold-silver alloy that survived Pizarro's melting frenzy.

34. Diego Velázquez's portrait of Juan de Pareja, a man who knew his dignity because he also knew it was a gift (see p. 354).

riches in Chile. The last thing he needed was any kind of friction with the Sapa Inka. As soon as he heard about the latter's rebellion and siege of Cusco, therefore, he began to communicate with him, making many conciliatory gestures.[32] Before approaching Cusco itself, Almagro tried to reach the Sapa Inka in Ullantaytampu, but was prevented by the ferocious Inca resistance mounted at Calca by the young commander Paukar. Almagro managed to escape with some difficulty and was forced to take refuge in Cusco, entering the city on 18 April. His enemies there were no longer the Inca, but Hernando and Gonzalo Pizarro, the brothers of his old partner, whom he soon put under arrest. After all, if Cusco was in the south, then no Pizarro should have any business there. No sooner had he imprisoned the brothers, however, than he needed to confront Francisco Pizarro's relief army, now making its way down from Jauja under Alvarado. Almagro was fortunate to have the support of Rodrigo Orgóñez, a veteran of the battle of Pavia that had led to the capture of the King of France, Francis I, in 1525, and a military strategist of genius. Orgóñez planned a night attack on Alvarado's forces and won an easy victory at Abancay on 12 July, not only routing Alvarado but also winning the support of a substantial proportion of his troops, rather like Cortés had done with Narváez.[33]

Orgóñez returned to Cusco in high spirits and tried to sell a tempting anti-Pizarro plan to Almagro: he urged him to order the execution of Hernando and Gonzalo before leading a campaign against Lima to capture Francisco, thereby leaving the whole of Tawantinsuyu in their hands. Almagro opted for caution. He feared that committing his forces to Lima would allow Manqo Inka to launch another attack on Cusco. Since the Sapa Inka had not shown any sign of being even remotely tempted by Almagro's offers of peace, the conquistador concluded that Orgóñez should first eliminate Manqo. Once this threat was removed, then they could think about Lima. Reluctantly, but persuaded that Almagro really was determined to launch an attack on his old partner as soon as Manqo was defeated, Orgóñez set off from Cusco a few days after his triumph at Abancay in pursuit of the Sapa Inka. He was unable to capture Manqo, but he did force him to flee his headquarters in Ullantaytampu by way of the inhospitable tropical swamps of the Urubamba to the secluded town of Vitcos in the Vilcabamba valley.[34]

With Manqo now an implacable enemy, Almagro decided that the Sapa Inka's half-brother, Paullu Tupaq, should take his place. Accordingly, he organized Paullu's formal enthronement to take place in Cusco at the end of July, to the general approval of the indigenous peoples of all the surrounding areas. Although Paullu had been a staunch supporter of Manqo, he had stayed loyal to Almagro throughout the Chilean expedition, sticking with him even when he could easily, as some witnesses attested, have finished him off.[35] On their return to Cusco, Paullu had been Almagro's main source of intelligence: he had reported on the advance of the young Alvarado's forces, and had made thousands of Inca warriors available to Almagro in the run-up to the battle of Abancay.[36]

This otherwise puzzling behaviour responded to a neat though complex logic. The arrival of the conquistadores in the wake of the bitter confrontation between Atawallpa and Waskhar had brought to light fundamental weaknesses that had irreparably upset the delicate balance of power in Tawantinsuyu: its use of the ascending decimal structure described in the previous chapter[37] had a clear theoretical efficiency, but this was not necessarily reflected in practice. Each of the four quarters (*suyu*) of Tawantinsuyu was administered by a great lord (*apu*), a title that could sometimes be conferred also on army commanders. But each of the four *suyu* was also made up of districts (*wamani*) that corresponded roughly to pre-Inca tribal jurisdictions. These *wamani* were controlled by provincial governors, *tokrikoq*, whose powers largely involved the collection of tribute and the choosing of candidates for military service – meaning that they inevitably came into conflict with the tribal chiefs of their provinces, who had other priorities. The demands of the central Inca court and government, in other words, constantly came up against local interests.

Now all these tensions had increased. After the enthronement of Manqo Inka, the *tokrikoq* attempted to reassert central authority in their various districts but were faced with the opposition of local tribal chiefs who resented Inca impositions and wanted to revitalize the tribal forms of association, always related to particular deities and *wak'a*. In the years of expansion, the Inca had cemented this system with the use of colonists (*mitmaqkuna* – the plural form of *mitmaq*) who formed an Inca nucleus of loyalty that in some regions amounted to as much as a third of the population. During the civil war, however, the *mitmaqkuna* developed much closer ties with the regions. This was even more evident among the personal servants of Inca nobles (*yanakuna* – the plural form of *yana*), who attached themselves to the Spaniards as readily as they had previously done to the Inca, and whom the Spaniards in turn rewarded by continuing their exemption from tribute and allowing them ample opportunities for plunder.[38]

Manqo understood the situation only too well. Barely five months after his rebellion he had fallen foul of these tensions and himself become a fugitive. By contrast, Almagro saw no immediate cause for concern: not only had Paullu continued to support him and pass on vital information, but he was also now in undisputed control of Cusco, with more than 800 Spaniards at his disposal and the two Pizarro brothers as useful trump cards to use against his former partner in Lima. Under the circumstances, Francisco Pizarro had little choice but to seek a compromise. He sent his trusted lawyer Gaspar de Espinosa to Cusco with the task of negotiating a temporary agreement with Almagro regarding a boundary between the two regions of Tawantinsuyu allotted to them by Charles V. At the same time Espinosa was to persuade Hernando and Gonzalo to give Almagro every impression of wanting a peaceful solution to their differences and eschewing any thought of revenge. Pizarro had made a wise choice of envoy: Espinosa was not only well honed in legal arguments but also a persuasive rhetorician. Although he met stubborn intransigence on both sides, in the course of a few weeks he prudently drove his point home. What would a confrontation achieve? Did they not know that Rome had never been threatened as perilously by powerful enemies such as Pyrrhus and Hannibal as by its own citizens? Was it not clear to them that seven centuries of warfare had been less harmful to Rome than the comparatively petty confrontations of Sulla and Marius, or Pompey and Caesar? Would they want posterity to remember them, not as the great heroes that they were, but as the men who began a shameful war of Spaniards against Spaniards?[39]

Almagro, now sixty-three and feeling increasingly frail, was persuaded. Orgóñez, on the other hand, could not have been more appalled. He is said to have grabbed his beard with his left hand and, raising his head, to have made a gesture with his right hand as if to cut his own throat while lamenting that his loyalty to Almagro would now cost him his life.[40] His words would soon prove prophetic: no sooner had the Pizarro brothers been released than the petty confrontation that Espinosa had tried to avoid became inevitable. The odds were now clearly against Almagro. Although he was firmly in control of Cusco and in charge of a substantial army, he was landlocked. The Pizarros, by contrast, continued to benefit from a steady flow of immigrants and reinforcements. When, on 26 April 1538, the two armies confronted each other at Las Salinas in the outskirts of Cusco, Almagro's 500 men paled next to Hernando Pizarro's 900 much better equipped troops. Orgóñez fought bravely but was soon captured and beheaded. Realizing the inevitable, Almagro escaped to the relative safety of the fortress of Saqsaywaman. Then, to Almagro's deep chagrin, Paullu opportunistically switched sides and ordered his men to attack his partner's troops. The battle of Las Salinas, as it came to be known, was a complete rout. Cusco was in Pizarro's hands once again.[41]

When, shortly afterwards, Almagro decided to give himself up, Hernando Pizarro was in no mood for magnanimity. He imprisoned his rival in the very same place that he had been held by Almagro the year before. There he kept him guessing for more than two months before cruelly announcing that the death sentence had been passed against him. Almagro was aghast. Had he forgotten, he asked Hernando, how graciously he had spared his life against the advice of most of his advisors? On 8 July, to the profound consternation of most of the Spaniards in Peru, Hernando Pizarro ignored Almagro's further pleas for mercy and, after a rushed judicial condemnation, had the sixty-three-year-old conquistador garrotted in his cell. Pedro Cieza de León, clearly with the benefit of hindsight, later claimed that Almagro had explained to the mayor of Cusco and his executioner that Peru belonged to the king, and that even if they thought he was too far away or that he did not even exist, they had better believe that there is a God. Thus, he continued, ended the life of a man of a background so humble and obscure that 'it could be said of him that in his very person his lineage began and ended'.[42]

With Almagro out of the picture, Manqo was back in the game. Constantly on the run, he had been badly shaken by the ease with which Orgóñez had driven him out of Ullantaytampu, and had even for a while flirted with the idea of accepting an invitation from the chiefs of the Chachapoyas, recently conquered by the Inca but still deeply resentful of them, to travel 1,300 miles north and take refuge at Kuélap, a superbly defended fortress on a ridge overlooking the Utcubamba valley.[43] As soon as Manqo heard about the growing divisions on the Spanish side, however, he settled for the relative security of Vilcabamba's forested crags rather than risk the long journey and the possible duplicity of the Chachapoyas. The news of Almagro's death emboldened him to raise a second rebellion: almost immediately his forces began to terrorize any Spaniards they could capture by taking them back to Vitcos and subjecting them to horrendous torture.[44] Manqo could even afford to show off. When, for instance, Francisco Pizarro dispatched a large contingent to deal with him in autumn 1538, Manqo was well prepared. He cut the water supply that fed the steep path to his headquarters; then, as the exhausted and thirsty Spaniards approached, he ambushed them on horseback in the company of three other chiefs of royal blood, also mounted on Spanish horses they had captured and riding with surprising agility while wielding steel lances. Twenty-four Spaniards were killed. The rest fled in horror.[45]

Manqo was on a roll. Heading to Jauja, he punished the Wanka tribesmen who had refused to join his rebellion, preferring to side with the conquistadores: 'Now, get your friends to help you!' Manqo apparently told them. When they did, Manqo inflicted a further defeat on a large contingent of Spaniards and Wanka allies at Yuramayo, to the east of Jauja, before desecrating Wari Willka, the Wanka's most important shrine, executing its priests and plunging its stone idol into a deep river, rather than following the old convention of taking it hostage as a means of ensuring subjection. It was an unprecedented act of humiliation.[46]

Further south, Manqo's commanders were equally active. The indomitable Willaq Umu, ensconced in the mountains to the south of Cusco, was busy inciting the natives to rebel. But in the area of the Tiwanaku, around Lake Titicaca, things were not so straightforward for Manqo. The region had been brought under Inca control only a few decades before the arrival of the Spaniards. Inca domination had been violently opposed by the surrounding tribes of the region, especially the Lupaqa and the Qolla. As Manqo's commanders persuaded the Lupaqa to attack the Qolla as a punishment for their collaboration with the Spaniards, the Qolla begged the Spaniards for help. Hernando Pizarro set off at once with a large force that included his young brother Gonzalo, and his new ally, Paullu, still rather ignobly claiming to be the Sapa Inka. They reached the Desaguadero river, where the Lupaqa were expecting them. They had removed the bridge, forcing the Spaniards to cross the river on a raft made of balsa-wood logs. As the first crossing was attempted, the Lupaqa unleashed a barrage of stone and arrow fire on the exposed Spaniards on the raft; when a group of eight horsemen attempted to come to their aid, they were swept away by the river. After this traumatic experience two larger rafts were successfully taken across the river by the Pizarro brothers, with Hernando in charge of forty men and Gonzalo of several horses. Once on the other side, as soon as the Spaniards could mount their horses, the fate of the Lupaqa was sealed. Town after town fell to the Spaniards with such ease that Hernando soon felt free to return to Cusco to appease his older brother who had recently arrived in the old Inca capital, still appalled by the execution of his admittedly difficult former partner, Almagro.[47]

Meanwhile, Gonzalo began a slow advance into the mild and fertile valley of Cochabamba, where Manqo had sent his uncle Tisoq, the most able survivor of Wayna Qhapaq's generals, to organize a resistance. Tisoq had had ample opportunity to observe the Spaniards in action and was quick to demonstrate how much he had learned. As Gonzalo's force of seventy Spaniards and thousands of Inca allies under Paullu's command moved into the valley, they found it surrounded and the passes blocked. When, the following morning, Gonzalo gave the order to attack, his men were heavily outnumbered and unable to take advantage of their horses: Tisoq's forces had surrounded their camp with 'an innumerable number of heavy poles' that impeded their mobility.[48] It was here that Paullu proved his generalship, keeping control of his men and preventing them from defecting. His organization allowed the Spanish and their allies to demolish enough barricades to give a clear passage for the horsemen, whose appearance achieved the predictable result. The battle ended with a brutal chase that left several hundred of Tisoq's men dead.[49] While Tisoq still had plenty of reinforcements, Hernando and Francisco Pizarro – the latter fresh from his expedition to found the city of Huamanga, between Jauja and Vilcas, specifically to protect communications between Lima and Cusco – sent a constant stream of troops to bolster Gonzalo's men until, after several weeks of relentless fighting, the tide began to turn in their favour. One after another, the native chiefs of the whole region expressed their willingness to pay homage to the Holy Roman Emperor. Finally, even Tisoq, recognizing the inevitable, decided to join them. When Gonzalo's triumphant troops marched back into Cusco on the feast of St Joseph, 19 March 1539, the Dominican friar Vicente de Valverde, now bishop of the city, candidly described Paullu and Tisoq as 'quite at peace with one another and firmly in our friendship'.[50]

These developments were observed with a combination of disgust and trepidation by the resilient Willaq Umu. Resolutely loyal to Manqo, he realized his own resistance was now doomed, but he was still in control of the Cuntisuyu, whose landscape was his greatest ally. As Bishop Valverde explained to Charles V, native leaders 'shall never lack wings to give flight to their evil thoughts, especially because the landscape itself furnishes them with countless subterfuges for their purposes, its very ruggedness turning it into a veritable fortress'.[51] Nor was Willaq Umu alone in his determination. To the north, the entire region stretching from Jauja to Huánuco remained unsubdued. It had even managed to survive the legendary brutality of Francisco de Chaves, 'el pizarrista', who led a savage campaign of unparalleled cruelty throughout the territory in the summer of 1539, brutal enough to horrify Charles V into ordering a substantial compensation to the natives of the region, all to be taken from Chaves's estate: the most unspeakable of his many crimes had been his order to massacre 600 children.[52] Manqo himself also managed to evade the fury of the conquistadores, retreating once more to Vitcos from where he began to plan the construction of Vilcabamba. Like Willaq Umu, Manqo used the Andean landscape wisely, adjusting his strategy of resistance accordingly. When Gonzalo Pizarro set off in April 1539 at the head of a contingent of 300 Spaniards chosen among the 'most distinguished captains', as one of his relatives put it, he was confident that Manqo's days were numbered.[53] But the terrain was impenetrable and totally unsuited to horses. Manqo's men reverted to the well-worn tactic of ambushing the Spaniards and hurling huge boulders at them from great heights. For over two months and suffering many casualties, the Spaniards fruitlessly tried to find and capture Manqo. Their feelings of frustration were intense.[54]

Their failure to penetrate Vilcabamba had not prevented the Spaniards from establishing contact with potential allies in the enemy camp. Among them were Huaspar and Inquill, half-brothers of Manqo and Paullu and brothers of Manqo's wife, the remarkable Cura Ocllo who, in traditional Inca fashion, was also Manqo's sister. When Gonzalo sent Huaspar and Inquill to negotiate a peace treaty with Manqo, the latter was enraged, reminding everyone that he had recently issued a decree whereby anyone who collaborated with the Spaniards in any way was to be summarily executed. Ignoring the desperate pleas of Cura Ocllo, Manqo decapitated both men, their executions plunging his wife into a deep grief that made her determined to remain on the spot where they were killed, even after Manqo and his entourage had taken flight from the approaching conquistadores. In his frustration at having failed to capture Manqo yet again, Gonzalo allowed the Spaniards to abuse the captured Inca queen. According to Manqo's son, Titu Cusi, they even tried to rape her. When the returning expedition reached Ullantaytampu, an eager Francisco Pizarro was waiting. He had been given a message, most likely false, that Manqo wanted to negotiate a peace treaty. Francisco therefore sent Manqo a good assortment of silk clothes and an imported horse with some indigenous envoys. After Manqo spurned the gifts, killing the whole party, including the horse, Francisco once again vented his fury on the ill-fated queen. Whether he and his secretary, Antonio Picado, actually managed to have sexual intercourse with her, as was later alleged, we will never know. But her execution reached levels of cruelty that shocked even the most heartless conquistadores. Having stripped her and tied her to a stake, Pizarro ordered a group of his Cañari allies first to beat her and then to impale her limbs with arrows. Once dead, her body was placed in a large basket and floated down the Urubamba river where it was bound to be found by Manqo's men. A few days later Manqo was shown the body. 'He wept and agonized over her, for he loved her very much', and returned to Vilcabamba bearing the late queen's remains.[55]

The insufferably cruel murder of this dignified queen was not the behaviour of a man in control of the situation. Nor was it, as Antonio de Herrera put it, 'worthy of a Christian man in full use of his senses'.[56] It was, however, consistent with the grotesquely disproportionate punishments that Pizarro seemed determined to inflict upon unruly indigenous leaders. When, in October 1539, Willaq Umu finally surrendered to the relentless pursuit of the Spaniards, Pizarro had him burned alive despite the prevailing opinion that, due to his great authority, he would be far more useful alive.[57] Pizarro also burned Tisoq, who had given no sign of anti-Spanish animosity since being taken to Cusco nearly a year earlier. According to Luis de Morales, the vicar-general of Cusco, Pizarro murdered sixteen of Manqo's commanders after promising them grants of land if they complied with his orders.[58] Many of Pizarro's followers began to wonder whether the title of Marquis recently conferred upon him by Charles V was at all appropriate.

It is just possible that Pizarro's excessive actions were motivated by the threat still posed by Manqo, whose men continued to frustrate the efforts of the conquistadores wherever possible and whose influence extended far and wide. In January 1540, for instance, an expedition led by Pedro de Valdivia, the man who would eventually manage to subdue large swathes of what is now Chile, set off from Cusco to the far south. His aim was to bring Almagro's failed efforts to conquer the region five years earlier to their desired conclusion. More than a year later, after a laborious march that took Valdivia and his men to what is present-day Santiago, the conquistadores heard that Manqo had already warned the leaders of the region to hide their gold, clothes and food, and to organize a concerted resistance. They accordingly attacked the conquistadores at Santiago in their tens of thousands and burned the town to ashes, killing many Spaniards and horses.[59] Closer to home, Manqo seemed tireless in his harassment and slaughter of the Spaniards and their indigenous allies. Taking advantage of Spanish divisions, he focused his efforts on the systematic destruction of crops. As a result a general famine struck the whole of southern Peru in 1540–41, claiming the lives of some 30,000 people. Raids, particularly in the neighbourhood of Huamanga, increased in intensity. The situation became so critical that it reached the attention of Charles V, who addressed a request to Manqo in 1540 urging him to heed the authority of the newly appointed governor, Cristóbal Vaca de Castro. In return for his compliance, Charles V invited Manqo to Spain, where he might spend the rest of his life in peace and luxury.[60] In spring 1541 this was the issue at the top of Pizarro's agenda: 'If a solution is not found,' he wrote to Garcí Manuel de Carvajal, the lieutenant-general of Arequipa, in a letter dated 7 May, 'these misdemeanours will only get worse.' Unlike Charles V, however, Pizarro saw war as the only solution: the situation would not improve until Manqo was dead.[61]

Absorbed in these concerns, Pizarro seemed blissfully oblivious to the dangerous forces gathering against him. These focused on a group of disgruntled Spanish settlers who began to see eye to eye with the *Almagristas*, the supporters of the faction loyal to the murdered Almagro and his cause. Many of them had been involved in the ill-fated expedition to Chile and the humiliating defeat at the battle of Las Salinas. The few who had managed to make it back to Spain had launched a concerted campaign against Hernando Pizarro, whom they would never forgive for the murder of their champion.

Before Hernando managed to obtain an audience with the emperor, he found himself in prison, where he would remain for the next two decades. We can get a flavour of the bitterness of the accusations against him from the testimony given by Alonso Enríquez de Guzmán, who had fought alongside Hernando during Manqo's siege of Cusco. As he wrote to the Royal Council, Diego de Almagro had given his life to the service of Charles V and had been callously betrayed by Hernando Pizarro who, 'moved by envy, hatred . . . greed and self-interest', had persuaded Manqo Inka to rebel against the emperor. This had led to the loss of the kingdom of Peru and of all the rents and royal fifths to which the emperor was entitled. And if this was not enough, Hernando had also chosen to forget Almagro's magnanimity in releasing him from prison by having him most ignominiously strangled, telling him that he was 'no *adelantado* but a castrated moor'. This atrocious act was tantamount to treason and deserved the most severe 'civil, military and capital penalties'.[62]

The *Almagristas* in Peru therefore knew that the tide of opinion at court was beginning to turn against the Pizarros, and they were determined to use this changing situation to their best advantage. Barred from political office by Pizarro, they found themselves in the same situation as the bulk of recent arrivals. At least the latter could justify their relative poverty by having arrived too late. But this was emphatically not the case of the *Almagristas*, who felt a zealous and frustrated entitlement to the honours of conquest. As long as Francisco Pizarro remained in power, however, they had practically no hope of bettering themselves. The Marquis seemed to take pride in doing absolutely nothing to help them. 'Those poor devils,' he was often heard to say, 'have had such bad fortune, and now they are disgraced, defeated and destitute.'[63] In their growing frustration a group of approximately twenty *Almagristas* gathered in Lima made up their minds to murder the Marquis in the summer of 1541. They chose Sunday 26 June, planning to surprise Pizarro on his way to Mass, which he was known to attend unarmed. That particular morning, however, the Marquis stayed at home, a sign that the plot had somehow been discovered. This put the conspirators in an impossible situation: it was either kill or be killed. As Juan de Herrada, the leader of the group, explained, they were left with no choice but to assassinate Pizarro that same day; any sign of weakness or hesitation on their part would lead to their 'heads being hung from the gallows of the square'.[64] Armed with two crossbows, an arquebus and a collection of swords and halberds, they made for Pizarro's home, a two-storey building on the main square, directly opposite the cathedral. Breaking into the house, they killed a page, and rushed up the stairs where they met Francisco de Chaves, the brutal slayer of the 600 children, who had been dining with Pizarro and a number of guests, most of whom had fled in a panic when they heard the commotion. Chaves had decided to face the aggressors, thinking that he could persuade them to desist. Instead, he was summarily stabbed to death. The conspirators then moved towards the dining room where they found Pizarro with his breastplates only half-buckled, brandishing a large sword. With him were two pages, his half-brother, Francisco Martín de Alcántara, and the one guest who had chosen to stay, Gómez de Luna. In the fight that followed, the *Almagristas* overwhelmed Pizarro and his supporters. Francisco Martín and Gómez de Luna were killed. Surrounded, Pizarro was stabbed repeatedly and viciously, slipping in a pool of his own blood while attempting to make the sign of the cross and calling for a confessor. The coup de grâce was said to have come when one of the conspirators, Juan Rodríguez Barragán, bashed Pizarro's head in with a water jar, yelling 'you can go to hell to make your confession!'[65]

16

The End of an Era

Pizarro's dramatic assassination confirmed all the suspicions in Castile about the wisdom of supporting any further expeditions of conquest anywhere in the New World. It had become clear that any such expedition would from now on be difficult to justify and a likely source of international embarrassment. Castilian preoccupations with the unpredictable independence of the conquistadores were not, of course, new. As early as 1499, Columbus himself had been stripped of his vice-regal title in response to his perceived incompetence in the government of Hispaniola. More recently, Atawallpa's murder by Francisco Pizarro had triggered fresh questions over the legality and justice of Spain's presence in the New World. Still, Charles V had increasingly come to rely on the fruits of such expeditions: they had produced great riches, which helped satisfy the emperor's never-ending financial needs. Whatever the Spanish Crown's qualms, the expeditions continued. Contracts with individual explorers were still seen as valuable tools for promoting conquest and settlement without the need to incur undue expenditure, while ensuring, through the granting of a number of political and military privileges known as *mercedes*, that any new territories remained, to all intents and purposes, the undisputed possessions of the Crown.[1] Unsurprisingly, the years leading up to Pizarro's assassination were marked by a flurry of such activity.

In the months leading up to the rebellion of Manqo Inka a crucial role was played by Hernando de Soto. After Pizarro appointed him governor of Cusco in 1534, Soto took care of the day-to-day minutiae of government with exemplary dedication, overseeing matters that ranged from the distribution of *encomiendas* to the punishment of one Juan García Gaitero for allowing his horse to defecate in one of the city's streams.[2] Comfortably ensconced in the sumptuous Amarukancha palace, Soto surrounded himself with an inner circle of supporters. His situation was more fragile than appearances suggest, for Pizarro had allowed many of Soto's most loyal supporters to return to Spain shortly after the distribution of bullion. Crucial posts in Soto's administration, therefore, had to be filled by Almagro's troops and from groups of recent arrivals. Tensions grew after Pizarro decided to replace Soto with Almagro as governor of Cusco, partly as a reward for the latter's role in securing Quito, and partly as a tactic, playing off against each other his two potential rivals for power. This politicking, however, only served to plunge Cusco into a delicate crisis of loyalties. Then, when Pizarro persuaded Almagro to conquer Chile, Soto angled for a place as his second in command, but was passed over. When the expedition set off in July 1535, therefore, Soto had managed to fall out with the two most powerful men in Peru. Unsurprisingly, he chose to follow the example of many of his supporters and sailed back to Spain in the last days of 1535, taking his astonishing wealth with him.[3]

After a twenty-two-year absence from his native Andalusia, the thirty-six-year-old conquistador returned to a hero's welcome. Buying a mansion in Seville that required a vast household worthy of a noble-man (including pages, footmen, an equerry, a majordomo, a grand master of ceremonies and a chamberlain),[4] Soto then pushed his way into the higher echelons of the Castilian nobility, securing the hand of the aristocratic Isabel de Bobadilla in marriage. Soto's first biographer, the Inca Garcilaso de la Vega, wrote that most men in his circum-stances would have chosen to settle down and live in luxury. Instead, 'raising his thoughts and his spirit with the memory of the feats he had achieved in Peru, not satisfied with what he had already laboured and obtained but wishing to undertake equal or better feats, if, indeed, bet-ter ones could be imagined', and driven by 'a generous envy and a magnanimous zeal' for the deeds of Cortés, Pizarro and Almagro, his 'liberal and generous soul' could not bear the thought of being inferior to them, either 'in valour and energy for war' or 'in prudence and dis-cretion for peace'.[5] Put in plain English, Soto never managed to shake off the conquistador bug. Cultivating networks of noblemen and cour-tiers, he secured an audience with Charles V.

Soto played his cards ably: on 20 April 1537, Charles V signed a *capitulación* allowing Soto to explore and conquer his own territory. The choice of region came as something of a surprise to Soto. With present-day Colombia – which Soto had for good reasons regarded as a logical continuation of his adventures in the Andes – already granted to others, the *capitulación* instead gave him the right to 'conquer and settle' those territories that had previously been allocated to the ill-fated Pánfilo de Narváez: the elusive region that, back in 1513, Juan Ponce de León had named Florida.[6]

The scheme worked for both parties. The emperor and his advisors were well aware that, in the intervening decades, the region had become a haven for French and British pirates who preyed on vulnerable Spanish vessels passing the coastline of Florida as they rode the Gulf Stream back to Spain. For Soto, the region had clear attractions: not only was it believed to be the location of the fabled city of Cíbola, with its enticing golden treasures, but the scholar Peter Martyr, writing about the adventures of Ponce de León, had also portrayed it as an earthly paradise, populated by women whose bodies never aged and fountains of rejuvenating waters.[7] The *capitulación* also granted Soto the governorship of Cuba, which he could use as a base for his expeditions. To boot, Soto was also made a knight of Santiago, at that time Castile's most revered military order.[8]

If any doubts remained in Soto's mind about the wisdom of Charles V's choice of region, they were soon put to rest by the arrival in Spain of his fellow Andalusian, Alvar Núñez Cabeza de Vaca, fresh from his extraordinary adventures – which included Florida. Inviting Cabeza de Vaca to his Seville mansion, Soto quizzed him thoroughly about his adventures. Cabeza de Vaca patiently answered Soto's questions, but he was frustratingly evasive and often blatantly contradictory about the most persistent one: where was the gold? At one point he told Soto that Florida was a wretched wasteland where one could only expect tedious hardships; on another, that any man who sold his possessions and joined Soto's expedition would be acting 'wisely'.[9] As is often the case when a group of ambitious men have fixed their minds on an illusion, such contradictions were construed as evidence that Cabeza de Vaca was hiding something. Soon, the fanciful claim that Florida was the richest land in the New World began to be attributed to him.[10] This illusion became so pervasive that Soto's expedition was substantially oversubscribed: many men who had sold their estates in order to join it found themselves forced to stay behind, frustrated and disillusioned. The cost of the operation was more than six times that of the legendary Pedrarias expedition twenty-three years earlier.[11]

Departing Sanlúcar de Barrameda on 7 April 1538, the huge fleet dropped anchor four days later off La Gomera, one of the Canary Islands. Soto managed to persuade the governor there, a cousin of his wife Isabel, to allow his teenage daughter, Leonor de Bobadilla, to join the expedition to keep his wife company. (The arrangement became a source of some embarrassment to Soto, for Leonor became pregnant by one Nuño de Tobar, who happened to be one of Soto's most trusted officers.)[12] The fleet was seaborne again on 28 April, though Soto's decision to sail westward, directly to Cuba, rather than taking the faster currents to the south, made the crossing frustratingly slow. Then, as the fleet approached the southern bay of Santiago in the first days of June, Soto's men noticed a Spaniard riding along the shore on a nimble horse and gesticulating insistently. He seemed to be instructing the fleet to bear left, but just as it began to do so the man incongruously changed his mind and instructed it to bear right. In the confusion, Soto's vessel, the San Cristóbal, struck hard against one of the many treacherous shoals that over the centuries have proved so lethal to mariners. As luck would have it, there was no major damage. Then the acting governor, sending all the help he could muster to get Soto and his entourage safely onto dry land, apologized for the false directions. He explained that he had assumed the San Cristóbal was yet another vessel of the French corsairs that had been attacking the island for weeks.[13]

Happy with this explanation, Soto wasted no time in presenting his credentials to the cabildo (city council), which immediately accepted him as governor. He assumed his new post with characteristic flamboyance, staging round after round of lavish celebrations that went on for days, with balls and masquerades held at night, often culminating in a bullfight held the following day.[14] It was not long before Spanish officials in Cuba began to express their concern at Soto's extravagance to the emperor and the Council of the Indies. In particular, they complained that Soto's fondness for tournaments and riding contests was a ruse to tempt established breeders to bring out their best horses, which the new governor was buying by the dozen. He was busy persuading the dwindling numbers of young Spaniards who had not managed to go to Peru or Nicaragua to join his expedition.[15] What would be left of Cuba, the officials asked, if Soto continued to use it as a ready milch cow for his personal ambitions? Even one of the island's richest landowners, Vasco Porcallo de Figueroa, was offering Soto his personal services and his best horses.

That autumn, Soto left Santiago for Havana, by then relocated to the north of the island, in the company of Vasco and 150 horsemen. Sending his wife Isabel and the infantry by sea, Soto went overland, keen to exercise his role as governor by visiting each town along the way. Of course, his intention was not exclusively political: going by land allowed Soto to continue to purchase horses and supplies as he went, and to harden his horsemen.[16]

Once in Havana, which was undergoing reconstruction after being targeted by French corsairs, Soto installed himself and his wife in luxurious comfort, and sent an expedition to the Florida coast, in order to find a suitable port to make a landing. Meanwhile, in the early months of 1539, he continued his preparations: to the dozens of horses, he added a plentiful supply of piglets, to be slaughtered for food as and when need arose. He also heard news that the viceroy in New Spain, Don Antonio de Mendoza, was raising an army to explore the vast northern territories of the viceroyalty. If, as Garcilaso later claimed, the news was alarming to Soto – for the plan might potentially create a situation analogous to the one that had so damaged the relationship between Pizarro and Almagro – it was also proof that he was not the only one to believe the rumours of the wealth of the region.[17] Finally, Soto signed a power of attorney to his wife, made his will and, on 18 May, set sail in pursuit of what he firmly believed to be the richest land in the New World.

The crossing from Cuba was unusually slow: it was a week before Soto's fleet set eyes on the Florida coastline. The explorers soon found a broad natural harbour that Soto named Bahía del Espíritu Santo (Bay of the Holy Spirit), suggesting that they landed on or around the Feast of Pentecost, which in 1539 fell on 28 May. From the vague descriptions, the likeliest candidate is present-day Tampa Bay. Their immediate impressions of the place fell far short of their expectations. The area seemed more or less deserted, the only signs of human activity coming from distant signs of smoke that led them to a hamlet of about half a dozen timber huts. This was their first encounter with the Timucua, and it was not encouraging: a sudden, nervous skirmish saw a horse killed instantly by an arrow. Then, the Timucua fled into surrounding woods and swamps that proved impenetrable on horseback.[18]

To see a horse killed by an arrow was a new experience: Garcilaso describes the perplexity that the men felt at the instantaneous death of 'so fierce and brave an animal'. They then discovered that the arrow had 'entered through the chest, passed through the heart and stomach and guts and stopped at the very end of the intestines'.[19] These 'arrows' were in fact 'as thick as an arm, six or seven feet long' and – according to the testimony of Cabeza de Vaca – supremely accurate from as far as 'two hundred paces'.[20] It soon dawned on the Spaniards that the Timucua were the most dangerous warriors they had yet encountered in the New World, especially in such constrained and unfamiliar surroundings. Soto and his men were more aware than ever of the importance of enticing their enemies into open territory, where the speed and strength of their horses would give them the advantage.

A few days later, Soto and his men were startled to hear a man shouting at the top of his voice in Castilian, pleading with the Spaniards to spare his life and that of his indigenous friends to whom he owed his life. This was Juan Ortiz, a Sevillian *hidalgo* who had first come to Florida with Pánfilo de Narváez and had been sent back there from Cuba by Narváez's wife on a mission to look for her missing husband. There, he had been captured and enslaved by a local *cacique* called Ocita.[21] He had managed to escape – with the help of a kind-hearted Timucua girl who would capture Garcilaso's chivalric imagination – to a nearby village where another local *cacique*, Mocoso, welcomed him and treated him with respect. Relieved, and conscious that he was unlikely to come across Spaniards again, Ortiz had gone completely native, learning to use the lethal longbow and even tattooing his body.[22]

The encounter with Ortiz seemed providential to Soto – comparable, indeed, to Cortés's encounter with Gerónimo de Aguilar in Yucatan two decades earlier. From the information Ortiz could provide, Soto and his men formed a picture of a region dominated by independent *caciques* who ruled clusters of villages from which they exacted tribute, and who were in constant conflict with each other. Such a situation played to the well-tested Spanish strategy of fomenting divisions in order to establish overall dominance. In other respects, however, Ortiz's information was not so agreeable: he had seen no gold (though, admittedly, he had not travelled far from the immediate area). Besides – a crucial piece of information – he knew that both Mocoso and Ocita paid tribute to a much more important *cacique* called Urriparacoxi. With the thought of gold, Soto's spirits soared at the news and he set about arranging a meeting with Mocoso. If we are to believe the sources, the *cacique* was most accommodating: he complained bitterly about the savagery of his rivals and proposed an alliance with the Spanish against them. Whether or not the conquistadores trusted him, they were clearly swayed by rumours – real or imagined – of great wealth to the north. Nothing speaks more eloquently about the state of mind of Soto and his men at this time than a report that Soto penned to the *cabildo* (town hall) of Havana. He mentions fields of maize, beans, exotic fruits and signs of highly sophisticated peoples only a few days away, where plentiful gold, silver and pearls awaited them. 'May it please God,' Soto concluded in lines that make painful reading (these being the last words by him that have come down to us), 'that this may be so; for of what these Indians say I believe nothing but what I see, and must well see; although they know, and have it for a saying, that if they lie to me it will cost them their lives.'[23] In other words, Soto saw no alternative but to believe the Timucua.

By mid-July the expedition was on the move again. It made its way slowly through the thick forests and swamps towards Luca and Ocale in a fruitless search for any wealth other than fields of maize. On the way the conquistadores spread mayhem: both violence and disease. (In 1984 archaeologists unearthed a mass grave near the Withlacoochee Swamp, which revealed several skeletons with deep cuts made by steel swords next to dozens of unwounded ones; they had died within weeks of each other, suggesting the spread of a European disease to which the natives had no immunity.)[24] Just north of the river Santa Fe, to the north-west of present-day Gainsville, they captured seventeen natives, among them the daughter of the local *cacique*, Aguacaleyquen, whom Soto decided to use as a bait to capture the *cacique* himself. He succeeded and was immediately pursued by enraged warriors demanding the release of the *cacique* and his daughter. At a place called Napituca, Soto, affronted by having been punched in the face by one of the *caciques*, ordered the mass execution of all the captured warriors by tying them to stakes and having them shot by a squad of indigenous allies with their lethal longbows. From there the expedition moved to Uzachile with about 200 captured natives who served as porters and servants.[25]

The Spaniards were now entering Apalachee territory. The Apalachee remembered the Narváez expedition and had learned their lessons well, taking care to confront the Spaniards in surprise attacks, well away

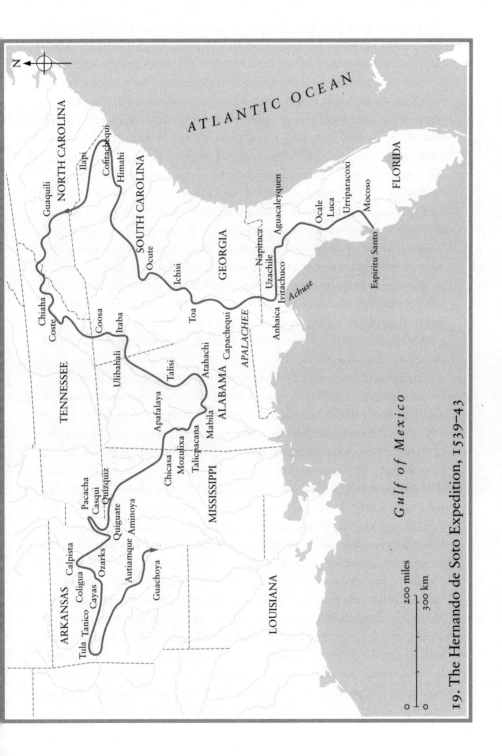

19. The Hernando de Soto Expedition, 1539–43

from open country. It was difficult for the Spanish to avoid significant casualties and the march was frustratingly slow. After resting for a few days in a village called Ivitachuco, which the Apalachee had set on fire as part of a scorched-earth policy, the Spaniards reached the capital, Anhaica, on 6 October. Although it had been abandoned, the city was nonetheless a very gratifying sight: graced with more than 200 houses that the Spaniards were only too glad to occupy, it would clearly make an excellent fortress, and Soto set about reinforcing it. After establishing that there was a good bay at Achuse, a few days' ride to the south of Anhaica, he dispatched one of his commanders back to Espíritu Santo to sail the ships up to it, where they would be more easily accessible in the event of an emergency. In the meantime, Soto set about learning as much as he could about the settlements in the region. The sight of mountains in the distance made him think that gold would be in abundance there, intimations confirmed by the testimony of a young lad the Spanish had captured, who claimed to come from a very rich land to the north called Yupaha. When the inevitable question about gold was put to him, the lad confirmed that there was plenty of it at a place called Cofitachequi.[26]

The Spaniards spent the winter months in Anhaica, setting off again in early spring, on 3 March 1540. The expedition headed north towards the river Flint, which was in full flow and extremely difficult to cross. On 11 March they reached Capachequi, a small enclave of huts nestling in an insalubrious swamp infested with alligators, coral snakes, leeches, ticks and hordes of mosquitoes. To their great relief they soon reached the comparatively peaceful and advanced region of what is present-day Georgia, where they were well received. Marching into the capital, Toa, on 23 March, they found it to be the most impressive settlement they had yet come across – which only made Soto anxious to move on as soon as possible, convinced that he was approaching a very rich kingdom. He was so eager that he set off with a small contingent that very evening, reaching the border of Ichisi the following morning; the rest of the expedition caught up with him on 29 March. Shortly afterwards, the *cacique* of Ichisi himself came to greet the Spaniards and informed them that there was a great lord to the north called Ocute. Before leaving, Soto erected a large cross, 'very high in the centre of the middle of the public place'. He then explained to the *cacique* that he and his subjects should revere it, for Christ, 'who was God and man, and created the heavens and the earth, and had suffered to save us', had died on it.[27]

On 3 April, as they approached the river Oconee, Soto and his men were met by ambassadors from a territory called Altamaha. From there, Soto moved on to Ocute, where he erected another cross in the central plaza. This pattern repeated itself in such a way that suggests all these natives were keen to help the Spaniards in their march towards Cofitachequi. Indeed, the natives of the region seemed to dread the fierce warriors of that legendary territory, who apparently lived in great cities filled with gold – or so the Spaniards stubbornly wanted to believe.[28]

Reassured by the captured lad, by now widely known among the Spaniards as Perico (little Peter), that Cofitachequi was only 'four days' journey thence towards the rising sun',[29] the expedition pressed on. The Spaniards did not want to believe the other indigenous allies, most of whom insisted that Cofitachequi was much further than a mere four days' journey, that the approach was by way of a dense wilderness with no trails, and that there was no gold or silver anywhere in the region. The 'lie of the Indian', as the chronicler Luis Hernández de Biedma called it,[30] began to dawn on the Spaniards after a long week of struggling to cut a trail through forest thickets and swamps, punctuated by crossings of rivers in full flow.[31] Nearly ten days had passed since their departure and there was no trace of any city, or any treasure. With supplies running low, Soto erupted in anger, threatening to throw Perico to the dogs for daring to deceive him. He soon came to his senses: no matter how misleading Perico's advice might have been, he was bilingual in Timucua (with which he could communicate with Juan Ortiz) and Muskogean (the language of the region they had now entered), so he was hardly an expendable commodity. Besides, he seemed to have befriended enough Spaniards to be able to pick up much more than the rudiments of Castilian, and enough Christian culture with which to convince the Spaniards that he was not responsible for having deceived them. It was all, he theatrically claimed, the fault of the devil! According to the chronicler known as the gentleman of Elvas, Perico even foamed at the mouth and threw himself into convulsions, convincing everyone that he was possessed. Exorcizing him, the expedition's friars decided to baptize him there and then, to keep the fiend at bay.[32]

It was late April before the desperate Spaniards saw any sign of hope. They approached a village called Himahi where they found corn flour, an abundance of mulberries and other fruits – some of them, according to Rodrigo Ranjel, Soto's secretary, 'like delicious and very fragrant strawberries' – and a wealth of roses, similar to those in Castile though 'rather more delicate and mellow'.[33] Finally, on 1 May, Soto laid eyes – or believed he did – on the fabled Queen of Cofitachequi herself. She received him graciously and offered to feed and house the whole expedition generously. Despite Garcilaso's romantic evocation of the episode – in which he compared the queen to Cleopatra when she crossed the river Cydnus in Cilicia to meet Mark Antony[34] – the experience left a lot to be desired. Although there were signs of some sophistication – the queen was carried in a litter and greeted Soto with a long string of pearl beads that she delicately placed around his neck; the people were dressed in 'very excellent hides' and were 'well set up and proportioned, and more well-mannered and civilized than any who had been seen in all the land'; the towns and houses were more elaborate[35] – there was no sign of any gold. Although the queen assured Soto that she would bring precious metals to him in a few days, the gold proved to be copper and the silver objects, which were 'very light', were in fact thick boards of mica that 'crumbled like a bundle of dried earth'.[36]

Ever the optimist, when Soto heard rumours of a 'great king' that ruled a country called Chiaha some twelve days' march away, he urged the expedition on once more. Not everyone was happy with his characteristically impulsive decision-making. Despite its obvious disappointments, Cofitachequi was a rich land and was strategically placed at a point near the Atlantic where the Gulf Stream carried fleets on their way back to Spain. 'All the ships from New Spain, and those from Peru, Santa Marta and Tierra Firme,' wrote Elvas, 'would come to take advantage of the stop here.' There was, besides, an abundance of pearls. Could it be, they wondered, that Soto was losing his mind?[37]

Whatever the case, the expedition was on the move again on 13 May. When Soto heard that the queen was refusing to provide porters, he took the brusque decision – perhaps with the examples of the imprisonment of Moctezuma and Atawallpa respectively by Cortés and Pizarro in mind – to place her under heavy guard and to inform her that she would be going with them.[38] Making good progress, they reached a place called Guaquili on 18 May. They then entered a land of mountains interspersed with limestone crags and waterfalls, supporting an astonishing profusion of plant life.[39] By late May they were approaching the Broad river, which marked the limits of the queen's domain. Wisely she planned an escape – and succeeded. On 5 June, crossing the river, the expedition entered Chiaha, which, according to Ranjel, was 'on an island of the same river'.[40] It had, alas, no gold. With the obvious exception of Soto, no one seemed to mind: the place was blessed with an abundance of good food provided generously by its very affable inhabitants. Even the emaciated horses grew fat 'because of the luxuriance of the land'.[41]

After four weeks, rested, replenished and refreshed, the expedition was ready to set off again on 28 June. The plan was to move south, towards the coast, where Soto's fleet was now likely to have arrived, perhaps even with reinforcements from Cuba. With a solid base in the Gulf, Soto could realistically plan further expeditions to the interior, and arrange for the construction of viable settlements. They therefore moved down towards Coste, where the *cacique*, outraged when the Spaniards began to plunder the area around his palace, seized and beat some of the looters. Aware of the danger they were in – having grown used to the peaceable nature of the area, the Spaniards had entered the town unprepared for battle – Soto pretended to be incensed with his men for daring to abuse the people, even beating some of them himself, while reassuring the *cacique* of his friendship and good intentions. The ruse paid off and the *cacique* offered to accompany the Spaniards to their camp. Then, as soon as Soto could reassure himself that they were out of range of the lethal longbows, he seized the *cacique* together with 'ten or twelve of his principals', put them in chains, and informed them that 'he would burn all of them because they had laid their hands on the Christians'.[42] Perhaps Soto only meant to intimidate his hosts, for there is no record of any punishment.

Eager to reach the Gulf, the Spaniards moved on fast through the kingdom of Coosa, whose capital they entered on 16 July. The *cacique* of this substantial Mississippian territory came to greet them in an impressive litter carried, according to Ranjel, by 'sixty or seventy of his principal Indians'.[43] As usual, Soto arrested the potentate in order to secure adequate supplies of food and servants. The place itself was obviously most agreeable, for the Spaniards stayed there for over a month. On 20 August they departed, together with the imprisoned *cacique*, continuing southwards towards Itaba, which Ranjel described as 'a large town alongside a good river'. There, they waited for the seasonal torrential rains to subside.[44] They reached a walled city called Ulibahali on 31 August, from which they continued the march south across ridges and valleys, arriving at the first villages of the large province called Talisi on 16 September. Two days later they entered the town, where they were met by a group of ambassadors sent by Tascalusa, the powerful lord of a tribe called the Atahachi, renowned for their ferocity.[45]

The Atahachi displayed all the attributes of a military enclave in a process of expansion. According to Garcilaso, the *cacique* of Talisi was in the process of switching allegiances from Coosa to their Atahachi neighbours. If this was really the case, then he is likely to have passed on valuable information about the Spaniards to his new sovereign, who therefore had plenty of time to prepare himself for their arrival. Their capital was also called Atahachi, and Soto's expedition arrived there on 10 October. The accounts of the meeting with Tascalusa are as embellished as they are contradictory. By all accounts, however, Tascalusa was a huge man. It is likely that, for reasons that will become clear, the chroniclers were keen to exaggerate this attribute. Yet even the measured Luis Hernández de Biedma called him 'a giant'.[46] Garcilaso claimed that, since none of the saddle horses at their disposal could cope with the weight of the *cacique*, the Spaniards fetched a very large packhorse for him to ride; even when mounted on such a large animal, Tascalusa's feet almost touched the ground.[47]

Despite his intimidating size, Tascalusa went out of his way to give the Spanish every indication that the Atahachi were yet one more in a chain of friendly and cooperative peoples. Civil as he was, he also cut a haughty, regal figure in the midst of prolonged celebrations.[48] His courtesy, too, only went so far: when Soto made his customary demand for food, servants and women, Tascalusa replied that 'he was not accustomed to serving anyone'.[49] Nevertheless, he allowed himself to be arrested, placed 400 of his men at the expedition's service, and reassured Soto that food and women – the latter of whom, according to Ranjel, would include 'those which they most desired' – would be much more plentiful at a nearby town called Mabila.[50] They departed the next day in good spirits, with the inscrutable Tascalusa, still a prisoner, riding Soto's largest packhorse. As it turned out, he had played Soto at his own game.

A week later, on the morning of 18 October, the Spanish entered Mabila to a festive reception, 'with many Indians playing music and singing'.[51] Distracted and seduced by the beauty and grace of a group of dancing girls, the Spaniards did not notice Tascalusa's swift escape into a hut, where his allies were planning an attack. From there he gave the order to kill all the Spaniards. It was only now that Soto and his men realized all the houses in Mabila were full of Atahachi warriors, who swarmed into the streets brandishing longbows, maces and clubs. There were thousands of them, and they caught the Spaniards unprepared and on foot.[52] Many were struck down by arrows or crushed by maces. In the chaos Rodrigo Ranjel managed to fight his way to a horse across the plaza and to rear it up against the warriors, forcing them to pause long enough for Soto to do the same. Once mounted, Soto was in his element. He battled his way to the gate, allowing the few Spaniards who survived the attack to escape and raise the alarm among the rest of the army, which lay in wait on the bank of the Alabama river. The majority, however, were native auxiliary troops – including the 400 servants that Tascalusa had given them a week earlier. Realizing what was going on, they quickly abandoned the Spanish and convinced a good number of Timucua and Apalachees to do the same. To add insult to injury, they took with them all the Spanish equipment, clothing and provisions.

Meanwhile, Soto busied himself organizing his troops to encircle the town. As the Castilian soldiers fought back in a prolonged and bloody counter-attack that went on until dusk, a few Spaniards eventually managed to breach the wall and set some houses on fire. The flames took hold of the cane-thatched roofs and burned hundreds of natives, forcing the others out into the open where they had no choice but to face Spanish horses, swords and lances. By nightfall, Soto and his men had prevailed. It was a sad and very costly victory.[53]

The losses were devastating for Tascalusa. Virtually every warrior in the region was dead or badly injured. Tascalusa's son was 'found lanced'. As for Tascalusa himself, 'nothing was ever learned of the *cacique* either dead or alive'.[54] But Soto had also lost dozens of men, among them his nephew Diego de Soto, and his niece's husband, the aristocratic and hugely popular Don Carlos Enríquez. Half the army had sustained wounds. Many more men and horses would die in the ensuing weeks, while practically all their clothes and equipment, including the pearls from Cofitachequi, had burned to ashes.[55] With winter almost upon them, Soto's mind turned away from the ships on the coast. Thinking that they would prove too much of a temptation for his dwindling army to return home, he decided that, as soon as his men had gathered enough strength, the expedition should again turn inland, thus trumping any possibility of desertion.[56] Astonishing as this unstinting determination might seem, it also pointed to a worrying illusory fixation.

In mid-November, Soto's weary and battered men set off again, heading north-west. It was cold, and soon began to snow. The expedition was a pitiful sight: Don Antonio Osorio, a brother of the Marquis of Astorga and one of the many rich noblemen whom Soto had seduced with his 'sweet talk', was now reduced to wearing a set of native blankets torn at the sides, and went 'bare-headed, bare-footed', carrying a scabbardless sword.[57] Hungry and exhausted, the expedition reached Talicpacana, a town in the region of Apafalaya. Finding little by way of sustenance, the Spaniards marched on towards Mozulixa; there the natives had retreated with all the available provisions across a river (probably the Black Warrior), daring the emaciated Spaniards to cross it. In a feat of endurance that scarcely needed any embellishment from Garcilaso, the Spaniards built a vessel in four days, and made a successful crossing. Once across, they feasted on the heaps of grain, fruits and vegetables they could secure to accompany the meat of their dwindling supply of piglets.[58] After crossing another challenging river (probably the Tombigbee), they arrived at Chicasa, 'a small town of twenty houses', on 18 December and settled down to endure a harsh winter.[59]

As ever, Soto was anxious to continue the journey, but the snow did not clear until early March. As they were getting ready to leave, they found themselves surrounded by Chicasa warriors who set the huts on fire and forced the Spaniards out into the open, unarmed. The whole town was burned to ashes, together with fifty-seven horses, eleven Spaniards and 400 piglets. In what Hernández de Biedma called 'a great mystery of God', the warriors, who could have finished the Spaniards off quite comprehensively, then withdrew for at least a week. When they returned, they found the Spaniards ready to chase them out on horseback to a flat plain where they vented their rage in a savage slaughter.[60]

Despite this seemingly providential escape, the dwindling expedition was more demoralized than ever. Soto and his men headed north-west along a gloomy trail that was humid by day and cold by night, swimming across thick swamps, before stumbling upon a small town called Quizquiz, which they seized in a surprise attack.[61] Reaching the Mississippi river, only a few miles distant, the Spaniards saw hundreds of 'large and well-built' vessels that seemed to them like a 'beautiful fleet of galleys': an intimidating sight, for the vessels carried thousands of warriors. Ever the optimist, Soto predictably saw this as a good omen: it signalled, surely, that their golden destination was only a short distance away. Accordingly, over the next month, the Spaniards set about building enough vessels to carry what remained of the expedition across the mighty river.[62]

They crossed on the night of 17 June 1541, Soto using the darkness in order to avoid an enemy attack. It was a swift and remarkably skilful operation: not a single person, horse or piglet was lost. Shortly afterwards they came across a fertile, heavily populated area nestling the large town of Casqui, whose *cacique* gave every sign of wanting to befriend the Spaniards. It soon became evident that he wanted their help against the rival city of Pacacha which, Soto had been told, had plenty of gold. Reaching Pacacha on 29 June, they found that its inhabitants had anticipated the attack: the place was empty. There was, of course, no gold, but the Spaniards were glad to be able to collect plenty of blankets and animal skins with which they made much-needed shirts, leggings and shoes. They stayed at Pacacha for almost a month, using it as a base to explore the surrounding area. Interestingly, Soto thought he was very near the 'South Sea', the Pacific Ocean. Although he was mistaken, his reasoning was good: the longitude of Pacacha is roughly the same as the Pacific coast off Nicaragua.[63]

The expedition was on its way again in late July, this time heading south. They reached Quiguate on 5 August and stayed there for three weeks. Failing to recruit either servants or guides, they were off again on 26 August heading north-west – hoping, perhaps, to stumble across the Pacific. Instead they found a succession of mud-drenched crossings and swamps that left them on the verge of despair. They reached Coligua on 4 September, seizing the town by surprise and availing themselves of as many clothes and as much food and salt as they could lay their hands on. A few days later, at Calpista, they decided to head south, away from the marshes and into the altogether more salubrious hardwood forests of the Ozarks. By early September they were approaching the Arkansas river valley, reaching the tilled fields and small villages of Cayas. On 15 September they halted at a village called Tanico. Flanked to the north and south by mountains and hills, it was an ideal place to rest and recover. Even the horses 'grew fat and thrived'.[64] From the friendly natives, Soto learned about a rich province to the north-west called Tula and, inevitably, set off to investigate. He soon ran into ferocious resistance; ten horses and eight Spaniards were wounded. According to Ranjel, the weapons their attackers used were 'long poles like lances, the points fire-hardened', which they commonly used to kill buffaloes. They were the fiercest people the Spaniards had come across, and the strangest. Hunter-gatherers rather than agriculturalists, they spoke a strange language that none of the guides could understand, and their domain consisted of flat expanses of arid land with little vegetation. There was no sign of the South Sea.[65]

Even without knowing that Francisco Vázquez de Coronado was already on his way back to Mexico City to inform his viceroy that there was no gold or anything of interest in the region, Soto had made up his mind that further searches to the west were pointless. To the north were impenetrable marshes; Soto had explored the east, so a southern march towards the Gulf was the only sensible option. But in 1541 winter set in early, and it was even harsher than the previous one. One of its first, tragic victims was the indispensable Juan Ortiz, who fell ill and died at Autiamque. As soon as the first signs of spring came, the despondent expedition renewed its southern march. In mid-April, Soto halted at a town called Guachoya; there he fell ill and took to his bed; he was, the sources suggest, deeply depressed. He even named Luis de Moscoso as his successor, a clear sign that he knew he was dying, and asked his men to forgive any offence they might have received from him.[66] Then a strong fever set in. After five days, on 21 May 1542, this 'magnanimous and unconquered knight' commended his soul to God and died, aged forty-two, 'a Catholic Christian' – having first asked 'for the mercy of the Blessed Trinity and invoked the help of the blood of Our Lord Jesus Christ, the intercession of the Virgin, of all the celestial court – in the faith of the Roman Church'.[67]

In his last days, and perhaps often during his fruitless search for gold, Soto must have wondered what would have happened had he left Peru earlier and secured a royal *capitulación* to explore the region of what is present-day Colombia. Settlements there were concentrated mainly along the coast, around the port cities of Santa Marta and Cartagena, but there had long been a Spanish interest in exploring the interior, especially if a link could be found to the fabled treasures of Peru. As early as 1528 the then governor of Santa Marta, Rodrigo Álvarez Palomino, had put together a contingent of 300 foot soldiers and fifty horsemen charged with locating the source of some intriguing objects he had seen on a vessel bound for Seville, which had docked briefly at Santa Marta. Among these objects, which suggested a high level of sophistication, there were also some 'strange sheep', which cannot have been anything but llamas.[68] This was none other than the vessel sent by Pizarro to Spain, after his explorations of the Andean Pacific coast with Bartolomé Ruiz de Estrada in 1527.[69]

Governor Álvarez Palomino died unexpectedly before the exploration could set out, and subsequent efforts only led to unedifying confrontations with increasingly hostile indigenous tribes. When in 1533 news of Pizarro's success in Peru began to spread, growing numbers of settlers abandoned the city and migrated to Peru, with the result that most efforts at exploration in Colombia ceased. As in the rest of the Caribbean, Santa Marta was in danger of being abandoned altogether. The remedy to this depopulation came from a quite unexpected quarter. The sixty-year-old governor of the Canaries, Pedro Fernández de Lugo – clearly well informed about the crisis from the various accounts he heard by Spaniards on their way back to Spain – decided to send his son Alonso to Castile. His remit was to persuade the Council of the Indies of the urgent need to remedy the worrying depopulation of Santa Marta by promoting further explorations into the interior. Initially sceptical, the Council eventually granted a *capitulación*: signed on 22 January 1535, it gave generous concessions to Fernández de Lugo, including the governorship of any new lands conquered between Santa Marta and the Pacific Ocean (still called 'the South Sea'). The quid pro quo was that Fernández de Lugo would put together a force of 1,700 men, build three fortresses in the city to protect it from attack, and assemble six brigantines to explore the source of the Magdalena river.[70]

This huge force eventually arrived in Santa Marta on 2 January 1536.[71] Fernández de Lugo's lieutenant-general there, Gonzalo Jiménez de Quesada, had been given this title even before the fleet sailed from Tenerife – so it is likely that the two men knew each other well, or that

Fernández de Lugo had been given the best references of the man he would appoint to lead the expedition into the interior.[72] Installing himself in Santa Marta, Fernández de Lugo wasted little time: the following April, Jiménez de Quesada (or plain Jiménez, as most of the sources call him) was already following the trail of the Magdalena. Fernández de Lugo's instructions to him were quite revealing. Omitting all mention of Peru and the South Sea – the lure for all ambitious explorers – they focused on the need to treat any indigenous peoples with justice, and on the manner in which any gold or booty should be recorded and distributed. Rather than establishing a line of communication with Peru, the members of the expedition were clearly enticed by the prospect of acquiring new lands and riches of their own.[73]

Leading a force of about 500 men – including 100 horsemen – divided into eight companies, Jiménez departed Santa Marta on 5 April 1536, heading for a small settlement on the Magdalena called Sampollón. There they planned to rendezvous with five brigantines – each carrying about forty men – which were due to depart two weeks later, on Easter Sunday. As the brigantines approached the mouth of the Magdalena, the plan went awry: they were hit by a heavy storm that sank two vessels and damaged the others beyond repair. Acting quickly, Fernández de Lugo fitted out a further five brigantines, which caught up with Jiménez's forces at Sampollón by the end of July. Resuming his journey upriver, Jiménez soon realized why previous expeditions had been so unsuccessful: the constant torrential rains led to flooding and treacherous currents, and the merciless mud and thick jungle vegetation made progress frustratingly slow. It was not until October that they reached nearby La Tora (present-day Barrancas Bermejas), where they decided to overwinter 'because the river was raging with such fury that they could go no further'.[74]

The situation was bleak. Some hundred or so men had died on the way to Sampollón; many more died on the way to La Tora. Those who were strong survived by eating lizards and snakes. The low morale was captured by two of the expedition's captains, who explained in a long letter to Charles V that by the time the expedition reached La Tora 'the majority of the people ... had died, both from hunger and because most were newcomers from Spain'. The sporadic exploratory missions that Jiménez dispatched from La Tora did not bring cheery news: the flooding was relentless and the terrain quite impenetrable. Missions

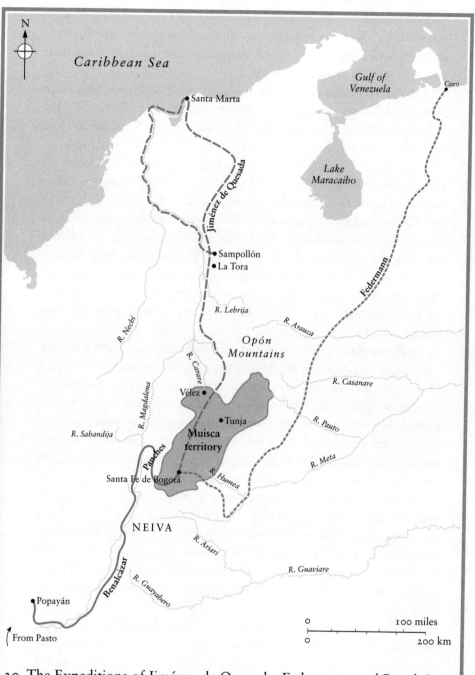

N

Caribbean Sea

Santa Marta

Gulf of
Venezuela

Coro

Jiménez de Quesada

Lake
Maracaibo

Sampollón
La Tora

Federmann

R. Lebrija

R. Nechi

R. Arauca

Opón
Mountains

R. Carare

R. Casanare

Vélez

R. Magdalena

Tunja

R. Pauto

R. Sabandija

Muisca
territory

R. Meta

Panches

Santa Fe de Bogotá

R. Humea

NEIVA

R. Ariari

R. Guaviare

Benalcázar

R. Guayabero

Popayán

From Pasto

0   100 miles
0   200 km

20. The Expeditions of Jiménez de Quesada, Federmann and Benalcázar

returned, speaking 'only of worse conditions, of land on which it was nearly impossible even to walk on account that the river had flooded everything'.[75] With dwindling provisions and rising mortality the situation became unbearable; it was compounded by attacks from local warriors who 'killed many people'.[76]

The explorers agreed to make one final effort to determine a route onward, with the unanimous agreement that, if unsuccessful, the expedition should return to Santa Marta and acknowledge failure. Led by Captain Juan de San Martín, a small force of about twenty men set out in two canoes, searching for a route into the mountains. Although they found nothing, on their way back to La Tora one of their number, Bartolomé Camacho – who later claimed to have felt 'a strong desire to serve Your Majesty' – swam across the river to the far bank, where he discovered some storehouses filled with large blocks of salt, very different from the granular type manufactured on the coast, and cloths of rich cotton.[77] The natives of the region were reported to believe that these items were made in 'a great land, with enormous riches, ruled by an extremely powerful lord whose excellence and superiority was widely regarded'.[78]

This information was enough to persuade Jiménez to take a further force up the eastern highlands. Falling ill near the base of the Opón Mountains, he sent his captains Juan de Céspedes and Antonio de Lebrija onward. It took them three weeks to cross the 'rough mountainous terrain', but at last they saw evidence of dense settlements nestling in rich lands and hurried back to inform Jiménez, who was overjoyed at the news.[79] Returning at once to La Tora – where his force had shrunk to a mere 200 men out of an original total of about 800 – Jiménez recruited the strongest and healthiest men, and set off again on 28 December 1536.[80] It is likely that, at La Tora, he received the news that Fernández de Lugo had died on 15 October. There is no record of his reaction to the news, but his growing confidence and determination suggest that Jiménez knew himself to be in full command of the venture and with no obligation to report to anyone but the king.

On the gruelling journey across the Opón Mountains and 'vast uninhabited lands', Jiménez and his men suffered 'such hunger that they were forced to eat a leather shield, as well as some mangy, crippled dogs'. Another twenty Spaniards died on the way; many more fell ill.

Eventually, in early March 1537, the 180 weary explorers caught sight of the Grita valley, home to the Muisca people. Over the next fortnight, they passed through 'many large settlements with abundant foodstuffs' including 'maize ... as well as deer ... [and] a great abundance of *curíes* [guinea pigs]', making their way to a town they had spotted from the mountains. The Muisca, meanwhile, stood off and watched. As the Spanish approached the town, 'leaving no one in the rear guard but Captain Cardoso, four or five horsemen, and many sick and injured on horseback', the Muisca saw their chance and 'attacked and killed many of the Christians in the rear guard, which we know because Captain Cardoso later was rescued by those who were up ahead'. Continuing warily, the Spanish began to notice a change in the local architecture: though made of thatch, the houses were among the very best buildings they had seen in 'the Indies'. They were 'well fenced, with walls made from cane stalks, elegantly crafted. Each house had ten or twelve doors, with twisting and turning walls to protect each entrance. Two walls enclosed the entire town, and between them was a great plaza. And between the inner wall and the houses was another beautiful plaza.' They had entered the territory of 'the most important lord in the land', whom the natives called 'Bogotá'.

According to local report, Bogotá had 'conquered and tyrannized a great part of this land' and was apparently enormously wealthy. The Spaniards grew in confidence on hearing this, for they thought the Muisca would welcome them as a liberating force against Bogotá in the same way as the Tlaxcalteca had welcomed Cortés as a liberating force against Moctezuma. Sometime in April 1537, Captain Cardoso then led a small expedition 'with four horsemen and up to twenty-five foot soldiers; they could not send more because so many Spaniards had fallen ill or were too exhausted'. They returned in triumph, accompanied by about 300 women and children, who had offered their services to them, thus 'helping to compensate many Spaniards who enjoyed no help whatsoever, and who barely could afford clothing'. From these people they also learnt that the great 'Bogotá' was only about ten miles away, in a town also called Bogotá. When they got there in late April, however, the Spaniards found that the great chief had fled, 'together with many other leaders and all of his gold, to a steep and craggy mountain, where no harm can come to him without a great amount of effort from Spaniards'. After several expeditions had tried fruitlessly to prise him out, the Spaniards focused their attention on rumours of emerald mines that were not far away. Unaware that the willingness of the Muisca to lead them to the mines was probably a ruse to escort them into the land of Bogotá's great enemy, whom the Muisca called Tunja, Jiménez sent Captain Pedro de Valenzuela to confirm what the Muisca were telling him about the source of these precious stones. Towards the end of May, after a six-day journey, Valenzuela and his companions reached 'a very high and sparse mountain range' located about fifty miles from a place they called 'the Valley of the Trumpet' and 'watched the Indians extract the emeralds from below the ground, and they witnessed such strange new things'. Whether or not the Muisca ploy had been a ruse, the emeralds certainly existed. The mines were located in a place where 'the soil contains certain sticky clay veins, which turn the colour of sky blue. Inside these veins the emeralds grow. They are all born so perfectly eight-sided, that no lapidary could carve them better.' Some emeralds were found in isolation, but others were 'together in clusters, shooting out like little branches from vines that grow out of trunks of slate'. In addition, the views were utterly breathtaking. The mines were so high up that 'from the top, the flat plains below look like the sea'. These 'great plains [*llanos*]' were 'so marvellous that nothing like them had ever been seen'.[81]

The excitement of Jiménez at the news would be difficult to exaggerate. At once he decided to move his camp nearer the mines, which they reached in August 1537, and then sent Juan de San Martín to explore the haunting and enticing *llanos*. The route proved impenetrable, 'either because of the steepness of the terrain or on account of the great rivers that descended into the *llanos*'.[82] Yet there was no doubt in anyone's mind by now that all the sacrifices and labours they had endured had not been in vain. In the hyperbolic words of one of the participants, the 'discovery of this New Kingdom must be considered the greatest thing to have happened in all the Indies; we know of no other Christian prince, nor infidel, who possesses what has been discovered in this New Kingdom. . . . And we know of no other mines anywhere in the world that are equal to these mines.'[83] Following the example of their predecessors in Mexico and Peru, they arrested Tunja and confiscated his riches, then set off to plunder the wealth of two other nearby *caciques*, Duitama and Sogamoso. When they returned to Tunja the treasure was weighed; it amounted to 191,294 pesos of fine gold, 37,288 pesos of low-grade ore and 1,815 emeralds.[84] Although this was only a fraction of the treasure collected in Peru, the conquistadores were convinced that they were in a land of 'grandeur and incredible riches' and they were soon on their way back to Bogotá, believing that it must be even richer, given the city's widely acknowledged predominance. Informed about their recent exploits, however, Bogotá himself had come out of hiding and was preparing to confront the intruders. He was soon killed in the ensuing skirmishes, in circumstances that remain mysterious. According to one account, he was killed by mistake, since he was in disguise and was not recognized; other accounts point to the clear involvement of a number of Spaniards, who knew full well the identity of their victim.[85]

The conquistadores soon learned that Bogotá's successor would be his nephew Sagipa,[86] who had allegedly gone into hiding in the mountains to guard his uncle's treasure. Knowing that there were many *caciques* in the region who were subservient to Bogotá, Jiménez made it widely known that they should all come forward and befriend the Spaniards. If they did not, then war would be waged against them until they were all dead. Sagipa himself soon turned up. Claiming to have come in peace, he asked the Spaniards for help against his deadly enemies, the Panches, who lived in a region about thirty miles west of Bogotá and were described in the anonymous *Relación de Santa Marta* as 'a fierce people who eat human flesh'. Jiménez agreed and accompanied Sagipa to engage the Panches, on whom they inflicted a comprehensive defeat at the battle of Tocarema on 20 August 1538. On their triumphant return, Jiménez pointed out to Sagipa, with what he probably saw as impeccable logic, that, since Bogotá had been killed as an enemy, all his treasure now belonged to Charles V. He added that 'he was not asking Sagipa to relinquish any of his own possessions; instead, the Christians only wanted what had belonged to Bogotá.'[87] To this Sagipa replied that, unfortunately, Bogotá had distributed the treasure in many parts of the region before he was killed. Suspicious at inconsistencies in Sagipa's account, however, Jiménez had him put in chains and then claimed to depart for Santa Marta, appointing his brother Hernán to take his place during his absence.[88]

There is no evidence that Jiménez actually left the region at this time; but, for some reason, he seemed keen to give that impression.

Some sources claim that he had given the order to torture Sagipa, with his body bound tightly, his feet put to the torch, and boiling animal fat poured over his chest, all of which led to the *cacique*'s slow and agonizing death. If this was really true, it was a scandal of a magnitude that would not serve Jiménez at all well back in Spain, where he would be found guilty, fined, stripped of his title of captain and forbidden to return to the New World.[89] He always protested his innocence, claiming that, by the time of the *cacique*'s death, he was already on his way back to Spain with the intention of claiming the new territories legitimately on behalf of the Crown. He had called them the New Kingdom of Granada because of their similarity with the Andalusian kingdom: 'both are situated among hills and mountains, both have climates that are colder than they are hot, and they differ little in size'.[90] Besides, they were 'a healthy place, and extremely so because in more than two years since we first arrived, we have not lost a single man to illness'. The whole area was also well stocked with a good range of fruits; maize was harvested every eight months; there was a wealth of deer and of other animals that could be hunted for meat; and there was a growing supply of pork brought by them and other Spaniards. The rivers had fish aplenty, and Spanish crops would 'grow well because of the temperate and cool climate'.[91]

Jiménez was clearly twisting the evidence. According to two of his captains who returned to Spain with him, just at the time when Jiménez claimed to be sailing back to Spain, he was in fact very distracted by reports of the existence of 'a nation of women, who live alone, without the presence of any Indian men', whom the Spaniards, with a good dose of wishful thinking, called 'the Amazons', and who were believed to possess an 'incalculable' amount of gold.[92] Such wishful thinking had been evident in Jiménez's expedition against the Panches. There the Spaniards had been struck by some 'high, snow-capped mountains' across a river they had discovered near a place called Neiva, whose inhabitants 'were said to be very rich because the vessels they use, as well as their other domestic service items, were all made of gold and silver. The Indians with us insisted that this was true, and we believed them because there is much fine gold along this river.' Surely, the two captains explained to Charles V, the need 'to investigate these places and bring Your Majesty a much more reliable account, even if it meant postponing our return for another year', had been a noble and sensible decision.[93]

A much more serious distraction had been in Jiménez's mind since the middle of 1538, when some 'strange news' had reached him about a group of 'Christians' who were making their way up the Magdalena river. By the time he agreed to help Sagipa against the Panches, Jiménez had discovered that these 'Christians' were a group of settlers 'from the governorship of Don Francisco Pizarro' under the leadership of the great conquistador's former deputy, Sebastián de Benalcázar. Uncannily, on the same day that Jiménez heard that Benalcázar and his men had crossed the Magdalena and were making their way up to the valley of Bogotá, he received even more startling news: another group of 'Christians' was approaching from the region of the *llanos*, 'the same region we have been unable to reach, which is in the direction of the rising sun'.[94]

The 'Christian' approaching from the *llanos* was Nikolaus Federmann, a German explorer who had moved to Hispaniola after Charles V granted the agents of the Welser company of Augsburg a monopoly to send 4,000 African slaves to the region of 'Tierra Firme' in return for a payment of 20,000 ducats to the imperial treasury.[95] After various uneventful expeditions, Federmann returned to Europe and was appointed captain and lieutenant to Georg von Speyer (often referred to in the sources as Jorge de la Espira), the governor of the province of Venezuela, in July 1534. Soon after returning to Venezuela, Federmann made up his mind to set off on an extensive journey of discovery. Leaving in February 1536, he followed the shores of Lake Maracaibo, passing treacherous marshes in which men and horses often vanished. Keeping the Andes always in sight to guide himself by, he struggled on for a whole year. Game was scarce and hunger was on the rise. Hearing that game would be more abundant in the *llanos*, Federmann plunged from the foothills of the Andes into the vast and grassy *llanos* of Casanare, which Jiménez's men had observed from the highlands while fishing for emeralds and had described as stretching out 'like the sea'. The whole region was bisected by innumerable rivers in all directions and by marshes whose paths were only known to wandering herdsmen. Keeping one's sense of direction was almost impossible. Often losing its way, Federmann's expedition made slow progress for long, dreary months. Many of his men wandered aimlessly until their horses dropped dead with fatigue. Forced to continue on foot, they were never seen again. A few of them were found, years later, as dried-up mummies shrivelled by the sun.[96] How Federmann himself managed to navigate his way out of the *llanos* seemed like a miracle. Jiménez and Benalcázar could at least follow the Magdalena, but Federmann, when he lost the Andes from view, was like a shipwrecked sailor. His journey had taken three years and of an original force of over 400 men only about 100 had survived. When they at long last limped into Bogotá, one veteran eyewitness of the Jiménez expedition wrote that the men were 'totally befuddled and decimated, ill and naked, wearing nothing but make-shift deerskins'.[97]

Benalcázar, on the other hand, had continued to move northward after his success in the conquest of Quito. Founding the cities of Santiago de Cali in 1536 and Pasto and Popayán in 1537, he made his way up to Neiva with comparative ease. When the natives brought the news to Jiménez, they said that 'the newcomers were far better dressed and armed than he was and far more numerous'.[98] That Bogotá should be the meeting point for these three entirely separate expeditions, however, seemed astonishing. Jiménez's captains wrote to Charles V that it had caused them 'great wonder and amazement . . . that people could come together from three separate governorships, as are the governorships of Peru, Venezuela and Santa Marta, in a place so far from the sea, as distant from the South Sea as it is from the North Sea'. With all three camps in a triangle and messengers moving from one camp to the other, 'it was Our Lord's will that in His service, and in the service of Your Majesty, our lieutenant came to an accord with Nicolás Federmán and Sebastián de Benalcázar'. They agreed that all the people who had come with Federmann from Venezuela and many of those who had come from Peru with Benalcázar were to remain 'in this New Kingdom of Granada and governorship of Santa Marta, with one person given judicial authority in order to maintain the peace'. Benalcázar also brought a wealth of experience, not least the need to establish properly constituted municipalities, which would act as the linchpin of any appeals to the Crown that might have a solid legal basis. What remained of 1538 was therefore spent on building 'three illustrious cities'. The first in Bogotá, which was called Santa Fé. 'The other was given the name Tunja, the same name as the land in which it is located. And he [Jiménez] called the other Vélez, which is located next to where Jiménez and his men had [first] entered this kingdom.'[99]

Meanwhile, the three captains agreed to go to Spain together, in order personally to provide Charles V with 'a full account of everything that had happened on their respective expeditions, and what services each had performed on Your behalf'. In particular, Jiménez's captains were keen to emphasize the high spirits of the people in the area and to reassure the emperor that Federmann and Benalcázar carried 'wonderful news of the riches of this New Kingdom. And Your Majesty can trust that these rich lands indeed exist, and that others will be found because at present this kingdom is at peace, and there are enough Spaniards and horses to send out to search and discover'.[100]

There was a note of desperation in these reassurances. Their tone belied a sense of urgency about the need to reassure a monarch who had grown increasingly disappointed and sceptical about the wisdom of encouraging, let alone supporting, further expeditions of conquest in the Americas. The emperor's doubts had increased after the return to Spain, in 1540, of the indefatigable Dominican friar Bartolomé de Las Casas. After his failure to evangelize the region of Cumaná in the early 1520s, Las Casas had undergone a second conversion.[101] Entering the Dominican order, he had devoted himself for a full decade to study and to the painstaking gathering of the copious materials that would go into his monumental histories of the events he had witnessed. Then news of events in Peru stirred Las Casas once more into action. In 1534 he set off on a mission to the newly conquered kingdom but was forced to turn back because of adverse sailing conditions and the news of Peru's worrying instability under Pizarro's unsteady rule. His attention then turned to Guatemala, Oaxaca and, finally, to Mexico City, where he arrived in 1538.[102]

It was at this time that Las Casas composed one of his most attractive treatises: *De unico vocationis modo omnium gentium ad veram religionem* ('On the only way of attracting all peoples to the true religion'). Firmly rooted in Patristic theology, especially St Augustine and St John Chrysostom, its central premise was founded upon the Aristotelian conviction, endorsed by Aquinas, that all human minds are the same in essence and that all human beings, regardless of background and external appearance, are innately susceptible to moral training. After his return to Spain in 1540, Las Casas continued to campaign at court for the complete reform of the systems of government that the conquistadores had established in the New World. His polemical tracts were consciously aimed at horrifying the emperor and his advisors into implementing reform. This tactic soon bore fruit in a set of legislative measures known as 'The New Laws', promulgated in 1542. Unmistakably indebted to Las Casas's findings, the initiative was a determined attempt to curtail the power and influence of the conquistadores and to assert direct royal authority in the New World. Among other things, the New Laws deprived all abusive *encomenderos* of their native labourers, denied the granting of *encomiendas* to any royal officials or members of the clergy, and forbade any further grants of *encomienda* by the stipulation that, on the death of the current incumbents, all their indigenous subjects should automatically revert to the Crown.[103]

From the perspective of the conquistadores, this royal initiative was an attack on the fundamentally seigneurial characteristics of the society they were hoping to create. Unsurprisingly, it met with fierce opposition. The royal representative in Mexico, Viceroy Antonio de Mendoza, adopted the practice of *obedezco pero no cumplo*, arguing that the laws could not be implemented before the Crown was made aware of the very reasonable complaints of the landowners, and even of the mendicant orders, including Las Casas's own Dominicans, all of whom urged caution. In Peru the immediate result was a violent rebellion led by Gonzalo Pizarro that culminated in the defeat and subsequent decapitation of Peru's first viceroy, Blasco Núñez Vela. Nor did the rebels harbour any doubts about the legitimacy of their actions. They confidently asserted that the conquistadores had established a contract with the Crown that would render any new law – especially one touching on the rights of property – utterly invalid until ratified by the leading citizens of the various kingdoms.[104]

If anything, such violent reactions made the Crown even more determined to oppose the ambitions of the conquistadores. As Charles V himself put it, 'the kingdoms of New Spain and Peru are to be ruled and governed by viceroys, who shall represent our royal person . . .

do and administer justice equally to all our subjects and vassals, and concern themselves with everything that will promote the calm, peace, ennoblement and pacification of those provinces'.[105] The viceroy, in other words, would be the alter ego of the monarch, taking his place at the heart of a system in which ritual and etiquette faithfully replicated the royal court in Madrid. Although not allowed to intervene directly in judicial affairs, the viceroy was president of the *audiencias* or judicial courts, head of the treasury and captain-general. His ample powers of patronage and appointment laid the foundations of a style of government that was directly dependent on the control of the Crown through a chain of command running from the Council of the Indies down (at the executive level) to the treasury, the local officials and the town governors, and (at the judicial level) to the *audiencias* and the judges.[106] There could be no clearer signal of the Crown's determination to frustrate the ambitions of the conquistadores, a trend that culminated in Philip II's 1573 promulgation of the *Ordenanzas para descubrimientos* ('Ordinances for discoveries'), in which the term 'conquest' was tellingly replaced by 'pacification'. This was no mere terminological sophistry: the ordinances stringently prohibited any armed expeditions. As far as the Spanish Crown was concerned, the ordinances were nothing other than a confirmation of the trend that had begun in the 1540s, whereby any further expansion was to be entrusted to missionaries. If, for any reason, this was not possible, explorers were expressly forbidden to engage in any act of war. Nor could they support one group of natives against another or become involved in any local disagreement or dispute.[107]

In practice, of course, the new viceroyalties were so far from Castile that it was easy to ignore such stipulations if the circumstances so dictated. Indigenous societies would continue to be attacked and even decimated in 'just wars' in the following decades. But the context in which these abusive developments would now take place had changed inexorably. By the time of Francisco Pizarro's assassination the conquistadores had already settled most regions formerly controlled by sedentary indigenous peoples and graced by mineral wealth; elsewhere, the land tended to languish in neglect.[108] Subsequently, whenever interest arose in unconquered territories, they usually became missions administered by the mendicant orders and, from the late 1560s, increasingly by the Jesuits. These were generally frontier areas that attracted little interest from explorers and settlers because they were poor in natural resources and usually occupied by nomadic tribes notoriously hostile to intruders. The few exceptions of areas rich in natural resources, such as the gold-rich Chocó in western Colombia, were now approached by much more carefully regulated expeditions in which the Crown's preference for 'pacification' and conversion was predominant.[109]

By the time that Jiménez, Benalcázar and Federmann returned to Spain, even Cortés was failing to defend his reputation against the endless lawsuits that his many disgruntled followers had amassed against him. After investing heavily in Charles V's ill-fated expedition to Algiers in 1541, in which he almost lost his life while pursuing the notorious Ottoman corsair Hayreddin Barbarossa, Cortés was subsequently cold-shouldered in Castile until, frustrated, he decided to return to Mexico. On his way to take ship he was struck down with dysentery and died aged sixty-two in Castilleja la Vieja, near Seville, on 2 December 1547, a wealthy but embittered and disappointed man. Meanwhile, Cortés's impetuous friend Pedro de Alvarado had been the latest to take on the challenge of sailing to China and the Spice Islands. Before he set sail, his horse took fright and ran amok; the conquistador was thrown and crushed under the weight of his horse, dying a few days later, on 4 July 1541 at fifty-six years old.[110] Nor was Jiménez, conqueror of the Muisca, able to capitalize on his successes. After returning to Spain and wandering aimlessly through the courts of Europe for twelve years, he was allowed to return to New Granada as a mere colonist. His subsequent attempt to conquer the *llanos* was a frustrating and expensive disaster that left him 'poor and weighed down with debt to the last day of his life'.[111] He died in old age in Suesca, Colombia. For his part, Federmann was accused of breach of contract by the Welser family, and died in February 1542 aged thirty-seven in a Valladolid prison. Of the three conquistadores who tried to lay claim to Bogotá, Benalcázar was the most successful: managing to catch Charles V in 1540, before Las Casas had had his say, he secured the title of governor of Popayán, the city he himself had founded on his way to Bogotá in 1536. Still, this was much less than he had hoped for. Once back in Popayán, he became embroiled in land feuds and vendettas lingering from the Pizarro and Almagro disputes. He was then sentenced to death and died in 1551 at fifty-six years old, before he had a chance to sail back to Spain to appeal against the decision.

This was an ignoble end for a group of men who – whatever their myriad faults and crimes – had succeeded, more or less through their own agency, in fundamentally transforming Spanish, and European, conceptions of the world in barely half a century.

Reassessment

In the 1590s the disillusionment of the conquistadores was summed up in Gonzalo Gómez de Cervantes's advice to Charles V's son and heir, Philip II. In 'all your kingdoms,' Gómez de Cervantes told the king, 'the principal source of strength available to Your Majesty consists in the virtue and nobility of knights' whose only interest is to 'maintain, preserve and increase' the domains of the monarchy. Rather than being rewarded, however, these 'knights' were systematically overlooked in favour of parvenus who went to the New World only to make a quick fortune and return home. 'The most impertinent thing imaginable,' Gómez de Cervantes lamented, was that those in charge of government were 'people without merit' who fawningly attached themselves to the servile entourages of the viceroys while flouting their contempt for 'the old settlers of these lands' – those virtuous men who served 'the king and the Republic with much greater love' than anyone else. It was indeed a scandal that 'those who but yesterday served in stores and taverns . . . are today in possession of the best and most honourable posts in the land, while the descendants of those who conquered and settled it are impoverished, humiliated, out of favour and ostracized.'[1]

This assessment reads like the last cry of a dying breed. As a descendant of the *corregidor* of Cádiz who had masterminded Nicolás de Ovando's fleet back in 1503,[2] Gómez de Cervantes still echoed the characteristic complaints of the ancient medieval nobility against upstart new men. Of course, he harboured no high hopes that his advice would be heeded – not for nothing had the Crown given every indication that there was no going back to the seigneurial arrangements he was proposing. Yet the tone of his memorandum leaves us in no doubt that Gómez de Cervantes was convinced he had a solid basis for voicing his displeasure. This conviction highlights a fascinating paradox: just as the descendants of the conquistadores realized they had been displaced by grasping royal officials, so they began to turn, with surprising approval, to the denunciations of their old enemy, Bartolomé de Las Casas, complete with their acerbic descriptions of Spanish cruelty. In the process they grew closer to their place of birth, the Americas, and increasingly resentful of the distant metropolis across the Atlantic.[3]

The figure who best captured this ambiguity was 'the Inca' Garcilaso de la Vega, the illegitimate son of a conquistador and an Inca princess, who in his literary works struck a subtle balance between the evocation of the high level of culture and nobility of the Inca past and the heroic bravery and chivalry of the conquistadores. His most bitter vitriol was reserved for one of Spain's most successful viceroys, Don Francisco de Toledo, who was put in charge of the viceroyalty of Peru in 1569 with the specific aim of frustrating the ambitions of those conquistadores who had rebelled against the imposition of the New Laws of 1542. Toledo's rule was marked by draconian efficiency. By the time he stepped down in 1581, any hopes that the descendants of the conquistadores might have had of being able to defend their seigneurial ambitions were in tatters. To Garcilaso's deep chagrin, Toledo's success had opened the doors of the viceroyalty to hordes of venal peninsular officials. His assessment could have been penned by Gómez de Cervantes himself: all these officials, Garcilaso lamented, were bent on giving their own relatives and friends that which belonged by right to a group of men now forced 'to beg for alms in order to eat, or to rob on the highways and then die on the gallows'.[4]

In this way, just at the time when, as we saw in the Introduction, William the Silent was composing his anti-Spanish *Apology*,[5] there emerged a complementary image of an unjust and unpopular Spanish monarchy across the Americas. This image would become a powerful tool in the hands of nineteenth-century nationalist historians bent on painting the wars of Independence against Spain as bitter rejections of what they saw as 300 years of obscurantist oppression. Such views chime well with the modern tendency to favour an approach to political history that centres on the nation state as the dominant political expression, but they do nothing to explain the various ways in which the political culture of the conquistadores and their descendants was rooted in a mutual agreement between the monarchy and the various regions.

As we have repeatedly seen, this agreement recognized diversity as a necessary condition for efficient government. The success of Viceroy Toledo in Peru was in fact the exception that proved the rule. Much more common than direct rule was the reliance of viceroys on the fostering of a community of interests with the various localities, all acutely jealous of their rights and privileges – their *fueros*. These regions understood themselves not as 'colonies' ruled by a distant metropolis, but as autonomous 'kingdoms' that, as everybody knew, worked best under the legitimizing aegis of the monarchy. For their part, the viceroys took good care to dispense justice with a view to turning the various local power brokers into their clients. These clients, of course, included all indigenous communities, which is why the use of indigenous languages was preserved and the collection of tribute was not assessed per capita but after a process of negotiation that led to the development of conventions for determining policies in local ways that were not even referred to the Council of the Indies.[6]

It was this very looseness, in other words, that invested the Spanish American viceroyalties with their surprising longevity and resilience. By guaranteeing to each province the continued enjoyment of its privileges, while making it aware of the benefits it could derive from its participation in the wider association represented by the monarchy, the vice-regal system succeeded in holding a loose amalgamation of autonomous 'kingdoms' together with the minimum of repression.[7] This was achieved not through the imposition of laws and regulations but through the sharing of a common mindset, a process that went hand in hand with the sharing of a common religious culture.

From a modern perspective, it is difficult to give this achievement its due. We find it hard to imagine a world where religious culture was at the centre of political affairs. Modern notions of statehood take for granted an understanding of sovereignty as indivisible – a notion first put forward by Jean Bodin in the late sixteenth century that became deeply entrenched in the post-1648 international system. Following the Treaty of Westphalia, all sovereign states were granted equal legal status regardless of their size or relative influence and importance. This was clearly not fertile ground for non-unitary political associations like the post-conquistador domains of the Americas, which came under increasing pressure to recognize claims to national autonomy within their borders.[8]

The settlement at Westphalia came after a century of appalling European warfare had exposed the futility of religious interference in politics. Although convinced secularists were still negligible in number, they hardly needed to make their case against religious believers who almost invariably did their work for them. All the secularists needed to do was to point out the incongruities and contradictions in the arguments, not to mention the behaviour, of the defenders of religion. Even a self-confessed Catholic like Michel de Montaigne had begun to do this in the late sixteenth century. By the time Thomas Hobbes and then Pierre Bayle and the English Deists took up their pens, the influence of religion on politics could already be denounced with a vigour and a confidence that reached a literary highpoint in Jonathan Swift's satire *A Tale of a Tub*. Thereafter, the theological field became a battleground of controversy and a source of antagonism rather than understanding.

Most attempts to explain how this situation had come about were carried out on the basis of an artificial separation between ecclesiastical and political history. The latter developed as the history of the unitary nation state and the balance of power in Europe; the former dealt exhaustively with heresies and theological controversies and impasses. Neither side paid any attention to the development of the new forms of religious culture that replaced medieval Christendom, and which persisted well into the nineteenth century. It is only recently that historians have begun to accept that religious warfare did not lead inevitably to secularism; that the seventeenth century was an intensely religious age when the materialism of a Hobbes or the monism of a Spinoza weighed lightly against the overwhelming mass of theologians and preachers who were almost solely responsible for popular instruction; and that as recently as the eighteenth century, the increasing prestige of the culture of the Enlightenment owed a great deal to the channels of international diffusion that it had acquired among the educated elites but which rarely reached the rest of the population. The majority of eighteenth-century Europeans still lived in economically self-contained regional units with their own laws and institutions. Voltaire and Viscount Bolingbroke were the contemporaries of John Wesley and St Paul of the Cross, and Edward Gibbon and Adam Smith composed their great works at the same time as St Benedict Joseph Labre led the life of a widely admired miracle worker.[9]

The neglect of this tradition is at the centre of the misunderstandings that plague the history of the conquistadores. Their exploits are invariably seen as part of a political culture whose eventual exhaustion demonstrates its worthlessness. Indeed, when seen through the prism of nationalism, any supranational association encompassing different peoples and geographical areas can only be described in terms of oppression.[10] But this does nothing to explain the remarkably long survival of what is commonly but misleadingly called the 'Spanish Empire'. Naples, Sicily, Sardinia and Milan were part of the Spanish Monarchy for longer than they have been part of the unified modern Italian state. How did Naples remain a kingdom and Milan a duchy? How could Spanish Americans insist that 'the Indies' were not 'colonies' but 'kingdoms'? And within the Spanish peninsula itself, how did the kingdoms of Aragon and Navarre – and, between 1580 and 1640, Portugal – remain separate from Castile, each subject to a different Council of State? None of these developments would have been possible without the concern that the Spanish Habsburgs showed for regional rights and privileges. Even Philip II, in sharp contrast to the dominant image of him as an obsessive centralizer, took particular care to highlight this principle. To give but one example, in a typical amendment to an ambassadorial instruction Philip wrote: 'This warrant saying: "from here [Lisbon] to Madrid and from there to Barcelona" will not do. It must read "from here [Lisbon] to the frontier of the kingdoms of Portugal and Castile to Madrid, and from there to the frontier of the kingdoms of Castile and Aragon, and from there to Barcelona". Let it be done that way.'[11]

This vignette is a reminder that the Spanish Habsburgs had the deepest respect for the local traditions, laws and privileges of the diverse components of the monarchy. In tune with this political culture, the conquistadores were conscious of belonging, first and foremost, not to a sovereign nation state but to a wider community in which the status of the various 'nations'[12] did not so much depend on their military and economic resources as on their historic rights and cultural achievements. Loyalty was owed first and foremost to the sovereigns, of course; but only insofar as the latter fulfilled their role as guarantors of the laws and customs of each constituent locality.

To realize this is to call the bluff of the persistent but radically mistaken idea that the achievements of the conquistadores came to a premature end in the middle of the sixteenth century, after which the Spanish 'colonies' were exploited by an oppressive Spanish monarchy until they managed to break their shackles in the insurgency wars.[13] A good way to begin to correct this perspective is to remember the testimony of Alexander von Humboldt. Travelling through the Americas in the first years of the nineteenth century, this extraordinary German polymath startled his European readers with an imposing portrait of a kingdom stretching from Costa Rica to Oregon. With nearly six million inhabitants, a thriving mining industry, and an overseas trade that linked the Atlantic to the Pacific, New Spain seemed destined to become a major global player. Its capital, Mexico City, was more than ten times the size of Philadelphia, Boston or New York. Adorned with buildings worthy of the streets of Rome or Naples, the 'City of Palaces', as Humboldt famously called it, was also home to countless intellectuals whom he praised for their ground-breaking contributions to scientific discovery. There was no doubt in Humboldt's mind that New Spain was the centre of the Enlightenment in the New World.[14]

Humboldt's portrait, however, tells us much more through its blind spots than through its praise. There is practically no mention in his account of the hundreds of churches, colleges and convents that less than a century before had captured the imagination of the Italian Giovanni Francesco Gemelli Careri.[15] About the only reference Humboldt ever made to anything similar was his puzzled description of the exquisite sacristy chapel of the Metropolitan Cathedral as 'Moorish or Gothic'. Nevertheless, it was precisely there, into the world of Baroque splendour, that much of the wealth that Humboldt had considered essential to New Spain's commercial prosperity was being poured. By Humboldt's time, however, European sensibilities were no longer attuned to the Baroque, and the nationalistic histories that were soon to emerge would take good care to consign it to oblivion.

Yet the many cultural expressions that ushered in the Baroque were remarkably resilient. They can be seen, not only in the persistence of the various forms of political organization that we have highlighted – reflected in the widespread use of the principle *obedezco pero no cumplo* – but also, and much more importantly, in the encouragement that the conquistadores gave to the early mendicant friars and their methods of evangelization. As we saw in chapter 11, the seeds planted by these men led to the emergence of religious cultures that were neither a covert survival of pre-Hispanic religions nor a pessimistic surrender to conquest. They were Christian cultures fed by the vibrant liturgical imagination of people who used indigenous metaphors, symbols and values to encourage a rich transfusion of the Christian message into the very essence of each local culture.

It is often thought that this development was short-lived, soon replaced by disillusionment leading to violence and resistance. Indeed, there is ample documentary evidence to support this claim and it has been extensively used. The most obvious instances are the various campaigns launched to 'extirpate idolatry'. These sources give the impression that Christianity continued to float like a layer of oil on the waters of pre-Hispanic religions throughout the Americas, leading to the common perception that behind every altar there is a pagan idol. The reality is entirely different: just like the draconian policies of Viceroy Toledo, these campaigns were the exception that proved the rule – they were sporadic and largely ineffectual initiatives. The typical scenario was the arrival of a new bishop who became concerned about reports of alleged 'idolatry' and then launched a campaign of 'extirpation'. Invariably, the campaigners would arrive at the appointed place only to become aware, from what they observed and from conversations with the local authorities and priests, that there was actually very little to worry about.[16]

It is obvious from these examples that the seeds sown by the early mendicants flourished among their successors – particularly the Jesuits, from the 1570s, but also the majority of parish priests.[17] They all continued to see the New World, not as a place infested with demonic forces but as a faithful echo of the wisdom of the Creator in whom they believed. They inhabited a symbolic cosmos where every created thing – every stone, every mountain, every river – both existed in its own right and symbolized some aspect of the divinity. In this sense, the entire natural world was 'sacramental' – a symbolic system that constantly communicated spiritual realities. Light and darkness, wind and fire, water and earth, the tree and its fruit, all spoke about the sacred by symbolizing both the greatness and the nearness of God. Just as in medieval Europe the new churches deliberately preserved earlier sacred sites, so throughout the Americas there was a profusion of churches, pilgrimage sites and sacred places where the creative imagination of the indigenous peoples was given free rein.[18] Humboldt's otherwise ecstatic description of New Spain somehow failed to appreciate this aspect of what has come to be known as the Baroque. The very term speaks for itself: coined as a pejorative adjective to describe a popular religiosity that, from the middle of the eighteenth century, had come to be widely despised as vulgar and tasteless, the Baroque has recently made a vigorous comeback. Could something similar be expected in relation to the conquistadores? This is too broad and speculative a question and this is not the place to address it. There is one Baroque artist, however, whose trajectory parallels the reception of the conquistadores in a way that can only shed light on the question.

Diego Velázquez (1599–1660) – not to be confused with the conquistador of Cuba, who was probably no relation – is nowadays widely regarded as one of the greatest painters of all time. Although his genius was never in question, it is startling to realize that he left no artistic followers: his successors throughout Spain turned to other models, notably Rubens, and painted as if Velázquez had never existed. Posterity was even more unkind to him. Any attempt to review the literature of art between the artist's death in 1660 and the early nineteenth century will struggle to find Velázquez mentioned among any painters considered to have achieved greatness. This puzzling trend was no doubt influenced by the fact that European travellers in search of art seldom considered Spain. Those who did – like Anton Mengs, who was in Madrid for two extended stays (1761–9 and 1774–6) – did not fail to notice the quality of what they saw, but they did so with the typical reservations of those who considered Spain to be strictly outside the orbit of any art that mattered. Mengs could only see Velázquez as a slavish imitator of nature who never attempted to 'improve' on what he saw, so he lumped Velázquez with all 'the other painters of the Spanish school', who 'did not have an exact idea of the merit of Greek things, nor of beauty or the ideal; they went on imitating each other.'[19]

It was not until the nineteenth century that, as we saw in the Introduction, Spain began to attract European travellers in search of the exotic. The Romantic sensibilities of the age were much more receptive to Velázquez, whose paintings had begun to arrive in France and England as a result of the plundering by soldiers and art dealers during the Peninsular War of 1807–14. By mid-century, Velázquez's reputation was second to none. 'My dear friend, what a painter!' wrote Alfred Dehodencq to one Monsieur Dubois in December 1850. 'It is nature done right there: the most subtle observations, the truest types, exquisite colour harmonies. Everything is there, thrown in profusion on the canvas.'[20] 'No man could draw the *minds* of men, or paint the air we breathe, better than he,' wrote Richard Ford.[21] But no one did more to advance the reputation of Velázquez than Edouard Manet, who thought just one of his paintings, the full-length portrait of the actor Pablo de Valladolid, was alone worth the long trip to Madrid. 'He is the painter of painters!' Manet wrote to Henri Fantin-Latour in 1865. Next to him everyone looked like a faker. 'He has astonished me; he has ravished me.'[22]

There is a curious parallel between these two contrasting perceptions and the two interpretative myths about the conquistadores that we considered in the Introduction – the one, influenced by the anti-Spanish 'Black Legend', leading to a thorough condemnation; the other, influenced by the Romantic imagination, leading to an exalted evocation.[23] Might there be another way that can get us closer to the mysteries of 'the Baroque'?

Scholars in search of such a way still find themselves mesmerized by Velázquez's astonishing manner of placing simple specks of white to ignite strings of glints across pale silk, or simple dabs of blue or grey to convey the tranquil translucence of gauze. He could paint eyes that see us while remaining themselves indistinct. He could create hazes that seem to come out of nowhere. He could make a casual dab of red read perfectly as an ear. The puzzle, we are sometimes told, becomes clear when we realize that the paintings are not imitations of reality but exercises in which the artist is mimicking the experience of seeing itself. This is a fascinating insight, but it does not shed much light upon the mystery behind the execution. By focusing unduly on the technique, such critics often miss the real depths of Velázquez's art. So, for example, Pablo de Valladolid, the character who so transfixed Manet, is often mistaken for a mere court jester or a buffoon. But anyone who looks at these paintings from a broader perspective knows at once that Velázquez was singling out the uniqueness of his sitters. Take the astonishing portrait of Juan de Pareja, the slave who was granted his freedom in Rome in 1650 but chose to remain by Velázquez's side until his death. That strong, proud and handsome face is magnificently poised and profoundly expressive. The look is that of a man who knows his dignity because he also knows it is a gift. Even the most sympathetic observers of what is justifiably Velázquez's best-known painting, *Las Meninas*, often seem unaware of the overwhelming human sympathy that imbues the piece: servants shine next to monarchs and monarchs pale next to children. Whatever their size or position, the characters have an equal dignity. Nobody ever appears as an ornament or a device. No one is superfluous. And this is true of all Velázquez's paintings.[24]

There are many specks and dabs in the canvas of our story that have also begun to attract attention. What is still conspicuously lacking is any consistent effort to understand the wider context. This requires a perspective that avoids the tendency to give pride of place to the unitary nation state in our understanding of politics, and to technique and empirical efficiency in our understanding of knowledge.[25] For it is only by placing the conquistadores in their pre-nationalist and pre-empirical context that we can have any hope of appreciating the medieval religious culture that motivated them and which, in turn, laid the foundations of a non-unitary system of government that survived for three centuries without a standing army or police force and with no major rebellions.

This was a remarkable achievement by any standards. Its badly needed re-evaluation should also allow us to see through the persistent condemnations of the legacy of the conquistadores as directly responsible for the ills that afflict modern Latin America. 'Let's Sue the Conquistadors' was the title of a recent article – in a publication otherwise renowned for its balanced judgements – about the plight of the peasants of Peru. 'Scattered across rural Peru are the ruins of *casas hacienda* (estate houses), reduced to broken porticoes and crumbled walls.' The scene, the article explains, recalls the heavy-handed land reforms undertaken in the 1970s in reaction to 'gross inequality in landholding and near-servile labour relations that stemmed from the Spanish conquest'.[26] This opinion is so widespread that the majority of readers will think it almost axiomatic. One of the most influential recent explorations of why nations 'fail', for instance, begins with an intriguing analysis of the city of Nogales, situated on the frontier of the Mexican state of Sonora and the American state of Arizona. While the Nogales of Arizona is prosperous, the Nogales of Sonora is poor. Why? Because of a mere 'institutional' difference, the authors assert: Arizona's Nogales has had the benefit of a pluralist and democratic system, while Sonora's Nogales still struggles under the weight of the conditions established when the conquistadores imposed their authority over a mass of indigenous peoples that have ever since been the victims of violence and exploitation. Arizona's Nogales has managed to develop 'inclusive' institutions which allow for an equitable sharing of power and encourage productivity, education, technological advancement and general well-being. Sonora's Nogales, by contrast, has stagnated under the weight of an 'extractive' model in which the sole aim is to acquire wealth through the ruthless exploitation of the majority for the sole benefit of an abusive and corrupt minority.[27]

This argument follows the still-influential view propagated by the nationalist histories of the nineteenth century, all of which condemned the vice-regal period as guilty of inflicting three hundred years of retrograde and obscurantist oppression. The reality, of course, is that the conditions of Sonora's Nogales, like those of the rest of Latin America, stem from the liberal reforms implemented in the nineteenth century by republican governments – reforms that abolished the legislative measures established, precisely, by the conquistadores and their successors. As we have seen, these measures succeeded in creating a moral climate in which the Spanish Crown was constantly reminded of its obligations towards the indigenous peoples, so much so that the latter felt empowered to fight for their rights all the way to the top of the judicial system.[28] The abolition of this set of legislative measures in favour of the 'universal' rights of 'man' in the abstract, left the Latin American indigenous communities totally defenceless against speculators for whom money was the only criterion. It also brought to an end a system of government dominated by a religious culture which has only recently begun to be properly evaluated, and which – it is now clear – allowed for a high level of local autonomy and regional diversity under a monarchy that was always deeply respectful of the local rights and privileges – the *fueros* – of its various kingdoms. The result, to cut a long story short, was three centuries of stability and prosperity. Of course, this was not the kind of prosperity that we would nowadays find readily comprehensible, accustomed as we are to insist on the need for relentless economic growth. But the vice-regal system, curiously enough, is much closer to the many and increasingly persuasive attempts to find solutions to the environmental crisis, a crisis brought about precisely by our obsession with continual economic growth.[29] From this viewpoint, there is still a lot to be learned from the legacy of a group of men who, whatever their myriad failures and shortcomings, deserve to be judged from a more sympathetic perspective than the one that has hitherto condemned them uncritically and on the basis of simplistic and even mendacious caricatures.

Notes

LIST OF ABBREVIATIONS

AGI   Archivo General de Indias, Seville
(IG) Indiferente General
(E)   Escribanía
(J)   Justicia
(P)   Patronato
(PR) Patronato Real

INTRODUCTION

1. Fernando de Herrera, *Poesía castellana original completa*, ed. Cristóbal Cuevas, 4th edn (Madrid, 2018), p. 807: 'No ciudad, eres orbe'.
2. *Critical and Historical Essays contributed to the Edinburgh Review*, 3 vols (London, 1843), vol. iii, p. 109.
3. On this often-neglected tradition see Gesa Mackenthun, *Metaphors of Dispossession: American Beginnings and the Translation of Empire, 1492–1637* (Norman, OK, 1997), p. 66: Mackenthun writes that, up until the beginning of the seventeenth century, Spain was not so much a rival as 'a precursor and model of English colonial action and ideology'.
4. *Tales of the Alhambra*, ed. W. T. Lenehan and A. B. Myers (Boston, MA, 1983), p. 8.
5. See Prescott's classic works, *The History of the Conquest of Mexico* (1843) and *A History of the Conquest of Peru* (1847).
6. It was almost thirty years before Shackleton returned his proposal to Patrick Leigh Fermor. 'The rather feeble publishers I was working with did not take to your proposal,' he wrote. 'This was their loss for I think it would have been a marvellous book.' I am very grateful to Adam Sisman for allowing me to see his transcription of this letter, found recently by him among Patrick Leigh Fermor's papers in the National Library of Scotland.

7. W. Wasink, ed., *The Apologie of Prince William of Orange against the Proclamation of the King of Spaine, edited after the English edition of 1581* (Leiden, 1969), p. 44. Such allegations would provide a wealth of detail to generations of dramatists and composers, most famously Friedrich Schiller's *Don Karlos* (1787), upon which Giuseppe Verdi based his famous opera. The very year in which Verdi's *Don Carlos* was first staged in Paris (1867), the American historian of the Netherlands J. L. Motley confidently asserted that, if Philip 'possessed a single virtue', it had 'eluded' his 'conscientious research'. 'If there are vices,' he continued, '– as possibly there are – from which he was exempt, it is because it is not permitted by human nature to attain perfection even in evil.' See his *History of the United Netherlands*, 4 vols (New York, 1868), vol. iii, p. 535.

8. J. H. Elliott, *Spain and Its World, 1500–1700* (New Haven, CT, 1989), pp. 217–61.

9. In the last few decades the image of a bigoted and obscurantist early modern Spain has been largely dispelled by historians. Even that most maligned and misunderstood of early modern institutions, the Spanish Inquisition, has emerged from recent investigations as a comparatively benign body, managing to bring about a relative degree of moderation by comparison with other judicial institutions of the time. Among recent studies see Francisco Bethencourt, *The Inquisition: A Global History* (Cambridge, 2009); Henry Kamen, *The Spanish Inquisition: An Historical Revision* (London, 1998); John Edwards, *The Spanish Inquisition* (Stroud, 1999); Helen Rawlings, *The Spanish Inquisition* (Oxford, 2008); Richard Kagan and Abigail Dyer, eds, *Inquisitorial Inquiries: Brief Lives of Secret Jews and Other Heretics* (Baltimore, MD, 2011); and Lu Ann Homza, *The Spanish Inquisition 1478–1614: An Anthology of Sources* (Indianapolis, IN, 2006). For the New World, see Solange Alberro, *Inquisición y Sociedad en México, 1571–1700* (Mexico City, 1988). Despite all these efforts, the overwhelmingly negative perceptions of the Inquisition are unlikely to subside. There is no dearth of modern monographs that thrive on blanket interpretations and attacks on opposing schools. See, for example: (a) for the view that, due to the circumstances in which inquisitors derived their information, the available evidence is only useful for revealing the anti-Jewish prejudices of the interrogators, Benzion Netanyahu, *The Origins of the Inquisition in Fifteenth-Century Spain* (New York, 1995), and Norman Roth, *Conversion, Inquisition and the Expulsion of the Jews from Spain* (Madison, WI, 1995); and (b) for the opposing view that, given that inquisitorial evidence reveals a deep religious and social affinity between Jews and Jewish converts to Christianity, the inquisitors were correct in their assumptions that most Jewish converts were in fact 'Judaizers', Yitzhak Baer, *A History of the Jews in Christian Spain*, 2 vols (Philadelphia, PA, 1992), and Haim Beinart, *Conversos on Trial: The Inquisition in Ciudad Real* (Jerusalem, 1981).

10. J. H. Elliott, *Imperial Spain* (Aylesbury, 1970), p. 65.

CHAPTER 1: THE OCEAN SEA

1. Maurice Lombard, 'Caffa et la fin de la route mongole', *Annales*, 5e année, no. 1 (1950), pp. 100–103.

2. For the Portuguese maritime development see especially the splendid study by Vitorino Magalhães Godinho, *A economia dos descobrimentos henriquinos* (Lisbon, 1962). For the Bristol connection, see Evan T. Jones and Margaret M. Condon, *Cabot and Bristol's Age of Discovery* (Bristol, 2016), pp. 4–8.

3. The classic study is by P. E. Russell, *Prince Henry 'the Navigator': A Life* (New Haven, CT, 2000).

4. On the legendary island of Brazil see T. J. Westropp, 'Brasil and the Legendary Islands of the North Atlantic: Their History and Fable. A Contribution to the "Atlantis" Problem', *Proceedings of the Royal Irish Academy*, 30 (1912), pp. 223–60; and Barbara Freitag, *Hy Brasil: The Metamorphosis of an Island: From Cartographic Error to Celtic Elysium* (Amsterdam, 2013).

5. Consuelo Varela Bueno, ed., *Cristóbal Colón, Textos y documentos completos* (Madrid, 1982), pp. 219, 357.

6. Varela Bueno, ed., *Cristóbal Colón*, p. 306.

7. Varela Bueno, ed., *Cristóbal Colón*, pp. 363, 167. Bartolomé de Las Casas, *Historia de las Indias*, ed. Agustín Millares Carló, 3 vols (Mexico City, 1951), vol. i, pp. 66–9.

8. Varela Bueno, ed., *Cristóbal Colón*, pp. xxxiv–xl, 1–2, 167. The viability of Columbus's claim to have sailed to Iceland is hotly disputed. For a meticulous discussion, see Alwyn A. Ruddock, 'Columbus and Iceland: New Light on an Old Problem', *Geographical Journal*, 136:2 (June 1970), pp. 177–89. I thank my colleague Evan T. Jones for alerting me to this item.

9. See John Day, 'The Great Bullion Famine in the Fifteenth Century', *Past & Present*, 79 (May 1978), pp. 3–54.

10. John Larner, *Marco Polo and the Discovery of the World* (New Haven, CT, 1999), pp. 152–6.

11. Cesare de Lollis et al., eds, *Raccolta di documenti e studi pubblicati della Reale Commissione Colombiana*, 14 vols (Rome, 1892–6), vol. i, p. iii, pl. CI.

12. Felipe Fernández-Armesto, *Columbus* (Oxford, 1991), p. 41.

13. Varela Bueno, ed., *Cristóbal Colón*, pp. 268, 277, 329, 357.

14. Miguel Ángel Ladero Quesada, 'Los genoveses en Sevilla y su región (siglos XIII–XVI): elementos de permanencia y arraigo', in idem, *Los mudéjares de Castilla y otros estudios de historia medieval andaluza* (Granada, 1989), pp. 293–312.

15. Juan Gil Fernández and Consuelo Varela Bueno, eds, *Cartas particulares a Colón y relaciones coetáneas* (Madrid, 1984), pp. 142–3.

16. A. Muro Orejón et al., eds, *Pleitos colombinos*, 4 vols (Seville, 1964–89), vol. iii, p. 390.

17. See Joaquim Carreras i Artau, *Relaciones de Arnau de Vilanova con los reyes de la casa de Aragón* (Barcelona, 1955), pp. 43–50.

18. Alain Milhou, *Colón y su mentalidad mesiánica en el ambiente franciscanista español* (Valladolid, 1983), pp. 361–400. See also Carol Delaney, *Columbus and the Quest for Jerusalem* (New York, 2011), passim.

19. Ronda was described as 'perched upon an isolated rock, crested by a strong citadel, with triple walls and towers'. See Washington Irving, ed., *A Chronicle of the Conquest of Granada, from the Manuscript of Antonio Agapida* (London, 1829), pp. 269–70.

20. 'Epístola que Mosén Diego de Valera enbió al rey don Fernando Nuestro Señor, después que ovo tomado la cibdad de Ronda', in *Prosistas castellanos del siglo xv*, ed. M. Penna, *Biblioteca de Autores Españoles*, vol. 116 (Madrid, 1959), p. 31.

21. Fernández-Armesto, *Columbus*, p. 50.

22. Pedro Mártir de Anglería, *Epistolario*, in *Documentos inéditos para la historia de España*, 113 vols (Madrid, 1953), vol. ix, p. 91.

23. See William Prescott, *History of the Reign of Ferdinand and Isabella the Catholic*, ed. John Foster Kirk (London, n.d.), pp. 205, 210, 224–9. Describing Ponce de León's funeral (pp. 302–3), Prescott writes: 'The banners have long since mouldered into dust; the very tomb which contained his ashes has been sacrilegiously demolished; but the fame of the hero will survive as long as anything like respect for valour, courtesy, unblemished honour, or any other attribute of chivalry, shall be found in Spain.'

24. *Epistolario*, vol. xi, p. 120.

25. J. H. Elliott, *Imperial Spain* (Aylesbury, 1970), p. 46.

26. *Don Quixote*, [i, 6], ed. Francisco Rico, 2 vols (Barcelona, 1998), vol. i, p. 83, where the *cura* refers to it as 'for its style, the best book in the world'.

27. David Crouch, *The English Aristocracy, 1070–1272: A Social Transformation* (New Haven, CT, 2011), pp. 248–9.

28. Christopher Dawson, *Religion and the Rise of Western Culture* (London, 1950), pp. 168–9.

29. See, for example, Nigel Saul, *For Honour and Fame: Chivalry in England, 1066–1500* (London, 2011), pp. 337–8.

30. On this see St Thomas Aquinas, *Summa Theologiae*, IIa–IIae, 161, 1 resp.; 162, 3 ad. 2; 161, 1 resp. 3.

31. *The Works of Geoffrey Chaucer*, ed. F. N. Robinson, 2nd edn (Oxford, 1957), pp. 167–88. The work by Buonaccorso is *De Nobilitate*. It became widely influential throughout Europe soon after it was written in the 1420s. It was translated into Italian, first by Giovanni Aurispa and then by Angelo Decembrio (the latter specifically for the Marquis of Santillana, Iñigo López de Mendoza, through whom it became widely known in fifteenth-century Spain due to the translation by Carlos de Viana). The first French translation was completed in 1449 by Jean Mielot (published in 1478); it was upon

this translation and the Latin original that John Tiptopf translated it into English in 1459–60 (printed by William Caxton in 1481). The first German translation was done by Niclas von Wyle in 1470. See Arsenio Dacosta Martínez and Carlos Mota Placencia, 'Un tratado inédito sobre la idea de nobleza atribuido a Francisco de Rades y Andrada', *Studia Aurea*, 8 (2014), pp. 417–54, at p. 436.

32. Irving A. Leonard, *Books of the Brave, being an account of books and of men in the Spanish Conquest and settlement of the sixteenth-century New World*, with a new introduction by Rolena Adorno (Berkeley, CA, 1992), p. 13.

33. Fernández-Armesto, *Columbus*, p. 17.

34. Gil Vicente, *Obras Completas*, ed. Álvaro Júlio da Costa Pimpão (Barcelos, 1956), p. 55. The influential work by Díez de Games is *El Vitorial*. I have used the edition by Rafael Beltrán Llavador (Salamanca, 1997).

35. Numbers are impossible to establish accurately, but Jews are generally acknowledged to have constituted between 3 per cent and 5 per cent of the population – that is, between 200,000 and 400,000.

36. Luis Suárez Fernández, *Les juifs espagnols au Moyen Âge* (Paris, 1983), p. 113.

37. Philippe Wolff, 'The 1391 Pogrom in Spain: Social Crisis or Not?', *Past & Present*, 50 (February 1971), pp. 4–18.

38. David Abulafia, *The Discovery of Mankind: Atlantic Encounters in the Age of Columbus* (New Haven, CT, 2008), pp. 22–3.

39. Angus MacKay, 'The Hispanic-Converso Predicament', *Transactions of the Royal Historical Society*, ser. 5, xxxv (1985), pp. 159–79; John Edwards, 'Religious Belief and Social Conformity: The *converso* Problem in Late Medieval Córdoba', *Transactions of the Royal Historical Society*, ser. 5, xxxi (1981).

40. David Abulafia, *Spain and 1492* (Dorchester, 1992), p. 38.

41. Henry Kamen, *The Spanish Inquisition: An Historical Revision* (London, 1997), pp. 28–65.

42. This had been a view central to the thirteenth-century Mongol Mission, led by Franciscan and Dominican friars, and it was still dominant in the millenarian literature that so attracted Columbus. On the Mongol Mission see Christopher Dawson, ed., *The Mission to Asia: Narratives and Letters of the Franciscan Missionaries in Mongolia and China in the Thirteenth and Fourteenth Centuries*, translated by a nun of Stanbrook Abbey (London, 1955).

43. The anti-feudal policies of Isabel and Fernando are lucidly analysed by Stephen Haliczer in *The Comuneros of Castile: The Forging of a Revolution, 1475–1521* (Madison, WI, 1981), pp. 31–65.

44. Varela Bueno, ed., *Cristóbal Colón*, p. 15.

45. Francisco López de Gómara, *Primera y segunda parte de la Historia General de las Indias con todo el descubrimiento y cosas notables que han acaecido desde que se ganaron hasta el año de 1551. Con la Conquista de Méjico de la Nueva España* (Zaragoza, 1552), unpaginated introduction.

CHAPTER 2: THE ADMIRAL

1. Felipe Fernández-Armesto, *Columbus* (Oxford, 1991), pp. 72–3.
2. Consuelo Varela Bueno, ed., *Cristóbal Colón: Textos y documentos completos* (Madrid, 1982), pp. 17–19.
3. Rolando Laguarda Trías, *El enigma de las latitudes de Colón* (Valladolid, 1974), pp. 13–28.
4. See the discussion in Laguarda Trías, *El enigma*, pp. 24–7.
5. Varela Bueno, ed., *Cristóbal Colón*, pp. 23–4.
6. Varela Bueno, ed., *Cristóbal Colón*, pp. 22, 27. See also Francisco Morales Padrón, 'Las relaciones entre Colón y Martín Alonso Pinzón', *Revista de Indias*, 21 (1961), pp. 95–105.
7. Varela Bueno, ed., *Cristóbal Colón*, pp. 27–30.
8. Varela Bueno, ed., *Cristóbal Colón*, pp. 31–2.
9. Varela Bueno, ed., *Cristóbal Colón*, pp. 33–4.
10. Varela Bueno, ed., *Cristóbal Colón*, pp. 35–44, 50–53.
11. Varela Bueno, ed., *Cristóbal Colón*, pp. 118–19, 141; Juan Gil Fernández and Consuelo Varela Bueno, eds, *Cartas de particulares a Colón y relaciones coetáneas* (Madrid, 1984), p. 260.
12. See Arthur Davies, 'The Loss of the *Santa Maria* Christmas Day, 1492', *American Historical Review*, 58:4 (July 1953), pp. 854–65.
13. Varela Bueno, ed., *Cristóbal Colón*, pp. 97–101; Rinaldo Caddeo, ed., *Le historie della vita e dei fatti di Cristoforo Colombo, per D. Fernando Colombo suo figlio*, 2 vols (Milan, 1958), vol. i, pp. 136–7; Bartolomé de Las Casas, *Historia de las Indias*, ed. Agustín Millares Carlo, 3 vols (Mexico City, 1951), vol. i, pp. 270–85.
14. Las Casas, *Historia de las Indias*, vol. i, p. 313.
15. *Memorias del reinado de los reyes católicos*, ed. Juan de Mata Carriazo y Arroquia (Madrid, 1962), pp. 308–10.
16. Pedro Mártir de Anglería, *Décadas*, ed. Edmundo O'Gorman, 2 vols (Mexico City, 1964), vol. i, 1; Martín Fernández de Navarrete, *Colección de los viajes y descubrimientos que hicieron por mar los españoles*, 4 vols (Madrid, 1954), vol. i, pp. 361–2.
17. The origin of the name is clearly phonetic. The Latin for St James, Sant Iacob, became Santiago, shortened to Tiago, which became Diego.
18. Gil Fernández and Varela Bueno, eds, *Cartas*, p. 183.
19. Gil Fernández and Varela Bueno, eds, *Cartas*, pp. 159–60.
20. Valera Bueno, ed., *Cristóbal Colón*, p. 144; Andrés Bernáldez, *Memorias del reinado de los reyes católicos*, ed. Juan de Mata Carriazo y Arroquia (Madrid, 1962), p. 295; Las Casas, *Historia de las Indias*, vol. i, pp. 358–9.
21. Varela Bueno, ed., *Cristóbal Colón*, p. 154. On the enslavement of cannibals see Antonio Rumeu de Armas, *La política indigenista de Isabel la Católica* (Valladolid, 1969); Felipe Fernández-Armesto, *Before Columbus:*

Exploration and Colonization from the Mediterranean to the Atlantic, 1229–1492 (Philadelphia, PA, 1987), pp. 232–3.

22. Las Casas, *Historia de las Indias*, vol. i, p. 358; Varela Bueno, ed., *Cristóbal Colón*, p. 150.

23. Las Casas, *Historia de las Indias*, vol. i, pp. 358–9.

24. Varela Bueno, ed., *Cristóbal Colón*, pp. 147–62.

25. Gil Fernández and Varela Bueno, eds, *Cartas*, pp. 217–23.

26. Gil Fernández and Varela Bueno, eds, *Cartas*, pp. 264–5.

27. Gil Fernández and Varela Bueno, eds, *Cartas*, p. 258.

28. Las Casas, *Historia de las Indias*, vol. i, pp. 416–20. This was a typical Lascasian exaggeration, but it is telling that even his enemy, Gonzalo Fernández de Oviedo, spoke of 'countless victims'; cf. *Historia general y natural de las Indias*, ed. Juan Pérez de Tudela Bueso, *Biblioteca de Autores Españoles*, 5 vols [cvii–cxxi] (Madrid, 1959), vol. i, pp. 64–8.

29. Consuelo Varela Bueno, *La caída de Cristóbal Colón: El juicio de Bobadilla*, ed. and trans. Isabel Aguirre (Madrid, 2006), pp. 28–9.

30. Fernández de Navarrete, *Colección de los viajes*, vol. i, p. 408.

31. Fernández de Navarrete, *Colección de los viajes*, vol. i, pp. 399–401. The decree was signed on 10 April 1495.

32. On this see Juan Pérez de Tudela y Bueso, *Las armadas de Indias y los orígenes de la política de colonización* (Madrid, 1956), p. 103.

33. Fernández de Navarrete, *Colección de los viajes*, vol. i, p. 406.

34. 'Instructions to Columbus and Antonio de Torres, 15 June 1497', in Christopher Columbus, *Libro de los privilegios del almirante don Cristóbal Colón (1498)*, ed. and trans. Ciriaco Pérez Bustamante (Madrid, 1951), doc. 8.

35. 'Instruction of 22 July 1497', in Columbus, *Libro de los privilegios*, doc. 22.

36. Helen Nader, *Liberty in Absolutist Spain: The Habsburg Sale of Towns, 1516–1700* (Baltimore, MD, 1990), p. 93. Nader's source is Demetrio Ramos, 'Colón y el enfrentamiento de los caballeros: Un serio problema del segundo viaje, que nuevos documentos ponen al descubierto', *Revista de Indias*, 39 (1979), pp. 9–88.

37. See, for example, Las Casas, *Historia de las Indias*, vol. ii, p. 90.

38. Pérez de Tudela, *Las armadas*, p. 259.

39. See the splendid study by Nader, *Liberty in Absolutist Spain*, p. 92.

40. Pedro Mártir de Anglería, *Epistolario*, in *Documentos inéditos*, vol. ix, p. 316.

41. Varela Bueno, ed., *Cristóbal Colón*, p. 204.

42. Varela Bueno, ed., *Cristóbal Colón*, pp. 179–85.

43. Varela Bueno, ed., *Cristóbal Colón*, p. 203.

44. I have used the 1611 King James version.

45. Gil Fernández and Varela Bueno, eds, *Cartas*, pp. 267–9.

46. Varela Bueno, ed., *Cristóbal Colón*, pp. 215–17.

47. Varela Bueno, ed., *Cristóbal Colón*, p. 218. It is difficult to capture the freshness of the Spanish phrase, *andando más, más se sabe*.

48. Antonio Rumeu de Armas, *Itinerario de los Reyes Católicos, 1474–1516* (Madrid, 1974), pp. 235–6.

49. Fernández de Navarrete, *Colección de los viajes*, vol. i, p. 222.

50. Varela Bueno, ed., *Cristóbal Colón*, pp. 190–99.

51. Varela Bueno, ed., *Cristóbal Colón*, p. 221; Las Casas, *Historia de las Indias*, vol. i, p. 498.

52. Varela Bueno, ed., *Cristóbal Colón*, p. 222.

53. Las Casas, *Historia de las Indias*, vol. ii, p. 9.

54. Fernández-Armesto, *Columbus*, p. 126.

55. Varela Bueno, ed., *Cristóbal Colón*, p. 208.

56. Varela Bueno, ed., *Cristóbal Colón*, p. 238.

57. Varela Bueno, ed., *Cristóbal Colón*, p. 216.

58. Varela Bueno, ed., *Cristóbal Colón*, pp. 212–16.

59. Las Casas, *Historia de las Indias*, vol. ii, p. 69.

60. Las Casas, *Historia de las Indias*, vol. ii, p. 70.

61. Gil Fernández and Varela Bueno, eds, *Cartas*, pp. 271–6.

62. Varela Bueno, *Caída de Colón*, p. 39. This version of events comes from Peter Martyr, see Gil Fernández and Varela Bueno, eds, *Cartas*, pp. 95–8.

63. Quoted in Varela Bueno, *Caída de Colón*, p. 40.

64. Gil Fernández and Varela Bueno, eds, *Cartas*, pp. 278–9.

65. Varela Bueno, *Caída de Colón*, pp. 41, 45.

66. Varela Bueno, *Caída de Colón*, p. 45.

67. Duquesa de Berwick y Alba, *Autógrafos de Cristóbal Colón y papeles de América* (Madrid, 1892), pp. 25–38.

68. Varela Bueno, *Caída de Colón*, p. 48.

69. The complete document is transcribed and edited by Isabel Aguirre, and published as *Pesquisia del Comendador Francisco de Bobadilla*, in Varela Bueno, *Caída de Colón*, pp. 181–257.

70. Varela Bueno, ed., *Cristóbal Colón*, pp. 263, 270.

71. Varela Bueno, ed., *Cristóbal Colón*, p. 244.

72. Varela Bueno, ed., *Cristóbal Colón*, p. 265.

73. Andrés Bernáldez, *Memorias*, p. 335. On the anti-Genoese feeling see Felipe Fernández-Armesto, *The Canary Islands after the Conquest: The Making of a Colonial Society in the Early Sixteenth Century* (Oxford, 1981), pp. 23–30.

74. Fernández de Navarrete, *Colección de los viajes*, vol. i, p. 443. The point is also made by Las Casas, *Historia de las Indias*, vol. ii, p. 176.

75. Fernández de Navarrete, *Colección de los viajes*, vol. i, p. 222.

76. *The 'Book of Prophecies' edited by Christopher Columbus* (Los Angeles, CA, 1997), pp. 66, 68, 70.

77. *Psalterium Hebraeum, Graecum, Arabicum, et Chaldaeum, cum Tribus Latinis interpretationibus et glossis* (Genoa, 1516), note D. The psalm concerned is no. 19.4–5: 'Non sunt loquelæ, neque sermones, quorum non audiantur voces eorum. In omnem terram exivit sonus eorum, et in fines orbis terræ verba eorum', which the 1611 King James Version renders thus: 'There is no speech nor language where their voice is not heard. Their line is gone out through all the earth, and their words to the end of the world.' And see also J. S. Cummins, 'Christopher Columbus: Crusader, Visionary and *Servus Dei*', in *Medieval Hispanic Studies Presented to R. Hamilton*, ed. A. D. Deyermond (London, 1976), p. 45.

78. The biblical references for these associations are Genesis 10:4 and Isaiah 23:12. See Felipe Fernández-Armesto, ed., *Columbus on Himself* (Indianapolis, IN, 2010), p. 266, fn. 210.

79. Fernández-Armesto, ed., *Columbus on Himself*, pp. 159–60.

80. Varela Bueno, ed., *Cristóbal Colón*, pp. 308–15.

81. Fernández de Navarrete, *Colección de los viajes*, vol. i, p. 224.

82. Varela Bueno, ed., *Cristóbal Colón*, p. 298.

83. Fernández de Navarrete, *Colección de los viajes*, vol. i, pp. 223–5.

84. Varela Bueno, ed., *Cristóbal Colón*, p. 317; Fernández de Oviedo, *Historia General*, vol. i, p. 72.

85. Varela Bueno, ed., *Cristóbal Colón*, pp. 324–5.

86. Caddeo, ed., *Le historie della vita e dei fatti di Cristoforo Colombo*, vol. ii, p. 93.

87. Pedro Mártir de Anglería, *Epistolario*, in *Documentos inéditos*, vol. ix, pp. 261, 307.

88. Varela Bueno, ed., *Cristóbal Colón*, p. 320.

89. Varela Bueno, ed., *Cristóbal Colón*, pp. 323–4.

90. Varela Bueno, ed., *Cristóbal Colón*, p. 329.

91. Varela Bueno, ed., *Cristóbal Colón*, pp. 320, 327.

92. A point well made by Fernández-Armesto, *Columbus*, p. 191.

93. Varela Bueno, ed., *Cristóbal Colón*, pp. 319–20.

94. Varela Bueno, ed., *Cristóbal Colón*, p. 341.

95. Varela Bueno, ed., *Cristóbal Colón*, p. 358.

CHAPTER 3: HISPANIOLA

1. Angus MacKay, *Spain in the Middle Ages: From Frontier to Empire, 1000–1500* (London, 1977), p. 32.

2. J. H. Elliott, *Imperial Spain, 1469–1716* (Aylesbury, 1990), p. 32; Teófilo F. Ruiz, *Spanish Society, 1400–1600* (Harlow, 2001), pp. 79–81. See also Jesús D. Rodríguez Velasco, *El debate sobre la caballería en el siglo XV: la tratadística caballeresca castellana en su marco europeo* (Salamanca,

1996), and Martín de Riquer, *Caballeros andantes españoles* (Madrid, 1967).

3. Stephen Haliczer, *The Comuneros of Castile: The Forging of a Revolution, 1475–1521* (Madison, WI, 1981), p. 31.

4. These developments need to be understood in the context of the sharp depopulation that the Black Death caused in rural areas which, in the fifteenth century, developed into a welcome asset. This was in large measure the result of the indirect, long-term effects that the medieval English policy of taxation on raw wool had in Castile. As English wool merchants came to realize that it was more economically viable to produce cloth than to sell heavily taxed raw wool, Flanders and France began to turn their attention to the growing Castilian raw-wool industry. This contributed enormously to the growth of old Castilian cities like Burgos, Segovia and Soria, and it fuelled a slow but steady expansion in the luxury textile industries created in Andalusian cities like Seville and Córdoba. The classic work on the English wool industry is by Eileen Power, *The Wool Trade in English Medieval History* (Oxford, 1941); on the effects of English wool taxation on the Iberian economy see Hilario Casado Alonso and Flávio Miranda, 'The Iberian Economy and Commercial Exchange with North-Western Europe in the Later Middle Ages', in Evan T. Jones and Richard Stone, *The World of the Newport Medieval Ship* (Cardiff, 2018), pp. 214–21. For the general effects in the late fifteenth century see Haliczer, *Comuneros*, pp. 12–23.

5. Haliczer, *Comuneros*, pp. 24–7.

6. Elliott, *Imperial Spain*, pp. 86–99; Haliczer, *Comuneros*, pp. 36–8.

7. A mere glance at the magnificent alabaster tomb of Cardinal Juan de Cervantes (1382–1453) – the only one of its kind in Seville Cathedral, preserved in the chapel of St Hermenegild – is immediately evocative of that chivalric ethos where the code of honour is inseparable from a spirit of service. Its disarmingly simple coat of arms, consisting of two austere deer (*cervus* in Latin, from which the family derived its name) evokes a spirit in which the duties of warfare found their natural completion in service. Any excessive accumulation of wealth was accordingly seen as an ignoble affront on the rights of the poor. On Don Diego's ancestors, see Rodrigo Méndez Silva, *Ascendencia ilustre, gloriosos hechos y posteridad noble del famoso Nuño Alfonso, Alcaide de la imperial ciudad de Toledo, Príncipe de su milicia, Ricohome de Castilla* (Madrid, 1648). The distinguished Cordoban poet Juan de Mena (1411–56) wrote about 'the lineage of Cervantes and Cervatos . . . stem from the Munios and Aldefonsos; . . . they are Galicians and descend from Gothic kings . . . They took part in the capture of Toledo and, having settled in the village of Cervatos, took that as their new name.' A branch of the Cervatos later called itself Cervantes and the name is mentioned in connection with the capture of Seville. See Luis Astrana Marín,

Vida ejemplar y heroica de Miguel de Cervantes Saavedra, 7 vols (Madrid, 1948–58), vol. i, ch. 4.

8. Cervantes, *Don Quijote* [ii, 36], ed. Francisco Rico, 2 vols (Barcelona, 1998), vol. i, p. 935. It is impossible to capture the disarming charm of the original: '. . . los extraordinariamente afligidos y desconsolados, en casos grandes y en desdichas enormes, no van a buscar su remedio a las casas de los letrados . . . ni al caballero que nunca ha acertado a salir de los términos de su lugar, ni al perezoso cortesano que antes busca nuevas para referirlas y contarlas que procura hacer obras y hazañas para que otros las cuenten y las escriban . . .'

9. Cervantes, *Don Quijote* [ii, 1], vol. i, pp. 633–4.

10. On the *quinto real* see Martín Fernández de Navarrete, *Colección de viajes y descubrimientos que hicieron por mar los españoles*, 4 vols (Madrid, 1954), vol. i, p. 546.

11. The Franciscans would found their first official presence on the island in 1505, the Province of the Holy Cross, with its headquarters in Santo Domingo; five convents were subsequently established: Santo Domingo, Concepción de la Vega, Vera Paz de Jaraguá, Villa de Buenaventura, and Mejorada in Cotuy; see Antonine S. Tibesar, 'The Franciscan Province of the Holy Cross of Española, 1509–1559', *The Americas*, 13:4 (April 1957), pp. 377–89; José Torrubia, *Crónica de la Provincia Franciscana de Santa Cruz de la Española y Caracas* (Caracas, 1972), p. 319.

12. Joaquín Pacheco and Francisco Cárdenas, eds, *Colección de documentos inéditos relativos al descubrimiento, conquista y organización de las posesiones españolas en América y Oceanía*, 42 vols (Madrid, 1864–84), vol. xxxi, pp. 13–25.

13. On this see Juan Pérez de Tudela y Bueso, *Las armadas de Indias y los orígenes de la política de colonización* (Madrid, 1956), passim.

14. Francisco López de Gómara, *La Conquista de México*, ed. José Luis Rojas (Madrid, 1987), p. 36. As Christian Duverger has pointed out (*Hernán Cortés: Más allá de la leyenda* [Madrid, 2013], p. 81), the story might contain an element of fantasy resulting from an image that Cortés was interested in promoting years later with the benefit of hindsight. However that may be, the incident is not at all out of character.

15. Bartolomé de Las Casas, *Historia de las Indias*, ed. Agustín Millares Carló, 3 vols (Mexico City, 1951), vol. ii, p. 215.

16. On this, see the opinion of Columbus's companion, Michele de Cuneo, in Juan Gil Fernández and Consuelo Varela Bueno, eds, *Cartas particulares a Colón y relaciones coetáneas* (Madrid, 1984), p. 257.

17. Las Casas, *Historia de las Indias*, vol. ii, p. 249.

18. Las Casas, *Historia de las Indias*, vol. ii, p. 226.

19. Hugh Thomas, *Rivers of Gold: The Rise of the Spanish Empire* (London, 2003), pp. 190–91.

20. Cándido Ruiz Martínez, *Gobierno de Frey Nicolás de Ovando en la Española* (Madrid, 1892), pp. 14–15; Ursula Lamb, *Frey Nicolás de Ovando* (Madrid, 1956), p. 130.

21. Bartolomé de Las Casas, *Brevísima Relación de la destrucción de las Indias*, various editions. There is a good English version in Penguin by Nigel Griffin: *A Short Account of the Destruction of the Indies* (Harmondsworth, 1992), see pp. 11, 129.

22. Las Casas, *Historia de las Indias*, vol. ii, p. 214.

23. Earl J. Hamilton, *American Treasure and the Price Revolution in Spain* (Cambridge, MA, 1934), p. 123. The *marvedí* was the most commonly used copper coin in Castile. Its value fluctuated so much in the sixteenth century that equivalences often prove misleading. Still, when we consider that Ovando's annual salary was 360,000 *marvedís*, these figures are substantial.

24. Antonio Rumeu de Armas, *Itinerario de los Reyes Católicos, 1474–1516* (Madrid, 1974), pp. 157–64, 179–83.

25. On Philip and Juana's sojourn in England, see the gripping reconstruction in Thomas Penn, *Winter King: The Dawn of Tudor England* (London, 2012), pp. 213–26.

26. Whether Juana was actually mad is a difficult question. Henry VII of England had thought her perfectly sane despite rumours to the contrary; cf. Penn, *Winter King*, p. 223. Her deep consciousness of her proprietary rights and their key role in securing the legitimacy, first of her father Fernando and then of her son Charles, is the topic of Bethany Aram, *Juana the Mad: Sovereignty and Dynasty in Renaissance Europe* (Baltimore, MD, 2005).

27. José Enrique Ruiz-Domènech, *El Gran Capitán* (Barcelona, 2002), pp. 401–16.

28. Penn, *Winter King*, p. 220.

29. Manuel Fernández Álvarez, *Corpus documental de Carlos V*, 5 vols (Salamanca, 1973), vol. i, p. 139.

30. *The Prince*, ch. xxi.

31. Thomas, *Rivers of Gold*, pp. 226–8.

32. Martín Fernández de Navarrete, *Colección de viajes y descubrimientos que hicieron por mar los españoles*, 4 vols (Madrid, 1954), vol. i, pp. 498–504.

33. Thomas, *Rivers of Gold*, p. 256.

34. Consuelo Varela Bueno, ed., *Cristóbal Colón: Textos y documentos completos* (Madrid, 1982), p. 18, fn. 4.

35. C. H. Haring, *The Spanish Empire in America* (New York, 1947), p. 16.

CHAPTER 4: A QUESTION OF JUSTICE

1. Bartolomé de Las Casas, *Historia de las Indias*, ed. Agustín Millares Carló, 3 vols (Mexico City, 1951), vol. ii, p. 440.

2. Las Casas, *Historia de las Indias*, quoted in Daniel Ulloa, *Los predicadores divididos: los Dominicos en Nueva España, siglo XVI* (Mexico City, 1977), p. 54, fn. 23.

3. Las Casas, *Historia de las Indias*, vol. ii, p. 441.

4. See above, p. 63.

5. Lewis Hanke, *Bartolomé de Las Casas: An Interpretation of his Life and Writings* (The Hague, 1951), p. 18. Montesinos, Hanke remarked, 'had come as near to convincing his hearers . . . as would a theological student in our day who delivered a soapbox philippic in Wall Street on the Biblical text "Sell whatsoever thou hast and give it to the poor, and thou shalt have treasure in heaven." '

6. Las Casas, *Historia de las Indias*, quoted in Ulloa, *Los predicadores*, p. 54.

7. Las Casas, *Historia de las Indias*, vol. ii, p. 443.

8. León Lopetegui and Félix Zubillaga, *Historia de la Iglesia en América Española*, 2 vols (Madrid, 1965), vol. i, p. 257, fn. 41.

9. José María Chacón y Calvo, ed., *Cedulario Cubano (Los Orígenes de la Colonización)* (Madrid, 1929), pp. 444–7. See also Manuel Serrano y Sanz, *Orígenes de la dominación española en América*, in *Biblioteca de Autores Españoles*, vol. xxv (Madrid, 1918), p. 348.

10. See, for example, *Le Orazioni di S. Caterina da Siena*, a cura di Giuliana Cavallini (Rome, 1978), IV, ll. 95–117.

11. *Il Dialogo della Divina Providenzia di S. Caterina da Siena*, a cura di Giuliana Cavallini (Rome, 1968), Prologue. For the 'divinization' of humanity see *Orazioni*, XXI, ll. 90–95, 104–9, 117–20. I draw on Kenelm Foster's introduction to *I Catherine: Selected Writings of St Catherine of Siena*, edited and translated by Kenelm Foster OP and Mary John Ronayne OP (London, 1980), pp. 30–39.

12. *Dialogo*, LXIV; *Orazioni*, XXI, ll. 80–89; *I Catherine*, pp. 172, 196.

13. Thomas Ripoll and Antonin Bremond, *Bullarium Ordinis Fratrum Praedicatorum*, 8 vols (Rome, 1729–40), vol. ii, p. 415.

14. Ripoll and Bremond, *Bullarium*, vol. ii, p. 445.

15. *Archivum Fratrum Praedicatorum*, vol. 7 (Rome, 1937), pp. 227, 230.

16. Ripoll and Bremond, *Bullarium*, vol. iv, p. 44.

17. Cajetan used the formula *gravioris culpae*. See Albertus de Meyer, ed., *Registrum Litterarum Fr Thomae de Vio Caietano OP Mag. Ordinis (1508–1513)*, in *Monumenta Ordinis Praedicatorum Historica*, 29 vols (Rome, 1896–2005), vol. xvii (Rome 1935), p. 7, n. 29.

18. Vicente Beltrán de Heredia, *Historia de la Reforma de la Provinicia de España (1450–1550)*, in *Dissertationes Historicae. Instituto Storico Domenicano*, 74 vols (Rome 1931–2007), vol. xi (Rome, 1939), pp. 108–23.

19. See Alain Milhou, *Colón y su mentalidad mesiánica en el ambiente franciscanista español* (Valladolid, 1983), pp. 349–449.

20. On this see Marcel Bataillon, *Erasmo y España: Estudios sobre la historia espiritual del siglo xvi*, trans. Antonio Alatorre (Mexico City, 1950), pp. 67–71.

21. Juan de Vallejo, *Memorial de la vida de fray Francisco Jiménez de Cisneros*, ed. Antonio de la Torre y del Cerro (Madrid, 1913), pp. 73–85.

22. Jodi Bilinkoff, 'A Spanish Prophetess and Her Patrons: The Case of María de Santo Domingo', *Sixteenth Century Journal*, 23:1 (Spring 1992), pp. 21–34.

23. Beltrán de Heredia, *Historia de la Reforma*, p. 38.

24. Alexander VI's bulls, all signed in 1493, are: *Inter cetera* and *Eximie devotionis* (3 May), *Piis fildelium* (23 June), *Inter cetera* (late June) and *Dudum siquidem*; all printed in Manuel Giménez Fernández, 'Nuevas consideraciones sobre la historia, sentido y valor de las bulas alejandrinas de 1493 referentes a las Indias', *Anuario de estudios americanos*, I (1944), pp. 173–429. For the 1504 pronouncement, see Chacón y Calvo, ed., *Cedulario*, p. 429.

25. Chacón y Calvo, ed., *Cedulario*, p. 447.

26. Cédula, April 1495, Richard Konetzke, ed., *Colección de documentos para la historia de la formación social de Hispanoamérica, 1493–1810*, 5 vols (Madrid, 1953/63), vol. i, p. 2.

27. Instrucción, September 1501, Konetzke, ed., *Colección*, vol. i, p. 5. The opinion was famously echoed in the 1530s by the great Dominican theologian, Francisco de Vitoria, when he wrote to Miguel de Arcos that making war on the natives of America was like making war on the inhabitants of Seville. See Francisco de Vitoria, *Relectio 'De Indis'*, ed. L. Pereña and J. M. Pérez Prendes (Madrid, 1967), pp. 136–9.

28. Ronald D. Hussey, 'Text of the Laws of Burgos (1512–1513) Concerning the Treatment of the Indians', *Hispanic American Historical Review*, 12:3 (August 1932), pp. 306–21.

29. Our only source is Las Casas. Here I have followed the summary by Hussey, 'Text of the Laws of Burgos', pp. 301–26, at pp. 303–5.

30. 'Libellus de insulanis oceanis quas vulgus Indias apelat per Ioannem Lopez de Palacios Ruvios decretorum doctorem regiumque consiliarum editus', *Biblioteca Nacional de Madrid*, MS 17641 (1513), fol. 4ʳ.

31. 'Libellus de insulanis', fols 13ʳ, 4ʳ.

32. 'Libellus de insulanis', fols 4ʳ⁻ᵛ.This opinion was almost certainly derived from the work *Mundus novus* (1505) attributed to Amerigo Vespucci; see Luigi Firpo, ed., *Colombo, Vespucci, Verazzano* (Turin, 1966), p. 88.

33. 'Libellus de insulanis', fols 5ʳ – 7ʳ, 15ᵛ. It is difficult to render the full force of the original: '. . . eorum ita sunt inepti et imbeciles, qui se nullo modo gubernare sciunt; quapropter largo modo possunt dici servi, *quasi* nati ad serviendum . . .' [my emphasis].

34. 'Libellus de insulanis', fol. 15^v.

35. Anthony Pagden, *The Fall of Natural Man: The American Indian and the Origins of Comparative Ethnology* (Cambridge, 1982), pp. 55–6.

36. 'El Requerimo q se ha de hazer a los indios de terra firme', *Archivo General de Indias*, Seville, Panamá 233, lib. I, fols 49^r–50^v. A good transcription was printed in Manuel Orozco y Berra, *Historia antigua y de la conquista de México*, 4 vols (Mexico City, 1880), vol. iv, pp. 85–6.

37. Sir Arthur Helps, to whom we owe the most famous rendering of the document in English, referred to it as 'an illustration of how long foolish conceits linger in the halls of learning', while admitting that its 'comicality' had often cheered him 'in the midst of the tedious research'. 'The logic,' Helps continued, 'the history, even the grammatical construction, are all, it seems to me, alike in error.' *The Spanish Conquest in America, and its Relation to the History of Slavery and the Government of Colonies*, 4 vols (London, 1856–68), vol. i, p. 267.

38. *Historia general y natural de las Indias*, ed. Juan Pérez de Tudela Bueso, *Biblioteca de Autores Españoles*, 5 vols [cvii–cxi] (Madrid, 1959), vol. cix, p. 230.

39. Las Casas, *Historia de las Indias*, vol. iii, p. 31. The characteristically Lascasian flurry of adjectives is quoted in Lewis Hanke, 'The "Requerimiento" and its Interpreters', *Revista de Historia de América*, 1 (March 1938), pp. 25–34, at pp. 32–3.

40. This was the opinion of the renowned Sevillian canon lawyer and politician Manuel Giménez Fernández (1896–1968), quoted in Juan Friede and Benjamin Keen, *Bartolomé de Las Casas in History* (DeKalb, IL, 1971), pp. 149–50.

41. Walter Ullmann, *Medieval Papalism* (London, 1949), pp. 10, 14.

42. Pope Innocent IV, *Commentaria in quinque libros decretalium* (Turin, 1581), ad 3, 34, 8, fol. 176. On the Mongol Mission see Christopher Dawson, ed., *The Mission to Asia: Narratives and Letters of the Franciscan Missionaries in Mongolia and China in the Thirteenth and Fourteenth Centuries*, translated by a nun of Stanbrook Abbey (London, 1955).

43. Hostiensis, *Lectura quinque decretalium* (Paris, 1512), ad 3, 34, 8, fol. 124.

44. See the excellent discussion in James Muldoon, 'John Wyclif and the Rights of the Infidels: The *Requerimiento* Re-Examined', *The Americas*, 36:3 (January 1980), pp. 301–16, at 305–11.

45. For example, when one of the most renowned modern historians of the age edited a critical edition of Palacios Rubios's treatise on the rights of the Spanish Crown in the New World, he candidly endorsed Las Casas's judgement that the Spanish canonist had followed 'the error of Hostiensis'. Juan López de Palacios Rubios, *De las Islas del Mar Océano*, ed. Silvio Zavala (Mexico City, 1954), p. xc.

46. Las Casas himself admitted to being deeply puzzled by Palacios Rubios's apparent willingness to follow such a doctrine, cf. *Historia de las Indias*, iii, pp. 25–8.

47. J. H. Elliott, *Empires of the Atlantic World: Britain and Spain in America 1492–1830* (New Haven, CT, 2006), p. 77.

48. Mario Góngora, *Studies in the Colonial History of Spanish America* (Cambridge, 1975), pp. 68–79.

49. Bartolomé Clavero, *Derecho de los reinos (Temas de historia del derecho)* (Seville, 1977), pp. 125–30.

50. *Recopilación de las leyes de los reynos de las Indias, mandadas a imprimir, y publicar por la Magestad Católica del Rey Don Carlos II nuestro señor*, 5th edn, 4 vols (Madrid, 1841), vol. i, p. 148, ley xxii: 'Los ministros y jueces obedezcan y no cumplan nuestras cédulas y despachos en que intervinieren los vicios de obrepción y subrepción, y en la primera ocasión nos avisen de la causa por que no lo hicieren.'

51. On the continuation of slave raids in the Caribbean see Enrique Otte, 'Los jerónimos y el tráfico humano en el caribe: una rectificación', *Anuario de estudios atlánticos*, 32 (1975), pp. 187–204. An illustrative example of non-compliance with royal edicts is the letter of Francisco Tello de Sandoval (November 1543), explaining to Charles V that despite his order to send any natives who had been shipped to Spain back to the Indies, their owners had opted to keep them by taking them from Seville to places where they would not be noticed. AGI (IG), 1095, ramo 6, no. 161.

52. *La historia general de las Indias, primera parte* (Seville, 1535), fol. lviii^v.

53. Ortiz is quoted by Pedro Mártir de Anglería, *Opus epistoralum* (Alcalá de Henares, 1530), fol. xcv^r.

54. 'Memorial de Fray Bernardino de Manzanedo sobre el buen régimen y gobierno de los indios', in Manuel Serrano y Sanz, *Orígenes de la dominación española en América*, in *Biblioteca de Autores Españoles*, vol. xxv (Madrid, 1918), p. dlxv.

55. A well-documented case is that of the Franciscan mission stations in eighteenth-century California. See Sherbourne F. Cook, *The Conflict between the California Indian and the White Civilization* (Berkeley, CA, 1976), pp. 135–57. For a comparative perspective focusing on modern India see Stephanie Thiel, 'Global Anomie and India: A Conceptual Approach', *Indian Journal of Asian Affairs*, 24:1–2 (June – December 2011), pp. 11–34.

56. Enrique Otte, *Las Perlas del Caribe* (Caracas, 1977), pp. 118–19.

57. Felipe Fernández-Armesto, *Amerigo: The Man who Gave his Name to America* (London, 2006), pp. 64, 68, 88–9, 182, 192.

58. Carl Ortwin Sauer, *The Early Spanish Main* (Berkeley, CA, 1966), pp. 104–19, 161–77.

59. Sauer, *Early Spanish Main*, p. 225.

60. Joaquín Pacheco and Francisco Cárdenas, eds, *Colección de documentos inéditos relativos al descubrimiento, conquista y organización de las posesiones españolas en América y Oceanía*, 42 vols (Madrid, 1864–84), vol. xxxix, p. 241.

61. Las Casas, *Historia de las Indias*, vol. iii, p. 15. The rumours were confirmed, in what is clearly a more ironic tone, by Pedro Mártir de Anglería: 'Spain no longer needs . . . to pierce mountains' and expose herself 'to a thousand dangers to make the earth yield its riches. She now finds them floating on the surface . . .'. *Décadas del Nuevo Mundo*, ed. Ramón Alba (Madrid, 1989), pp. 34, 37.

62. Miguel Ángel Ladero Quesada, *La Hacienda Real de Castilla. Rentas y Gastos de la Corona al morir Isabel I* (Seville, 1976), p. 326.

63. Miguel Ángel Ladero Quesada, *El primer oro de América* (Madrid, 2002), p. 62.

64. Carmen Mena García, *Sevilla y las flotas de Indias* (Seville, 1998), p. 73.

65. Pedro Mártir de Anglería, *Décadas*, p. 140.

66. Pedro Mártir de Anglería, *Décadas*, p. 166.

67. J. H. Elliott, *The Old World and the New, 1492–1650* (Cambridge, 1970), pp. 15–16.

68. Quoted in Fernández-Armesto, *Amerigo*, p. 100.

69. William Shakespeare, *Othello*, I, 3, 144–6.

70. Las Casas, *Historia de las Indias*, vol. iii, p. 175.

71. Hugh Thomas, *Rivers of Gold: The Rise of the Spanish Empire* (London, 2003), p. 437.

72. Las Casas, *Historia de las Indias*, vol. iii, p. 105. For the mention of the strait see Solís's 'Instructions' in Pacheco and Cárdenas, eds, *Colección de documentos*, vol. xxxix, pp. 325–7.

73. Thomas, *Rivers of Gold*, p. 438.

CHAPTER 5: CUBA

1. Juan Beltrán, *Bojeo de Cuba por Sebastián de Ocampo* (Havana, 1924), pp. 1–24.

2. See Santiago Otero Enríquez, *Noticias genealógicas de la familia Velázquez Gaztelu* (Madrid, 1916).

3. AGI (IG), leg. 419, lib. 5, fol. 94ᵛ.

4. I. A. Wright, *The Early History of Cuba, 1492–1586* (New York, 1916), pp. 24–45.

5. Las Casas, *Historia de las Indias*, ed. Agustín Millares Carlo, 3 vols (Mexico City, 1951), vol. ii, p. 524.

6. Las Casas, *Historia de las Indias*, vol. ii, pp. 536–9.

7. D. A. Brading, *The First America: The Spanish Monarchy, Creole Patriots and the Liberal State, 1492–1867* (Cambridge, 1991), p. 59.

8. Brading, *First America*, p. 60; Hugh Thomas, *Rivers of Gold: The Rise of the Spanish Empire* (London, 2003), p. 279.

9. Joaquín Pacheco and Francisco Cárdenas, eds, *Colección de documentos inéditos relativos al descubrimiento, conquista y organización de las posesiones españolas en América y Oceanía*, 42 vols (Madrid, 1864–84), vol. vii, p. 427. See also the discussion in Luis Arranz Márquez, *Don Diego Colón: almirante, virrey y gobernador de las Indias* (Madrid, 1982), p. 371.

10. Ecclesiasticus (Sirach), 34. 20–22. I have used Ronald Knox's evocative translation, though the Latin text from the Vulgate version available to Las Casas is rather more forceful: 'Qui offert sacrificium ex substantia pauperum, quasi qui victimat filium in conspectu patris sui. Panis egentium vita pauperum est: qui defraudat illum homo sanguinis est. Qui aufert in sudore panem, quasi qui occidit proximum suum. Qui effundit sanguinem, et qui fraudem facit mercenario, fratres sunt.'

11. Las Casas, *Historia de las Indias*, vol. iii, p. 95.

12. Luis Arranz Márquez, *Repartimientos y encomiendas en la isla Española: el Repartimiento de Albuquerque, 1514* (Madrid, 1992), pp. 36–40. More flexible calculations, allowing for higher estimates, rarely go above 300,000 Indians at the time of contact. See Massimo Livi Bacci, *Conquest: The Destruction of the American Indios* (Cambridge, 2008), pp. 95–105.

13. This was the *Memorial de remedios* of 1516, printed in Bartolomé de Las Casas, *Obras escogidas*, ed. Juan Pérez de Tudela Bueso, *Biblioteca de Autores Españoles* (Madrid, 1958), vol. cx, pp. 3–39.

14. Las Casas, *Obras escogidas*, pp. 12–24.

15. Ramón Pané, *An Account of the Antiquities of the Indians*, ed. J. J. Arrom, trans. S. C. Griswold (Durham, NC, 1999), Introduction.

16. I have used David Abulafia's excellent summary in *The Discovery of Mankind: Atlantic Encounters in the Age of Columbus* (New Haven, CT, 2008), pp. 137–44.

17. R. W. Southern, *Western Views of Islam in the Middle Ages* (Cambridge, MA, 1962), p. 72. The episode, Southern explains, turned into one of those frequent ironies in which promising intellectual movements get official recognition at the very moment when 'they cease to have any weight in the counsels of the world'.

18. David Abulafia, *The Western Mediterranean Kingdoms: The Struggle for Dominium, 1200–1500* (London, 1997), pp. 91–4.

19. See Francisco Javier Martínez Medina and Martin Biersack, *Fray Hernando de Talavera: Primer Arzobispo de Granada. Hombre de Iglesia, estado y letras* (Granada, 2011).

20. Segovia wrote about it in detail to his friend Nicholas of Cusa, one of the earliest practitioners of historical criticism, who had already demonstrated that the Donation of Constantine was a forgery. Cusa's argument, which preceded Lorenzo Valla's more famous claim, was first put forward in *De Concordantia Catholica*, vol. iii, 2. There is a good English translation by Paul E. Sigmund, *Nicholas of Cusa: The Catholic Concordance* (Cambridge, 1991).

21. Segovia coined this interesting neologism to distinguish the confrontational approach from the, originally monastic, friendly meeting associated with 'conferentia' and 'collatio'. See Southern, *Western Views of Islam*, p. 91, n. 39. Segovia's letter has yet to find an editor, but the list of contents and conclusions can be consulted in Darío Cabanelas Rodríguez, *Juan de Segovia y el problema islámico* (Madrid, 1952), pp. 303–10.

22. *Libro Copiador de Cristóbal Colón*, ed. Antonio Rumeu de Armas, 2 vols (Madrid, 1989), vol. ii, p. 463.

23. Pacheco and Cárdenas, eds, *Colección de documentos inéditos*, vol. xi, p. 428.

24. *Décadas del nuevo mundo*, ed. Ramón Alba (Madrid, 1989), p. 294; Leonardo Olschki, 'Ponce de León's Fountain of Youth: History of a Geographical Myth', *Hispanic American Historical Review*, 21:3 (August 1941), pp. 361–85.

25. Columbus's anxieties about food can be read in his Memorial to the Catholic Monarchs of 30 January 1494, printed in *Los cuatro viajes del almirante y su testamento*, ed. Ignacio Anzoátegui (Madrid, 1971), pp. 155–68. They reflected a much wider and hitherto underestimated preoccupation. Take, for instance, Pedrarias de Benavídez's opinion that Indians 'don't have the same humours as us because they don't eat the same foods', or Agustín de Vetancurt's argument that 'by eating new foods, people from different climates who come here create new blood, and this produces new humours and the new humours give rise to new abilities and conditions'. Both cited in Rebecca Earle, *The Body of the Conquistador: Food, Race and the Colonial Experience in Spanish America, 1492–1700* (Cambridge, 2012), p. 5.

26. Wright, *Early History*, p. 49.

27. Pacheco and Cárdenas, eds, *Colección de documentos inéditos*, vol. ix, pp. 412–29.

28. San Salvador was not quite where present-day Bayamo is located, and Havana was originally on the south coast, close to the present-day Batabanó. Its move to the north coast happened sometime after the conquest and settlement of Mexico created the need for a more strategically located port to cater for the return of ships from the gulf to Spain via the Bahamas.

29. Thomas, *Rivers of Gold*, p. 276.

30. Pacheco and Cárdenas, eds, *Colección de documentos inéditos*, vol. xxxii, p. 369.

31. Garci Rodríguez de Montalvo, *Amadís de Gaula*, ed. Juan Bautista Avalle-Arce (Madrid, 2015).

32. Irving A. Leonard, *Books of the Brave: Being an Account of Books and of Men in the Spanish Conquest and Settlement of the Sixteenth-Century New World*, introduction by Rolena Adorno (Berkeley, CA, 1992), p. 17.

33. Pascual de Gayangos y Arce, ed., *Sergas, Libros de Caballerías* (Madrid, 1950), pp. 505–6.

34. Gayangos y Arce, *Sergas*, p. 455.

35. Gayangos y Arce, *Sergas*, pp. 540–48.

CHAPTER 6: IMPERIAL DESIGNS

1. Hugh Thomas, *Rivers of Gold: The Rise of the Spanish Empire* (London, 2003), p. 317.

2. J. H. Elliott, *Imperial Spain 1469–1716* (Aylesbury, 1990), p. 135. The members of the Regency Council in Castile wrote to Charles as soon as they heard he had been proclaimed king in Brussels, warning him that 'wicked people in these kingdoms have always complained about whomever is ruling, and tried to make friends with whomever is about to succeed, so as to create discord and more easily tyrannize the kingdom'. Quoted in Geoffrey Parker, *Emperor: A New Life of Charles V* (New Haven, CT, 2019), p. 57.

3. Manuel Fernández Álvarez, ed., *Corpus documental de Carlos V*, 5 vols (Salamanca, 1973), vol. i, pp. 48–9.

4. Letter to his cousin, the Bishop of Tuy, quoted in Fernando Martínez Laínez, *Fernando el Católico: Crónica de un Reinado* (Madrid, 2016). 'Allí quedó muerto, en una casita desguarnecida e indecorosa'.

5. Sancho Cota, *Memorias*, ed. Hayward Keniston (London, 1964), p. 77.

6. Jerónimo López de Ayala, *El cardenal Cisneros, gobernador del reino: estudio histórico*, 2 vols (Madrid, 1921), vol. ii, p. 99.

7. Alonso de Santa Cruz, *Crónica del emperador Carlos V*, ed. Ricardo Beltrán y Rózpide and Antonio Blázquez y Delgado-Aguilera, 5 vols (Madrid, 1920–5), vol. i, pp. 106–10. See also Parker, *Emperor*, p. 57.

8. Jorge Varacaldo to Diego López de Ayala, September 1516, in Vicente de la Fuente, ed., *Cartas de los secretarios del Cardenal D. Fr. Francisco Jiménez de Cisneros* (Madrid, 1875), p. 29.

9. On this see Federico Chabod, *Carlos Quinto y su imperio*, trans. Rodrigo Ruza (Madrid, 1992), p. 64.

10. AGI (PR), 252, R.1, 12^v: '. . . dezimos que este clerigo es persona liviana de poca abtoridad e credito habla en lo que no sabe ni vio por razones quellas mismas se contradicen'.

11. Manuel Giménez Fernández, *Bartolomé de las Casas*, 2 vols (Seville, 1953), vol. i, p. 220.

12. José de Sigüenza, *Historia de la Orden de San Jerónimo*, 2 vols (Madrid, 1909), vol. i, pp. 6, 29, 198; Marcel Bataillon, 'L'Espagne religieuse et son histoire', *Bulletin Hispanique*, lii (1952), p. 20.

13. J. K. McConica, *English Humanists and Reformation Politics under Henry VIII and Edward VI* (Oxford, 1965), pp. 18–23.

14. First published in 1503, the *Enchiridion* was reprinted in 1509 and in 1515. In the next six years there were twenty-three editions; see P. S. Allen, ed., *Opus Epistolarum Des. Erasmi Roterodami*, 12 vols (Oxford, 1906–58), vol. i, epistle no. 373. In Spain it was reprinted every year between 1526 and 1531 and there are six more editions between 1533 and 1556; see Marcel Batallion, *Erasmo y España: Estudios sobre la historia espiritual del siglo xvi*, trans. Antonio Alatorre (Mexico City, 1950), p. lvi.

15. Charles F. Fraker Jr., 'Gonçalo Martínez de Medina, the Jerónimos and the Devotio Moderna', *Hispanic Review*, 34:3 (July 1966), pp. 197–217, at pp. 204–5.

16. Bartolomé de Las Casas, *Historia de las Indias*, ed. Agustín Millares Carlo, 3 vols (Mexico City, 1951), p. 138.

17. Las Casas, *Historia de las Indias*, vol. iii, p. 138.

18. Thomas, *Rivers of Gold*, p. 333.

19. Giménez Fernández, *Bartolomé de las Casas*, vol. i, p. 373. The evidence was confirmed by Alonso de Zuazo in his *residencia*, where he described the involvement of judges in the raids; foremost among them was Lucas Vázquez de Ayllón; see AGI (J), 43. 4.

20. Las Casas, *Historia de las Indias*, vol. iii, p. 154.

21. Las Casas, *Historia de las Indias*, vol. iii, p. 166; Parker, *Emperor*, p. 76.

22. The legend that it was the letter that prompted the cardinal's swift death is not entirely fanciful. See Elliott, *Imperial Spain*, p. 144, which takes a different view.

23. Elliott, *Imperial Spain*, p. 145; Parker, *Emperor*, pp. 82–7.

24. Las Casas, *Historia de las Indias*, vol. iii, p. 168.

25. Thomas, *Rivers of Gold*, pp. 361–3.

26. Manuel Serrano y Sanz, ed., *Orígenes de la dominación española en América*, in *Biblioteca de Autores Españoles* (Madrid, 1918), vol. xxv, pp. 580–82.

27. Las Casas, *Historia de las Indias*, vol. iii, pp. 168–87.

28. Las Casas, *Historia de las Indias*, vol. iii, pp. 190–93.

29. Paul J. Alexander 'The Medieval Legend of the Last Roman Emperor and its Messianic Origins', *Journal of the Warburg and Courtauld Institutes*, 41 (1978), pp. 1–15; Marie Tanner, *The Last Descendant of Aeneas: The Hapsburgs and the Mythic Image of the Emperor* (New Haven, CT, 1993), pp. 120–30. See also John M. Headley, *The Emperor and his Chancellor: A Study of the Imperial Chancellery under Gattinara* (Cambridge, 1983), pp. 140–43.

30. Mercurino di Gattinara, *Oratio Supplicatoria*, British Library, MS 18008, fol. 7ʳ. The document was unearthed by John Headley in 1990 and used by Rebecca Boone in 'Empire and Medieval Simulacrum: A Political Project of Mercurino di Gattinara, Grand Chancellor of Charles V', *Sixteenth Century Journal*, 42:4 (2011), pp. 1,027–49, at pp. 1,036–8.

31. The fourteenth-century Ghibellines, as the supporters of emperors against popes were known in the Italian city states, boasted a distinguished list of supporters that included Dante Alighieri and Bartolo da Sassoferrato.

32. It is impossible to capture the somewhat deranged tone of the original: 'Ascendet tunc Rex Romanorum sursum in Golgata, in quo confixum est lignum sanctae crucis, in quo loco pro nobis dominus mortem sustrinuit, et tollet Rex coronam de capitae sua, et ponet eam super crucem, et expandet manus suas in coelum, et tradet regnum Christianorum Deo Patri . . .' Gattinara, *Oratio*, fol. 93ᵛ.

33. See above, p. 13. Gattinara cited a long passage from a well-known prophecy associated with Vilanova known as the *Vae mecum*; see Boone, 'Empire and Medieval Simulacrum', pp. 1,043–4.

34. Anthony Pagden, *Lords of All the World: Ideologies of Empire in Spain, Britain and France c. 1500 – c.1800* (New Haven, CT, 1995), pp. 42–3.

35. Giménez Fernández, *Bartolomé de las Casas*, vol. ii, p. 259.

36. Frances Yates, *Astraea: The Imperial Theme in the Sixteenth Century* (London, 1975), p. 23. Ariosto's lines are quoted below, pp. 195–6.

37. Giménez Fernández, *Bartolomé de las Casas*, vol. ii, p. 730.

38. Las Casas, *Historia de las Indias*, vol. iii, pp. 242–4.

39. Marcel Bataillon, *Estudios sobre Bartolomé de las Casas* (Barcelona, 1976), p. 232.

40. Las Casas, *Historia de las Indias*, vol. iii, p. 361.

41. Hernán Cortés, *Cartas de Relación*, ed. Manuel Alcalá (Mexico City, 1978), p. 18.

42. See above, pp. 93–4.

43. Cortés, *Cartas*, pp. 12, 14, 15, 17, 18.

44. Thomas, *Rivers of Gold*, p. 385.

45. A widely popular refrain alluding to the good fortune of anyone in Castile who had not fallen into Chièvres's hands spoke for itself: 'Doblón de a dos, norbuena estedes / Pues con vos no topó Xevres.' Quoted in Elliott, *Imperial Spain*, p. 145. The best study of the *comunero* revolt is by Stephen Haliczer, *The Comuneros of Castile: The Forging of a Revolution* (Madison, WI, 1981); see also Parker, *Emperor*, pp. 108–15.

46. '. . . magro al posibile, palido, molto melincolico, porta la boca sempre cazuda et aperta, et cosi li occhi cazudi che par il stagino atacati et non sieno soi'. Marino Sanuto, *I diarii di Marino Sanuto*, ed. F. Stefani, G. Berchet and N. Barozzi, 58 vols (Venice, 1879–1903), vol. xx, p. 422. I am grateful to my Bristol colleagues, Ruth Glynn and Mair Parry, for their help with the translation.

47. Elliott, *Imperial Spain*, p. 153.

48. Las Casas, *Historia de las Indias*, vol. iii, pp. 361–3. Las Casas knew that these proposals would be irresistible to Adrian, who was increasingly frustrated by the lack of response to his letters to Charles. As Geoffrey Parker has recently observed, 'scarcely any of the 105 original letters sent by Adrian to Charles during the Comunero crisis contain annotations or comments by the recipient and his advisers'. Parker has established that many of the marginal annotations found in the letters are in the hand of nineteenth-century historians; see *Emperor*, pp. 110, 611–12, n. 28.

49. Robert H. Fuson, *Juan Ponce de León and the Discovery of Puerto Rico and Florida* (Blacksburg, VA, 2000), pp. 159–75.

50. Las Casas, *Historia de las Indias*, vol. iii, p. 379.

51. Las Casas, *Historia de las Indias*, vol. iii, p. 386.

52. Karl Brandi, *Carlos V: vida y fortuna de una personalidad y de un imperio mundial* (Madrid, 1937), p. 169.

53. Albrecht Dürer, *Diary of His Journey to the Netherlands, 1520–1521*, eds J.-A. Goris and G. Marlier (Greenwich, CT, 1971), pp. 53–4.

CHAPTER 7: THE LURE OF CHINA

1. Hernán Cortés, *Cartas de Relación*, ed. Manuel Alcalá (Mexico City, 1978), p. 20.

2. José Luis Martínez, *Documentos Cortesianos*, 4 vols (Mexico City, 1990–1), vol. i, pp. 45–57.

3. Peter Martyr, *De Orbe Novo: The Eight Decades of Peter Martyr D'Anghera*, ed. and trans. F. A. MacNutt, 2 vols (New York, 1912), vol. ii, p. 27.

4. Joaquín Pacheco and Francisco Cárdenas, eds, *Colección de documentos inéditos relativos al descubrimiento, conquista y organización de las posesiones españolas en América y Oceanía*, 42 vols (Madrid, 1864–84), vol. xxvii, p. 318; vol. xxviii, p. 124.

5. Hugh Thomas, *The Conquest of Mexico* (London, 1993), p. 162.

6. *Oration in Praise of Constantine*, [trans. http://www.newadvent.org/fathers/2504.htm, accessed 16 October 2016], xvi.4.

7. Christopher Dawson, ed., *The Mission to Asia: Narratives and Letters of the Franciscan Missionaries in Mongolia and China in the Thirteenth and Fourteenth Centuries*, translated by a nun of Stanbrook Abbey (London, 1955), pp. 220, 75.

8. More than a century later the Augustinian chronicler Antonio de la Calancha could still insist on this very point. After he came across evidence of a great bearded white sage called Tunupa who had set up a famous cross at Carabuco, he concluded that this must have been none other than St Thomas the Apostle. His logic was impeccable: given Christ's injunction to his

apostles, it would surely be contrary to divine mercy and natural justice to leave any member of humanity to languish for so long in darkness and sin. *Crónica moralizada del orden de San Agustín en el Perú* , ed. Ignacio Prado Pastor, 6 vols (Lima 1974), vol. ii, pp. 701–69; see also Adolph F. Bandelier, 'The Cross of Carabuco in Bolivia', *American Anthropologist*, 6:5 (October – December, 1904), pp. 599–628, at p. 612. I have written more extensively on this topic in 'The Bible in European Colonial Thought *c.* 1450–1750', *The New Cambridge History of the Bible*, vol. iii (1450–1750), ed. Euan Cameron (Cambridge, 2016), pp. 805–27.

9. Thomas, *Conquest*, p. 163. This is the testimony given by several witnesses and preserved in AGI (J), leg. 223, pt. 2, fols 227^r, 309^v, 424^v.

10. Thomas, *Conquest*, p. 164.

11. At least this is what Cortés recounted to his humanist biographer; see Francisco López de Gómara, *La Conquista de México*, ed. José Luis Rojas (Madrid, 1987), p. 61.

12. D'Anghera, *De Orbe Novo*, vol. ii, pp. 33–4.

13. Pacheco and Cárdenas, *Colección de documentos inéditos*, vol. xxvii, p. 325. According to Demetrio Ramos, this was probably not the *Requerimiento* of Palacios Rubios, but a document written for the purpose by Godoy himself. See his *Hernán Cortés* (Madrid, 1992), p. 67.

14. Pacheco and Cárdenas, *Colección de documentos inéditos*, vol. xxvii, pp. 325–9; Bernal Díaz del Castillo, *Historia verdadera de la conquista de la Nueva España*, ed. Miguel León Portilla, 2 vols (Madrid, 1984), vol. i, pp. 142–5.

15. The name did not survive, and it is now impossible to give the exact location of Potonchan.

16. Pacheco and Cárdenas, *Colección de documentos inéditos*, vol. xxviii, pp. 130–31.

17. Díaz del Castillo, *Historia verdadera*, vol. i, p. 152; Pacheco and Cárdenas, *Colección de documentos inéditos*, vol. xxvii, p. 333; Ramos, *Hernán Cortés*, p. 89; D'Anghera, *De Orbe Novo*, vol. ii, p. 35; Pacheco and Cárdenas, *Colección de documentos inéditos*, vol. xxvii, pp. 229–332; López de Gómara, *Conquista*, pp. 65–9; Thomas, *Conquest*, p. 171, again, using the evidence from AGI (J), leg. 223.

18. Thomas, *Conquest*, p. 172. On Marina, see Camilla Townsend, *Malintzin's Choices: An Indian Woman in the Conquest of Mexico* (Albuquerque, NM, 2006).

19. A point well made by Stephen Greenblatt, *Marvellous Possessions: The Wonder of the New World* (Chicago, IL, 1992), p. 145.

20. See Michael A. Ohnersorgen, 'Aztec Provincial Administration at Cuetlaxtlan, Veracruz', *Journal of Anthropological Archaeology*, 25 (2006), pp. 1–32.

21. Bernardino de Sahagún, *Florentine Codex: The General History of the Things of New Spain*, trans. Charles E. Dibble and Arthur J. Anderson, 12 vols (Santa Fe, NM, 1951–5), vol. xii, p. 20.

22. Sahagún, *Florentine Codex*, vol. xxi, pp. 19–20.

23. 'Historia de los mexicanos por sus pinturas', c. 1535, in Joaquín García Icazbalceta, ed., *Nueva Colección de documentos para la historia de México* (Mexico City, 1941), p. 253.

24. Codex Chimalpopoca, in John Bierhorst, *Four Masterworks of American Indian Literature* (New York, 1974), p. 37.

25. See for example, the opinions of Fray Toribio de Motolinía, in Joaquín García Icazbalceta, ed., *Colección de documentos inéditos para la historia de México*, 3 vols (Mexico City, 1858–66), vol. i, p. 65; Gonzalo Fernández de Oviedo, *Historia General y Natural de las Indias*, ed. Juan Pérez de Tudela Bueso, 5 vols [*Biblioteca de autores españoles*, vols cvii–cxi] (Madrid, 1959), vol. iv [vol. cxx], p. 252; Diego Durán, *Historia de las Indias de Nueva España*, ed. Ángel María Garibay, 2 vols (Mexico City, 1967), vol. i, p. 507; Jerónimo de Mendieta, *Historia Eclesiástica Indiana*, ed. Joaquín García Icazbalceta (Mexico City, 1870), p. 92; Sahagún, *Florentine Codex*, vol. i, pp. 11–12.

26. Sahagún, *Florentine Codex*, vol. i, p. 5; H. B. Nicholson, 'Religion in Pre-Hispanic Central Mexico', in *Handbook of Middle American Indians* (Austin, TX, 1971), vol. x, p. 402.

27. They included golden jewels, quetzal feathers, elaborate objects of obsidian, turquoise and jade, golden sculptures of exotic animals, headdresses, fans and plenty of decorative clothing. See the descriptions in Sahagún, *Florentine Codex*, vol. xii, p. 13; Díaz del Castillo, *Historia verdadera*, vol. i, p. 161; D'Anghera, *De Orbe Novo*, vol. ii, pp. 45–6.

28. Durán, *Historia de las Indias*, vol. ii, p. 508.

29. *Florentine Codex*, vol. xii, p. 21.

30. López de Gómara, *Conquista*, p. 87.

31. On this see Frances Berdan, *The Aztecs of Central Mexico: An Imperial Society* (New York, 1982), p. 38.

32. Fernando de Alba Ixtlilxochitl, *Historia de la Nación Chichimeca*, ed. Germán Vázquez Chamorro (Madrid, 1985), p. 232.

33. Pacheco and Cárdenas, *Colección de documentos inéditos*, vol. xxvii, pp. 334–5.

34. I follow the revised chronology suggested by John F. Schwaller in his splendid edition of 'the lost petition' of 20 June. See John F. Schwaller with Helen Nader, *The First Letter from New Spain: The Lost Petition of Cortés and his Company, June 20, 1519* (Austin, TX, 2014), p. 52.

35. D'Anghera, *De Orbe Novo*, vol. ii, p. 37; Francisco Cervantes de Salazar, *Crónica de la Nueva España* (Madrid, 1914), pp. 141, 188–91.

36. Thomas, *Conquest*, p. 201.

37. Salvador de Madariaga, *Hernán Cortés* (Buenos Aires, 1951), p. 183; Manuel Giménez Fernández, *Hernán Cortés y su revolución comunera en la Nueva España* (Seville, 1948), p. 91.

38. Richard Konetzke, 'Hernán Cortés como poblador de la Nueva España', in *Estudios Cortesianos: IV Centenario de Hernán Cortés* (Madrid, 1948), p. 369. The author intriguingly links Cortés's idea with the political philosophy of Carl Schmitt!

39. For what follows, I have shamelessly plundered Víctor Frankl's exhaustive (and exhausting) demonstration, 'Hernán Cortés y la tradición de las Siete Partidas', in *Revista de Historia de América*, 53:4 (June – December, 1962), pp. 9–74.

40. '. . . personas nobles, caballeros hijosdalgo, celosos del servicio de Nuestro Señor y de vuestras reales altezas, y deseosos de ensalzar su corona real, de acrecentar sus señoríos y de aumentar sus rentas . . .' Cortés, *Cartas*, p. 18.

41. 'Honrados deben ser mucho los caballeros . . . et por ende los reyes los deben honrar como á aquellos con quien han de facer su obra, guardando et honrando á sí mismos con ellos et acrescentando su poder et su honra.' *Las Siete Partidas del Rey Don Alfonso el Sabio, cotejadas con varios códices antiguos por la Real Academia de la Historia*, 3 vols (Madrid 1802), vol. ii, p. 216.

42. '. . . nos respondió diciendo que su voluntad estaba más inclinada al servicio de vuestras majestades que a otra cosa alguna, y que no mirando al interese que a él se le siguiera si prosiguiera en el recate que traía presupuesto de rehacer . . . le placía . . . de hacer lo que por nosotros le era pedido, pues que tanto convenía al servicio de vuestras reales altezas.' Cortés, *Cartas*, p. 19.

43. '. . . ca non serie guisada cosa que por el pro de todos los homes comunalmente se destorvase por la pro de algunos', *Las Siete Partidas*, vol. ii, p. 712.

44. 'Desatadas non deben seer las leyes por ninguna manera, fueras ende si ellas fuesen tales que desataren el bien que deben facer. . . . Et porque el facer es muy grave cosa, et el desfacer muy ligera, por ende el desatar de las leyes et tollerlas del todo que non valan, non se debe facer sinon con el grant consejo de todos los homes buenos de la tierra, los mas buenos et honrados et mas sabidores . . . Et . . . si fallaren las razones de las leyes que tiran mas á mal que á bien, puedenlas desfacer ó desatar del todo.' *Las Siete Partidas*, vol. i, p. 25.

45. According to Francisco Cervantes de Salazar, this very sentiment was echoed by Pedro de Alvarado when he exclaimed that any show of respect for Velázquez's instructions would run directly against the interests of God and the monarchs. Laws that have been promulgated for good reasons, he explained, do not necessarily work in different circumstances, and therefore anyone who breaks them 'does a good deed, because their principal purpose is the common good, and if this is absent and evil ensues they [the laws] are no longer valid'. The original is more forceful; '. . . porque muchas vezes acontece que cuando se haze la ley es necesaria, y andando el tiempo, según lo que se ofresce, no haze mal el que la quebranta, porque el principal motivo d'ella es el bien común, y quando falta y se sigue daño cesa su vigor',

Crónica de Nueva España, vol. i, fol. 62ʳ (as cited by Frankl, 'Hernán Cortés', p. 37).

46. '. . . lo mejor que a todos nos parecía era que en nombre de vuestras reales altezas se fundase y poblase allí un pueblo en que hubiese justicia, para que en esta tierra tuviesen señorío, como en sus reinos y señoríos lo tienen . . .' Cortés, *Cartas*, p. 18.

47. '. . . dos tiempos han de catar los grandes señores . . . el uno en tiempo de guerra de armas et de gente contra los enemigos de fuera fuertes et poderosos, et el otro en tiempo de paz de leyes et de fueros derechos contra los de dentro torticeros et soberbiosos, de manera que siempre ellos sean vencedores, lo uno con esfuerzo et con armas, et lo al con derecho et con justicia', *Las Siete Partidas*, vol. ii, p. 349.

48. 'Pareciéndonos . . . que para la pacificación y concordia entre nosotros y para nos gobernar bien, convenía poner una persona para su real servicio que estuviese en nombre de vuestras majestades . . . por justicia mayor y capitán y cabeza a quien todos acatásemos hasta hacer relación de ello a vuestras reales altezas para que en ello proveyese lo que más servido fuesen . . .' Cortés, *Cartas*, p. 19.

49. '. . . ius gentium en latin tanto quiere decir como derecho comunal de todas las gentes, et qual conviene a los homes et non a las otras animalias, et esto fue fallado con razon . . . porque los homes non podrien vevir entre si en concordia et en paz, si todos non usasen dél; ca por tal derecho como este cada un home conosce lo suyo apartadamente, et son departidos los campos et los términos de las villas', *Las Siete Partidas*, vol. i, p. 12.

50. 'Dios . . . dió en las palabras para facer departimiento entre la mentira que es amarga, que aborrece la natura que es sana et complida, de la verdad et lealtad de que se paga el entendimiento del home bueno . . . Et por ende el pueblo . . . debe siempre decir palabras verdaderas al rey, et guardarse de mentirle . . . ; ca el que dixiese mentira a sabiendas al rey por que hobiese á prender á alguno, ó á facerle mal en el cuerpo . . . debe haber en el suyo tal pena qual feciere haber al otro por la mentira que dijo.' *Las Siete Partidas*, vol. ii, p. 106. 'Onde los que á sabiendas le aconsejan malfaciéndole entender una cosa por otra . . farien grant yerro et deben haber muy grant pena; ca si fuese home honrado el que lo feciese, debe ser echado de la tierra et perder lo que ha; et si fuese de menor guisa debe morir por ello.' *Las Siete Partidas*, vol. ii, p. 108.

51. '. . . no son ni han podido ser ciertas porque nadie hasta ahora las ha sabido como será ésta que nosotros a vuestras reales altezas escribimos y contaremos aquí desde el principio que fue descubierta de esta tierra hasta el estado en que al presente está . . .' Cortés, *Cartas*, p. 7.

52. For example, law iv of the third 'title' of the second *Partida*: 'la cobdicia es muy mala cosa, asi que dixieron por ella que es madre et raiz de todos los males; et aun dixieron más, que el home que cobdicia allegar grandes

tesoros para non obrar bien con ellos ... que non es ende señor, más siervo ... que es grant pecado mortal quanto á Dios, et grant malestanza al mundo.' *Las Siete Partidas*, vol. ii, p. 19; or law ii of the ninth 'title' of the second *Partida*: '... pobredat trae á los homes á grant cobdicia, que es raíz de todo mal ... lo que non conviene á los homes que han á servir al rey; ca non podrie ser que si atales fuesen, que non recebiese el rey mal dellos ... viniéndole daño de su cobdicia', *Las Siete Partidas*, vol. ii. p. 58.

53. '... movido más a codicia que a otro celo', Cortés, *Cartas*, p. 8.

54. '... que en ninguna manera den ni hagan merced en estas partes a Diego Velázquez ... de adelantamiento ni gobernación ... ni de cargos de justicia, y si alguna se tuviere hecha la manden revocar porque no conviene al servicio de su corona real ...' Cortés, *Cartas*, p. 23.

55. The document mentioned is the recently found 'lost petition' of 20 June. See n. 34 above.

56. Thomas, *Conquest*, pp. 222–3.

57. Pacheco and Cárdenas, *Colección de documentos inéditos*, vol. xxvii, pp. 204–5. Some readers might be surprised that Cortés did not in fact burn the ships, a supposition so influential that it has even become proverbial. It was first made by Francisco Cervantes de Salazar when he dedicated his *Diálogo de la dignidad del hombre* (Alcalá de Henares, 1546) to Cortés, and misread the term used in the early handwritten document for 'breaking' – *quebrando* – for *quemando*, which means 'burning'.

58. These were allegedly Cortés's very words, according to question 89 in the *residencia* against him; he told his followers that 'ya no les quedaba otro remedio sino ... vencer e ganar la tierra o morir', Pacheco and Cárdenas, *Colección*, vol. xxvii, p. 337.

59. For illuminating short biographies of each of the signatories of the 20 June petition see Schwaller (with Nader), *The First Letter from New Spain*, pp. 160–240.

60. Francisco López de Gómara, *La Conquista de México*, ed. José Luis Rojas (Madrid, 1987), p. 93.

61. Known to the Mexica as Chalchiuhtlicue, she was the second wife of Tlaloc, the god of rain, whose first wife had been stolen by Tezcatlipoca, leaving Tlaloc so bereft that his depression had brought about a drought. See Burr Cartwright Brundage, *The Fifth Sun: Aztec Gods, Aztec World* (Austin, TX, 1979), pp. 156–9. See also Camilla Townsend, *Fifth Sun: A New History of the Aztecs* (New York, 2020), p. 35.

62. So claimed Andrés de Tapia; see Germán Vázquez Chamorro, ed., *La Conquista de Tenochtitlán* (Madrid, 1988), p. 86.

63. Díaz del Castillo, *Historia verdadera*, vol. i, p. 224.

64. Cortés, *Cartas*, p. 35; the testimony was confirmed by Andrés de Tapia; see Vázquez Chamorro, ed., *Conquista*, p. 86.

65. López de Gómara, *Conquista*, pp. 120–22.

66. Díaz del Castillo, *Historia verdadera*, vol. i, pp. 225–6.
67. Ixtilxochitl, *Historia*, p. 238; Cortés, *Cartas*, p. 36.
68. Cortés, *Cartas*, p. 36.
69. Many insisted on going to confession. This is the testimony of Francisco de Aguilar (then still called Alonso – Francisco was the name he took after joining the Dominican order in 1529); see Vázquez Chamorro, ed., *Conquista*, p. 167.
70. Thomas, *Conquest*, p. 237.
71. Cortés, *Cartas*, p. 41. In similar vein Peter Martyr wrote to Pope Leo X that Tlaxcallan resembled Rome 'when it was a republic, before it became a despotic kingdom', *De Orbe Novo*, vol. ii, p. 77. For Tlaxcallan see Charles Gibson, *Tlaxcala in the Sixteenth Century* (New Haven, CT, 1952), pp. 9–13.
72. López de Gómara, *Conquista*, p. 126.
73. Cortés, *Cartas*, p. 42.
74. Cortés, *Cartas*, p. 42. The quotation actually conflates the gospels of Matthew (12:25), *Omne regnum divisum contra se desolabitur*, and Luke (11.17), *Omne regnum in se ipsum divisus desolabitur*.
75. Vázquez Chamorro, ed., *Conquista*, p. 90; Díaz del Castillo, *Historia verdadera*, vol. i, p. 252. In the 1580s, Michel de Montaigne, using Cortés's humanist biographer as his source, wrote: 'They offered him three sorts of gifts in this wise: Lord, here are five slaves; if thou art a fierce god who feedest of flesh and blood, eat them and we shall bring thee more. If thou art a kindly god, here are feathers and incense; if thou art human, accept these birds and these fruits.' 'On Moderation', *The Complete Essays*, trans. M. A. Screech (London, 1993), p. 227. Montaigne's source is López de Gómara, *Conquista*, p. 131, which he most probably read in the Italian translation by A. de Cravaliz, *Historia del Capitano Fernando Cortes* (Rome, 1556).
76. For Xicotencatl's alleged speech see Diego Muñoz Camargo, *Historia de Tlaxcala*, ed. Germán Vázquez Chamorro (Madrid, 1986), p. 192. Hints of the deal can be gauged in *Relación del origen de los indios que habitan esta Nueva España según sus historias* (aka Tovar Codex and Ramírez Codex), Museo Nacional de Antropología e Historia, Mexico City, fols 137^{r-v}, and Bernardino de Sahagún, *The Conquest of New Spain*, trans. Howard Cline, introduction by S. L. Cline (Salt Lake City, UT, 1989), p. 54. The negotiations were probably very complex. Thomas, *Conquest*, p. 241, proposes Temilotecatl, 'leader of the third district', as the main broker; but it is likely that many more leaders were involved. According to Peter Gerhard, 'Atlihuetzian, Quiahuixtlan, Tecoac, Tepetípcac, Topoyanco, and Tzompantzinco were each ruled separately, as were other places, perhaps as many as sixty political entities altogether.' See *A Guide to the Historical Geography of New Spain* (Cambridge, 1972), p. 324. His sources are Gibson, *Historia*, pp. 9–13, and Antonio de Herrera, *Historia general de los hechos de los castellanos en las islas y tierra firme del mar océano*, 4 vols (Madrid, 1601–15), vol. i, p. 360.

77. Díaz del Castillo, *Historia verdadera*, vol. i, p. 271.

78. Ixtilxochitl, *Historia*, p. 241; Díaz del Castillo, *Historia verdadera*, vol. i, p. 264.

79. Muñoz Camargo, *Historia*, p. 197.

80. Díaz del Castillo, *Historia verdadera*, vol. i, p. 276: '... los cabellos muy largos y engreñados, que no se pueden desparcir si no se cortan, y llenos de sangre, que les salía de las orejas, que en aquel día se habían sacrificado ... y traían las uñas de los dedos de las manos muy largas'.

81. Thomas, *Conquest*, pp. 255–6.

82. See James Lockhart, *The Nahuas after the Conquest: A Social and Cultural History of the Indians of Central Mexico, Sixteenth through Eighteenth Centuries* (Stanford, CA, 1992), pp. 14–58.

83. I draw on Matthew Restall's subtle analysis in *When Montezuma Met Cortés: The True Story of the Meeting that Changed History* (New York, 2018), pp. 200–205.

84. Exact numbers are impossible to fathom. The ones given in the sources are clear exaggerations, characteristic of the time. Andrés de Tapia, for instance, claims there were 40,000 Tlaxcalteca with them, in Vázquez Chamorro, ed., *Conquista*, p. 99.

85. Cortés, *Cartas*, p. 44: '... con muchas trompetas y atabales ...'

86. Cortés, *Cartas*, p. 45: '... está asentada en un llano, y tiene hasta veinte mil casas dentro, en el cuerpo de la ciudad, y tiene de arrabales otras tantas. Es señorío por sí ... no obedece a señor ninguno, excepto que se gobiernan como estos otros de Tlascaltecal. La gente de esta ciudad es más vestida ... [E]s muy fértil de labranzas ... y aun es la ciudad más hermosa de fuera que hay en España, porque es muy torreada y llana, y certifico a vuestra alteza que yo conté desde una mezquita cuatrocientas treinta y tantas torres ... Es la ciudad más a propósito de vivir los españoles ...'

87. Cortés, *Cartas*, p. 45: 'Todos ellos han sido y son después de este trance pasado, muy ciertos vasallos se vuestra majestad y muy obedientes a lo que yo en su real nombre les he requerido y dicho, y creo que lo serán de aquí adelante.'

88. Rojas, *Relación de Cholollan*, p. 160; for the attributes, see Muñoz Camargo, *Historia*, p. 210.

89. Pacheco and Cárdenas, *Colección*, xxvii, p. 386; Vázquez Chamorro, ed., *Conquista*, p. 96; López de Gómara, *Conquista*, p. 125; Díaz del Castillo, *Historia verdadera*, vol. ii, pp. 5–9; Juan Ginés de Sepúlveda, *Historia del Nuevo Mundo*, ed. Antonio Ramírez de Verger (Madrid, 1987), p. 141. The latter's testimony is of special significance because it is based on Cortés's verbal account.

90. This is the testimony of Andrés de Tapia; see Vázquez Chamorro, ed., *Conquista*, p. 100.

91. Sahagún, *Florentine Codex*, vol. xii, p. 30.

92. Thomas, *Conquest*, p. 261.

93. *Brevísima relación de la destrucción de las Indias*, ed. Gregorio Weinberg (Buenos Aires, 1966), p. 59: '. . . estando metiendo a espada los cinco o seis mil hombres en el patio, estaba cantando el capitán de los españoles: "Mira Nero de Trapeya a Roma cómo ardía; gritos dan niños y viejos y él de nada se dolía." '

94. AGI (J), leg. 223, pt. 1, fol. 722^r; pt. 2, fols 511^{r-v}, 584^v.

95. Thomas, *Conquest*, pp. 263–4.

96. Restall, *When Montezuma Met Cortés*, pp. 208–11.

97. *Cartas*, p. 47 '. . . y vinieron muy alegres por haber descubierto tan buen camino, y Dios sabe cuánto holgué yo de ello'.

98. Díaz del Castillo, *Historia verdadera*, vol. ii, pp. 28–9.

99. Sahagún, *Florentine Codex*, vol. xii, pp. 31–2.

100. Durán, *Historia de las Indias*, vol. ii, p. 535.

101. Díaz del Castillo, *Historia verdadera*, vol. ii, pp. 31–2.

102. So claimed Andrés de Tapia; see Vázquez Chamorro, ed., *Conquista*, p. 101.

103. *Cartas*, p. 50: '. . . son tan buenas como las mejores de España, digo de grandes y bien labradas, así de obra de cantería como de carpintería . . .'

104. *Cartas*, p. 51: '. . . y en todas muy buenos edificios de casas y torres, en especial las casas de los señores y personas principales, y de sus mezquitas y oratorios donde ellos tienen sus ídolos'.

105. Sahagún, *Florentine Codex*, vol. xii, pp. 39–41.

106. A summary of the available evidence suggests that there may have been between 70,000 and 100,000 canoes in the lake, most of which were in constant use for fishing, transporting food and collecting tribute. See C. Harvey Gardiner, *Naval Power in the Conquest of Mexico* (Austin, TX, 1958), p. 54. On comparisons between Tenochtitlan and Venice see Peter Martyr d'Anghera , *De Orbe Novo*, vol. ii, pp. 108, 192; also, 'Relazione di Gasparo Contarini ritornato ambasciatore da Carlo V, leta in Senato a dì 16 Novembre 1525', in Eugenio Albèri, ed., *Relazioni degli ambasciatori veneti al senato* Serie I.^{a} – Volume II.º (Florence, 1840), p. 53: 'Questa città è meravigliosa e di grandeza e di sitio e di artifizj, posta in mezzo un lago di acqua salsa . . . e da un capo si congiunge con un altro lago d'acqua dolce . . . come fa qui a Venezia.'

107. Durán, *Historia de las Indias*, vol. i, p. 20. Durán got this description from Alonso de Aguilar, who took the name Francisco after he joined the Dominican order.

108. Restall, *When Montezuma Met Cortés*, p. 117.

109. On this see Barbara E. Mundy, 'Mapping the Aztec Capital: The 1524 Nuremberg Map of Tenochtitlan, its Sources and Meaning', *Imago Mundi* 50 (1998), and Elizabeth H. Boone, 'This New World Now Revealed:

Hernán Cortés and the Presentation of Mexico to Europe', *World & Image*, 27:1 (January – March 2011).

110. The description is Alonso (later Francisco) de Aguilar's; see Vázquez Chamorro, ed., *Conquista*, p. 178.

111. Díaz del Castillo, *Historia verdadera*, vol. ii, p. 42.

112. Ignacio López Rayón, ed., *Proceso de residencia instruido contra Pedro de Alvarado y Nuño de Guzmán* (Mexico City, 1847), p. 126; Díaz del Castillo, *Historia verdadera*, vol. i, p. 314.

113. Durán, *Historia de las Indias*, vol. i, p. 20.

114. Díaz de Castillo, *Historia verdadera*, vol. i, pp. 314–15.

CHAPTER 8: TENOCHTITLAN

1. Alonso (by then called Francisco, the name he took after joining the Order of Preachers) de Aguilar, in Germán Vázquez Chamorro, ed., *La conquista de Tenochtitlán* (Madrid, 1988), p. 180.

2. Hernán Cortés, *Cartas de relación*, ed. Manuel Alcalá (Mexico City, 1978), p. 63; Bernal Díaz del Castillo, *Historia verdadera de la conquista de la Nueva España*, ed. Miguel León Portilla, 2 vols (Madrid, 1984), vol. i, p. 335; see also Joaquín García Icazbalceta, ed., *Colección de documentos inéditos para la historia de México*, 3 vols (Mexico City, 1858–66), vol. i, p. 392, where the anonymous conquistador describes the market as being three times the size of the great square in Salamanca.

3. Cortés, *Cartas*, p. 63: 'Finalmente ... se venden todas cuantas cosas se hallan en toda la tierra, que demás de las que he dicho, son tantas y de tantas calidades, que por la prolijidad y por no me ocurrir tantas a la memoria, y aun por no saber poner los nombres, no las expreso.'

4. Esther Pasztory, *Aztec Art* (New York, 1983), p. 155.

5. Vázquez Chamorro, ed., *Conquista*, p. 107; Diego Durán, *Historia de las Indias de Nueva España*, ed. Ángel María Garibay, 2 vols (Mexico City, 1967), vol. i, p. 81. These accounts are difficult to verify and might well contain elements of fantasy and exaggeration. Jorge Gurría Lacroix goes so far as to suggest that the description of the temple is closer to the one in Tlatelolco; see his 'Andrés de Tapia y la Coatlicue', *Estudios de Cultura Náhuatl*, 13 (1978), pp. 23–34; but see Elizabeth Boone's rebuttal, 'Incarnations of the Aztec Supernatural: Representations of Huitzilopochtli in Mexico and Europe', *Transactions of the American Philosophical Society*, 79:2 (1989), pp. 1–107, at p. 47.

6. Díaz del Castillo, *Historia verdadera*, vol. i, p. 336: 'Señor Montezuma: no sé yo cómo un tan gran señor e sabio varón como vuestra majestad es no haya colegido en su pensamiento cómo no son estos vuestros ídolos dioses, sino cosas malas, que se llaman diablos ...'

7. Cortés, *Cartas*, p. 52.

8. Quoted in D. A. Brading, *The First America: The Spanish Monarchy, Creole Patriots and the Liberal State* (Cambridge, 1991), p. 35. For more recent views expressing scepticism see Camilla Townsend, *Malintzin's Choices: An Indian Woman in the Conquest of Mexico* (Albuquerque, NM, 2006), p. 86; Serge Gruzinski, *The Eagle and the Dragon: Globalization and European Dreams of Conquest in China and America* (Cambridge, 2014), p. 114; and Peter B. Villella, *Indigenous Elites and Creole Identity in Colonial Mexico, 1500–1800* (Cambridge, 2016), p. 52.

9. See Matthew Restall's suggestive analysis in *When Montezuma Met Cortés: The True Story of the Meeting that Changed History* (New York, 2018), pp. 16–17. Restall underlines that Cortés chose to introduce the speech with the words, as they appear in the first edition of 1522, 'ppuso eñsta manera', rendered as 'prepuso en esta manera' in 1528, and as 'propuso en esta manera' in most subsequent editions. Most modern historians have accepted 'propuso', meaning 'proposed' or 'suggested'. In the legal context that interested Cortés, however, it is clear that 'prepuso', meaning 'to place in front' or 'prioritize', as rendered in the 1528 edition, might well be more accurate. Ibid., p. 381, fn. 21.

10. On this see Esther Pasztory, 'El arte mexica y la conquista española', *Estudios de cultura Náhuatl*, 17 (1984), pp. 101–24, at pp. 115–17.

11. Bernardino de Sahagún, *Florentine Codex: The General History of the Things of New Spain*, trans. Charles E. Dibble and Arthur J. Anderson, 12 vols (Santa Fe, NM, 1951–5), vol. xii, p. 47.

12. Díaz del Castillo, *Historia verdadera*, vol. i, pp. 344–8; Vázquez Chamorro, *Conquista*, pp. 102–3, 182.

13. Vázquez Chamorro, ed., *Conquista*, p. 103. The testimony is Andrés de Tapia's.

14. Vázquez Chamorro, ed., *Conquista*, p. 182. The testimony is Alonso (by then Francisco) de Aguilar's.

15. Díaz del Castillo, *Historia verdadera*, vol. i, pp. 348–50. Vázquez de León spoke 'con voz algo alta y espantosa', saying 'o le llevamos preso o dalle hemos de estocadas'.

16. Joaquín F. Pacheco and Francisco de Cárdenas, eds, *Colección de documentos inéditos relativos al descubrimiento, conquista y colonización de las posesiones españolas en América y Oceanía*, 42 vols (Madrid, 1864–84), vol. xxviii, pp. 139–40.

17. Sahagún, *Florentine Codex*, vol. xii, p. 45.

18. Cortés, *Cartas*, pp. 53–5. Restall argues forcefully that the whole incident was embellished by Cortés and that it in fact makes far better sense in the context of a 'non-Cortesian power jostling among the three kings that underpinned the alliance'. The situation was rendered all the more acute after the death of Nezahualpilli, lord of Tetzcoco, who had died four years

previously leaving behind him an impossibly complicated succession crisis. Although the conquistadores undoubtedly benefited from Mesoamerican dynastic crises, Restall concludes that 'in the early months of 1520 they were a long way from understanding its [*sic*] complexities, let alone controlling them', *When Montezuma Met Cortés*, pp. 218–19.

19. Not many sources coincide with Cortés's account of Cohualpopocatzin's execution. The *Relación del origen de los indios que habitan esta Nueva España según sus historias* (aka Tovar Codex and Ramírez Codex), for example, affirms that he was hanged (fol. 221), and Fernando Alvarado Tezozomoc agrees; see *Crónica mexicana* (Mexico City, 1975), p. 36. The *Anales de Tlatelolco* state that he was killed during the Templo Mayor massacre (see above, pp. 163–4), quoted in Miguel León Portilla, ed., *Crónicas indígenas: la visión de los vencidos* (Madrid, 1985), p. 150. Diego Durán claims that he was torn to pieces by order of Moctezuma himself; see *Historia de las Indias de Nueva España*, ed. Ángel María Garibay, 2 vols (Mexico City, 1967), vol. ii, p. 528. The fact that only Bernal Díaz del Castillo coincides with Cortés's account might lend some weight to Christian Duverger's intriguing claim that Cortés was in fact the author of the *Historia verdadera*; see his *Crónica de la eternidad: ¿quién escribió la Historia verdadera de la conquista de la Nueva España?* (Madrid, 2013), but the evidence is still overwhelmingly against the French scholar's thesis; see, for example, María José Rodilla León, 'Novela sobre la paternidad de un manuscrito mestizado', in *Iberoamericana (2001 –)*, 13:52 (December 2013), pp. 173–80.

20. Pacheco and Cárdenas, eds, *Colección de documentos inéditos*, vol. xxviii, pp. 140–41.

21. Francisco López de Gómara, *La Conquista de México*, ed. José Luis Rojas (Madrid, 1987), p. 193; Díaz del Castillo, *Historia verdadera*, vol. i, p. 390.

22. Sahagún, *Florentine Codex*, vol. xii, pp. 47, 65.

23. Sahagún, *Florentine Codex*, vol. vi, pp. 50, 241–60. Here I draw on Thelma D. Sullivan's helpful elucidation of the text, with her own translations; see her 'Tlatoani and Tlatocayotl in the Sahagún Manuscripts', *Estudios de Cultura Náhuatl*, 14 (1980), pp. 225–39, at pp. 227–8, 237.

24. *Florentine Codex*, vol. xii, p. 47.

25. Díaz del Castillo, *Historia verdadera*, vol. i, p. 363: '. . . había de matar hombres y muchachos para hacer su sacrificio, y no podíamos en aquella sazón hacer otra cosa sino disimular con él, porque estaba muy revuelto Méjico y otras grandes ciudades con los sobrinos del Montezuma, como adelante diré'.

26. Hugh Thomas, *The Conquest of Mexico* (London, 1993), p. 310.

27. Antonio de Solís, *Historia de la conquista de México*, 2 vols (Madrid, 1783), vol. i, p. 79.

28. L. P. Harvey, *Islamic Spain, 1250–1500* (Chicago, IL, 1990), pp. 332–9.

29. Pacheco and Cárdenas, eds, *Colección de documentos inéditos*, vol. xxvii, p. 344.

30. Cortés, *Cartas*, p. 65: 'y todos, en especial el dicho Mutezuma, me respondieron que ya me habían dicho que ellos no eran naturales de esta tierra, y que había muchos tiempos que sus predecesores habían venido a ella, y que bien creían que podían estar errados en algo de aquello que tenían, por haber tanto tiempo que salieron de su naturaleza, y que yo, como más nuevamente venido, sabría las cosas que debían tener y creer mejor que no ellos; que se las dijese e hiciese entender, que ellos harían lo que yo les dijese que era lo mejor'.

31. Thomas, *Conquest*, p. 315.

32. Sahagún, *Florentine Codex*, vol. xii, pp. 47–8.

33. Thomas, *Conquest*, p. 331.

34. Sahagún, *Florentine Codex*, vol. i, pp. 39–40; vol. ii, pp. 44–57.

35. Pacheco and Cárdenas, eds, *Colección de documentos inéditos*, vol. xxvii, p. 352: '. . . quel dicho Pánfilo de Narváez imbió a decir a Montezuma . . . quel dicho don Hernando Cortés le abia venido a matar e a quitarle la Tierra e quel vernia a rrestituirle en sus estados, e dexalle libre, e irse, porque ansí lo mandaba el Rey'.

36. Vázquez Chamorro, ed., *Conquista*, p. 113.

37. Cortés, *Cartas*, p. 70: '. . . que . . . por merced me hiciesen saber quién eran y si eran vasallos naturales de los reinos y señoríos de vuestra alteza . . . Donde no . . . los prendería y mataría como extranjeros que se querían entremeter en los reinos y señoríos de mi rey y señor.'

38. Díaz del Castillo, *Historia verdadera*, vol. i, p. 399.

39. Díaz del Castillo, *Historia verdadera*, vol. i, p. 400: '. . . que donde venían muy bravosos leones volvieron muy mansos'. The testimony of Hernando de Caballos (Pacheco and Cárdenas, eds, *Colección de documentos inéditos*, vol. xxvii, p. 108) contradicts this, claiming that in fact Cortés had the prisoners confined to a dungeon ('pierde-amigos'). But he was not an eyewitness and he was writing on behalf of Narváez with a clear aversion to Cortés, whom he calls 'traydor e alevoso, omicida, rrobador e saqueador'.

40. Pacheco and Cárdenas, eds, *Colección de documentos inéditos*, vol. xxvii, p. 483; Cortés, *Cartas*, pp. 73–5.

41. Pacheco and Cárdenas, eds, *Colección de documentos inéditos*, vol. xxvii, p. 349.

42. Camilo García de Polavieja y del Castillo, ed., *Hernán Cortés: copias de documentos existentes en el archivo de Indias y en su palacio de Castilleja de la Cuesta sobre la conquista de Méjico* (Seville, 1889), p. 255.

43. Cortés, *Cartas*, pp. 71–2.

44. Vázquez Chamorro, ed., *Conquista*, p. 115.

45. Díaz del Castillo, *Historia verdadera*, vol. i, pp. 431–2.

46. Pacheco and Cárdenas, eds., *Colección de documentos inéditos*, vol. xvii, pp. 205–6: 'que nunca el dicho Hernando Cortés sopo quel dicho Narváez

truxiese Provisiones de Su Magestad ... e que puesto caso que las viera e sopiera ... fuera obligado a obedecerlas e las obedeciera como del Rey Nuestro Señor ... pero que ... estaba claro, que si Vuestra Magestad la verdad sopiera, no le diera tal Provision, si alguna le dio ...'

47. Thomas, *Conquest*, pp. 375–82.

48. The source is the *Codex Borgia*.

49. Emily Umberger, 'Events Commemorated by Date Plaques at the Templo Mayor: Further Thoughts on the Solar Metaphor', in Elizabeth H. Boone, *The Aztec Templo Mayor* (Washington D.C., 1987), pp. 411–49.

50. *The Conquest of Mexico*, 2 vols (London, 1922), vol. ii, p. 58.

51. Ignacio López Rayón, ed., *Proceso de residencia instruido contra Pedro de Alvarado y Nuño de Guzmán* (Mexico City, 1847), p. 118.

52. Fernando de Alba Ixtlilxochitl, *Historia de la nación chichimeca*, ed. Germán Vázquez Chamorro (Madrid, 1985), p. 260; López Rayón, ed., *Proceso*, pp. 37, 65, 66, 113, 126, 130, 134, 144.

53. Samuel Martí and Gertrude P. Kurath, *Dances of Anáhuac: The Choreography and Music of Precortesian Dances* (Chicago, IL, 1964), p. 15.

54. Or at least this is what Cortés later recounted to his humanist biographer; see López de Gómara, *Conquista*, p. 208.

55. Sahagún, *Florentine Codex*, vol. xii, pp. 54–5.

56. Ross Hassig, *Aztec Warfare: Imperial Expansion and Political Control* (Norman, OK, 1995), p. 61.

57. López Rayón, ed., *Proceso*, pp. 36–8.

58. Sahagún, *Florentine Codex*, vol. xii, p. 57.

59. Thomas, *Conquest*, pp. 392–3.

60. Manuel Orozco y Berra, *Historia Antigua de la Conquista de México*, 4 vols (Mexico City, 1880), vol. iv, p. 409.

61. Sahagún, *Florentine Codex*, vol. xii, p. 57.

62. Thomas, *Conquest*, p. 397.

63. López de Gómara, *Conquista*, pp. 210–11.

64. Vázquez Chamorro, ed., *Conquista*, pp. 145, 189; Gonzalo Fernández de Oviedo, *Historia general y natural de las Indias*, ed. Juan Pérez de Tudela Bueso, *Biblioteca de Autores Españoles*, 5 vols [*Biblioteca de autores españoles*, vols cvii–cxi] (Madrid, 1959), vol. iv [vol. cx], p. 262; on Alonso (Francisco) de Aguilar see Patricia de Fuentes, *The Conquistadors: First-Person Accounts of the Conquest of Mexico* (Norman, OK, 1993), p. 134; on Leonel de Cervantes's family, see above, p. 58 and p. 366, fn.7; Fernando de Alba Ixtlilxochitl, *Obras Históricas*, ed. Edmundo O'Gorman, 2 vols (Mexico City, 1975), vol. i, p. 390; on Moctezuma's death at the hands of the Spaniards, see Sahagún, *Florentine Codex*, vol. xii, p. 65, and Diego Durán, *Historia de las Indias de Nueva España*, ed. Ángel María Garibay, 2 vols (Mexico City, 1967), vol. ii, p. 556.

65. Sahagún, *Florentine Codex*, vol. xii, pp. 35, 68; Thomas, *Conquest*, p. 412. Figures are difficult to establish with any precision. A native source speaks

of 400 Spaniards including a grossly exaggerated 200 horsemen (cf. Juse Tudella and José Corona Núñez, eds., *Relación de las ceremonias y ritos y población y gobierno de los indios de la provincia de Michoacán* [1541] (Madrid, 1977), p. 123). For the various sources and conflicting figures see Thomas, *Conquest*, pp. 734–5, fns 63–5.

CHAPTER 9: DEFEAT AND VICTORY

1. '¡Vamos, que nada nos falta!' Quoted in Hugh Thomas, *The Conquest of Mexico* (London, 1993), p. 412.
2. For this, and what follows, see J. H. Elliott, 'Cortés, Velázquez and Charles V', in Hernán Cortés, *Letters from Mexico*, trans. and ed. Anthony Pagden (New Haven, CT, 2001), pp. xxiv–xxix.
3. Francisco del Paso y Troncoso, ed., *Epistolario de la Nueva España, 1505–1818*, 16 vols (Mexico City, 1939–42), vol. vii, p. 34.
4. Hernán Cortés, *Cartas de Relación*, ed. Manuel Alcalá (Mexico City, 1978), p. 85: '. . . íbamos muy cansados y casi todos heridos y desmayados de hambre'.
5. Joaquín Pacheco and Francisco Cárdenas, eds., *Colección de documentos inéditos relativos al descubrimiento, conquista y organización de las posesiones españolas en América y Oceanía*, 42 vols (Madrid, 1864–84), vol. xxvii, pp. 222–3, 366, vol. xviii, pp. 160–61; Bernal Díaz del Castillo, *Historia verdadera de la conquista de la Nueva España*, ed. Miguel León Portilla, 2 vols (Madrid, 1984), vol. i, p. 472; Alfredo Chavero, *Lienzo de Tlaxcala* (Mexico City, 1892), pls 27 and 28; Fernando de Alva Ixtlilxochitl, *Historia de la Nación Chichimeca*, ed. Germán Vázquez Chamorro (Madrid, 1985), p. 266.
6. Diego Muñoz Camargo, *Historia de Tlaxcala*, ed. Germán Vázquez Chamorro (Madrid, 1986), p. 230.
7. The document is elegantly summarized by Francisco Cervantes de Salazar, who gives every sign of having had a copy of the original to hand; see *Crónica de la Nueva España* (Madrid, 1914), pp. 516–17.
8. Juan Ginés de Sepúlveda, *Historia del Nuevo Mundo*, ed. Antonio Ramírez de Verger (Madrid, 1987), p. 177.
9. Cortés, *Cartas*, pp. 87–8: 'acordándome que siempre a los osados ayuda la fortuna, y que eramos cristianos y confiando en la grandísima bondad y misericordia de Dios . . . que yo no había de desamparar esta tierra, porque . . . demás de ser vergonzoso a mi persona y a todos muy peligroso, a vuestra majestad hacíamos muy gran traición'.
10. See Edward Calnek, 'The Internal Structure of Tenochtitlan', in E. R. Wolf, ed., *The Valley of Mexico* (Albuquerque, NM, 1976), pp. 287–302.
11. See Edward Calnek, 'Patterns of Empire Formation in the Valley of Mexico, Late Postclassic Period, 1200–1521', in George A. Collier, Renato

I. Rosaldo and John D. Wirth, eds, *The Inca and Aztec States, 1400–1800: Anthropology and History* (New York, 1982), pp. 43–62. The same theme is developed for the post-conquest period by James Lockhart, 'Views of Corporate Self and History in Some Valley of Mexico Towns', in eadem, pp. 367–93.

12. Inga Clendinnen, *Aztecs: An Interpretation* (Cambridge, 1991), pp. 26, 28.

13. Pacheco and Cárdenas, eds, *Colección de documentos inéditos*, vol. xxvii, pp. 501–3.

14. Peter Gerhard, *A Guide to the Historical Geography of New Spain* (Cambridge, 1972), p. 278.

15. Cortés, *Cartas*, pp. 88–9.

16. This evidence would be used against him by his enemies for years to come. When the very long investigation [*residencia*] concluded in 1548, a year after Cortés's death, Charles V was left with no option but to condemn the conquistador posthumously for the mass subjugation of indigenous peoples – something which 'no person in good conscience and title can do' – and to order all the surviving vassals in Cortés's estates to be freed immediately, 'together with their children and the descendants of any subjugated women'. *Libro Quarto de Provisiones, Cédulas, Capítulos, de ordenanças, instrucciones, y cartas* (Madrid, 1596), pp. 369–70. The estates of Cortés continued to flourish and the free natives were being paid directly and by the week by the 1580s, with plentiful free-wage employment strengthened by the growth of a mulatto labour force. See Bernardo García Martínez, *El Marquesado del Valle: tres siglos de régimen señorial en Nueva España* (Mexico City, 1969), and Lolita Gutiérrez Brockington, *The Leverage of Labor: Managing the Cortés Haciendas in Tehuantepec* (Durham, NC, 1989).

17. Cervantes de Salazar, *Crónica*, pp. 53–4.

18. Ixtlilxochitl, *Historia*, p. 270.

19. Thomas, *Conquest*, pp. 445–6.

20. Bernardino de Sahagún, *Florentine Codex: The General History of the Things of New Spain*, trans. Charles E. Dibble and Arthur J. Anderson, 12 vols (Santa Fe, NM, 1951–5), vol. xii, p. 83.

21. Díaz del Castillo, *Historia verdadera*, vol. ii, p. 286.

22. Thomas, *Conquest*, p. 450.

23. Ixtlilxochitl, *Historia*, pp. 272–3. Intriguingly, Cortés says this was Cohuanacoch, called by him Guanacacin, who did not come in person but sent some messengers; cf. *Cartas*, pp. 108–9.

24. Cortés, *Cartas*, p. 108.

25. According to Michael E. Smith, the city spread across 450 hectares and had a population of just over 24,000; cf. 'City-Size in Late Post-Classic Mesoamerica', *Journal of Urban History*, 31:4 (May 2005), pp. 403–34, at p. 422.

26. William E. Doolittle, *Canal Irrigation in Prehistoric Mexico: The Sequence of Technological Change* (Austin, TX, 1990), esp. chapter 5.

27. Pacheco and Cárdenas, eds, *Colección de documentos inéditos*, vol. xxvii, p. 245; Cortés, *Cartas*, p. 109.

28. Pacheco and Cárdenas, eds, *Colección de documentos inéditos*, vol. xxvii, pp. 243–7; Ángel María Garibay K., *Historia de la literatura náhuatl*, 2 vols (Mexico City, 1953), vol. i, pp. 26–7.

29. Cortés, *Cartas*, pp. 109–10.

30. See Rudolph van Zantwijk, *The Aztec Arrangement: The Social History of Pre-Spanish Mexico* (Noman, OK, 1985), p. 130.

31. Ixtlilxochitl, *Historia*, pp. 220–23; Ross Hassig, *Polygamy and the Rise and Demise of the Aztec Empire* (Albuquerque, NM, 2016), pp. 132–3; Bradley Benton, *The Lords of Tetzcoco: The Transformation of Indigenous Rule in Postconquest Central Mexico* (Cambridge, 2017), pp. 25–8.

32. Matthew Restall, *When Montezuma Met Cortés: The True History of the Meeting that Changed History* (New York, 2018), p. 260.

33. Francisco López de Gómara, *La Conquista de México*, ed. José Luis Rojas (Madrid, 1987), pp. 266–8; Díaz del Castillo, *Historia verdadera*, vol. i, pp. 520–21.

34. Ixtlilxochitl, *Historia*, p. 278; Restall, *When Montezuma Met Cortés*, pp. 262–3.

35. Thomas, *Conquest*, p. 464.

36. Cortés, *Cartas*, pp. 118–19. The words Cortés puts in the mouths of the indigenous peoples are: '¿Pensáis que hay ahora otro Mutezuma, para que haga todo lo que vosotros quisiéredes?'

37. Ruth Pike, *Enterprise and Adventure: The Genoese in Seville and the Opening of the New World* (Ithaca, NY, 1966), p. 141.

38. Gonzalo Fernández de Oviedo, *Historia general y natural de las Indias*, ed. Juan Pérez de Tudela Bueso, *Biblioteca de Autores Españoles*, 5 vols [*BAE*, cvii–cxi] (Madrid, 1959), vol. iv [xx], p. 260; see also the illuminatingly unambiguous explanation in 'Relación de la genealogía y linaje de los señores que han señoreado esta tierra de la Nueva España', in Joaquín García Icazbalceta, ed., *Nueva Relación de documentos para la historia de México, III: Pomar, Zurita, Relaciones antiguas (Siglo XVI)* (Mexico City, 1891), p. 280: 'El hijo varon legítimo llamado Axayacaci, que había de ser Señor, á él y á su padre bien saben los españoles cristianos que le mataron los mexicanos, porque el padre se dio de paz; y el padre muerto, el hijo quizo seguir la voluntad del padre por obedecerlo, que ansí se lo había mandado, que fuese amigo de los españoles, y obedeciese al Emperador y á su capitán en su nombre.' On Cuauhtemoc more generally, see the valuable study by Héctor Pérez Martínez, *Cuauhtémoc: vida y muerte de una cultura* (Buenos Aires, 1948).

39. Díaz del Castillo, *Historia verdadera*, vol. ii, p. 35.

40. Díaz del Castillo, *Historia verdadera*, vol. i, p. 533.

41. Cortés, *Cartas*, p. 130: '. . . fue obra grandísima y mucho para ver'.

42. Manuel Orozco y Berra, *Historia antigua y de la conquista de México*, 4 vols (Mexico City, 1880), vol. iv, p. 526.

43. Cervantes de Salazar, *Crónica*, pp. 600–601.

44. Cortés, *Cartas*, p. 131, gives Alvarado 25,000, Olid 20,000 and Sandoval 30,000, but these numbers are likely to be gross exaggerations.

45. Cortés, *Cartas*, p. 131; Díaz del Castillo gives very similar figures; cf. *Historia verdadera*, vol. ii, p. 123.

46. Cortés, *Cartas*, p. 131.

47. Cortés, *Cartas*, p. 132.

48. Cortés, *Cartas*, p. 133: '. . . y en este combate me hirieron veinte y cinco españoles, pero fue muy hermosa victoria'.

49. Cortés kept mysteriously quiet about the key role played by Martín López in the battle; cf. Thomas, *Conquest*, pp. 495–6.

50. C. Harvey Gardiner, *Naval Power in the Conquest of Mexico* (Austin, TX, 1958), p. 166.

51. Diego Durán, *Historia de las Indias de Nueva España*, ed. Ángel María Garibay Kintana, 2 vols (Mexico City, 1967), vol. ii, p. 564.

52. Díaz del Castillo, *Historia verdadera*, vol. ii, p. 61.

53. Whether Cortés had in mind the Spanish refrain, 'Al enemigo que huye puente de plata' ('a silver bridge for the enemy that flees'), often attributed to Gonzalo Fernández de Córdoba, is an intriguing question. As with all refrains, the origins of this one are impossible to trace, but it was certainly in common use in early modern Spain. Don Quixote uses it to disagree with it: '¡Deteneos y esperad, canalla malandrina; que un solo caballero os espera, el cual no tiene condición ni es de parecer de los que dicen que al enemigo que huye, hacerle la puente de plata!' Miguel de Cervantes, *Don Quijote de la Mancha* [II, lviii], ed. Francisco Rico, 2 vols (Barcelona, 1998), vol. i, p. 106. By that time the saying was often attributed to Julius Caesar; e.g. Luis Vélez de Guevara: 'No sigáis a quien huye,/que hacerle puente de plata/Julio César aconseja.' Cf. *Cumplir dos obligaciones y duquesa de Saxonia* (Valencia, 1768), 2b. Jean Plattard wrote that the refrain is 'un mot d'Alphonse d'Aragon, rapporté par Erasme', *Apophthegms*, VIII, 14: 'Magnopere audare solet dictum nescio cuius, hostibus fugientibus pontem argenteum extruendum esse'; cf. his note on Rabelais, I, xliii, *Oeuvres*, ed. Abel Lefranc (Paris, 1913), vol. ii, p. 356.

54. Cortés, *Cartas*, p. 136.

55. Cortés recounted these incidents in meticulous detail; cf. *Cartas*, pp. 136–43.

56. Cortés, *Cartas*, p. 143.

57. Cervantes de Salazar, *Crónica*, p. 688. The story is confirmed by a native source: cf. Sahagún, *Florentine Codex*, vol. xii, p. 99.

58. Edward Calnec, 'The Calmecac and the Telpochcalli in Pre-Conquest Tenochtitlan', in *The Work of Bernardino de Sahagún: Pioneer Ethnographer of*

Sixteenth-Century Aztec Mexico, ed. J. Jorge Klor de Alva et al. (Albany, NY, 1988), pp. 169–77.

59. Sahagún, *Florentine Codex*, vol. vi, p. 215. The Nahua glyph for the *calmecac* can be seen in the Codex Mendoza with the following extraordinary description: 'Mosque called *calmecac*'. Next to the glyph are two human figures with the following, no less extraordinary descriptions: 'Youth of fifteen, whose father hands over to the chief alfaqui to receive him as alfaqui.' And '*Tlamcazqui*, that is, chief alfaqui'. Cf. José Ignacio Echeagaray, ed., *Códice Mendocino o Colección de Mendoza: Manuscrito mexicano del siglo xvi que se preserva en la Biblioteca Bodleiana de Oxford* (Mexico City, 1979), p. 173.

60. Sahagún, *Florentine Codex*, vol. x, p. 173.

61. Sahagún, *Florentine Codex*, vol. xii, p. 93.

62. Cortés, *Cartas*, p. 144. According to Bernal Díaz del Castillo, Cortés was not as opposed to the idea as he later claimed to have been; cf. *Historia verdadera*, vol. ii, pp. 76–7.

63. Cortés, *Cartas*, p. 146.

64. Sahagún, *Florentine Codex*, vol. xii, pp. 103–4. The same scene was described in much more chilling detail by Bernal Díaz del Castillo: '. . . placing them on their backs, on top of some rather thin planks of stone that they had specially made for their sacrifices, with some large stone knifes they sawed their chest and extracted the palpitating hearts and they offered them to their idols . . . and they kicked the bodies down the stairs of the temple where other butchering Indians awaited them, who cut their arms and legs, flayed their faces, dried them like glove leather and kept them, still with their beards on, to party with them during their drunken orgies, and they ate the flesh with chilli sauce [*chimole*] and they sacrificed all the others in like manner, eating their legs and arms, offering the hearts and blood to the idols . . . and the bodies, which were the guts and feet, they fed to the tigers and lions . . .' *Historia verdadera*, vol. ii, p. 86. Cortés also recounted the episode, though understandably in more measured terms, to Charles V; cf. *Cartas*, p. 148.

65. Thomas, *Conquest*, p. 511.

66. Díaz del Castillo, *Historia verdadera*, vol. ii, p. 94; Durán, *Historia de las Indias*, vol. ii, p. 567.

67. Cortés, *Cartas*, pp. 147–8; López de Gómara, *Conquista*, p. 303.

68. Cortés, *Cartas*, p. 148.

69. Cortés, *Cartas*, pp. 149–53. Cervantes de Salazar, *Crónica*, p. 700. On Matlacingo see Nigel Davies, *The Toltec Heritage: From the Fall of Tula to the Rise of Tenochtitlan* (Norman, OK, 1980), pp. 135–9.

70. Sahagún, *Florentine Codex*, vol. xii, p. 114.

71. Vicente Murga Sanz, *Juan Ponce de León: fundador y primer gobernador del pueblo puertorriqueño* (San Juan, 1971), pp. 236–40.

72. Sahagún, *Florentine Codex*, vol. xii, pp. 104–5.

73. Cortés, *Cartas*, p. 154: '. . . y aquella noche tuvieron bien que comer nuestros amigos, porque todos los que se mataron, tomaron y llevaron hechos piezas para comer'.

74. Cortés, *Cartas*, p. 155.

75. Sahagún, *Florentine Codex*, vol. xii, p. 113. For Cortés's comment see *Cartas*, p. 157: '. . . no había maestros que supiesen hacerle'.

76. Cortés, *Cartas*, p. 157.

77. Cortés, *Cartas*, pp. 157–158. For Cortés's genuine desire for peace see the, admittedly partisan, account of Juan Ginés de Sepúlveda, *Historia del Nuevo Mundo*, ed. Antonio Ramírez de Verger (Madrid, 1987), p. 218.

78. Sahagún, *Florentine Codex*, vol. xii, p. 117.

79. Sahagún, *Florentine Codex*, vol. xii, p. 118.

80. Cortés, *Cartas*, p. 160: '. . . y ya nosotros teníamos más que hacer en estorbar a nuestros amigos que no matasen ni hiciesen tanta crueldad que no en pelear con los indios; la cual crueldad nunca en generación tan recia se vió, ni tan fuera de toda orden de naturaleza como en los naturales de estas partes.'

81. Sahagún, *Florentine Codex*, vol. xii, p. 120.

82. I draw on Josefina Muriel's cautious analysis: 'Divergencias en la biografía de Cuauhtémoc', *Estudios de Historia Novohispana*, 1 (1966), pp. 53–114, at p. 97.

83. For the name of the owner of the rooftop and the description of the canopy see Sahagún, *Florentine Codex*, vol. xii, p. 119; its careful preparation is described in Díaz del Castillo, *Historia verdadera*, vol. ii, p. 114.

84. Díaz del Castillo, *Historia verdadera*, vol. ii, p. 114.

85. Díaz del Castillo, *Historia verdadera*, vol. ii, pp. 112–14. See also López de Gómara, *Conquista*, p. 311.

86. Cortés, *Cartas*, p. 162.

CHAPTER 10: THE GRAND CHANCELLOR'S DREAM

1. José Luis Martínez, *Documentos Cortesianos*, 4 vols (Mexico City, 1990–91), vol. i, pp. 242–53. For the actual figures see the calculations done by C. H. Haring in 'Ledgers of the Royal Treasures in Spanish America in the Sixteenth Century', *Hispanic American Historical Review*, II (1919), pp. 173–87. The taste for the exotic became fashionable in court circles. Charles V, in particular, often requested to be sent 'exotic' items from America to lift his spirits. From his retirement home in Yuste, he raved about 'two bedspreads lined with feathers' from America and ordered 'dressing gowns and sheets for his bedroom made of the same material'. See Geoffrey Parker, *Emperor: A New Life of Charles V* (New Haven, CT, 2019), p. 343.

2. Peter Martyr, *De Orbe Novo: The Eight Decades of Peter Martyr D'Anghera*, ed. and trans. F. A. MacNutt, 2 vols (New York, 1912), vol. ii, p. 178.

3. Bernal Díaz del Castillo, *Historia verdadera de la conquista de la Nueva España*, ed. Miguel León Portilla, 2 vols (Madrid, 1984), vol. ii, p. 143.

4. Quoted in Stephen C. Neff, *Justice among Nations: A History of International Law* (Cambridge, MA, 2014), p. 127. For Fleury and Ango, see Eugène Guénin, *Ango et ses pilotes*, 2 vols (Paris, 1901).

5. Hugh Thomas, *The Conquest of Mexico* (London, 1993), pp. 536–7.

6. Lyndal Roper, *Martin Luther: Renegade and Prophet* (London, 2016), p. 99. For a full discussion see Volker Leppin, *Martin Luther: Gestalten des Mittelalters und der Renaissance* (Darmstadt, 2006), pp. 117–26.

7. *The New Shorter Oxford English Dictionary*.

8. David Nirenberg, *Anti-Judaism: The History of a Way of Thinking* (New York, 2013), p. 247.

9. A. G. Dickens, *The German Nation and Martin Luther* (London, 1974), pp. 112–13.

10. Nirenberg, *Anti-Judaism*, p. 248.

11. Thomas, *Conquest*, p. 538.

12. AGI (J), leg. 4, lib. 1, fols 132^r–147^v.

13. Joaquín F. Pacheco and Francisco de Cárdenas, eds, *Colección de documentos inéditos relativos al descubrimiento, conquista y organización de las posesiones españolas en América y Oceanía*, 42 vols (Madrid, 1864–84), vol. xxvii, pp. 16–17.

14. See above, pp. 132–4.

15. Ignacio López Rayón, ed., *Archivo Mexicano: Documentos para la historia de México. Sumario de la residencia tomada a Don Fernando Cortés, gobernador y capitán general de la Nueva España* (Mexico City, 1852), p. 365.

16. Thomas, *Conquest*, p. 551. The negotiations can be read in Pacheco and Cárdenas, eds, *Colección de documentos inéditos*, vol. xxvi, p. 30. See also Hernán Cortés, *Cartas de Relación*, ed. Manuel Alcalá (Mexico City, 1978), pp. 166–7.

17. Cortés, *Cartas*, p. 168: 'Allegados a donde el dicho Tapia estaba . . . todos juntos se volvieron a la ciudad de Cempoal, y allí el dicho Cristóbal de Tapia presentó las provisiones de vuestra majestad, las cuales todos *obedecieron* con el acatamiento que a vuestra majestad se debe; y en cuanto al *cumplimiento* de ellas dijeron que suplicaban para ante vuestra majestad, porque así convenía a su real servicio por las causas y razones de la misma suplicación que hicieron . . . y . . . lo llevan signado de escribano público' (my emphasis).

18. Pacheco and Cárdenas, eds, *Colección de documentos inéditos*, vol. xxvi, pp. 126, 548; vol. xxvii, p. 228; vol. xviii, p. 100. See also Cortés, *Cartas*, p. 168.

19. There is, as far as I can establish, no single study of this formula, which was incorporated into the laws of the Indies as early as 1528 (e.g. *Recopilación*

de las leyes de los reynos de las Indias, mandadas a imprimir, y publicar por la Magestad Católica del Rey Don Carlos II nuestro señor, 5th edn, 4 vols [Madrid, 1841], vol. i, p. 148, ley xxii: 'Los ministros y jueces obedezcan y no cumplan nuestras cédulas y despachos en que intervinieren los vicios de obrepción y subrepción, y en la primera ocasión nos avisen de la causa por que no lo hicieren'). See also Bartolomé Clavero, *Derecho de los Reinos: temas de historia de derecho* (Seville, 1977), pp. 125–30; José Manuel Pérez Prendes, *La monarquía indiana y el estado de derecho* (Valencia, 1989), pp. 167–8; Víctor Frankl, 'Hernán Cortés y la tradición de las *Siete Partidas*', *Revista de Historia de América*, 53/4 (June – December, 1962), pp. 9–74; Mario Góngora, *Studies in the Colonial History of Spanish America* (Cambridge, 1975), pp. 68–79; and J. H. Elliott, *Empires of the Atlantic World: Britain and Spain in America, 1492–1830* (New Haven, CT, 2006), pp. 131–2. On the late-medieval understanding of obedience I draw on Herbert McCabe's perceptive elucidation in *God Matters* (London, 1987), pp. 226–34.

20. Díaz del Castillo, *Historia verdadera*, vol. ii, p. 131: '. . . antes que de Santo Domingo saliese para venir a la Nueva España le habían mandado expresamente que en aquella sazón no curase de venir, porque sería causa de venir daño y quebrar el hilo de conquistas de Méjico . . .'

21. Thomas, *Conquest*, p. 554.

22. On this see John Lynch, *Spain, 1516–1598: From Nation State to World Empire* (Oxford, 1991), pp. 61–83; and J. H. Elliott, *Imperial Spain, 1469–1714* (Aylesbury, 1990), pp. 170–81.

23. Louis-Prosper Gachard, *Correspondance de Charles-Quint et d'Adrien VI publiée pour la première fois par M. Gachard* (Brussels, 1859), pp. 24–5.

24. Gachard, *Correspondance*, pp. 26–30, 33–46, 50–54, 59, 71–9, 92–5, 99, 100–109, and passim.

25. The bull was reprinted in Jerónimo de Mendieta, *Historia eclesiástica Indiana*, ed. Joaquín García Icazbalceta (Mexico City, 1870), pp. 128–9.

26. *Orlando Furioso*, trans. Barbara Reynolds (Harmondsworth, 1973), canto XV, stanza 25, p. 453.

27. Frances Yates, *Astraea: The Imperial Theme in the Sixteenth Century* (London, 1975), p. 23. See above, pp. 113–14.

28. Earl Rosenthal, '*Plus Ultra* and the Columnar Device of Emperor Charles V', *Journal of the Warburg and Courtauld Institutes*, 34 (1971), pp. 204–28. It is not often realized that the twin-pillar emblem of the Spanish gold *real* is the ancestor of the dollar sign.

29. See Peter Burke, 'Presenting and Re-Presenting Charles V', in Hugo Soly, ed., *Charles V, 1500–1558, and His Time* (Antwerp, 1999), pp. 422–5.

30. See, for example, P. S. Allen, *Opus Epistolarum Desiderii Erasmi Roterodami*, 12 vols (London, 1906–58), vol. ix, p. 254; see also James D. Tracy, *Erasmus of the Low Countries* (Berkeley, CA, 1996), pp. 171–4.

31. See Paul J. Alexander 'The Medieval Legend of the Last Roman Emperor and its Messianic Origins', *Journal of the Warburg and Courtauld Institutes*, 41 (1978), pp. 1–15; and Marie Tanner, *The Last Descendant of Aeneas: The Hapsburgs and the Mythic Image of the Emperor* (New Haven, CT, 1993), pp. 120–30 and passim.

32. See above, p. 113.

33. Antonio Fontán and Jerzy Axer, eds, *Españoles y polacos en la corte de Carlos V: Cartas del embajador Juan Dantisco* (Madrid, 1994), p. 153.

34. Eulàlia Duran and Joan Requesens, eds, *Profecia i poder al renaixement: texts profètics catalans favorables a Ferran el Catòlic* (Valencia, 1997), p. 376. I draw on Rebecca Boone, 'Empire and Medieval Simulacrum: A Political Project of Mercurino di Gattinara, Grand Chancellor of Charles V', *Sixteenth Century Journal*, 42:4 (2011), pp. 1,027–49.

35. On this see J. H. Elliott, 'Cortés, Velázquez and Charles V', in *Hernán Cortés: Letters from Mexico*, trans. and ed. Anthony Pagden (New Haven, CT, 2001), p. xxvii.

36. Elliott, *Imperial Spain*, p. 163.

37. Luigi Avonto, *Mercurino Arborio di Gattinara e l'America* (Vercelli, 1981), pp. 49–50.

38. Beatriz Arteaga Garza and Guadalupe Pérez San Vicente, eds, *Cedulario Cortesiano* (Mexico City, 1949), pp. 49–52.

CHAPTER 11: THE WORLD OF THE MENDICANTS

1. This was the Bull *Alias felicis recordationis*, printed in Francisco Javier Hernáez, ed., *Colección de Bulas y otros documentos de la iglesia de América y Filipinas*, 2 vols (Brussels, 1879), vol. i, pp. 377–81.

2. Hugolin Lippens, 'Jean Glapion, défenseur de la réforme de l'Observance, conseiller de l'empereur Charles-Quint', *Archivum Franciscanum Historicum*, XLIV (1951), pp. 3–70; XLV (1952), pp. 3–71.

3. See the entry for Francis Quiñones in *The Catholic Encyclopaedia*, www.newadvent.org/cathen/12613c.htm(accessed 4 November 2017).

4. Pedro Torres, *La Bula Omnímoda de Adriano VI* (Madrid, 1948), p. 71.

5. Hernán Cortés, *Cartas de Relación*, ed. Manuel Alcalá (Mexico City, 1978), pp. 203–4.

6. 'Carta de fray Pedro de Gante a los padres y hermanos de la provincia de Flandes, 27 de junio de 1529', printed in Ernesto de la Torre Villar, 'Fray Pedro de Gante, maestro y civilizador de América,' *Estudios de Historia Novohispana*, 5 (1974), pp. 9–77, at pp. 40–43.

7. Juan Meseguer Fernández, 'Contenido Misionológico de la Obediencia e Instrucción de Fray Francisco de los Ángeles a los Doce Apóstoles de México,' *The Americas*, 11:3 (January, 1955), pp. 473–500.

8. D. A. Brading, *The First America: The Spanish Monarchy, Creole Patriots and the Liberal State, 1492–1867* (Cambridge, 1991), p. 102.

9. Cortés explained and justified his decision to Charles V in his fifth letter, dated 3 September 1526. See *Cartas*, pp. 221–83.

10. Robert Bontine Cunninghame Graham, *The Horses of the Conquest*, ed. Robert Moorman Denhardt (Norman, OK, 1949), pp. 34–6.

11. See Antonio Rubial García, *La hermana pobreza: el franciscanismo de la edad media a la evangelización novohispana* (Mexico City, 1996), pp. 42–3.

12. This was especially the case among the early Franciscans influenced by Gerardo di Borgo San Donnino and John of Parma – the latter even becoming minister-general of the Order between 1247 and 1257. But these Joachimist prophecies were condemned: John of Parma was forced to resign in favour of the most outstanding Franciscan intellectual of the age, St Bonaventure, who became minister-general of the Order in 1258, thereafter devoting his prodigious intellectual gifts to a convincing refutation of Joachimism. I draw on Elsa Cecilia Frost's perceptive study, *La historia de Dios en las Indias: visión franciscana del nuevo mundo* (Mexico City, 2002), pp. 64–76. I am grateful to Jaime Cuadriello and Iván Martínez for making the text available to me.

13. Admittedly, there is a section in Friar Francisco de Los Ángeles's set of instructions that a candid reader might feel tempted to interpret as Joachimist: 'Now that the day of the world is declining at the eleventh hour, you have been called . . . to go to the vineyard . . . so that . . . being true children . . . you should be the last to come.' But the section is in fact a reference to the parable of the workers sent to the vineyard in the Gospel of Matthew (20:1–16), and it is much closer to Augustine of Hippo's teaching that the world (*saeculum*) had already entered the final age, but that this did not enable anyone to fathom its end. See Frost, *Historia de Dios*, p. 168.

14. See above, pp. 71–6.

15. As David Knowles once wrote, other saints 'are of a school and of a date', whereas 'the most characteristic utterances of St Francis have something of the dateless purity of the gospels'. See Knowles, 'St Francis of Assisi', in M. W, Sheenan, ed., *Francis of Assisi: Essays in Commemoration* (New York, 1982), p. 7, cited in Paul Murray OP, *God's Spies: Michelangelo, Shakespeare and Other Poets of Vision* (London, 2019); I am grateful to Fr Murray for allowing me to read the manuscript. St Francis's first biographer, Thomas of Celano, leaves us in no doubt about the sentiment: 'Who could ever express the deep affection he bore for all things that belong to God? Or who would be able to tell of the sweet tenderness he enjoyed while contemplating in creatures the wisdom, power and goodness of the Creator? From this reflection he often overflowed with amazing, unspeakable joy as he looked at the sun, gazed at the moon, or observed the stars in the sky.' Regis J. Armstrong, ed., *Francis of Assisi: Early Documents*, 3 vols (New York, 1999), vol. i, p. 250.

16. See above, pp. 108–9.

17. It is true that the alleged 'Erasmianism' of 'the Twelve' has been the subject of heated debate, and it would be a brave undertaking to attempt to establish it with any precision. The most influential thesis, dealing not with the Franciscans but with the Bishop of Michoacán, Don Vasco de Quiroga, is by Silvio Zavala, *La Utopía de Tomás Moro en la Nueva España* (Mexico City, 1937). See also Pablo Arce Gargollo, *La vida santa de Vasco de Quiroga y su proceso de canonización* (Mexico City, 2015).

18. Gerónimo de Mendieta, *Historia eclesiástica Indiana*, ed. Joaquín García Icazbalceta (Mexico City, 1870), pp. 651–3, 222, 250.

19. Toribio de Motolinía, *Historia de los Indios de la Nueva España*, ed. Joaquín García Icazbalceta (Mexico City, 1858), pp. 67–98, 106, 115.

20. The classic and still fundamental study is Robert Ricard, *La 'Conquête spirituelle' du Mexique: essai sur l'apostolat et les méthodes missionnaires des ordres mendicants en Nouvelle Espagne de 1523/24 à 1572* (Paris, 1933).

21. 'Relatio Vera de Novis Insulis', printed in Antonine Tibesar, *Franciscan Beginnings in Colonial Peru* (Washington D.C., 1953), pp. 101–2.

22. See George Kubler, *Mexican Architecture in the Sixteenth Century*, 2 vols (New Haven, CT, 1948), passim.

23. On this see Serge Gruzinski, *The Conquest of Mexico: The Incorporation of Indian Societies into the Western World, 16th–18th Centuries*, trans. E. Corrigan (Cambridge, 1993), pp. 58–9.

24. Francisco del Paso y Troncoso, ed., *Papeles de Nueva España*, 7 vols (Madrid, 1905–8), vol. iv, p. 236.

25. Diego Muñoz Camargo, *Historia de Tlaxcala*, ed. Germán Vázquez Chamorro (Madrid, 1986), p. 176; Juse Tudella and José Corona Núñez, eds, *Relación de las ceremonias y ritos y población y gobierno de los indios de la provincia de Michoacán*, facsimile of *El Escorial* Ms c. IV.5 (Morelia, 1977), pp. 265–7.

26. Luis González Obregón, ed., *Procesos de indios idólatras y hechiceros* (Mexico City, 1912), p. 23. For a chilling description of *tzitzimime*, see Bernardino de Sahagún, *Historia general de las cosas de Nueva España*, ed. Ángel María Garibay Kintana, 6th edn (Mexico City, 1985), pp. 317, 439.

27. Motolinía, *Historia*, pp. 15–28, 206–7.

28. Toribio de Motolinía, *Memoriales ó libro de las cosas de la Nueva España y de los naturales de ella*, ed. Edmundo O'Gorman (Mexico City, 1971), pp. 85–6, 237–42.

29. See Georges Baudot, *Utopie et histoire au Mexique* (Toulouse, 1977), pp. 122–36, 182–4, 237–8.

30. See Patricia Lopes Don, *Bonfires of Culture: Franciscans, Indigenous Leaders, and the Inquisition in Early Mexico, 1524–1540* (Norman, OK, 2010).

31. Sahagún, *Historia general*, pp. 704–5. I draw on my study *The Devil in the New World: The Impact of Diabolism in New Spain* (New Haven, CT, 1994), pp. 13–16.

32. D. A. Brading, 'Images and Prophets: Indian Religion and the Spanish Conquest', in Arij Ouweneel and Simon Miller, eds, *The Indian Community of Colonial Mexico* (Amsterdam, 1990), p. 185.
33. Louise M. Burkhart, *The Slippery Earth: Nahua-Christian Moral Dialogue in Sixteenth-Century Mexico* (Tucson, AZ, 1989), pp. 37–8, 124.
34. Nancy M. Farriss, *Maya Society under Colonial Rule: The Collective Enterprise of Survival* (Princeton, NJ, 1984), p. 287.
35. González Obregón, ed., *Procesos de indios*, pp. 9, 75, 123. On Mixcoatl see Serge Gruzinski's perceptive study, *Man-Gods in the Mexican Highlands: Indian Power and Colonial Society, 1520–1800*, trans. E. Corrigan (Stanford, CA, 1989), pp. 36–62.
36. Cervantes, *The Devil in the New World*, p. 47.
37. James Lockhart, *The Nahuas after the Conquest: A Social and Cultural History of the Indians of Central Mexico, Sixteenth Through Eighteenth Centuries* (Stanford, CA, 1992), p. 4.
38. On this see Jaime Cuadriello, 'Winged and Imagined Indians', in Fernando Cervantes and Andrew Redden, eds, *Angels, Demons and the New World* (Cambridge, 2013), pp. 211–48.
39. *Historia de las Indias de Nueva España e Islas de Tierra Firme*, ed. Ángel María Garibay Kintana, 2 vols (Mexico City, 1967), vol. i, p. 273.
40. Sahagún, *Coloquios y Doctrina Cristiana*, ed. Miguel León Portilla (Mexico City, 1986), pp. 146–55.
41. See above, pp. 82–3, 162, 193.
42. John Lynch, *New Worlds: A Religious History of Latin America* (New Haven, CT, and London, 2012), p. 172. For what follows I draw heavily on my essay 'How to See Angels: The Legacy of Mendicant Spirituality', in Cervantes and Redden, eds, *Angels, Demons*, pp. 69–97.
43. For a splendid evocation of this awareness see Christopher Dawson, *The Making of Europe: An Introduction to the History of European Unity* (London, 1932), pp. 103–22. On Byzantium, a good recent survey is Averil Cameron, *The Byzantines* (Oxford, 2010), esp. pp. 96–115.
44. Cf. Henri de Lubac, 'Remarques sur l'histoire du mot "surnaturel"', *Nouvelle revue théologique*, 61 (1934), p. 357.
45. Epistola 76, PL 77: 1215–1216: www.fordham.edu/halsall/source/greg1-mellitus.text (accessed 6 January 2018).
46. Joaquín García Icazbalceta, *Don Fray Juan de Zumárraga: primer obispo y arzobispo de México*, eds Rafael Aguayo Spence and Antonio Castro Leal, 4 vols (Mexico City, 1947), vol. iii, p. 153.
47. Jaime Lara, *City, Temple, Stage: Eschatological Architecture and Liturgical Theatrics in New Spain* (Notre Dame, IN, 2004), p. 11.
48. See Jaime Lara, *Christian Texts for Aztecs: Art and Liturgy in Colonial Mexico* (Notre Dame, IN, 2008), p. 87. Durán called many Indian practices

that show similarities with Christianity 'pagan sacraments'; Lara, *Christian Texts*, p. 81.

49. Quoted by Lara, *Christian Texts*, p. 82.

50. On this see David Albert Jones, *Angels: A History* (Oxford, 2010), pp. 29–31. The Cupid that sends St Teresa of Avila into ecstasy in Bernini's famous sculpture is as far removed from the Mendicant angels in New Spain as it is from the visions of Ezekiel (Ezekiel 10) or the descriptions of angels in the Temple of Jerusalem (e.g. 1 Kings 6:24).

51. Lara, *Christian Texts*, p. 185.

52. Lara, *Christian Texts*, pp. 201–2.

53. Lara, *City, Temple, Stage*, p. 109.

54. See Craig H. Russell, *From Serra to Sancho: Music and Pageantry in the California Missions* (Oxford, 2009), pp. 27, 258–75.

55. B. Stross, 'Mexican Copal Resins', *U-Mut Maya*, 6 (1993), pp. 177–86.

56. Genesis 58–12; John 1:51.

57. José A. Llaguno, *La personalidad jurídica del indio y el III Concilio Provincial Mexicano* (Mexico City, 1963), pp. 17–18, 34, 134, 140, 176, 286.

58. On the College of Santa Cruz see José María Kobayashi, *La educación como conquista: empresa franciscana en México* (Mexico City, 1974), pp. 207–84; Michael W. Mathes, *Santa Cruz de Tlatelolco: la primera biblioteca académica de las Américas* (Mexico City, 1982); and more generally, Baudot, *Utopie et histoire*.

59. Ángel María Garibay K., *Poesía náhuatl*, 3 vols (Mexico City, 1964–68), vol. i, p. x.

60. Francisco del Paso y Troncoso, ed., *Papeles de Nueva España*, 3 vols (Madrid, 1914–36), vol. ii, p. 46.

61. Pilar Gonzalbo Aizpuru, 'Del tercero al cuarto concilio provincial mexicano, 1585–1771', *Historia Mexicana*, 35:1 (1986), pp. 6–7.

62. See William A. Christian Jr., *Local Religion in Sixteenth-Century Spain* (Princeton, NJ, 1981).

63. See David Ewing Duncan, *Hernando de Soto: A Savage Quest in the Americas* (New York, 1995), p. 216.

64. Rolena Adorno and Patrick Charles Pautz, eds, *Alvar Núñez Cabeza de Vaca: His Account, His Life, and the Expedition of Pánfilo de Narváez*, 3 vols (Lincoln, NB, 1999), vol. i, pp. 113, 115.

65. I draw on David J. Weber, *The Spanish Frontier in North America* (New Haven, CT, 1992), pp. 42–4.

66. Adorno and Pautz, eds, *Alvar Núñez*, vol. i, p. 245.

67. Andrés Pérez de Ribas, quoted by Nicholas Griffiths, *Sacred Dialogues: Christianity and Native Religions in the Colonial Americas, 1492–1700*, 2nd edn (Lulu, 2017), p. 30.

68. Adorno and Pautz, eds, *Alvar Núñez*, vol. i, pp. 249–51 (my emphasis).

69. Adorno and Pautz, eds, *Alvar Núñez*, vol. i, pp. 255–7.

70. It might be thought that the use of a powerful native sacred symbol to convert indigenous peoples to Christianity is a rather incongruous development, but that would leave historians of Christianity with the embarrassing problem of explaining a great deal of Christian symbolism, not least the cross, a pagan instrument of death as repugnant as it is possible to get but which has been given a place of unparalleled honour. On this see Nicholas Boyle, *Sacred and Secular Scriptures: A Catholic Approach to Literature* (London, 2004), pp. 104–5: '. . . the presence of what is alien, pagan, unholy, unclean at the heart of the church is essential to its nature'. The nations 'she brings to mount Zion will come bearing gifts from their own lands' and they may 'take strange forms'.

71. Maureen Ahern, 'The Cross and the Gourd: The Appropriation of Ritual Signs in the *Relaciones* of Alvar Núñez Cabeza de Vaca and Fray Marcos de Niza', in Jerry M. Williamson and Robert E. Lewis, eds, *Early Images of the Americas: Transfer and Invention* (Tuscson, AZ, 1993), pp. 224–32; Jacques Lafaye, *Mesías, cruzadas, utopías: el judeo-cristianismo en las sociedades iberoamericanas*, 2nd edn (Mexico City, 1997), pp. 83–4.

72. Christian, *Local Religion*, pp. 33, 97, 124, 142, 174–7.

73. Eamon Duffy, *The Stripping of the Altars: Traditional Religion in England c. 1400 – c. 1580* (New Haven, CT, 1992), p. 279.

74. The term was coined by Richard White in *The Middle Ground: Indians, Empires, and Republics in the Great Lakes Region, 1650–1815* (Cambridge, 1991), but it was Nancy Farriss who first pointed to the limitations of a two-tiered model that presented Christianity and indigenous religions as mutually exclusive alternatives; see *Maya Society under Colonial Rule: The Collective Enterprise of Survival* (Princeton, NJ, 1984), esp. chapters 10 and 11. For the same development in Late Antiquity and the early Middle Ages, see Peter Brown, *Authority and the Sacred: Aspects of the Christianisation of the Roman World* (Cambridge, 1995); idem, *Power and Persuasion in Late Antiquity: Towards a Christian Empire* (Madison, WI, 1992); and, more generally, idem, *The Cult of the Saints: Its Rise and Function in Latin Christianity* (London, 1981).

75. The point was made by St Augustine in his explanation of the Christian notion that the lowest degree of grace in a human being was of far greater value than the natural goodness of the whole universe, both visible and invisible. Also, perhaps even more clearly, in his refutation of the inference that if angels had always existed, they were therefore co-eternal with God. As logical as it may sound, Augustine replied that God could be said both to have existed before the angels and to have never been without them, for he preceded them not 'in temporal space' but 'in the stability of eternity'. *De Civitate Dei*, xii.9: 'simul eis . . . condens naturam et largiens gratiam'; and xii.15.3: 'non eam spatio transcurrente, sed manente perpetuitate praecedens'. I have used

J. Morán's bilingual edition *Obras de San Agustín*, vols xvi – xvii, conflated in one tome (Madrid, 1958), pp. 808, 822–3. The notion is also found throughout Patristic thought, particularly in Irenaeus of Lyons, Clement of Alexandria and Eusebius of Caesarea who, in the words of Henri de Lubac, found in the Scriptures 'a discourse on universal history'; see his *Catholicisme: Les aspects sociaux du dogme* (Paris, 1938), p. 119.

76. This process could have either an upward direction, where the natural world is endowed with a symbolic character that points to the supernatural, or a downward one, where the mystery of the Incarnation endows the created world with its sacramental character. From these two movements stem the contrasting, but ultimately complementary, methods called 'apophatic' and 'cataphatic' in Christian mystical theology. The first method stresses the dissimilarity between God and his creatures; the second stresses the continuity between them, leading to the possibility of divine revelation in the Scriptures and in the *Logos* (suggestively meaning *both* the Word of God *and* human reason). See Denys Turner, *The Darkness of God: Negativity in Christian Mysticism* (Cambridge, 1995).

77. On this see Cornelius Ernst, *Multiple Echo*, eds Fergus Kerr and Timothy Radcliffe (London, 1979), pp. 200–201.

78. See Osvaldo Pardo's suggestive analysis, *The Origins of Mexican Catholicism: Nahua Rituals and Christian Sacraments in Sixteenth-Century Mexico* (Ann Arbor, MI, 2004), esp. pp. 20–48.

79. Fray Juan de Zumárraga, *Regla christiana breve para ordenar la vida y el tiempo del christiano que se quiere salvar y tener su alma dispuesta para que Jesu Christo more en ella*, ed. Ildefonso Adeva (Pamplona, 1994), pp. 71–4, 79, 104, 112, 119.

80. Zumárraga, *Regla christiana*, pp. 127–8.

81. Sahagún, *Psalmodia Christiana*, pp. 129, 83 (my emphasis).

82. Sahagún, *Psalmodia*, p. 201; Agustín Dávila Padilla, *Historia de la fundación y discurso de la provincia de Santiago de México, de la orden de predicadores* (Mexico City, 1595), pp. 615–16.

83. *Doctrina christiana en lengua mexicana* [1553], quoted and translated by Louise Burkhart, *Before Guadalupe: The Virgin Mary in Early Colonial Nahuatl Literature* (Albany, NY, 2001), p. 121.

84. 'In festo assuptionnis Virginis. m.ae. p. mo der secunda. eius. exaltatione. super omnes cellos [*sic*]', in 'Doctrina, evangelios y epístolas en Nahuatl', *Codex Indianorum 7*, the John Carter Brown Library; quoted and translated by Burkhart, *Before Guadalupe*, pp. 102–8, at 107; Sahagún, *Psalmodia*, p. 279.

85. Lara, *Christian Texts*, p. 196.

86. I draw on Étienne Gilson's classic study, *The Philosophy of St Bonaventure*, trans. Illtyd Trethowan and F. J. Sheed (London, 1938), pp. 261–70.

87. The city of Puebla, for example, was built on a site revealed to the Dominican Bishop of Tlaxcala, Fray Julián de Garcés, who in 1531 had a dream in which

he saw angels measuring cords to delineate the foundations of the city. (See Lara, *City, Temple, Stage*, pp. 104–5. The description is reminiscent of a similar phenomenon recounted in the book of the prophet Ezekiel, chapter 40. It is an obscure and difficult chapter, but it was well known to the friars through the detailed commentary of St Gregory the Great, who dedicated the ten homilies of his second book on Ezekiel entirely to an elucidation of this chapter. I have used the Spanish edition, *Obras de San Gregorio Magno*, trans. Paulino Gallardo, ed. Melquíades Andrés [Madrid, 1958], pp. 392–532.) More than a century later, and in a very different spirit, the controversial Aragonese visitor-general and Bishop of Puebla, Juan de Palafox y Mendoza, lent his enthusiastic support to the devotion of the archangel St Michael who, according to a local tradition, had miraculously appeared to an Indian called Diego Lázaro. (See Francisco de Florencia, *Narración de la maravillosa aparición que hizo el arcángel san Miguel a Diego Lázaro de San Francisco, indio feligrés del pueblo de San Bernardo, de la jurisdicción de Santa María Nativitas* [Seville, 1692].) Palafox's enthusiasm, expressed in a letter to King Philip IV, is in perfect tune with the methods of the early friars: he assured the king that the devotion to St Michael, following such a 'happy circumstance', would help the process of ethnic integration throughout the diocese. (See Juan de Palafox to Philip IV [16 February, 1645], *Biblioteca Nacional de Madrid*, MS 8865, fols 110ᵛ–111ᵛ. Palafox's angelic devotion was reflected in his proposal that the municipal coat of arms in Mexico City, which bore the image of an eagle and serpent, should be replaced by a more obviously Christian image, among which he suggested an angel bearing a cross [cf. *Actas del cabildo de la ciudad de México*, 54 vols (Mexico City, 1889–1916)], vol. xxxi, pp. 353–60. He was not alone in this: his famous contemporary, the Jesuit Juan Eusebio Nieremberg – who was Philip IV's confessor – had recently expounded his devotion to St Michael in *Devoción y patrocinio de san Miguel, príncipe de los ángeles, antiguo tutelar de los godos, y protector de España* [Madrid, 1643].) The Augustinian notion of one city of angels and humans could not be more in evidence here, and it is expressed with the same sense of realism that had, a few decades earlier, allowed the Dominican Gregorio García to explain the re-population of the world after the Great Flood by suggesting that God had entrusted angels with the transportation of humans to faraway places. (See Gregorio García, *Origen de los indios del nuevo mundo, e indias occidentales* [Valencia, 1607], pp. 68–71.)

88. Miguel Sánchez, *Imagen de la Virgen María, Madre de Dios de Guadalupe, Milagrosamente aparecida en la ciudad de México: Celebrada en su historia, con la profecía del capítulo doce del Apocalipsis* (Mexico City, 1648), pp. 177–91.

89. Lisa Sousa, Stafford Poole and James Lockhart, eds and trans., *The Story of Guadalupe: Luis Lasso de la Vega's* Huei tlamahuiçoltica *of 1649* (Stanford, CA, 1998).

90. Manuel Loayzaga, *Historia de la Milagrosissima Imagen de N^{ra} S^{ra} de Occotlan que se venera extramuros de la ciudad de Tlaxcala* (Mexico City, 1750), pp. 21–8: 'Ven tras mi, que yo te daré otra agua, con que se extinga ese contagio, y sanen, no solo tus Parientes; sino quantos bebieren de ella: porque mi Corazon siempre inclinado a favorecer desvalidos, y ya no me sufre ver entre ellos tantas desdichas sin remediarlas' (p. 22); 'le notició que antes de mucho, en aquel proprio sitio encontrarian en una imagen suya, un verdadero Retrato, así de sus perfecciones, como de du piedad, y clemencia: que avissare à los Padres de San Francisco, la colocaran en dicha Iglesia . . .' (p. 24).

91. The likely forgery is a document allegedly written by the Franciscan Martín Sarmiento de Hojacastro. It was made available to the anthropologist Hugo Nutini in the 1970s by its private owner. Unfortunately, all subsequent attempts to consult it have been in vain. The advice given by the friar to encourage such developments wherever possible struck Nutini as interesting given that, in the neighbouring areas of Tianguismanalco and Chiautempan respectively, St John the Apostle was identified with the youthful manifestation of Tezcatlipoca, and St Anne, the mother of the Virgin Mary, took the place of the grandmother goddess Toci. See Hugo G. Nutini, 'Syncretism and Acculturation: The Historical Development of the Cult of the Patron Saint in Tlaxcala, Mexico, (1519–1670)', *Ethnology*, 15:3 (July 1976), pp. 306–17.

92. Sahagún, *Historia general*, pp. 705: '. . . y ahora que está allí edificada la Iglesia de Ntra. Señora de Guadalupe, también la llaman *Tonantzin* . . . y es cosa que se debía remediar porque . . . parece . . . invención satánica para paliar su idolatría debajo de la equivocación de este nombre . . . porque en todas partes hay muchas iglesias de Nuestra Señora y no van a ellas, y vienen de lejas tierras a esta *Tonantzin*, como antiguamente.'

93. The best study is by D. A. Brading, *Mexican Phoenix. Our Lady of Guadalupe: Image and Tradition across Five Centuries* (Cambridge, 2002); see also Stafford Poole, *Our Lady of Guadalupe: The Origins and Sources of a Mexican National Symbol, 1531–1797* (Tucson, AZ, 1995). On the role of the Virgin Mary as Conqueror, see Amy G. Remensnyder, *La Conquistadora: The Virgin Mary at War and Peace in the Old and New Worlds* (Oxford, 2014), pp. 294–329.

94. It is no accident that every time this tradition was attacked, leading to a clash, it was invariably at the level of religious practice rather than religious belief that the battles were waged. See Alan Knight, 'Rethinking the Tomóchic Rebellion', *Mexican Studies/Estudios Mexicanos*, 15:2 (1999), pp. 382–3. I have dealt with this resilience in 'Mexico's Ritual Constant: Religion and Liberty from Colony to Post-Revolution', in Matthew Butler, ed., *Faith and Impiety in Revolutionary Mexico* (New York, 2007). For some highly suggestive examples of traditional resistance to Bourbon reformist zeal, see D. A. Brading, 'Tridentine Catholicism and Enlightened Despotism in Bourbon Mexico', *Journal of Latin American Studies*, 15 (1983).

95. The classic account of the growing separation of the natural and the supernatural in the Christian tradition is Henri de Lubac, *Le mystère du surnaturel: Augustinisme et théologie moderne* (Paris, 1965). A suggestive interpretation of the shift from communal to individual forms of religious expression in the early modern period is John Bossy, *Christianity in the West, 1400–1700* (Oxford, 1985).

CHAPTER 12: SPICES AND GOLD

1. Bernal Díaz del Castillo, *Historia verdadera de la conquista de la Nueva España*, ed. Miguel León Portilla, 2 vols (Madrid, 1984), vol. ii, p. 512.
2. Diego Durán, quoted in Hugh Thomas, *The Golden Age: The Spanish Empire of Charles V* (London, 2011), p. 67.
3. Eugene R. Craine and Reginald C. Reindorp, eds, *Chronicles of Michoacán: The Description of the Ceremonies, Rites, Population, and Government of the Indians of the Province of Michoacán, 1540–1541* (Norman, OK, 1970), pp. 70–71. See also J. Benedict Warren, *The Conquest of Michoacán: The Spanish Domination of the Tarascan Kingdom in Western Mexico, 1521–1530* (Norman, OK, 1985), pp. 53–69.
4. Hernán Cortés, *Cartas de Relación*, ed. Manuel Alcalá, 10th edn (Mexico City, 1978), p. 281.
5. Harry Kelsey, 'Finding the Way Home: Spanish Exploration of the Round-Trip Route across the Pacific Ocean', *Western Historical Quarterly*, 17:2 (April 1986), pp. 145–64, at p. 151.
6. Kelsey, 'Finding the Way Home', p. 152. This was actually the instruction given to the second expedition that set off in 1526 under the command of Sebastian Cabot, but the first one was more than likely given a similar remit.
7. Cortés, *Cartas*, pp. 281–2.
8. Cortés, *Cartas*, p. 184.
9. Adrián Recinos, Delia Goetz and Sylvanus G. Morley, eds, *Popol Vuh: The Sacred Book of the Ancient Quiché Maya* (Norman, OK, 1950), p. 219.
10. Judith Maxwell and Robert M. Hill II, eds, *Kaqchikel Chronicles: The Definitive Edition* (Austin, TX, 2006), pp. 238–44.
11. George W. Lovell and Christopher H. Lutz, 'Pedro de Alvarado and the Conquest of Guatemala, 1522–1524', in John M. Weeks, ed., *The Past and the Present Maya: Essays in Honour of Robert M. Carmack* (Lancaster, CA, 2001), p. 48.
12. Lovell and Lutz, 'Pedro de Alvarado', pp. 50–51.
13. Matthew Restall and Florine Asselbergs, *Invading Guatemala: Spanish, Nahua, and Maya Accounts of the Conquest Wars* (Pennsylvania, PA, 2007), p. 10.

14. Adrián Recinos, *Pedro de Alvarado: Conquistador de México y Guatemala*, 2nd edn (Guatemala City, 1986), p. 93.

15. Restall and Asselbergs, *Invading Guatemala*, pp. 11–13.

16. It was Wendy Kramer who first drew attention to this anomaly. See *Encomienda Politics in Early Colonial Guatemala, 1524–1544: Dividing the Spoils* (Boulder, CO, 1994), p. 46.

17. Lisa Sousa and Kevin Terrenciano, 'The "Original Conquest" of Oaxaca: Nahua and Mixtec Accounts of the Spanish Conquest', *Ethnohistory*, 50:2 (Spring 2003), pp. 353–4. When the Dominican friars began to arrive in the early 1530s, they were glad to be able to use Nahuatl as the lingua franca while relying on bilingual Zapotec and Mixtec interpreters. See Francisco de Burgoa, *Geográfica descripción de la parte septentrional del Polo Ártico de la América y nueva iglesia de las Indias Occidentales y sitio astronómico de esta provincia de predicadores de Antequera, Valle de Oaxaca*, 2 vols (Mexico City, 1989), vol. i, p. 42.

18. William Taylor, *Landlord and Peasant in Colonial Oaxaca* (Stanford, CA, 1972), p. 23.

19. Thomas, *Golden Age*, pp. 68–70.

20. Thomas, *Golden Age*, pp. 101–2, 107. Disraeli's comment, transcribed by Thomas on p. 607, fn. 16, is from Robert Blake, *Disraeli* (London, 1966).

21. Kramer, *Encomienda Politics*, pp. 63–122; Florine G. L. Asselbergs, *Conquered Conquistadors: The Lienzo de Quauhquechollan: A Nahua Vision of the Conquest of Guatemala* (Leiden, 2004), pp. 87–91.

22. Bartolomé de Las Casas, *Brevísima relación de la destrucción de las Indias*, ed. Gregorio Weinberg (Buenos Aires, 1966), pp. 65–70.

23. Restall and Asselbergs, *Invading Guatemala*, p. 16.

24. Restall and Asselbergs, *Invading Guatemala*, pp. 17–18, 94–8.

25. The document is transcribed in Vicente Francisco de Cadenas y Vicent, *Carlos I de Castilla, Señor de las Indias* (Madrid, 1988), pp. 28–33.

26. Antonio Rodríguez Villa, *El Emperador Carlos V y su corte según las cartas de don Martín de Salinas, embajador del infante don Fernando, 1522–1539* (Madrid, 1903), p. 327.

27. *I diarii di Marino Sanuto*, ed. F. Stefani, G. Brechet and N. Barozzi, 58 vols (Venice, 1879–1903), vol. xxxviii, cols 205–7.

28. Geoffrey Parker, *Emperor: A New Life of Charles V* (New Haven, CT, 2019), pp. 141–8.

29. Alonso de Valdés, *Relación de las nuevas de Italia: sacada de las cartas que los capitanes y comisarios del Emperador y rey nuestro señor han escripto a su magestad: assi de la victoria contra el rey de Francia como de otras cosas allá acaecidas: vista y corregida por el señor gran Chanciller e consejo de su magestad* (Madrid, 1525), fols A vii – A viii.

30. Pierantonio Serassi, *Delle lettere del conte Baldessar Castiglione, ora per la prima volta date in luce*, 2 vols (Padua, 1769–71), pp. 125–7.

31. Cortés, *Cartas*, p. 279.
32. See above, pp. 167–8.
33. Francisco del Paso y Troncoso, *Papeles de Nueva España*, 2nd series, 7 vols (Madrid, 1905–8), vol. i, p. 57.
34. These included Azcapotzalco, Chila and Matlactlan; see Peter Gerhard, *A Guide to the Historical Geography of New Spain* (Cambridge, 1972), pp. 249, 391.
35. Joaquín Pacheco and Francisco Cárdenas, eds., *Colección de documentos inéditos relativos al descubrimiento, conquista y organización de las posesiones españolas en América y Oceanía*, 42 vols (Madrid, 1864–84), vol. xxii, pp. 201–23.
36. Antonio Fontán and Jerzy Axer, eds, *Españoles y polacos en la corte de Carlos V: Cartas del embajador Juan Dantisco* (Madrid, 1994), p. 167.
37. Paso y Troncoso, *Papeles*, vol. i, p. 78.
38. Robert Himmerich y Valencia, *The Encomenderos of New Spain, 1521–1555* (Austin, TX, 1991), p. 170; Donald E. Chipman, *Nuño de Guzmán and the Province of Pánuco in New Spain* (Glendale, CA, 1967), pp. 59–65, 149–54, 225.
39. Geoffrey Parker, *Emperor: A New Life of Charles V* (New Haven, CT, 2019), p. 351.
40. Judith Hook, *The Sack of Rome*, 2nd edn (London, 2004), pp. 156–80.
41. James D. Tracy, *Emperor Charles V, Impresario of War: Campaign Strategy, International Finance, and Domestic Politics* (Cambridge, 2002), p. 47.
42. Maurizio Arfaioli, *The Black Bands of Giovanni: Infantry and Diplomacy during the Italian Wars, 1526–1528* (Pisa, 2005), p. 165.
43. 'Cédula de Carlos V nombrando a Hernán Cortés Gobernador de las islas que descubriese en el mar del Sur', 5 November 1529, in Martín Fernández de Navarrete, Miguel Salvá and Pedro Sainz de Baranda, eds, *Colección de documentos históricos para la historia de España*, 113 vols (Madrid, 1842–95), vol. ii, pp. 401–5; Hugh Thomas, *The Conquest of Mexico* (London, 1993), p. 598.
44. Jean Babelon, 'Un retrato verdadero de Hernán Cortés', in *Memorias de la Academia Mexicana de la Historia*, 13 (July – August, 1954), pp. 173–8.
45. The curious (and heroically patient) reader can consult the prolix investigations in Ignacio López Rayón, 'Sumario de la residencia tomada a D. Fernando Cortés, gobernador y Capitán General de la N. E., y a otros gobernadores y oficiales de la misma', in *Archivo Mexicano: Documentos para la historia de México*, 2 vols (Mexico City, 1852–3).
46. See W. Michael Mathes, *The Conquistador in California 1535: The Voyage of Fernando Cortés to Baja California in Chronicles and Documents* (Los Angeles, CA, 1973).
47. Gonzalo Fernández de Oviedo, *Historia general y natural de las Indias*, ed. Juan Pérez de Tudela Bueso, 5 vols (Madrid, 1959), vol. iii, p. 398.

48. Despite its age, Robert S. Chamberlain's *The Conquest and Colonization of Yucatan, 1517–1550* (Washington D.C., 1948), remains the most reliable guide; see pp. 49–54, 60–72. The description of the meeting with Guerrero is in Fernández de Oviedo, *Historia general*, vol. iii, pp. 404–5.

49. All these hubs of activity were controlled by the Chontal of Campeche, those 'Phoenicians of the New World', as they were once called, who traded goods between Yucatan and the rest of the mainland. J. Eric Thompson, *Maya History and Religion* (Norman, OK, 1970), p. 7.

50. Nancy M. Farriss, *Maya Society under Colonial Rule: The Collective Enterprise of Survival* (Princeton, NJ, 1984), pp. 12–16.

51. Pacheco and Cárdenas, eds, *Colección de documentos inéditos*, vol. xiii, pp. 86–91.

52. Thomas, *Golden Age*, pp. 194–200.

53. See above, p. 88.

54. María del Carmen Mena García, *Pedrarias Dávila o la ira de Dios: una historia olvidada* (Seville, 1992), p. 160.

55. José Antonio del Busto Duthurburu, *La Conquista del Perú* (Lima, 2011), p. 26.

56. Pedro Cieza de León, *Descubrimiento y Conquista del Perú*, ed. Carmelo Sáenz de Santa María (Madrid, 1986), pp. 74–6.

57. Raúl Porras Barrenechea, *Pizarro* (Lima, 1978), p. 5.

58. Thomas, *Golden Age*, pp. 128–9.

59. Parker, *Emperor*, pp. 186–6.

60. Pacheco and Cárdenas, eds, *Colección de documentos inéditos*, vol. xix, pp. 5–18.

61. Thomas, *Golden Age*, p. 146.

CHAPTER 13: CAJAMARCA

1. Pedro Pizarro, *Relación del Descubrimiento y Conquista de los Reinos del Perú, y el gobierno y órden que los naturales tenían, y tesoros que en ella se hallaron*, in Martín Fernández de Navarrete, ed., *Colección de documentos inéditos para la historia de España*, 113 vols (Madrid, 1842–95), vol. v, pp. 210–12. It is difficult to establish how much gold the Spaniards seized. Estimates from contemporary sources range from 15,000 pesos of gold and 1,500 pesos of silver (Francisco de Jerez) to a grossly exaggerated 200,000 pesos of gold (Pedro Pizarro). For details see the indispensable study by James Lockhart, *The Men of Cajamarca: A Social and Biographical Study of the First Conquerors of Peru* (Austin, TX, 1972), p. 7, fn. 8.

2. Pizarro, *Relación*, p. 212; Pedro Cieza de León, *Descubrimiento y Conquista del Perú*, ed. Carmelo Sáenz de Santa María (Madrid, 1986), p. 154. This was more than likely a form of Carrion's disease, also known as Oroya fever.

3. Cieza de León, *Descubrimiento*, p. 150.

4. Again, the numbers vary in the sources; see Lockhart, *Men of Cajamarca*, p. 7, fn. 9.

5. Lockhart, *Men of Cajamarca*, p. 9.

6. Cieza de León, *Descubrimiento*, p. 159.

7. I draw mainly on Terrence N. D'Altroy's cautious synthesis: *The Incas*, 2nd edn (Oxford, 2015), pp. 91–102.

8. D'Altroy, *Incas*, pp. 103–4.

9. Hugh Thomas speculates that this might have been syphilis: see *The Golden Age: The Spanish Empire of Charles V* (London, 2011), p. 218.

10. See María Rostworowski de Diez Canseco, *History of the Inca Realm*, trans. Harry B. Iceland (Cambridge, 1999), pp. 106–7.

11. Lockhart, *Men of Cajamarca*, p. 8, fn. 10.

12. Pizarro, *Relación*, p. 213.

13. David Ewing Duncan, *Hernando de Soto: A Savage Quest in the Americas* (New York, 1995), p. 113.

14. Lockhart, *Men of Cajamarca*, p. 8.

15. El Inca Garcilaso de la Vega, *Royal Commentaries of the Incas*, ed. Harold Livermore, 2 vols (Austin, TX, 1966), vol. ii, p. 663.

16. Cieza de León, *Descubrimiento*, p. 176.

17. Francisco de Jerez, *Verdadera relación de la conquista del Perú y provincia del Cusco, llamada la Nueva Castilla*, in Enrique de Vedia, ed., *Historiadores primitivos de Indias*, 3 vols (Madrid, 1852–57), vol. ii (1853), p. 325.

18. Pizarro, *Relación*, pp. 219–20.

19. Pedro Ruiz Naharro, *Relación de los hechos de los españoles en el Perú desde su descubrimiento hasta la muerte del marqués Francisco Pizarro*, in Fernández de Navarrete, ed., *Colección*, vol. xxvi, pp. 232–56, at p. 241; Fernando Montesinos, *Anales del Perú*, 2 vols (Madrid, 1906), vol. i, p. 72; Garcilaso, *Royal Commentaries*, vol. ii, p. 665.

20. Jerez, *Verdadera relación*, p. 330.

21. John Hemming, *The Conquest of the Incas* (New York, 1970), pp. 37–8.

22. Thomas, *The Golden Age*, p. 238. Thomas writes that 'Felipillo' was the name given to the interpreter by El Inca Garcilaso de la Vega; 'Martinillo' was Pedro Pizarro's attribution. But 'Felipillo' also appears in Pizarro's account, which suggests that the Spaniards took more than one interpreter, thus adding to the confusion.

23. Hemming, *Conquest*, pp. 34–5.

24. Felipe Guaman Poma de Ayala, *El primer nueva corónica y buen gobierno*, online facsimile with parallel transcription (Copenhagen, Det Kongelige Bibliotek, GKS 2232 4°), http://www.kb.dk/permalink/2006/poma/titlep age/en/text (accessed 16/02/2018), fol. 383. It is impossible to render the ungrammatical and garbled charm of the original: 'todos trayýan bonetes

colorados y calsones chupados, jubón estofados y manga larga y un capo-
tillo con su manga larga, como caci a la byscaynada'.

25. See George Kubler, 'A Peruvian Chief of State: Manco Inca (1515–1545)',
    Hispanic American Historical Review, 24:2 (May 1944), pp. 253–76, at
    p. 253.
26. Pizarro, *Relación*, p. 225: '. . . el Atabalipa mandó matar á estos indios que
    se levantaron y tuvieron miedo, y á sus caciques que ahí estaban y sus hijos
    y mugeres, por poner temor a su gente, y que no huyese ninguno al tiempo
    del pelear con los cristianos'.
27. Pizarro, *Relación*, p. 224.
28. Estete, *Noticia*, p. 30 [fol. 8ʳ].
29. This is Garcilaso's account, written many years later and unashamedly
    embellished, but it captures something of the message that Fr Valverde tried,
    and failed, to transmit. *Royal Commentaries*, vol. ii, p. 687.
30. The sources differ widely in the details. The figures of native casualties tend
    to rise as time passes. The lowest is 2,000 (Francisco de Xerez); the highest
    is 8,000 (Diego de Trujillo). Garcilaso settles for a compromise of 5,000. All
    these figures are, typically, gross exaggerations. Hemming provides a bal-
    anced summary of the tragic episode, but still goes with a higher figure than
    is believable for an episode that lasted a mere two hours: *Conquest*, pp.
    39–45. Juan Ruiz de Arce claims that Atawallpa himself had estimated the
    dead at 7,000; see 'Relación de los servicios en Indias', *Boletín de la Real
    Academia de la Historia*, 102 (1933), pp. 327–84, at p. 361.
31. Francisco de Xerez, *Verdadera relación de la conquista del Perú y provincia
    del Cusco*, in *Biblioteca de Autores Españoles*, vol. xxvi (Madrid, 1947),
    pp. 320–46, at p. 334.
32. Pizarro, *Relación*, pp. 230–31.
33. 'Carta del Lycenciado Espinosa al Comendador Francisco de los Cobos . . .',
    Panama, 1 August 1533, in Joaquín F. Pacheco and Francisco de Cárdenas,
    eds, *Colección de documentos inéditos relativos al descubrimiento, con-
    quista y organización de las posesiones españolas en América y Oceanía*,
    42 vols (Madrid, 1864–84), vol. xlii, p. 70.
34. Hemming, *Conquest*, pp. 53–4.
35. Hemming, *Conquest*, p. 90.
36. See Brian Bauer, *Ancient Cuzco: Heartland of the Inca* (Austin, TX, 2004),
    p. 109. The information is from Xerez, *Verdadera relación*.
37. Xerez, *Verdadera relación*.
38. Hemming, *Conquest*, pp. 64–70, 72–3.
39. I have not been able to find evidence for Hugh Thomas's suggestive specula-
    tion that it was Felipillo, the native interpreter, who peddled this idea in the
    hope of getting Atawallpa executed as a traitor because he had fallen in love
    with Cuxirimay, one of the Inca's favourite wives and the future concubine
    of Francisco Pizarro; see his *The Golden Age*, p. 249.

40. Pizarro, *Relación*, pp. 245–6; Ruiz Naharro, *Relación*, pp. 249–50; Montesinos, *Anales*, vol. i, pp. 77–8.

41. Pedro Sancho de la Hoz, *Relación para S. M. de lo que sucedió en la conquista y pacificación de estas provincias de la Nueva Castilla y de la calidad de la tierra, después que el capitán Hernando Pizarro se partió y llevó a Su Majestad la relación de la victoria de Caxamalca y de la prisión del Cacique Atabalipa* (Lima, 1968), p. 280.

42. See D'Altroy, *Incas*, p. 459.

43. Pizarro, *Relación*, p. 247.

44. Hemming, *Conquest*, pp. 84–5.

45. See *Verdadera relación*, pp. 345–6.

46. Thomas, *Golden Age*, p. 253.

47. Garcilaso, *Royal Commentaries*, vol. ii, p. 709.

48. Raúl Porras Barrenechea, ed., *Colección de documentos inéditos para la historia del Perú*, 3 vols (Lima, 1944–59), vol. iii, p. 64.

49. Francisco de Vitoria, *Political Writings*, ed. and trans. Anthony Pagden and Jeremy Lawrance (Cambridge, 1991), p. 331.

50. On this see Ramón Menéndez Pidal, *El Padre Las Casas y Vitoria con otros temas de los siglos xvi y xvii* (Madrid, 1958), pp. 30–31.

51. Vitoria, *Political Writings*, pp. 332–3.

52. As Melchor Cano once stated in relation to Vitoria: 'Insofar as we are learned, prudent and elegant, we are so because we follow this outstanding man ... and emulate his precepts and his example.' Quoted by Pagden, *Burdens of Empire*, p. 46.

53. Vitoria, *Political Writings*, pp. 237–8.

54. St Thomas Aquinas, *Summa Theologiae*, Blackfriars edn, 61 vols (Cambridge, 2006), vol. xxxvii, pp. 20–21 [IIa–IIae, 58.1]: 'perpetua et constans voluntas jus suum unicuique tribuendi'.

55. Plato, *Republic*, 331e–332c. I have used *The Collected Dialogues, including the letters*, Edith Hamilton and Huntington Cairns, eds (Princeton, NJ, 1961), pp. 580–81.

56. St Thomas Aquinas, *Summa contra gentiles*, 2, 28.

57. Plato, *Gorgias*, 508c. *Collected Dialogues*, p. 290.

58. See above, pp. 82–3.

59. Vitoria, *Political Writings*, p. 85.

60. Vitoria, *Political Writings*, pp. 264, 246, 250.

61. Vitoria, *Political Writings*, pp. 252–77, quotation at pp. 276–7.

62. Aquinas, *Summa* I–II. 91. 2 in *c*.

63. Quoted by Pagden, *Burdens of Empire*, p. 53. On Soto see the excellent discussion by David A. Lupher, *Romans in a New World: Classical Models in Sixteenth-Century Spanish America* (Ann Arbor, MI, 2003), pp. 61–8. For the wider context the best study is by Quentin Skinner, *The Foundations of*

Modern Political Thought: Vol II, The Age of Reformation (Cambridge, 1978), pp. 113–84.

64. See, for example, Josef Pieper, *The Four Cardinal Virtues*, trans. Richard and Clara Winston, Lawrence E. Lynch and Daniel F. Coogan (South Bend, IN, 1966).

65. Vitoria, *Political Writings*, p. 291.

66. Vitoria, *Political Writings*, p. 40. Cicero's opinion is from *De Officis*, iii, 69.

67. See the discussion in Martti Koskenniemi, *From Apology to Utopia: The Structure of International Legal Argument* (Cambridge, 2006), p. 98, fn. 95.

68. Vitoria, *Political Writings*, pp. 278–87.

69. 'Los reyes piensan a las veces del pie a la mano y más los de consejo.' Quoted by Pagden, *Burdens of Empire*, pp. 46, 68 fn. 9 (I have amended Pagden's rather free translation).

CHAPTER 14: CUSCO

1. Pedro Sancho de la Hoz, *Relación para S. M. de lo que sucedió en la conquista y pacificación de estas provincias de la Nueva Castilla y de la calidad de la tierra, después que el capitán Hernando Pizarro se partió y llevó a Su Majestad la relación de la victoria de Caxamalca y de la prisión del Cacique Atabalipa* (Lima, 1968), pp. 281–3.

2. Sancho de la Hoz, *Relación*, pp. 284–5.

3. See above, pp. 122–4.

4. '. . . siendo el trecho grande se dobla el puente cuando pasa uno por el, que siempre va uno bajando hasta el medio, y desde allí subiendo hasta que acaba de pasar a la otra orilla, cuando se pasa tiembla muy fuerte, de manera que al que no está a ello acostumbrado se le va la cabeza'. Sancho de la Hoz, *Relación*, p. 296.

5. Enrique Torres Saldamando, ed., *Libro Primero de Cabildos de Lima*, 3 vols (Paris, 1888–1900), vol. iii, p. 2.

6. Sancho de la Hoz, *Relación*, pp. 286–7.

7. Sancho de la Hoz, *Relación*, p. 288.

8. Terrence N. D'Altroy, *The Incas*, 2nd edn (Oxford, 2015), p. 335.

9. Sancho de la Hoz, *Relación*, p. 289.

10. D'Altroy, *Incas*, p. 343.

11. Sancho de la Hoz, *Relación*, p. 290; Juan Ruiz de Arce, 'Relación de los servicios en Indias', *Boletín de la Real Academia de la Historia*, 102 (1933), pp. 327–84, at p. 365; Miguel de Estete, *Noticia del Peru*, in Carlos A. Romero and Horacio H. Urteaga, eds, *Colección de libros y documentos referentes a la historia del Perú*, 2nd series, 22 vols (Lima, 1916–36), vol. viii, pp. 3–56, at p. 43.

12. Ruiz de Arce, *Relación*, p. 365; John Hemming, *The Conquest of the Incas* (New York, 1970), p. 95.

13. D'Altroy, *Incas*, pp. 322, 334.

14. D'Altroy, *Incas*, pp. 323–4.

15. John H. Rowe, 'Inca Culture at the Time of the Spanish Conquest', *Handbook of South American Indians* 143.2, ed. Julian Stewell (Washington, 1946), pp. 183–330, at p. 280.

16. Bernabé Cobo, *Inca Religion and Customs*, trans. and ed. Ronald Hamilton (Austin, TX, 1990), p. 216.

17. Mariusz S. Ziółkowski, *La guerra de los Wawqi: los objetivos y los mecanismos de la rivalidad dentro de la élite inka, siglos XV–XVI* (Quito, 1996), pp. 136–40.

18. Peter Gose, 'Oracles, Divine Kingship, and Political Representation in the Inka State', *Ethnohistory*, 43:1 (1996), pp. 1–32, at p. 4.

19. Felipe Guaman Poma de Ayala, *El primer nueva corónica y buen gobierno*, ed. John v. Murra, Rolena Adorno and Jorge Urioste (Mexico City, 1980), p. 287.

20. Torres Saldamando, ed., *Libro Primero*, vol. iii, p. 3; Sancho de la Hoz, *Relación*, p. 293.

21. Pedro Pizarro, *Relación del Descubrimiento y Conquista de los Reinos del Perú*, in Martín Fernández de Navarrete, ed., *Colección de documentos inéditos para la historia de España*, 113 vols (Madrid, 1842–95), vol. v (1844), pp. 201–388, at pp. 252–3; Fray Antonio, *Discurso sobre la descendencia y gobierno de los Incas*, in *Colección de libros y documentos referentes a la historia del Perú* (Lima, 1920), pp. 1–53, at p. 32.

22. D'Altroy, *Incas*, pp. 326–8; Charles Gibson, *The Inca Concept of Sovereignty and the Spanish Administration in Peru* (Austin, TX, 1948), pp. 10–11, 16, 97.

23. See above, p. 259.

24. Hernando Pizarro, 'Carta a los oidores de Santo Domingo, 23 November 1533', in Gonzalo Fernández de Oviedo *Historia general y natural de las Indias*, ed. Juan Pérez de Tudela Bueso, *Biblioteca de Autores Españoles*, 5 vols [cxvii–cxxi] (Madrid, 1959), vol. v [cxxi], pp. 84–90, at p. 88.

25. Diego de Trujillo, *Relación del descubrimiento del reyno del Perú*, ed. Raúl Porras Berrenechea (Seville, 1948), p. 61; Pizarro, *Relación*, p. 256.

26. '. . . fue cosa notable . . . que jamás después acá se ha visto, especialmente en el Apurímac'. Antonio de Herrera y Tordesillas, *Historia general de los hechos de los castellanos en las Islas y Tierra Firme del Mar Oceano*, 4 vols (Madrid, 1601–15), vol. iv, p. 136. The successor of this very bridge would be immortalized by Thornton Wilder in a 1927 classic, where he described a friar who 'stopped to wipe his forehead and to gaze upon the scenery of snowy peaks in the distance, then into the gorge below him filled with the dark plumage of green trees and green birds and traversed by its ladder of

osier'. After a contemplative moment, 'his glance fell upon the bridge, and at that moment a twanging noise filled the air, as when the string of some musical instrument snaps in a disused room, and he saw the bridge divide and fling five gesticulating ants into the valley below'. *The Bridge of San Luis Rey* (London, 2000), pp. 8–9.

27. José Antonio del Busto Duthurburu, 'Los caídos de Vilcaconga', *Historia y Cultura: Órgano del Museo Nacional de Historia* (Lima, 1965), vol. i, pp. 115–25; Estete, *Noticia*, p. 44; Pizarro, *Relación*, pp. 256–8; Ruiz de Arce, *Relación*, p. 367.

28. 'One rides through them huddled against the cold, longing for the Andean sun to break through the cloud, to glisten on the damp grasses and shine with dazzling brilliance on the snows of Soray and Salcantay.' John Hemming, *The Conquest of the Incas* (New York, 1970), p. 108.

29. Sancho de la Hoz, *Relación*, pp. 308–9.

30. Hemming, *Conquest*, p, 109.

31. Ruiz de Arce, *Relación*, p. 368; Sancho de la Hoz, *Relación*, pp. 311–12.

32. Sancho de la Hoz, *Relación*, p. 312.

33. See above, pp. 252–3, 258.

34. Some scholars believe that these revelations preceded Pizarro's decision to execute Challcochima (e.g. D'Altroy, *Incas*, pp. 460–61), but it is impossible to draw such a conclusion from the available evidence. The one document that implies it, Pizarro's *Relación* (pp. 261–2), is so badly damaged in that section that nothing certain can be derived from it.

35. Cristóbal de Molina, *Relación de muchas cosas acaescidas en el Perú* (Madrid, 1968), p. 80; Trujillo, *Relación*, p. 63; Pizarro, *Relación*, p. 261; Sancho de la Hoz, *Relación*, p. 311.

36. Hemming, *Conquest*, p. 126.

37. Hemming, *Conquest*, p. 127. The quotations are all from Estete, *Noticia*, pp. 54–6 (I have kept Hemming's translation).

38. Hemming, *Conquest*, p. 128.

39. The approximate figure for the totality of the bullion is a staggering 1.5 billion *marvedís*. Actual figures are as follows: 697,994,930 *marvedís* at Cajamarca and 700,113,880 *marvedís* at Cusco. The gold at Cajamarca amounted to 596,942,550 *marvedís* while at Cusco it was 264,719,700 *marvedís*. Conversely the silver at Cajamarca was 101,052,380 *marvedís* while at Cusco it was 435,394,180 *marvedís*. For details see Rafael Loredo's admirable reconstruction in *Los repartos: bocetos para la nueva historia del Perú* (Lima, 1958), pp. 95–130.

40. Loredo, *Los repartos*, pp. 102–3.

41. Torres Saldamando, ed., *Libro Primero*, vol. iii, p. 4.

42. Steve Kosiba and Andrew M. Bauer, 'Mapping the Political Landscape: Toward a GIS Analysis of Environmental and Social Difference', *Journal of Archaeological Method and Theory*, 20:1 (March, 2013), pp. 61–101, at pp. 67–83.

43. D'Altroy, *Incas*, p. 202.
44. Craig Morris and Ariana von Hagen, *The Incas: Lords of the Four Quarters* (New York, 2011), p. 33. It has been estimated that there were about 2,000 *tampu* in Tawantinsuyu at the time of the conquest; see John Hyslop, *The Inka Road System* (New York, 1984), pp. 277–9.
45. Santiago Agurto Calvo, *Cuzco: Traza urbana de la ciudad Inca* (Cusco, 1980), pp. 122–8.
46. Brian S. Bauer, 'The Legitimization of the Inca State in Myth and Ritual', *American Anthropologist*, 98:2 (June 1996), pp. 327–37.
47. D'Altroy, *Incas*, pp. 214, 245.
48. Jesús Arriaga, *Apuntes de arqueología Cañar* (Cuenca, 1965), p. 24. On the shifting balance of power see John Hyslop *Inka Settlement Planning* (Austin, TX, 1990), pp. 291–309.
49. Torres Saldamando, ed., *Libro Primero*, vol. iii, p. 5.
50. For details of the battle see Torres Saldamando, ed., *Libro Primero*, vol. iii, p. 6, and Sancho de la Hoz, *Relación*, pp. 316–18.
51. Hemming, *Conquest*, pp. 141–2.
52. Porras Barrenechea, ed., *Colección de documentos inéditos para la historia del Perú*, 3 vols (Lima, 1944–59), vol. iii, p. 100.
53. Hemming, *Conquest*, p. 149.

CHAPTER 15: MANQO INKA

1. Raúl Porras Barrenechea, ed., *Colección de documentos inéditos para la historia del Perú*, 3 vols (Lima, 1944–59), vol. iii, pp. 97, 102–3, 106; José Toribio Medina, ed., *Colección de documentos inéditos para la historia de Chile desde el viaje de Magellanes hasta la batalla de Maipo, 1518–1818*, 30 vols (Santiago, 1888–1902), vol. iv, p. 172; Joaquín F. Pacheco and Francisco de Cárdenas, eds, *Colección de documentos inéditos relativos al descubrimiento, conquista y organización de las posesiones españolas en América y Oceanía*, 42 vols (Madrid, 1864–84), vol. x, p. 139, vol. xlii, p. 93; Enrique Torres Saldamando, ed., *Libro primero de cabildos de Lima*, 3 vols (Paris, 1888–1900), vol. iii, p. 2.
2. Pedro Sancho de la Hoz, *Relación para S. M. de lo que sucedió en la conquista y pacificación de estas provincias de la Nueva Castilla y de la calidad de la tierra, después que el capitán Hernando Pizarro se partió y llevó a Su Majestad la relación de la victoria de Caxamalca y de la prisión del Cacique Atabalipa* (Lima, 1968), pp. 323–4; Pacheco and Cárdenas, eds, *Colección*, vol. x, p. 142; Torres Saldamando, ed., *Libro primero*, vol. iii, p. 6; Medina, ed., *Colección*, vol. iv, p. 220.
3. After they were defeated, Atawallpa ordered his commanders to slaughter all the Cañari men they could lay their hands on, and even the boys who had

come to beg for mercy. Fifteen years later, Pedro Cieza de León made the chilling observation that the women outnumbered the men by fifteen to one in the region. See John Hemming, *The Conquest of the Incas* (New York, 1970), p. 156, and the footnote on p. 568.

4. Hemming, *Conquest*, p. 156.

5. Hemming, *Conquest*, p. 156.

6. Antonio de Herrera y Tordesillas, *Historia general de los hechos de los castellanos en las islas y tierra firme del mar océano*, 4 vols (Madrid, 1601–15), vol. iii, pp. 127–9.

7. Gonzalo Fernández de Oviedo, *Historia general y natural de las Indias*, ed. Juan Pérez de Tudela Bueso, *Biblioteca de Autores Españoles*, 5 vols [cxvii – cxxi] (Madrid, 1959), vol. v [cxxi], p. 111.

8. Hemming, *Conquest*, p. 159.

9. Francisco López de Gómara, *Primera y segunda parte de la Historia General de las Indias con todo el descubrimiento y cosas notables que han acaecido desde que se ganaron hasta el año de 1551. Con la Conquista de Méjico de la Nueva España*, 2 vols (Zaragoza, 1552), vol. ii, p. 40.

10. Pacheco and Cárdenas, eds, *Colección*, vol. iv, pp. 219–20.

11. Jacinto Jijón y Caamaño, *Sebastián de Benalcázar*, 2 vols (Quito, 1936–8), vol. i, p. 67.

12. Hemming, *Conquest*, p. 164.

13. Medina, ed. *Colección*, vol. vii, p. 338.

14. Pedro Pizarro, *Relación del descubrimiento y conquista de los reinos del Perú*, in Martín Fernández de Navarrete, ed., *Colección de documentos inéditos para la historia de España*, 113 vols (Madrid, 1842–95), vol. v, p. 199.

15. Juan de Velasco, *Historia del reino de Quito en la América Meridional*, ed. Agustín Yerovi, 3 vols (Quito, 1841–4), vol. ii, p. 121.

16. Pizarro, *Relación*, pp. 196, 200; Herrera y Tordesillas, *Historia general*, vol. iii, pp. 138–42; Medina, ed., *Colección*, vol. iv, p. 60.

17. The priest Cristóbal de Molina 'El Almagrista' was in the expedition and described the cruelties in great detail. See his *Relación de muchas cosas acaescidas en el Perú* (Madrid, 1968), pp. 155–67.

18. Fernández de Oviedo, *Historia general*, vol. v [cxxi], p. 134.

19. Martín de Murúa, *Historia general del Perú: Origen y descendencia de los Incas*, ed. Manuel Ballesteros Gaibrois, 2 vols (Madrid, 1962–4), vol. i, pp. 196–7.

20. Juan de Matienzo, *Gobierno del Perú*, ed. Guillermo Lohmann Villena (Paris, 1967), p. 301.

21. Agustín de Zárate, *Historia del descubrimiento y conquista del Perú*, in *Biblioteca de Autores Españoles*, vol. xxvi (Madrid, 1946), p. 486; Pizarro, *Relación*, p. 201.

22. Hemming, *Conquest*, pp. 187–8.

23. Pizarro, *Relación*, p. 289. The numbers of native troops are impossible to fathom with certainty. Figures range from 50,000 to 400,000. The generally accepted number is somewhere around 150,000. See Hemming, *Conquest*, p. 190 and the footnote on pp. 572–3.

24. *Relación del sitio de Cuzco y principio de las guerras civiles del Perú hasta la muerte de Diego de Almagro*, in *Colección de libros españoles raros ó curiosos*, 25 vols (Madrid, 1871–96), vol. xiii, pp. 1–195, at pp. 19–20.

25. *Relación de los sucesos del Perú con motivo de las luchas de los Pizarros y los Almagros*, in Roberto Levillier, ed., *Gobernantes del Perú: Cartas y Papeles, siglo XVI*, 14 vols (Madrid, 1921–26), vol. ii, pp. 389–419, at p. 392.

26. *Relación del sitio de Cuzco*, pp. 26–7; Pizarro, *Relación*, p. 293; Murúa, *Historia general*, pp. 198–9.

27. Pizarro, *Relación*, pp. 294–6; Murúa, *Historia general*, p. 200; Hemming, *Conquest*, pp. 198–201.

28. George Kubler, 'A Peruvian Chief of State: Manco Inca (1515–1545)', *Hispanic American Historical Review*, 24:2 (May 1944), pp. 253–76, at p. 261.

29. Jijón y Caamaño, *Sebastián de Benalcázar*, vol. i, pp. 173–6.

30. Hemming, *Conquest*, pp. 209–20.

31. Porras Barrenechea, ed., *Colección*, vol. iii, p. 272.

32. Fernández de Oviedo, *Historia general*, vol. v [cxxi], pp. 151–4.

33. Hemming, *Conquest*, pp. 227–8; for Cortés and Narváez see above, pp. 160–62.

34. Kim MacQuarrie, *The Last Days of the Incas* (London, 2007), pp. 286–90.

35. Medina, ed., *Colección*, vol. v, p. 351.

36. Pedro Cieza de León, *Guerras civiles del Perú. Tomo Primero: Guerra de las Salinas* (Alicante, 2005), pp. 73–80.

37. See above, p. 279.

38. John H. Rowe, 'Inca Culture at the Time of the Spanish Conquest', *Handbook of South American Indians*, 143:2, ed. Julian Stewell (Washington, DC, 1946), pp. 183–330, at p. 263; Charles Gibson, *The Inca Concept of Sovereignty and the Spanish Administration in Peru* (New York, 1969), pp. 32–45.

39. Cieza de León, *Guerras*, p. 102.

40. Cieza de León, *Guerras*, p. 266.

41. Cieza de León, *Guerras*, pp. 318–29; see also MacQuarrie's vivid account in *Last Days*, pp. 294–300.

42. Cieza de León, *Guerras*, pp. 351–6, quotation at p. 356: '. . . nacido de tan bajos padres que se puede decir de él principiar y acabar en él su linaje'.

43. See the account of Manqo's son, Titu Cusi, in Carlos A. Romero and Horacio H. Urteaga, eds, *Colección de libros y documentos referentes a la historia del Perú*, 12 vols (Lima, 1916–19), vol. ii, p. 83.

44. Cieza de León, *Guerras*, p. 424.

45. See the account of Titu Cusi in Romero and Urteaga, eds, *Colección*, vol. ii, p. 85; *Relación del sitio de Cuzco*, p. 190; Torres Saldamando, ed., *Libro primero*, vol. iii, p. 107.

46. Romero and Urteaga, eds, *Colección*, vol. ii, pp. 86–8.

47. Hemming, *Conquest*, p. 244.

48. Murúa, *Historia general*, vol. i, p. 217.

49. *Relación del sitio de Cuzco*, pp. 188–9. The numbers of dead natives are difficult to fathom. Hemming gives a realistic figure of 800, *Conquest*, p. 246.

50. Pacheco and Cárdenas, eds, *Colección*, vol. iii, p. 121.

51. Pacheco and Cárdenas, eds, *Colección*, vol. iii, p. 121: '. . . teninedo algún caudillo destos [i.e. Willaq Umu – referred to by Valverde as Vilaoma, 'who is like a pope here'] en la tierra, siempre ternán alas para sus malos pensamientos, principalmente dándoles la tierra tantos aparejos para sus propósitos, que toda es fortaleza por ser tan doblada como es'.

52. Pacheco and Cárdenas, eds, *Colección*, vol. xviii, p. 481.

53. Pizarro, *Relación*, p. 341.

54. Hemming, *Conquest*, p. 255.

55. For Titu Cusi's detailed testimony see Romero and Urteaga, eds, *Colección*, vol. ii, pp. 89–90; I draw on MacQuarrie's reconstruction in *Last Days*, pp. 328–30.

56. Herrera y Tordesillas, *Historia General*, vol. iii, p. 145: 'cosa, que pareciò mui indigna de Hombre cuerdo, i Christiano'.

57. See, for example, the dispatch of Illán Suárez de Carvajal, dated 3 November 1539, in Pacheco and Cárdenas, eds, *Colección*, vol. xlii, p. 173.

58. Hemming, *Conquest*, p. 255.

59. See Valdivia's letter to Hernando Pizarro, dated 4 September 1545, in Sarah de Laredo, ed., *From Panama to Peru: The Conquest of Peru by the Pizarros, the Rebellion of Gonzalo Pizarro, and the Pacification of La Gasca* (London, 1925), p. 66.

60. Fernando Montesinos, *Anales del Perú*, 2 vols (Madrid, 1906), vol. i, pp. 114, 122; Herrera y Tordesillas, *Historia General*, vol. iii, p. 187.

61. Romero and Urteaga, eds, *Colección*, vol. ii, pp. 115–17.

62. *Libro de la Vida y Costumbres de Don Alonso Enríquez de Guzmán, Caballero noble desbaratado*, in Martín Fernández de Navarrete, ed., *Colección de documentos inéditos para la historia de España*, 113 vols (Madrid, 1842–95), vol. lxxxv, pp. 390–95.

63. Agustín de Zárate, *Historia del descubrimiento y conquista del Perú*, in *Biblioteca de Autores Españoles*, vol. xxvi (Madrid, 1946), p. 496.

64. Pedro Cieza de León, *Guerras civiles del Perú. Tomo Segundo: Guerra de Chupas* (Alicante, 2005), p. 115.

65. MacQuarrie, *Last Days*, pp. 342–3. Rodríguez Barragán's words are from a study by Raúl Porras Barrenechea quoted in Antonio San Cristóbal Sebastián, *La Ficción del esqueleto de Pizarro* (Lima, 1986), p. 30, which I have been unable to consult.

CHAPTER 16: THE END OF AN ERA

1. Mario Góngora, *Studies in the Colonial History of Latin America* (Cambridge, 1975), p. 30.

2. Raúl Rivera Serna, ed., *Libro Primero de Cabildos de la Ciudad del Cuzco* (Lima, 1965), pp. 31, 32–7, 42.

3. David Ewing Duncan, *Hernando de Soto: A Savage Quest in the Americas* (New York, 1995), pp. 195–200.

4. Duncan, *Hernando de Soto*, p. 202.

5. Garcilaso de la Vega, 'El Inca', *La Florida del Inca* (Amazon imprint for Plaza Editorial, 2011), p. 12. It is impossible to render the rich chivalric flavour of the original: '. . . levantando los pensamientos y el ánimo con la recordación de las cosas que por él habían pasado en el Perú, no contento con lo ya trabajado y ganado mas deseando emprender otras hazañas iguales o mayores, si mayores podían ser . . . movido de generosa envidia y celo magnánimo de las hazañas [de Cortés etc.] . . . como en su ánimo libre y generoso no cupiese súbdito, ni fuese inferior a los ya nombrados en valor y esfuerzo para la guerra ni en prudencia y discreción para la paz . . .'

6. A transcription of the *capitulación* was printed in Antonio del Solar y Taboada and José de Rújula y de Ochotorena, *El Adelantado Hernando de Soto* (Badajoz, 1929), pp. 119–22.

7. See above, p. 99.

8. Duncan, *Hernando de Soto*, p. 211.

9. Duncan, *Hernando de Soto*, p. 219.

10. At least this is what the gentleman of Elvas reported; see *True Relation of the Hardships Suffered by Governor Don Hernando de Soto and Certain Portuguese Gentlemen in the Discovery of the Province of Florida. Now Newly Set Forth by a Gentleman of Elvas*, trans. James Alexander Robertson, in Lawrence A. Clayton, Vernon James Knight Jr and Edward C. Moore, eds, *The De Soto Chronicles: The Expedition of Hernando de Soto to North America, 1539–1453*, vol. 1 (Gainesville, FL, 1993), pp. 48, 136.

11. See above, pp. 87.

12. Duncan, *Hernando de Soto*, p. 225.

13. Garcilaso, *Florida*, p. 25–7.

14. Garcilaso, *Florida*, pp. 29–30.

15. See, for example, the letters of Gonzalo de Guzmán and the royal treasurer, Lope Hurtado, to Charles V in Ángel de Altolaguirre y Duvale and Adolfo Bonilla y San Martín, eds, *Colección de documentos inéditos relativos al descubrimiento, conquista y organización de las antiguas posesiones españolas de Ultramar*, 25 vols (Madrid, 1885–1932), vol. vi, pp. 2, 337.

16. Duncan, *Hernando de Soto*, pp. 230–38.

17. Garcilaso, *Florida*, p. 33.

18. Elvas, *True Relation*, p. 57.

19. Garcilaso, *Florida*, p. 75.

20. Quoted in Duncan, *Hernando de Soto*, p. 258.

21. The term *cacique* is so consistently used in the sources that, although clearly inaccurate when referring to Florida and the other regions explored by Soto (or, for that matter, any other region outside the Caribbean), it is quite useful as a generic term; on this see Richard Conway, 'Caciques', in J. Michael Francis, ed., *Iberia and the Americas: Culture, Politics and History*, 3 vols (Santa Barbara, CA, 2006), vol. i, pp. 167–9.

22. Garcilaso, *Florida*, pp. 43–4; Luis Hernández de Biedma, *Relation of the Island of Florida*, trans. John Worth, in Clayton et al., eds, *The De Soto Chroniclers* [as above, fn. 22], p. 225.

23. Quoted in Duncan, *Hernando de Soto*, p. 266.

24. Jerald T. Milanich and Charles Hudson, *Hernando de Soto and the Indians of Florida* (Gainesville, FL, 1993), pp. 103–4.

25. Elvas, *True Relation*, pp. 69–70.

26. Duncan, *Hernando de Soto*, pp. 306–13.

27. Elvas, *True Relation*, p. 77.

28. Duncan, *Hernando de Soto*, pp. 328–9.

29. Elvas, *True Relation*, p. 80; Hernández de Biedma claimed that Perico said the journey was three days; *Relation*, p. 229.

30. Hernández de Biedma, *Relation*, p. 229.

31. From the descriptions – 'extremely large ... divided into two branches, broader than a shot of an arquebus ... [with] many bad fords of flat stones, and it came up to the stirrups, and in places to the saddle pads [and] the current was very strong ...' (Rodrigo Ranjel, *Account of the Northern Conquest and Discovery of Hernando de Soto*, trans. John Worth, in Clayton, et al., eds, *The De Soto Chroniclers* [as above, fn. 22], p. 274) – these were almost certainly the Savannah and the Broad. See Duncan, *Hernando de Soto*, p. 509, fn. 332 (4).

32. Elvas, *True Relation*, p. 80; Garcilaso, *Florida*, p. 100.

33. Hernández de Biedma, *Relation*, p. 230; Ranjel, *Account*, p. 275.

34. *Florida*, p. 110. Admittedly, Garcilaso qualifies his hyperbolic comparison by saying that it was 'inferior in greatness and majesty'.

35. Elvas, *True Relation*, p. 83; Ranjel, *Account*, p. 280.

36. Garcilaso, *Florida*, p. 117: '... no pesaban cosa alguna, y manoseadas se desmoronaban como un terrón de tierra seca'.

37. Elvas, *True Relation*, pp. 84–5.

38. Elvas, *True Relation*, p. 85; Ranjel, *Account*, p. 281. Both of them clearly disapproved of Soto's rash decision. Ranjel sarcastically remarks that the queen's arrest was 'in payment' for the good treatment she had given them.

39. Duncan, *Hernando de Soto*, p. 346.

40. Ranjel, *Account*, pp. 281–2.

41. Elvas, *True Relation*, pp. 88–9.
42. Ranjel, *Account*, pp. 283–4.
43. Ranjel, *Account*, p. 284.
44. Ranjel, *Account*, p. 285.
45. Ranjel, *Account*, p. 288; Garcilaso, *Florida*, pp. 138–9.
46. *Relation*, p. 232.
47. *Florida*, p. 139: 'En todos los caballos que en el ejército llevaban no se halló alguno que pudiese sufrir y llevar a Tacazula, según la grandeza de su cuerpo, y no porque era gordo . . . Los castellanos . . . hallaron un rocín . . . que por ser tan fuerte, servía de llevar carga. Este pudo sufrir a Tacazula, el cual era tan alto que, puesto encima del caballo, no le quedaba una cuarta de alto de sus pies al suelo.'
48. For a good summary see Duncan, *Hernando de Soto*, p. 375.
49. *Relation*, p. 232.
50. Ranjel, *Account*, p. 291.
51. Elvas, *True Relation*, p. 98.
52. The figures given by the chroniclers range from 3,000 to 11,000 warriors. These are obvious exaggerations, but since Mabila had about eighty large houses that could accommodate at least thirty warriors each, the figure was likely close to 2,500 warriors.
53. Hernández de Biedma, *Relation*, p. 235; Garcilaso, *Florida*, pp. 143–53.
54. Ranjel, *Account*, p. 294.
55. Duncan, *Hernando de Soto*, pp. 389–90 and 518, fn. 389[1].
56. Garcilaso, *Florida*, pp. 158–61.
57. Quoted in Duncan, *Hernando de Soto*, p. 393.
58. Garcilaso, *Florida*, pp. 164–8.
59. Elvas, *True relation*, p. 105.
60. Elvas, *True Relation*, pp. 108–9; Hernández de Biedma, *Relation*, p. 237; Garcilaso, *Florida*, pp. 190–3.
61. Duncan, *Hernando de Soto*, pp. 401–2.
62. Elvas, *True Relation*, pp. 112–13; Ranjel, *Account*, p. 300.
63. Hernández de Biedma, *Relation*, p. 240.
64. Elvas, *True Relation*, p. 124.
65. Ranjel, *Account*, p. 305; Elvas, *True Relation*, p. 126.
66. Elvas, *True Relation*, pp. 133–4.
67. Garcilaso, *Florida*, p. 221.
68. AGI(P), 27, R9, fol. 3^v.
69. See above, pp. 246–7.
70. The various negotiations are in AGI (P) 27, R15, bl. 6, fols 3^r – 6^r; bl 4, fols 8^r – 9^v; and R12, fols 1^v – 4^v. They have all been transcribed, translated and edited by J. Michael Francis in his pioneering study, *Invading Colombia: Spanish Accounts of the Gonzalo Jiménez de Quesada Expedition of*

Conquest (Pennsylvania, PA, 2007), pp. 20–33. It is worth noting that the Crown's officials took special care to protect the rights of individuals granted previous *capitulaciones*; among them they single out the German commercial house of Welser, granted the governorship of Venezuela in 1528 – on which see José Ignacio Avellaneda Navas, *The Conquerors of the New Kingdom of Granada* (Albuquerque, NM, 1995), pp. 14–19 – and Pedro de Heredia, granted the province of Cartagena in 1532 – on which see María del Carmen Gómez Pérez, *Pedro de Heredia y Cartagena de Indias* (Seville, 1984), pp. 10–11.

71. Fernández de Lugo actually fell short of the agreed number and was granted a two-year extension on that commitment. The exact number is unknown, but it was likely to be close to 1,200, transported in approximately ten vessels. See Avellaneda Navas, *Conquerors*, pp. 7–10.

72. Avellaneda Navas, *Conquerors*, pp. 9–10.

73. Fernández de Lugo's instructions to Jiménez de Quesada are printed in Juan Friede, ed., *Documentos inéditos para la historia de Colombia*, 10 vols (Bogotá, 1955–60), vol. iv, pp. 75–9.

74. 'Epítome de la conquista del Nuevo Reino de Granada'. The only surviving copy is in the Archivo Histórico Nacional, Madrid, Sección Documentos de Indias, 27. I have used J. Michael Francis's transcription and translation in idem, *Invading Colombia*, p. 43.

75. This was what captains Juan de San Martín and Antonio de Lebrija related subsequently to Charles V. 'Relación del Nuevo Reino', AGI(P) 27, R14, fol. 1^v (Francis, *Invading Colombia*, p. 59).

76. 'Carta del Cabildo de Santa Marta, 20 November 1537', AGI(P) 197, R13, fols 59^r–60^r (Francis, *Invading Colombia*, p. 46).

77. Francis, *Invading Colombia*, p. 56. The information comes from Camacho's *probanza de mérito* – a petition to 'prove his merit' compiled in 1565 and preserved in AGI(P) 160 N1 R6.

78. 'Epítome', in Francis, *Invading Colombia*, p. 44.

79. 'Relación del Nuevo Reino' AGI(P) 27 R14, fol. 1^r (Francis, *Invading Colombia*, p. 59).

80. José Ignacio Avellaneda Navas, *La expedición de Gonzalo Jiménez de Quesada al Mar del Sur y la creación del Nuevo Reino de Granada* (Bogotá, 1995), p. 24.

81. These descriptions combine information from 'Relación del Nuevo Reino', AGI(P) 27 R14, fols 1^v – 3^v, and the anonymous 'Relación de Santa Marta', c. 1545, in AGI(P) 27 R9, fols 12^v – 13^v (both in Francis, *Invading Colombia*, pp. 58–62, 63–8).

82. 'Relación del Nuevo Reino', AGI(P) 27 R14, fol. 3^v (Francis, *Invading Colombia*, p. 58).

83. 'Epítome', in Francis, *Invading Colombia*, p. 70.

84. These are the figures given by San Martín and Lebrija, who also mention 18,390 pesos of 'old jewellery' (*chafolanía*), 'Relación del Nuevo Reino', AGI(P) 27 R14, fol. 3^v; those given in the expedition's official logbook are lower, and probably refer only to the loot of Tunja: 136,000 pesos of fine gold, 14,000 pesos of low-grade ore and 280 emeralds, AGI(E) 1006A, 5, fol. 7^r.

85. On this see Francis, *Invading Colombia*, p. 88, fn. 14.

86. This, at least, is what San Martín and Lebrija claimed. Other sources, such as the anonymous 'Relación de Santa Marta', claim that Sagipa was a mere war captain who usurped the title. See Francis, *Invading Colombia*, p. 104.

87. 'Relación de Santa Marta', AGI(P) 267 R9, fol. 16^r (Francis, *Invading Colombia*, pp. 109–10); 'Relación del Nuevo Reino' AGI(P) 27 R14, fol. 6^r (Francis, *Invading Colombia*, p. 99).

88. 'Relación del Nuevo Reino', AGI(P) 27 R14, fols 4^v – 5^v (Francis, *Invading Colombia*, pp. 92–3).

89. Testimonies against Jiménez can be read in AGI(E) 1006A, fols 26^r – 49^v.

90. 'Epítome', in Francis, *Invading Colombia*, p. 103.

91. 'Relación del Nuevo Reino', AGI(P) 27 R14, fols 5^v – 6^r (Francis, *Invading Colombia*, pp. 98–9).

92. 'Relación del Nuevo Reino', AGI(P) 27 R14, fols 4^r, 5^r (Francis, *Invading Colombia*, pp. 90, 93).

93. 'Relación del Nuevo Reino', AGI(P) 27 R14, fols 5^r – 5^v (Francis, *Invading Colombia*, pp. 95, 94).

94. 'Relación del Nuevo Reino', AGI(P) 27 R14, fol. 6^r (Francis, *Invading Colombia*, p. 96).

95. Geoffrey Parker, *Emperor: A New Life of Charles V* (New Haven, CT, 2019), pp. 343–4.

96. Robert Bontine Cunninghame Graham, *The Conquest of New Granada, Being the Life of Gonzalo Jiménez de Quesada* (Boston, MA, 1922), pp. 175–6. This is the same writer who traced the route of Cortés to Honduras. He also did this on horseback following Federmann's route.

97. This was the testimony of Francisco de Tordehumos in the *probanza* of Hernando Hierro Maldonado, AGI(P) 160, 1 R9, fol. 378^v. For a recent study of the Federmann expedition see José Ignacio Avellaneda Navas, *Los compañeros de Féderman. Cofundadores de Santa Fé de Bogotá* (Bogotá, 1990).

98. Cunninghame Graham, *The Conquest of New Granada*, p. 167.

99. 'Epítome', in Francis, *Invading Colombia*, p. 101.

100. 'Relación del Nuevo Reino', AGI(P) 27 R14, fol. 6^r (Francis, *Invading Colombia*, pp. 96–7).

101. See above, p. 118.

102. Henry Raup Wagner and Helen Rand Parish, *The Life and Writings of Bartolomé de Las Casas* (Albuquerque, NM, 1967), pp. 70–85.

103. Lewis Hanke, *The Spanish Struggle for Justice in the Conquest of America* (Philadelphia, PA, 1949), p. 92.

104. Wagner and Parish, *Life and Writings*, pp. 118–19; D. A. Brading, *The First America: The Spanish Monarchy, Creole Patriots and the Liberal State, 1492–1867* (Cambridge, 1991), p. 68.

105. *Recopilación de las leyes de los reynos de las Indias*, lib. iii, tit. 3, ley 1, cited in J. H. Elliott, *Empires of the Atlantic World: Britain and Spain in America, 1492–1830* (New Haven, CT, 2006), p. 125 (Elliott's translation).

106. Elliott, *Empires of the Atlantic*, pp. 125–7.

107. Richard Konetzke, ed., *Colección de documentos para la historia de la formación social de Hispanoamérica, 1493–1810*, 5 vols (Madrid, 1953–62), vol. i, pp. 471–8. For the entrusting of expansion to the religious orders, primarily mendicants and, from the late 1560s, also Jesuits, see C. R. Boxer, *The Church Militant and Iberian Expansion, 1440–1770* (Baltimore, MD, 1978), pp. 71–2.

108. James Lockhart and Stuart B. Schwartz, *Early Latin America: A History of Colonial Spanish America and Brazil* (Cambridge, 1983), p. 60.

109. For pioneering studies of such *entradas*, see Grant D. Jones, *Maya Resistance to Spanish Rule: Time and History on a Colonial Frontier* (Albuquerque, NM, 1989); David Block, *Mission Culture in the Upper Amazon: Native Tradition, Jesuit Enterprise, and Secular Policy in Moxos, 1660–1880* (Lincoln, NB, 1994); and Caroline A. Williams, *Between Resistance and Adaptation: Indigenous Peoples and the Colonisation of the Chocó* (Liverpool, 2005).

110. Bernal Díaz del Castillo, *Historia verdadera de la conquista de la Nueva España*, ed. Miguel León Portilla, 2 vols (Madrid, 1984). ch. 103.

111. Cunninghame Graham, *The Conquest of New Granada*, p. 236.

REASSESSMENT

1. 'Memorial de Don Gonçalo Gómez de Cervantes del modo de vivir que tienen los indios, y del beneficio de las minas de la plata, y de la cochinella.' *British Library*, MS Am2006, Drg.210, fols 132^v, 133^r, 138^v, 141^r: '. . . pues en todos sus Reynos la principal fuerça que su magestad tiene consiste en la virtud ynobleça de los caballeros y gente noble que tienenvassallos y posibilidad Por quelos tales como miembros principales de lacaueça siempre tienen respecto de acudir ala conservacion y ahumento della [132^v] los otros . . . son gente sin meritos, que es la cossa mas impertinente del mundo [138^v] . . . siendo como son todos u los mas descendientes de los conquistadores hombres virtuosos de entendimiento y capacidad para administrar maiores y mas grandes cargos [139^r] . . . con mas amor a su rrey y rreppu^{ca} acudirían y mirarían las cossas y su magestad les pagaria sus meritos y

servicios con que siempre se yrian animando mas y no que los que ayer esta-
ban entiendas y tabernas y enottros exercicios viles estenoy puestos y
constituidos en los [139ᵛ] mejores y mas calificados officios delatierra y los
cavalleros y descendientes de aquellos que laconquistaron y ganaron pobres
avatidos desfavorecidos y arrinconados y a la reppublica es a quien cave
maior parte deste daño . . . [141ʳ]'.

2. See above, p. 58.

3. The classic study of this process is D. A. Brading, *The Origins of Mexican
   Nationalism* (Cambridge, 1985), pp. 4–9.

4. Inca Garcilaso de la Vega, *Historia General de Perú*, 3 vols (Buenos Aires,
   1944), vol. iii, pp. 244–5.

5. See above, p. xvii.

6. For New Spain, see José-Juan López-Portillo, *'Another Jerusalem': Political
   Legitimacy and Courtly Government in the Kingdom of New Spain (1535–
   1568)* (Leiden, 2018).

7. See J. H. Elliott, 'A Europe of Composite Monarchies', *Past and Present*,
   137 (November 1992), pp. 48–71, at pp. 68–9.

8. On this see Robert Frost, *The Oxford History of Poland-Lithuania, Vol. I:
   The Making of the Polish-Lithuanian Union, 1385–1569* (Oxford, 2015), p.
   44.

9. See, for example, William J. Bulman and Robert G. Ingram, eds, *God in the
   Enlightenment* (Oxford, 2016).

10. There is a helpful introduction to the negative nationalist historiographies
    dealing with Spanish rule in Milan in Stefano D'Amico, *Spanish Milan: A
    City within the Empire* (New York, 2012), pp. 1–7. See also Aurelio Espi-
    nosa, *The Empire of the Cities: Emperor Charles V, the Comunero Revolt,
    and the Transformation of the Spanish System* (Leiden, 2009), pp. 1–34. On
    the debate of the Spanish Black Legend, see the classic works by William
    S. Maltby, *The Black Legend in England: The Development of Anti-
    Spanish Sentiment, 1558–1660* (Durham, NC, 1971), and Philip Wayne
    Powell, *Tree of Hate: Propaganda and Prejudices Affecting United States
    Relations with the Hispanic World* (New York, 1971), as well as the admit-
    tedly partisan but enlightening work by María Elvira Roca Barea, *Imperiofobia
    y Leyenda Negra: Roma, Rusia, Estados Unidos y el Imperio español*
    (Madrid, 2016). This idea still pervades the writings of some Spanish
    authors of different nationalist backgrounds who insist on using the old and
    modern uses of the term 'nation' as synonymous. See, for instance, Jaume
    Sobrequés i Callicó, 'Nació, nacionalisme i ordre constitucional català
    durant la guerra civil del segle XV', in his *Estudis d'historia de Catalunya*,
    vol. i (Barcelona, 2008), pp. 259–83. The idea of the decline of Spain as the
    result of the temperament of the Spanish people, imagined to be more
    inclined to conquest than conservation, was most famously developed in the
    works of W. H. Prescott. For their effect in subsequent North American

interpretations of Spanish history, see Richard L. Kagan, 'Prescott's Paradigm: American Historical Scholarship and the Decline of Spain', *American Historical Review*, 101:2 (April 1996), pp. 423–46. I am grateful to Dr Gonzalo Velasco Berenguer for his help with some of these sources.

11. Geoffrey Parker, 'Philip II and his World in the 1580s', in Richard Kagan and Geoffrey Parker, eds, *Spain, Europe and the Atlantic World: Essays in Honour of John H. Elliott* (Cambridge, 1995), p. 252; I have slightly amended Parker's translation. For more examples see Parker's monumental study, *Felipe II: la biografía definitiva* (Barcelona, 2015), published in an abridged and more accessible English version as *Imprudent King: A New Life of Philip II* (New Haven, CT, 2014).

12. I have placed the word in inverted commas because its meaning in the medieval and early modern periods was fundamentally different from the way in which we understand the term today. The root is the Latin *natio* – place of birth. It referred to a particular region that kept its privileges and rights – what in Spanish law is called *fueros* – and was especially resentful of any outside imposition.

13. The snag in this interpretation is that exactly the same views were widely expressed in Spain itself at precisely this time, complete with references to 300 years of alleged tyranny and exploitation. This can only mean that Napoleon's invasion of Spain triggered a dilution of power that sought its natural expression in the traditional, contractual understanding of the monarchy as an organic community. Some hints of this development were already discernible in areas of Spanish America before 1808, when various groups had been reacting against what they saw as the ill-advised and intrusive reforms that centralizing Bourbon ministers had been implementing since the middle of the eighteenth century. (See, for example, John Fisher, Allan Kuethe and Anthony McFarlane, eds, *Reform and Insurrection in Bourbon New Granada and Peru* [Baton Rouge, FL, 1990]; and Anthony McFarlane, *Colombia before Independence: Economy, Society and Politics under Bourbon Rule* [Cambridge, 1993], pp. 251–71.) But in 1808 the crisis was brought about by the absence rather than the perceived abuse of the monarchy. This is why the first responses were dictated by a search for legitimacy, *not* independence, a search that found its natural home in medieval Spanish political thought. (See Mario Góngora, *Studies in the Colonial History of Spanish America* [Cambridge, 1975], pp. 68–79.) Indeed, the origins of the insurgent movement were never marked by any of the anti-Spanish feeling that nationalist histories try to promote but, rather, by a fervent anti-absolutism that was deeply monarchical and part of a wider movement that included Spain itself. (See Tamar Herzog, *Defining Nations: Immigrants and Citizens in Early Modern Spain and Spanish America* [New Haven, CT, 2003], pp. 144–5.) In 1809, for example, the Spanish Junta had declared that 'the Indies' were not 'colonies . . . like those of other nations, but an

essential and integral part of the Spanish monarchy' and that, consequently, all Spanish American kingdoms should send representatives to the peninsula. (See Manuel Chust, *La cuestión nacional americana en las Cortes de Cádiz* [Valencia, 1999], pp. 32–3.) Clearly, the framers of the Constitution were aware that Spain and Spanish America were afflicted by the same ills which required the same treatment. It should hardly surprise us, in this context, that the Liberal Constitution filtered down to the Spanish American kingdoms through the same ritual channels that had characterized traditional official and religious functions, being accompanied by a profusion of feasts, processions, symbols, allegories and images of saints. (See Annick Lempérière, '¿Nación moderna o república barroca? México 1823–1857', in François-Xavier Guerra and Mónica Quijada, eds, *Imaginar la Nación* [Münster, 1994], pp. 135–77.)

14. Alexander von Humboldt, *Ensayo político sobre el reino de la Nueva España*, ed. Juan A. Ortega y Medina (Mexico City, 1966), pp. 79–82, 121–2.

15. *Viaje a la Nueva España*, ed. Francisca Perujo (Mexico City, 2002).

16. On this see Kenneth Mills, 'The Limits of Religious Coercion in Mid-Colonial Peru', *Past & Present*, 145 (November 1994), pp. 84–121; idem, *Idolatry and its Enemies: Colonial Andean Religion and Extirpation* (Princeton, NJ, 1997). See also Nicholas Griffiths, *The Cross and the Serpent: Religious Repression and Resurgence in Colonial Peru* (Norman, OK, 1996).

17. For New Spain see the exhaustive investigation by William Taylor, *Magistrates of the Sacred: Priests and Parishioners in Eighteenth-Century Mexico* (Stanford, CA, 1996).

18. The process is most eloquently expressed in art. For New Spain, see Jaime Cuadriello, *Las glorias de la república de Tlaxcala, o la conciencia como imagen sublime* (Mexico City, 2004); for Peru, see Ramón Mujica Pinilla, *Ángeles apócrifos en la América virreinal* (Mexico City, 1996), and *Rosa Limensis: mística, política e iconografía en torno a la patrona de América* (Mexico City, 2005).

19. Quoted in Jonathan Brown, *Velázquez: Painter and Courtier* (New Haven, CT, 1986), pp. 267–8.

20. Gabriel Séailles, *Alfred Dehodencq: L'homme et l'artiste* (Paris, 1910), p. 32.

21. *A Handbook for Travellers in Spain*, quoted in Laura Cumming, *Vanishing Man: In Pursuit of Velázquez* (London, 2016), p. 18.

22. Étienne Moreau-Nélaton, *Manet raconté par lui-même*, 2 vols (Paris, 1926), vol. i, pp. 71–2.

23. See above, pp. xv–xvii.

24. Readers who know her work will have noticed that I have been rather liberal with my borrowings – and the occasional outright steal – from Laura Cumming's deliciously perceptive *Vanishing Man*. For the wider picture see Brown, *Velázquez*, and Javier Portús's many works, especially *Velázquez: su mundo y el nuestro* (Madrid, 2018).

25. See the splendid study by Iain McGilchrist, *The Master and his Emissary: The Divided Brain and the Making of the Western World* (New Haven, CT, 2009).

26. *Economist*, 16 July 2016, p. 42.

27. Daren Acemoglu and James A. Robinson, *Why Nations Fail: The Origins of Power, Prosperity, and Poverty* (London, 2012), pp. 7–44.

28. See above. See also J. H. Elliott's measured assessment in *Empires of the Atlantic*, pp. 77–8: The Spanish Crown's commitment to ensuring justice, Elliott writes, is one which, 'in its continuity and strength, is not easy to find parallels in the history of other colonial empires.... Spanish judges ... showed a flexibility in their approach to crime ... that contrasted sharply with the severity of New England's courts.... In so far as an [John] Eliot played the part of a [Bartolomé de] Las Casas, there was no one prepared to give him a hearing.' All this sheds an interesting light on the confusion expressed by the English colonists sent to Jamaica by Oliver Cromwell in the 1650s. Rather than finding oppressed populations to welcome them as liberators, they found groups of 'Spanish Negroes', who had secured their freedom, lived in thriving communities, and demanded a concerted agreement. See David Horspool, 'Total Rout: How Cromwell Tried to Conquer the Caribbean'; review of Carla Gardina Pestana's *The English Conquest of Jamaica*, in *The Times Literary Supplement*, 5970, 1 September 2017, pp. 28–9.

29. See, for example, Kate Raworth, *Doughnut Economics: Seven Ways to Think Like a 21st Century Economist* (London, 2017), and Mariana Mazzucato, *The Value of Everything: Making and Taking in the Global Economy* (London, 2018).

Bibliography

MANUSCRIPTS

Gattinara, Mercurino Arborio di, *Oratio Supplicatoria* addressed to Charles of Ghent in 1516, British Library, MS 18008.

Gómez de Cervantes, Gonzalo, 'Memorial de Don Gonçalo Gómez de Cervantes del modo de vivir que tienen los indios, y del beneficio de las minas de la plata, y de la cochinella', British Library, MS Am2006, Drg.210.

Palacios Rubios, Juan López de, 'Libellus de insulanis oceanis quas vulgus Indias apelat per Ioannem Lopez de Palacios Ruvios decretorum doctorem regiumque consiliarum editus', Biblioteca Nacional de Madrid, MS 17641 (1513).

'El Requerimo q se ha de hazer a los indios de terra firme', Archivo General de Indias, Seville, Panamá 233, lib I, fols. 49^r–50^v (1513).

Palafox y Mendoza, Juan de, 'Juan de Palafox to Philip IV (16 February 1645)', Biblioteca Nacional de Madrid, MS 8865.

Relación del origen de los indios que habitan esta Nueva España según sus historias (aka Tovar Codex and/or Ramírez Codex), Museo Nacional de Antropología e Historia, Mexico City.

PRIMARY PRINTED WORKS

Adorno, Rolena, and Patrick Charles Pautz, *Alvar Núñez Cabeza de Vaca: His Account, His Life, and the Expedition of Pánfilo de Narváez*, 3 vols (Lincoln, NB, 1999).

Adrian VI, Pope, *Charissimo in Christo*, Bull of 9 May 1522, reprinted in Jerónimo de Mendieta, *Historia eclesiástica indiana*, ed. Joaquín García Icazbalceta (Mexico City, 1870), pp. 128–9.

Aguirre, Isabel, ed., *Pesquisia del Comendador Francisco de Bobadilla*, in Consuelo Varela, *La Caída de Cristóbal Colón. El juicio de Bobadilla* (Madrid, 2006), pp. 181–257.

Allen, P. S., ed., *Opus Epistolarum Desiderii Erasmi Roterodami*, 12 vols (Oxford, 1906–58).

Altolaguirre y Duvale, Ángel de, and Adolfo Bonilla y San Martín, eds, *Colección de documentos inéditos relativos al descubrimiento, conquista y organización de las antiguas posesiones españolas de Ultramar*, 25 vols (Madrid, 1885–1932).

Anglería, Pedro Mártir de, *Opus epistolarum* (Alcalá de Henares, 1530).

——*Epistolario*, in *Documentos inéditos para la historia de España*, 113 vols (Madrid, 1953), vols ix–xii.

——*Décadas*, ed. Edmundo O'Gorman, 2 vols (Mexico City, 1964).

——*Décadas del Nuevo Mundo*, ed. Ramón Alba (Madrid, 1989).

Antonio, Fray, *Discurso sobre la descendencia y gobierno de los Incas*, in *Colección de libros y documentos referentes a la historia del Perú* (Lima, 1920).

Aquinas, St Thomas, *Summa Theologiae*, Blackfriars edn, 61 vols, reprinted by Cambridge University Press (Cambridge, 2006).

——*Summa contra gentiles*; https://dhspriory.org/thomas/ContraGentiles.htm

Archivum Fratrum Praedicatorum, vol. 7 (Rome, 1937).

Ariosto, Ludovico, *Orlando Furioso*, trans. Barbara Reynolds (Harmondsworth, 1973).

Armstrong, Regis J., ed., *Francis of Assisi: Early Documents*, 3 vols (New York, 1999).

Arteaga Garza, Beatriz, and Guadalupe Pérez San Vicente, eds, *Cedulario Cortesiano* (Mexico City, 1949).

Augustine of Hippo, St, *De Civitate Dei*, in J. Morán, ed., *Obras de San Agustín*, vols xvi–xvii, conflated in one tome (Madrid, 1958).

——*On the Trinity*, ed. Gareth B. Matthews (Cambridge, 2002).

Bauer, Wilhelm et al., eds, *Die Korrespondenz Ferdinands I*, 4 vols (Vienna, 1912–73).

Bernáldez, Andrés, *Memorias del reinado de los reyes católicos*, ed. Juan de Mata Carriazo y Arroquia (Madrid, 1962).

Berwick y Alba, Duquesa de, *Autógrafos de Cristóbal Colón y papeles de América* (Madrid, 1892).

Burgoa, Francisco de, *Geográfica descripción de la parte septentrional del Polo Ártico de la América y nueva iglesia de las Indias Occidentales y sitio astronómico de esta provincia de predicadores de Antequera, Valle de Oaxaca*, 2 vols (Mexico City, 1989).

Caddeo, Rinaldo, ed., *Le historie della vita e dei fatti di Cristoforo Colombo, per D. Fernando Colombo suo figlio*, 2 vols (Milan, 1958).

Calancha, Antonio de la, *Crónica moralizada del orden de San Agustín en el Perú*, ed. Ignacio Prado Pastor, 6 vols (Lima 1974).

Catherine of Siena, St, *Il Dialogo della Divina Providenzia di S. Caterina da Siena*, a cura di Giuliana Cavallini (Rome, 1968).

——*Le Orazioni di S. Caterina da Siena*, a cura di Giuliana Cavallini (Rome, 1978).

—— *I Catherine: Selected Writings of St Catherine of Siena*, ed. and trans. Kenelm Foster OP and Mary John Ronayne OP (London, 1980).

Cervantes, Miguel de, *Don Quijote de la Mancha*, ed. Francisco Rico, 2 vols (Barcelona, 1998).

Cervantes de Salazar, Francisco, *Crónica de la Nueva España* (Madrid, 1914).

—— *Diálogo de la dignidad del hombre* (Alcalá de Henares, 1546).

Chacón y Calvo, José María, ed., *Cedulario Cubano: Los Orígenes de la Colonización* (Madrid, 1929).

Chaucer, Geoffrey, *The Works of Geoffrey Chaucer*, ed. F. N. Robinson, 2nd edn (Oxford, 1957).

Chavero, Alfredo, ed., *Lienzo de Tlaxcala* (Mexico City, 1892).

Cieza de León, Pedro, *Descubrimiento y Conquista del Perú*, ed. Carmelo Sáenz de Santa María (Madrid, 1986).

—— *Guerras civiles del Perú. Tomo Primero: Guerra de las Salinas* (Alicante, 2005).

—— *Guerras civiles del Perú. Tomo Segundo: Guerra de Chupas* (Alicante, 2005).

Cobo, Bernabé, *Inca Religion and Customs*, trans. and ed. Ronald Hamilton (Austin, TX, 1990).

Columbus, Christopher, *Libro de los privilegios del almirante don Cristóbal Colón (1498)*, trans. and ed. Ciriaco Pérez Bustamante (Madrid, 1951).

—— *Los cuatro viajes del almirante y su testamento*, ed. Ignacio Anzoátegui (Madrid, 1971).

—— *Libro Copiador de Cristóbal Colón*, ed. Antonio Rumeu de Armas, 2 vols (Madrid, 1989).

—— *The 'Book of Prophecies' edited by Christopher Columbus* (Los Angeles, CA, 1997).

Contarini, Gasparo, 'Relazione di Gasparo Contarini ritornato ambasciatore da Carlo V, leta in Senato a dì 16 Novembre 1525', in Eugenio Albèri, ed., *Relazioni degli ambasciatori veneti al senato*, series I.ª, vol. II (Florence, 1840).

Cortés, Hernán, *Cartas de Relación*, ed. Manuel Alcalá, 10th edn (Mexico City, 1978).

Cota, Sancho, *Memorias*, ed. Hayward Keniston (London, 1964).

Craine, Eugene R., and Reginald C. Reindorp, eds, *Chronicles of Michoacán: The Description of the Ceremonies, Rites, Population, and Government of the Indians of the Province of Michoacán, 1540–1541* (Norman, OK, 1970).

Cusa, Nicholas of, *The Catholic Concordance*, trans. and ed. Paul E. Sigmund (Cambridge, 1991).

D'Anghera, Peter Martyr, *De Orbe Novo: The Eight Decades of Peter Martyr D'Anghera*, ed. and trans. F. A. MacNutt, 2 vols (New York, 1912).

Dávila Padilla, Agustín, *Historia de la fundación y discurso de la Provincia de Santiago de México, de la Orden de Predicadores, por las vidas de sus varones insignes y casos notables de Nueva España* (Mexico City, 1595).

Dawson, Christopher, ed., *The Mission to Asia: Narratives and Letters of the Franciscan Missionaries in Mongolia and China in the Thirteenth and Fourteenth Centuries*, trans. by a nun of Stanbrook Abbey (London, 1955).

Díaz de Castillo, Bernal, *Historia verdadera de la conquista de la Nueva España*, ed. Miguel León Portilla, 2 vols (Madrid, 1984).

Díez de Games, Gutierre, *El Victorial*, ed. Rafael Beltrán Llavador (Salamanca, 1997).

Durán, Diego, *Historia de las Indias de Nueva España e islas de Tierra Firme*, ed. Ángel María Garibay Kintana, 2 vols (Mexico City, 1967).

Duran, Eulàlia, and Joan Requesens, eds, *Profecia i poder al renaixement: texts profètics catalans favorables a Ferran el Catòlic* (Valencia, 1997).

Dürer, Albrecht, *Diary of His Journey to the Netherlands, 1520–1521*, eds J.-A. Goris and G. Marlier (Greenwich, CT, 1971).

Echeagaray, José Ignacio, ed., *Códice Mendocino o Colección de Mendoza: Manuscrito mexicano del siglo xvi que se preserva en la Biblioteca Bodleiana de Oxford* (Mexico City, 1979).

Elvas, Gentleman of, *True Relation of the Hardships Suffered by Governor Don Hernando de Soto and Certain Portuguese Gentlemen in the Discovery of the Province of Florida. Now Newly Set Forth by a Gentleman of Elvas*, trans. James Alexander Robertson, in Lawrence A. Clayton, Vernon Jones Knight Jr and Edward C. Moore, eds, *The De Soto Chronicles: The Expedition of Hernando de Soto to North America, 1539–1453*, vol. 1 (Gainsville, FL, 1993).

Enríquez de Guzmán, Alonso, *Libro de la Vida y Costumbres de Don Alonso Enríquez de Guzmán, Caballero noble desbaratado*, in Martín Fernández de Navarrete, ed., *Colección de documentos inéditos para la historia de España*, 113 vols (Madrid, 1842–95), vol. lxxxv.

Estete, Miguel de, *Noticia del Peru*, in Carlos A. Romero and Horacio H. Urteaga, eds, *Colección de libros y documentos referentes a la historia del Perú*, 2nd series, 22 vols (Lima, 1916–36), vol. viii, pp. 3–56.

Eusebius of Caesarea, *Oration in Praise of Constantine* (trans. http://www.newadvent.org/fathers/2504.htm).

Ferber, Nicolaus, 'Relatio Vera de Novis Insulis', printed in Antonine Tibesar, *Franciscan Beginnings in Colonial Peru* (Washington DC, 1953), pp. 101–2.

Fernández-Armesto, Felipe, ed., *Columbus on Himself* (Indianapolis, IN, 2010).

Fernández Álvarez, Manuel, ed., *Corpus documental de Carlos V*, 5 vols (Salamanca, 1973).

Fernández de Navarrete, Martín, ed., *Colección de documentos inéditos para la historia de España*, 113 vols (Madrid, 1842–95).

——*Colección de los viajes y descubrimientos que hicieron por mar los españoles*, 4 vols (Madrid, 1954).

Fernández de Oviedo, Gonzalo, *La historia general de las Indias, primera parte* (Seville, 1535).

Historia general y natural de las Indias, ed. Juan Pérez de Tudela Bueso, *Biblioteca de Autores Españoles*, 5 vols [cxvii–cxxi] (Madrid, 1959).

Firpo, Luigi, ed., *Colombo, Vespucci, Verazzano* (Turin, 1966).

Florencia, Francisco de, *Narración de la maravillosa aparición que hizo el arcángel san Miguel a Diego Lázaro de San Francisco, indio feligrés del pueblo de San Bernardo, de la jurisdicción de Santa María Nativitas* (Seville, 1692).

Fontán, Antonio, and Jerzy Axer, eds, *Españoles y polacos en la corte de Carlos V: Cartas del embajador Juan Dantisco* (Madrid, 1994).

Fuente, Vicente de la, ed., *Cartas de los secretarios del Cardenal D. Fr. Francisco Jiménez de Cisneros* (Madrid, 1875).

Fuentes, Patricia de, *The Conquistadors: First-Person Accounts of the Conquest of Mexico* (Norman, OK, 1993).

Gachard, Louis-Prosper, *Correspondance de Charles-Quint et d'Adrien VI, publiée pour la première fois par M. Gachard* (Brussels, 1859).

Gante, Pedro de, *Doctrina christiana en lengua mexicana* (Mexico City, 1553).

——'Carta de fray Pedro de Gante a los padres y hermanos de la provincia de Flandes, 27 de junio de 1529', printed in Ernesto de la Torre Villar, 'Fray Pedro de Gante, maestro y civilizador de América', *Estudios de Historia Novohispana*, vol. v (1974), pp. 9–77, at pp. 40–43.

García, Gregorio, *Origen de los indios del nuevo mundo, e indias occidentales* (Valencia, 1607).

García Icazbalceta, Joaquín, ed., *Colección de documentos inéditos para la historia de México*, 3 vols (Mexico City, 1858–66).

——*Nueva Colección de documentos para la historia de México, III: Pomar, Zurita, Relaciones Antiguas (Siglo XVI)* (Mexico City, 1891).

——*Nueva Colección de documentos para la historia de México* (Mexico City, 1941).

Garcilaso de la Vega, El Inca, *Historia General de Perú*, 3 vols (Buenos Aires, 1944).

——*Royal Commentaries of the Incas*, ed. Harold Livermore, 2 vols (Austin, TX, 1966).

——*La Florida del Inca* (Amazon imprint for Plaza Editorial, 2011).

Gayangos y Arce, Pascual de, ed., *Sergas, Libros de Caballerías* (Madrid, 1950).

Gemelli Careri, Giovanni Francesco, *Viaje a la Nueva España*, ed. Francisca Perujo (Mexico City, 2002).

Gil Fernández, Juan, and C. Varela Bueno, eds, *Cartas de particulares a Colón y relaciones coetáneas* (Madrid, 1984).

Giustiniani, Agostino, *Psalterium Hebraeum, Graecum, Arabicum, et Chaldaeum, cum Tribus Latinis interpretationibus et glossis* (Genoa, 1516).

Gregory the Great, Pope, St, *Obras de San Gregorio Magno*, trans. Paulino Gallardo, ed. Melquíades Andrés (Madrid, 1958).

Hernáez, Francisco Javier, ed., *Colección de Bulas y otros documentos de la iglesia de América y Filipinas*, 2 vols (Brussels, 1879).

Herrera, Fernando de, *Poesía castellana original completa*, ed. Cristóbal Cuevas, 4th edn (Madrid, 2018).

Herrera y Tordesillas, Antonio de, *Historia general de los hechos de los castellanos en las islas y tierra firme del mar océano*, 4 vols (Madrid, 1601–15).

Homza, Lu Ann, ed., *The Spanish Inquisition, 1478–1614: An Anthology of Sources* (Indianapolis, IN, 2006).

Hostiensis (Henry of Susa), *Lectura quinque decretalium* (Paris, 1512).

Humboldt, Alexander von, *Ensayo político sobre el reino de la Nueva España*, ed. Juan A. Ortega y Medina (Mexico City, 1966).

Hussey, Ronald D., ed., 'Text of the Laws of Burgos (1512–1513) Concerning the Treatment of the Indians', *Hispanic American Historical Review*, 12:3 (August 1932), pp. 301–26.

Innocent IV, Pope, *Commentaria in quinque libros decretalium* (Turin, 1581).

Irving, Washington, ed., *A Chronicle of the Conquest of Granada, from the Manuscript of Antonio Agapida* (London, 1829).

Ixtlilxochitl, Fernando de Alva, *Obras históricas*, ed. Edmundo O'Gorman, 2 vols (Mexico City, 1975).

—— *Historia de la Nación Chichimeca*, ed. Germán Vázquez Chamorro (Madrid, 1985).

Jerez, Francisco de, *Verdadera relación de la conquista del Perú y provincia del Cuzco, llamada la Nueva Castilla*, in Enrique de Vedia, ed., *Historiadores primitivos de Indias*, 3 vols (Madrid, 1852–7), vol. ii (1853), pp. 319–46.

Kagan, Richard, and Abigail Dyer, eds, *Inquisitorial Inquiries: Brief Lives of Secret Jews and Other Heretics* (Baltimore, MD, 2011).

Konetzke, Richard, ed., *Colección de documentos para la historia de la formación social de Hispanoamérica, 1493–1810*, 5 vols (Madrid, 1953–62).

Laredo, Sarah de, ed., *From Panama to Peru: The Conquest of Peru by the Pizarros, the Rebellion of Gonzalo Pizarro, and the Pacification of La Gasca* (London, 1925).

Las Casas, Bartolomé de, *Historia de las Indias*, ed. Agustín Millares Carlo, 3 vols (Mexico City, 1951).

—— *Obras escogidas*, ed. Juan Pérez de Tudela Bueso, *Biblioteca de Autores Españoles*, vol. cx (Madrid, 1958).

—— *Brevísima relación de la destrucción de las indias*, ed. Gregorio Weinberg (Buenos Aires, 1966).

—— *Del único modo de atraer a todos los pueblos a la verdadera religión* (Mexico City, 1975).

—— *A Short Account of the Destruction of the Indies*, trans. Nigel Griffin (Harmondsworth, 1992).

Las Siete Partidas del Rey Don Alfonso el Sabio, cotejadas con varios códices antiguos por la Real Academia de la Historia, 3 vols (Madrid 1802).

León Portilla, Miguel, ed., *Crónicas indígenas: la visión de los vencidos* (Madrid, 1985).

Levillier, Roberto, ed., *Gobernantes del Perú: Cartas y Papeles, siglo XVI*, 14 vols (Madrid, 1921–6).

Loayzaga, Manuel, *Historia de la Milagrosissima Imagen de N^{ra} S^{ra} de Occotlan que se venera extramuros de la ciudad de Tlaxcala* (Mexico City, 1750).

Lollis, Cesare de, et al., eds., *Raccolta di documenti e studi pubblicati della Reale Commissione Colombiana*, 14 vols (Rome, 1892–6).

López de Gómara, Francisco, *Primera y segunda parte de la Historia General de las Indias con todo el descubrimiento y cosas notables que han acaecido desde que se ganaron hasta el año de 1551. Con la Conquista de Méjico de la Nueva España*, 2 vols (Zaragoza, 1552).

—— *Historia del Capitano Fernando Cortes*, trans. A. de Cravaliz (Rome, 1556).

——*La Conquista de México*, ed. José Luis Rojas (Madrid, 1987).

López Rayón, Ignacio, ed., *Proceso de residencia instruido contra Pedro de Alvarado y Nuño de Guzmán* (Mexico City, 1847).

——'Sumario de la residencia tomada a D. Fernando Cortés, gobernador y Capitán General de la N. E., y a otros gobernadores y oficiales de la misma', in *Archivo Mexicano: Documentos para la historia de México*, 2 vols (Mexico City, 1852–3).

Machiavelli, Niccolò, *The Prince* (various editions).

Manzanedo, Bernardino de, 'Memorial de Fray Bernardino de Manzanedo sobre el buen régimen y gobierno de los indios', in Manuel Serrano y Sanz, *Orígenes de la dominación española en América* (Madrid, 1918).

Martínez, José Luis, ed., *Documentos Cortesianos*, 4 vols (Mexico City, 1990–1).

Martínez Luza, Abel, 'Un memorial de Hernán Cortés', *Anuario de Estudios Americanos*, 45, Supplement (1988).

Matienzo, Juan de, *Gobierno del Perú*, ed. Guillermo Lohmann Villena (Paris, 1967).

Maxwell, Judith, and Robert M. Hill II, eds, *Kaqchikel Chronicles: The Definitive Edition* (Austin, TX, 2006).

Toribio Medina, José ed., *Colección de documentos inéditos para la historia de Chile desde el viaje de Magallanes hasta la batalla de Maipo, 1518–1818*, 30 vols (Santiago, 1888–1902).

Méndez Silva, Rodrigo, *Ascendencia ilustre, gloriosos hechos y posteridad noble del famoso Nuño Alfonso, Alcaide de la imperial ciudad de Toledo, Príncipe de su milicia, Ricohome de Castilla* (Madrid, 1648).

Mendieta, Jerónimo de, *Historia eclesiástica indiana*, ed. Joaquín García Icazbalceta (Mexico City, 1870).

Meyer, Albertus de, ed., *Registrum Litterarum Fr Thomae de Vio Caietano OP Mag. Ordinis (1508–1513)*, in *Monumenta Ordinis Praedicatorum Historica*, 29 vols (Rome, 1896–2005), vol. xvii (Rome, 1935).

Molina, Cristóbal de ('El Almagrista'), *Relación de muchas cosas acaescidas en el Perú* (Madrid, 1968).

Montaigne, Michel de, *The Complete Essays*, trans. M. A. Screech (London 1993).

Montesinos, Fernando, *Anales del Perú*, 2 vols (Madrid, 1906).

Motolinía, Fray Toribio de, *Historia de los Indios de la Nueva España*, ed. Joaquín García Icazbalceta (Mexico City, 1858).

——*Memoriales ó libro de las cosas de la Nueva España y de los naturales de ella*, ed. Edmundo O'Gorman (Mexico City, 1971).

Muñoz Camargo, Diego, *Historia de Tlaxcala*, ed. Germán Vázquez Chamorro (Madrid, 1986).

Muro Orejón, A. et al., eds., *Pleitos colombinos*, 4 vols (Seville, 1964–89).

Murúa, Martín de, *Historia general del Perú: Origen y descendencia de los Incas*, ed. Manuel Ballesteros Gaibrois, 2 vols (Madrid, 1962–4).

Nieremberg, Juan Eusebio, *Devoción y patrocinio de san Miguel, príncipe de los ángeles, antiguo tutelar de los godos, y protector de España* (Mardid, 1643).

Pacheco, Joaquín F., and Francisco de Cárdenas, eds, *Colección de documentos inéditos relativos al descubrimiento, conquista y organización de las posesiones españolas en América y Oceanía, sacados en su mayor parte del Archivo de Indias, bajo la dirección de los señores D. Joaquín F. Pacheco y D. Francisco de Cárdenas, miembros de varias reales academias científicas; y D. Luis Torres de Mendoza, abogado de los Tribunales del Reino, con la cooperación de otras personas competentes*, 42 vols (Madrid, 1864–84).

Palacios Rubios, Juan López de, *De las Islas del Mar Océano*, ed. Silvio Zavala (Mexico City, 1954).

Pané, Ramón, *An account of the antiquities of the Indians*, ed. J. J. Arrom, trans. S. C. Griswold (Durham, NC, 1999).

Paso y Troncoso, Francisco del, ed., *Papeles de Nueva España*, 2nd series, 7 vols (Madrid, 1905–8).

——*Papeles de Nueva España*, 3 vols (Madrid, 1914–36).

—— *Epistolario de la Nueva España, 1505–1818*, 16 vols (Mexico City, 1939–42).

Pizarro, Hernando, 'Carta a los oidores de Santo Domingo, 23 November 1533', in Gonzalo Fernández de Oviedo, *Historia General y Natural de las Indias*, ed. Juan Pérez de Tudela Bueso, *Biblioteca de Autores Españoles*, 5 vols [cxvii–cxxi] (Madrid, 1959), vol. v [cxxi], pp. 84–90.

Pizarro, Pedro, *Relación del descubrimiento y conquista de los reinos del Perú*, in Martín Fernández de Navarrete, ed., *Colección de documentos inéditos para la historia de España*, 113 vols (Madrid, 1842–95), vol. v (1844), pp. 201–388.

Plato, *The Collected Dialogues, including the letters*, Edith Hamilton and Huntington Cairns, eds (Princeton, NJ, 1961).

Polavieja y del Castillo, Camilo García de, ed., *Hernán Cortés: copias de documentos existentes en el archivo de Indias y en su palacio de Castilleja de la Cuesta sobre la conquista de Méjico* (Seville, 1889).

Poma de Ayala, Felipe Guaman, *El primer nueva corónica y buen gobierno*, online facsimile with parallel transcription (Copenhagen, Det Kongelige Bibliotek, GKS 2232 4°). http://www.kb.dk/permalink/2006/poma/titlepage/en/text

—— *El primer nueva corónica y buen gobierno*, ed. John V. Murra, Rolena Adorno and Jorge Urioste (Mexico City, 1980).

Porras Barrenechea, Raúl, ed., *Colección de documentos inéditos para la historia del Perú*, 3 vols (Lima, 1944–59).

Raymond of Capua, Bl., *Life of St Catherine of Siena*, trans. G. Lamb (London, 1960).

Recinos, Adrián, Delia Goetz and Sylvanus G. Morley, eds, *Popol Vuh: The Sacred Book of the Ancient Quiché Maya* (Norman, OK, 1950).

Recopilación de las leyes de los reynos de las Indias, mandadas a imprimir, y publicar por la Magestad Católica del Rey Don Carlos II nuestro señor, 5th edn, 4 vols (Madrid, 1841).

'Relación de la genealogía y linaje de los señores que han señoreado esta tierra de la Nueva España', in Joaquín García Icazbalceta, ed., *Nueva Colección de documentos para la historia de México, III: Pomar, Zurita, Relaciones Antiguas (Siglo XVI)* (Mexico City, 1891).

Relación del sitio de Cuzco y principio de las guerras civiles del Perú hasta la muerte de Diego de Almagro, in *Colección de libros españoles raros ó curiosos*, 25 vols (Madrid, 1871–96), vol. xiii, pp. 1–195.

Relación de los sucesos del Perú con motivo de las luchas de los Pizarros y los Almagros, in Roberto Levillier, ed., *Gobernantes del Perú: Cartas y Papeles, siglo XVI*, 14 vols (Madrid, 1921–6), vol. ii, pp. 389–419.

Ripoll, Thomas, and Antonin Bremond, eds, *Bullarium Ordinis Fratrum Praedicatorum*, 8 vols (Rome, 1729–40).

Rivera Serna, Raúl, ed., *Libro Primero de Cabildos de la Ciudad del Cuzco* (Lima, 1965).

Rodríguez de Montalvo, Garci, *Amadís de Gaula*, ed. Juan Bautista Avalle-Arce (Madrid, 2015).

Rojas, Gabriel de, 'Relación de Cholula, 1582', ed. Fernando Gómez de Orozco, *Revista Mexicana de Estudios Históricos*, I:5 (September–October 1927).

Romero, Carlos A., and Horacio H. Urteaga eds, *Colección de libros y documentos referentes a la historia del Perú*, 12 vols (Lima, 1916–19).

Ruiz de Arce, Juan, 'Relación de los servicios en Indias', *Boletín de la Real Academia de la Historia*, 102 (1933), pp. 327–84.

Ruiz Naharro, Pedro, *Relación de los hechos de los españoles en el Perú desde su descubrimiento hasta la muerte del marqués Francisco Pizarro*, in Martín Fernández de Navarrete, ed., *Colección de documentos inéditos para la historia de España*, 113 vols (Madrid, 1842–95), vol. xxvi, pp. 232–56.

Sahagún, Bernardino de, *Florentine Codex: The General History of the Things of New Spain*, trans. Charles E. Dibble and Arthur J. Anderson, 12 vols (Santa Fe, NM, 1951–5).

—— *Historia General de las cosas de Nueva España*, ed. Ángel María Garibay Kintana, 6th edn (Mexico City, 1985).

—— *Coloquios y Doctrina Cristiana*, ed. Miguel León Portilla (Mexico City, 1986).

—— *The Conquest of New Spain*, trans. Howard Cline, intro. S. L. Cline (Salt Lake City, UT, 1989).

—— *Psalmodia Christiana*, trans. A. J. O. Anderson (Salt Lake City, UT, 1993).

—— *Adiciones, Apendice a la Postilla y Ejercicio Cotidiano*, ed. A. J. O. Anderson (Mexico City, 1993).

Sánchez, Miguel, *Imagen de la Virgen María, Madre de Dios de Guadalupe, Milagrosamente aparecida en la ciudad de México: Celebrada en su historia, con la profecía del capítulo doce del Apocalipsis* (Mexico City, 1648).

Sancho de la Hoz, Pedro, *Relación para S. M. de lo que sucedió en la conquista y pacificación de estas provincias de la Nueva Castilla y de la calidad de la tierra, después que el capitán Hernando Pizarro se partió y llevó a Su Majestad la relación de la victoria de Caxamalca y de la prisión del Cacique Atabalipa* (Lima, 1968).

Santa Cruz, Alonso de, *Crónica del emperador Carlos V*, ed. Ricardo Beltrán y Rózpide and Antonio Blázquez y Delgado-Aguilera, 5 vols (Madrid, 1920–25).

Sanuto, Marino, *I diarii di Marino Sanuto*, ed. F. Stefani, G. Berchet and N. Barozzi, 58 vols (Venice, 1879–1903).

Sepúlveda, Juan Ginés de, *Historia del Nuevo Mundo*, ed. Antonio Ramírez de Verger (Madrid, 1987).

Serassi, Pierantonio, *Delle lettere del conte Baldessar Castiglione, ora per la prima volta date in luce*, 2 vols (Padua, 1769–71).

Serrano y Sanz, Manuel, ed., *Orígenes de la dominación española en América*, in *Biblioteca de Autores Españoles*, vol. xxv (Madrid, 1918).

Shakespeare, William, *The Tragedy of Hamlet, Prince of Denmark*.

—— *The Tragedy of Othello, the Moor of Venice*.

Sigüenza, José de, *Historia de la Orden de San Jerónimo*, 2 vols (Madrid, 1909).

Solís, Antonio de, *Historia de la conquista de México*, 2 vols (Madrid, 1783).

Tezozomoc, Fernando Alvarado, *Crónica mexicana* (Mexico City, 1975).

Torquemada, Juan de, *Los ventiún libros rituales y monarquía indiana*, 7 vols (Mexico City, 1975–83).

Torres Saldamando, Enrique, ed., *Libro Primero de Cabildos de Lima*, 3 vols (Paris, 1888–1900).

Torrubia, José, *Crónica de la Provincia Franciscana de Santa Cruz de la Española y Caracas* (Caracas, 1972).

Trujillo, Diego de, *Relación del descubrimiento del reyno del Perú*, ed. Raúl Porras Berrenechea (Seville, 1948).

Tudella, Juse, and José Corona Núñez, eds, *Relación de las ceremonias y ritos y población y gobierno de los Indios de la Provincia de Michoacán* [1541], facsimile of *El Escorial* Ms c. IV.5 (Morelia, 1977).

Valdés, Alonso de, *Relación de las nuevas de Italia: sacada de las cartas que los capitanes y comisarios del Emperador y rey nuestro señor han escripto a su magestad: assi de la victoria contra el rey de Francia como de otras cosas allá acaecidas: vista y corregida por el señor gran Chanciller e consejo de su magestad* (Madrid, 1525).

Valera, Mosén Diego, 'Epístola que Mosén Diego de Valera enbió al rey don Fernando Nuestro Señor, después que ovo tomado la cibdad de Ronda', in *Prosistas castellanos del siglo xv*, ed. M. Penna, *Biblioteca de Autores Españoles*, vol. cxvi (Madrid, 1959).

Vallejo, Juan de, *Memorial de la vida de fray Francisco Jiménez de Cisneros*, ed. Antonio de la Torre y del Cerro (Madrid, 1913).

Varela Bueno, Consuelo, ed., *Cristóbal Colón, Textos y documentos completos* (Madrid, 1982).

Vázquez Chamorro, Germán, ed., *La Conquista de Tenochtitlán* (Madrid, 1988).

Velasco, Juan de, *Historia del reino de Quito en la América Meridional*, ed. Agustín Yerovi, 3 vols (Quito, 1841–4).

Vélez de Guevara, Luis, *Cumplir dos obligaciones y duquesa de Saxonia* (Valencia, 1768).

Vicente, Gil, *Obras Completas*, ed. Álvaro Júlio da Costa Pimpão (Barcelos, 1956).

Vitoria, Francisco de, *Relectio 'De Indis'*, ed. L. Pereña and J. M. Pérez Prendes (Madrid, 1967).

—— *Political Writings*, ed. and trans. Anthony Pagden and Jeremy Lawrance (Cambridge, 1991).

Xerez, Francisco de, *Verdadera relación de la conquista del Perú y provincia del Cuzco*, in *Biblioteca de Autores Españoles*, vol. xxvi (Madrid, 1947), pp. 320–46.

Zárate, Agustín de, *Historia del descubrimiento y conquista del Perú*, in *Biblioteca de Autores Españoles*, vol. xxvi (Madrid, 1946).

Zumárraga, Juan de, *Regla christiana breve para ordenar la vida y el tiempo del christiano que se quiere salvar y tener su alma dispuesta para que Jesu Christo more en ella*, ed. Ildefonso Adeva (Pamplona, 1994).

SECONDARY WORKS

Abulafia, David, *Spain and 1492* (Dorchester, 1992).

—— *The Western Mediterranean Kingdoms: The Struggle for Dominion, 1200–1500* (London, 1997).

——*The Discovery of Mankind: Atlantic Encounters in the Age of Columbus* (New Haven, CT, 2008).

Acemoglu, Daren, and James A. Robinson, *Why Nations Fail: The Origins of Power, Prosperity, and Poverty* (London, 2012).

Agurto Calvo, Santiago, *Cuzco: traza urbana de la ciudad Inca* (Cuzco, 1980).

Ahern, Maureen, 'The Cross and the Gourd: The Appropriation of Ritual Signs in the *Relaciones* of Alvar Núñez Cabeza de Vaca and Fray Marcos de Niza', in Jerry M. Williamson and Robert E. Lewis, eds, *Early Images of the Americas: Transfer and Invention* (Tucson, AZ, 1993).

Alberro, Solange, *Inquisición y Sociedad en México, 1571–1700* (Mexico City, 1988).

Alexander, Paul J., 'The Medieval Legend of the Last Roman Emperor and its Messianic Origins', *Journal of the Warburg and Courtauld Institutes*, 41 (1978).

Aram, Bethany, *Juana the Mad: Sovereignty and Dynasty in Renaissance Europe* (Baltimore, MD, 2005).

Arce Gargollo, Pablo, *La vida santa de Vasco de Quiroga y su proceso de canonización* (Mexico City, 2015).

Arfaioli, Maurizio, *The Black Bands of Giovanni: Infantry and Diplomacy during the Italian Wars, 1526–1528* (Pisa, 2005).

Arranz Márquez, Luis, *Don Diego Colón: almirante, virrey y gobernador de las Indias* (Madrid, 1982).

——*Repartimientos y Encomiendas en la isla Española: el Repartimiento de Albuquerque, 1514* (Madrid, 1992).

Arriaga, Jesús, *Apuntes de arqueología Cañar* (Cuenca, 1965).

Asselbergs, Florine G. L., *Conquered Conquistadors: The Lienzo de Quauhquechollan; a Nahua Vision of the Conquest of Guatemala* (Leiden, 2004).

Astrana Marín, Luis, *Vida ejemplar y heroica de Miguel de Cervantes Saavedra*, 7 vols (Madrid, 1948–58).

Avonto, Luigi, *Mercurino Arborio di Gattinara e l'America* (Vercelli, 1981).

Babelon, Jean, 'Un retrato verdadero de Hernán Cortés', in *Memorias de la Academia Mexicana de la Historia*, 13 (July–August 1954).

Baer, Yitzhak, *A History of the Jews in Christian Spain*, 2 vols (Philadelphia, PA, 1992).

Ballesteros Beretta, Antonio, *Cristóbal Colón y el descubrimiento de América*, 2 vols (Barcelona, 1945).

Bandelier, Adolph F., 'The Cross of Carabuco in Bolivia', *American Anthropologist*, 6:5 (October–December, 1904), pp. 599–628.

Bataillon, Marcel, *Erasmo y España: Estudios sobre la historia espiritual del siglo xvi*, trans. Antonio Alatorre (Mexico City, 1950).

——'L'Espagne religieuse et son histoire', *Bulletin Hispanique*, vol. lii (1952).

——*Estudios sobre Bartolomé de las Casas* (Barcelona, 1976).

Baudot, Georges, *Utopie et histoire au Mexique* (Toulouse, 1977).

Bauer, Brian S., 'The Legitimization of the Inca State in Myth and Ritual', *American Anthropologist*, 98:2 (June 1996), pp. 327–37.

——*Ancient Cuzco: Heartland of the Inca* (Austin, TX, 2004).

Bayerri y Bertomeu, Enrique, *Colón tal cual fue* (Barcelona, 1961).

Beinart, Haim, *Conversos on Trial: The Inquisition in Ciudad Real* (Jerusalem, 1981).

Beltrán, Juan, *Bojeo de Cuba por Sebastián de Ocampo* (Havana, 1924).

Beltrán de Heredia, Vicente, *Historia de la Reforma de la Provincia de España (1450–1550)*, in *Dissertationes Historicae. Instituto Storico Domenicano*, 74 vols (Rome, 1931–2007), vol. xi (Rome, 1939).

Berdan, Frances, *The Aztecs of Central Mexico* (New York, 1982).

Bethencourt, Francisco, *The Inquisition: A Global History, 1478–1834*, trans. Jean Birrell (Cambridge, 2009).

Bierhorst, John, *Four Masterworks of American Indian Literature* (New York, 1974).

Bilinkoff, Jodi, 'A Spanish Prophetess and Her Patrons: The Case of María de Santo Domingo', *The Sixteenth Century Journal*, 23:1 (Spring 1992), pp. 21–34.

Block, David, *Mission Culture in the Upper Amazon: Native Tradition, Jesuit Enterprise, and Secular Policy in Moxos, 1660–1880* (Lincoln, NB, 1994).

Boone, Elizabeth H., 'Incarnations of the Aztec Supernatural: Representations of Huitzilopochtli in Mexico and Europe', *Transactions of the American Philosophical Society*, 79:2 (1989), pp. 1–107.

——'This New World Now Revealed: Hernán Cortés and the Presentation of Mexico to Europe', *World & Image*, 27:1 (January–March, 2011), pp. 31–46.

Boone, Rebecca, 'Empire and Medieval Simulacrum: A Political Project of Mercurino di Gattinara, Grand Chancellor of Charles V', *Sixteenth Century Journal*, 42:4 (2011), pp. 1,027–49.

Bossy, John, *Christianity in the West, 1400–1700* (Oxford, 1985).

Boxer, C. R., *The Church Militant and Iberian Expansion, 1440–1770* (Baltimore, MD, 1978).

Boyle, Nicholas, *Sacred and Secular Scriptures: A Catholic Approach to Literature* (London, 2004).

Brading, D. A., 'Tridentine Catholicism and Enlightened Despotism in Bourbon Mexico', *Journal of Latin American Studies*, 15 (1983).

——*The Origins of Mexican Nationalism* (Cambridge, 1985).

——'Images and Prophets: Indian Religion and the Spanish Conquest', in Arij Ouweneel and Simon Miller, eds, *The Indian Community of Colonial Mexico* (Amsterdam, 1990).

——The First America: The Spanish Monarchy, Creole Patriots and the Liberal State, 1492–1867 (Cambridge, 1991).

—— Mexican Phoenix. Our Lady of Guadalupe: Image and Tradition across Five Centuries (Cambridge, 2002).

Brandi, Karl, Carlos V: vida y fortuna de una personalidad y de un imperio mundial (Madrid, 1937).

Brown, Jonathan, Velázquez: Painter and Courtier (New Haven, CT, 1986).

Brown, Peter, The Cult of the Saints: Its Rise and Function in Latin Christianity (London, 1981).

——Authority and the Sacred: Aspects of the Christianisation of the Roman World (Cambridge, 1995).

—— Power and Persuasion in Late Antiquity: Towards a Christian Empire (Madison, WI, 1992).

Brundage, Burr Cartwright, The Fifth Sun: Aztec Gods, Aztec World (Austin, TX, 1979).

Bulman, William J., and Robert G. Ingram, eds, God in the Enlightenment (Oxford, 2016).

Burke, Peter, 'Presenting and Re-Presenting Charles V', in Hugo Soly, ed., Charles V, 1500–1558, and His Time (Antwerp, 1999).

Burkhart, Louise M., The Slippery Earth: Nahua-Christian Moral Dialogue in Sixteenth-Century Mexico (Tucson, AZ, 1989).

——Before Guadalupe: The Virgin Mary in Early Colonial Nahuatl Literature (Albany, NY, 2001).

Busto Duthurburu, José Antonio del, 'La marcha de Francisco Pizarro de Cajamarca al Cusco', Revista Histórica, 26 (1962–3).

—— 'Los caídos de Vilcaconga', Historia y Cultura: Órgano del Museo Nacional de Historia, vol. i (Lima, 1965), pp. 115–25.

——La Conquista del Perú (Lima, 2011).

Cabanelas Rodríguez, Darío, Juan de Segovia y el problema islámico (Madrid, 1952).

Cadenas y Vicent, Vicente Francisco de, Carlos I de Castilla, Señor de las Indias (Madrid, 1988).

Calnek, Edward, 'The Internal Structure of Tenochtitlan', in E. R. Wolf, ed., The Valley of Mexico (Albuquerque, NM 1976), pp. 287–302.

—— 'Patterns of Empire Formation in the Valley of Mexico, Late Postclassic Period, 1200–1521', in George A. Collier, Renato I. Rosaldo and John D. Wirth, eds, The Inca and Aztec States, 1400–1800: Anthropology and History (New York, 1982), pp. 43–62.

—— 'The Calmecac and the Telpochcalli in Pre-Conquest Tenochtitlan', in The Work of Bernardino de Sahagún: Pioneer Ethnographer of Sixteenth-Century Aztec Mexico, ed. J. Jorge Klor de Alva et al. (Albany, NY, 1988).

Cameron, Averil, The Byzantines (Oxford, 2010).

Carreras i Artau, Joaquim, *Relaciones de Arnau de Vilanova con los reyes de la casa de Aragón* (Barcelona, 1955).

Casado Alonso, Hilario, and Flávio Miranda, 'The Iberian Economy and Commercial Exchange with North-Western Europe in the Later Middle Ages', in Evan T. Jones and Richard Stone, eds, *The World of the Newport Medieval Ship: Trade, Politics and Shipping in the Mid-Fifteenth Century* (Cardiff, 2018), pp. 207–27.

Cervantes, Fernando, *The Devil in the New World: The Impact of Diabolism in New Spain* (New Haven, CT, 1994).

—— 'Mexico's Ritual Constant: Religion and Liberty from Colony to Post-Revolution', in Matthew Butler, ed., *Faith and Impiety in Revolutionary Mexico* (New York, 2007).

—— 'How to See Angels: The Legacy of Mendicant Spirituality', in Fernando Cervantes and Andrew Redden, eds, *Angels, Demons and the New World* (Cambridge, 2013).

—— 'The Bible in European Colonial Thought c. 1450–1750', *The New Cambridge History of the Bible*, vol. iii (1450–1750), ed. Euan Cameron (Cambridge, 2016), pp. 805–27.

Chabod, Federico, *Carlos Quinto y su imperio*, trans. Rodrigo Ruza (Madrid, 1992).

Chamberlain, Robert S., *The Conquest and Colonization of Yucatan, 1517–1550* (Washington DC, 1948).

Chipman, Donald E., *Nuño de Guzmán and the Province of Pánuco in New Spain* (Glendale, CA, 1967).

Christian Jr, William A., *Local Religion in Sixteenth-Century Spain* (Princeton, NJ, 1981).

Chust, Manuel, *La cuestión nacional americana en las Cortes de Cádiz* (Valencia, 1999).

Clavero, Bartolomé, *Derecho de los reinos: temas de historia de derecho* (Seville, 1977).

Clendinnen, Inga, *Aztecs: An Interpretation* (Cambridge, 1991).

Cook, Sherburne F., *The Conflict between the California Indian and the White Civilization* (Berkeley, CA, 1976).

Crouch, David, *The English Aristocracy, 1070–1272: A Social Transformation* (New Haven, CT, 2011).

Cuadriello, Jaime, *Las glorias de la República de Tlaxcala, o la conciencia como imagen sublime* (Mexico City, 2004).

—— 'Winged and Imagined Indians', in Fernando Cervantes and Andrew Redden, eds, *Angels, Demons and the New World* (Cambridge, 2013).

Cumming, Laura, *Vanishing Man: In Pursuit of Velázquez* (London, 2016).

Cummins, J. S., 'Christopher Columbus: Crusader, Visionary and *Servus Dei*', in *Medieval Hispanic Studies Presented to R. Hamilton*, ed. A. D. Deyermond (London, 1976).

Dacosta Martínez, Arsenio, and Carlos Mota Placencia, 'Un tratado inédito sobre la idea de nobleza atribíudo a Francisco de Rades y Andrada', *Studia Aurea*, 8 (2014), pp. 417–54.

D'Altroy, Terrence N., *The Incas*, 2nd edn (Oxford, 2015).

D'Amico, Stefano, *Spanish Milan: A City within the Empire* (New York, 2012).

Davies, Arthur, 'The Loss of the *Santa Maria* Christmas Day, 1492', *American Historical Review*, 58:4 (July 1953), pp. 854–65.

Davies, Nigel, *The Toltec Heritage: From the Fall of Tula to the Rise of Tenochtitlan* (Norman, OK, 1980).

Dawson, Christopher, *The Making of Europe: An Introduction to the History of European Unity* (London, 1932).

——*Religion and the Rise of Western Culture* (London, 1950).

Day, John, 'The Great Bullion Famine in the Fifteenth Century', *Past and Present*, 79 (May 1978), pp. 3–54.

Delaney, Carol, *Columbus and the Quest for Jerusalem* (New York, 2011).

Dickens, A. G., *The German Nation and Martin Luther* (London, 1974).

Don, Patricia Lopes, *Bonfires of Culture: Franciscans, Indigenous Leaders, and the Inquisition in Early Mexico, 1524–1540* (Norman, OK, 2010).

Doolittle, William E., *Canal Irrigation in Prehistoric Mexico: The Sequence of Technological Change* (Austin, TX, 1990).

Duffy, Eamon, *The Stripping of the Altars: Traditional Religion in England c.1400–c.1580* (New Haven, CT, 1992).

Duncan, David Ewing, *Hernando de Soto: A Savage Quest in the Americas* (New York, 1995).

Duverger, Christian, *Hernán Cortés: Más allá de la leyenda* (Madrid, 2013).

——*Crónica de la eternidad: ¿quién escribió la Historia verdadera de la conquista de la Nueva España?* (Madrid, 2013).

Earle, Rebecca, *The Body of the Conquistador: Food, Race and the Colonial Experience in Spanish America, 1492–1700* (Cambridge, 2012).

Edwards, John, 'Religious Belief and Social Conformity: The *converso* Problem in Late Medieval Córdoba', *Transactions of the Royal Historical Society*, series 5, xxxi (1981).

——*The Spanish Inquisition* (Stroud, 1999).

Elliott, J. H., *The Old World and the New, 1492–1650* (Cambridge, 1970).

——*Imperial Spain 1469–1716* (Aylesbury, 1990).

——'A Europe of Composite Monarchies', *Past and Present*, 137 (November 1992).

——'Cortés, Velázquez and Charles V', in Hernán Cortés, *Letters from Mexico*, trans. and ed. Anthony Pagden (New Haven, CT, 2001), pp. xi–xxxvii.

——*Empires of the Atlantic World: Britain and Spain in America 1492–1830* (New Haven, CT, 2006).

Ernst, Cornelius, *Multiple Echo*, eds Fergus Kerr and Timothy Radcliffe (London, 1979).

Espinosa, Aurelio, *The Empire of the Cities: Emperor Charles V, the Comunero Revolt, and the Transformation of the Spanish System* (Leiden, 2009).

Farriss, Nancy M., *Maya Society under Colonial Rule: The Collective Enterprise of Survival* (Princeton, NJ, 1984).

Fernández-Armesto, Felipe, *The Canary Islands after the Conquest: The Making of a Colonial Society in the Early Sixteenth Century* (Oxford, 1981).

——*Before Columbus: Exploration and Colonization from the Mediterranean to the Atlantic, 1229–1492* (Philadelphia, PA, 1987).

——*Columbus* (Oxford, 1991).

——*Amerigo: The Man Who Gave his Name to America* (London, 2006).

Fisher, John, Allan Kuethe and Anthony McFarlane, eds, *Reform and Insurrection in Bourbon New Granada and Peru* (Baton Rouge, LO, 1990).

Foster, Kenelm, 'Introduction', *I Catherine: Selected Writings of St Catherine of Siena*, ed. and trans. Kenelm Foster OP and Mary John Ronayne OP (London, 1980), pp. 11–50.

Fraker, Charles F. Jr., 'Gonçalo Martínez de Medina, the Jerónimos and the Devotio Moderna', *Hispanic Review*, 34:3 (July 1966), pp. 197–217.

Frankl, Víctor, 'Hernán Cortés y la tradición de las Siete Partidas', *Revista de Historia de América*, 53:4 (June – December, 1962), pp. 9–74.

Freitag, Barbara, *Hy Brasil: The Metamorphosis of an Island: From Cartographic Error to Celtic Elysium* (Amsterdam, 2013).

Friede, Juan, and Benjamin Keen, *Bartolomé de Las Casas in History* (DeKalb, IL, 1971).

Frost, Elsa Cecilia, *La historia de Dios en las Indias: visión franciscana del nuevo mundo* (Mexico City, 2002).

Frost, Robert, *The Oxford History of Poland-Lithuania, Volume I: The Making of the Polish-Lithuanian Union, 1385–1569* (Oxford, 2015).

Fuson, Robert H., *Juan Ponce de León and the Discovery of Puerto Rico and Florida* (Blacksburg, VA, 2000).

García Icazbalceta, Joaquín, *Don Fray Juan de Zumárraga: primer obispo y arzobispo de México*, eds Rafael Aguayo Spence and Antonio Castro Leal, 4 vols (Mexico City, 1947).

García Oro, José, *La Reforma de los religiosos en tiempo de los Reyes Católicos* (Valladolid, 1969).

Gardiner, C. Harvey, *Naval Power in the Conquest of Mexico* (Austin, TX, 1958).

Garibay Kintana, Ángel María, *Historia de la literatura náhuatl*, 2 vols (Mexico City, 1953).

Gerhard, Peter, *A Guide to the Historical Geography of New Spain* (Cambridge, 1972).

Gibson, Charles, *Tlaxcala in the Sixteenth Century* (New Haven, CT, 1952).
—— *The Inca Concept of Sovereignty and the Spanish Administration in Peru* (New York, 1969).
Gilson, Étienne, *The Philosophy of St Bonaventure*, trans. Illtyd Trethowan and F. J. Sheed (London, 1938).
—— *God and Philosophy* (New Haven, CT, 1941).
Giménez Fernández, Manuel, 'Nuevas consideraciones sobre la historia, sentido y valor de las bulas alejandrinas de 1493 referentes a las Indias', *Anuario de estudios americanos*, vol. i (1944), pp. 173–429.
—— *Hernán Cortés y su revolución comunera en la Nueva España* (Seville, 1948).
—— *Bartolomé de las Casas*, 2 vols (Seville, 1953).
Góngora, Mario, *Studies in the Colonial History of Spanish America* (Cambridge, 1975).
Gonzalbo Aizpuru, Pilar, 'Del tercero al cuarto concilio provincial mexicano, 1585–1771', *Historia Mexicana*, 35:1 (1986).
Gose, Peter, 'Oracles, Divine Kingship, and Political Representation in the Inka State', *Ethnohistory*, 43:1 (1996), pp. 1–32.
Greenblatt, Stephen, *Marvellous Possessions: The Wonder of the New World* (Chicago, IL, 1992).
Griffiths, Nicholas, *The Cross and the Serpent: Religious Repression and Resurgence in Colonial Peru* (Norman, OK, 1996).
—— *Sacred Dialogues: Christianity and Native Religions in the Colonial Americas, 1492–1700*, 2nd edn (Lulu, 2017).
Gruzinski, Serge, *Man-Gods in the Mexican Highlands: Indian Power and Colonial Society, 1520–1800*, trans. E. Corrigan (Stanford, CA, 1989).
—— *The Conquest of Mexico: The Incorporation of Indian Societies into the Western World, 16th – 18th Centuries*, trans. E. Corrigan (Cambridge, 1993).
—— *The Eagle and the Dragon: Globalization and European Dreams of Conquest in China and America* (Cambridge, 2014).
Guénin, Eugène, *Ango et ses pilotes*, 2 vols (Paris, 1901).
Gurría Lacroix, Jorge, 'Andrés de Tapia y la Coatlicue', *Estudios de Cultura Náhuatl*, 13 (1978), pp. 23–34.
Haliczer, Stephen, *The Comuneros of Castile: The Forging of a Revolution, 1475–1521* (Madison, WI, 1981).
Hamilton, Earl J., *American Treasure and the Price Revolution in Spain* (Cambridge, MA, 1934).
Hanke, Lewis, 'The 'Requerimiento' and its Interpreters', *Revista de Historia de América*, 1 (March 1938), pp. 25–34.
—— *The Spanish Struggle for Justice in the Conquest of America* (Philadelphia, PA, 1949).
—— *Bartolomé de las Casas: An Interpretation of his Life and Writings* (The Hague, 1951).

Haring, C. H., *The Spanish Empire in America* (New York, 1947).

—— 'Ledgers of the Royal Treasures in Spanish America in the Sixteenth Century', *Hispanic American Historical Review*, II (1919), pp. 173–87.

Harvey, L. P., *Islamic Spain, 1250–1500* (Chicago, IL, 1990).

Hassig, Ross, *Aztec Warfare: Imperial Expansion and Political Control* (Norman, OK, 1995).

Headley, John M., *The Emperor and his Chancellor: A Study of the Imperial Chancellery under Gattinara* (Cambridge, 1983).

Helps, Arthur, *The Spanish Conquest in America, and its Relation to the History of Slavery and the Government of Colonies*, 4 vols (London, 1856–68).

Hemming, John, *The Conquest of the Incas* (New York, 1970).

Henige, David, *Numbers from Nowhere: The American Indian Contact Population Debate* (Norman, OK, 1998).

Herzog, Tamar, *Defining Nations: Immigrants and Citizens in Early Modern Spain and Spanish America* (New Haven, CT, 2003).

Himmerich y Valencia, Robert, *The Encomenderos of New Spain, 1521–1555* (Austin, TX, 1991).

Hook, Judith, *The Sack of Rome*, 2nd edn (London, 2004).

Horspool, David, 'Total Rout: How Cromwell Tried to Conquer the Caribbean', *The Times Literary Supplement* 5970 (1 September 2017).

Hussey, Ronald D., 'Text of the Laws of Burgos (1512–1513) Concerning the Treatment of the Indians', *Hispanic American Historical Review*, 12:3 (August 1932), pp. 301–26.

Hyslop, John, *The Inka Road System* (New York, 1984).

—— *Inka Settlement Planning* (Austin, TX, 1990).

Jijón y Caamaño, Jacinto, *Sebastián de Benalcázar*, 2 vols (Quito, 1936–8).

Jones, David Albert, *Angels: A History* (Oxford, 2010).

Jones, Evan T., and Margaret Condon, *Cabot and Bristol's Age of Discovery* (Bristol, 2016).

Jones, Evan T., and Richard Stone, eds, *The World of the Newport Medieval Ship: Trade, Politics and Shipping in the Mid-Fifteenth Century* (Cardiff, 2018).

Jones, Grant D., *Maya Resistance to Spanish Rule: Time and History on a Colonial Frontier* (Albuquerque, NM, 1989).

Kagan, Richard L., 'Prescott's Paradigm: American Historical Scholarship and the Decline of Spain', *American Historical Review*, 101:2 (April 1996).

Kamen, Henry, *The Spanish Inquisition: An Historical Revision* (London, 1997).

—— *Philip of Spain* (New Haven, CT, 1997).

Kelsey, Harry, 'Finding the Way Home: Spanish Exploration of the Round-Trip Route across the Pacific Ocean', *Western Historical Quarterly*, 17:2 (April 1986).

Knight, Alan, 'Rethinking the Tomóchic Rebellion', *Mexican Studies/Estudios Mexicanos*, 15:2 (1999).

Knowles, David, 'St Francis of Assisi', in M. W. Sheenan, ed., *Francis of Assisi: Essays in Commemoration* (New York, 1982).

Konetzke, Richard, 'Hernán Cortés como poblador de la Nueva España', in *Estudios Cortesianos: IV Centenario de Hernán Cortés* (Madrid, 1948).

Kosiba, Steve, and Andrew M. Bauer, 'Mapping the Political Landscape: Toward a GIS Analysis of Environmental and Social Difference', *Journal of Archaeological Method and Theory*, 20:1 (March 2013), pp. 61–101.

Koskenniemi, Martti, *From Apology to Utopia: The Structure of International Legal Argument* (Cambridge, 2006).

Kramer, Wendy, *Encomienda Politics in Early Colonial Guatemala, 1524–1544: Dividing the Spoils* (Boulder, CO, 1994).

Kubler, George, *Mexican Architecture in the Sixteenth Century*, 2 vols (New Haven, CT, 1948).

—— 'A Peruvian Chief of State: Manco Inca (1515–1545)', *Hispanic American Historical Review*, 24:2 (May 1944), pp. 253–76.

Ladero Quesada, Miguel Ángel, *La Hacienda Real de Castilla. Rentas y Gastos de la Corona al morir Isabel I* (Seville, 1976).

—— 'Los genoveses en Sevilla y su región (siglos XIII–XVI), elementos de permanencia y arraigo', in idem, *Los mudéjares de Castilla y otros estudios de historia medieval andaluza* (Granada, 1989), pp. 283–312.

—— *El primer oro de América* (Madrid, 2002).

Lafaye, Jacques, *Mesías, cruzadas, utopías: el judeo-cristianismo en las sociedades iberoamericanas*, 2nd edn (Mexico City, 1997).

Laguarda Trías, Rolando, *El enigma de las latitudes de Colón* (Valladolid, 1974).

Lamb, Ursula, *Frey Nicolás de Ovando* (Madrid, 1956).

Lara, Jaime, *City, Temple, Stage: Eschatological Architecture and Liturgical Theatrics in New Spain* (Notre Dame, IN, 2004).

—— *Christian Texts for Aztecs: Art and Liturgy in Colonial Mexico* (Notre Dame, IN, 2008).

Larner, John, *Marco Polo and the Discovery of the World* (New Haven, CT, 1999).

Lempérière, Annick, '¿Nación moderna o república barroca? México 1823–1857', in François-Xavier Guerra and Mónica Quijada, eds, *Imaginar la Nación* (Münster, 1994).

Leonard, Irving A., *Books of the Brave, being an account of books and of men in the Spanish Conquest and settlement of the sixteenth-century New World*, introduction by Rolena Adorno (Berkeley, CA, 1992).

Leppin, Volker, *Martin Luther: Gestalten des Mittelalters und der Renaissance* (Darmstadt, 2006).

Lippens, Hugolin, 'Jean Glapion, défenseur de la réforme de l'Observance, conseiller de l'empereur Charles-Quint', *Archivum Franciscanum Historicum*, xliv (1951), pp. 3–70; xlv (1952), pp. 3–71.

Livi Bacci, Massimo, *Conquest: The Destruction of the American Indios* (Cambridge, 2008).

Llaguno, José A., *La personalidad jurídica del indio y el III Concilio Provincial Mexicano* (Mexico City, 1963).

Lockhart, James, *The Men of Cajamarca: A Social and Biographical Study of the First Conquerors of Peru* (Austin, TX, 1972).

—— 'Views of Corporate Self and History in some Valley of Mexico Towns', in George A. Collier, Renato I. Rosaldo and John D. Wirth, eds, *The Inca and Aztec States, 1400–1800: Anthropology and History* (New York, 1982), pp. 367–93.

—— *The Nahuas after the Conquest: A Social and Cultural History of the Indians of Central Mexico, Sixteenth Through Eighteenth Centuries* (Stanford, CA, 1992).

Lockhart, James, and Stuart B. Schwartz, *Early Latin America: A History of Colonial Spanish America and Brazil* (Cambridge, 1983).

Lombard, Maurice, 'Caffa et la fin de la route mongole', *Annales*, 5e Année, no. 1 (1950), pp. 100–103.

Lopetegui, León, and F. Zubillaga, *Historia de la Iglesia en América Española*, 2 vols (Madrid, 1965).

López de Ayala, Jerónimo, *El cardenal Cisneros, gobernador del reino: estudio histórico*, 2 vols (Madrid, 1921).

López-Portillo, José-Juan, *'Another Jerusalem': Political Legitimacy and Courtly Government in the Kingdom of New Spain (1535–1568)* (Leiden, 2018).

Loredo, Rafael, *Los repartos: bocetos para la nueva historia del Perú* (Lima, 1958).

Lovell, George W., and Christopher H. Lutz, 'Pedro de Alvarado and the Conquest of Guatemala, 1522–1524', in John M. Weeks, ed., *The Past and the Present Maya: Essays in Honour of Robert M. Carmack* (Lancaster, CA, 2001).

Lubac, Henri de, 'Remarques sur l'histoire du mot "surnaturel"', *Nouvelle revue théologique*, 61 (1934).

—— *Catholicisme: Les aspects sociaux du Dogme* (Paris, 1938).

—— *Le mystère du surnaturel: Augustinisme et théologie moderne* (Paris, 1965).

Lupher, David A., *Romans in a New World: Classical Models in Sixteenth-Century Spanish America* (Ann Arbor, MI, 2003).

Lynch, John, *Spain, 1516–1598: From Nation State to World Empire* (Oxford, 1991).

—— *New Worlds: A Religious History of Latin America* (New Haven, CT, and London, 2012).

MacKay, Angus, *Spain in the Middle Ages: From Frontier to Empire, 1000–1500* (London, 1977).

—— 'The Hispanic-*Converso* Predicament', *Transactions of the Royal Historical Society*, series 5, xxxv (1985), pp. 159–67.

MacQuarrie, Kim, *The Last Days of the Incas* (London, 2007).

Madariaga, Salvador de, *Hernán Cortés* (Buenos Aires, 1951).

Magelhães Godinho, Vitorino, *A Economia dos descubrimentos henriquinos* (Lisbon, 1962).

Maltby, William S., *The Black Legend in England: The Development of Anti-Spanish Sentiment, 1558–1660* (Durham, NC, 1971).

Martí, Samuel, and and Gertrude P. Kurath, *Dances of Anáhuac: The Choreography and Music of Precortesian Dances* (Chicago, IL, 1964).

Martínez Laínez, Fernando, *Fernando el Católico: Crónica de un Reinado* (Madrid, 2016).

Martínez Medina, Francisco, and Javier and Martin Biersack, *Fray Hernando de Talavera: Primer Arzobispo de Granada. Hombre de Iglesia, estado y letras* (Granada, 2011).

Mathes, W. Michael, *The Conquistador in California 1535: The Voyage of Fernando Cortés to Baja California in Chronicles and Documents* (Los Angeles, CA, 1973).

Mazzucato, Mariana, *The Value of Everything: Making and Taking in the Global Economy* (London, 2018).

McCabe, Herbert, *God Matters* (London, 1987).

McConica, James K., *English Humanists and Reformation Politics under Henry VIII and Edward VI* (Oxford, 1965).

McFarlane, Anthony, *Colombia before Independence: Economy, Society and Politics under Bourbon Rule* (Cambridge, 1993).

McGilchrist, Iain, *The Master and his Emissary: The Divided Brain and the Making of the Western World* (New Haven, CT, 2009).

Medina, Miguel Ángel, *Una comunidad al servicio del indio. La obra de fray Pedro de Córdoba OP, 1482–1521* (Madrid, 1983).

Mena García, María del Carmen, *Pedrarias Dávila o la ira de Dios: una historia olvidada* (Seville, 1992).

—— *Sevilla y las flotas de Indias* (Seville, 1998).

Menéndez Pidal, Ramón, *El Padre Las Casas y Vitoria con otros temas de los siglos xvi y xvii* (Madrid, 1958).

Meseguer Fernández, Juan, 'Contenido misionológico de la obediencia e instrucción de Fray Francisco de los Ángeles a los Doce Apóstoles de México', *Americas*, 11:3 (January 1955), pp. 473–500.

Milhou, Alain, *Colón y su mentalidad mesiánica en el ambiente franciscanista español* (Valladolid, 1983).

Mills, Kenneth, 'The Limits of Religious Coercion in Mid-Colonial Peru, *Past & Present*, 145 (November 1994), pp. 84–121.

—— *Idolatry and its Enemies: Colonial Andean religion and Extirpation* (Princeton, NJ, 1997).

Morales Padrón, Francisco, 'Las relaciones entre Colón y Martín Alonso Pinzón', *Revista de Indias*, 21 (1961).

Moreau-Nélaton, Étienne, *Manet raconté par lui-même*, 2 vols (Paris, 1926).

Morris, Craig, and Ariana von Hagen, *The Incas: Lords of the Four Quarters* (New York, 2011).

Mujica Pinilla, Ramón, *Ángeles apócrifos en la América virreinal* (Mexico City, 1996).

—— *Rosa Limensis: Mística, política e iconografía en torno a la patrona de América* (Mexico City, 2005).

Muldoon, James, 'John Wyclif and the Rights of the Infidels: The *Requerimiento* Re-Examined', *Americas*, 36:3 (January 1980), pp. 301–16.

Mundy, Barbara E., 'Mapping the Aztec Capital: The 1524 Nuremberg Map of Tenochtitlan, its Sources and Meaning', *Imago Mundi*, 50 (1998), pp. 11–33.

Murga Sanz, Vicente, *Juan Ponce de León: fundador y primer gobernador del pueblo puertorriqueño* (San Juan, 1971).

Muriel, Josefina, 'Divergencias en la biografía de Cuauhtémoc', *Estudios de Historia Novohispana*, 1 (1966), pp. 53–114.

Murray, Paul OP, *God's Spies: Michelangelo, Shakespeare and Other Poets of Vision* (London, 2019).

Nader, Helen, *Liberty in Absolutist Spain: The Habsburg Sale of Towns, 1516–1700* (Baltimore, MD, 1990).

Neff, Stephen C., *Justice among Nations: A History of International Law* (Cambridge, MA, 2014).

Netanyahu, Benzion, *The Origins of the Inquisition in Fifteenth-Century Spain* (New York, 1995).

Nicholson, H. B., 'Religion in pre-Hispanic Central Mexico', in *Handbook of Middle American Indians*, vol. x (Austin, TX, 1971).

Nirenberg, David, *Anti-Judaism: The History of a Way of Thinking* (New York, 2013).

Nutini, Hugo G., 'Syncretism and Acculturation: The Historical Development of the Cult of the Patron Saint in Tlaxcala, Mexico, (1519–1670)', *Ethnology*, 15:3 (July 1976).

Ohnersorgen, Michael A., 'Aztec Provincial Administration at Cuetlaxtlan, Veracruz', *Journal of Anthropological Archaeology*, 25 (2006), pp. 1–32.

Olschki, Leonardo, 'Ponce de León's Fountain of Youth: History of a Geographical Myth', *Hispanic American Historical Review*, 21:3 (August 1941), pp. 361–85.

Orozco y Berra, Manuel, *Historia antigua y de la conquista de México*, 4 vols (Mexico City, 1880).

Otero Enríquez, Santiago, *Noticias genealógicas de la familia Velázquez Gaztelu* (Madrid, 1916).

Otte, Enrique, 'Los jerónimos y el tráfico humano en el caribe: una rectificación', *Anuario de estudios atlánticos*, 32 (1975).

—— *Las Perlas del Caribe* (Caracas, 1977).

Pagden, Anthony, *The Fall of Natural Man: The American Indian and the Origins of Comparative Ethnology* (Cambridge, 1982).

——*Lords of All the World: Ideologies of Empire in Spain, Britain and France c. 1500–c. 1800* (New Haven, CT, 1995).

——*The Burdens of Empire: 1539 to the Present* (Cambridge, 2015).

Pardo, Osvaldo, *The Origins of Mexican Catholicism: Nahua Rituals and Christian Sacraments in Sixteenth-Century Mexico* (Ann Arbor, MI, 2004).

Parker, Geoffrey, 'Philip II and his World in the 1580s', in Richard Kagan and Geoffrey Parker, eds, *Spain, Europe and the Atlantic World: Essays in Honour of John H. Elliott* (Cambridge, 1995).

——*Imprudent King: A New Life of Philip II* (New Haven, CT, 2014).

——*Felipe II: la biografía definitiva* (Barcelona, 2015).

——*Emperor: A New Life of Charles V* (New Haven, 2019)

Pasztory, Esther, *Aztec Art* (New York, 1983).

—— 'El arte mexica y la conquista española', *Estudios de cultura Náhuatl* (1984).

Penn, Thomas, *Winter King: The Dawn of Tudor England* (London, 2012).

Pérez de Tudela y Bueso, Juan, *Las armadas de Indias y los orígenes de la política de colonización* (Madrid, 1956).

Pérez Martínez, Héctor, *Cuauhtemoc: vida y muerte de una cultura* (Buenos Aires, 1948).

Pérez Prendes, José Manuel, *La monarquía indiana y el estado de derecho* (Valencia, 1989).

Phelan, John Leddy, *The Millennial Kingdom of the Franciscans in the New World: A Study of the Writings of Gerónimo de Mendieta* (Berkeley, CA, 1956).

Pieper, Josef, *The Four Cardinal Virtues*, trans. Richard and Clara Winston, Lawrence E. Lynch and Daniel F. Coogan (South Bend, IN, 1966).

Pike, Ruth, *Enterprise and Adventure: The Genoese in Seville and the Opening of the New World* (Ithaca, NY, 1966).

Poole, Stafford, C. M., *Our Lady of Guadalupe: The Origins and Sources of a Mexican National Symbol* (Tucson, AZ, 1995).

Porras Barrenechea, Raúl, *Pizarro* (Lima, 1978).

Portús, Javier, *Velázquez: su mundo y el nuestro* (Madrid, 2018).

Powell, Philip Wayne, *Tree of Hate: Propaganda and Prejudices Affecting United States Relations with the Hispanic World* (New York, 1971).

Power, Eileen, *The Wool Trade in English Medieval History* (Oxford, 1941).

Prescott, W. H., *The Conquest of Mexico*, illustrated by Keith Henderson, with an introduction by T. A. Joyce, 2 vols (London, 1922).

Ramos, Demetrio, 'Colón y el enfrentamiento de los caballeros: Un serio problema del segundo viaje, que nuevos documentos ponen al descubierto', *Revista de Indias*, 39 (1979), pp. 9–88.

——*Hernán Cortés* (Madrid, 1992).

Ratzinger, Joseph, *La théologie de l'histoire de saint Bonaventure*, trans. Robert Givord (Paris, 2007).

Rawlings, Helen, *The Spanish Inquisition* (Oxford, 2008).

Raworth, Kate, *Doughnut Economics: Seven Ways to Think Like a 21st Century Economist* (London, 2017).

Recinos, Adrián, *Pedro de Alvarado: Conquistador de México y Guatemala*, 2nd edn (Guatemala City, 1986).

Reeves, Marjorie, *The Influence of Prophecy in the Later Middle Ages: A Study in Joachimism* (Oxford, 1969).

Remensnyder, Amy G., *La Conquistadora: The Virgin Mary at War and Peace in the Old and New Worlds* (Oxford, 2014).

Restall, Matthew, *When Montezuma Met Cortés: The True Story of the Meeting that Changed History* (New York, 2018).

Restall, Matthew, and Florine Asselbergs, *Invading Guatemala: Spanish, Nahua, and Maya Accounts of the Conquest Wars* (Pennsylvania, PA, 2007).

Ricard, Robert, *La 'Conquête spirituelle' du Mexique: essai sur l'apostolat et les méthodes missionnaires des ordres mendiants en Nouvelle Espagne de 1523/24 à 1572* (Paris, 1933).

Riquer, Martín de, *Caballeros andantes españoles* (Madrid, 1967).

Roca Barea, María Elvira, *Imperiofobia y Leyenda Negra: Roma, Rusia, Estados Unidos y el Imperio español* (Madrid, 2016).

Rodilla León, María José, 'Novela sobre la paternidad de un manuscrito mestizado', *Iberoamericana*, 13:52 (December 2013), pp. 173–80.

Rodríguez Velasco, Jesús D., *El debate sobre la caballería en el siglo XV: la tratadística caballeresca castellana en su marco europeo* (Salamanca, 1996).

Rodríguez Villa, Antonio, *El Emperador Carlos V y su corte según las cartas de don Martín de Salinas, embajador del infante don Fernando, 1522–1539* (Madrid, 1903).

Roper, Lyndal, *Martin Luther: Renegade and Prophet* (London, 2016).

Rosenthal, Earl, '*Plus Ultra* and the Columnar Device of Emperor Charles V', *Journal of the Warburg and Courtauld Institutes*, 34 (1971), pp. 204–28.

Rostworowski de Diez Canseco, María, *History of the Inca Realm*, trans. Harry B. Iceland (Cambridge, 1999).

Roth, Norman, *Conversion, Inquisition and the Expulsion of the Jews from Spain* (Madison, WI, 1995).

Rowe, John H., 'Inca Culture at the Time of the Spanish Conquest', *Handbook of South American Indians*, 143:2, ed. Julian Stewell (Washington DC, 1946), pp. 183–330.

Rubial García, Antonio, *La hermana pobreza: el franciscanismo de la edad media a la evangelización novohispana* (Mexico City, 1996).

Rubio Mañé, José Ignacio, *Introducción al estudio de los virreyes de la Nueva España, 1535–1746*, 3 vols (Mexico City, 1955).

Ruddock, Alwyn A., 'Columbus and Iceland: New Light on an Old Problem', *Geographical Journal*, 136:2 (June 1970), pp. 177–89.

Ruiz, Teófilo F., *Spanish Society, 1400–1600* (Harlow, 2001).

Ruiz-Domènech, José Enrique, *El Gran Capitán* (Barcelona, 2002).

Ruiz Martínez, Cándido, *Gobierno de Fray Nicolás de Ovando en La Española* (Madrid, 1892).

Rumeu de Armas, Antonio, *La política indigenista de Isabel la Católica* (Valladolid, 1969).

——*Itinerario de los Reyes Católicos, 1474–1516* (Madrid, 1974).

Russell, Craig H., *From Serra to Sancho: Music and Pageantry in the California Missions* (Oxford, 2009).

Russell, Peter, *Prince Henry 'the Navigator': A Life* (New Haven, CT, 2000).

Saladini, Lucien, *Les origines de Christophe Colomb: Informations complémentaires* (Broché, 1988).

Saranyana, José Ignacio, *Joaquín de Fiore y Tomás de Aquino: historia doctrinal de una polémica* (Pamplona, 1979).

Sauer, Carl Ortwin, *The Early Spanish Main* (Berkeley, CA, 1966).

Saul, Nigel, *For Honour and Fame: Chivalry in England, 1066–1500* (London, 2011).

Schwaller, John F., with Helen Nader, *The First Letter from New Spain: The Lost Petition of Cortés and his Company, June 20, 1519* (Austin, TX, 2014).

Séailles, Gabriel, *Alfred Dehodencq: L'homme et l'artiste* (Paris, 1910).

Skinner, Quentin, *The Foundations of Modern Political Thought: Vol II, The Age of Reformation* (Cambridge, 1978).

Smith, Michael E., 'City-Size in Late Post-Classic Mesoamerica', *Journal of Urban History*, 31:4 (May 2005), pp. 403–34.

Sobrequés i Callicó, Jaume, 'Nació, nacionalisme i ordre constitucional català durant la guerra civil del segle XV', in *Estudis d'historia de Catalunya*, vol. I (Barcelona, 2008).

Solar y Taboada, Antonio del, and José de Rújula y de Ochotorena, *El Adelantado Hernando de Soto* (Badajoz, 1929).

Sousa, Lisa, and Kevin Terrenciano, 'The "Original Conquest" of Oaxaca: Nahua and Mixtec Accounts of the Spanish Conquest', *Ethnohistory*, 50:2 (Spring 2003).

Sousa, Lisa, Stafford Poole, and James Lockhart, eds and trans., *The Story of Guadalupe: Luis Lasso de la Vega's Huei tlamahuiçoltica of 1649* (Stanford, CA, 1998).

Southern, R. W., *Western Views of Islam in the Middle Ages* (Cambridge, MA, 1962).

Strieder, Jacob, *Jacob Fugger the Rich: Merchant and Banker of Augsburg, 1459–1525* (Washington DC, 1931).

Stross, B., 'Mexican Copal Resins', *U-Mut Maya*, 6 (1993).

Suárez Fernández, Luis, *Les juifs espagnols au Moyen Âge* (Paris, 1983).

Sullivan, Thelma D., 'Tlatoani and Tlatocayotl in the Sahagún Manuscripts', *Estudios de Cultura Náhuatl*, 14 (1980), pp. 225–39.

Tanner, Marie, *The Last Descendant of Aeneas: The Hapsburgs and the Mythic Image of the Emperor* (New Haven, CT, 1993).

Taylor, William, *Landlord and Peasant in Colonial Oaxaca* (Stanford, CA, 1972).

——*Magistrates of the Sacred: Priests and Parishioners in Eighteenth-Century Mexico* (Stanford, CA, 1996).

Thiel, Stephanie, 'Global Anomie and India: A Conceptual Approach', *Indian Journal of Asian Affairs*, 24:1–2 (June–December 2011).

Thomas, Hugh, *The Conquest of Mexico* (London, 1993).

——*Rivers of Gold: The Rise of the Spanish Empire* (London, 2003).

——*The Golden Age: The Spanish Empire of Charles V* (London, 2011).

Thompson, J. Eric, *Maya History and Religion* (Norman, OK, 1970).

Tibesar, Antonine S., *Franciscan Beginnings in Colonial Peru* (Washington DC, 1953).

—— 'The Franciscan Province of the Holy Cross of Española, 1509–1559', *Americas*, 13:4 (April 1957), pp. 377–89.

Torre Villar, Ernesto de la, 'Fray Pedro de Gante, maestro y civilizador de América', *Estudios de Historia Novohispana*, 5 (1974), pp. 9–77.

Torres, Pedro, *La Bula Omnímoda de Adriano VI* (Madrid, 1948).

Townsend, Camilla, *Fifth Sun: A New History of the Aztecs* (New York, 2020).

Townsend, Camilla, *Malintzin's Choices: An Indian Woman in the Conquest of Mexico* (Albuquerque, NM, 2006).

Tracy, James D., *Erasmus of the Low Countries* (Berkeley, CA, 1996).

——*Emperor Charles V, Impresario of War: Campaign Strategy, International Finance, and Domestic Politics* (Cambridge, 2002).

Turner, Denys, *The Darkness of God: Negativity in Christian Mysticism* (Cambridge, 1995).

Ullmann, Walter, *Medieval Papalism* (London, 1949).

Ulloa, Daniel, *Los predicadores divididos: los dominicos en Nueva España, siglo xvi* (Mexico City, 1977).

Umberger, Emily, 'Events Commemorated by Date Plaques at the Templo Mayor: Further Thoughts on the Solar Metaphor', in Elizabeth H. Boone, *The Aztec Templo Mayor* (Washington DC, 1987), pp. 411–49.

Varela, Consuelo, *La Caída de Cristóbal Colón: El Juicio de Bobadilla*, ed. and trans. Isabel Aguirre (Madrid, 2006).

Villella, Peter B., *Indigenous Elites and Creole Identity in Colonial Mexico, 1500–1800* (Cambridge, 2016).

Wagner, Henry Raup, and Helen Rand Parish, *The Life and Writings of Bartolomé de Las Casas* (Albuquerque, NM, 1967).

Warren, J. Benedict, *The Conquest of Michoacán: The Spanish Domination of the Tarascan Kingdom in Western Mexico, 1521–1530* (Norman, OK, 1985).

Watts, Pauline Moffitt, 'Prophecy and Discovery: On the Spiritual Origins of Christopher Columbus's "Enterprise of the Indies"', *American Historical Review*, 90:1 (1985).

Weber, David J., *The Spanish Frontier in North America* (New Haven, CT, 1992).

Westropp, T. J., 'Brasil and the Legendary Islands of the North Atlantic: Their History and Fable. A Contribution to the "Atlantis" Problem', *Proceedings of the Royal Irish Academy*, 30 (1912), pp. 223–60.

Wilder, Thornton, *The Bridge of San Luis Rey* (London, 2000).

Williams, Caroline A., *Between Resistance and Adaptation: Indigenous Peoples and the Colonisation of the Chocó* (Liverpool, 2005).

Wolff, Philippe, 'The 1391 Pogrom in Spain: Social Crisis or Not?', *Past and Present*, 50 (February 1971), pp. 4–18.

Wright, I. A., *The Early History of Cuba, 1492–1586* (New York, 1916).

Yates, Frances, *Astraea: The Imperial Theme in the Sixteenth Century* (London, 1975).

Zantwijk, Rudolph van, *The Aztec Arrangement: The Social History of Pre-Spanish Mexico* (Norman, OK, 1985).

Zavala, Silvio, *La Utopía de Tomás Moro en la Nueva España* (Mexico City, 1937).

Ziółkowski, Mariusz S., *La guerra de los Wawqi: los objetivos y los mecanismos de la rivalidad dentro de la élite inka, siglos XV – XVI* (Quito, 1996).

Acknowledgements

It would never have occurred to me to write this book had it not been for a telephone call I received sometime in 2015 from the late Felicity Bryan. She told me that it was high time to have a proper book on the Conquistadores and that I was the obvious person to write it. Naturally I expressed some reservations, but Felicity was characteristically undeterred. Her contagious enthusiasm, sharp intelligence and good humour soon won me over. She mercilessly savaged many of my proposals, each time giving me invaluable advice and making me even more determined to come up trumps. She was a model agent who became a dear friend and who has left an enormous gap in the world of publishing.

At that early stage I also received very helpful advice from Joy de Menil and George Lucas, and I was encouraged and given much-needed confidence by Diarmaid MacCulloch.

Much of the drafting was done during quite a difficult period, when I was looking after my frail and confused father after my mother's death. Without the support of my brother Ignacio, who took three years off to come to Bristol to help, I would have had to abandon the project. This is a debt that I will never be able to repay.

I have been fortunate to be surrounded by brilliant and supportive colleagues in the History Department at Bristol. In various and often unexpected ways, I have benefited from conversations with Kenneth Austin, Fanny Bessard (now in Oxford), Robert Bickers, Hilary Carey, Peter Coates, Tim Cole, Juliane Fürst (now in Potsdam), Anke Holdenried, Ronald Hutton, Evan Jones, Josie McLellan, Noah Millstone (now in Birmingham), Ben Pohl, John Reeks, Richard Stone and Ian Wei. Amy Edwards kindly offered to take a good look at chapter 11 and reassured me that it was fine for non-specialists. One colleague went well beyond what could reasonably be expected of a friend, even a diehard *compadre*, and it is a very special pleasure to dedicate this book to him and his wife.

Many other friends have given me their encouragement and support.

I am grateful to James Alison, Ignacio Almada, Francisco Arce, Luz Arce, John Battle, William and Karena Batstone, Roger Bird, David and Celia Brading, María Inés Camarena, Federico Castillo, Carlos Cervantes, Lourdes María Cervantes RJM, Jaime Cuadriello, Frank Deane, Bill and Christine Doyle, Eamon Duffy, George Eccles, Sir John Elliott, John Farrell OP, Alison Fincham, Richard Finn OP, Kieran Flanagan, Bob Fowler, Christopher Francis, Rob and Sue Gore-Langton, Mary Gormaly, Cathy Hallam, Andrew Hegarty, Hugh Herzig, Richard Holmes, Gregor McLennan, Iván Martínez, Michael Oborne, Robert Ombres OP, Anthony Pagden, Timothy Radcliffe OP, Andrew Redden, Matthew Restall, Pia de Richemont, Blanche Ridge, the late Rupert Ridge, Isabel de Salis, the late David Sanders OP, Tim Sheehy, Adam Sisman, Quentin Skinner, Domingo Tortonese, Gonzalo Velasco Berenguer, the late Caroline Williams and Paul Williams. Paul Murray OP kindly read and commented on the section relating to the influence of St Catherine of Siena on Dominican reform. My former colleague and friend Clare Flanagan was enthusiastic and supportive throughout. A very special word of gratitude is due to Jonathan Scherer and to Miko and Dorothee Giedroyć.

The first six chapters were read by Georgia Bodnar who tactfully exposed my many 'academic tics', as she quaintly called them, and gave me excellent suggestions about how to avoid them. Her advice allowed me to revise the manuscript, which was then read with keen interest, meticulous care and sheer love of the subject by Tom Penn: his enormously helpful and wise suggestions have vastly improved the book; no author could wish for a better editor. I was also very fortunate to have Richard Mason, eagle-eyed and good-humoured, as my copy-editor, and Cecilia Mackay's expert help with the illustrations. It was a wonderful surprise to be contacted by Ania Gordon, and to confirm that she was indeed the same Ania Gordon who took my course 'Aztecs, Incas and Evangelizers' at Bristol. She reminded me of the many generations of Bristol undergraduates who have taken that course in the last few years, and who have taught me far more than I could possibly hope to have taught them. Ania has joined a wonderful team at Penguin Press, among whom Richard Duguid and Eva Hodgkin have repeatedly demonstrated that the book could not have been in better hands.

Needless to say, my greatest debt, in this as in everything else, is to my family, especially my wife Annabelle.

FC, Bristol, June 2020

Index

Abancay 303, 304
Abancay, River 282
Abravanel, Isaac 19
Abulafia, Samuel 19
Acachinanco 149, 180, 182
Acalán 245
Acosta, José de 210
Adrian of Utrecht (Pope Adrian VI)
    106, 107, 112, 115, 116, 117,
    191, 195, 199, 236, 379 n.48;
    influenced by 'Devotio
    moderna' 107; as Cardinal and
    Grand Inquisitor 112; won
    over by Las Casas 112;
    appointed Regent in
    Charles's absence 115;
    elected Pope, 195
Adrian VI, pope, see Adrian of
    Utercht
Agramonte, Juan de 68
Aguacaleyquen 320
Aguado, Juan 34
Aguilar, Count of 240
Aguilar, Fray Francisco de (formerly,
    Alonso) 154, 165, 385 n.69,
    387 n.107
Aguilar, Gerónimo de 125, 126, 127,
    130, 163, 243, 255, 319
Ahuitzotl 178, 231
Alabama 216
Alabama, River 327

Alanus Anglicus 81
Álavez Palomino, Rodrigo 331
Alcalá de Henares 108
Alcántara, Francisco Martín de 313
Alcázar, Rodrigo del 60
Aldeanueva 74, 75
Alderete, Julián de 178
Alexander the Great 37
Alexander VI, Pope 30, 39, 48, 76,
    78, 266, 370 n.24
Alfonso V 'the Magnanimous', King
    of Aragon 13, 396 n.53
Alfonso X 'the Wise', King
    of Castile 132
Algiers 344
Alhama 14
Alhambra 15, 235
Almagristas 311–13
Almagro, Diego de 247, 260, 261,
    277, 281, 282, 283, 287, 290,
    293, 296, 297, 298, 301, 305–8,
    311, 312, 315, 318, 344;
    allotted the South of
    Tawantinsuyu by Charles V
    297; betrayed by Paullu 306;
    garrotted by Hernando
    Pizarro, 306; praised by
    Alonso Enríquez de
    Guzmán 312
Almanach Perpetuum (Zacuto) 38
Alvarado, Alonso de 301, 303, 304

Alvarado, Jorge de 230, 232, 233, 234; depicted in the *Lienzo de Quauhquechollan* 234

Alvarado, Pedro de xvii, 126, 135, 141, 142, 146, 161–4, 174, 179, 180, 182, 183, 184, 187, 193 194, 227, 228, 231, 232, 233, 245, 257, 293, 296, 297, 301, 344; nicknamed 'Tonatiuh' 162; described by Prescott 162; invades Guatemala 228–30; sails back to Spain 230; plans expedition to China and the Spice Islands 344; dies after being crushed by his horse 344

Álvarez Chanca, Dr Diego 30

Álvarez Chico, Rodrigo 131

Álvarez de Pineda, Alonso 135

Amadís de Gaula 89, 102

Amarukancha 314

Amazon Basin 259, 282, 300

Amazons 8, 12, 53, 88, 99, 122, 262, 338

Anacaona 45, 62

Andalusia 3, 8, 10, 14, 58, 61,174, 202, 211, 214, 315, 316, 338, 366 n.4

Andes 252, 259, 282, 301, 316, 339–40

Andorga, Pascual de 87

angelic hierarchies 220; *see also* angels; archangels; principalities; seraphim; thrones; virtues

angels 207, 208, 210, 213, 219, 220, 405 n.50, 406 n.75, 407–8 n.87; *see also* angelic hierarchies

Ango, Jean 190

Anhaica 322

Antequera *see* Oaxaca

anthropophagy 31, 88, 216, 275, 337; *see also* Cannibalism

Antipodes 8, 12, 42, 268

Antisuyu 252, 288

Apalachee 216, 320, 322, 327

Apoo 254, 257, 258

apostasy 207, 208

Apulco Valley 138

Apulco, River 137

Apurímac, Canyon 282, 283

Apurímac, River 282–3, 290, 300, 418 n.26

Aquinas, Friar St Thomas 264–5, 267, 341–2

Aragon, Crown of 10, 12, 65, 108, 113, 114, 196–7, 350

Arborio, Mercurino, *see* Gattinara

archangels 219, 220, 407–8 n.87; *see also* angelic hierarchies

Arcos, Friar Miguel de 263, 269, 370 n.27

Arequipa 250, 311

Arimaspi 88

Ariosto, Ludovico 114, 196–7

Aristotle 79, 265, 341–2

Arkansas, River Valley 329–30

arquebuses 122, 148, 160, 165, 178, 179, 180, 182, 296, 313, 425 n.31

Asia 5, 8, 9, 12, 20, 23, 26, 29, 31, 32, 35, 36, 37, 38, 39, 41, 42, 49, 53, 81, 88, 93, 103, 226, 245

Astomi 88

Atahachi 326, 327

Atawallpa (Atahualpa) xv, 250, 252, 253, 254, 255–9 *passim*, 260, 261, 262, 263, 273, 274, 275, 277, 280, 281, 282, 283, 285, 293, 295, 297, 299, 304, 314, 324, 415 n.30, 420 n.3

Atemoztli ('The Descent of the Waters') 157

Atlantic Ocean xv, 3, 6, 7, 8, 20, 28, 29, 30, 39, 40, 50, 53, 58, 197, 198, 200, 226, 324, 340, 347, 351

audiencia (court of justice) 68, 195,
    196, 343; Santo Domingo 68,
    195; Mexico City 233, 244
Augustine of Canterbury, St 209,
    210, 213
Augustine of Hippo, St 38, 82, 265,
    341, 402 n.13, 406 n.75
Augustinian Order 208
Augustus 114, 197
Aukaypata ('terrace of repose',
    Cusco) 288
Austria 237, 247
Austria, House of 114, 196
Autiamque 330
Auwera, Johann van der 200, 201,
    202, 203
Ávila, Alonso de 135
Ávila, Antonio de 245
Ávila, Gil González de 245
Ávila, Pedro Arias de, *see* Dávila,
    Pedrarias
Axayacatl, Palace 150, 154, 164
Ayllu 252; *see also Panaqa*
Aymara 250
Azcapotzalco 177
Azores 6, 7, 28, 42, 189
Aztecs (Mexica) xv; *see also* Mexica
    (Aztecs)

Bahía del Espíritu Santo
    see Tampa Bay
Balboa *see* Núñez de Balboa
Baracoa (Asunción) 94, 101
Barbarossa, Hayreddin 344
Barcelona 29, 64, 112, 114, 167, 168,
    247, 248, 350
Baroque 223, 351, 352–3, 354
Barrancas Bermejas *see* La Tora
Bastidas, Rodrigo de 84, 178
Bayle, Pierre 349
Bede, the Venerable, St 208
Béjar, Duke of 110, 240
Belize 50, 51, 52, 53

Benalcázar, Sebastián de 253, 293,
    295, 296, 297, 339, 340,
    341, 344; governor of
    Popayán 344
Benavente, Friar Toribio de,
    see Motolinía
Benincasa *see* Catherine of Siena
Bernal *see* Díaz del Castillo
Bernáldez, Andrés 14, 29
Bernini, Gian Lorenzo 405 n.50
Betanzos, Friar Domingo de 118
Black Death 6, 18, 73, 366 n.4
Bobadilla, Francisco de 46, 47, 50,
    62, 87
Bobadilla, Isabel de 87, 315, 317
Bobadilla, Leonor de 317
Bodin, Jean 348
Boethius 205
Bogotá (*cacique*) 335, 336
Bogotá, Santa Fe de 335, 337, 340,
    341, 344
Bolingbroke, Viscount 349
Bombón 277, 299
Bonaventure, St 220, 402 n.12
Boniface IV, Pope 210
Boniface of Crediton, St 210, 213
Boston 351
Boyle, Nicholas 406 n.70
Brazil 39, 48, 52, 53
Brazil (legendary island) 7
brigantines 126, 127, 131, 158, 160,
    173, 174, 179, 180, 182, 183,
    185, 188, 331, 332
Briones, Pedro de 225
Bristol 6, 7, 8, 38
Broad, River 325, 425 n.31
Brussels 105, 106, 118, 130, 190,
    196, 200, 238, 376 n.2
Bueno, Martín 259, 260, 285
Buil, Friar Bernardo 29, 31, 32, 33,
    35, 60
Buonaccorso da Montemagno,
    Giovane 17, 361 n.31

Burgos 35, 37, 64–5, 75, 77, 167, 366 n.4

Burgundy 16, 53, 104, 105, 106, 108, 110

Byzantium 209, 211

Cabeza de Vaca, Alvar Núñez 214, 216–18, 316, 319

Cabot, John 38

Cabot, Sebastian 410 n.6

Cacama 150, 164, 175, 176

cacique 27, 30, 31, 34, 60, 62, 67, 86, 93, 94, 125, 137, 138, 243, 319, 320, 322, 325, 326, 327, 329, 336, 337, 338, 415, n.26, 425, n.21

Cádiz 10, 34, 35, 40, 58, 346

Caesar *see* Julius Caesar

Caguax 94

Cajamarca 254–8, 259, 260, 261, 273, 275, 280, 281, 286, 287, 419 n.39

Cajamarca Massacre 257, 415 n.30

Cajatambo 277

Cajetan, Friar Tomas de Vio 74, 369 n.17

Calafia 103

Calancha, Antonio de la 379–80 n.8

Calca 303

Cali (Santiago de) 340

Calicut 32, 39

Callicles 265

calmecac 183, 397 n.59

Camacho, Bartolomé 334, 427 n.77

Camagüey (Santa María del Puerto Príncipe) 94

Campeche 243, 245, 413 n.49

Cañari 295, 310, 420–21 n.3

Canaries 6, 7, 10, 11, 21, 23, 36, 40, 50, 98, 317, 331

Cannibalism 30, 31, 88, 109, 137, 172, 186, 206, 235, 337, *Among Spaniards* 216

Cannons 126, 138, 148, 165, 166, 179, 180, 189, 225

Cano, Friar Melchor 264, 416 n.52

Caonao 94, 95

Caonaobó 30, 34

Capachequi 322

Cape Verde Islands 6, 39, 40, 226

capitulación (pl. *capitulaciones*) 21, 22, 238, 248, 315, 316, 330, 331, 426–7 n.70

cardinal virtues 268; *see also* justice

Cardoso, Captain 335

Caribbean xv, 30, 51, 53, 63, 98, 126, 131, 211, 252, 291, 293, 301, 331, 372 n.51, 425 n.21

Carrion's disease (Oroya fever) 413 n.2

Casa de Contratación de Indias 64, 111

Casa del Cordón 35

Casana 286

Cassava 52, 96, 99, 162

Castiglione, Bladassare 237

Castile 3, 10, 11, 12, 15, 20, 21, 27, 28, 33–4, 43, 50, 53, 57, 58, 61, 66, 74, 75, 86, 93, 101, 102, 104, 105, 106, 110, 111, 112, 116, 117, 118, 179, 190, 191, 195, 200, 218, 297, 314, 316, 324, 331, 343, 344, 350, 368 n.23, 376 n.2, 378 n.45; exclusive rights to the New World 59; wary of Aragonese intrusions 104–5

Castilla del Oro 87, 128, 245

Castillo Maldonado, Alonso del 216

Cathay 26, 27, 226

Catherine of Siena, St 71–3, 74, 76, 202

'Caxtilteca' 142, 143, 148, 155, 163

Celano, Friar Thomas of 402 n.15

Cempoala *see* Cempohuallan (Cempoala)

Cempohuallan (Cempoala) 130, 135, 161, 162, 173, 193
Cempohualteca 138, 139, 140, 143, 145, 161
Centla 126
Centurione firm 7
Cervantes de Salazar, Francisco 213, 384 n.57, 393 n.7
Cervantes, Cardinal Juan de 366, n.7
Cervantes, Leonel de 165
Cervantes, Miguel de 15, 58–9
Cervantes family 58, 366–7, n.7; see also Gómez de Cervantes
Céspedes, Juan de 334
chac-mool 151
Chachapoyas 281, 306–7
Chahuaca. 243, 244
Chalchicueyecan see Veracruz
Chalchiuhtlicue 384 n.61; see also Matlacueitl
Chalco 146, 147, 173, 175, 177, 178, 185
Challcochima 253, 259, 274, 275, 277, 278, 280, 281, 282, 283, 285, 290, 419 n.34
Champotón 245
Chanca see Álvarez Chanca
Chapultepec 180
Charissimo in Christo, Papal Bull 196
Charlemagne 114
Charles III of Bourbon, Duke 236, 239
Charles of Ghent, see Charles V
Charles V (Holy Roman Emperor) xv, 89, 104–18 passim, 122, 132, 139, 140, 142, 144, 147, 148, 151, 152, 155, 156, 158, 160, 161, 162, 164, 167, 168, 171, 172, 174, 175, 176, 177, 179, 180, 183, 184, 185, 186, 187, 190, 191–9 passim, 200, 201, 206, 226, 227, 235–41 passim, 244, 247, 257, 262, 263, 268, 274, 287, 292, 297, 299, 301, 305, 308, 309, 311, 312, 314, 315, 316, 317, 332, 337, 338, 339, 340, 341, 344, 346; warned by the Regency Council in Castile 376 fn.2; influenced by 'devotio moderna' 107; seen as 'last world emperor' 113; described by Piero Pasqualigo 117; elected Holy Roman Emperor 144; condemns Cortés posthumously 394 n.16; penchant for exotic items from the Americas 398 n.1; hailed by Ariosto 196–7; compared to Charlemagne, 197; plans to play Cortés off against Nuño de Guzmán 240; grants Pizarro title of Adelantado Mayor of Peru 248; conquers Tunis from the Ottomans 262; asks Manqo Inka to heed the authority of the Spanish governor, 311; invites Manqo Inka to Spain 311; allows Soto to conquer Florida 315–16; expedition to Algiers 344
Chaucer, Geoffrey 17
Chaves, Francisco de ('El Pizarrista') 309, 313
Chetumal 243
Chiaha 324, 325
Chiapas 225, 227, 230, 244, 245
Chicasa 328
Chicha 286
Chichimecatecle 170, 184, 185
Chièvres, Sieur de (Guillaume II de Croÿ) 105, 110–11, 113, 378 n.45
Chile 226, 250, 252, 298, 301, 303, 304, 311, 312, 315

Chimaltenango 233
Chimor 255
Chimú 255
China 9, 27, 32, 53, 120, 130, 131,
    225, 227, 241
Chincha, River 247
Chinchaysuyu 252, 290, 293, 297
Chios 5, 6
Chiquián 277
chivalry 7, 14, 16, 17, 55, 99, 102,
    103, 197, 347, 360 n.23;
    romances of 15, 16, 57, 101–3,
    148; moral code of 16–17
Chocó 344
Cholollan (Cholula) 129, 138, 142,
    143, 144, 145, 146, 153, 154,
    161, 170, 176, 241
Chololteca 143, 144, 145, 146
Cholula *see* Cholollan
Choromandae 88
Chrétien de Troyes 16
Christendom xv, 5, 7, 15, 53, 72, 102,
    113, 114, 124, 197, 198, 349
Christian universalism 123
Chrysostom, St John 341
chunka kamayuq 279
Cibao 62
Cíbola 316
Cicero 205, 265, 269, 417 n.66
Cieza de León, Pedro 306, 421 n.3
Cipangu 9, 26, 27, 48, 226
Cisneros *see* Jiménez de Cisneros
citizenship 36, 131, 254, 430 n.10
Citlaltépetl (Star Mountain), *see* Pico
    de Orizaba
Ciudad de los Reyes *see* Lima
Civil War (1474–9) 10, 11, 19, 21,
    57–8, 93
Clement VII, Pope 196, 236, 237,
    239, 247
Coanacoch 175, 176
Coaque 249
Coatepec 137, 174, 175

Coatlinchan 174, 175
Coatzacoalcos 225, 227
Cobán 233
Cobo, Bernabé 279
Cochabamba 308
Cochuah 244
Cofitachequi 322, 323, 324, 328
Cofitachequi, Queen of 324
Cofre de Perote 137
Cohualpopocatzin (Qualpopoca)
    153, 155
Colmerares, Rodrigo de 80
Colombia 80, 84, 246, 250, 252,
    315–16, 331, 344
Colón, Diego (Columbus's son) 8,
    66, 67, 68, 69, 70, 71, 76, 77,
    84, 94, 115; reinstated as
    governor of Hispaniola after
    being deposed by Fonseca 155;
    invests in Las Casas's Cumaná
    project 115
Colón, Diego (Giacomo, Columbus's
    brother) 29, 43, 44, 46
Colón, Fernando (Columbus's son)
    45, 51
Columbus, Bartolomé 11, 32, 34, 40,
    43, 94
Columbus, Christopher xv, 3, 7, 8,
    11, 17, 20–22, 23–52 *passim*,
    64, 69, 75, 93, 99, 113, 314;
    first voyage 23–7; second
    voyage 30–35; third voyage
    39–47; fourth voyage 50–53;
    Commitment to the conquest of
    Jerusalem 14; 'Prologue' to his
    account of the First Voyage 22;
    ideals of nobility 22, 39; 'map
    of islands' 26; manipulates the
    ship's log to confirm his
    erroneous theories 25; uses
    'natural Law' theories to justify
    enslavement of cannibals 31;
    dresses up as Franciscan Friar

34–5; draws up an entail 39;
exaggerated monetary
ambitions 39; cryptic signature
39; millenarianism 47–8;
dubbed 'the Pharaoh' 52;
Mourns Queen Isabel's death
53; loses confidence in King
Fernando 53; anxieties about
diet 375 n.25; death 54
comunero revolt 117, 168, 191, 192,
195, 198, 236, 238, 379 n.48
Concepción de la Vega 34, 43, 61,
62, 69, 367 n.11
Conchillos y Quinatana, Lope 106
Congregation of Lombardy 73, 74
Conil 243
Constantinople 5, 102, 103, 151,
198, 237
conversos 18, 19, 20, 33, 60, 106
Coosa 325, 326
copal 211–13
Córdoba, Friar Pedro de 69, 71, 77,
95, 96, 111, 112, 202
Coronado see Vázquez de Coronado
corregidores 58, 117, 131, 346
corsairs 317, 318; see also piracy
cortes 116, 117, 196
Cortés, Hernán xv, xvi, 61, 93–4,
101, 116, 118, 120–22, 123,
124, 125, 126–34, 135, 136,
137, 138, 139, 140–49 passim,
151–7, 159, 160, 161, 162, 163,
164, 165, 166, 167, 168, 169,
170–74, 176–89 passim, 190,
191, 192, 193, 194, 195, 196,
198, 199, 201, 202, 225, 226,
227, 228, 230, 237, 238, 239,
240, 242, 243, 244, 247, 248,
249, 255, 257, 258, 267, 275,
291, 293, 303, 315, 319, 324,
335, 344, 367 n.14, 380 n.11,
382 n.38, 390 n.19, 392 n.54,
394 n.16, 402 n.9; appointed
chief justice and captain-
general after crafted resignation
132; knowledge of the 'Siete
Partidas' 132–4; orders his
ships to be dismantled 135, 384
n.57; first Meeting with
Moctezuma 149; visit to
Tlatelolco 150–51; visit to the
Great Temple 152; forced to
turn a blind eye to the sacrifices
157; applies the principle of
'obedezco pero no cumplo'
162; outmanoeuvres Narváez
162; weeps under an ahuehuetl
tree after the Noche Triste 167;
captures Tepeaca (Segura de la
Frontera) 172; merciless
brutality 172, 394 n.16;
appointed Governor of New
Spain 199; support for
Franciscan mission 201;
expedition to Honduras 202;
sails back to Spain in 1528 239;
received magnanimously by
Charles V and made Marquis
of the Valley of Oaxaca 240;
marries Juana Ramírez de
Arellano 240; sails back to
New Spain to face Guzmán's
investigation against him 241;
sets off on a quest for islands in
the Pacific 241; discovers Baja
California 241; invests in
Charles V's expedition to
Algiers 344; pursues Hayreddin
Barbarossa 344; dies in
Castilleja la Vieja 344
Corunna see La Coruña
Cosmographia (Münster) 3
Council of the Indies 87, 199, 202,
235, 317, 331, 343, 348
Coyoacán (Coyohuacan) 148, 180,
182, 189, 201, 231

Coyohuacan *see* Coyoacán

Cozumel 122, 123, 125, 173, 241

Creation 22, 69, 72, 73, 203, 207, 267

Cromwell, Oliver 433 n.27

crossbows 122, 148, 160, 174, 179, 180, 182, 186, 225, 296, 301, 313

Cuauhnahuac (Cuernavaca) 178, 179, 185, 240

Cuauhtemoc 178, 179, 182, 184, 185, 186, 187, 188, 189, 190, 395 n.38

Cuauhxicalli 151, 210, 218

Cuba (Fernandina) 26, 27, 32, 42, 52, 53, 93–5, 99–101, 103, 106, 107, 116, 120, 122, 131, 132, 135, 162, 173, 174, 195, 316, 317, 318, 319, 325

Cuchumatanes, Sierra de los 232

Cuéllar, Cristóbal de 60, 101

Cuéllar, Sancho de 261

Cuernavaca *see* Cuauhnahuac

Cuetlaxtlan *see* Cotaxtla

Cuitlahuac 164, 165, 170, 173, 178

Culhuacan 148

Culoa Tlaspicue 208

Cumaná 112, 114, 115, 118, 341

Cunningham Graham, Robert Bontine 202, 428 n.96

Cuntisuyu 252, 288, 309

Cupids 211

Cura Ocllo 309, 310

Curaçao 84

curíes (Guinea pigs) 335

Cusa, Nicholas of 375 n.20

Cuscatlán 230

Cusco 252, 254, 258, 259, 261, 273, 275, 277, 278, 280, 281, 283, 284, 285, 286, 287, 288, 289, 290, 291, 292, 293, 297, 298, 299, 300, 301, 303, 305, 308, 310, 312, 315

Cusco Valley 250

Cydnus, River 342

Cynocephali 88

D'Ailly, Pierre 9, 25, 38, 41–2

D'Anghera, Peter Martyr 14, 44, 51, 96, 99, 105, 122, 126, 316, 373 n.61, 385 n.71

Dabeiba 86

Dame Prudence 17; *see also* cardinal virtues

Dante Alighieri 378 n.31

Dantiscus, Johannes 198, 238, 240

Darién 84, 86, 115, 125, 128, 247

Dávila, Pedrarias 81, 87, 245, 246, 247, 316

De unico vocationis modo omnium gentium ad veram religionem 341

Dehodencq, Alfred 353

Dekkers, Johann 200, 201, 202

demonization 208

Desaguadero, River 307

Desdemona 88

Devil, the 71, 151, 201, 204, 206, 207, 208, 323, 352

devotio moderna 107, 108, 200

Deza, Friar Diego de 12

Díaz de Solís, Juan 89

Díaz del Castillo, Bernal 152, 225, 397 n.64

Díaz, Rui 295

Díez de Games, Gutierre 17

Disraeli, Benjamin 232

divine law 267, 268, 269

dogs 34, 87, 128, 148, 172, 323

Dominica (island) 30

Dominican Order 68, 69, 71, 73–5, 203, 208, 220, 233, 235, 264, 342

Dominions *see* angelic hierarchies

dominium 9, 81, 82, 266, 267, 268, 274

Don Quixote (M. de Cervantes)
58–9, 396 n.53
Donatists 82
Dorantes de Carranza, Andrés 216
Doria, Andrea 239–40, 247
drugs 183
Duero, Andrés de 161
Duitama 336
Durán, Friar Diego 129, 208, 210,
217, 404–5 n.48
Durand, Guillaume 211
Dürer, Albrecht 118–19, 120, 130,
132, 191, 196, 200, 232, 238
Dutch Revolt xvii

Ecclesiasticus (Sirach) 95, 374 n.10
Ecuador 250, 252, 253, 290
Eden, Garden of 42, 48, 52
Eguía, Francisco de 173
Egypt 204, 206
El Hierro, Port of 25, 30
El Pinar, Battle 228
'El Pizarrista' *see* Chaves, Francisco de
El Salvador 230
Elisena, mythical Princess 102
Elliott, J. H. xviii
Elvas, gentleman of 323, 425 n.38
emeralds 249, 257, 258, 336, 337
empiricism 355
Enchiridion militis Christiani
(Erasmus) 109, 377 n.14
encomienda system 61, 62, 95, 195,
238, 246, 254, 314, 342; *see
also* Laws of Burgos; New Laws
England 6, 7, 10, 11, 18, 32, 38, 65,
110, 112, 168, 200, 210, 213,
232, 236, 353, 368 n.25
Enlightenment 349, 351
Enríquez de Guzmán, Alonso 312
Enríquez, Don Carlos 327
entradas 429 n.109
entropy 207
Erasmianism 108–9, 203, 403 n.17

Erasmus of Rotterdam, Desiderius
108, 109, 197, 203, 205
Erotes 211
Esmeraldas, River 249
Espinar, Friar Alonso de 77
Espinosa y Luna, Gaspar de
246, 305
Espira, Jorge de la, *see* Speyer
Esplandián 102, 103
esse (ens; 'being') 265
Estete, Miguel de 260
Estevanico 216
Estrada *see* Ruiz de Estrada
eternal law *see* divine law
Eusebius of Caesarea 123
exempla 220
exorcism 323
extirpation 209, 214, 352;
see also idolatry
Extremadura 30, 60, 87, 104, 109,
201, 202, 232, 248
Ezekiel 405 n.50, 409 n.87

'famous thirteen' 246, 250
Fantin-Latour, Henri 354
Farriss, Nancy 406 n.74
Federmán, Nicolás 340; *see also*
Federmann, Nikolaus
Federmann, Nikolaus 339, 341, 344
Felipillo/Martinillo 253, 255,
414 n.22
Ferber, Friar Nicolaus 205
Ferdinand of Aragon *see* Fernando II,
King of Aragon
Fermor, Patrick Leigh xvi, 357 n.6
Fernández de Córdoba, Gonzalo
396 n.53
Fernández de Lugo, Alonso 331,
332, 334
Fernández de Lugo, Pedro 331
Fernández de Oviedo, Gonzalo 60,
80, 81, 82, 83, 115, 152
Fernandina *see* Cuba (Fernandina)

Fernando II, King of Aragon 3, 7,
10, 11, 12, 14, 15, 17, 18, 20,
21, 23, 28, 29, 36, 39, 43, 46,
47, 48, 49, 55, 57, 59, 63, 64,
65, 66, 71, 74, 74, 75, 77, 84,
86, 87, 89, 93, 95, 99, 101, 102,
103, 104–5, 106, 108, 113, 116,
117, 195, 202, 235, 266;
interest in the trade routes to
the Orient 12, 13; heir to the
Kingdom of Jerusalem 13; seen
as last world emperor 13;
frictions with Columbus 22;
appointed 'Vicar Apostolic of
the Indies' by pope Alexander
VI 30; appointed
'administrator and governor' of
Castile after Isabel's death 65;
to be declared 'permanent
regent' of Castile in the event of
Juana's incapacity 65; and
Kingdom of Naples 65–6;
interest in the Beata of
Piedrahíta 75; supports the first
Dominican friars sent to
Hispaniola 76; in Chivalric
Romance 102: last confession
104; death 103, 104–5
Fernando, *Infante* Don 104, 106;
shipped to Flanders by Charles
110; claims crown of Hungary
after Suleiman's triumph at
Mohács 236
Ferrer, *see* Vincent Ferrer, St
feudalism 16, 20, 21, 362 n.43
Figueroa, Rodrigo de 111
Fiore, Joachim of 13, 47, 203,
402 n.12
Flanders 6, 16, 108, 110, 195, 200,
366 n.4
Fleury, Jean 190
Florida 26, 99, 118, 186, 216, 316,
318, 319, 379

Foix, Germaine de, *see* Germaine
de Foix
Foix, Odet de, Viscount of Lautrec
239, 240
Fonseca *see* Rodríguez de Fonseca
Ford, Richard 354
France 10, 11, 18, 32, 65, 240, 353,
366 n.4
Francis I, King of France 105, 112,
114, 190–91, 236, 237, 239,
247, 303; imprisoned in Madrid
by Charles V 237; and
Ottoman Turks 239, 247; and
Lutheran Princes 247
Francis of Assisi, St 204, 220, 402 n.15
Franciscan Order 60, 77, 196, 199,
200–224 *passim*, 203, 367 n.11
Franciscan spirituality 13, *Links to
Hieronymites in Spain* 107
Francisco, Nahua interpreter 163
Fredrick III, Elector of Saxony 112
fueros (laws and privileges) 193–4,
348, 431 n.12
Fugger, Jakob 114

Galata 5
Gallo (island) 246, 249
Galway 8
Gama, Vasco da 50
Ganges, River 52
Gante, Pedro de, *see* Peter of Ghent
Garay, Francisco de 135
Garcés, Friar Julián de 407, n.87
García de Salazar, Lope 7
García Gaitero, Juan 314
García, Alejo 89
García, Friar Gregorio 408 n.87
Garcilaso de la Vega, El Inca 315,
318, 319, 324, 326, 347,
424 n.5
Gattinara, Mercurino Arborio,
Marquis of 113, 114, 115, 116,
197–8, 199, 236, 237, 240

Gemelli Careri, Giovanni Francesco 351
Genesis 42
Geneva, Lake 259
Genoa 3, 6, 49, 139, 236, 240, 247
Genoese 5, 7, 10, 12, 35, 47, 49, 59, 111, 178, 240, 262
Geoffrey of Monmouth 16
Georgia 322
Germaine de Foix 65, 104, 105
Germany 210, 213
Ghana 8, 11, 40
Ghibellines 378 n.31
Gibbon, Edward 349
Gibraltar 197
Gideon 237
Giustiniani, Agostino 48
Glapion, Friar Jean 200
God 10, 13, 72, 73, 113, 122, 124, 132, 134, 135, 155, 158, 171, 204, 207, 217, 219, 267, 268, 306, 322–3, 330; see also Providence
Godoy, Diego de 126, 225
gold 6, 8, 9, 11, 12, 26, 27, 28, 33, 36, 40, 48, 49, 50, 51, 52, 53, 59, 62, 64, 67, 84, 86, 87, 93, 95, 130, 131, 159, 161, 166, 216, 227, 230, 235, 243, 245, 246, 247, 249, 254, 258, 259, 262, 287, 288, 296, 299, 311, 316, 319, 322, 323, 324, 325, 329, 330, 331, 335, 337, 338, 344, 413 n.1, 419 n.39
Gold Coast of Africa 8
Golden Chersonese (Peninsula of Malaysia) 51
Golden Fleece, Order of the 114
Golden Spur, Order of 115
Golgotha 113
Gómez de Cervantes, Don Diego 58
Gómez de Cervantes, Don Gonzalo 346, 347

González de Mendoza, Cardinal Pedro 35
Good Hope, Cape of 6, 8
Gorrevod, Laurent 111
grace see nature and grace
Gracias a Dios, Cape of 51
Gran Canaria 10, 50, 51
Granada xvii, 3, 5, 10, 11, 13, 14, 15, 18, 19, 20, 21, 33, 46, 57, 235, 238, 300; conquest of 15, 48, 101, 158, 211
Great Khan 26
Greenland 6
Gregorio, Pedro 249
Gregory the Great, Pope St 209, 210, 408 n.87
griffins 32, 88, 103
Grijalva, Juan de 101, 120, 122, 127, 129
Grijalva, River 126, 245
Grimaldi, Jerónimo 64
Grita Valley 335
Guacanagarí 27, 30, 31, 32, 34
Guachoya 300
Guadalajara 238
Guadalquivir, River 41, 262
Guadalupe (island) 30
Guadalupe, Extremadura 30
Guadalupe, Our Lady of, see Our Lady of Guadalupe
Guadeloupe, see Guadalupe . . .
Guahabá 93
Guanahaní 26
Guaraní 89
Guasco 250
Guatemala 225, 227–30, 232, 233, 244, 246, 262, 279, 296
Guatemalans 293, 296
Guayaquil 253, 296
Guerrero, Gonzalo 125, 243
Guevara, Fernando de 45, 62
Guillaume II de Croÿ, see Chièvres
Guinea, Gulf of 10

Gulf of Mexico 99,127, 325, 330
gunpowder 186
Gutiérrez de Valdelomar, Pedro 154
Gutiérrez, Pero 127
Guzmán, Nuño Beltrán de 238, 240,
    241, 244

Habsburg Dynasty xv, xvii, 113,
    114, 350
Haiti 27, 28, 93, 118
hallucinogens 153, 183, 208; see also
    peyote; mushrooms
Hanan ('upper sector', Cusco) 288
Hannibal 88, 305
Hatuey 93, 94
Hatun ayllu 252
Hatun runa 279
Havana 101, 318, 320, 375 n.28
Henry 'the Navigator', Prince 6
Henry II, King of Castile 57
Henry IV, King of Castile 10
Henry VII, King of England 65
Henry VIII, King of England 110,
    112, 236, 237, 239
Henry of Susa see Hostiensis
hermandades (brotherhoods) 58
Hernández de Biedma, Luis 323,
    326, 328
Hernández de Córdoba, Francisco 122
Hernández Puertocarrero, Alonso
    167, 192
Herod 145
Herrada, Juan de 313
Herrera, Antonio de 310
Herrera, Fernando de xv
hidalguía 55, 60, 84, 116, 132, 133
Hieronymite Order 107, 108, 109,
    110, 111,
Higueymota 45
Himahi 324
Hispania 113
Hispaniola 27, 30, 32, 34, 35, 36, 37,
    39, 40, 41, 42, 43, 44, 45, 46,

48, 49, 50, 51, 52, 55–68
passim, 69, 70, 74, 76, 77, 79,
    84, 87, 93, 94, 95, 98, 101, 106,
    107, 110, 111, 112, 132, 173,
    178, 192, 194, 195, 203, 235,
    314, 339
Hobbes, Thomas 349
Hojacastro, Friar Martín Sarmiento
    de 409 n.91
Hojeda, Alonso de 31, 34, 44, 45,
    84, 86
Hojeda, Friar Alonso de 19
Holguín, Garci 188
Holy Grail, Quest of 16
Holy League of Cognac 239
Holy Roman Empire 113, 145,
    152–3, 154, 155, 198, 309
Holy Spirit 47, 170, 203
Honduras 201, 202, 239,
    244, 246
horses 126, 128, 138, 148, 173, 174,
    182, 183, 184, 185, 217, 233,
    243, 253, 256, 282, 283, 284,
    291, 293, 295, 296, 297, 299,
    300, 307, 308, 309, 317, 318,
    319, 325, 327, 328, 329, 332,
    339–40, 341, 344
Hostiensis (Henry of Susa) 81, 82,
    372 n.45
Huaca, see wak'a
Huamachuco 275
Huamanga 301, 308, 311
Huánuco 309
Huáscar see Waskhar
Huascarán see Waskaran
Huaspar 309
Huatanay, River 286, 287, 288
Huaura, River 277
Huaylas 277
Huehuecalco 147
Huejotzingo, see Huexotzingo
Huelva 23
Huexola 175

Huexotzingo (Huejotzingo) 142, 144, 146, 147, 176, 184
huey tlahtoani 156
Hueyohtiplan 170
Huitzilopochtli 128–9, 151, 154, 157
human law *see* positive law
human sacrifice 125, 127, 128, 129, 137, 141, 150, 157, 179, 183, 184, 201, 206, 228, 231, 275; of young children 159
Humboldt, Alexander von 351
Hundred Years' War 6, 18
Hungary 237
hunu kuraka 279
Hurin ('lower sector', Cusco) 288
Hus, Jan 82, 266

Iceland 6, 7, 8
Ichisi 322
idolatry 206, 213, 214, 223, 275, 352; *see also* extirpation
Imitation of Christ (Kempis) 107, 200
Inca warfare 279–80, 303, 304
incarnation 22, 72, 81, 407 n.76
Incas xv, 89, 247, 250–53, 263, 275, 278, 279, 280, 281, 283–4, 291, 295, 298, 299, 300, 301, 347
Independence, Spanish American wars of 347, 431 n.13
India xv, 3, 8, 29, 50, 51, 52, 71
'Indies' xviii, 14, 29, 30, 35, 38, 47, 49, 64, 66, 67, 70, 74, 79, 83, 107, 109, 111, 113, 115, 190, 191, 198, 201, 233, 235, 263, 264, 287, 335, 336; seen as kingdoms, not colonies 350
Innocent IV, Pope 81, 124
Innocent VIII, Pope 13
Inquill 309
Inquisition 19, 20, 33, 206–7, 358 n.9; excluded from Granada 33

Insurgency Wars 351; *see also* Independence, Spanish American wars of
Inter caetera, papal bull 39
Ireland 6, 7, 8
Irving, Washington xvi
Isabel I, Queen of Castile 3, 7, 10, 11, 12, 13, 14, 15, 17, 18, 19, 20, 21, 23, 26, 28, 29, 30, 32, 33, 34, 35, 36, 37, 39, 43, 46, 47, 48, 49, 53, 55, 57, 58, 59, 60, 61, 63, 64, 65, 66, 74, 77, 84, 102, 105, 108, 113, 117, 127, 195, 202, 235, 266; frictions with Columbus 22, 33, 34; bans the enslavement of Taínos 77; in chivalric romance 102; death 53, 64, 66
Isabela (island) 26
Isabela (town in Hispaniola) 43
Isabella, Queen, *see* Isabel I, Queen of Castille
Isaiah 38, 70
Isla Mujeres 123, 124, 125
Islam 15, 20, 21, 55, 97, 98, 113, 114, 197
Israel 204, 206
Istanbul 237; *see also* Constantinople
Italy 6, 65, 73, 88, 112, 247
Itzquauhtzin 150, 156, 164
Itztlolinqui, Don Juan de Guzmán 142, 145–6
ius (justice) 264, 265, 266, 269; *see also* justice
ius gentium (law of nations) 133, 269
Ivitachuco 322
Ixguacan (Ixhuacán) 137
Ixhuacán *see* Ixguacan
Iximche' (Santiago) 230
Ixtacamaxtitlan 138
Ixtapalapa *see* Iztapallapan
Ixtlilxochitl 130, 174, 175, 179, 180, 184

Izalco 230
iztac teteo ('white gods') 213
Iztaccihuatl ('White Woman') 146
Iztapallapan 147–8, 165, 176, 177, 180, 182

Jacobita, Martín 205
Jagua Tree 97
jaguars 190
Jalapa 135
Jamaica 32, 52, 53, 63, 94, 125, 135, 195, 433 n.27
Jánico 31
Janus (Ianos) 3
Jaquijahuana 283
Jaraguá 44, 61, 62, 63 *massacre* 63
Jauja 253, 277, 278, 280, 281, 282, 287, 290, 291, 292, 293, 298–9, 301, 307, 308, 309
Jerez de la Frontera 214
Jerome, St 38
Jerusalem 13, 14, 20, 32, 48, 53, 75, 113, 197, 210, 211, 237, 405 n.50; surrogate Jerusalems 211
Jesuits 344, 352
Jesus 27, 123, 139, 156, 213
Jews xvii, 18, 19, 20, 33, 67, 80, 361 n.35; pogrom of 1391 18; expulsion from Spain xvii, 18, 20, 33; expulsion from England and France 18; fifteenth-century pogroms against 19; forbidden to travel to the New World 67
Jiménez de Cisneros, Cardinal Francisco 36, 43, 66, 75, 76, 95, 105, 106, 107, 108, 109, 110, 111, 202, 211; appointed Regent of Castile after Philip I's death 66, and after Fernando II's death in 1516 105; interest in St Catherine of Siena and the Beata of Pierdrahíta 75; plans crusade against the Moors 75; supports Charles of Ghent's succession 106; supports Las Casas's campaign 107; death 110, 377 n.22
Jiménez de Quesada, Gonzalo 331, 332, 334, 336, 337, 340, 341; failed attempt to conquer the Llanos 344
Jiménez de Quesada, Hernán 337
Joachimism 13, 402 n.12
João II, King 7, 8, 28, 40–41
John II, King of Aragon 10
Juan Diego 221
Juan, Prince 12
Juana 'the Mad', Queen of Castile 53, 65, 66, 104, 110, 132, 368 n.2; her rights defended by the Council of the Realm in Castile 105
Juana, 'la Beltraneja' 10
Judaism 98
Judaizing 20
Julius Caesar 135, 396 n.53
Julius II, Pope 74
Junín, Lake 277
'just war' theory 78, 269, 343
justice 57–8, 70, 95, 195, 238, 262, 263–9, *see also ius*
Juvenal 205

K'iche' 228, 230, 231, 232, 233
Kaqchikel 228, 230, 232, 233, 234
Karankawa 216, 217
Kempis, Thomas à 107, 200
khipu kamayuc 278
khipus 278
knight-errantry 59, 102
Knowles, Dom David 402 n.15
Kollasuyu 252, 297, 298, 299
Kónoj 255, 256, 257, 273
Kublai Khan 9
Kuélap 306

Kusi Yupanki 252, 284
Kusipata ('terrace of fortune', Cusco) 288

La Chaulx, Charles de Poupet, Seigneur de 196
La Coruña 65, 115, 116, 168, 226
La Cosa, Juan de 45, 84
La Gomera 317
La Hoz, Pedro Sancho de 277
La Isabela 31
La Malinche, *see* Marina
La Mejorada 38–9
La Palma 10
La Rábida (ship) 61
La Rábida (convent) *see* Santa María de la Rábida
La Tora (Barrancas Bermejas) 332
Labre, St Benedict Joseph 349
'Land of War' 233
Lannoy, Charles de 111
Laredo 262
Las Casas, Bartolomé de xvii, 31, 34, 41, 43, 45, 46, 60–61, 62, 63, 68, 69, 70, 77, 79, 81, 82, 86, 89, 94, 95–6, 99, 106–11 *passim*, 114, 115 117, 118, 145, 233, 235, 266; 341–2, 344, 347; first priest to be ordained in the New World 94; acquires an 'encomienda' 95; engages in gold mining and turtle farming 95; proposes abolition of the 'encomienda' 95–6; proposes the import of African slaves to the Caribbean 96; clashes with Hieronymite mission 109–10; fiasco in Cumaná 118, 341; enters the Order of Preachers 118, 341; on the Massacre in Cholollan 145; sets off to Peru in 1534, 341; in Guatemala, Oaxaca and Mexico City, 1539 341; The New Laws 342

Las Casas, Pedro de 61
Las Meninas (Velázquez) 354–5
Las Salinas, Battle of 306, 312
Laso de la Vega, Luis 221
Last Judgement 70, 197
Laudi (da Todi) 107
Lautrec, Viscount of, *see* Foix, Odet de
Laws of Burgos, 78, 84, 235, 266; *see also* 'Ordinances'
Lázaro Cárdenas 225
Lebrija, Antonio de 334
Leo III, Pope 197
Leo X, Pope 112, 196, 200
Leonorina, mythical Byzantine princess 102, 103
Lérida 112
liberalism 355–6
Lidamor de Escocia (de Córdoba) 262
Lienzo de Quauhquechollan 234
Lima (Ciudad de los Reyes) 247, 259, 292, 297, 300, 305, 308, 312, 313
Lisbon 6, 7, 28, 350
liturgy 209, 211, 213, 218, 219, 223, 224, 351–2
Livy 205
llamas 247, 255, 262, 331
llanos (plains) 336, 339, 340
llautu (headband) 256, 273, 274
Loaísa, García Joffre de 226
Loaysa, Friar Alonso de 71
local privileges 134; *see also fueros*
'local' religion 214, 217
Loché 243
Lombardy 236, 239
Lomellini family 6
López de Recalde, Juan 111
López, Martín 167, 173, 174, 179, 396 n.49
lordship 134, 152, 193, 217, 227
Los Ángeles, Friar Francisco de 200, 201
Louis II, King of Hungary

Louise of France 105
Louise of Savoy 236
Louisiana 216
Lugo, see Fernández de Lugo, Alonso;
    Fernández de Lugo, Pedro
Lugo, Francisco de 177, 225
Lull, Friar Raymond 97
Luna, Gómez de 313
Lupaqa 250, 307–8
Luque, Hernando de 247
Luther, Martin 191–2, 266

Mabila 326–7, 426 n.52
Macaulay, Thomas Babington xv
Machiavelli, Nicolò 66
Macul, River 296
Madeira 6, 7
Madrid 237, 343, 350, 353, 354
Madrid, Treaty of 237
Madrigalejo 104
Magdalena (fortress in Hispaniola) 43
Magdalena, River 331, 332, 339
Magellan, Ferdinand 88, 226
Magellan, Strait of 226
Maguana 34
Malacca, Strait of 51
Malaysia 51
Maldonado de Talavera, Rodrigo 11
Maldonado, Alonso de 60
Malinalco 185
Malinali see Marina
Mam 228
Mandeville, Sir John 9, 31, 99
Manet, Edouard 354
Maní 244
Manqo Inka 284–5, 286, 290, 291,
    298, 299, 300, 301, 303, 304,
    305, 306–7, 309, 310, 311,
    312, 314
Manrique, Alonso 105
Mantanaro, River 278, 282
Mantanaro, Valley 278
Manzanedo, Friar Bernardino de 83

'map of islands' (Columbus) 26
Mapuche 250
Maracaibo, Lake 339
Marchena, Friar Antonio de 8, 12
Marco Polo 9, 51, 99
Marcus Aurelius 114, 197
Margaret of Austria, Archduchess 196
Margarit, Pedro 31, 32
Margarita (island) 41, 112
Marina (La Malinche) 127, 144, 153,
    154, 163, 255
Marinus of Tyre 9
Mark Antony 324
Márquez, Diego 60
Martial 205
Martín, Benito 167
Martinillo see also Felipillo/
    Martinillo
Martinique 50, 51
Martorell, Joanot 15
marvedí (coin) 368 n.23
Mary Magdalen, St 220
Massagetans 52
Matienzo, Friar Tomás de 74, 104
Matininó 97, 99
Matlacueitl 137; see also
    Chalchiuhtlicue
Maule, Battle of 152
Maximilian I (Holy Roman Emperor)
    112, 113
Maxixcatzin 140, 141, 170, 173
Mayas 123, 124, 227, 234, 275
Maztalán 245
Mecca 39, 47
Medellín see Nahutla
Medina del Campo 36, 39
Medina Sidonia, Duke of 11
Medinaceli, Count of 11
Mediterranean 3, 262
Megasthenes 88
Mela, Pomponius 88
Melchor (Maya interpreter) 122,
    125, 126

Melibee 17
Mellitus, Abbot 209
Mena, Cristóbal de 262
Méndez de Salcedo, Diego 52, 63
Mendicant Orders 196, 199,
    200–224 passim, 343, 351-2
Mendieta, Friar Gerónimo de 204
Mendoza, Don Antonio de (Viceroy
    of New Spain) 318, 342
Mengs, Anton 353
mercedes (rewards) 21, 314
Mexía, Gonzalo de 159
Mexica (Aztecs) 138, 146, 147, 150,
    152, 154-5, 163, 165, 169, 170,
    171, 175, 178, 179, 180, 185,
    188, 257; astonishing resilience
    183-4, 186
Mexico 116, 120, 264, 274-5,
    279, 336
Mexico City 202, 230, 232, 240,
    244, 330, 351; called the City
    of Palaces by Alexander von
    Humboldt 351
Michael, Archangel 408 n.87
Michoacán 173, 225
Midianites 237
Milan 236, 239, 350
Millenarianism 13, 202, 203
miracles 219
Miraflores, Carthusian monastery 66
Mississippi 135, 216
Mississippi, River 329
Mitla 231-2
mitmaq (Inca colonist; pl.
    mitmaqkuna) 304
Mixcoatl, Andrés 208
Mixcoatl-Camaxtli 157
Mixtecs 231-2
Mochí 243
Mocoso 319
Moctezuma (Montezuma) xv, 127-8,
    137, 138, 139, 140, 142, 145,
    147, 152, 153-7, 158, 159, 161,

164, 165, 170, 173, 175, 176,
    178, 187, 231, 239, 249, 258,
    324, 335; in Itzlolinqui's version
    142-3; as surrogate of the gods
    and keeper of the universe 156;
    decides to make war on the
    Spaniards 159; death 165
Moere, Pieter van der, see Peter
    of Ghent
Mogrovejo de Quiñones,
    Francisco 301
Moguer, Pedro de 259, 260, 285
Mohács 236, 237, 239
Mojos 250
Molina, Cristóbal de ('El
    Almagrista') 421 n.17
Molina, Luis de 264
Moluccas 89, 226, 227
Mongol mission, 81, 123-4, 361 n.42
Mongols 124
Moniz Perestrelo, Filipa 8, 17
Monroy, Francisco de 60
Montaigne, Michel de 349, 385 n.75
Montalvo see Rodríguez de Montalvo
Monte Albán 231
Montejo, Francisco de 131, 167,
    237-8, 241-5 passim
Montesinos, Friar Antonio de 68,
    70, 73, 76, 77, 203; Advent
    sermon 70
Montezuma see Moctezuma
Morales, Luis de 310
Moscoso, Luis de 330
Motley, John Lothrop 358 n.7
Motolinía, Friar Toribio de 204
Motux 255
Mount Zion 48
Mozarabic Rite 211
Muisca 335, 336, 344
municipal government 35-6, 192,
    194-5, 280, 296, 340-41, 342
Münster, Sebastian 3, 5
mushrooms 153, 183, 208

Muskogean 323
Muslims 18, 33, 158; forbidden to
    travel to the New World 67
Múxica, Adrián de 45
Mystical Theology (Bonaventure) 220

Nahuas 128, 228, 231, 234
Nahuatl 127, 156, 209, 214, 219,
    221, 222, 231
Napituca 320
Naples (city) 66, 351
Naples (kingdom) 13, 65, 66, 239,
    240, 247, 350
Narváez, Diego de 287
Narváez, Pánfilo de 94, 107, 160,
    161, 162, 164, 168, 173, 174,
    216, 303, 316, 319
Nasamones 88
Nasrid kingdom 15
nation state 347, 350, 355
Nnationalism 347, 350, 351, 430
    n.10, 431 n.12
Natural Law 31, 267, 268, 269
nature and grace 81–2, 124, 203,
    219, 266, 341–2
Nature and the Supernatural 223–4,
    410 n.95
Nauhtla (Medellín) 153, 192
Navarre 350
Navarro, Antonio 249
Navidad, *see* Puerto Navidad
Nazca 250
Nebrija, Antonio de 127, 205
Neiva 338, 340
Neo-Platonism 108
Nepantla, Nepantlism 208–9
Nero 145
Netherlands 105, 192
New England 433 n.27
New Granada, Kingdom of 338,
    340, 344
New Laws 342, 347; *see also* Laws
    of Burgos; *encomienda* system

New Spain 192, 195, 199, 200, 204,
    318, 324, 351
New York 351
Newfoundland 38
Nezahualcoyotl 175
Nezahualpilli 175
Nican mopohua 221, 222
Nicaragua 51, 99, 245, 246, 249,
    253, 262, 279, 301, 317, 329
Nicuesa, Diego de 84
Nieremberg, Juan Eusebio 408 n.87
Niña (ship) 23, 25, 28, 29, 34
Ninan Cuyuchi 252
Nobility 16, 22, 58–9, 347, 366 n.7
Noche Triste 167, 168, 176, 178, 184
Nonalco 182
North Sea 340; *see also*
    Atlantic Ocean
Núñez de Balboa, Vasco 86, 87, 88
Núñez Vela, Blasco
    (Viceroy of Peru) 342
Núñez, Francisco 168
Nuremberg Map 149
Nutini, Hugo G. 409 n.91

Oaxaca (Huaxayacac) 231
'obedezco pero no cumplo' ('I obey
    but I do not implement') 82–3,
    162, 193, 209, 214, 342,
    351, 372 n.50, 399 n.17,
    399–400 n.19
obedience 194, 214, 399–400 n.19
Ocampo, Sebastián 93
Ocita 319
Ocotelulco 140
Ocute 322, 323
Olid, Cristóbal de 135, 174, 179,
    180, 182, 202, 225
Olintecle 137, 138
Olintepeque 228, 233
Ollantaytambo *see* Ullantaytampu
Olmedo, Friar Bartolomé de 157, 179
Olmos 255

Olmos, Friar Andrés de 206
Ometochtzin, Don Carlos 206
Omnimoda, Papal bull 200
Ophaz 48
Ophir 48, 226
Opón Mountains 334
Oran, Port of 75
Oratio Supplicatoria (Gattinara) 113
Ordenanzas para descubrimientos
   (Ordinances for discoveries) 343
Order of Preachers
   see Dominican Order
'Ordinances' 77, 78; *see also*
   Law of Burgos
Orduña, Francisco de 233
Orejón(es) 254, 258
Orgóñez, Rodrigo 303, 305, 306
Oriana, mythical Scottish Princess 102
Orinoco 41
Orlando Furioso (Ariosto) 196
Oroya fever *see* Carrion's disease
Orozco, Francisco de 174, 231
Orteguilla 156
Ortiz, Friar Tomás de 83
Ortiz, Juan 319, 330
Osorio, Don Antonio 328
Othello 88
Otomí 138, 139
Otoncalpulco 168
Ottoman Empire 5, 11, 20, 191,
   197, 237
Ottomans 5, 247, 262
Otumba 146, 170
Our Lady of Guadalupe 221, 222
Our Lady of Ocotlán 222, 223
Ovando, Nicolás de 49, 50, 52, 55,
   58, 59, 60–64 *passim*, 66, 67,
   70, 77, 109, 199, 346
Oviedo *see* Fernández de Oviedo
Oyón 277

Pachacamac 253, 254, 259
pachaka kuraka 279

Pachakuti Inka Yupanki 286
Pacific Ocean (South Sea) 51, 85, 88,
   225, 226, 227, 228, 232, 240,
   241, 245, 246, 249, 250, 259,
   277, 288, 293, 295, 297, 329,
   330, 331, 351
pacification 343, 344
Palacios Rubios, Juan López de
   78–80, 81, 82, 372 fn.45,
   372 n.46
Palafox y Mendoza, Juan 408 n.87
Palma de Mallorca 64
Palmerín de Oliva 99
Palos de la Frontera, port of 23, 28
Pampas, River 282, 291
Panama 51, 68, 86, 87, 245, 246,
   247, 249, 252, 253, 260, 261,
   262, 279, 291, 292, 301
panaqa 252
Panches 337, 338, 339
Pané, Friar Ramón 96–7, 98
Panquetzaliztli ('the Raising of
   Banners') 157
Panticalla Pass 300
Pánuco 217, 238
Papal Schism (1378–1417) 73, 82
Papaloapan 231
Paqoman 228
Parcos 281, 282
Pareja, Juan de 354
Paria, Gulf of 41, 42
Paris University 97
Parker, Geoffrey 379 n.48
Pasamonte, Miguel de 67, 70, 71, 76,
   77, 93, 109
Paso de Cortés 146, 174
Pasto (Colombia) 340
Patagonia 226
Pativilca, River 277
patristics 109, 203, 205, 209, 211,
   220, 341, 407 n.75
Patronato Real 13, 48
Paukar 303

Paul of the Cross, St 349
Paullu Tupaq 298, 303–4, 305, 306, 307, 308, 309
Pavia, Battle of 236, 237, 239, 240, 247, 303; described by Alfonso de Valdés 237
Paz, Matías de 78–9
pearl fisheries 28, 68, 84, 178, 235
pearls 9, 68, 115, 149, 178, 235, 312, 320, 324, 328
Peninsular War 353
Perestrelo, Bartolomeo 17
Perestrelo, Filipa see Moniz Perestrelo
Pérez del Pulgar, Hernán (el de las hazañas) 14
Pérez, Friar Juan 12
Perico 323
Perion, mythical King of Wales 102
Pero Niño, Count 17
Peru 261, 264, 274, 278, 280, 291, 292, 301, 324, 330, 331, 332, 337, 340, 355
Petén 232
Peter Martyr see D'Anghera, Peter Martyr
Peter of Ghent (Pedro de Gante) 200, 201, 204–5, 220
Peter, St 80, 81
peyote (peyotl) 183
Philadelphia 351
Philip 'the Handsome', King Philip I of Castile 53, 65, 66, 104
Philip II, King xvii, 343, 346, 350
Philosophia Naturalis (Albert) 38
Picado, Antonio 310
Piccolomini, Enea Silvio de' (Pope Pius II) 9, 38, 71, 74
Pico de Orizaba (Citlaltepetl) 120, 137, 172
Piedrahíta 74, 75
Piedrahíta, Beata of 74; and the Conquest of Jerusalem 75; and the Expedition to Oran 75–6

piglets 318, 327, 328, 329
Piis fidelium, papal bull 29
Pike's Peak 259
Pillars of Hercules 5, 197
Pinelli family 12
Pinta (ship) 23, 25, 26, 28
Pinzón, Martín Alonso 23, 26, 27, 28
Pinzón, Vicente Yáñez 48
Pinzón brothers 23, 28, 48
Pipil 228, 230
piracy 189, 244, 316, 317
Piura see San Miguel
Pius II, Pope, see Piccolomini
Pizarro, Francisco xv, xvi, 88, 245, 246, 247, 249–50, 253, 254–9 passim, 260, 273, 274, 275, 277, 280, 281, 282, 284, 285, 287, 290, 291, 292, 293, 296, 297, 298, 301, 305, 306, 307, 308, 310, 314, 315, 324, 331, 339, 343, 344; sails to Spain 247–8; seizes Atawallpa 257; melts down Qorikancha treasure 260; executes Atawallpa as a traitor 261; appalled at Almagro's execution 308; made a marquis 311; cruelty 310–11; despises the Almagristas, 312; assassinated 313
Pizarro, Gonzalo 298, 299, 303, 305, 306, 307–8, 310, 342
Pizarro, Hernando 253, 255, 256, 259, 260, 261, 262, 282, 297, 299, 303, 305, 306, 307–8; accused of treason 312
Pizarro, Juan 298, 299, 300
Plano Carpini, John of 123
Plato 265
Pliny the Elder 31, 88, 205
Pole Star 25, 42
Polemarchus 265

polytheism 96, 97, 124, 204–7
passim
Ponce de León, Juan 99, 118, 186, 316
Ponce de León, Rodrigo (Duke of
Cádiz) 14
Popayán 340
Popocatepetl 146, 172, 178
Popol Vuh 228, 232
Popotla 166
Porcallo de Figueroa, Vasco 317, 318
Porco 250
Porto Santo 17
Portugal 5, 6, 7, 8, 10, 39, 48, 50, 64,
89, 137, 226, 227, 350
Positive Law 267, 268
Potonchan (Santa María de la
Victoria) 126, 128
Poupet, Charles de, see La Chaulx
Powers 220, see also Angelic
Hierarchies
Prescott, William xvi, 162, 360 n.23
Prester John 20, 32
Principalities see angelic hierarchies
printing press 108, 191–2
Protestantism 191–2, 197, 236
Providence 144, 203, 209, 283,
319, 328
prudence see cardinal virtues
Ptolemy, Claudius 8, 9, 88
Pucará 282
Puebla 407–8 n.87
Puerto Navidad 27, 30, 31, 33, 34
Puerto Plata 62
Puerto Rico 30, 99, 101, 117–18, 292
Puerto Viejo 250
Puertocarrero see Hernández
Puertocarrero
Puná (island) 253, 254
Pyrrhus 305

Qhapac ayllu 252
Qolla 250, 281, 307
Qorikancha 259, 285

Qualpopoca see Cohualpopocatzin
Quauhpopocatzin 142
Quauhquechollan, see Lienzo de
Quauhquechollan
Quecholli ('Precious feather') 157
Quechua 279
Quetzal-Owl Warrior 187
Quetzalcoatl 128–9, 144, 150,
153, 159
Quetzaltenango 228
Quevedo, Friar Juan de 115
Quiahuiztlan 135
Quibdó 86
Quiñones, Enrique de, see Los
Ángeles, Francisco de
Quintanilla, Alonso de 12
quinto real (royal 'fifth') 59, 262
Quiroga, Vasco de 403 n.17
Quisquis 253, 275, 278, 282, 283, 284,
285, 290, 291, 293, 297, 298
Quito (San Francisco de) 253, 260,
275, 281, 284, 290, 291, 293,
295, 296, 297, 315, 340
Quitttim 48
Quizquiz see Quisquis

Ramírez de Arellano, Juana 240
Rangel, Rodrigo 161, 231
Ranjel, Rodrigo 323, 325, 326, 327,
330, 425 n.38
Raphael (Archangel) 219
Rationale divinorum officiorum 211
Raymond of Capua 73
Recife (Brazil) 48
Reconquista, 21, 36, 55, 93, 113, 143
Recuay 277
Relectio de Indis 264
relics 219, 286
religious culture 348, 351–2, 355,
431–2 n.13
Renaissance 16, 17, 88, 102, 108,
142, 190, 211
Republic (Plato) 265

republicanism 355–6
Requerimiento 80–82, 87, 266, 274, 286, 371 n.37
Restall, Matthew 389–90 ns.9, 18
Rimac, River 292
Riobamba 295
Riquelme, Alonso 249, 287, 291, 293
Rivarolo, family 12
River Plate 89
Rocky Mountains 259
Rodríguez Barragán, Juan 313
Rodríguez de Fonseca, Juan 35, 36, 37, 45, 48, 66, 77, 87, 107, 111, 112, 114, 115, 116, 168, 178, 190, 192; and Castilla del Oro 87; clashes with Las Casas 107, 112; bribes Chièvres 111,; and Comunero Revolt, 192; and Critóbal de Tapia 192
Rodríguez de Montalvo, Garci 102, 103
Rojas, Gabriel de 291, 293
Roldán, Francisco 43, 44, 45, 46, 50, 62
Roman Empire 123, 267, 269
Roman Law 265
Romans 36, 197, 268
Romanticism xvi, 253, 254
Rome 114, 135, 239, 305, 351
Ronda 13
Royal Council 195, 312
Rubens, Peter Paul 353
Rubicon 135
Rubruck, William of 124
Ruiz de Estrada, Bartolomé 246, 247, 331
Rumiñawi 253, 260, 261, 275, 290, 293, 295, 296, 297, 298

Sack of Rome 239, 247
sacramentality 210, 219, 404–5 n.48, 407 n.76
Sagipa 337, 338, 339

Sahagún, Friar Bernardino de 128, 153, 158, 163, 209, 219–20, 222
Saint Anne 409 n.91
Saint John the Apostle 409 n.91
Saint Mary of the Victory, monastery of 6
Saint Thomas the Apostle 29
saints 217, 218, 219, 223–4, 286
Salamanca 99, 132, 151
Salamanca (Yucatan) 241
Salamanca University 11, 93, 97, 98, 132, 274; see also Vitoria, Friar Francisco de
Sallust 205
Salvador (Brazil) 48
Samalá, River 227
Sampollón 332
San Buenaventura, Pedro de 205
San Cristóbal (ship) 317
San Cristóbal (Chiapas) 245
San Francisco see Quito
San Gabriel de Extremadura (Franciscan Province) 202, 203
San Giorgio (Genoa) 49
San Juan (ship) 109
San Juan (Puerto Rico) 30
San Juan de Ulúa (island) 127, 131, 135
San Juan, River see Atrato
San Martín, Juan de 334, 336
San Mateo, Bay 249, 252
San Miguel (Piura) 254, 293, 296
San Salvador (island) 26
San Salvador de Bayamo 101, 375
San Vicente de la Barquera 110
Saña 255
Sánchez, Miguel 221, 223
Sánchez de Carvajal, Alonso 44
Sancta Maria Rotunda 210
Sancti Spiritus 95, 101
Sandoval, Gonzalo de 109, 135, 160, 176, 177, 178, 179, 180, 182, 183, 184, 187, 188, 192, 193, 194, 225, 227

Sanlúcar de Barrameda 40, 53, 87, 238, 247, 248, 317

Santa Cruz de Tlatelolco (College) 213

Santa Fé (Andalusia) 14, 15

Santa María (Azores) 28

Santa María (ship) 23, 27

Santa María de la Concepción (island) 26

Santa María de la Encarnación (Santa Fé, Andlausia) 14

Santa María de la Rábida (Franciscan Convent) 3, 8, 12, 13, 17

Santa María de la Victoria, *see* Potonchan

Santa María la Antigua 86, 246

Santa María la Redonda 210

Santa Marta (Colombia) 80, 324, 331, 332, 334, 337, 340

Santa, River 277

Santángel, Luis de 12

Santiago (ship) 226

Santiago (Chile) 311

Santiago (Hispaniola) 61

Santiago de Compostela 116

Santiago de Cuba 101, 103, 122, 317

Santo Domingo 61, 62, 63, 64, 67, 68, 69, 70, 73, 84, 86, 109, 118, 125, 161, 189, 245, 246

Santo Domingo of Piedrahíta 74

Santo Domingo, María de, *see* Piedrahíta, *Beata* of

Santo Tomás (Jánico) 31

São Francisco, River 48

São Jorge da Mina 8

São Tiago 40

Saona 62

Sapa Inka 252, 255, 256, 257, 258, 260, 261, 262, 273, 274, 275, 277, 279, 280, 281, 285, 290, 293, 298, 299, 303, 307

Saphy *see* Huatanay

Saqsaywaman 300, 306

Saragossa *see* Zaragoza

Sardinia 7, 112, 350

Sarrán 255

Sassoferrato, Bartolo da 378 n.31

Satan *see* Devil, the

Saucedo, Francisco de 135

Sauvage, Jean 89, 111, 113

Savannah, River 425 n.31

Savoy 98

Schiller, Friedrich 358 n.7

Segovia 87, 93, 106

Segovia, Juan de 97

Segura de la Frontera 172–3, 174, 191; *see also* Tepeaca

Seneor, Abraham 19

Sergas de Esplandián 102, 103

Serrano, Francisco 89

Severus 114, 196

Seville xv, 3, 10, 35, 94, 104, 109, 115, 117, 167, 178, 262, 263, 315, 331

Sforza, Francesco, Duke of Milan 239

Shackleton, Edward xvi, 357 n.6

Sheba 27

Sicily 5, 7, 112, 350

Siena 71

Sierra de Puebla 208

Siete Partidas 132–4, 192, 382–4, ns. 39–53

Sigismund I, King of Poland 198

silver 9, 249, 254, 258, 259, 262, 287, 288, 296, 320, 323, 338, 413 n.1, 419 n.39

Simonides 265

Sinsimato 243

slavery 6, 31, 32, 34, 62, 67, 68, 76, 77, 84, 95, 109, 178, 238, 246, 254, 339, 372 n.51; *in Aristotle* 79; *endorsed by Las Casas* 95; *endorsed by Hieronymites* 110; *encouraged by Chièvres* 111

Smallpox 111, 173, 252

Smith, Adam 349

Soconusco 227
Socrates 265
Sogamoso 336
Solís *see* Díaz de Solís
Solomon 36, 48, 52
Soto, Diego de 327
Soto, Friar Domingo de 264, 268
Soto, Hernando de 253, 254, 255,
    256, 257, 260, 261, 277, 281,
    282, 283, 285, 290, 297, 298,
    314, 315, 316–30 *passim*;
    appalled at execution of
    Atawallpa 261; governor of
    Cusco 314; sails back to Spain
    315; 'capitulación' to conquer
    Florida 315; governor of Cuba
    316; knight of Santiago 316;
    obsession with gold 316–39
    passim; thought to be losing his
    mind 324; seizes Queen of
    Cofitachequi 324; names his
    successor and dies 330
South Sea 240, 329, 330, 331, 332,
    340; *see also* Pacific Ocean
sovereignty 348, 350
Spain, 10, 18, 32, 33, 37, 38, 43, 46,
    53, 73, 74, 89, 104, 105, 109,
    117, 137, 156, 167, 170, 192,
    196, 218, 274, 287, 300, 327,
    301, 311, 316, 331, 338, 344,
    353; in Isaiah's prophecies 38;
    as Tarshish 38; receptive to
    Erasmianism 109; local
    Religion 218,; tensions with
    Portugal 226
Speyer, Georg von 339
Spice Islands 226–7
Spices 12, 28, 33, 35, 50, 89, 225, 226
Spinoza, Baruch 349
Statehood 348
Strabo 88
Suárez, Francisco 264
Suesca (Colombia) 344

Suleiman the Magnificent 236,
    237, 247
suum cuique 264
suyu (división) 304
Swift, Jonathan 349
syphilis 414 n.9

Tabasco 244, 245
Tacaetl 208
Tacuba *see* Tlacopan
Taínos 30, 33, 34, 41, 43, 44, 52, 60,
    61, 62, 67, 69, 76, 79, 93, 94,
    95, 96, 106, 110, 111, 112, 11;
    mythology 96–7; demographic
    decline 109
Talavera, Friar Hernando de 11,
    33, 98
Tale of a Tub, A (Swift) 349
Talisi 326
Tallahassee 216
Tampa 216, 318
tampu 288, 295, 420 n.44
Tapia, Andrés de 154, 185
Tapia, Cristóbal de 61, 192, 193,
    194, 195
Tapia, Gonzalo de 301
Tarapacá 250
Tarma 299
Tarma, Valley 277, 291
Tarshis 38, 226
Tartars 98, 124
Tascalusa 326, 327
Tawantinsuyu 252, 253, 256, 257, 258,
    273, 275, 287, 288, 290, 297,
    298, 299, 301, 303, 304, 305
Teapa 245
Techcatl 151
Tecún Umán 228, 233
Tehuantepec 227
Telpochcalli 183
temperance *see* cardinal virtues
Tenayuca 177
Tendile 127–8

Tenerife 10, 331

Tenochtitlan 127, 128, 129, 130, 135, 138, 139, 142, 144, 145, 146, 148–9, 150–52, 159, 160, 162, 163, 164, 167, 168, 170, 171, 174, 176, 177, 178, 180–89 *passim*, 193, 199, 211, 221, 225, 230, 231, 239, 243, 244, 257, 287, 291; weaknesses 171–2; re-named Mexico City 202

Teocajas 295

Teocalhueycan 168

Teoctlamacazqui 129

Tepanecs 168–70

Tepeaca 172, 174, 175, 241; *see also* Segura de la Frontera

Tepepolco 180

Tepeyac 182, 221

Tepotzotlan 170

Teresa of Ávila, St 405 n.50

Tetzcoca 176, 177

Tetzcoco (Texcoco) 130, 150, 174, 175, 176, 178, 179, 184, 206

Texcoco *see* Tetzcoco

Tezcatlipoca 129, 151, 409 n.91

Teziutlan 137

Travels of Marco Polo, The 38

'The Twelve' 201, 202, 203, 204, 207; *see also* Franciscan Order

Thomas the Apostle, St 379 n.8

Thupa Inka Yupanki 252

Thupa Wallpa 273, 274, 275, 280, 285

Tianguismanalco 409 n.91

Timucua 216, 318, 319, 320, 327

Tirant lo Blanch (Martorell) 15

Tisoq Yupanki 298, 299, 308, 309

Titian (Tiziano Vecelli) 114

Titicaca, Basin 250

Titicaca, Lake 250, 281, 307

Tititl ('the Stretching') 157

Titu Cusi 310

Tiwanaku 307

Tizoc 175

Tlacaxipehualitzli ('the Flaying of Men') 159

Tlachiac 144

Tlacochcalcatl 161

Tlacopan (Tacuba) 150, 164, 165, 168, 173, 175, 176, 180, 182

Tlaloc 157, 159

Tlaquiach 144

Tlatelolco 150, 151, 156, 182, 184, 186, 187

Tlatlauquitepec 137

Tlaxcala *see* Tlaxcallan

Tlaxcallan (Tlaxcala) 138, 141, 142, 144, 146, 170, 173, 174, 176, 179, 185, 222, 225, 239

Tlaxcalteca 138, 139, 140, 141, 143, 144, 146, 163, 166, 170, 171, 174, 176, 177, 178, 179, 184, 185, 188, 275, 291, 335

Toa 322

tobacco 27

Tobar, Nuño de 317

Tobias 219

Tocarema, Battle of 337

Toci 409 n.91

Todi, Friar Iacapone da 107

tokrikoq (provincial governors) 304

Toledo 106, 247

Toledo, Archbishopric of 35, 111, 264

Toledo, Francisco de (Viceroy of Peru) 347, 348, 352

Toledo y Rojas, María de 66

Tollan (Tula) 128, 185

Tomas de Vio *see* Cajetan, Friar Tomas de Vio

Tombigbee, River 328

Tonantzin 221, 223

Tonatiuh 162, 163

Tordesillas 36, 110, 168

Tordesillas, Junta of 117

Tordesillas, Treaty of 39, 226

Torquemada, Cardinal Juan de 73

Torrella, Jeroni 198

Torres de Ávila, Juana 12
Torrid Zone 8
Totocalli 158
Totonacs 127, 130, 135, 153, 161,
    173, 192
Totoquihuatzin 150
Toxcatl 163
Trajan 114, 197
Transcendence 219
Trastámara, House of 57
Trier, Archdiocese of 112
Trinidad (Cuba) 101
Trinidad (island) 41
Trinidad (ship) 109, 226
Triple Alliance 128, 130
Tristán de Leonís el Joven 262
Trujillo 87, 248
Tula (Arkansas) 330
Tula, *see* Tollan (Tula)
Tulum 244
Tumbes 247, 249, 250, 253, 254,
    255, 284
Tumbez *see* Tumbes
Tumipampa 290, 293, 295, 297
Tunis 262
Tunja 337, 340–41
Tunja (*cacique*) 336
Tunupa 379 n.8
Tuxtepec 225
Tyrrhenian Sea 7
Tz'utujil 228, 230
tzitzimiml (plural *tzitzimite*) 205,
    403 n.26
Tzompachtepetl 139

Ulibahali 326
Ullantaytampu 300, 303, 310
Ulúa 120
Urabá, Gulf of 84, 86, 112, 178
Urriparacoxi 319
Urubamba, River 300, 303
Usumacinta, River 126
Utalán 228

Utcubamba 306
Uzachile 320

Vaca de Castro, Cristóbal 311
Valdés, Alfonso de 236
Valdivia, Pedro de 311
Valencia, Friar Martín de 201
Valenzuela, Captain Pedro de 336
Valeriano, Antonio 205, 221
Valla, Lorenzo 375 n.20
Valladolid 36, 54, 74, 78, 89, 93,
    110, 116, 168, 344
Valladolid, Pablo de 354
Valverde, Friar Vicente de 257, 261,
    287, 309–10, 415 n.29
Vázquez de Ayllón, Lucas 161
Vázquez de Coronado, Francisco 330
Vázquez de Tapia, Bernardino
    142, 146
Vejerano, Antonio 205
Velázquez de Cuéllar, Diego 63, 93,
    94, 99, 101, 103, 116, 120, 122,
    130, 131, 132, 133, 134, 135,
    152, 162, 167, 168, 192, 199, 23;
    accused of greed 134; appoints
    Narváez Captain-General 160
Velázquez de León, Juan 131, 135,
    141, 154, 159, 161
Velázquez, Antonio 107
Velázquez, Diego Rodríguez de Silva y
    353–5
Vélez de Mendoza, Luis 48
Venezuela 41, 43, 84, 339, 340
Venice 6, 139, 236, 239
Veracruz 127, 186, 189, 192, 193,
    195, 225, 238
Veragua 51
Verdi, Giuseppe 358 n.7
Vespucci, Amerigo 45, 84, 89
Vetancurt, Agustín de 375 n.25
Viceregal Government 342–3, 348
Vienne, Council of 97
Vigo 28

Vilanova, Arnau de 13, 113
Vilcabamba 306–7, 309
Vilcabamba Valley 303
Vilcaconga 283, 284, 287
Vilcanota *see* Urubamba
Vilcas 254, 308
Vilcashuaman 281, 282
Villa de la Concepción 226
Villa Rica de la Vera Cruz 116, 131,
    132, 134, 153, 160, 162
Villacorta, Rodrigo de 60
Vincent Ferrer, St 18
Viracocha *see* Wiracocha
Virgin Mary 122, 220, 221, 222, 330
virtue 16, 17, 57, 114, 263
Virtues *see* angelic hierarchies
Vitcos 303, 307, 309
Vitoria, Friar Francisco de 263–9,
    370 n.27
Vives, Juan Luis 205
Vlissingen 65
Volta, River 11, 40
Voltaire 349

wak'a 279–80, 288, 304
Waldseemüller, Martin 89
Wanakawri 288
Wanka 291, 301, 307
waranka kuraka 279
Wari Willka 307
Waskaran 277
Waskhar 250, 252, 253, 254, 258,
    260, 273, 275, 277, 280, 285,
    290, 295, 304
Wayna Qhapaq 250, 252, 255, 273,
    284, 286, 290, 298, 299, 308
Weiditz, Christoph 240
Welser Company 339, 344
Wesley, John 349
West African Coast 6, 7, 28
Westphalia, Treaty of 348, 349
White, Richard 406 n.74
Wilder, Thornton 418–19 n.26

Willaq Umu 298, 299, 307, 309, 310
William the Silent, Prince of Orange
    xvii, 347
Windisheim reform 108
Wiracocha 255, 279
Withlacoochee 320
Wyclif, John 82, 266

Xalacingo 137
Xaltepec-Apan Pass 174
Xaltocan 177
Xamanzana 125
Xerez, Francisco de 262
Xicochimalco 137
Xicotencatl the elder 140, 141,
    170, 185
Xicotencatl the younger 140, 170,
    385 n.76
Xipe Totec 159
Xochimilco 179, 185
Xochiquetzalli 222
Xoloc 180, 182

Yana (pl. *Yanacuna*) 304–5
Yanamarca 278
Yáquimo 118
Ymago Mundi, Pierre d'Ailly's 25
Yucatan 99, 116, 120–26, 128, 173,
    225, 238, 241–5, 262, 275,
    279, 319
Yucay Valley 299, 300
Yupaha 322
Yuramayo 307

Zacatula 225
Zacuto, Abraham 38
Zapotecs 231
Zaragoza 102, 112, 134, 196
Zárate, Juan de 259, 260, 285
Zautla 137, 138
Zemís 96, 97
Zumárraga, Friar Juan de 206, 207,
    208, 219, 221, 222